Analysis of Changes

NEC - 2014

Analysis of Changes
NEC - 2014

International Association of Electrical Inspectors
Richardson, Texas

International Association of Electrical Inspectors
901 Waterfall Way, Suite 602
Richardson, TX 75080-7702

 First edition published 1978
Printed in the United States of America
17 16 15 14 13 5 4 3 2 1

ISBN-10: 1-890659-64-9
ISBN-13: 978-1-890659-64-6

Library of Congress Control Number: 2010930805

Photos used in this book were shot *in situ* or at tradeshows. Use of the photos does not imply endorsement by IAEI of the manufacturers or the products. Photos without a credit line are from IAEI Archives.

Notice to the Reader

This book has not been processed in accordance with NFPA Regulations Governing Committee Projects. Therefore, the text and commentary in it shall not be considered the official position of the NFPA or any of its committees and shall not be considered to be, nor relied upon as a formal interpretation of the meaning or intent of any specific provision or provisions of the 2014 edition of NFPA 70, *National Electrical Code*.©[1]

Publishers do not warrant or guarantee any of the products described herein or perform any independent analysis in connection with any of the product information contained herein. Publisher does not assume, and expressly disclaims, any obligation to obtain and include information referenced in this work.

The reader is expressly warned to consider carefully and adopt all safety precautions that might be indicated by the activities described herein and to avoid all potential hazards. By following the instructions contained herein, the reader willingly assumes all risks in connection with such instructions.

[1]*National Electrical Code* and *NEC* are registered trademarks of the National Fire Protection Association, Inc., Quincy, MA 02169

This book conveys the information related to each change as of July 1, 2013, but does not reflect any subsequent appeal or action taken by the NFPA Standards Council.

Table of Contents

Entire Code, Code-Wide Changes

8 New Articles for the 2014 *NEC*
10 Code Wide Changes
12 Code Wide Changes for Voltage Threshold

Introduction, Article 90

14 90 Introduction

Chapter 1: General, Articles 100 – 110

16 100 Definitions
32 110 Requirements for Electrical Installations

Chapter 2: Wiring and Protection, Articles 200 – 285

45 200 Use and Identification of Grounded Conductors
48 210 Branch Circuits
76 220 Branch-Circuit, Feeder, and Service Calculations
78 225 Outside Branch Circuits and Feeders
79 230 Services
84 240 Overcurrent Protection
88 250 Grounding and Bonding
113 285 Surge-Protective Devices (SPDs), 1000 Volts or Less

Chapter 3: Wiring Methods, Articles 300 – 399

115 300 Wiring Methods and Materials
122 310 Conductors for General Wiring
130 314 Outlet, Device, Pull, and Junction Boxes; Conduit Bodies; Fittings; and Handhole Enclosures
136 324 Flat Conductor Cable: Type FCC
137 330 Metal-Clad Cable: Type MC
139 334 Nonmetallic-Sheathed Cable: Types NM, NMC, and NMS
141 344 Rigid Metal Conduit: Type RMC
142 348 Flexible Metal Conduit: Type FMC
143 350 Liquidtight Flexible Metal Conduit: Type LFMC
144 356 Liquidtight Flexible Nonmetallic Conduit: Type LFNC
145 370 Cablebus
147 376 Metal Wireways
151 386 Surface Metal Raceways
152 392 Cable Trays
157 393 Low-Voltage Suspended Ceiling Power Distribution Systems
159 399 Outdoor Overhead Conductors Over 1000 Volts

Chapter 4: Equipment for General Use, Articles 400 – 480

160 400 Flexible Cords and Cables
165 404 Switches
169 406 Receptacles, Cord Connectors, and Attachment Plugs (Caps)
180 408 Switchboards, Switchgear, and Panelboards
185 409 Industrial Control Panels
186 410 Luminaires, Lampholders, and Lamps
191 422 Appliances
200 424 Fixed Electric Space-Heating Equipment
204 430 Motors, Motor Circuits, and Controllers
211 440 Air-Conditioning and Refrigerating Equipment
213 445 Generators
219 450 Transformers and Transformer Vaults (Including Secondary Ties)
222 480 Storage Batteries
223 490 Equipment over 1000 Volts, Nominal

Chapter 5: Special Occupancies, Articles 500 – 590

225 501 Class I Locations
226 504 Intrinsically Safe Systems
227 514 Motor Fuel Dispensing Facilities
228 516 Spray Application, Dipping, and Coating Processes
229 517 Health Care Facilities
242 520 Theaters, Audience Areas of Motion Picture and Television Studios, Performance Areas, and Similar Locations
243 547 Agricultural Buildings
245 550 Mobile Homes, Manufactured Homes, and Mobile Home Parks
247 551 Recreational Vehicles and Recreational Vehicle Parks
248 555 Marinas and Boatyards
251 590 Temporary Installations

Chapter 6: Special Equipment, Articles 600 – 695

256 600 Electric Signs and Outline Lighting
261 610 Cranes and Hoists
263 620 Elevators, Dumbwaiters, Escalators, Moving Walks, Platform Lifts, and Stairway Chairlifts
266 625 Electric Vehicle Charging System
268 630 Electric Welders
269 645 Information Technology Equipment
272 646 Modular Data Centers
273 680 Swimming Pools, Fountains, and Similar Installations
290 690 Solar Photovoltaic (PV) Systems
309 694 Wind Electric Systems

Chapter 7: Special Conditions, Articles 700 – 770

310 700 Emergency Systems

319 702 Optional Standby Systems

323 705 Interconnected Electric Power Production Sources

325 708 Critical Operations Power Systems (COPS)

327 725 Class 1, Class 2, and Class 3 Remote-Control, Signaling, and Power-Limited Circuits

334 728 Fire-Resistive Cable Systems

335 750 Energy Management Systems

336 760 Fire Alarm Systems

338 770 Optical Fiber Cables and Raceways

Chapter 8: Communications Systems, Articles 800 – 830

344 800 Communications Circuits

350 810 Radio and Television Equipment

352 820 Community Antenna Television and Radio Distribution Systems

355 830 Network-Powered Broadband Communication Systems

Chapter 9: Tables

357 900 Notes to Tables

Colophon

368 Credits

Code Wide

Change at a Glance

New articles for the 2014 *NEC*

See proposals with associated new articles

See comments with associated new articles

All changes in code language are highlighted in gray, and the strike-throughs indicate deletions. This is the same procedure that is followed in the *NEC*.

Code-Wide Changes: (4) New Articles

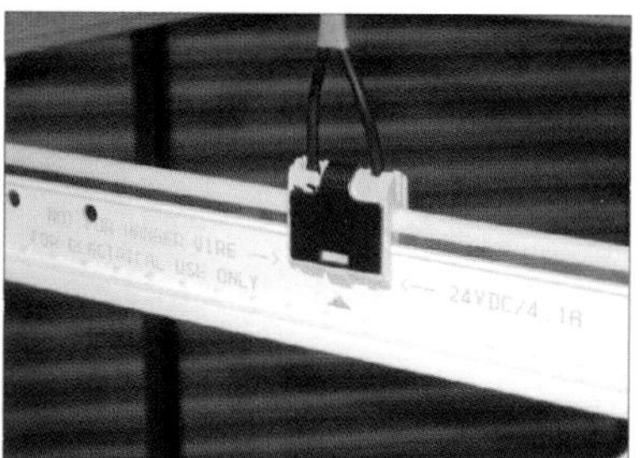

Article 393 Low-Voltage Suspended Ceiling Power Distribution Systems

Article 646 Modular Data Centers

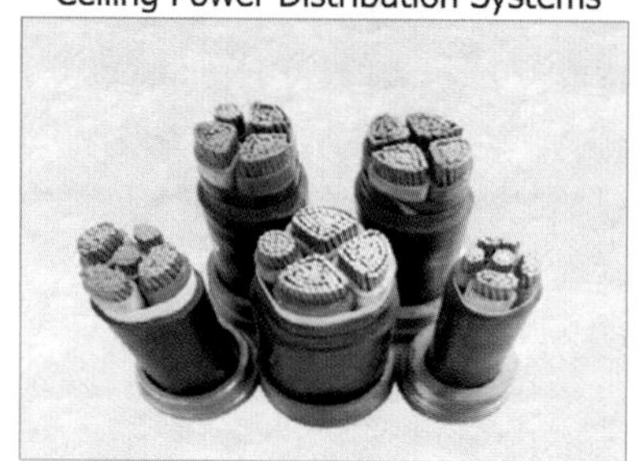

Article 728 Fire-Resistive Cable Systems

Article 750 Energy Management Systems

Analysis of Change

Article 393 Low-Voltage Suspended Ceiling Power Distribution Systems. A new article was added to address low-voltage Class 2 ac and dc volt equipment connected to ceiling grids, and walls built specifically for this type of power distribution system. The growing interest in alternative energy sources (e.g., photovoltaics, wind turbines, batteries, fuel cells, etc.) and the proliferation of low-voltage, low-power devices (sensors, LV lighting, IT equipment, AV equipment, etc.) have created a significant need for adequate language supporting the practical safeguarding of circuits and electrical equipment operating at 30 volts ac, or 60 volts dc, or less. This new article addresses equipment with similar characteristics to track lighting, but includes the wiring and power supply requirements as well. It also provides the specific requirements for the safe installation of low-voltage, power-limited power distribution providing power to lighting and non-lighting loads. See Proposal 18-10a and Comments 18-7, 18-8, 18-9, 18-10, and 18-10a.

Article 646 Modular Data Centers. This new article was added in Chapter 6 to distinguish between data centers that currently fall under the scope of Article 645, Information Technology Equipment. Modular Data Centers (MDCs) are an important emerging trend in data center architecture. Their construction, installation and use result in a unique hybrid piece of equipment that falls somewhere in-between a large enclosure and a prefabricated building. The contained equipment in the enclosures or prefabricated buildings would be fully customizable and scalable to provide data center operations but, typically, would not be permanently installed. Article 645 is applicable only to installations that meet the criteria of 645.4. Otherwise, Article 645 would not be applicable to these products and the other articles of the *Code* would have to be applied. However, it is not always obvious which requirements of the *NEC* are applicable, or how they should be applied given the complexity,

customization and scalability of modular data centers. This article identifies those areas of the *NEC* that should be applied to MDCs and also includes additional new requirements where necessary. See Proposal 12-147 and Comments 12-71, 12-72, 12-74, 12-75, 12-76, 12-77, 12-78, 12-80, 12-81, 12-82, and 12-83.

Article 728 Fire-Resistive Cable Systems. A new article has been added to address installations of fire-resistive cables. The installations of these cables are critical to their ability to function during a fire. These cable systems must be installed in accordance with very specific materials, supports, and requirements and are critical for the survivability of life safety circuits. There are diverse details for installing fire-rated cables that differ from other type cables. Some of these variances pertain to conduit, conduit supports, type of couplings, vertical supports and boxes and splices. Without these details being included in the *NEC*, the installer and the enforcement community can be left uninformed. See Proposal 3-170 and Comments 3-79, 3-80, 3-81, 3-82, 3-83, 3-83a, and 3-83b.

Article 750 Energy Management Systems. A new article was added to provide some general requirements to address the types of loads permitted to be controlled through energy management. Energy management has become commonplace in today's electrical infrastructure through the control of utilization equipment, energy storage and power production. Installation codes currently establish requirements for utilization equipment, for energy storage, and for power production that serve to address facility and personnel safety. However, limited consideration has been given in installation codes to actively managing these systems as a means to reduce energy cost or to support peak power needs for a much broader electrical infrastructure demand. This article resulted from the work of the Smart Grid Task Group appointed by the NEC Correlating Committee. This task group identified two key areas of focus: interconnection and energy management systems. This article includes such things as definitions, requirements for alternative power sources, load-management provisions and field-marking requirements. See Proposal 13-180.

Code Wide

Change at a Glance

Code Wide Changes

See proposals with associated new articles

See comments with associated new articles

Code-Wide Changes

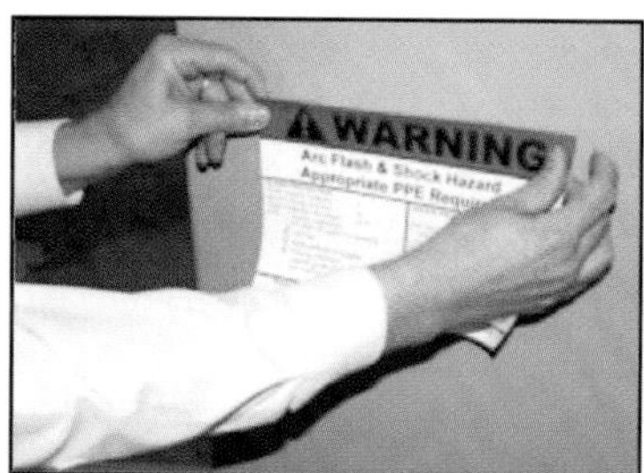

Field-Applied Hazard Markings

Lockable Disconnecting Means

Direct Current (dc) Circuits

Switchgear

Analysis of Change

Field-Applied Hazard Markings. A new 110.21(B) lists specific requirements for warning labels and similar markings where required or specified elsewhere in the *Code*. The *NEC* contains several requirements for labels to be installed on wiring methods and equipment. These required labels or markings typically include one of the following hazard commands: DANGER, WARNING, or CAUTION. This new requirement will incorporate consistent uniformity to rules where additional direction and guidance were needed. These markings, signs or labels should meet ANSI Z535.4 for suitable font sizes, words, colors, symbols and location requirements. Coordinated companion proposals and comments were submitted where caution, warning, and danger markings or signs are required throughout the *NEC* with reference to this new requirement in Article 110.

Lockable Disconnecting Means in Article 110. A new 110.25 was added to deliver a one-stop location providing consistent requirements for a lockable disconnecting means. Forty-six companion proposals were submitted throughout the *NEC* to reference this new requirement and to send users of the *Code* back to one location for lockable disconnecting means requirements. These companion proposals were submitted by a Usability Task Group assigned by the NEC Correlating Committee (NEC CC) to look at the numerous locations in the 2011 *NEC* that referenced lockable disconnecting means requirements.

Requirements for dc Systems Integrated throughout the *NEC*. Direct current (dc) applications are experiencing a re-emergence because of such things as electric vehicle charging, solar photovoltaic (PV) systems, microgrids, wind-generated electric systems, etc. In a great number of cases, these dc systems can achieve greater efficiencies and energy savings than their conventional alternating current (ac) contemporaries. The industry trades installing these different dc applications have been known to use inconsistent polarity identification schemes, particularly with regard to whether or not the grounded conductors of

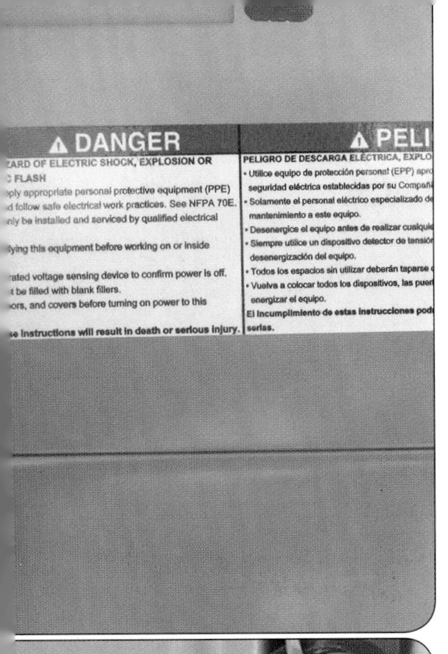

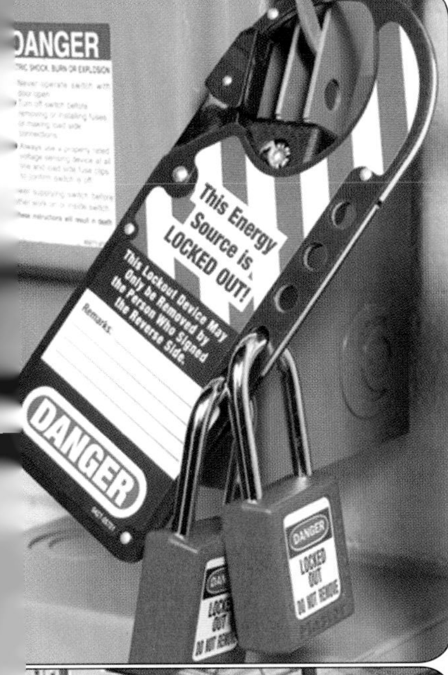

negatively-grounded or positively-grounded two-wire dc systems are actually identified as such. Such inconsistency can result in risk and confusion to installers and service personnel where the branch circuits of these various applications, as well as branch circuits of conventional ac circuits, come together. These inconsistencies are the backdrop for the need to have consistent and reliable rules throughout the *NEC* for these dc systems. Several of the proposals for expanding these dc system requirements were developed and submitted by a subgroup of the NEC DC Task Force of the NEC Correlating Committee.

Use of the Term *Switchgear* Incorporated throughout the *NEC*. The existing definition for *metal-enclosed power switchgear* was modified and retitled to simply *switchgear* to make it inclusive of all types of switchgear under the purview of the *NEC*. This revised definition created the opportunity to utilize this generic term in all locations where the term *switchboard* is already mentioned, and where the use of the term *switchgear* is appropriate. The term *switchgear* includes all types of switchgear such as *metal-enclosed low-voltage power circuit breaker switchgear, metal-clad switchgear,* and *metal-enclosed interrupter switchgear.*

Definitions Relocated to Article 100. Several existing definitions which appeared in the definitions of a particular article have been relocated to Article 100 as these terms are also found in other articles, not just in the article where the previous definition was located. An example of this would be the definition of *effective ground-fault current path* relocated from 250.2 to Article 100. The *NEC Style Manual* at section 2.2.2.1 generally requires that Article 100 contain definitions of terms that appear in two or more other articles of the *NEC*.

Code Wide

Change at a Glance

Numerous changes were made throughout the *NEC* from the 600 volts threshold to 1000 volts.

Code Language

See *NEC* for complete text

Numerous.
See ROP for complete list

Numerous.
See ROC for complete list

Code-Wide Changes

- 120 proposals submitted to raise the 600 volt threshold to 1000 volts
- Resulted in numerous changes throughout the *NEC*
- Proposals were submitted by the High Voltage Task Group (HVTG)

Numerous changes throughout the *NEC* from the 600 volts threshold to 1000 volts

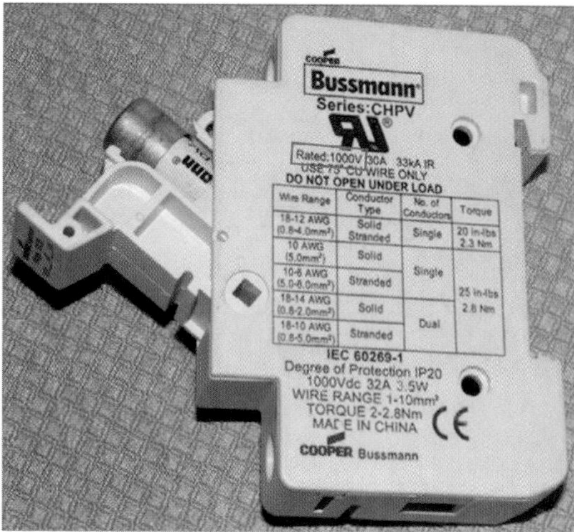

2011 *NEC* Requirement

Voltage threshold was 600 volts in the 2011 *NEC*.

2014 *NEC* Change

Voltage threshold has been moved from 600 volts to 1000 volts in several locations throughout the *NEC*.

Analysis of Change

There were 120 proposals submitted to raise the 600 volt threshold in the *NEC* to 1000 volts. This resulted in numerous changes throughout the *NEC*. These proposals were submitted by the High Voltage Task Group (HVTG), which was appointed by the NEC Correlating Committee. The HVTG was charged to review all *NEC* requirements and/or the lack of requirements for circuits and systems operating at over 600 volts. The origin of this task group began at the end of the 2008 *NEC* cycle when a fine print note (FPN) [now Informational Notes] referencing the *National Electrical Safety Code* (NESC) was deleted from 90.2(A)(2). The substantiation provided in the proposal to delete the FPN stated that "conductors on the load side of the service point are under the purview of the *NEC*, and the FPN sending *NEC* users to the NESC creates serious confusion for designers, installers and the authority having jurisdiction (AHJ) working on premises wiring at voltage levels over 600 volts." The proposal was supported by comments that pointed out conflicts that place the AHJ in a very difficult position, and the FPN was deleted in the 2008 *NEC*. The NEC Correlating Committee then appointed the High Voltage Task Group to address issues with installations over 600 volts.

For the 2014 *NEC*, the work of the HVTG had the primary focus of raising the voltage threshold in the *NEC* from 600 to 1000 volts. This is not the first coordinated attempt to raise the voltage threshold in the *NEC*. The threshold was raised from 550 to 600 volts in the 1920 *NEC*. Finding substantiation on how

the *NEC* settled at 600 volts is difficult at best. In the 1990 *NEC* revision cycle, a NEC Correlating Committee task group tried unsuccessfully to raise the voltage threshold as it was difficult to substantiate a need to raise the voltage threshold at that time. Today, emerging technologies such as wind electric generating systems are operating at just over the 600-volt threshold. Solar photovoltaic (PV) systems are currently being installed at dc voltages over 600 volts up to and including 1000 volts, 1200 volts, 1500 volts, and 2000 volts dc. We need product standards and installation requirements to facilitate their safe installation. The electrical industry is changing rapidly and codes/standards must keep pace; otherwise, we could be faced with using the International Electrotechnical Commission (IEC) products and installation standards other than the *NEC*.

Moving the *NEC* threshold from 600 volts to 1000 volts will not, by itself, allow the immediate installation of systems at 1000 volts. Equipment must first be tested and found acceptable for use at the higher voltage(s). Nor will the testing and listing of equipment, by itself, allow for the installation of 1000-volt systems. The *NEC* must include prescriptive requirements to permit the installation of systems that operate over 600 but less than or equal to 1000 volts. It will take both tested/listed equipment and changes in the *NEC*, to meet the needs of these emerging technologies that society demands. Most *NEC* experts would agree that this is just the first step of many to recognize emerging technology with prescriptive requirements to ensure that these systems and products can be safely installed and inspected in accordance with the *NEC*.

Eighty-two percent of the proposals submitted to raise the voltage threshold were accepted in some form. Where a code-making panel felt there was a safety issue or where manufacturers did not want to pursue having their products evaluated at 1000 volts, the HVTG agreed to reject.

1

90.1(A)

Change at a Glance

Previous "Intention" of the *Code* was deleted and incorporated into "Purpose" of the *Code*.

Code Language

90.1 Purpose

(A) ~~**Practical Safeguarding**~~ **Purpose.** The purpose of this *Code* is the practical safeguarding of persons and property from hazards arising from the use of electricity. This *Code* is not intended as a design specification or an instruction manual for untrained persons.

(B) Adequacy. (Text unchanged; see *NEC* for complete text)

~~**(C) Intention.** This *Code* is not intended as a design specification or an instruction manual for untrained persons.~~

~~**(D)**~~ **(C) Relation to Other International Standards.** (Text unchanged; see *NEC* for complete text)

Proposal 1-3

Comment 1-1

90.1(A) Purpose (of the *Code*)

- The purpose of this *Code* is the practical safeguarding of persons and property from hazards arising from the use of electricity.
- This *Code* is not intended as a design specification or an instruction manual for untrained persons.
- Previous "Intention" of the *Code* was deleted and incorporated into "Purpose" of the *Code*.

2011 *NEC* Requirement

The "Practical Safeguarding" of the *Code* was covered in 90.1(A) with "Intention" of the *Code* covered at previous 90.1(C).

2014 *NEC* Change

Previous 90.1(C) dealing with the intent of the *Code* was deleted in its entirety and incorporated into 90.1(A), with this subsection being retitled "Purpose."

Analysis of Change

Section 90.1 relating the purpose of the *Code* was revised to contain a positive statement of the intent of the *Code*. By deleting subsection (C), which dealt with the intention of the *Code*, in its entirety and incorporating the deleted text into subsection (A), the purpose of the *Code* is consolidated into one paragraph that includes both its purpose and language limiting its intended use. The title of 90.1(A), was changed from "Practical Safeguarding," to "Purpose" to better reflect the objective of the *Code*. The previous language at 90.1(C) was a negative statement that told users of the *Code* what the *NEC* was not intended for. By combining the intent and the purpose of the *Code* into one subsection, there is a positive statement about the intention of the *NEC*.

90.8(B)

Change at a Glance

The words "in one circuit" in the last sentence has been deleted.

Code Language

90.8 Wiring Planning

(B) Number of Circuits in Enclosures. It is elsewhere provided in this *Code* that the number of wires and circuits confined in a single enclosure be varyingly restricted. Limiting the number of circuits in a single enclosure minimizes the effects from a short circuit or ground fault ~~in one circuit~~.

Proposal 1-19

2011 *NEC* Requirement

The previous language in 90.8(B) indicated that a short-circuit or ground-fault condition was limited to any one circuit within raceways or enclosures.

2014 *NEC* Change

The words "in one circuit" in the last sentence were deleted to clarify that a short-circuit or ground-fault condition is not limited to any one circuit within raceways or enclosures.

Analysis of Change

As previously written, 90.8(B) was misleading by indicating that a short-circuit or ground-fault condition was limited to just one circuit within a raceway or enclosure. The removal of the phrase "in one circuit" clarifies that a short-circuit or ground-fault condition is not limited to any one circuit within raceways or enclosures. The previous phrase "in one circuit" was excessive and unnecessary and added no clarity to the *Code*.

Article 100

Change at a Glance

Definitions of *adjustable speed drive* and *adjustable speed drive system* were relocated from 430.2 to Article 100 and revised for clarity.

Code Language

Article 100 Definitions: Adjustable Speed Drive and Adjustable Speed Drive System

Adjustable Speed Drive. Power conversion equipment that provides a means of adjusting the speed of an electric motor.

Informational Note: A variable frequency drive is one type of electronic adjustable speed drive that controls the rotational speed of an alternating current electric motor by controlling the frequency and voltage of the electrical power supplied to the motor.

Adjustable Speed Drive System. A combination of an adjustable speed drive, its associated motor(s), and auxiliary equipment.

Proposal 11-3, 11-75

2011 *NEC* Requirement

The existing definitions for *adjustable speed drive* and *adjustable speed drive system* were located at 430.2 in Article 430 for motors. An adjustable speed *drive* was defined as "A combination of the power converter, motor, and motor-mounted auxiliary devices such as encoders, tachometers, thermal switches and detectors, air blowers, heaters, and vibration sensors." An *adjustable-speed drive system* was defined as "An interconnected combination of equipment that provides a means of adjusting the speed of a mechanical load coupled to a motor. A drive system typically consists of an adjustable speed drive and auxiliary electrical apparatus."

2014 *NEC* Change

The definitions of *adjustable speed drive* and *adjustable speed drive system* were relocated from 430.2 to Article 100 and revised for clarity.

Analysis of Change

These terms were referenced in more locations in the *Code* than just Article 430; therefore, they needed to be defined in Article 100 rather than in 430.2. These definitions were also being proposed for Article 440 which deals with air conditioning and refrigeration equipment having adjustable speed drive systems (also known as variable speed drives) for use with hermetic refrigerant motor-compressors. These proposed revisions were being driven by technological advances in air-conditioning and refrigerating equipment to make the equipment more efficient. Electronic control and protection of motor compressors is becoming more common, while the use of traditional electromechanical control and protection of motor-compressors is becoming less desirable. CMP-11 revised the relocated definitions for completeness and clarity.

Article 100

Change at a Glance

Revision and relocation of the definitions of *motor control circuit* and *control circuit*.

Code Language

Article 100 Definitions: Control Circuit

~~Motor~~ Control Circuit. The circuit of a control apparatus or system that carries the electric signals directing the performance of the controller but does not carry the main power current.

Proposal 11-5, 11-8

Comment 15-79

Article 100 Definitions: Control Circuit

~~Motor~~ Control Circuit. The circuit of a control apparatus or system that carries the electric signals directing the performance of the controller but does not carry the main power current.

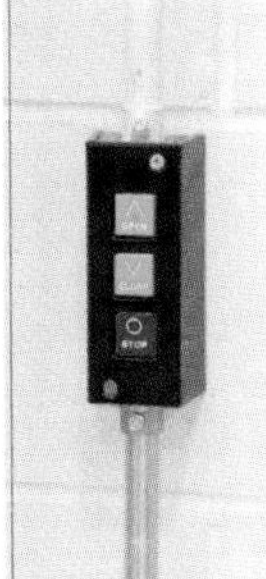

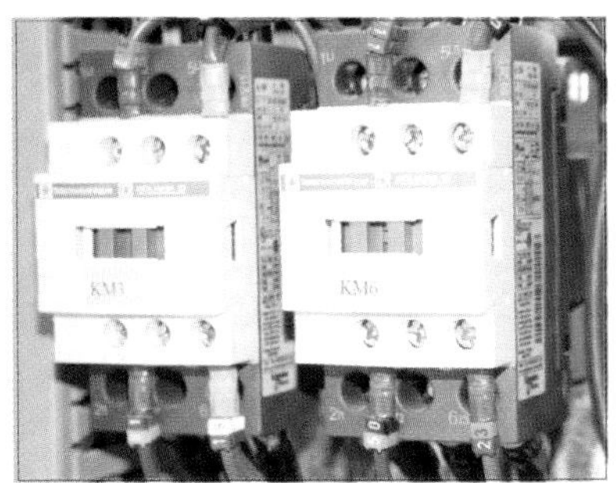

2011 *NEC* Requirement

The terms *motor control circuit* and *control circuit* were defined in three different articles of the *Code*.

409.2 Definitions: Control Circuit. The circuit of a control apparatus or system that carries the electric signals directing the performance of the controller but does not carry the main power current.

430.2 Definitions: Motor Control Circuit. The circuit of a control apparatus or system that carries the electric signals directing the performance of the controller but does not carry the main power current.

522.2 Definitions: Control Circuit. For the purposes of this article, the circuit of a control system that carries the electrical signals directing the performance of the controller but does not carry the main power current.

2014 *NEC* Change

The definition of *motor control circuit* was revised by removing the word "motor," making the term *control circuit,* which is now a new definition in Article 100 that applies to all control circuits, not just motor control circuits. The previous definitions in Article 409, Industrial Control Panels; Article 430, Motors, Motor Circuits, and Controllers; and Article 522, Control Systems for Permanent Amusement Attractions, have been removed.

Analysis of Change

These terms are referenced and used in several articles throughout the *NEC*; therefore, the definitions needed to be located in Article 100, as the *NEC Style Manual* directs that Article 100 shall contain definitions of terms that appear in two or more other articles of the *NEC*. CMP-11 removed the word "motor" from the definition for consistency and applicability with other sections of the *Code*.

Article 100

Change at a Glance

Definition of *selective coordination* was revised to improve clarity and readability.

Code Language

Article 100 Definitions: Coordination (Selective)

Localization of an overcurrent condition to restrict outages to the circuit or equipment affected, accomplished by the ~~choice~~ selection and installation of overcurrent protective devices and their ratings or settings for the full range of available overcurrents, from overload to the maximum available fault current, and for the full range of overcurrent protective device opening times associated with those overcurrents.

Proposal 10-5

Comment 10-2

Article 100 Definitions: Selective Coordination

Coordination (Selective). Localization of an overcurrent condition to restrict outages to the circuit or equipment affected, accomplished by the selection and installation of overcurrent protective devices and their ratings or settings for the full range of available overcurrents, from overload to the maximum available fault current, and for the full range of overcurrent protective device opening times associated with those overcurrents.

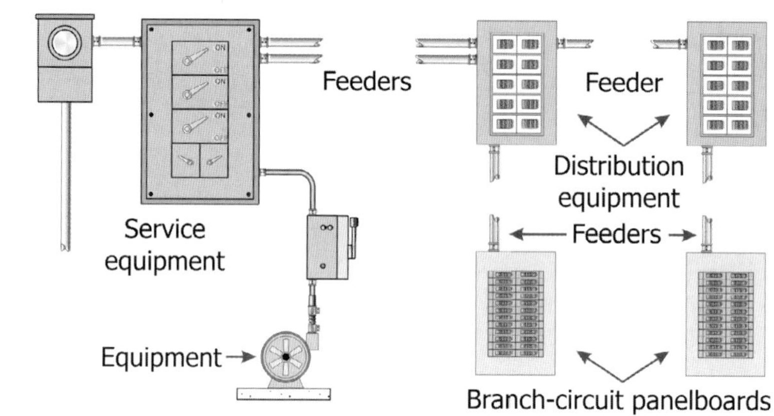

2011 *NEC* Requirement

The previous definition for *selective coordination* indicated to some users of the *Code* that selective coordination was a choice. It is not a choice that provides for a selectively coordinated system; rather, it's the "selection and installation" of the same.

2014 *NEC* Change

The word "choice" was replaced with "selection and installation" in the first part of the definition. Additional language was added to indicate that selective coordination is for the full range of overcurrents that the overcurrent protective devices could see and for whatever opening times it takes for the overcurrent protective devices to open at those overcurrent levels.

Analysis of Change

The definition of *selective coordination* was revised to improve clarity and readability by replacing the word "choice" with the phrase "selection and installation" of overcurrent protective devices and by adding the additional wording to the last part of the sentence. Equipment cannot be installed until it has been "selected," hence the word "selection" was added to clarify the importance of matching overcurrent protective device performance. This will allow for the interaction between two or among three or more overcurrent protective devices to properly isolate the faulted conditions without disrupting the total electrical system. The *NEC* needs to remain the quintessential document for the safety of an electrical installation. While the previous definition has served the electrical industry well for many years, it is now necessary to clarify the definition, not change the meaning. These changes to the definition add the specific clarity that is needed.

The new language accepted by CMP-10 is necessary to distinguish between the word "coordination" and the phrase "selective coordination." The word "coordination" is often used to describe the isolation of downstream overcurrent conditions over limited ranges of time and currents. At the same time, "selective coordination" is used to describe the isolation of downstream overcurrent conditions over the complete range of available overcurrents and the times associated with those overcurrents. In some situations covered by the *Code*, there is a need for "total" coordination for certain life-safety related loads, and it is for these life-safety related loads that some code-making panels have chosen to use the phrase "selective coordination" or "selectively coordinate," rather than simply the word "coordination" or "coordinate" (see 620.62, 700.27, 701.27, and 708.54 as examples). "Total coordination" is synonymous with the phrase "selective coordination." The words "coordinate" or "coordination" alone are simply not sufficiently specific enough to describe the concept as utilized in this revised definition.

Article 100

Change at a Glance

Definition of *device* was revised to indicate that a device is not a conductor.

Code Language

Article 100 Definitions: Device

A unit of an electrical system, other than a conductor, that carries or controls electric energy as its principal function.

Proposal 1-31a

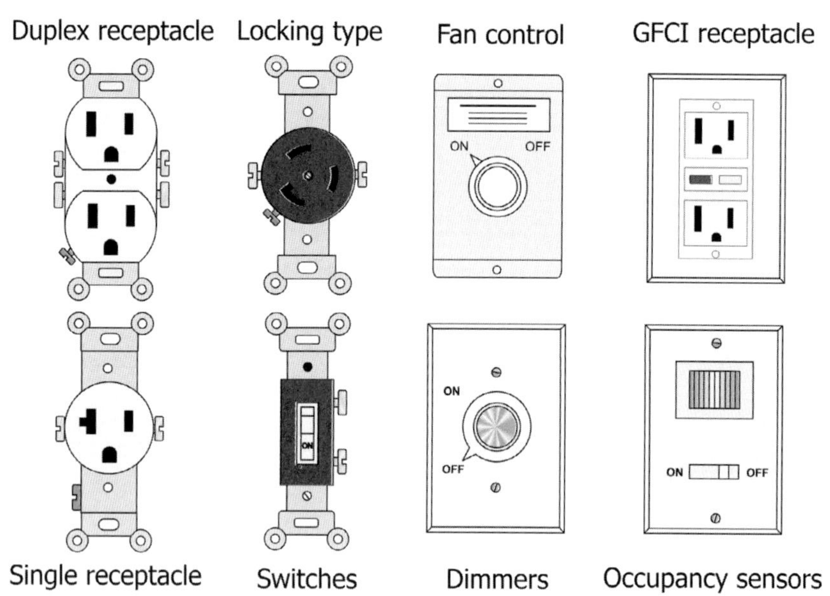

A device is a unit of an electrical system, other than a conductor, that carries or controls electric energy as its principal function.

2011 *NEC* Requirement

Previous definition could have indicated that a conductor is a device, as a conductor "carries or controls electric energy as its principal function."

2014 *NEC* Change

The phrase "other than a conductor" was inserted into the definition.

Analysis of Change

There are references to "devices" and references to "conductors" in several areas of the *Code*. The previous definition of device could have been interpreted as including a conductor as a device. While there are many devices that incorporate materials that serve as conductors (e.g., terminals), the ratings of devices are determined by their listing or markings, whereas the maximum useable ratings of a conductor is determined in accordance with the *NEC* and the allowable current or amperage ratings, etc. The revised language provides clear distinction between a device and a conductor.

Article 100

Change at a Glance

The definition for *effective ground-fault current path* was revised and relocated from 250.2 to Article 100.

Code Language

Article 100 Definitions: Effective Ground-Fault Current Path

An intentionally constructed, low-impedance electrically conductive path designed and intended to carry current under ground-fault conditions from the point of a ground fault on a wiring system to the electrical supply source and that facilitates the operation of the overcurrent protective device or ground-fault detectors ~~on high-impedance grounded systems~~.

Proposal 5-6, 5-46

Comment 5-14

Article 100 Definitions:
Effective Ground-Fault Current Path

Effective Ground-Fault Current Path. An intentionally constructed, low-impedance electrically conductive path designed and intended to carry current under ground-fault conditions from the point of a ground fault on a wiring system to the electrical supply source and that facilitates the operation of the overcurrent protective device or ground-fault detectors ~~on high-impedance grounded systems~~.

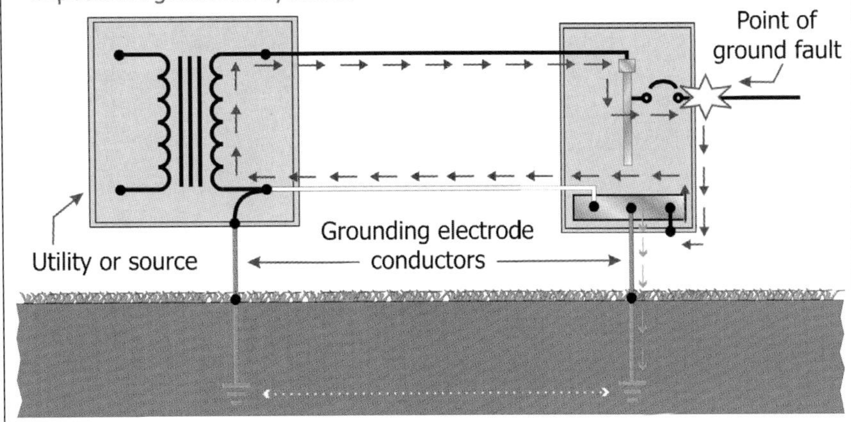

2011 *NEC* Requirement

The definition of *effective ground-fault current path* was located at 250.2 and indicated that an effective fault-current path facilitates ground-fault detector operation only on high-impedance grounded systems.

2014 *NEC* Change

The definition of an *effective ground-fault current path* was relocated to Article 100 and the phrase "on high-impedance grounded systems" was removed from the end of the previous definition.

Analysis of Change

The definition of *effective ground-fault current path* was relocated to Article 100 from 250.2 since the term is also found in other articles, not just in Article 250 [see 300.50(A)(1); 404.9(B); 427.23; 517.13(A); and 800.90(A)(1)(e) as examples]. At the end of the relocated definition, the phrase "on high-impedance grounded systems" was removed since an effective fault-current path facilitates ground-fault detector operation on systems other than just high-impedance grounded systems, such as ungrounded systems. Even though this deletion at the end of the definition was accepted, CMP-5 pointed out that an ungrounded system ground-fault detection system is based on magnitude and vector relationship at the source and not on the carrying of current from the location of ground fault to the source.

Article 100

Change at a Glance

Only intersystem bonding conductors are permitted to terminate on the *intersystem bonding termination.*

Code Language

Article 100 Definitions: Intersystem Bonding Termination

A device that provides a means for connecting intersystem bonding conductors for communications systems to the grounding electrode system.

Proposal 5-16

2011 *NEC* Requirement

The previous definition for *intersystem bonding termination* permitted *bonding conductors* to terminate on the intersystem bonding termination. This broad term of *bonding conductors* left users of the *Code* to speculate as to a wide variety of bonding conductors that could be terminated on the intersystem bonding termination.

2014 *NEC* Change

The term *bonding conductors* was revised to *intersystem bonding termination* to clarify the type of bonding conductors that are permitted to terminate on the intersystem bonding termination.

Analysis of Change

Revision to existing definition of *intersystem bonding termination* will make it clear that other bonding conductors should not be connected to the intersystem bonding termination. The revision provides clarity and correlation with the text of 250.94, Bonding of Other Systems. Not all types of bonding conductors should be connected to the intersystem bonding termination. The intersystem bonding termination is specifically for the connection of intersystem bonding conductors of such "other systems" as communication circuits.

Another proposal (Proposal 5-17) was submitted to CMP-5 seeking permission to terminate "other" bonding conductors — such as a bonding conductor for gas piping, or such as corrugated stainless steel tubing (CSST) — to the intersystem bonding termination. CMP-5 rejected this proposal citing that "this device (intersystem bonding termination) is intended for use with intersystem bonding conductors for communication systems only."

Article 100

Change at a Glance

New Informational Note was added to the existing definition to provide examples of premises wiring systems.

Code Language

Article 100 Definitions: Premises Wiring (System)

Interior and exterior wiring, including power, lighting, control, and signal circuit wiring together with all their associated hardware, fittings, and wiring devices, both permanently and temporarily installed. This includes (a) wiring from the service point or power source to the outlets or (b) wiring from and including the power source to the outlets where there is no service point. Such wiring does not include wiring internal to appliances, luminaires, motors, controllers, motor control centers, and similar equipment.

Informational Note: Power sources include, but are not limited to, interconnected or stand-alone batteries, solar photovoltaic systems, other distributed generation systems, or generators.

Proposal 1-61

2011 *NEC* Requirement

2011 *NEC* provided a definition of *premises wiring (system)* but did not include an Informational Note to provide examples of same.

2014 *NEC* Change

A new Informational Note was added after the existing definition to offer examples of premises wiring systems.

Analysis of Change

This note provides examples of premises wiring system for additional clarification such as batteries, photovoltaic systems, interconnected power sources, and stand-alone generators. According to the substantiation submitted, some members and contributors to Underwriters Laboratories (UL) Standards Technical Panel (STP) for UL 2201 *Portable Engine-Generator Assemblies* have contended that portable generators in stand-alone use are not premises wiring. This new Informational Note clarifies the premises wiring system definition and includes examples of power sources that might not be from a serving utility, including generators.

The definition of *premises wiring (system)* was revised in the 2008 *NEC* process to remove a list of example sources that was very similar to the list of examples in this new Informational Note. At that time, CMP-1 indicated in the panel statement that premises wiring can exist on the supply side of a separately derived system, such as supply conductors originating from another system. CMP-1 also indicated that if there is no service point, all wiring is premises wiring. This clarification more closely aligns with the Occupational Safety and Health Administration (OSHA) definition of a premises wiring system.

On the subject of portable stand-alone generators, portable generators are electrical equipment. As such, use of portable generators is included in the purpose of the *NEC* to provide practical safeguarding of persons and property from hazards arising from the use of electricity. Use of portable generators is also under the scope of the *NEC* based on 90.2(A), which covers the installation of electrical equipment. Additionally, 250.34, Portable and Vehicle-Mounted Generators and Article 590, Temporary Installations clearly contain requirements addressing the use of portable generators. These requirements clearly fall under the confines of the definition of premises wiring systems.

Article 100

Change at a Glance

The definition of *raceway* was revised by removing the laundry list of raceways listed in the previous definition.

Code Language

Article 100 Definitions: Raceway

An enclosed channel of ~~metal~~ metallic or nonmetallic materials designed expressly for holding wires, cables, or busbars, with additional functions as permitted in this *Code*. ~~Raceways include, but are not limited to, rigid metal conduit, rigid nonmetallic conduit, intermediate metal conduit, liquidtight flexible conduit, flexible metallic tubing, flexible metal conduit, electrical nonmetallic tubing, electrical metallic tubing, underfloor raceways, cellular concrete floor raceways, cellular metal floor raceways, surface raceways, wireways, and busways.~~

Informational Note: A raceway is identified within specific article definitions.

Proposal 8-24

Comment 8-3

2011 *NEC* Requirement

The definition of *raceway* included a list of wiring methods that are considered raceways.

2014 *NEC* Change

As the laundry list of wiring methods considered to be a raceway included in the previous definition was incomplete, this list of wiring methods was removed from the definition of a raceway. A new Informational Note was added to indicate that the definition of a raceway can be identified within the specific wiring method article definition.

Analysis of Change

The definition of *raceway* was revised by removing the laundry list of raceways from the previous definition as this list was incomplete. Identification of each individual raceway can be done in each raceway wiring method article and is not dependent on an incomplete list in this definition. The list of raceways in the previous definition was problematic in that specific raceways were identified as raceways, while other raceway systems were not identified (enclosed channel) for holding of conductors. Identification of a raceway within its own article will clarify what a raceway is and how it is to be applied to that particular article. This should also help the code-user to understand the differences between a raceway and a support system for a raceway or an area for supplemental wiring space.

In the definition, the word "metal" was changed to "metallic" for consistency throughout the *NEC*, because some locations use the word "metal" while other locations use the word "metallic." As an example, metallic is used at 366.2 to describe a metallic auxiliary gutter. It should be noted that metallic appeared in 375 locations in the 2011 *NEC*. CMP-8 issued a statement of support for the task group to correlate the words "metal" and "metallic" in the 2014 *NEC*.

The following is a list of article definitions that were changed or revised due to the revised definition of *raceway* in Article 100 of the 2014 *NEC*:

352.2
rigid polyvinyl chloride conduit (PVC) removed the word "conduit" and added *raceway* within the definition (ROP 8-63).

354.2
nonmetallic underground conduit with conductors (NUCC) removed the word "conduit" and added *raceway* in the definition (ROP 8-73)

355.2
reinforced thermosetting resin conduit (RTRC)] removed the word "conduit" and added *raceway* within the definition (ROP 8-75).

356.2
liquidtight flexible nonmetallic conduit (LFNC)] removed the word "conduit" and added *raceway* within the definition at (2) and (3) (ROP 8-80).

368.2
busway inserted the term "A *raceway* consisting of a…" at the beginning of the definition (ROP 8-105).

376.2
metal wireways removed the word "wireway" and inserted *raceway* for the housing and protection of electrical conductors (ROP 8-132).

378.2
nonmetallic wireways removed the word "wireway" and inserted *raceway* for the housing and protection of electrical conductors (ROP 8-144).

Article 100

Change at a Glance

Revised definition to prohibit "the use of tools" when equipment is required to be *readily accessible.*

Code Language

Article 100 Definitions: Accessible, Readily (Readily Accessible)

Capable of being reached quickly for operation, renewal, or inspections without requiring those to whom ready access is requisite to actions such as; to use tools, to climb over or remove obstacles, or to resort to portable ladders, and so forth.

Proposal 1-24

Comment 1-13

Article 100 Definitions: Readily Accessible

Accessible, Readily (Readily Accessible). Capable of being reached quickly for operation, renewal, or inspections without requiring those to whom ready access is requisite to use tools, to climb over or remove obstacles, or to resort to portable ladders, and so forth.

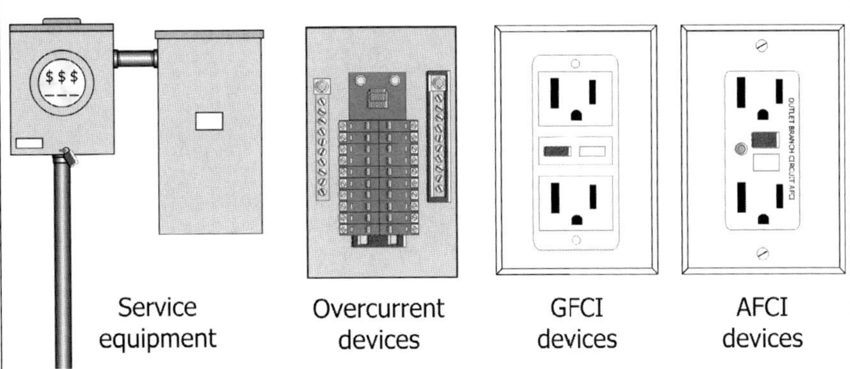

2011 *NEC* Requirement

The previous definition of *readily accessible* prohibited persons from having to resort to climb over or remove obstacles or resort to the use of portable ladders, etc., in order to gain access to *readily accessible* equipment.

2014 *NEC* Change

Having to resort to the use of tools was added to the prohibited provisions in order for someone to gain access to *readily accessible* equipment.

Analysis of Change

The *Code* makes a clear distinction between electrical equipment required to be *accessible* and equipment required to be *readily accessible*. In order for equipment to be *readily accessible*, a person should be able to walk right up to that piece of equipment and gain access without having to climb a ladder, remove a ceiling tile, crawl through an attic, etc. Furthermore, the need to use a tool to reach a piece of equipment for operation, renewal, or inspection may make it accessible, but not necessarily readily accessible. The need to use a tool, even one as simple as a screw driver, would add another level of action that would impede or delay this ready access.

One example given in the substantiation for this revision to this long-standing definition was an issue regarding the disconnecting means encountered on occasion for some types of built-in disconnect switch within different types of HVAC equipment. This built-in disconnect is sometimes located behind a panel that requires the use of a screwdriver to open. This type of situation can lead to debates as to whether or not this type of built-in disconnect meets the requirements of 440.14, which calls for a readily accessible disconnecting means to be located within sight from air-conditioning or refrigeration equipment. This revision to the definition of *readily accessible* should clarify that this type of built-in disconnect located behind an access panel would not meet the requirements for readily accessible equipment.

Article 100

Change at a Glance

A new definition for the term *retrofit kit* was added to Article 100.

Code Language

Article 100 Definitions:

Retrofit Kit

A general term for a complete subassembly of parts and devices for field conversion of utilization equipment.

Proposal 18-9

Comment 18-4, 18-5

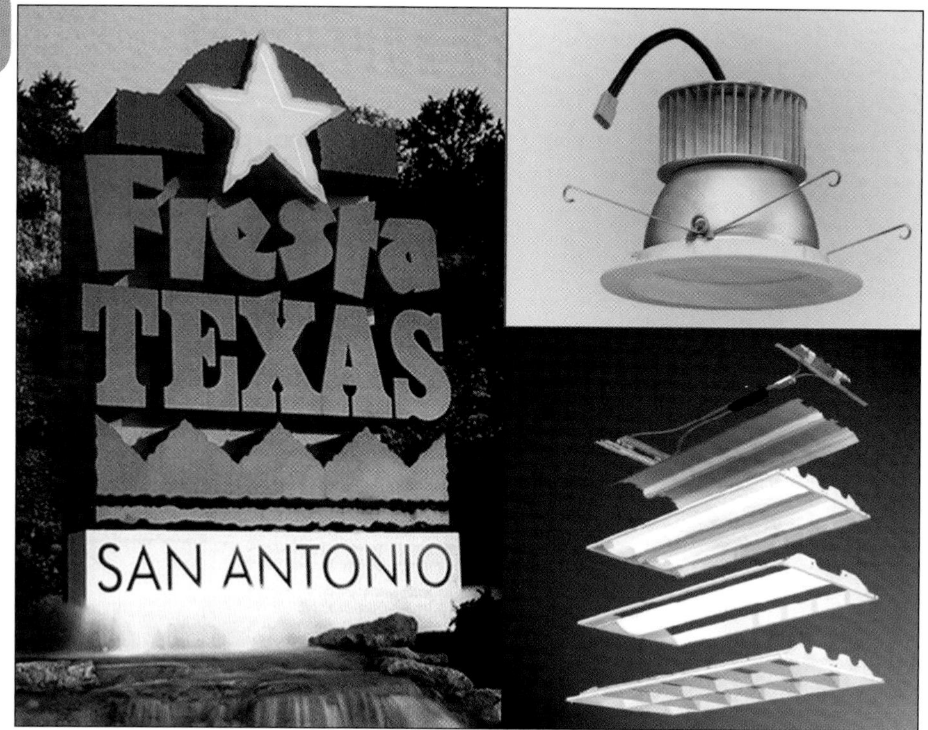

2011 *NEC* Requirement

Neither the term *retrofit kit* nor a definition of the same existed in the 2011 *NEC*.

2014 *NEC* Change

A new definition of the term *retrofit kit* was added to Article 100, as this term applies to LED listed retrofit kits used for luminaires and signs as referenced by new requirements in Articles 410 and 600.

Analysis of Change

Extensive upgrades are underway in the sign and lighting industries to achieve greater energy efficiency in signs and luminaires by replacing in-place illumination systems with light emitting diodes (LED) technology. This will incorporate field modifications of signs or luminaires. Field modifications of utilization equipment usually require a field evaluation by a qualified nationally recognized testing laboratory (NRTL). Testing laboratories have developed protocols for these field conversions, such that when done within the testing laboratory parameters, these field conversion *retrofit kits* do not compromise the safety profile of the listed sign or luminaire. As an example, to ensure that the parts are compatible with the field modification, UL requires all the parts for luminaire and sign conversions to be assembled into a kit that UL labels as Classified. A definition of *retrofit kits* in the *NEC* will provide a basis for, (1) use of conversion subassemblies, (2) inclusion in applicable ANSI / UL standards for manufacturers of the retrofit kits, (3) a basis for the AHJ to approve a field-modified field conversion in listed signs and luminaires, and (4) their use by the installer.

The original proposal for this definition was to limit these retrofit kits to signs and luminaires. CMP-18 correctly pointed out that retrofit kits are not unique to luminaires, signs and outline lighting.

Article 100

Change at a Glance

The definition of *separately derived system* was revised to clarify that the required grounding and bonding may create a connection between systems and that separately derived systems are not services.

Code Language

Article 100 Definitions: Separately Derived System

~~A premises wiring system whose power is derived from a source of electric energy or equipment~~ An electrical source, other than a service, having no direct connection(s) to circuit conductors of any other electrical source other than those established by grounding and bonding connections. ~~Such systems have no direct connection from circuit conductors of one system to circuit conductors of another system, other than connections through the earth, metal enclosures, metallic raceways, or equipment grounding conductors.~~

Proposal 5-20, 5-22, 5-23

Comment 5-6

Article 100 Definitions: Separately Derived System

Separately Derived System. An electrical source, other than a service, having no direct connection(s) to circuit conductors of any other electrical source other than those established by grounding and bonding connections.

Transformers

Generators

2011 *NEC* Requirement

The previous definition implied that any wiring system whose source is derived from a service cannot be considered a separately derived system and that another source would be needed in order to have a separately derived system. However, the fact is a wiring system supplied through a transformer that is not supplied by the utility but with its source derived from a service can indeed be a separately derived system if other requirements of separately derived system are met (i.e., no direct connection from circuit conductors of one system to circuit conductors of another system). The previous definition also described these "no direct connection from circuit conductors of one system to circuit conductors of another system" as being "the earth, metal enclosures, metallic raceways, or equipment grounding conductors."

2014 *NEC* Change

The revised definition was simplified and indicates that the required grounding and bonding may create a connection between systems and that this condition does not disqualify this system from being a separately derived system. This revised definition also clarifies that a separately derived systems is not a service but can have its source derived from a service.

Analysis of Change

The definition of *separately derived system* was revised to clarify that the required grounding and bonding may create a connection between systems and still qualify as a separately derived system, Further clarification states that separately derived systems are not services but can have their source derived from a service. For example, 250.30(A)(6) permits a common grounding electrode conductor to be installed for multiple separately derived systems. Under the previous definition, when the grounded conductors of two or more separately derived systems were connected together by the grounding electrode conductor, the separate systems are no longer separately derived systems. This revised definition is intended to correct that inaccuracy.

Article 100

Change at a Glance

The definition of *substation* was relocated from 225.2 to Article 100 and revised for clarity.

Code Language

Article 100 Definitions: Substation

An enclosed assemblage of equipment (e.g., switches, interrupting devices, circuit breakers, buses, and transformers) ~~under the control of qualified persons~~, through which electric energy is passed for the purpose of distribution, switching, or modifying its characteristics.

Proposal 4-9, 4-10, 4-13, 9-8a

Comment 9-5, 9-6, 9-7

2011 *NEC* Requirement

The definition of *substation* was located at 225.2 and applied only to outside branch circuits and feeders.

2014 *NEC* Change

The definition of *substation* was relocated to Article 100 as this term is used throughout numerous articles in the *NEC,* and the definition was revised for clarity.

Analysis of Change

The term and definition of *substation* apply to more than just outside branch circuits and feeders; thus, the definition was relocated from 225.2 to Article 100 as this term is used throughout numerous articles in the *NEC*. This relocation was a companion proposal to transfer the text in previous 225.70 for substations to Article 490 covering equipment over 1000 volts (previously 600 volts). By this transfer of text, the jurisdiction of the definition of *substation* is now assigned to CMP-9. CMP-9 has acted to include within Article 490 numerous substation provisions in the 2014 *NEC* code cycle. The wording of the revised and relocated definition is based on the text previously located at 225.2.

The phrase "under the control of qualified persons" was removed from the definition of *substation* as this phrase would constitute a requirement within a definition, which is in violation of the *NEC Style Manual.* The original proposal also would have limited the application of the term and definition of a substation to outdoor applications. CMP-9 disagreed as the term *substation* applies to prefabricated metal-enclosed equipment installed indoors as well as field fabricated outdoor equipment.

Article 100

Change at a Glance

The definition of *metal-enclosed power switchgear* was revised to *switchgear*.

Code Language

Article 100 Definitions:
~~Metal-Enclosed Power~~ Switchgear

An ~~A switchgear~~ assembly completely enclosed on all sides and top with sheet metal (except for ventilating openings and inspection windows) and containing primary power circuit switching, interrupting devices, or both, with buses and connections. The assembly may include control and auxiliary devices. Access to the interior of the enclosure is provided by doors, removable covers, or both. ~~Metal-enclosed power switchgear is available in non-arc-resistant or arc-resistant constructions.~~

Informational Note: All switchgear subject to *NEC* requirements is metal enclosed. Switchgear rated 1000 volts or less may be identified as "low-voltage power circuit breaker switchgear." Switchgear rated over 1000 volts may be identified as "metal-enclosed switchgear" or "metal-clad switchgear." Switchgear is available in non-arc-resistant or arc-resistant constructions.

Proposal 9-7

Comment 9-2, 9-3

2011 *NEC* Requirement

Article 100 included a definition for *metal-enclosed power switchgear.*

2014 *NEC* Change

A revision to the definition for *metal-enclosed power switchgear* removed the words "metal-enclosed power" to simplify the new term to simply *switchgear.* This new term will address all types of switchgear, and a new Informational Note includes a list of switchgear types to which the revised definition will apply.

Analysis of Change

The existing definition for *metal-enclosed power switchgear* was modified and retitled *switchgear* to make it inclusive of all types of switchgear under the purview of the *NEC*. This action allows the use of the generic term in all locations where *switchboard* is already mentioned and in other locations where it is appropriate. As required by the *NEC Style Manual*, explanatory material was removed from the definition and inserted into a new Informational Note that now follows the revised definition. *Switchgear* includes "metal-enclosed low-voltage power circuit breaker switchgear," "metal-clad switchgear," and "metal-enclosed interrupter switchgear" according to ANSI C37.20 documents. The listing mark on "metal-enclosed low-voltage power circuit breaker switchgear" reads "Low-Voltage Power Circuit Breaker Switchgear."

See also companion CMP-9 Proposal 9-152b to change references in Article 490 from "metal-enclosed" and "metal-clad" to just *switchgear*. There are also a large group of proposals from CMP-9 to change similar references in the remainder of the *Code*. For complete incorporation of the term *switchgear* within Article 408, see panel action on CMP-9 Proposal 9-103a. See also the panel statement and panel action on Proposal 9-104 and 9-104a.

110.16

Change at a Glance

Revision to Arc-Flash Hazard Warning adds the words "or factory" to the rule to clarify that the required arc-flash warning label could be applied in the field or at the factory by a manufacturer.

Code Language

110.16 Arc-Flash Hazard Warning

Electrical equipment, such as switchboards, switchgear, panelboards, industrial control panels, meter socket enclosures, and motor control centers, that are in other than dwelling units, and are likely to require examination, adjustment, servicing, or maintenance while energized shall be field or factory marked to warn qualified persons of potential electric arc flash hazards. The marking shall meet the requirements in 110.21(B) and shall be located so as to be clearly visible to qualified persons before examination, adjustment, servicing, or maintenance of the equipment.

Proposal 1-102, 1-105, 1-107, 1-108, 9-14a

Comment 1-47, 1-52, 1-53, 1-54, 1-56

110.16 Arc-Flash Hazard Warning

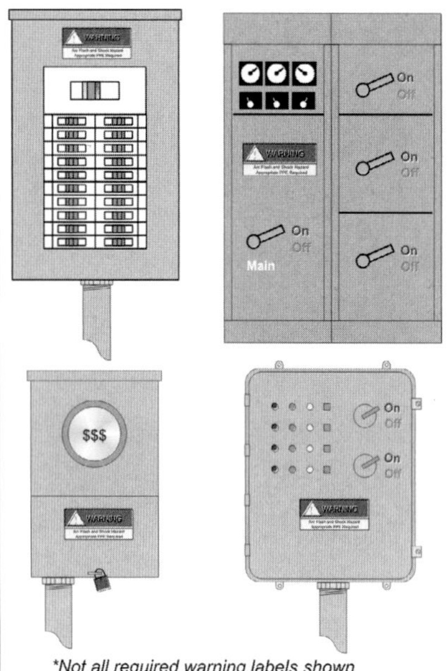

*Not all required warning labels shown

WARNING
Arc Flash and Shock Hazard
Appropriate PPE Required

- Arc-flash warning label is required to be applied in the field or factory.
- This rule applies to equipment such as: switchboards, switchgear, panelboards, motor control centers, industrial control panels, meter socket enclosures, and enclosed circuit breakers.
- Applies only to equipment in other than dwelling occupancies.

2011 *NEC* Requirement

This arc-flash warning label to be applied to electrical equipment that is likely to require examination, adjustment, servicing, or maintenance while energized was required to be a "field marking" to be applied by the installer.

2014 *NEC* Change

The words "or factory" were added to 110.16 to allow the required arc-flash warning label to be applied in the field by the installer or at the factory by a manufacturer.

Analysis of Change

The provisions at 110.16 to require a field marking or warning label on electrical equipment to warn qualified persons of the potential electrical arc-flash hazards involved when working on that electrical equipment while energized were added during the 2002 *NEC* code cycle. The requirement for this warning label to be applied in the field by the installer seemed to be related to industry concerns that electrical equipment manufacturers might not be able to include the required arc-flash markings in time for early adoptions of the 2002 *NEC*.

Currently, some electrical equipment manufacturers are providing the arc-flash warning labels on some of their products. When the arc-flash warning or marking is provided by the manufacturer, an additional "field marking" does not seem to add value or safety to the installation.

At the time this requirement was placed in the 2002 *NEC*, some *Code* authorities argued that this arc-flash warning had to be installed in the field as the manufacturer had no reasonable idea how or where their electrical equipment (such as a switchgear or panelboard) would be installed. Allowing field or factory marking to be an acceptable method of meeting this arc-flash warning does not place any additional burden or requirement on manufacturers while still allowing the

110.16

Continued

installer the ability to apply this warning label or marking indentifying any unique field provisions.

Switchgear was added to the list of likely electrical equipment requiring an arc-flash warning label. This action corresponds to the action taken by CMP-9 to place a revised definition of what used to be *metal-enclosed power switchgear* in Article 100. This change renamed the defined term as *switchgear* and resulted in numerous changes throughout the *Code,* revising or adding this newly defined term. A new reference to the code-wide warning label provisions at 110.21(B) was also added at 110.16.

110.21(B)

Change at a Glance

New subsection for Field-Applied Hazard Markings was added for specific requirements for warning labels and similar markings required elsewhere in the *Code*.

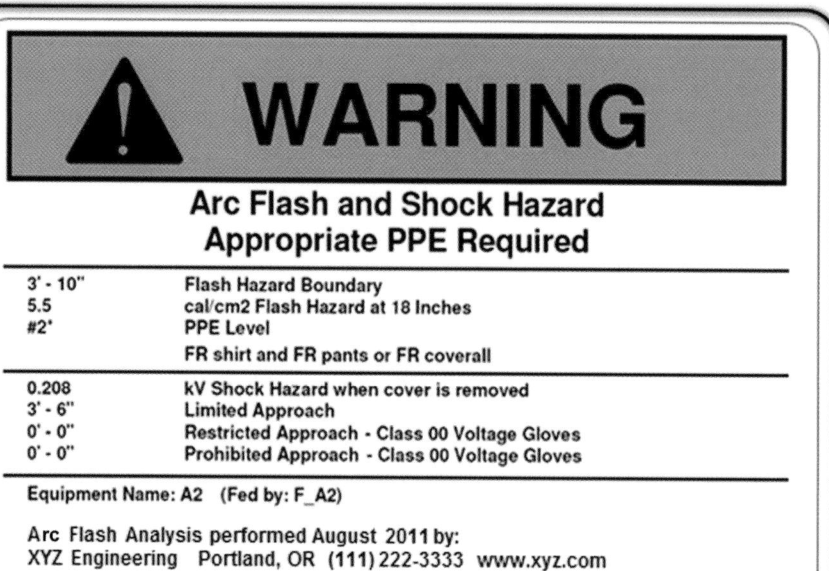

Code Language

110.21 Marking

(A) Manufacturer Markings. The manufacturer's name, trademark, or other descriptive marking by which the organization responsible for the product can be identified shall be placed on all electrical equipment. Other markings that indicate voltage, current, wattage, or other ratings shall be provided as specified elsewhere in this *Code*. The marking or label shall be of sufficient durability to withstand the environment involved.

(B) Field-Applied Hazard Markings. Where caution, warning, or danger signs or labels are required by this *Code*, the labels shall meet the following requirements:

(1) The marking shall adequately warn of the hazard using effective words and/or colors and/or symbols.

Informational Note: ANSI Z535.4-2011, Product Safety Signs and Labels, provides guidelines for suitable font sizes, words, colors, symbols, and location requirements for labels.

2011 *NEC* Requirement

The 2011 *NEC* contained several requirements for warning labels, caution and/or danger signs, and similar field-applied hazard markings throughout the *Code*. At the majority of these hazard markings, the requirements were the basically the same — such as permanently affixed, durability, etc. These hazard markings were repeated dozens of times throughout the 2011 *NEC*.

2014 *NEC* Change

A new 110.21(B), Field-Applied Hazard Markings, was added for specific one-stop requirements for warning labels and similar markings required elsewhere in the *Code*. Companion proposals and comments were submitted where the caution, warning, and danger markings or signs are required throughout the *NEC* with references back to this new hazard marking requirement in Article 110.

Analysis of Change

A new 110.21(B), Field-Applied Hazard Markings, adds specific requirements for warning labels and similar markings where required or specified elsewhere in the *Code*. The *NEC* contains several requirements for hazard markings to be installed on wiring methods and equipment. These required labels or markings typically include one of the following hazard commands: DANGER, WARNING, or CAUTION. This new requirement will incorporate uniformity to rules where additional direction and guidance were needed. These hazard markings, signs or labels should meet the requirements in ANSI Z535.4 for suitable font sizes, words, colors, symbols and location requirements for labels. This ANSI document is referenced in the new Informational Note following this new requirement.

The new exception to list item 2 is an effort to allow handwritten information to remain accurate on some labels or markings that may be subject to periodical change, such as labels required by 110.22 for series rated systems and by 110.24 for available fault current.

110.21(B)

Continued

Code Language
110.21 Marking

(A) Manufacturer Markings. The manufacturer's name, trademark, or other descriptive marking by which the organization responsible for the product can be identified shall be placed on all electrical equipment. Other markings that indicate voltage, current, wattage, or other ratings shall be provided as specified elsewhere in this *Code*. The marking or label shall be of sufficient durability to withstand the environment involved.

(B) Field-Applied Hazard Markings. Where caution, warning, or danger signs or labels are required by this *Code*, the labels shall meet the following requirements:
(1) The marking shall adequately warn of the hazard using effective words and/or colors and/or symbols.

110.21(B) Field-Applied Hazard Markings

DANGER indicates a hazardous situation which, if not avoided, will result in death or serious injury.

WARNING indicates a hazardous situation which, if not avoided, could result in death or serious injury.

CAUTION indicates a hazardous situation which, if not avoided, may result in minor or moderate injury.

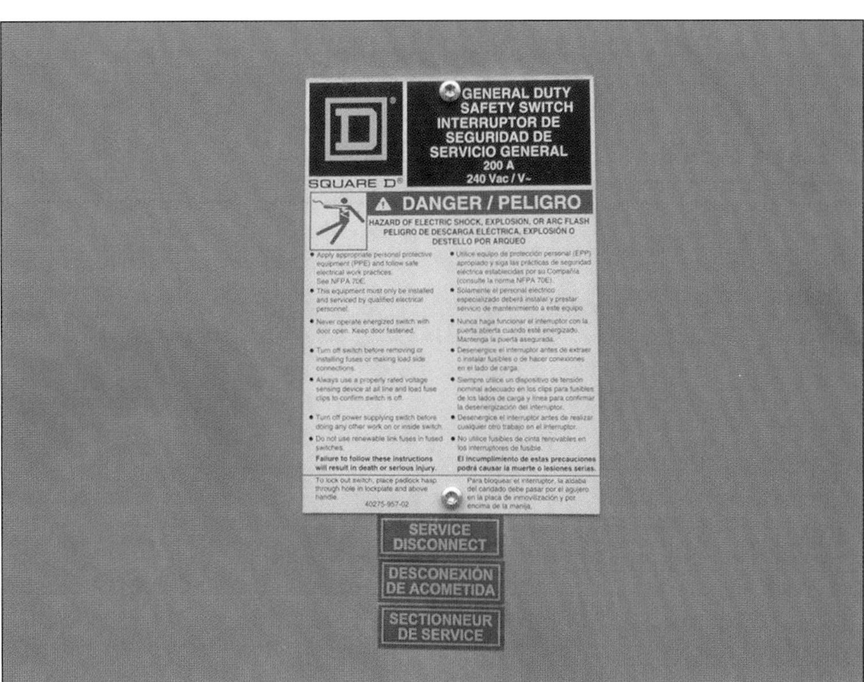

110.24(A)IN

Change at a Glance

New Informational Note was added to clarify that the available fault current markings are for equipment rating purposes and not for arc-flash hazard analysis as required by NFPA 70E.

Code Language

110.24 Available Fault Current

(A) Field Marking. Service equipment in other than dwelling units shall be legibly marked in the field with the maximum available fault current. The field marking(s) shall include the date the fault current calculation was performed and be of sufficient durability to withstand the environment involved.

Informational Note: The available fault current marking(s) addressed in 110.24 are related to required short-circuit current ratings of equipment. NFPA 70E-2012, *Standard for Electrical Safety in the Workplace*, provides assistance in determining severity of potential exposure, planning safe work practices, and selecting personal protective equipment.

Proposal 1-121, 1-124, 1-125

Comment 1-64, 1-66

110.24(A) Available Fault Current

Non-dwelling unit service equipment required to be field-marked with the amount of available fault current when installed or modified

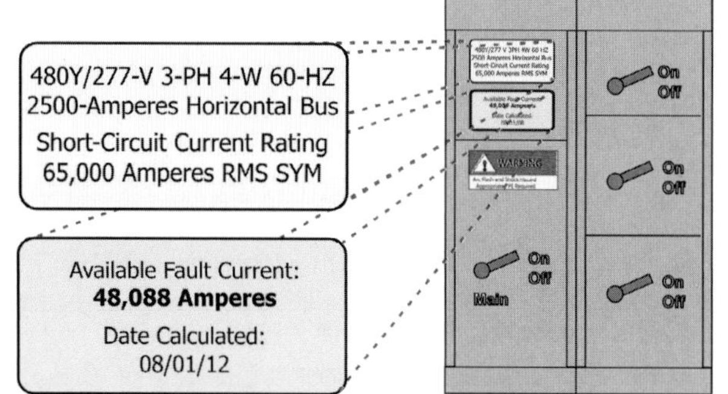

Service equipment in other than dwelling units shall be legibly marked in the field with the maximum available fault current

The field marking(s) shall include the date the fault current calculation was performed and be of sufficient durability to withstand the environment involved

Informational Note: The available fault current marking(s) are related to required short-circuit current ratings of equipment *(not NFPA 70E)*

2011 *NEC* Requirement

The requirement for nondwelling unit service equipment to be legibly marked with the maximum available fault current was added to the 2011 *NEC*. The field marking(s) are required to include the date the fault-current calculation was performed and to be of sufficient durability to withstand the environment involved.

2014 *NEC* Change

A new Informational Note was added to make it clear that the available fault current markings are for short-circuit current ratings and equipment rating purposes and not for arc-flash hazard analysis as required by NFPA 70E.

Analysis of Change

As noted above, maximum available fault-current markings were added in the 2011 *NEC* code cycle. During this same *Code* cycle, comments were submitted to address concerns about these available fault-current markings being used or required for arc-flash hazard analysis studies related to workplace safety as covered in NFPA 70E. This caused confusion for some users of the *Code* as to the intent of this requirement. Was this 110.24(A) requirement intended for maximum available fault current at a service, or for the calculation of energy that is used to apply rules in NFPA 70E?

This new Informational Note clarifies that the available fault-current markings required at 110.24 are related to proper application of electrical equipment with regard to the maximum level of available fault current. These markings are a starting point for installers and enforcers of the *Code* when they are selecting proper equipment with sufficient interrupting ratings and short-circuit ratings for the application involved. This value of available fault current marked on the equipment should not be used for arc-flash hazard analysis studies covered by NFPA 70E addressing workplace safety.

110.25

Change at a Glance

New 110.25 was added in Article 110 to provide consistent requirements at one location for lockable disconnecting means rules.

Code Language

110.25 Lockable Disconnecting Means

Where a disconnecting means is required to be lockable open, elsewhere in this *Code*, it shall be capable of being locked in the open position. The provisions for locking shall remain in place with or without the lock installed.

Exception: *Cord-and-plug connection locking provision shall not be required to remain in place without the lock installed.*

Proposal 1-130, 1-32, 1-112, 1-116, 1-119

Comment 1-76

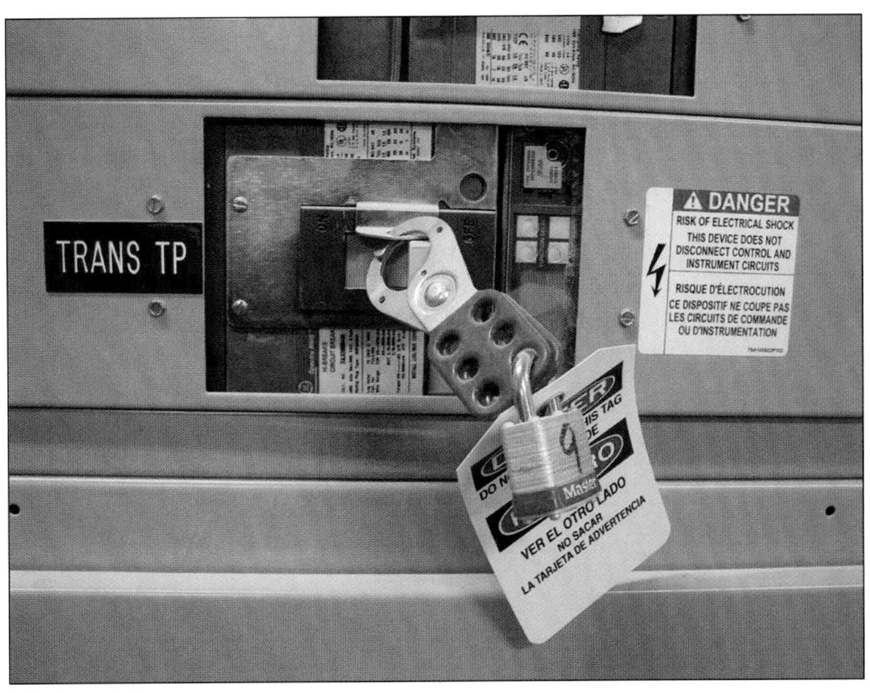

2011 *NEC* Requirement

Separate rules for lockable disconnecting means were located in several locations throughout the *Code*. These separate and individual lockable disconnecting means rules varied widely in their uniformity.

2014 *NEC* Change

A new 110.25, Lockable Disconnecting Means, was added to provide consistent requirements for a lockable disconnecting means.

Analysis of Change

A new section was added to Article 110 to provide a one-stop consistent requirement for rules pertaining to lockable disconnecting means. Requirements for a disconnecting means to be "lockable in the open position" existed in a number of locations in the 2011 *NEC*. This new section will consolidate these numerous requirements throughout the *Code* into one location in Article 110 for uniformity and clarity. This proposal had forty-six companion proposals to remove text from all sections that provide the specific requirements for lockable disconnecting means throughout the *Code*. The proposal along with the companion proposals were developed by a Usability Task Group assigned by the NEC Correlating Committee (NEC CC), with a proposed mission to identify the numerous locations in the 2011 *NEC* that referenced lockable disconnecting means requirements.

This requirement consists of more than just disconnecting and locking electrical power sources. It is intended to facilitate a lockout/tagout situation. It is equally important to ensure that the means for placing the lock remain in place, with or without the lock installed. The concept required by this new section is necessary to provide correlation throughout the *NEC* with respect to the capability of placing a lock on a disconnecting means to secure it in the open position. As stated above, several companion proposals were submitted throughtout the *NEC* containing references to this new requirement in Article 110.

110.25

Continued

A new exception was also added to distinguish between lockable disconnecting means for permanently connected equipment and lockable disconnecting means for cord- and plug-connected equipment where the attachment plug serves as the disconnecting means. Where the attachment plug serves as the disconnecting means, the provision for locking typically consists of a lockable "clamshell" that surrounds the attachment plug, thereby precluding energizing of the cord- and plug-connected equipment being serviced. When not locking out such equipment, the clamshell is stored on the flexible cord above the cord cap. This "provision for locking" therefore does not "remain in place ... without the lock installed." Many requirements for disconnecting means permit attachment plugs to serve as the disconnecting means for cord-and-plug-connected equipment.

110.26(C)(3)

Change at a Glance

The ampere value related to provisions for "Personnel doors" for "Entrance to and Egress from Working Space" was lowered to 800 amperes from 1200 amperes. The term *listed panic hardware* replaces the previous list of specific hardware provided at this requirement.

Code Language

110.26 Spaces About Electrical Equipment

Access and working space shall be provided and maintained about all electrical equipment to permit ready and safe operation and maintenance of such equipment.

(C) Entrance to and Egress from Working Space.

(3) Personnel Doors. Where equipment rated 800 ~~1200~~ A or more that contains overcurrent devices, switching devices, or control devices is installed and there is a personnel door(s) intended for entrance to and egress from the working space less than 7.6 m (25 ft) from the nearest edge of the working space, the door(s) shall open in the direction of egress and be equipped with listed panic hardware ~~bars, pressure plates, or other devices that are normally latched but open under simple pressure~~.

110.33 Entrance to Enclosures and Access to Working Space (Over 600 Volts, Nominal).

110.26(C)(3) Personnel Doors

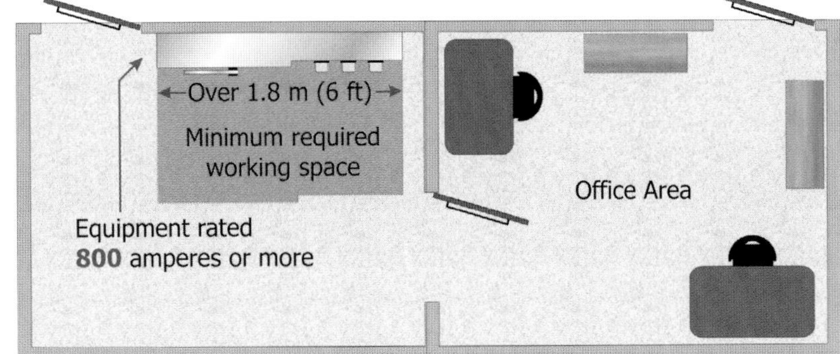

110.26(C)(3) Personnel Doors. Where equipment rated 800 A or more that contains overcurrent devices, switching devices, or control devices is installed and there is a personnel door(s) intended for entrance to and egress from the working space less than 7.6 m (25 ft) from the nearest edge of the working space, the door(s) shall open in the direction of egress and be equipped with listed panic hardware.

Note: Requirements for "Large Equipment" at 110.26(C)(2) still applies to equipment rated at 1200 A or more and over 1.8 m (6 ft) wide.

2011 *NEC* Requirement

This provision required any personnel doors located within 7.6 m (25 ft) of the working space for large electrical equipment to be provided with panic bars, pressure plates, or other devices that are normally latched but open under simple pressure. *Large equipment* was defined as "equipment rated 1200 amperes or more and over 1.8 m (6 ft) wide that contains overcurrent devices, switching devices, or control devices."

2014 *NEC* Change

For this provision for panic hardware for personnel doors, the ampere threshold was lowered from 1200 amperes to 800 amperes. Another revision involved the term *listed panic hardware*, which replaced the previous list of specific hardware provided at this requirement.

Analysis of Change

This personnel safety provision was added to the *NEC* in the 2002 *Code* cycle. In the event of an arc flash or arc blast, electrical installers and maintenance personnel need escape routes, such as doors to open in the direction of egress, with these doors provided with panic hardware in order to escape the extreme thermal energy, hazardous gases and other hazards that accompany an arc flash. These new personnel doors/panic hardware requirements for the 2002 *NEC* were not based on the 1200-ampere threshold; rather, these provisions were based on the panic hardware requirement for doors. The 2002 substantiation included personal experiences where a transformer exploded and a switchgear failure was accompanied by difficulty exiting the room containing this electrical equipment. These safety provisions were each accepted by CMP-1 recognizing the need for panic hardware and doors that open in the direction of egress. There was no substantiation or data provided that would mandate a 1200-ampere threshold. The requirement for doors and large equipment seemed the most likely place for this then-new requirement and the 1200-ampere threshold was already in place at 110.26(C).

110.26(C)(3)

Continued

(A) Entrance. At least one entrance to enclosures for electrical installations as described in 110.31 not less than 610 mm (24 in.) wide and 2.0 m (6 ½ ft) high shall be provided to give access to the working space about electrical equipment.

(3) Personnel Doors. Where there is a personnel door(s) intended for entrance to and egress from the working space less than 7.6 m (25 ft) from the nearest edge of the working space, the door(s) shall open in the direction of egress and be equipped with listed panic hardware ~~bars, pressure plates, or other devices that are normally latched but open under simple pressure~~.

Proposal 1-143a, 1-145, 1-169a

While the trigger of 1200 amperes for large equipment may be appropriate for the need for two doors at 110.26(C)(2), it is not substantiated with respect to personnel doors and personal safety at 110.26(C)(3). Serious injury and fatalities have and continue to occur involving electrical equipment rated at levels far below 1200 amperes. Moving the ampere threshold from 1200 amperes down to 800 amperes is not a burden on manufacturers or the enforcement community. Rather, this is a prudent step in the direction of electrical safety to allow electrical personnel unimpeded egress in the event of an arc fault resulting in an arc blast.

Another revision occurred with the panic hardware itself. The term *listed panic hardware* will replace the phrase "panic bars, pressure plates, or other devices that are normally latched but open under simple pressure." This revision will result in consistency with applicable building codes that use only the term *panic hardware*. Panic hardware is required to be "listed" under ANSI/UL 305.

This same panic hardware change occurred at 110.33(A)(3) for equipment with a voltage rating over 600 volts.

110.26(E)(2)(a)&(b)

Change at a Glance

Dedicated equipment space is now required for both outdoor installations and for indoor installations.

Code Language

110.26 Space about Electrical Equipment

(E) Dedicated Equipment Space. All switchboards, switchgear, panelboards, and motor control centers shall be located in dedicated spaces and protected from damage.

Exception: *Control equipment that by its very nature or because of other rules of the Code must be adjacent to or within sight of its operating machinery shall be permitted in those locations.*

(1) Indoor. (Text unchanged)

(2) Outdoor. Outdoor installations shall comply with 110.26(E)(2)(a) and (b).

(a) Installation Requirements. Outdoor electrical equipment shall be installed in suitable enclosures and shall be protected from accidental contact by unauthorized personnel, or by vehicular traffic, or by accidental spillage or leakage from piping systems. The working clearance space shall include the zone described in 110.26(A). No architectural appurtenance or other equipment shall be located in this zone.

2011 *NEC* Requirement

A space equal to the width and depth of the electrical equipment and extending from grade to a height of 1.8 m (6 ft) above all indoor switchboards, panelboards, and motor control centers is required to be located above and below such equipment. This space is known as *dedicated electrical or equipment space*. This space is to be dedicated to the electrical installation *(electrical conduits, cables, equipment, etc., only; no equipment foreign to the electrical installation)*. However, this dedicated electrical space requirement applied only to indoor installations in the 2011 *NEC*.

2014 *NEC* Change

A new 110.26(E)(2)(b), Dedicated Equipment Space, was added for outdoor installations of electrical equipment. This new requirement calls for the same basic dedicated equipment or electrical space for outdoor installations that has been in effect for indoor installations at 110.26 since the 1999 *NEC* (*prior to the 1999 NEC, this indoor dedicated equipment space was located at 384-4 for panelboards and motor control centers*). The term *switchgear* was added to the types of electrical equipment needing this dedicated equipment space resulting from code-wide actions taken by CMP-9 revising the term *switchgear* throughout the *Code*.

Analysis of Change

On indoor installations, the *Code* is clear as to the dedicated equipment space for electrical equipment; but for outdoor electrical installations, the *Code* was silent on this dedicated equipment space. Outdoors, some of same "equipment foreign to the electrical installation" is often present such as gas piping, water piping, mechanical refrigeration lines, irrigation equipment, phone and internet equipment, compressed air lines, and other non-electrical equipment. These foreign systems are often installed outdoors above or below the electrical equipment in what would be called the "dedicated equipment or electrical space" if

110.26(E)(2)(a)&(b)

Continued

(b) Dedicated Equipment Space. The space equal to the width and depth of the equipment and extending from grade to a height of 1.8 m (6 ft) above the equipment shall be dedicated to the electrical installation. No piping or other equipment foreign to the electrical installation shall be located in this zone.

Proposal 1-155, 9-14d

this same electrical equipment were installed indoors. This space above and below the electrical equipment should be dedicated to the electrician to install electrical conduits, cables, etc., in and out of panelboards, switchgears, etc. When installed in the dedicated electrical space, these foreign items impede access to the electrical equipment. This is true whether the electrical equipment is installed indoors or outdoors. When electrical equipment is installed outdoors, the *Code* already requires that nothing "foreign" be attached to a service mast (230.28), which is typically located in what should be defined as the dedicated electrical equipment space.

In many areas, the majority of the service equipment and HVAC equipment is installed outdoors. With designers and architects typically attempting to put all equipment in one location, the problem arises concerning other items being located in close proximity to the outdoor electrical equipment, which can create a safety hazard when attempting to service electrical equipment. The enforcement community along with the electrical installer/maintainer needs the ability to enforce a safe installation around electrical equipment regardless of its location. The new requirement for dedicated equipment space at outdoor installations correlates with the existing provisions at 110.26(E)(1)(a) for indoor installations.

110.27(A)(4)

Change at a Glance

Revision for "Guarding of Live Parts" increases the elevation of live parts against accidental contact to 2.6 m (8 ½ ft.) when voltages range from 301 to 600 volts.

Code Language

110.27 Guarding of Live Parts

(A) Live Parts Guarded Against Accidental Contact. Except as elsewhere required or permitted by this *Code*, live parts of electrical equipment operating at 50 volts or more shall be guarded against accidental contact by approved enclosures or by any of the following means:

(1) By location in a room, vault, or similar enclosure that is accessible only to qualified persons.

(2) By suitable permanent, substantial partitions or screens arranged so that only qualified persons have access to the space within reach of the live parts. Any openings in such partitions or screens shall be sized and located so that persons are not likely to come into accidental contact with the live parts or to bring conducting objects into contact with them.

(3) By location on a suitable balcony, gallery, or platform elevated and arranged so as to exclude unqualified persons.

2011 *NEC* Requirement

Live parts of electrical equipment operating at 50 volts or more are required to be guarded against accidental contact by approved enclosures or by 4 specific methods described at 110.27(A). Level 2 list item (4) permitted elevation of 2.5 m (8 ft) or more above the floor or other working surfaces. In the 2011 *NEC*, this elevation provision applied to all applications, regardless of the voltage involved.

2014 *NEC* Change

A revision to 110.27(A)(4) increased the elevation of live parts against accidental contact to 2.6 m (8 ½ ft.) when voltages range from 301 to 600 volts. Live parts of electrical equipment with 50 to 300 volts can still comply with this requirement with a minimum of 2.5 m (8 ft) above the floor or other working surface.

Analysis of Change

A revision to 110.27(A)(4) for elevation of live parts of electrical equipment operating at 50 volts or more to be guarded against accidental contact was raised to 2.6 m (8 ½ ft.) when voltages range from 301 to 600 volts. This 2.6 m (8 ½ ft) clearance corresponds with the National Electrical Safety Code (NESC) clearances for live exposed parts (*see NESC 124A3 and Table 124-1*). Table 124-1 of the NESC does separate voltages of 300 volts (phase-to-phase) and below from those 301 to 600 volts for clearances for live exposed parts.

Typically, clearances of any sort in the *NEC* are determined by different factors and conditions. One of these factors is a base reference of height for the activity involved in the vicinity of different components to be cleared. An example would be 230.24(B), which provides height requirements for 4 list items of specific types of "activities" that can be placed under overhead service conductors such as buildings, residential driveways, public streets,

110.27(A)(4)

Continued

(4) By elevation of ~~2.5 m (8 ft) or more~~ above the floor or other working surface as shown in (a) or (b) below:
(a) a minimum of 2.5 m (8 ft) for 50 – 300 volts
(b) a minimum of 2.6 m (8 ½ ft) for 301 to 600 volts.

Proposal 1-158

Comment 1-94

alleys, etc. The clearances for these overhead service conductors are different for each situation and in some instances different due to voltages involved. Depth of working space at Table 110.26(A)(1) and Table 110.34(A) are examples where the voltage of the live part is another component in required clearances; the higher the voltage, the greater the clearance required. Using only a straight 2.5 m (8 ft) for clearance of live parts above the floor or other working surface without consideration for the voltage involved would seem unreasonable in previous editions of the *Code*.

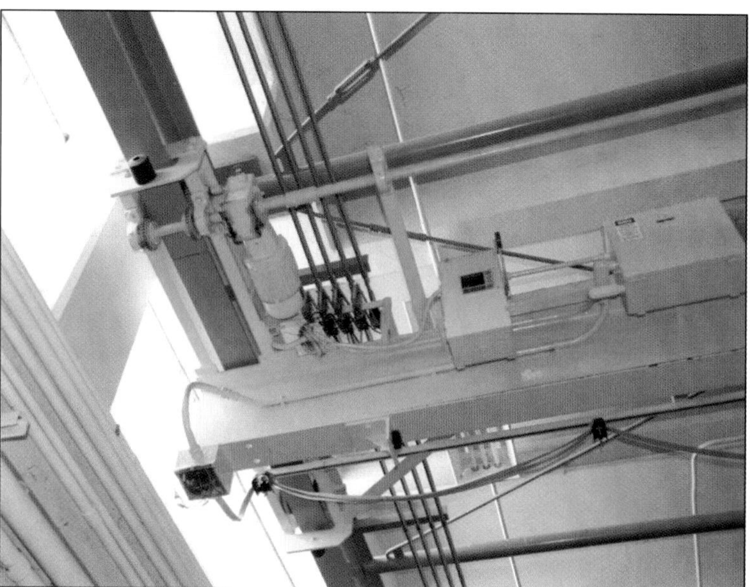

200.4(B)

Change at a Glance

New provisions require grouping the common neutral conductor for multiple circuits with its associated ungrounded conductors when contained in the same enclosure.

Code Language

200.4 Neutral Conductors

Neutral conductors shall be installed in accordance with (A) and (B).

(A) Installation. Neutral conductors shall not be used for more than one branch circuit, for more than one multiwire branch circuit, or for more than one set of ungrounded feeder conductors unless specifically permitted elsewhere in this *Code*.

(B) Multiple Circuits. If more than one neutral conductor associated with different circuits is in an enclosure, grounded circuit conductors of each circuit shall be identified or grouped to correspond with the ungrounded circuit

2011 *NEC* Requirement

Section 200.4, new for the 2011 *NEC*, prohibited a neutral conductor from being used for more than one branch circuit, multiwire branch circuit, or for more than one feeder.

2014 *NEC* Change

New 200.4(B), Multiple Circuits, requires grouping the common neutral conductor for multiple circuits with their associated ungrounded conductors when contained in the same enclosure. New exceptions were also added to relax this grouping requirement where the grouping is obvious or where looped conductors or conductors simply pass through the enclosure.

Analysis of Change

A new provision for grouping of neutral conductors to their associated ungrounded conductors of multiple circuits was added to 200.4, with similar provisions for grouping requirements for multiwire branch circuits located at 210.4(D). This new provision for multiple circuits requires this grouping of the neutral and ungrounded conductors "within the (each) enclosure," whereas 210.4(D) is for a specific application at the panelboard or point of supply where it is necessary to be able to identify the ungrounded conductors and associated neutral conductor of a multiwire branch circuit for safe disconnection. The new grouping requirement for multiple circuits seems to place a difficulty on the enforcement community, as all junction and splice points where there are multiple circuits with shared neutral conductors are present would have to be open for inspection of the grouping requirements. An additional inspection would then be required to assure all covers are in place.

The substantiation for this new provision pointed to the fact that unlike ungrounded conductors which can be traced back to the overcurrent protection

200.4(B)

Continued

conductor(s) by wire markers, cable ties, or similar means in at least one location within the enclosure.

Exception No. 1: *The requirement for grouping or identifying shall not apply if the branch circuit or feeder conductors enter from a cable or a raceway unique to the circuit that makes the grouping obvious.*

Exception No. 2: *The requirement for grouping or identifying shall not apply where branch circuit conductors pass through a box or conduit body without a loop as described in 314.16(B)(1) or without a splice or termination.*

Proposal 5-29

Comment 5-10, 5-11

device where these conductors are terminated, the neutral conductors are terminated on a common neutral terminal bar making tracing these neutral conductors more difficult.

200.6(A)(3)

Change at a Glance

Revision permits three continuous white "or gray" stripes along the grounded conductor's entire length on other than green insulation for identification of sizes 6 AWG or smaller.

REVISION

Code Language

200.6 Means of Identifying Grounded Conductors

(A) Sizes 6 AWG or Smaller. An insulated grounded conductor of 6 AWG or smaller shall be identified by one of the following means:

(1) A continuous white outer finish.

(2) A continuous gray outer finish.

(3) Three continuous white or gray stripes along the conductor's entire length on other than green insulation.

(4) Wires that have their outer covering finished to show a white or gray color but have colored tracer threads in the braid identifying the source of manufacture shall be considered as meeting the provisions of this section.

(5) The grounded conductor of a mineral-insulated, metal-sheathed cable (Type MI) shall be identified at the time of installation by distinctive marking at its terminations.

(See *NEC* for complete text.)

Proposal 5-31

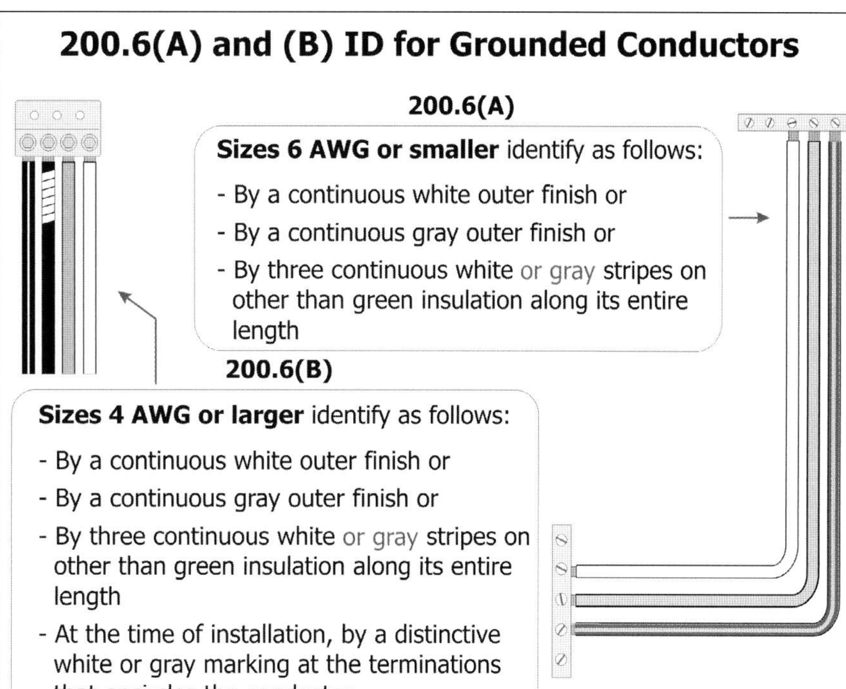
200.6(A) and (B) ID for Grounded Conductors
200.6(A)
Sizes 6 AWG or smaller identify as follows:
- By a continuous white outer finish or
- By a continuous gray outer finish or
- By three continuous white or gray stripes on other than green insulation along its entire length
200.6(B)
Sizes 4 AWG or larger identify as follows:
- By a continuous white outer finish or
- By a continuous gray outer finish or
- By three continuous white or gray stripes on other than green insulation along its entire length
- At the time of installation, by a distinctive white or gray marking at the terminations that encircles the conductor

2011 *NEC* Requirement

For sizes 6 AWG and smaller, 200.6(A) permits grounded conductors to be identified by a continuous white or gray outer finish. For the 2011 *NEC*, a grounded conductor could also be identified by three continuous white stripes along the conductor's entire length on other than green insulation.

2014 *NEC* Change

For the 2014 *NEC*, a grounded conductor can still be identified by a continuous white or gray outer finish or by three continuous white *or gray* stripes along the conductor's entire length on other than green insulation of sizes 6 AWG or smaller.

Analysis of Change

With improvements in compounds and coloring methods from conductor manufacturers, white and gray skim coats for insulation and stripes are now easily distinguishable. Gray coloring for grounded conductors is frequently requested for 277/480-volt circuits, making gray stripes a natural addition to the acceptable means of identification for grounded conductors. This addition of white or gray stripes will offer more choices to installers when complying with the requirements at 200.6(D), which requires grounded conductors of different systems to be identified by different identification means conforming to 200.6(A) or (B).

Companion proposals for additional changes were submitted for 200.6(B)(3); 200.6(E); 200.7; 200.7(A)(2); 200.7(C); 200.7(C)(1) and 200.7(C)(2) where white *or gray* stripes are now permitted for identification of grounded conductors.

210.5(C)(2)

Change at a Glance

New branch circuit identification requirements were added for dc systems. Sizes 6 AWG and smaller will be identified by red for positive dc conductors and by black for negative dc conductors.

Code Language

210.5 Identification for Branch Circuits

(A) Grounded Conductor. The grounded conductor of a branch circuit shall be identified in accordance with 200.6.

(B) Equipment Grounding Conductor. The equipment grounding conductor shall be identified in accordance with 250.119.

(C) Identification of Ungrounded Conductors. Ungrounded conductors shall be identified in accordance with 210.5(C)(1)~~;~~ or (2), ~~and (3)~~ as applicable.

(1) ~~Application~~ Branch Circuits Supplied From More Than One Nominal Voltage System. Where the premises wiring system has branch circuits supplied from more than one nominal voltage system, each ungrounded conductor of a branch circuit shall be identified by phase or line and system at all termination, connection, and splice points in compliance with 210.5(C)(1)(a) and (b).

(a) Means of Identification. The means of identification shall be permitted to be by separate color coding, marking tape, tagging, or other approved means.

(b) Posting of Identification Means. The method utilized for

210.5(C)(2) ID of Branch Circuits From DC Systems

New branch circuit identification requirements added for dc systems

+POSITIVE+

-NEGATIVE-

For sizes 6 AWG and smaller, red for positive dc conductors and black for negative dc conductors

2011 *NEC* Requirement

These identification means for conductors at 210.5(C) was applied only to ac system in the 2011 *NEC*.

2014 *NEC* Change

A new 210.5(C)(2), Branch Circuits Supplied from Direct-Current Systems, gives the new branch circuit identification requirements for dc circuits. For branch circuits supplied from a dc system operating at more than 50 volts, each ungrounded conductor of 4 AWG or larger is to be identified by polarity at all termination, connection, and splice points by marking tape, tagging, or other approved means. Ungrounded conductors of 6 AWG or smaller are required to be identified by polarity at all termination, connection, and splice points with a red identification means for positive conductors and marked "+" or the word "POSITIVE" or "POS" durably marked on the insulation, and by a black identification means for negative conductors with markings of "–" or the word "NEGATIVE" or "NEG" durably marked on the insulation.

Analysis of Change

Direct current (dc) applications are experiencing a re-emergence in the electrical industry because of such things as electric vehicle charging, solar photovoltaic (PV) systems, microgrids, wind generated electric systems, etc. These dc systems can achieve greater efficiencies and energy savings than their ac current colleagues. In the electrical installation and maintenance vocation worlds, these dc applications have experienced great inconsistencies in polarity identification schemes, particularly with the grounded conductors of negatively-grounded or positively-grounded two-wire direct-current systems. Such inconsistency often results in risk and confusion to installers and maintenance workers where the branch circuits of these various dc applications come together with branch circuits of conventional ac circuits.

Continued

conductors originating within each branch-circuit panelboard or similar branch-circuit distribution equipment shall be documented in a manner that is readily available or shall be permanently posted at each branch-circuit panelboard or similar branch-circuit distribution equipment.

(2) Branch Circuits Supplied From Direct Current Systems. Where a branch circuit is supplied from a dc system operating at more than 50 volts, each ungrounded conductor of 4 AWG or larger shall be identified by polarity at all termination, connection, and splice points by marking tape, tagging, or other approved means; each ungrounded conductor of 6 AWG or smaller shall be identified by polarity at all termination, connection, and splice points in compliance with 210.5(C)(2)(a) and (b). The identification methods utilized for conductors originating within each branch-circuit panelboard or similar branch-circuit distribution equipment shall be documented in a manner that is readily available or shall be permanently posted at each branch-circuit panelboard or similar branch-circuit distribution equipment.

(a) Positive Polarity, Sizes 6 AWG or Smaller. Where the positive polarity of a dc system does not serve as the connection point for the grounded conductor, each positive ungrounded conductor shall be identified by one of the following means:
(1) A continuous red outer finish.
(2) A continuous red stripe durably marked along the conductor's entire length on insulation of a color other than green, white, gray, or black.
(3) Imprinted plus signs "+" or the word "POSITIVE" or "POS" durably marked on insulation of a color other than green, white, gray, or black, and repeated at intervals not exceeding 610 mm (24 in.) in accordance with 310.120(B).

(b) Negative Polarity, Sizes 6 AWG or smaller. Where the negative polarity of a dc system does not serve as the connection point for the grounded conductor, each negative ungrounded conductor shall be identified by one of the following means:
(1) A continuous black outer finish.
(2) A continuous black stripe durably marked along the conductor's entire length on insulation of a color other than green, white, gray, or red.
(3) Imprinted minus signs "–" or the word "NEGATIVE" or "NEG" durably marked on insulation of a color other than green, white, gray, or red, and repeated at intervals not exceeding 610 mm (24 in.) in accordance with 310.120(B).9

Proposal 2-23

Comment 2-10

This new provision for dc circuits was developed by a subgroup of the NEC DC Task Force of the NEC Correlating Committee. A similar change occurred at 215.12(C) (*see Proposal 2-217*) to address this same dc circuit identification issue for feeders. A similar proposal for 690.4(B)(5) (*2011 NEC Code reference*) was submitted to CMP-4 specific to photovoltaic (PV) applications (*see Proposal 4-198*). This proposal was rejected by CMP-4 with a Panel Statement: "Circuit identification is critically important in the installation of a PV system. However, there are multiple marking schemes that will accomplish this. The proposed wiring method is too prescriptive and may disallow other legitimate marking methods."

A companion proposal was developed by the NEC DC Task Force of the NEC CC and submitted to CMP-2 (and accepted) at 215.12(C) for this same identification requirement for feeders supplied for dc systems (*see Proposal 2-217 and Comment 2-100*).

210.8(A)(7)

Change at a Glance

GFCI protection is required within 1.8 m (6 ft) of all dwelling unit sinks (including kitchen sinks).

Code Language

210.8 Ground-Fault Circuit-Interrupter Protection for Personnel

Ground-fault circuit-interrupter protection ~~interruption~~ for personnel shall be provided as required in 210.8(A) through (C). The ground-fault circuit-interrupter shall be installed in a readily accessible location.

Informational Note: See 215.9 for ground-fault circuit-interrupter protection for personnel on feeders.

(A) Dwelling Units. All 125-volt, single-phase, 15- and 20-ampere receptacles installed in the locations specified in 210.8(A) (1) through ~~(8)~~ (10) shall have ground-fault circuit-interrupter protection for personnel.

(7) Sinks — ~~located in areas other than kitchens~~ Where receptacles are installed within 1.8 m (6 ft) of the outside edge of the sink

---

Proposal 2-40, 2-27a

Comment 2-20

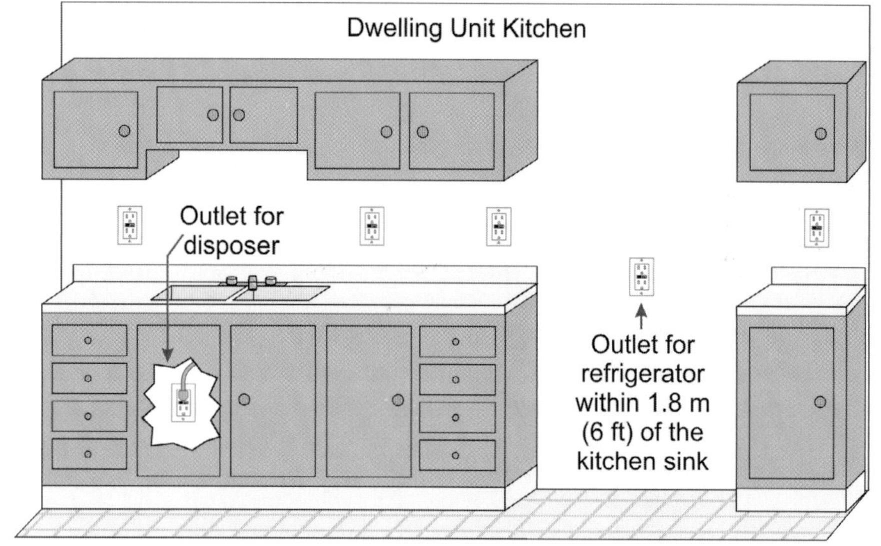

All 125-volt, single-phase, 15- and 20-ampere receptacles installed within 1.8 m (6 ft) of the outside edge of any dwelling unit sink now require GFCI protection.

2011 *NEC* Requirement

Section 210.8(A)(7) required all 125-volt, single-phase, 15- and 20-ampere receptacles installed within 1.8 m (6 ft) of the outside edge of dwelling unit sinks to be provided with GFCI protection. This requirement precluded dwelling unit kitchen sinks as it was felt that 210.8(A)(6) adequately covered GFCI protection pertaining to the dwelling unit kitchen sink. The device providing the GFCI protection for all of the list items in 210.8 had to be installed in a readily accessible location.

2014 *NEC* Change

A revision to 210.8(A)(7) for GFCI protection for dwelling unit sinks removes the words "located in areas other than kitchens" to require GFCI protection for all 125-volt, single-phase, 15- and 20-ampere receptacles installed within 1.8 m (6 ft) of the outside edge of dwelling unit sinks (including kitchen sinks).

Analysis of Change

The provisions of 210.8(A)(7) for GFCI protection within 1.8 m (6 ft) of the outside edge of dwelling unit sinks has seen substantial changes and revisions for the last five code cycles. For the 2002 *NEC*, this list item (7) pertained only to wet bar sinks with the receptacle being located within 1.8 m (6 ft) of the wet bar sink and "intended to serve the countertop." The 2005 *NEC* saw this requirement expanded to "laundry, utility, and wet bar sinks" with the provision that the receptacle be "intended to serve the countertop" removed. For the 2011 *NEC*, the title was simplified to just "Sinks," but excluded kitchen sinks as the GFCI provisions for kitchen sinks was covered at 210.8(A)(6) and this list item only required GFCI protection for receptacles that served a kitchen countertop and did not intend GFCI protection for such things as a receptacle under the kitchen sink for a garbage disposal, even though that garbage disposal receptacle might be within 1.8 m (6 ft) of the outside edge of dwelling unit kitchen sink. Now, for the 2014 *NEC*, this provision was expanded to all dwelling unit sinks (including the kitchen).

210.8(A)(7)

Continued

Some users of the *Code* felt that the 2011 *NEC* language at 210.8(A)(7) left a loop hole in the *Code* by not requiring GFCI protection for all 125-volt, single-phase, 15- and 20-ampere receptacles installed within 1.8 m (6 ft) of dwelling unit kitchen sinks. Examples of non-GFCI-protected receptacles located within 1.8 m (6 ft) of dwelling unit kitchen sinks under this 2011 *NEC* scenario would include the garbage disposal receptacle located in the cabinets under the kitchen sink, a receptacle located behind a refrigerator, or a general lighting branch-circuit living room receptacle located on the back side of a kitchen sink bar area.

By eliminating the phrase "located in areas other than kitchens" at 210.8(A)(7), this now requires all 125-volt, single-phase, 15- and 20-ampere receptacles installed within 1.8 m (6 ft) of any dwelling unit sink to be provided with GFCI protection. This change should bring some consistency to the "within 1.8 m (6 ft) of the outside edge of dwelling unit sink" requirements as a receptacle for such things as an appliance (refrigerator, washing machine, etc.) would require GFCI protection if it were located within 1.8 m (6 ft) of a wet bar sink; but under previous editions of the *Code*, these were not required to be GFCI-protected if this same receptacle were located within 1.8 m (6 ft) of a kitchen sink.

A collateral-damage situation to this change might need to be taken into consideration. As an example, GFCI protection will now be required for a receptacle outlet that supplies the kitchen disposal under the kitchen sink. This will create a unique situation considering the factor that AFCI protection is now required for branch circuits supplying outlets in dwelling unit kitchens. All AFCI and GFCI devices are also now required to be installed in a readily accessible location. Installers will be faced with the problem of how to provide two different means of protection without having to add additional outlets, considering this fact that both AFCI and GFCI devices will have to be readily accessible. Installers who choose to provide a combination AFCI device at the panelboard would now have to install an additional GFCI outlet device in a readily accessible location to provide the necessary GFCI protection to the garbage disposal receptacle outlet; a GFCI device could not be installed under the kitchen sink in the cabinets as this GFCI device would not be considered to be readily accessible.

210.8(A)(9)

Change at a Glance

GFCI protection is now required where receptacles are installed within 1.8 m (6 ft) of the outside edge of dwelling unit bathtubs or shower stalls.

Code Language

210.8 Ground-Fault Circuit-Interrupter Protection for Personnel

Ground-fault circuit-interrupter protection ~~interruption~~ for personnel shall be provided as required in 210.8(A) through (C). The ground-fault circuit-interrupter shall be installed in a readily accessible location.

Informational Note: See 215.9 for ground-fault circuit-interrupter protection for personnel on feeders.

(A) Dwelling Units. All 125-volt, single-phase, 15- and 20-ampere receptacles installed in the locations specified in 210.8(A)(1) through ~~(8)~~ (10) shall have ground-fault circuit-interrupter protection for personnel.

(9) Bathtubs or Shower Stalls — where receptacles are installed within 1.8 m (6 ft) of the outside edge of the bathtub or shower stall.

Proposal 2-46, 2-27a

210.8(A)(9) GFCI: Bathtubs or Shower Stalls

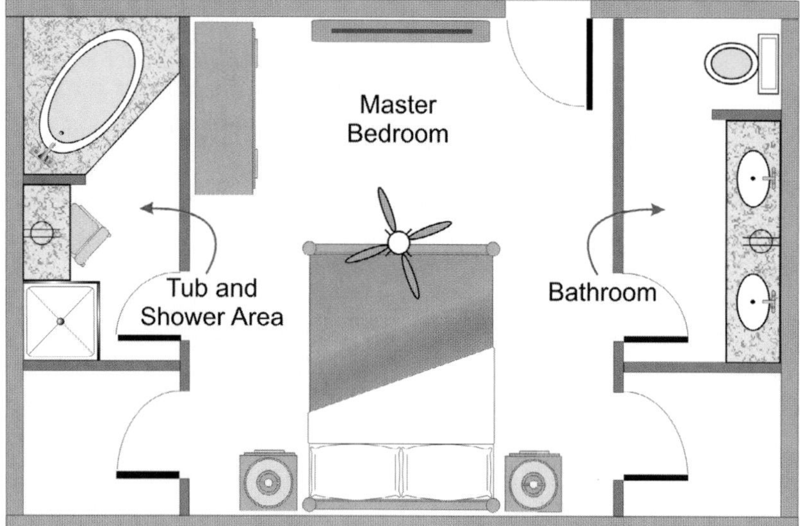

All 125-volt, single-phase, 15- and 20-ampere receptacles installed within 1.8 m (6 ft) of the outside edge of a dwelling unit bathtub or shower stall requires GFCI protection

2011 *NEC* Requirement

All 125-volt, single-phase, 15- and 20-ampere receptacles installed in dwelling unit bathrooms require GFCI protection. This would include bathtub or shower stall areas (*regardless of its distance from said tub or shower stall*), but only if the bathtub or shower stall was located in a bathroom as defined in Article 100.

2014 *NEC* Change

A new 210.8(A)(9) for bathtubs or shower stalls will now require GFCI protection for all 125-volt, single-phase, 15- and 20-ampere receptacles installed within 1.8 m (6 ft) of the outside edge of a dwelling unit bathtub or shower stall, even if these bathtub or shower stalls are not located in a defined bathroom.

Analysis of Change

This new GFCI provision for dwelling unit bathtub and shower stall areas is a logical expansion as bathtubs or shower stalls are not always located in an area that meets the Article 100 definition of a bathroom, and any receptacles in such areas might not require GFCI protection. An example of such an area would be a room or area connected to a dwelling unit bedroom with a bathtub or shower stall as the only plumbing fixture in that particular room or area, with a basin sink and toilet provided in another common area of the dwelling. The definition in Article 100 calls for a bathroom to be "an area including a basin with one or more of the following: a toilet, a urinal, a tub, a shower, a bidet, or similar plumbing fixtures." Without a basin and any of the other plumbing fixtures listed in the definition, present in one area, this area would not meet the definition of a bathroom. This new requirement will provide a better level of safety for occupants of the dwelling unit. This requirement is similar to the GFCI provisions found at 680.71 for hydromassage bathtubs.

210.8(A)(10)

Change at a Glance

All dwelling unit laundry areas now require GFCI protection for 125-volt, single-phase, 15- and 20-ampere receptacles, regardless of the presence of a sink or the distance from the same.

Code Language

210.8 Ground-Fault Circuit-Interrupter Protection for Personnel

Ground-fault circuit-interrupter protection ~~interruption~~ for personnel shall be provided as required in 210.8(A) through (C). The ground-fault circuit-interrupter shall be installed in a readily accessible location.

Informational Note: See 215.9 for ground-fault circuit-interrupter protection for personnel on feeders.

(A) Dwelling Units. All 125-volt, single-phase, 15- and 20-ampere receptacles installed in the locations specified in 210.8(A) (1) through ~~(8)~~ (10) shall have ground-fault circuit-interrupter protection for personnel.

(10) Laundry areas

Proposal 2-27a, 2-47

2011 *NEC* Requirement

125-volt, single-phase, 15- and 20-ampere receptacles installed in dwelling unit laundry areas required GFCI protection, but only those receptacles located within 1.8 m (6 ft) of the outside edge of a laundry room sink as required by 210.8(A)(7).

2014 *NEC* Change

A new 210.8(A)(10) for laundry areas which will now require GFCI protection for all 125-volt, single-phase, 15- and 20-ampere receptacles installed in a laundry room. The presence of a laundry room sink is no longer the driving factor as to whether GFCI protection is required or not.

Analysis of Change

Laundry areas typically involve electrical appliances and the presence of water, with a resulting increased risk of electric shock hazards. This action by CMP-2 to require GFCI protection of receptacles in laundry areas addresses this increased shock hazard risk and is consistent with other *NEC* requirements for GFCI protection of receptacles in areas in close proximity of water. As the requirements for GFCI protection have been expanded throughout the *NEC* over the last fifteen *Code* cycles, the number of electrical shock incidents related to consumer products has continued to decline over that time. Increased usage of GFCI protection for personnel at receptacles of residential homes is a highly effective means of further reducing the potential for electrical shock hazards.

210.8(B)(8)

Change at a Glance

GFCI protection is required for all 125-volt, single-phase, 15- and 20-ampere receptacles installed in all non-dwelling unit garages, service bays, and similar areas (other than vehicle exhibition halls and showrooms).

Code Language

210.8 Ground-Fault Circuit-Interrupter Protection for Personnel

Ground-fault circuit-interrupter protection ~~interruption~~ for personnel shall be provided as required in 210.8(A) through (C). The ground-fault circuit-interrupter shall be installed in a readily accessible location.

Informational Note: See 215.9 for ground-fault circuit-interrupter protection for personnel on feeders.

(B) Other Than Dwelling Units. All 125-volt, single-phase, 15- and 20-ampere receptacles installed in the locations specified in 210.8(B)(1) through (8) shall have ground-fault circuit-interrupter protection for personnel.

(8) Garages, service bays, and similar areas ~~where electrical diagnostic equipment, electrical hand tools, or portable lighting equipment are to be used~~ other than vehicle exhibition halls and showrooms.

Proposal 2-49, 2-50, 2-27a

Comment 2-27

2011 *NEC* Requirement

GFCI protection for personnel was required for all 125-volt, single-phase, 15- and 20-ampere receptacles installed in non-dwelling unit garages, service bays, and similar areas, but only in areas where electrical diagnostic equipment, electrical hand tools, or portable lighting equipment were to be used.

2014 *NEC* Change

The words "where electrical diagnostic equipment, electrical hand tools, or portable lighting equipment are to be used" were deleted. GFCI protection for personnel will now be required for all 125-volt, single-phase, 15- and 20-ampere receptacles installed in all non-dwelling unit garages, service bays, and similar areas (other than vehicle exhibition halls and showrooms).

Analysis of Change

Many commercial garages have receptacles installed for purposes other than the use of hand tools. In geographical areas that experience winter, many garages for cars, trucks and busses have 15- or 20-amp 120-volt receptacles at each stall for electric engine block heaters. Cord- and plug-connected engine block heaters may not be listed and, therefore, not subject to the maximum leakage current requirements of the standard for appliances. When these receptacles are not GFCI-protected, the frame of the vehicle can become energized, posing a hazard to personnel.

The words "other than vehicle exhibition halls and showrooms" were added in the Comment stage because a review of the definition of *garage* in Article 100 reveals that the auto dealer showroom floor area, for example, meets this definition. Potentially, the riding mower dealer showroom floor area also falls under the definition of garage. If the proposed language was accepted without this added phrase, GFCI protection would have been mandated for the receptacles at an automobile dealership's showroom floor area, which was not the intent of this revision.

210.8(D)

Change at a Glance

GFCI protection is now required for all outlets that supply dishwashers installed in dwelling units.

Code Language

210.8 Ground-Fault Circuit-Interrupter Protection for Personnel

Ground-fault circuit-interrupter protection ~~interruption~~ for personnel shall be provided as required in 210.8(A) through (C). The ground-fault circuit-interrupter shall be installed in a readily accessible location.

Informational Note: See 215.9 for ground-fault circuit-interrupter protection for personnel on feeders.

(D) Kitchen Dishwasher Branch Circuit. GFCI protection shall be provided for outlets that supply dishwashers installed in dwelling unit locations.

Proposal 2-58a, 2-27a

Comment 2-29

2011 *NEC* Requirement

GFCI protection was (and is) required for all 125-volt, single-phase, 15- and 20-ampere receptacles installed in dwelling unit kitchens where those receptacles serve a kitchen countertop. This provision was for receptacle outlets only and did not include hard-wired outlets and did not include receptacles that did not serve a kitchen countertop, such as a receptacle for a garbage disposal or a receptacle for a dishwasher installed behind the dishwasher under the countertop in the dishwasher space.

2014 *NEC* Change

A new 210.8(D) will now require GFCI protection for all outlets that supply dishwashers installed in dwelling units. This would include a receptacle outlet or a direct-wired outlet for a dishwasher.

Analysis of Change

Modern electronically controlled dishwashers have different failure modes than their electromechanical ancestors. End of life for today's dishwashers can result in increased risk of electrical shock, which can be mitigated by providing GFCI protection for outlets supplying dishwashers. As the requirement for ground-fault circuit interrupters has been expanded throughout the *NEC* for a number of Code cycles, the number of electrical shock hazards related to consumer products has continued to decline. Increased usage of GFCI protection within branch circuits of residential dwelling units is a highly effective means of further reducing the potential for electrical shocks.

Most of the substantiation to provide GFCI protection for dishwashers was related to concerns with an appliance. The submitter indicated the vast majority of failures have been related to either end-of-life component use for the dishwasher, unexplained electronic circuitry error, or poor quality control as indicated by chafed wiring.

210.8(D)

Continued

Article 210 contains rules for receptacle placement. Due to the unlimited possibilities of cord- and plug-connected equipment that can be supplied from those receptacles, the rules at 210.8(A) and (B) are appropriate. With the understanding that it would be unrealistic to address the many different types of portable appliances individually, it perhaps would make better sense to require GFCI protection for the 15- and 20-ampere, 125-volt receptacles in areas where they are most likely to be used. Appliances, such as dishwashers, washing machines, etc., and their GFCI protection requirements may be more appropriately covered in Chapter 4 of the *NEC*. The GFCI protection rules for cord- and plug-connected vending machines and electric drinking fountains already exist in Article 422. Leakage-current detector interrupter (LCDI) or arc-fault circuit interrupter (AFCI) rules for window air conditioner units are in Article 440. Boat hoists and their GFCI protection rules are also specific fixed equipment that may be more appropriately located in Chapter 4 as well.

210.12

Change at a Glance

New provision requires all AFCI devices mandated by 210.12 to be installed in a readily accessible location.

Code Language

210.12 Arc-Fault Circuit-Interrupter Protection

Arc-fault circuit-interrupter protection shall be provided as required in 210.12(A), (B), and (C). The arc-fault circuit interrupter shall be installed in a readily accessible location.

Proposal 2-116, 2-86, 2-99, 2-122, 2-124

Comment 2-60

210.12 Arc-Fault Circuit-Interrupters

AFCI devices are required to be installed in a readily accessible location.

2011 *NEC* Requirement

No provisions existed in the 2011 *NEC* to require AFCI devices to be installed in a readily accessible location.

2014 *NEC* Change

New language in the main body of 210.12 will now require all AFCI devices mandated by 210.12 to be installed in a readily accessible location.

Analysis of Change

This proposal seeks to align the readily accessible requirements for GFCI devices that are covered at the parent text of 210.8 with the rules for arc-fault circuit-interrupter (AFCI) protective devices required by 210.12. The 2011 *NEC* introduced the readily accessible language for GFCI devices at 210.8. Justification for the readily accessible rules for GFCI devices, and now for AFCI devices, is primarily related to occupant or user accessibility to the monthly testing and reset features of these devices. AFCI protection can be accomplished by circuit-breaker-type devices or outlet-type devices which have the same test and reset features and requirements for monthly testing as found at GFCI devices. Accessibility to AFCI protective devices should be the same as that for GFCI devices. With the option of a listed outlet branch-circuit type AFCI device, there is a possibility of these receptacle-type outlet devices being placed in a location that could easily place the AFCI device in a location that is not readily accessible. This readily accessible feature to this new requirement for AFCI devices will also facilitate the ability to reset the AFCI device in the event the AFCI trips.

There was a proposal submitted to CMP-1 that would have added a new section to Article 110 requiring all AFCI and GFCI receptacle outlet devices to be installed in a readily accessible location (*see Proposal 1-131 and Comment 1-46*). This proposed provision in Article 110 was rejected by CMP-1 in part due to the fact that this proposal for ready accessibility would only apply to outlet-type devices, whereas the wording accepted by CMP-2 at this new provision at 210.12 applies to all types of AFCI devices.

210.12(A)

Change at a Glance

Kitchens and laundry areas were added to the list of areas requiring AFCI protection. AFCI protection was also expanded from *outlets only* to *outlets or devices,* which would now include switches, etc.

Code Language

210.12 Arc-Fault Circuit-Interrupter Protection

Arc-fault circuit-interrupter protection shall be provided as required in 210.12(A),(B), and (C). The arc-fault circuit interrupter shall be installed in a readily accessible location.

(A) Dwelling Units. All 120-volt, single phase, 15- and 20-ampere branch circuits supplying outlets or devices installed in dwelling unit kitchens, family rooms, dining rooms, living rooms, parlors, libraries, dens, bedrooms, sunrooms, recreation rooms, closets, hallways, laundry areas, or similar rooms or areas shall be protected by ~~a listed arc-fault circuit interrupter, combination-type, installed to provide protection of the branch circuit~~ any of the following means described in 210.12(A)(1) through (6):

[See *Analysis of Changes* report for 210.12(A)(1) thru (A)(6) for complete Code text.]

Proposal 2-80, 2-82a, 2-85

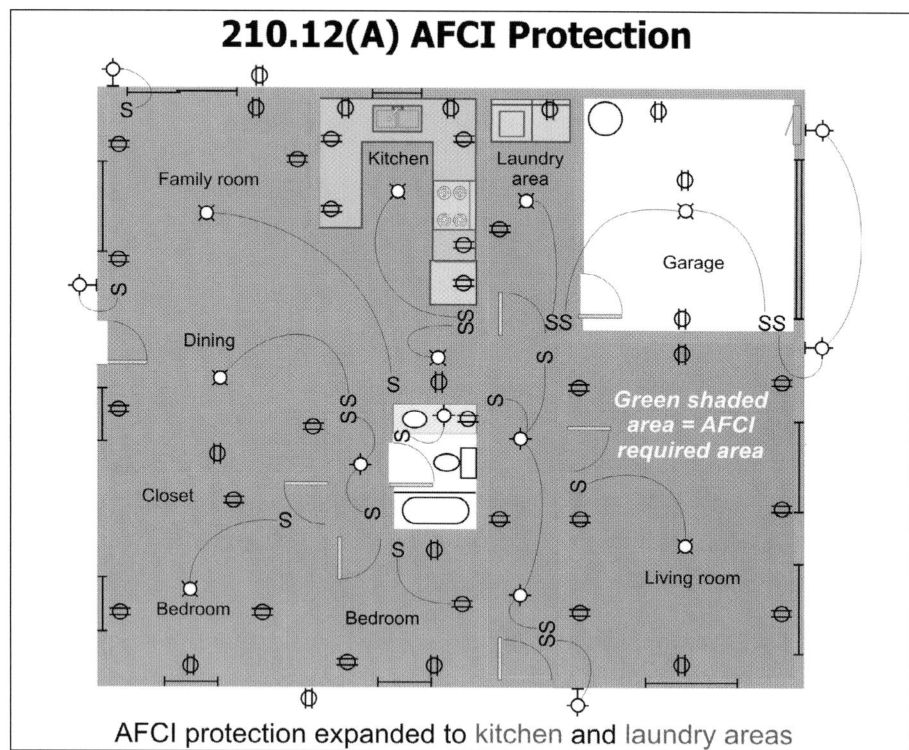

AFCI protection expanded to kitchen and laundry areas

2011 *NEC* Requirement

AFCI protection was required for all 120-volt, single-phase, 15- and 20-ampere branch circuits supplying *outlets* installed in dwelling unit family rooms, dining rooms, living rooms, parlors, libraries, dens, bedrooms, sunrooms, recreation rooms, closets, hallways, or similar rooms or areas.

2014 *NEC* Change

The list of areas in a dwelling unit that will now be required to be provided with AFCI protection was expanded to include kitchens and laundry areas. AFCI protection is now required for all 120-volt, single-phase, 15- and 20-ampere branch circuits supplying not just outlets but also devices installed in the list of areas requiring AFCI protection at 210.12(A).

Analysis of Change

AFCI protection has been required in the *Code* beginning in the 1999 *NEC*. At that time, AFCI protection was limited to branch circuits supplying receptacle outlets in dwelling unit bedrooms. For the 2002 *NEC*, the word "receptacle" was removed to require AFCI protection for all branch circuits supplying all "outlets" in dwelling unit bedrooms. The 2005 *NEC* saw "combination" type AFCI protection introduced with a future enforcement date of January 1, 2008. Combination AFCI protection being AFCI protection for both "Series" and "Parallel" arching events. The 2008 *NEC* brought about expansion of the rooms or areas where AFCI protection was required to more than just the bedrooms. Experience and information provided to CMP-2 over several code cycles indicates that AFCI technology provides protection against arcing incidents in the electrical system.

CMP-2 has taken an approach of incrementally expanding AFCI protection over several code cycles to provide increased safety by reducing the number of arcing events in dwellings. This stepped approach has given installers an opportunity to gain experience with what was at that time a new product, and for manufacturers to address any unforeseen problems with their designs. By the time the 2014 edition of the *NEC* is published, the industry will have over a decade of experience with the manufacture and installation of AFCI devices and over six years of experience with combination type AFCI devices. This expansion into the kitchens and laundry areas is another step in the incremental approach for AFCI protection at dwelling units.

Another change that occurred at 210.12(A) was requiring AFCI protection for all 120-volt, single-phase, 15- and 20-ampere branch circuits supplying not just outlets but also devices installed in the list of rooms or areas requiring AFCI protection. In Article 100, the definition of an *outlet* is "a point on the wiring system at which current is taken to supply utilization equipment." This would include receptacle outlets, lighting outlets, an outlet for a single-station, 120-volt smoke alarm, etc. This definition does not include a device such as a switch. At a switch location, current is not taken to supply utilization equipment, the switch allows current to *pass through* the switch to supply utilization equipment. Up until the 2014 *NEC,* a switch installed in a dwelling unit bedroom to supply outside lighting such as a flood light would not require AFCI protection. This switch is not an outlet, and the outlet the switch supplies is not located in any of the areas described at 210.12(A). This scenario will not hold true for the 2014 *NEC,* as AFCI protection has been expanded to devices as well. A *device* is defined in Article 100 as "a unit of an electrical system, other than a conductor, that carries or controls electric energy as its principal function." This definition would describe such things as a switch.

210.12(A)(1) thru (A)(6)

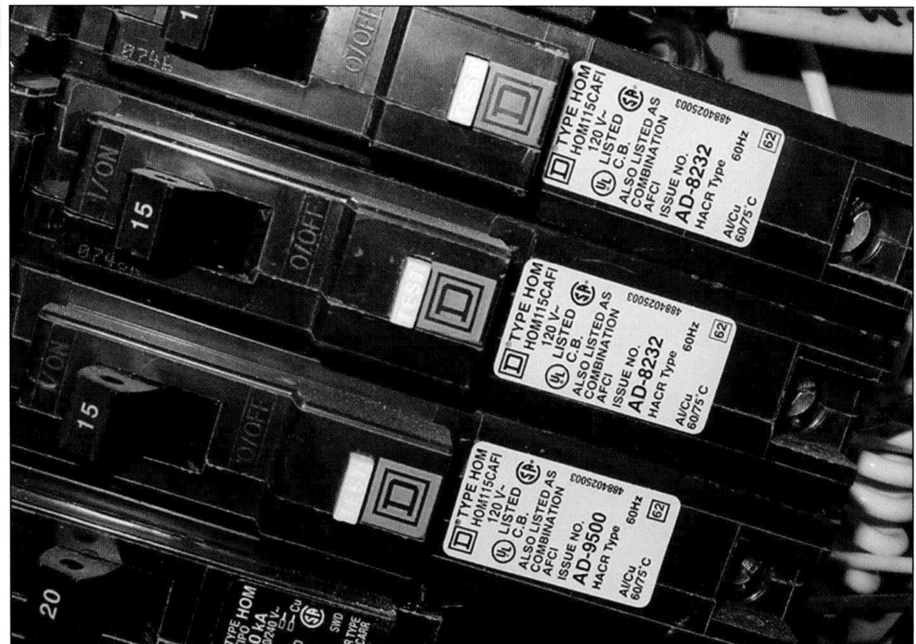

Change at a Glance

AFCI protection methods were expanded and language was put into a list format. Provisions for outlet branch circuit (OBC) AFCI devices were expanded.

Code Language

210.12 Arc-Fault Circuit-Interrupter Protection

Arc-fault circuit-interrupter protection shall be provided as required in 210.12(A),(B) and (C). The arc-fault circuit interrupter shall be installed in a readily accessible location.

(A) Dwelling Units. All 120-volt, single phase, 15- and 20-ampere branch circuits supplying outlets or devices installed in dwelling unit kitchens, family rooms, dining rooms, living rooms, parlors, libraries, dens, bedrooms, sunrooms, recreation rooms, closets, hallways, laundry areas, or similar rooms or areas shall be protected by ~~a listed arc-fault circuit interrupter, combination-type, installed to provide protection of the branch circuit~~ any of the means described in (1) through (6):

(1) A listed combination type arc-fault circuit interrupter, installed to provide protection of the entire branch circuit.

(2) A listed branch/feeder type AFCI installed at the origin of the branch circuit in combination with a listed outlet branch circuit type arc-fault circuit interrupter installed at the first outlet box on the

2011 *NEC* Requirement

AFCI protection was required for all 120-volt, single-phase, 15- and 20-ampere branch circuits supplying *outlets* installed in dwelling unit family rooms, dining rooms, living rooms, parlors, libraries, dens, bedrooms, sunrooms, recreation rooms, closets, hallways, or similar rooms or areas. There were three (3) exceptions to this rule and three (3) Informational Notes.

2014 *NEC* Change

The list of rooms in a dwelling unit that will now be required to be provided with AFCI protection was expanded to include kitchens and laundry areas. AFCI protection is now required for all 120-volt, single-phase, 15- and 20-ampere branch circuits supplying not just outlets but also *devices* that are installed in the list of rooms requiring AFCI protection at 210.12(A). The first two exceptions were revised to positive language and put into a list format of six provisions for providing AFCI protection to the branch circuit(s) involved. Provisions for the use and installation of outlet branch circuit (OBC) AFCI devices were greatly expanded. The three existing Informational Notes were revised and updated for clarity.

Analysis of Change

For the 2014 *NEC*, AFCI protection for dwelling units has taken another step forward with the continued incrementally approach to the expansion of this safety enhancing protection. This incremental approach holds true for the delivery methods for this AFCI protection as well. From the inception of AFCI protection in the 1999 *NEC*, the entire branch circuit was required to be protected with this AFCI protection being provided by a branch circuit/feeder type AFCI overcurrent device located at the origin of the branch circuit, typically, the panelboard. The 2005 *NEC* saw combination type AFCI protection introduced with a future enforcement date of January 1, 2008. Combination AFCI protection provided AFCI protection for both series and parallel arcing events. The 2005 *NEC* also introduced an exception to the location of the AFCI device at the origin of the branch circuit by allowing the AFCI device to be located at an outlet within 1.8 m (6 ft) of the point of origin

Continued

branch circuit. The first outlet box in the branch circuit shall be marked to indicate that it is the first outlet of the circuit.

(3) A listed supplemental arc protection circuit breaker installed at the origin of the branch circuit in combination with a listed outlet branch circuit type arc-fault circuit interrupter installed at the first outlet box on the branch circuit where all of the following conditions are met:

(a) The branch circuit wiring shall be continuous from the branch circuit overcurrent device to the outlet branch circuit arc-fault circuit interrupter.

(b) The maximum length of the branch circuit wiring from the branch circuit overcurrent device to the first outlet shall not exceed 15.2 m (50 ft) for a 14 AWG or 21.3 m (70 ft) for a 12 AWG conductor.

(c) The first outlet box in the branch circuit shall be marked to indicate that it is the first outlet of the circuit.

(4) A listed outlet branch circuit type arc-fault circuit interrupter installed at the first outlet on the branch circuit in combination with a listed branch circuit overcurrent protective device where all of the following conditions are met:

(a) The branch circuit wiring shall be continuous from the branch circuit overcurrent device to the outlet branch circuit arc-fault circuit interrupter.

(b) The maximum length of the branch circuit wiring from the branch circuit overcurrent device to the first outlet shall not exceed 15.2 m (50 ft) for a 14 AWG or 21.3 m (70 ft) for a 12 AWG conductor.

(c) The first outlet box in the branch circuit shall be marked to indicate that it is the first outlet of the circuit.

(d) The combination of the branch circuit overcurrent device and outlet branch circuit AFCI is identified as meeting the requirements for a "System Combination" type AFCI and is listed as such.

(5) If RMC, IMC, EMT, Type MC, or steel armored Type AC cables meeting the requirements of 250.118, metal wireways, metal auxiliary gutters and metal outlet and junction boxes are installed for the portion of the branch circuit between the branch-circuit overcurrent device and the first outlet, it shall be permitted to install ~~an~~ a listed outlet branch-circuit type AFCI at the first outlet to provide protection for the remaining portion of the branch circuit.

(6) Where a listed metal or nonmetallic conduit or tubing or Type MC cable is encased in not less than 50 mm (2 in.) of concrete for the portion of the branch circuit between the branch-circuit overcurrent device and the first outlet, it shall be permitted to install ~~an~~ a listed outlet branch circuit type AFCI at the first outlet to provide protection for the remaining portion of the branch circuit.

~~**Exception No. 1:** If RMC, IMC, EMT, Type MC, or steel armored Type AC cables meeting the requirements of 250.118 and metal outlet and junction boxes are installed for the portion of the branch circuit between the branch-circuit overcur-~~

with the portion of the branch circuit between the point of origin and the AFCI location having to be installed in a metal raceway or a metallic-sheathed cable. The 2008 *NEC* expanded the AFCI protection delivery method by removing the 1.8 m (6 ft) limitation on the unprotected portion of the branch circuit(s), allowing the AFCI device to be located at the first outlet with no length limitation as long as the unprotected portion was installed in a metallic wiring method.

For the 2014 *NEC*, the metallic wiring method provision between the origin of the branch circuit and the first outlet (home run) containing the AFCI device has been removed for specific installations involving a listed outlet circuit breaker (OBC) AFCI device at the first outlet and specific types of listed branch circuit overcurrent protective devices at the panelboard or origin of the branch circuit. According to discussions that took place at the ROP and ROC meetings, manufacturers of OBC-type AFCI devices will have to provide the installer and the inspection community information in their manufacturer's specifications as to the specific brand and type of overcurrent protective device that can be used in conjunction with their OBC-type AFCI device that would constitute a "system combination" type AFCI combination to meet the requirements of new 210.12(A)(4)(d).

A length limitation has been placed on the "home run" portions of the branch circuit from the panelboard to the first outlet of a maximum length of 15.2 m (50 ft) for a 14 AWG, or 21.3 m (70 ft) for a 12 AWG conductor. Substantiated evidence was presented to CMP-2 in the form of a report by Underwriters Laboratories (UL) entitled "Effectiveness of Circuit Breakers in Mitigating Parallel Arcing Faults in the Home Run" that provided significant statistical assurance (99%) that the "home run" portion of the branch circuit is protected from parallel arcing faults, which prompted the removal of the metallic wiring method. The AFCI protection can now be provided by a system consisting of a branch circuit overcurrent device (circuit breaker) having a specific instantaneous trip current, a branch circuit with a length limitation from the overcurrent protection device to the first outlet, and the installation of a listed outlet branch circuit (OBC) AFCI device at the first outlet on the circuit.

Continued

~~rent device and the first outlet, it shall be permitted to install an outlet branch-circuit type AFCI at the first outlet to provide protection for the remaining portion of the branch circuit.~~

~~**Exception No. 2:** Where a listed metal or nonmetallic conduit or tubing is encased in not less than 50 mm (2 in.) of concrete for the portion of the branch circuit between the branch-circuit overcurrent device and the first outlet, it shall be permitted to install an outlet branch-circuit type AFCI at the first outlet to provide protection for the remaining portion of the branch circuit.~~

Exception ~~No. 3~~: *Where an individual branch circuit to a fire alarm system installed in accordance with 760.41(B) or 760.121(B) is installed in RMC, IMC, EMT, or steel-sheathed cable, Type AC or Type MC, meeting the requirements of 250.118, with metal outlet and junction boxes, AFCI protection shall be permitted to be omitted.*

Informational Note No. 1: For information on ~~types of~~ combination type and branch/feeder type arc-fault circuit interrupters, see UL 1699-1999, *Standard for Arc-Fault Circuit-Interrupters*. For information on outlet branch-circuit type arc-fault circuit interrupters, see UL Subject 1699A *Outline of Investigation for Outlet Branch Circuit Arc-Fault Circuit-Interrupters*. For information on system combination AFCIs, see UL Subject 1699C *Outline of Investigation for System Combination Arc-Fault Circuit Interrupters*.

Informational Note No. 2: See 11.6.3(5) of NFPA 72-2010, *National Fire Alarm and Signaling Code*, for information related to secondary power supply requirements for smoke alarms installed in dwelling units.

Informational Note No. 3: See 760.41(B) and 760.121(B) for power-supply requirements for fire alarm systems.

Proposal 2-92, 2-65 thru 2-73, 2-79, 2-80, 2-82, 2-82a, 2-85, 2-86, 2-90, 2-93, 2-94, 2-95, 2-99, 2-102, 2-103, 2-109, 2-109a

Comment 2-52, 2-46, 2-40, 2-41, 2-42, 2-44, 2-54, 2-55, 2-59a

Some of the discussion pertaining to allowing a standard circuit breaker to protect the "home run" portion of the AFCI protected branch circuit centered around this circuit breaker having an instantaneous trip current of 300 amperes or less. It should be noted the requirement for circuit breakers to have an instantaneous trip current of 300 amperes or less is not part of the testing process under UL Product Standard 489 for circuit breakers. The circuit breakers tested by four of the major manufacturers under the UL report on the effectiveness of circuit breakers in mitigating parallel arcing faults in the home run did trip in the vicinity of 300 amperes. While the testing was effective in confirming that currently manufactured circuit breakers can be relied upon to protect from parallel faults of limited length, the testing also precludes many of the older, outdated overcurrent devices that exist in older dwellings from the benefits of these new provisions. Outdated overcurrent devices were not included in the UL study; in addition to the fact that since an instantaneous trip function is not a requirement of the UL 489 standard, certain manufacturers of outdated circuit breakers have no instantaneous function at all.

The main proposal (Proposal 2-92) that resulted on the majority of the new provisions at 210.12(A) was made on behalf of the Arc Fault Circuit Interrupter Wiring Device Joint Research and Development Consortium. The Consortium members consist of: Cooper Wiring Devices, Hubbell Incorporated (Delaware), Leviton Manufacturing Company, Inc., and Legrand/Pass and Seymour.

Continued

210.12(A) AFCI Protection

All 120-volt, single phase, 15- and 20-ampere branch circuits supplying outlets or devices installed in specified areas of dwelling unit shall be protected by any of the means described in (1) through (6):

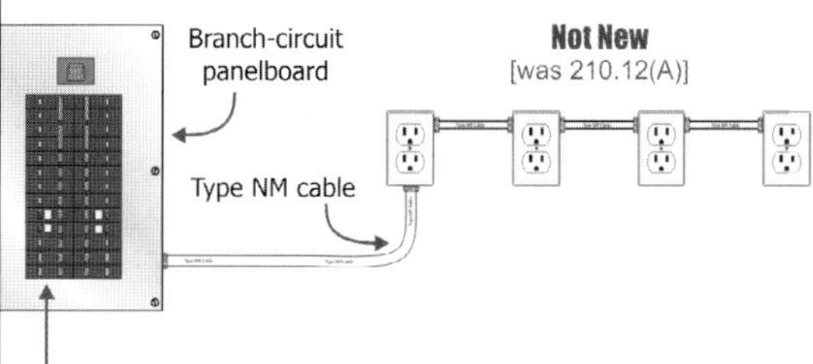

ombination AFCI circuit breaker

1) A listed combination type arc-fault circuit interrupter, installed to provide protection of the entire branch circuit

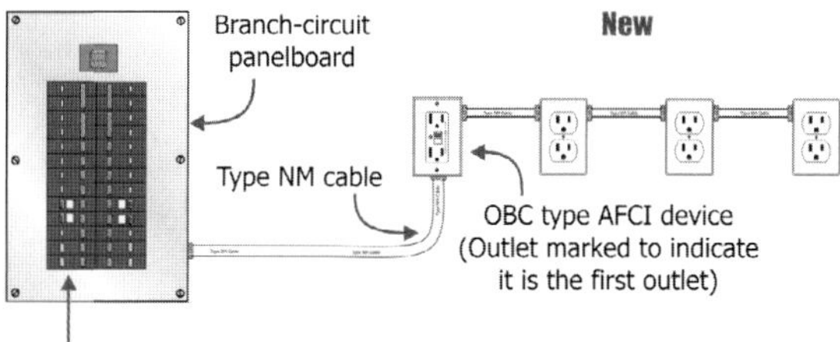

Branch/Feeder AFCI circuit breaker

(2) A listed branch/feeder type AFCI installed at the origin of the branch circuit in combination with a listed outlet branch circuit type AFCI installed at the first outlet box on the branch circuit (first outlet marked to indicate that it is the first outlet)

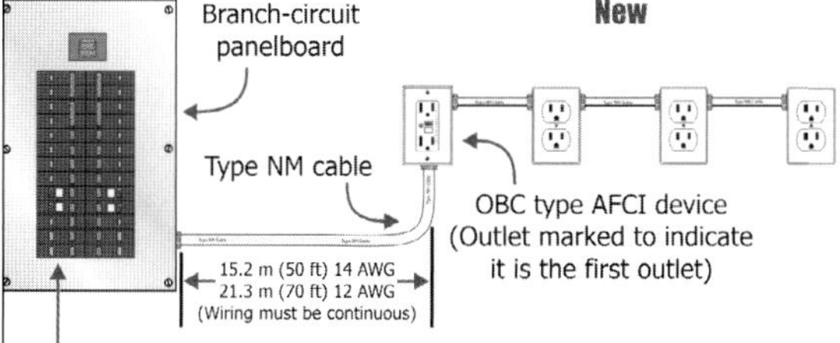

upplemental arc protection circuit breaker

3) A listed supplemental arc protection circuit breaker installed at the origin of the branch circuit in combination with a listed outlet branch circuit type AFCI installed at the first outlet box on the branch circuit (with three limiting conditions)

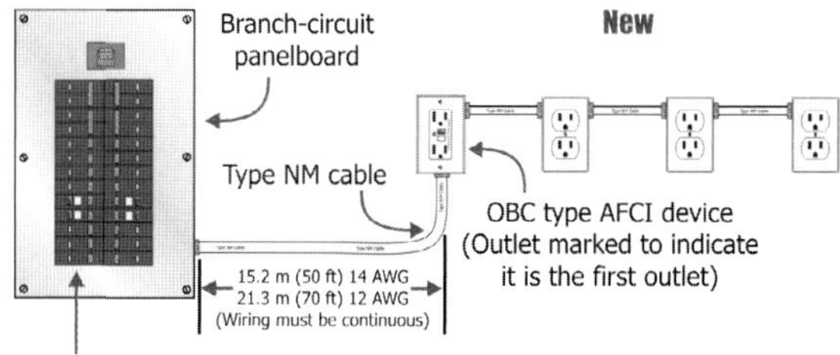

Listed branch circuit OCPD (circuit breaker or fuse)

(4) **System Combination Type AFCI.** A listed outlet branch circuit type AFCI installed at the first outlet in combination with a listed branch circuit over-current protective device (with four limiting conditions) (OCPD & OBC AFCI device must be identified and listed as "System Combination" type AFCI)

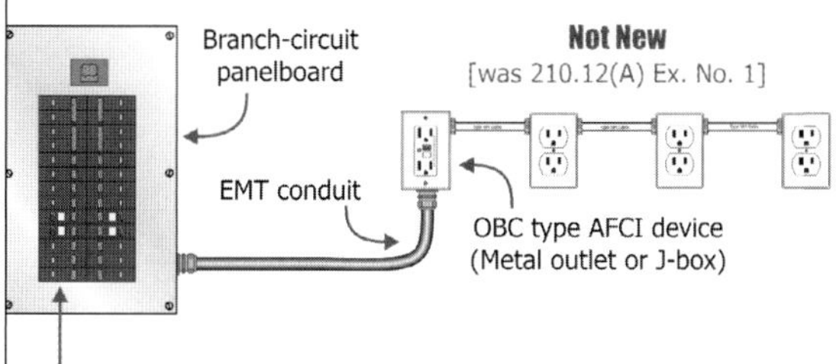

isted branch circuit OCPD (circuit breaker or fuse)

5) A listed outlet branch-circuit type AFCI device (first outlet) is permitted with RMC, IMC, EMT, Type MC, steel armored Type AC cables, metal wireways, or metal auxiliary gutters and metal outlet and junction boxes installed for the portion of the branch circuit between the OCPD and the first outlet

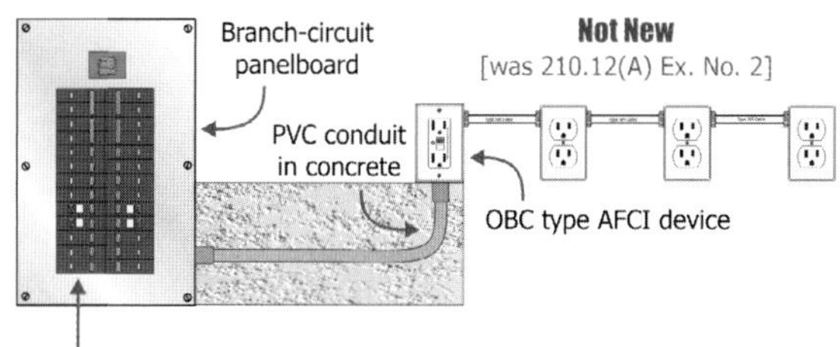

Listed branch circuit OCPD (circuit breaker or fuse)

(6) Where a listed metal or nonmetallic conduit or tubing or Type MC cable is encased in not less than 50mm (2 in.) of concrete for the portion of the branch circuit between the OCPD and the first outlet, it shall be permitted to install an a listed outlet branch circuit type AFCI at the first outlet

210.12(B) Exception

Change at a Glance

Existing branch circuit conductors can be extended up to 1.8 m (6 ft.) without AFCI protection where no additional outlets or devices are installed for when modified or extended.

Code Language

210.12 Arc-Fault Circuit-Interrupter Protection

Arc-fault circuit-interrupter protection shall be provided as required in 210.12(A),(B), and (C). The arc-fault circuit interrupter shall be installed in a readily accessible location.

(B) Branch Circuit Extensions or Modifications — Dwelling Units. In any of the areas specified in 210.12(A), where branch-circuit wiring is modified, replaced, or extended, the branch circuit shall be protected by one of the following:

(1) A listed combination-type AFCI located at the origin of the branch circuit

(2) A listed outlet branch-circuit type AFCI located at the first receptacle outlet of the existing branch circuit.

Exception: *AFCI protection shall not be required where the extension of the existing conductors is not more than 1.8 m (6 ft.) and does not include any additional outlets or devices.*

Proposal 2-115

210.12(B) AFCI - Extensions or Modifications

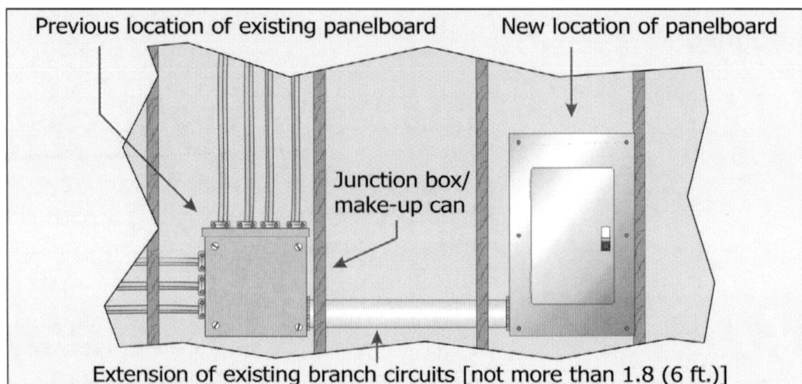

In any of the areas specified in 210.12(A), where branch-circuit wiring is modified, replaced or extended, the branch circuit shall be protected by:

(1) A listed combination AFCI located at the origin of the branch circuit, or

(2) A listed outlet branch-circuit AFCI located at the first receptacle outlet of the existing branch circuit

Exception: *AFCI protection is not required where the extension is not more than 1.8 m (6 ft.) and does not include any additional outlets or devices.*

2011 *NEC* Requirement

A provision was added at 210.12(B) requiring AFCI protection for branch-circuit wiring in areas of a dwelling unit specified at 210.12(A) when said wiring is modified, replaced, or extended. This AFCI protection can be provided by a listed combination-type AFCI overcurrent device or a listed outlet branch-circuit (OBC) AFCI device located at the first receptacle outlet of the existing branch circuit.

2014 *NEC* Change

A new exception to AFCI Branch Circuit Extensions or Modifications was added to indicate what is considered a "dwelling unit branch circuit extension" and to clarify that branch circuit conductors can be extended up to 1.8 m (6 ft.) without AFCI protection where no additional outlets or devices are installed.

Analysis of Change

There are times when a service upgrade occurs at dwelling units. This action can sometimes involve a panelboard relocation even a short distance from the original location. This situation can easily result in the existing branch circuit conductors being too short to reach their new location at the new panelboard. Often times, these branch circuits are spliced and extended using the old panelboard cabinet as a junction box, with the busbars removed. This is a good example of an extension or modification that will be exempted from AFCI protection with this new exception to 210.12(B). These type issues are often topics of discussion at IAEI meetings, as well as other educational meetings, and do need some clarification.

There has been varied interpretation and enforcement of situations like this over the past three years. This new exception will help clarify which extensions and modifications require AFCI protection and which ones will not. This will clarify that extending branch circuit conductors within an enclosure for the purposes of replacing a device or utilization equipment or for extending a branch circuit to

210.12(B) Exception

Continued

a panelboard being replaced or upgraded does not require an AFCI protective device to be installed. A distance of 1.8 m (6 ft) was chosen for branch circuit extensions in this exception as this length should provide a sufficient length for most applications where an existing panelboard is being relocated out of a clothes closet or to comply with readily accessible requirements, etc.

210.12(B) AFCI - Extensions or Modifications

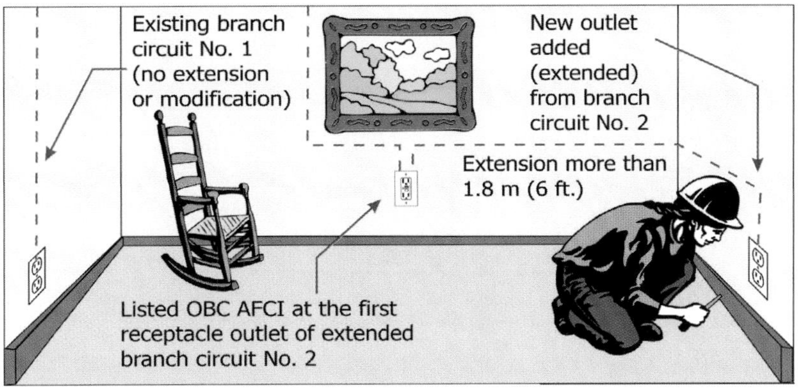

In any of the areas specified in 210.12(A), where branch-circuit wiring is modified, replaced or extended, the branch circuit shall be protected by:

(1) A listed combination AFCI located at the origin of the branch circuit, or

(2) A listed outlet branch-circuit AFCI located at the first receptacle outlet of the existing branch circuit

Exception: *AFCI protection is not required where the extension is not more than 1.8 m (6 ft.) and does not include any additional outlets or devices.*

210.12(C)

Change at a Glance

Dormitory units will now require AFCI protection.

Code Language

210.12 Arc-Fault Circuit-Interrupter Protection

Arc-fault circuit-interrupter protection shall be provided as required in 210.12(A),(B) and (C). The arc-fault circuit interrupter shall be installed in a readily accessible location.

(C) Dormitory Units. All 120-volt, single-phase, 15- and 20-ampere branch circuits supplying outlets installed in dormitory unit bedrooms, living rooms, hallways, closets, and similar rooms shall be protected by a listed arc-fault circuit interrupter meeting the requirements of 210.12(A)(1) through (6) as appropriate.

Proposal 2-78

Comment 2-37

2011 *NEC* Requirement

AFCI protection applied to dwelling units only. No provision existed to require AFCI protection at dormitory units.

2014 *NEC* Change

A new 210.12(C) requires all 120-volt, single-phase, 15- and 20-ampere branch circuits supplying outlets installed in dormitory unit bedrooms, living rooms, hallways, closets, and similar rooms to be provided with AFCI protection.

Analysis of Change

Many of today's dormitories more closely resemble an apartment building with suite style units that include a mini version of a kitchen. Currently, the distinction between apartments and dormitory units can become a bit confusing. Dormitories are sleeping areas that are usually inhabited by individuals who are not knowledgeable regarding the use of extension cords, outlet strips and electrical appliance loads. These confined living quarter conditions can lead to damage or misuse of the extension cords which in many cases are undersized for the applied load, such as a microwave oven. These facilities serve as dwelling units to those who reside in them and the occupants should be afforded the same level of protection provided by AFCI protection as those who reside in a dwelling unit.

210.13

Change at a Glance

GFP of equipment is now required for branch-circuit disconnects meeting provisions described at 230.95.

Code Language

210.13 Ground-Fault Protection of Equipment
Each branch-circuit disconnect rated 1000 amperes or more and installed on solidly grounded wye electrical systems of more than 150 volts to ground, but not exceeding 600 volts phase-to-phase, shall be provided with ground-fault protection of equipment in accordance with the provisions of 230.95.

Informational Note: For buildings that contain health care occupancies, see the requirements of 517.17.

Exception No. 1: *The provisions of this section shall not apply to a disconnecting means for a continuous industrial process where a nonorderly shutdown will introduce additional or increased hazards.*

Exception No. 2: *The provisions of this section shall not apply if ground-fault protection of equipment is provided on the supply side of the branch circuit and on the load side of any transformer supplying the branch circuit.*

Proposal 2-125

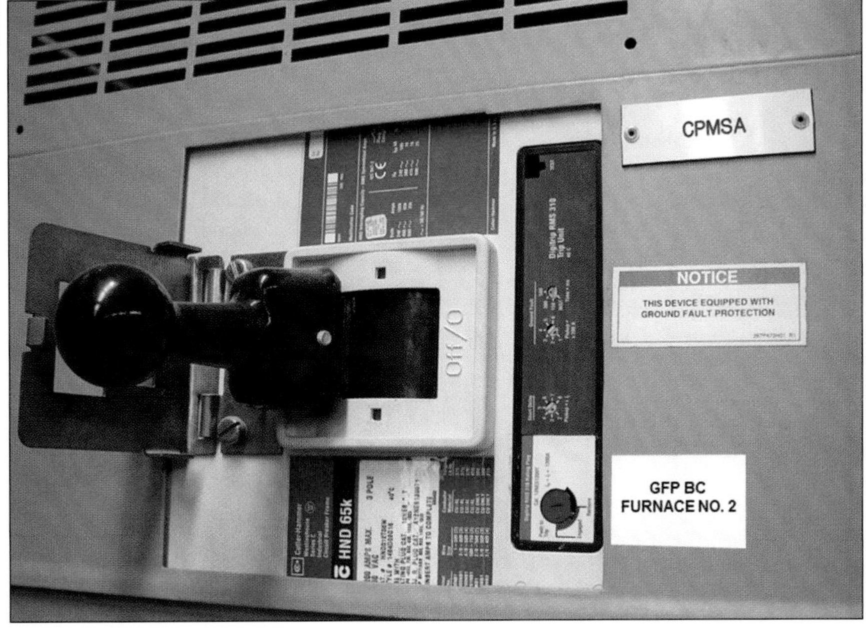

2011 *NEC* Requirement

Ground-fault protection of equipment is required at 230.95 for services and for feeders at 215.10. These GFP provisions are applicable when these service or feeder disconnecting means are rated at 1000 amperes or more and installed on solidly grounded wye electrical systems of more than 150 volts to ground, but not exceeding 600 volts phase-to-phase, with this GFP of equipment supplied in accordance with the provisions of 230.95. No provisions existed for GFP of branch-circuit equipment in the 2011 *NEC*.

2014 *NEC* Change

A new section for "Ground-Fault Protection of Equipment" was added to require each branch-circuit disconnect rated 1000 amperes or more and installed on solidly grounded wye electrical systems of more than 150 volts to ground, but not exceeding 600 volts phase-to-phase to be provided with GFP of equipment in accordance with the provisions of 230.95.

Analysis of Change

There are installations in industrial establishments where a separate transformer with a 480/277 secondary is used to supply some types of industrial machinery. Such machines can have 1000 amperes or larger overcurrent protection devices. This type of wiring would be considered a branch circuit by definition. This new requirement in Article 210 would require ground-fault protection of equipment for this type of application involving a branch circuit. There are applications where this can be applied and avoid confusion where the overcurrent protection is functioning as a branch-circuit overcurrent device directly supplying a load. This new language for branch circuits was crafted after the existing language at 215.10 for feeders, including the appropriate exceptions for GFP provisions creating additional or increased hazards, and GFP already provided on the supply side of the branch circuit.

Articles 215 and 230 have requirements for GFP of equipment for feeders and services. This new provision will bring the same GFP protection for equipment supplied by a branch circuit.

210.17

Change at a Glance

Outlet(s) installed for the purpose of charging electric vehicles are required to be supplied by a separate branch circuit with no other outlets.

Code Language

210.17 Electric Vehicle Branch Circuit

Outlet(s) installed for the purpose of charging electric vehicles shall be supplied by a separate branch circuit. This circuit shall have no other outlets.

Informational Note. See 625.2 for the definition of "Electrical Vehicle".

Proposal 2-128a

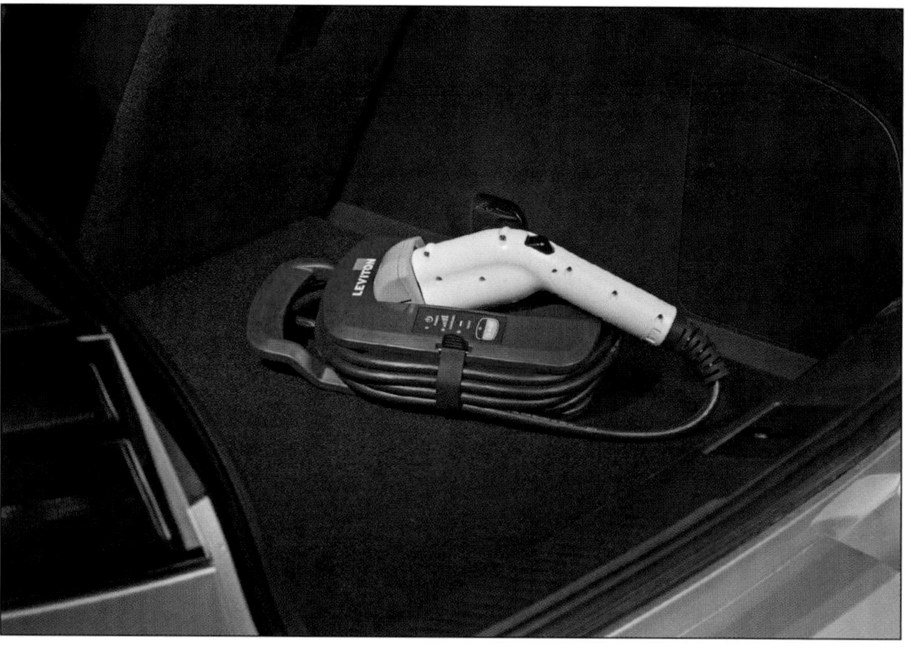

2011 *NEC* Requirement

The 2011 *NEC* had no provisions that required outlet(s) that provide power to electric vehicle charging stations to be on an individual or separate branch circuit.

2014 *NEC* Change

New provisions were added to require outlet(s) installed for the purpose of charging electric vehicles to be supplied by a separate branch circuit with no other outlets. A new Informational Note was also added to point users of the *Code* to 625.2 for the definition of an *electrical vehicle*.

Analysis of Change

With the growing trend toward seeking alternative energy sources combined with the rising cost of oil and gasoline prices, electric vehicles have become more popular than ever before over the last few years. Combining these newer and advanced technologies for electric vehicle charging demands with older and traditional wiring methods (*particularly at dwelling units*) can be challenging at best. Charging an electric vehicle (EV) by simply plugging into an existing 120-volt receptacle outlet that is more than likely supplied from a general lighting circuit can and will overload this existing general purpose branch circuit.

It should be noted that this new requirement does not demand that an outlet(s) for the specific and sole purpose of charging EV equipment be installed. This new requirement simply states that where such EV charging outlet(s) are installed (by choice), these outlet(s) must be supplied by a separate or individual branch circuit with no other outlets. This new provision for EV charging will go a long way in ensuring that EV charging can be completed safely and effectively without overloading an existing branch circuit.

A new Informational Note was also added giving guidance to 625.2 for the definition of an *electrical vehicle*. This should provide a link from this new requirement in Article 210 to the requirements in Article 625 for Electric Vehicle Charging Systems.

Change at a Glance

The requirements for outdoor receptacles at dwellings have been revised to permit the required receptacle outlets to be "readily accessible from grade."

Code Language

210.52 Dwelling Unit Receptacle Outlets

(E) Outdoor Outlets. Outdoor receptacle outlets shall be installed in accordance with (E)(1) through (E)(3). ~~[See 210.8(A)(3).]~~

Informational Note: See 210.8(A)(3).

(1) One-Family and Two-Family Dwellings. For a one-family dwelling and each unit of a two-family dwelling that is at grade level, at least one receptacle outlet readily accessible ~~while standing at~~ from grade ~~level~~ and ~~located~~ not more than 2.0 m (6 ½ ft) above grade level shall be installed at the front and back of the dwelling.

(2) Multifamily Dwellings. For each dwelling unit of a multifamily dwelling where the dwelling unit is located at grade level and provided with individual exterior entrance/egress, at least one receptacle outlet readily accessible from grade ~~level~~ and not more than 2.0 m (6 ½ ft) above grade level shall be installed.

Proposal 2-168, 2-169, 2-170

210.52(E)(1) and (E)(2) Outdoor Outlets

At least one receptacle outlet readily accessible from grade and not more than 2.0 m (6½ ft) above grade level shall be installed at the front and back of dwelling units

Same provision for multifamily dwellings where the dwelling unit is located at grade level and provided with individual exterior entrance/egress

2011 *NEC* Requirement

This section of the *Code* requires at least two outdoor receptacles at every single-family dwelling, one at the front and one at the back. The parent language at 210.52 clarifies that these receptacle outlets are to be rated at 125-volt, 15- or 20-amperes. This rule also applies at every two-family dwelling that is accessible at grade level. For the 2011 *NEC*, these outdoor receptacle outlets were required to be "accessible while standing at grade level and located not more than 2.0 m (6 ½ ft) above grade." At least one receptacle outlet is required at multifamily dwellings where an individual dwelling unit is located at grade level and provided with exterior entrance/egress from that individual unit.

2014 *NEC* Change

This provision for outdoor receptacles was revised by removing the "while standing at grade level" requirement for one- and two-family dwellings. The required outdoor receptacle outlet(s) was further revised by requiring these receptacle outlet(s) to be "readily accessible" rather than just "accessible" from grade level. The required outdoor receptacle outlet(s) now has the same requirement to be "readily accessible from grade" at one-family, two-family, and multifamily dwelling units.

Analysis of Change

The *NEC* requirement for outdoor receptacle outlets and their location and accessibility at dwelling units has gone through substantial changes over the past few *Code* cycles. In the 1996 *NEC*, these outdoor receptacle outlets were required to be "accessible at grade level." There were no provisions for outdoor receptacle outlets at multifamily dwellings until the 2005 *NEC*. The provisions for "accessible at grade level" stayed the same until the 2008 *NEC*, which saw the requirement for "accessible *while standing* at grade level" added to that *Code* cycle and remained the same for the 2011 *NEC*. Outdoor receptacle outlets at multifamily dwellings were required to be "accessible from grade level" from their inception in the 2005 *NEC* and remained the same until the 2011 *NEC*. The 2014 *NEC* experienced further revision to these provisions to now required outdoor receptacle outlet(s) to have the same necessity of being "readily accessible from grade" at one-family, two-family, and multifamily dwelling units.

Close interpretation to the literal text of the previous code requirement at 210.52(E)(1) disqualified an outdoor receptacle outlet installed at a low open deck or porch from serving as one of these required outdoor receptacle outlets for one- and two-family dwelling units, unless it was installed and located close enough to the edge so it can be reached "while standing at grade level." This change would allow the deck or porch receptacle outlet described above to serve as one of the required outdoor receptacle outlets if it were "readily accessible from grade" with the deck or porch permitted to serve as "grade." The safety justification for the receptacle outlet placement is clearly met provided there is unencumbered access to the receptacle outlet and as long as the receptacle outlet is located low enough so it will be routinely used for outdoor applications rather than resorted to for running extension cords through windows or doorways.

This revision changes the outdoor receptacle outlet(s) from having to be "accessible" to being "readily accessible." Caution should be exercised by both the installer and the enforcement community with this change as there is a momentous difference from "accessible" to "readily accessible." *Readily accessible* is defined as "capable of being reached quickly for operation, renewal, or inspections without requiring those to whom ready access is requisite to climb over or remove obstacles or to resort to portable ladders, and so forth."

This revision also removes the outdoor receptacle outlet requirement distinction between a one- and two-family dwelling and a multifamily dwelling. Individual units of multifamily dwellings (with individual exterior entrance/egress) required an outdoor receptacle outlet, but their decks or porches were not included in the equation for the accessibility of this required outdoor receptacle outlet until the 2014 *NEC*.

210.52(E)(3)

Change at a Glance

The requirement for a receptacle located at "Balconies, Decks, and Porches" has been revised to require the balcony, deck or porch to be attached to the dwelling, and to eliminate the requirements for the outdoor receptacle outlet to be installed "within the perimeter of the balcony, deck or porch."

Code Language

210.52 Dwelling Unit Receptacle Outlets

(E) Outdoor Outlets. Outdoor receptacle outlets shall be installed in accordance with (E)(1) through (E)(3). ~~[See 210.8(A)(3).]~~

Informational Note: See 210.8(A)(3).

(3) Balconies, Decks and Porches. Balconies, decks and porches that are attached to the dwelling unit and are accessible from inside the dwelling unit shall have at least one receptacle outlet ~~installed within the perimeter of~~ accessible from the balcony, deck or porch. The receptacle outlet shall not be located more than 2.0 m (6 ½ ft) above the balcony, deck, or porch walking surface.

Proposal 2-168, 2-169, 2-175, 2-176

Comment 2-80

210.52(E)(3) Balconies, Decks and Porches

Balconies, decks and porches that are attached to the dwelling unit and are accessible from inside the dwelling unit shall have at least one receptacle outlet accessible from the balcony, deck or porch.

The receptacle outlet shall not be located more than 2.0 m (6½ ft) above the balcony, deck, or porch walking surface.

2011 *NEC* Requirement

All balconies, decks, and porches that are accessible from inside the dwelling unit are required to have at least one 125-volt, 15- or 20-ampere receptacle outlet installed within the perimeter of the balcony, deck, or porch. The receptacle cannot be located more than 2.0 m (6 ½ ft) above the balcony, deck, or porch surface.

2014 *NEC* Change

The 2014 *NEC* clarified that this outdoor receptacle outlet requirement only applied to a balcony, deck or porch that is attached to the dwelling. Further revision to this requirement eliminated the requirements for the outdoor receptacle outlet(s) to be installed "within the perimeter of the balcony, deck or porch."

Analysis of Change

The requirement for a 125-volt, 15- or 20-ampere outdoor receptacle outlet to be installed at every balcony, deck or porch (*accessible from inside the dwelling unit*) was introduced into the 2008 edition of the *NEC*. At that time, there was an exception to this rule for balcony, deck or porch that was smaller than 1.86 m^2 (20 ft^2) to not be required to have a receptacle outlet installed. This outdoor receptacle outlet was required to be "installed within the perimeter of the balcony, deck or porch"; and this worked well with these smaller balconies, decks and porches (*simply in existence for decorative or architectural purposes*) being exempted from this requirement. For the 2011 *NEC*, this exception for smaller balconies, decks and porches was removed in favor of all balconies, decks and porches having an outdoor receptacle outlet for holiday lighting purposes, etc. It proved to be difficult in some situations to install an outdoor receptacle outlet "within the perimeter of the balcony, deck or porch" of these smaller esthetic balconies, decks and porches which, in some cases,

210.52(E)(3)

Continued

had an exterior double door or sliding glass door covering the entire width of the balcony, deck or porch. For the 2014 *NEC*, this requirement for the outdoor receptacle outlet to be installed within the perimeter of the balcony, deck or porch has been deleted.

This revised text further clarifies that this requirement for at least one 125-volt, 15- or 20-ampere outdoor receptacle outlet to be installed at every balcony, deck or porch that has access from inside the dwelling unit be limited to only those balconies, decks and porches that are "attached to the dwelling unit." No substantiation was given for this distinction in the proposal for this change, but one would surmise that these "detached" balconies, decks and porches do not pose the same threat of extension cords being run through windows and doorways as their "attached" counterparts might suggest. Is it possible to have a "detached" balcony?

210.52(G)

Change at a Glance

Receptacle provisions for basements, garages, and accessory buildings were revised into a list format. A branch circuit supplying garage receptacle(s) is to supply only the garage. Receptacles are required for each car space in a garage.

NEW

REVISION

Code Language:

210.52 Dwelling Unit Receptacle Outlets

(G) Basements, Garages, and Accessory Buildings. For a one-family dwelling, ~~the following provisions shall apply:~~ at least one receptacle outlet shall be installed in the following specified areas. These receptacles shall be in addition to receptacles required for specific equipment.

(1) Garages. In each attached garage and in each detached garage with electric power. The branch circuit supplying this receptacle(s) shall not supply outlets outside of the garage. At least one receptacle outlet shall be installed for each car space.

(2) Accessory Buildings. In each accessory building with electric power.

(3) Basements. In each separate unfinished portion of a basement.

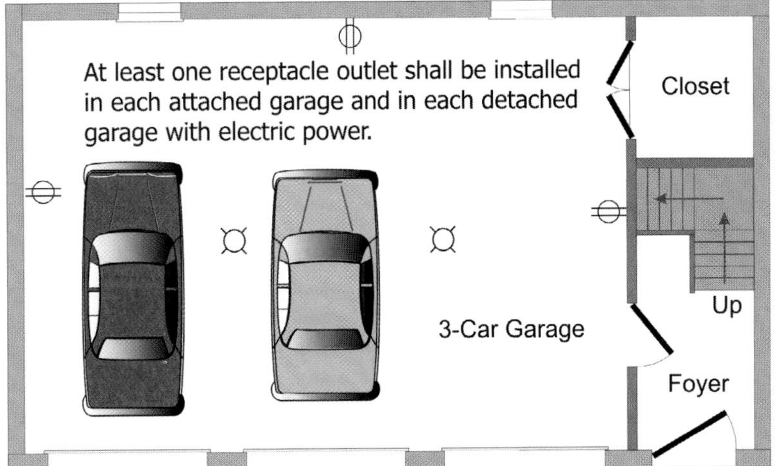

210.52(G)(1) Dwelling Unit Garages
At least one receptacle outlet shall be installed in each attached garage and in each detached garage with electric power.
Closet
3-Car Garage
Up
Foyer
The branch circuit supplying this receptacle(s) shall not supply outlets outside of the garage.
At least one receptacle outlet shall be installed for each car space.

2011 *NEC* Requirement

At least one 125-volt, 15- or 20-ampere receptacle outlet is required to be installed in every single-family dwelling basement, attached garage, and in each detached garage or accessory building with electric power. A receptacle is required in each separate unfinished portion of a basement.

2014 *NEC* Change

Receptacles are still required in the same locations at basements, garages, and accessory buildings as the 2011 *NEC* requirements, with revisions added to require the branch circuit(s) supplying garage receptacle(s) to supply only garage outlet(s). A receptacle is now required for each car space in a garage as well.

Analysis of Change

Section 210.52(G)(1) has been revised into appropriate list items to provide for greater clarity and added titles to the applicable list items of the subsection. The main changes occurred at (1) Garages. The garages encountered today at most dwelling units have gone from a simple place to park vehicles out of the elements in a bygone era to do-it-all locations where homeowners service their vehicles and/or convert a portion of the garage space to serve as a workshop. In previous editions of the *Code*, one convenience receptacle outlet was required in this garage location regardless of the size of the garage or the intended use of same. In many instances, this one required receptacle outlet may very well be located behind a large appliance such as a freezer or refrigerator. It is not uncommon in these situations for the homeowner to resort to running an extension cord from this receptacle outlet behind the appliance or from the garage door receptacle outlet, stapling the cord to the ceiling and down the wall to have an additional outlet for convenience use for such things as hand drills, car vacuum cleaners, etc. The majority of dwelling units built today are constructed with 2- or 3-car garages. This new provision

Continued

Proposal 2-178a, 2-179, 2-180, 2-181

Comment 2-82, 2-83, 2-84

which will now require an additional receptacle outlet for each car space will reduce the use of extension cords currently being used to extend the branch-circuit wiring and provide a safer environment for the homeowner.

Another provision added here will require the branch circuit(s) supplying garage receptacle(s) to supply only garage outlet(s). This is an effort to recognize the possibility of electric vehicle (EV) and plug-in hybrid electric vehicle (PHEV) charging that is becoming more and more of a possibility with the rise in popularity of EV technology and the continued search for alternative fuel sources. Having these branch circuits limited to just the garage will greatly assist in the ability of these garage receptacle outlets possessing enough capacity to handle a load such as an EV charging station. With this EV charging concept in mind, it makes sense to expand the requirements for receptacle outlets in dwelling unit garages to provide at least one receptacle outlet in each car parking space. It should be noted that this requirement limits the branch circuit(s) supplying garage receptacle(s) to "not supply outlets outside of the garage." This requirement does not prohibit switches and lighting outlets located in the garage form being supplied by these garage branch circuits.

210.64

Change at a Glance

New provision requires 125-volt, single-phase, 15- or 20-ampere receptacle outlet to be installed at electrical service areas.

Code Language

210.64 Electrical Service Areas

At least one 125-volt, single-phase, 15- or 20-ampere-rated receptacle outlet shall be installed within 15 m (50 ft) of the electrical service equipment.

Exception: *The receptacle outlet shall not be required to be installed in one- and two-family dwellings.*

Proposal 2-191

Comment 2-86

210.64 Electrical Service Areas

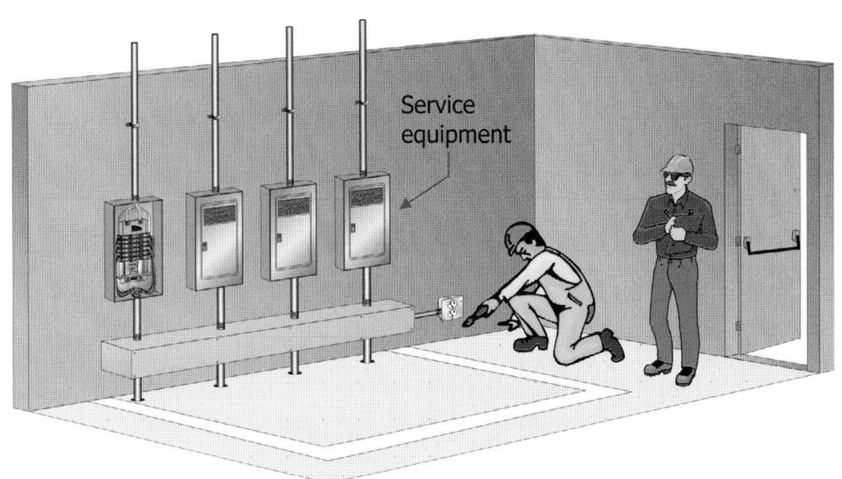

At least one 125-volt, single phase, 15 or 20 ampere rated receptacle outlet shall be installed within 15 m (50 ft) of the electrical service equipment.

Exception for one and two family dwellings

2011 *NEC* Requirement

There was no requirement for a 125-volt, single-phase, 15- or 20-ampere receptacle outlet to be installed at electrical service equipment areas or in service room areas.

2014 *NEC* Change

A new section entitled, "Electrical Service Areas" was added which will require at least one 125-volt, single-phase, 15- or 20-ampere receptacle outlet to be installed within 15 m (50 ft) of the electrical service area.

Analysis of Change

At least one 125-volt, single-phase, 15- or 20-ampere receptacle outlet is now required to be installed within 15 m (50 ft) of all electrical service areas. An exception was also added for this rule to exempt one- and two-family dwelling services from this requirement. This new rule is similar to the requirement for a service receptacle outlet to be installed within 7.5 m (25 ft) of all heating, air-conditioning, and refrigeration equipment at 210.63. At service equipment, there is sometimes a need for connecting portable electrical data acquisition equipment for the qualitative analysis of the electrical system. Test equipment is frequently needed for monitoring and servicing electrical equipment in service areas as well.

Extension cords were often used where they are run across the floor of a hallway into an adjoining electrical service roomThis new requirement does not go far enough to stop such practices. If the wording chosen for this requirement had said something like "within sight" or something similar, the receptacle would have had to be *visible* and not more than 15 m (50 ft) from the service equipment per the definition of *within sight* in Article 100. This rule simply states that the required receptacle "shall be installed within 15 m (50 ft) of the electrical service equipment." This can be accomplished with a receptacle outlet located in the next room down and across the hallway from the electrical service area employing an extension cord as long as the receptacle is "installed within 15 m (50 ft) of the electrical service equipment."

Table 220.3

Change at a Glance

A new line item was added to Table 220.3 for "Electric Vehicle Charging Equipment" and a reference to 625.14.

[See next page for Code Language]

Proposal 2-219

Table 220.3 Additional Load Calculation References (in part)

Calculation	Article	Section (or Part)
Air-conditioning and refrigerating equipment, branch-circuit conductor sizing	440	Part IV
Cranes and hoists, rating and size of conductors	610	610.14
Electric vehicle charging system branch circuit and feeder calculations	625	625.14
Electric welders, ampacity calculations	630	630.11, 630.31
Electrically driven or controlled irrigation machines	675	675.7(A), 675.22(A)

(Remainder of table unchanged, see NEC for complete table)

2011 *NEC* Requirement

Table 220.3 gives several references to calculations found throughout the *NEC*. Section 220.3 is titled, "Application of Other Articles." Electric vehicle charging equipment was not mentioned in the table.

2014 *NEC* Change

New line item was added to Table 220.3, Additional Load Calculation References. The new line item is titled "Electric vehicle charging system branch circuit and feeder calculations" with a reference to 625.14 also added to this table.

Analysis of Change

This new line item for Table 220.3 will help clarify the load calculation requirements for electric vehicle (EV) charging loads that are considered as continuous. The previous table references provide necessary correlation to other rules in the *Code*. This included factors that need to be included in the overall calculation for service conductors and equipment. Electric vehicles and their charging stations are a growing trend in our modern world. This change will give a direct and necessary link from Article 220 for calculations to Article 625 for electric vehicle charging systems.

220.12, Exception

Change at a Glance

New exception to "Lighting Loads for Specified Occupancies" will permit lighting loads to be calculated in accordance with locally adopted energy codes.

Code Language

220.12 Lighting Load for Specified Occupancies

A unit load of not less than that specified in Table 220.12 for occupancies specified therein shall constitute the minimum lighting load. The floor area for each floor shall be calculated from the outside dimensions of the building, dwelling unit, or other area involved. For dwelling units, the calculated floor area shall not include open porches, garages, or unused or unfinished spaces not adaptable for future use.

Exception: *Where the building is designed and constructed to comply with an energy code adopted by the local authority, the lighting load shall be permitted to be calculated at the values specified in the energy code where the following conditions are met:*

(1) *A power monitoring system is installed that will provide continuous information regarding the total general lighting load of the building.*

(2) *The power monitoring system will be set with alarm values to alert the building owner or manager if the lighting load exceeds the values set by the energy code.*

(3) *The demand factors specified in 220.42 are not applied to the general lighting load.*

Proposal 2-228

Comment 2-102

2011 *NEC* Requirement

Lighting loads were calculated using the unit load of not less than that specified in Table 220.12 for occupancies specified in the table.

2014 *NEC* Change

A new exception to "Lighting Loads for Specified Occupancies" was added that will permit lighting loads to be calculated in accordance with locally adopted energy codes where power monitoring systems are in place and the demand factors specified in 220.42 have not been applied to the general lighting load.

Analysis of Change

This new exception recognizes that there are calculations in Article 220 that can be adjusted to align with model energy code mandates. The three conditions stipulated in the new exception are necessary to alert the owners and maintenance personnel that might be monitoring the system that the energy code calculations are about to, or have been, exceeded. An example might be when subsequent expansions or renovations take place. This is a very significant change to industries and their occupancies, such as the education facilities industry. Several buildings could be affected by this allowance to substantially reduce the size of services, feeders, transformers, etc., to many of these educational buildings. The costs associated with increasing the size of the services, etc., only adds to the increasing financial burden on the student and the taxpayer. This also increases the amount of available fault current and arc flash energy, thereby decreasing safety. Using energy code values may result in smaller services, feeders, transformers and available fault-current values, which could result in significant cost savings for these educational locations.

225.52(A)

Change at a Glance

Revision correlates location and operating requirements for outside branch circuit and feeder disconnecting means operating at over 1000 volts with that of service disconnecting means.

Code Language

225.52 Disconnecting Means

(A) Location. A building or structure disconnecting means shall be located in accordance with 225.32, or, if not readily accessible, it shall be operable by mechanical linkage from a readily accessible point. For multibuilding industrial installations under single management, it shall be permitted to be electrically operated by a ~~similarly located,~~ readily accessible remote-control device in a separate building or structure.

Proposal 4-69

Comment 4-32

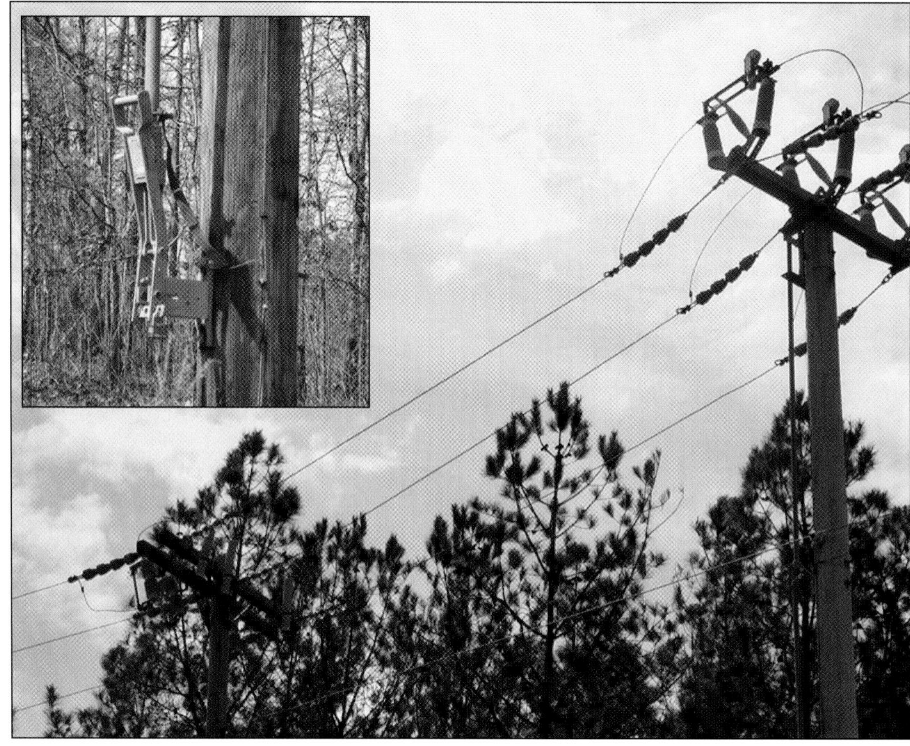

2011 *NEC* Requirement

For outside branch circuits and feeders rated over 600 volts, 225.52(A) generally allowed the disconnecting means to be installed either inside at a readily accessible location nearest the point of entrance of the conductors or outside of the building or structure served, or the disconnecting means was permitted to be electrically operated by a similarly located remote-control device.

2014 *NEC* Change

The requirements pertaining to the disconnection means for services rated over 1000 volts have been incorporated into the requirements for the disconnecting means of outside branch circuits and feeders.

Analysis of Change

Section 225.52(A) applies to the location of the disconnecting means for an outside branch circuit of feeder. There is a growing trend in the electrical industry to utilize more branch circuits and feeders rated over 1000 volts. This Level 1 subsection has been revised to incorporate the same language seen at 230.205(C) which deals with a service disconnecting means being able to be electrically operated by a readily accessible, remote-control device. This revised language in Article 225 correlates with the language at 230.205(A) for location requirements for medium voltage service disconnecting means when the service exceeds 1000 volts, nominal. Quite often, at campus-style industrial occupancies, a pole-mounted disconnect will be placed in an outdoor feeder location and not in service conductors supplied directly by the utility. The safety concerns for this type of feeder disconnecting means will be identical to those for a service disconnection means in Article 230.

230.30

Change at a Glance

Section 230.30 was divided into two sub-sections (A) Insulation and (B) Wiring Methods, and a list of acceptable wiring methods for underground service conductors was added.

Code Language

230.30 ~~Insulation~~ Installation. (Underground Service Conductors)

(A) Insulation. Underground service~~-lateral~~ conductors shall be insulated for the applied voltage.

See *NEC* for exceptions.

(B) Wiring Methods. Underground service conductors shall be installed in accordance with the applicable requirements of this *Code* covering the type of wiring method used and shall be limited to the following methods:
(1) Type RMC conduit
(2) Type IMC conduit
(3) Type NUCC conduit
(4) Type HDPE conduit
(5) Type PVC conduit
(6) Type RTRC conduit
(7) Type IGS cable
(8) Type USE conductors or cables
(9) Type MV or Type MC cable identified for direct burial applications
(10) Type MI cable, where suitably protected against physical damage and corrosive conditions

---

Proposal 4-115, 4-116

Comment 4-44, 4-45

230.30(B) Wiring Methods (Underground Service Conductors)

A list of acceptable wiring methods for "Underground Service Conductors" was added at 230.30(B).

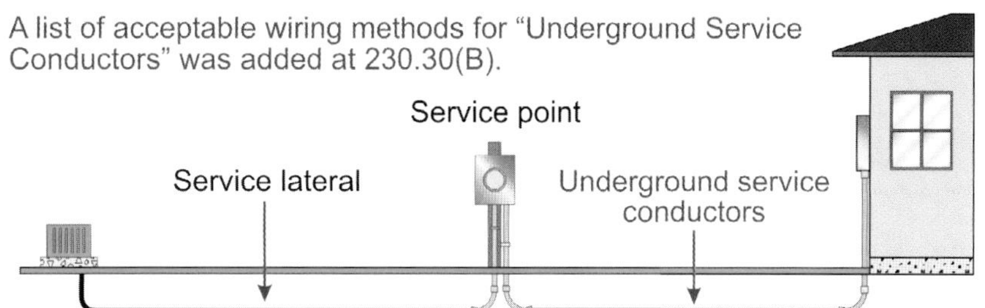

Underground service conductors are required to be installed in accordance with the applicable requirements of the *NEC* for the type of wiring method used and shall be limited to the following wiring methods:

(1) Type RMC conduit
(2) Type IMC conduit
(3) Type NUCC conduit
(4) Type HDPE conduit
(5) Type PVC conduit
(6) Type RTRC conduit
(7) Type IGS cable
(8) Type USE conductors or cables
(9) Type MV or Type MC cable identified for direct burial applications
(10) Type MI cable, where suitably protected against physical damage and corrosion

2011 *NEC* Requirement

This section was titled, "Insulation" and stated that service-lateral conductors had to be insulated for the applied voltage with an exception for the grounded conductor with conditions.

2014 *NEC* Change

This section was retitled, "Installation" and divided into two subsections. Section 230.30(A) is the previous language in 230.30 with the term *service-lateral conductors* changed to *service conductors* to recognize that the definition for *service lateral* (that was revised in the 2011 *NEC*) is the "underground conductors between the utility electric supply and the service point." This section is referring to "the conductors from the service point to the service disconnecting means," which is the definition of *service conductors*. New 230.30(B) was added to this section identifying a list of acceptable wiring methods permitted for underground service conductors.

Analysis of Change

Section 230.30(B) was added to provide a list of acceptable wiring methods to be utilized for the installation of underground service conductors. The list includes all the cables and conductors that are identified in Chapter 3 as suitable for use as both service conductors and for direct burial.

This new list of wiring methods for underground service conductors was conceived in the 2011 *NEC Code* process, but was placed on hold by the NEC CC, stating that, "The text added by the panel, 'listed direct burial cable,' permits any listed direct burial cable to be installed for use as underground service cables and is inconsistent with the requirements of Chapter 3 [e.g., UF cable as covered in 340.12(1)]. This action appeared as Proposal 4-93 and Comment 4-30 in the 2011 *NEC* process.

230.44

Change at a Glance

Cable trays containing service-entrance conductors are required to include warning labels, spaced at intervals not to exceed 3.0 m (10 ft).

Code Language

230.44 Cable Trays

Cable tray systems shall be permitted to support service-entrance conductors. Cable trays used to support service-entrance conductors shall contain only service-entrance conductors and shall be limited to the following methods:

(1) Type SE cable
(2) Type MC cable
(3) Type MI cable
(4) Type IGS cable
(5) Single ~~thermoplastic-insulated~~ conductors 1/0 and larger with CT rating

Such cable trays shall be identified with permanently affixed labels with the wording "Service-Entrance Conductors." The labels shall be located so as to be visible after installation with a spacing not to exceed 3.0 m (10 ft) ~~and placed~~ so that the service-entrance conductors are able to be readily traced through the entire length of the cable tray.

230.44 Service Conductors in Cable Trays

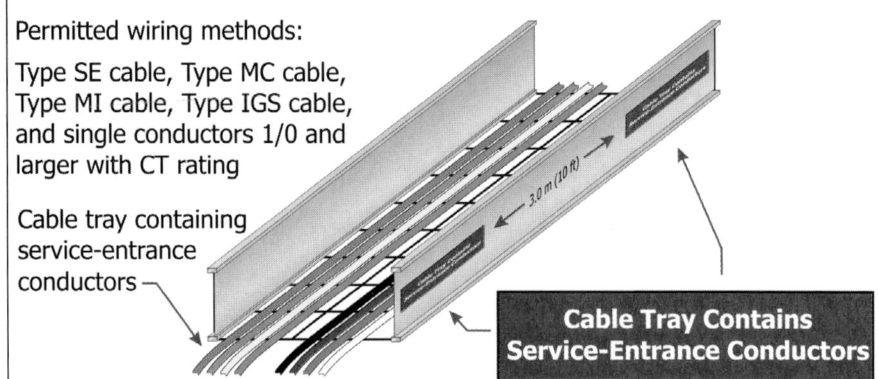

Cable trays containing service conductors shall be identified with permanently affixed labels with the wording "***Service-Entrance Conductors***".

Labels are to be located so as to be visible after installation with a spacing not to exceed 3.0 m (10 ft) so that the SE conductors are readily traceable through the entire length of the cable tray.

2011 *NEC* Requirement

Whenever a cable tray contained serviced-entrance conductors, the cable tray was required to be identified by a permanently affixed warning label with the words "Service-Entrance Conductors." There was no provision for spacing these warning label(s) any set distance apart, or to even have more than one warning label.

2014 *NEC* Change

Revision to this section added spacing intervals to now require these warning label(s) for cable trays containing service-entrance conductors to be affixed at intervals not to exceed 3.0 m (10 ft).

Analysis of Change

Provisions were added to the 2002 *NEC* to permit cable trays to contain service-entrance conductors. In the 2005 *NEC*, an exception was added to allow "other conductors" to be in the same cable tray as service-entrance conductors, provided a fixed barrier was in place within the cable tray to separate the service-entrance conductors from the other conductors in the cable tray. A labeling requirement was added to this exception in the 2008 *NEC* to identify a cable tray containing service conductors. This labeling requirement was intended to identify any cable tray containing service conductors (not just cable trays containing service conductors and other conductors). For the 2011 *NEC*, this labeling requirement was moved from the exception to the main body of 230.44 to identify a cable tray containing only service-entrance conductors as well as cable trays meeting the exception containing both service-entrance conductors and other conductors. For the 2014 NEC, a spacing interval provision was inserted to require these warning label(s) for cable trays containing service-entrance conductors to be affixed to the cable tray at least every 3.0 m (10 ft).

230.44

Continued

Exception: *Conductors, other than service-entrance conductors, shall be permitted to be installed in a cable tray with service-entrance conductors, provided a solid fixed barrier of a material compatible with the cable tray is installed to separate the service-entrance conductors from other conductors installed in the cable tray.*

Proposal 4-133, 4-134, 4-135

This spacing requirement for the warning labels is very similar to the requirement at 392.18(H) that requires a warning label at least every 3.0 m (10 ft) at cable trays containing conductors rated over 600 volts. This 3.0 m (10 ft) warning label spacing is reasonable as these service-entrance conductors do not have overcurrent protection ahead of these conductors and given the importance of these service-entrance conductors relative to the electrical system. This warning label spacing requirement will aid in the ability to trace the service-entrance conductors throughout the building.

One other revision at 230.44 removed the term *thermoplastic-insulated* from Item (5) for the allowable wiring methods for service-entrance conductors allowed in a cable tray. Item (5) now simply reads, "Single conductors 1/0 and larger with CT rating." When 230.44 was revised for the 2011 *NEC* to specify the allowable wiring methods in cable tray systems supporting service-entrance conductors, only thermoplastic-insulated single conductors were included. The limitation to thermoplastic-insulated conductors has resulted in an adverse impact on the allowable uses of thermoset-insulated CT-rated conductors. There was really no technical rationale for limiting the conductors utilized to those of the thermoplastic type. If a manufacturer produces conductors that meet the listing requirements required for CT rating, those conductors should also be allowed as service-entrance conductors in a cable tray.

230.82(3)

Change at a Glance

For "Equipment Connected to the Supply Side of Service Disconnect," provisions for a meter disconnect switch were revised by adding a label requirement to indicate "METER DISCONNECT NOT SERVICE EQUIPMENT."

Code Language

230.82 Equipment Connected to the Supply Side of Service Disconnect

Only the following equipment shall be permitted to be connected to the supply side of the service disconnecting means:

(1) Cable limiters or other current-limiting devices.
(2) Meters and meter sockets nominally rated not in excess of ~~600~~ 1000 volts, provided that all metal housings and service enclosures are grounded in accordance with Part VII and bonded in accordance with Part V of Article 250.
(3) Meter disconnect switches nominally rated not in excess of ~~600~~ 1000 volts that have a short-circuit current rating equal to or greater than the available short-circuit current, provided all metal housings and service enclosures are grounded in accordance with Part VII and bonded in accordance with Part V of Article 250. A meter disconnect switch shall be capable of interrupting the load served. A meter disconnect

230.82(3) Equipment Connected to the Supply Side of Service Disconnect

Meter disconnect switch are permitted on supply side of service disconnect under the following conditions:

- Rated 1000 volts or less
- Rated for at least the available short-circuit current
- Housing and enclosure grounded in accordance with Part VII and bonded in accordance with Part V of Article 250
- Capable of interrupting the load served
- Legibly field marked on its exterior (suitable for the environment) as follows: "METER DISCONNECT - NOT SERVICE EQUIPMENT"

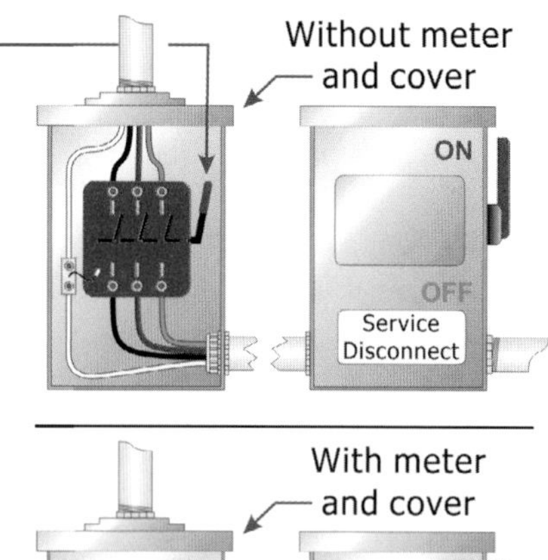

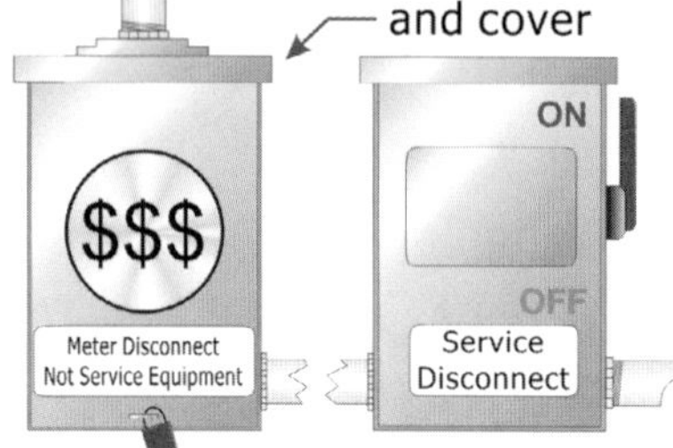

2011 *NEC* Requirement

A meter disconnect switch is one of the nine (9) items listed at 230.82 that was permitted to be installed on the line (or supply) side of a service disconnecting means. This meter disconnect switch had to be rated not in excess of 600 volts and have a short-circuit current rating equal to or greater than the available short-circuit current. The metal housings and service enclosures were required to be grounded in accordance with Part VII and bonded in accordance with Part V of Article 250. A meter disconnect switch located ahead of the service disconnect had to be capable of interrupting the load served.

2014 *NEC* Change

For the 2014 *NEC*, item (3), which addresses a *meter disconnect switch* ahead of the service disconnect was revised by adding a label requirement to indicate the following: "METER DISCONNECT - NOT SERVICE EQUIPMENT."

Analysis of Change

Section 230.82 lists several items that the *Code* permits to be installed ahead of, or on the line side of, a service disconnecting means. Three of these items are the electric utility meter and meter sockets as well as a meter disconnect switch. A meter disconnect switch is not the service disconnecting means. It is a simple load-breaking disconnect switch, sometimes located inside the meter socket enclosure, designed to interrupt or remove the load from the meter socket for the purpose of removing or changing the glass (some are now plastic) meter, maintenance, etc. Potential hazardous arcing can exist when attempting to change out a meter when the voltage involved exceeds 150 volts to ground, thus the need for a meter disconnect switch.

Because this meter switch is used to remove the load from the meter socket, it is required to have a short-circuit current rating equal to or greater than the available short-circuit current. Due in part to this equipment rating, meter disconnect

230.82(3)

Continued

shall be legibly field marked on its exterior in a manner suitable for the environment as follows: METER DISCONNECT NOT SERVICE EQUIPMENT.

(Remainder of text unchanged. See NEC for complete text.)

Proposal 4-156, 4-154

Comment 4-64

switches are often times confused with the service disconnecting means. Each service disconnecting means is required to be marked and identified as a service disconnect as required by 230.70(B). This service disconnect marking is sometimes placed at this meter disconnecting switch in error. This new labeling requirement involving the meter disconnect switch is intended to help solve this confusion concerning the service disconnecting means and the meter disconnect switch.

One of the most important areas of concern within the enforcement community is making sure that all parties involved (owner, electrical contractor, inspector, and utility personnel) are on the same page as far as exactly where the service disconnect(s) is located. This new requirement for a meter disconnect switch label will send a very clear message to all involved to look elsewhere for the service disconnecting means.

240.21(B)(1)

Change at a Glance

Tap conductor ampacity for feeder taps not over 3 m (10 ft) long is to be not less than the rating of the equipment containing an overcurrent device(s).

Code Language

240.21 Location in Circuit

Overcurrent protection shall be provided in each ungrounded circuit conductor and shall be located at the point where the conductors receive their supply except as specified in 240.21(A) through (H). Conductors supplied under the provisions of 240.21(A) through (H) shall not supply another conductor except through an overcurrent protective device meeting the requirements of 240.4.

(B) Feeder Taps. Conductors shall be permitted to be tapped, without overcurrent protection at the tap, to a feeder as specified in 240.21(B)(1) through (B)(5). The provisions of 240.4(B) shall not be permitted for tap conductors.

(1) Taps Not over 3 m (10 ft) Long. If the length of the tap conductors does not exceed 3 m (10 ft) and the tap conductors comply with all of the following:

(1) The ampacity of the tap conductors is

a. Not less than the combined calculated loads on the circuits supplied by the tap conductors, and

240.21(B)(1) Feeder Taps Not Over 3 m (10 ft)

Conductors are permitted to be tapped, without overcurrent protection at the tap, if the length of the tap conductors does not exceed 3 m (10 ft) and the tap conductors:

- Ampacity is not less than the combined calculated loads on the circuits supplied by the tap conductors
- Ampacity is not less than the rating of the equipment containing an overcurrent device(s) supplied by the tap conductors

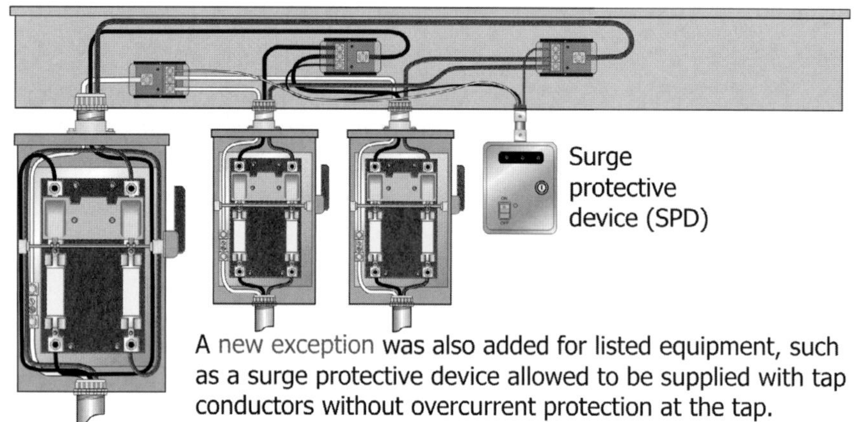

A new exception was also added for listed equipment, such as a surge protective device allowed to be supplied with tap conductors without overcurrent protection at the tap.

2011 *NEC* Requirement

The main rule at 240.21 states that all ungrounded conductors are to be provided with overcurrent protection, with that overcurrent protection located at the point where the conductors receive their supply. Eight conditions are then described at 240.21(A) through (H) to provided variances to this main rule. Section 240.21(B)(1) permits conductors to be tapped without overcurrent protection at the tap of a feeder tap not over 3.0 m (10 ft) long. There are four (4) specific conditions that this 3.0 m (10 ft) or less feeder tap must meet at this point. The fourth of these four specific conditions states that if the tap conductors leave the enclosure in which the tap is made, the ampacity of the tap conductors cannot be less than one-tenth of the rating of the overcurrent device protecting the feeder conductors. Generally, the tap conductors have to be enclosed in a raceway. The tap conductors do not extend beyond the panelboard, etc., they supply. And, finally, the ampacity of the tap conductors cannot be less than the combined calculated loads on the circuits supplied by the tap conductors, and they cannot be less than the rating of the "device" supplied by the tap conductors.

2014 *NEC* Change

In the fourth condition mentioned above, which is described at 240.21(B)(1), the "device" referred to has been clarified as the "equipment containing an overcurrent device(s)" supplied by the tap conductors. A new exception was also added at this location for listed equipment, such as surge protective device(s) (SPDs).

Analysis of Change

This revision to 240.21(B)(1) was meant to clarify the application of the previous requirement for 3.0 m (10 ft) or less feeder taps and to state the specific type of "device" as an overcurrent device. This clarification was needed since something as simple as a conductor would fit within the 2011 *NEC* definition of *device* in Article 100: "a unit of an electrical system that carries or controls electric energy as its principal function." This definition was revised in the 2014 *NEC* as "a unit

Continued

b. Not less than the rating of the equipment containing an overcurrent device(s) supplied by the tap conductors or not less than the rating of the overcurrent protective device at the termination of the tap conductors.

Exception to b.: *Where listed equipment, such as surge protective device(s) (SPDs), are provided with specific instructions on minimum conductor sizing, the ampacity of the tap conductors supplying that equipment shall be permitted to be determined based on the manufacturer's instructions.*

**(See NEC for remainder of Code text)*

Proposal 10-32

Comment 10-14

of an electrical system, *other than a conductor*, that carries or controls electric energy as its principal function." The new language of 240.21(B)(1) added as, "equipment containing an overcurrent device(s)" could be a main-lug panelboard, a fusible switch, a switchboard or switchgear, a motor control center, etc.

A new exception was also added after 240.21(B)(1)(1)(b) to address the installation of surge protective device(s) (SPD) and other non-energy consuming devices. This new exception will allow listed equipment such as surge protective devices, power monitoring equipment and metering equipment, etc., to be connected with tap conductors without overcurrent protection at the device, provided that the equipment has specific instructions included with its listing and labeling on the sizing of the tap conductors.

This same change also occurred at 240.21(C)(2) for transformer secondary conductors not over 3.0 m (10 ft) long (*see Proposal 10-39 and Comment 10-16*).

240.87

Change at a Glance

Title was changed to "Arc Energy Reduction" and the section was revised for usability and formatted into subdivisions.

Code Language

240.87 ~~Noninstantaneous Trip~~ Arc Energy Reduction ~~Where a circuit breaker is used without an instantaneous trip,~~ Where the highest continuous current trip setting for which the actual overcurrent device installed in a circuit breaker is rated or can be adjusted is 1200 amperes or higher then 240.87(A) and (B) shall apply.

(A) Documentation. Documentation shall be available to those authorized to design, install, operate, or inspect the installation as to the location of the circuit breaker(s).

(B) Method to Reduce Clearing Time. ~~Where a circuit breaker is utilized without an instantaneous trip,~~ One of the following or approved equivalent means shall be provided:

(1) Zone-selective interlocking

(2) Differential relaying

(3) Energy-reducing maintenance switching with local status indicator

(4) Energy-reducing active arc-flash mitigation system

(5) An approved equivalent means

240.87 Arc Energy Reduction

Clearing Time

150 ms

100 ms

50 ms

Courtesy of Eaton Corporation

Short Time Delay

Zone Selective Interlocking

Instantaneous Trip

Energy-Reducing Maintenance Switch

Current

Relative clearing times for electronic circuit breaker trip functions

2011 *NEC* Requirement

A new section was added to the 2011 *NEC* entitled "Noninstantaneous Trip" which provide one of the three arc-flash energy reducing methods (or approved equivalent means) when power circuit breakers without instantaneous trip are used. These new provisions identified three methods that can be utilized to limit energy levels within that equipment and included permission of other approved equivalent means: (1) zone-selective interlocking, (2) differential relaying, and (3) an energy reducing maintenance switch. These provisions did not require that power circuit breakers without instantaneous trip be used; but that when they were utilized, documentation had to be provided to designers, installers, and enforcement to indicate that option had been selected. One of the three arc-flash energy reducing methods (or approved equivalent means) had to be utilized as well.

2014 *NEC* Change

Title was changed to "Arc Energy Reduction" which better reflects the purpose for this code rule, and the entire section was revised for usability and formatted into subdivisions. The revision clarifies that this rule applies only to circuit breakers that are intentionally delayed under short-circuit conditions, and that these circuit breakers do not have an instantaneous trip setting. They also do not have an override setting higher than the potential arc current. A limitation to the size of breaker (1200 ampere) required to comply with this section was added. Two additional methods for reducing arc energy were added to the list of methods as well.

Analysis of Change

These revisions provide necessary clarity and usability to 240.87 which was added in the 2011 *NEC Code* cycle to limit the arc-flash energy to which a worker could be exposed when working on the load side of a circuit breaker with a built-in intentional delay under short-circuit conditions. The new and

240.87

Continued

Informational Note No. 1: An energy-reducing maintenance switch allows a worker to set a circuit breaker trip unit to "no intentional delay" to reduce the clearing time while the worker is working within an arc-flash boundary as defined in NFPA 70E-2012, *Standard for Electrical Safety in the Workplace,* and then to set the trip unit back to a normal setting after the potentially hazardous work is complete.

Informational Note No. 2: An energy-reducing active arc-flash mitigation system helps in reducing arcing duration in the electrical distribution system. No change in circuit breaker or the settings of other devices is required during maintenance when a worker is working within an arc-flash boundary as defined in NFPA 70E-2012, *Standard for Electrical Safety in the Workplace.*

Proposal 10-53a, 10-56

Comment 10-24, 10-20, 10-22, 10-23, 10-25

revised text is easier to read, easier to apply, and easier to enforce for the enforcement community. This new and revised text also clarifies that this requirement applies only to a circuit breaker that (1) is intentionally delayed under short-circuit conditions (short-time delay), and (2) does not have an instantaneous trip (that opens as quickly as possible under short-circuit conditions, typically 5 to 10 times the rating of the circuit breaker), and (3) does not have an instantaneous override (found on most insulated case circuit breakers), or the instantaneous override is set higher than the arcing current (so that the circuit breaker will not open as quickly as possible under arcing current conditions).

The requirements found at 240.87 are industry-proven methods to reduce arc-flash injuries. These are an installation requirement that provides a method to reduce the amount of time a fault will be permitted to exist. The amount of time that an arcing event lasts is directly proportional to the incident energy. The installation requirements of 240.87 provide a means to reduce the level of incident energy.

250.8(A)

Change at a Glance

The permitted methods for connecting equipment grounding conductors, bonding jumpers, etc., to such things as enclosures were expanded to one "or more" of the methods described at 250.8(A).

REVISION

Code Language

250.8 Connection of Grounding and Bonding Equipment.

(A) Permitted Methods. Equipment grounding conductors, grounding electrode conductors, and bonding jumpers shall be connected by one or more of the following means:

(1) Listed pressure connectors

(2) Terminal bars

(3) Pressure connectors listed as grounding and bonding equipment

(4) Exothermic welding process

(5) Machine screw-type fasteners that engage not less than two threads or are secured with a nut

(6) Thread-forming machine screws that engage not less than two threads in the enclosure

(7) Connections that are part of a listed assembly

(8) Other listed means

Proposal 5-53

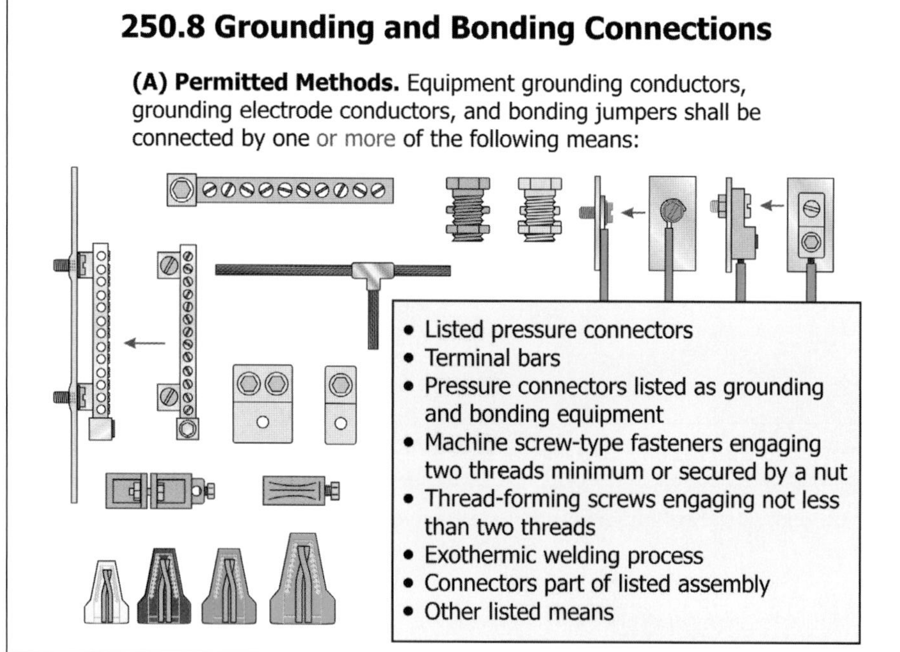

250.8 Grounding and Bonding Connections
(A) Permitted Methods. Equipment grounding conductors, grounding electrode conductors, and bonding jumpers shall be connected by one or more of the following means:
• Listed pressure connectors
• Terminal bars
• Pressure connectors listed as grounding and bonding equipment
• Machine screw-type fasteners engaging two threads minimum or secured by a nut
• Thread-forming screws engaging not less than two threads
• Exothermic welding process
• Connectors part of listed assembly
• Other listed means

2011 *NEC* Requirement

Equipment grounding conductors, grounding electrode conductors, and bonding jumpers were required to be connected by "one" of the eight methods described at 250.8(A).

2014 *NEC* Change

A revision occurred at 250.8(A) to permit one "or more" of the eight methods described in this subsection for connection of equipment grounding conductors, grounding electrode conductors, and bonding jumpers.

Analysis of Change

During the 2008 *NEC* code cycle, 250.8 was revised and rewritten from one long paragraph into two subsections and a list format incorporating acceptable concepts included in several proposals for the permitted methods of connection of grounding and bonding conductors. This 2008 *NEC* revision also removed the term *sheet metal screws* from this section, providing further emphasis that sheet metal screws were not an acceptable means of attaching equipment grounding conductors, grounding electrode conductors, and bonding jumpers or connection devices to enclosures. Connections of grounding conductors and bonding jumpers are an important element of the electrical wiring system. The path for ground-fault current must remain effective to ensure performance under all anticipated conditions. By providing an inclusive list of acceptable methods, 250.8(A) improved the clarity of the important element of the fault-return path.

A revision transpired at 250.8(A) for the 2014 *NEC* to allow more than one of the permitted methods for connection of equipment grounding conductors, grounding electrode conductors, and bonding jumpers to metal enclosures, etc. As previously written, only one of the eight methods listed was permitted to be used for making a connection in a panelboard, disconnect, etc. By the letter of the law, using a pressure connector to connect to a bonding jumper and using a machine screw to connect the pressure connector to an enclosure were literally not permitted by the previously written text at 250.8(A).

250.21(C)

Change at a Glance

Ungrounded systems are to be legibly marked "Caution Ungrounded System Operating —____ Volts Between Conductors."

REVISION

Code Language

250.21 Alternating-Current Systems of 50 Volts to ~~Less Than~~ 1000 Volts Not Required to Be Grounded

(C) Marking. Ungrounded systems shall be legibly marked "Caution Ungrounded System Operating — _____ Volts Between Conductors" at the source or first disconnecting means of the system. The marking shall be of sufficient durability to withstand the environment involved.

Proposal 5-66, 5-64, 5-65

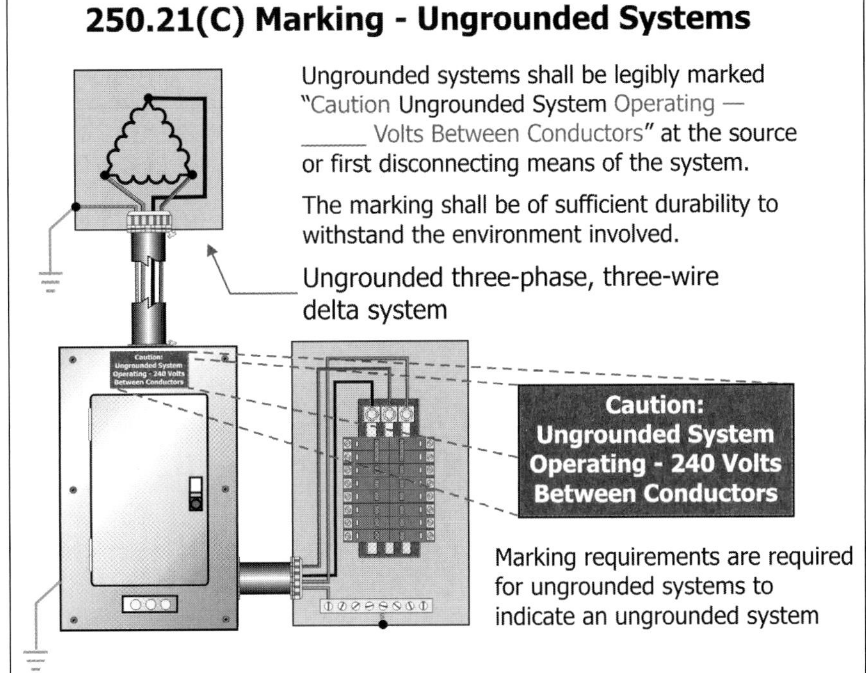
250.21(C) Marking - Ungrounded Systems
Ungrounded systems shall be legibly marked "Caution Ungrounded System Operating — _____ Volts Between Conductors" at the source or first disconnecting means of the system.
The marking shall be of sufficient durability to withstand the environment involved.
Ungrounded three-phase, three-wire delta system
Caution: Ungrounded System Operating - 240 Volts Between Conductors
Marking requirements are required for ungrounded systems to indicate an ungrounded system

2011 *NEC* Requirement

Ungrounded systems were to be legibly marked "Ungrounded System" at the source or first disconnecting means of the system, with the marking of sufficient durability to withstand the environment involved.

2014 *NEC* Change

The marking requirement for an ungrounded system in Article 250 was changed to "Caution Ungrounded System Operating — _____ Volts Between Conductors" to coincide with similar provisions at 408.3(F)(2) for a switchboard, switchgear, or panelboard.

Analysis of Change

Marking requirements for ungrounded systems were added in two separate places in the 2011 *NEC*. The first one was inserted at 250.21(C) where the *Code* discusses ac systems that are permitted to be grounded. If an ungrounded system is installed, 250.21(C) required a marking or label stating, "**Ungrounded System**." The second place where this marking requirement for ungrounded systems occurred was at 408.3(F)(2) for switchboard and panelboard identification. This provision requires a switchboard or panelboard containing an ungrounded electrical system (as permitted at 250.21) to be field marked, "**Caution Ungrounded System Operating — _____ Volts Between Conductors**." With the previous wording, if the ungrounded system disconnect was in the form of a panelboard or switchboard, two different labels stating two different phrases were required on said panelboard or switchboard. These two provisions for marking of ungrounded systems need to contain the same labeling requirements as both sections address the same issue. This revision is intended to incorporate the marking requirements from 408.3(F)(2) which are more complete than the previous marking requirements at 250.21(C).

250.24(A)(1)

Change at a Glance

References to *overhead service conductors* and *underground service conductors* have been added to sections where needed in Article 250.

REVISION

Code Language

250.24 Grounding Service-Supplied Alternating-Current Systems

(A) System Grounding Connections. A premises wiring system supplied by a grounded ac service shall have a grounding electrode conductor connected to the grounded service conductor, at each service, in accordance with 250.24(A)(1) through (A)(5).

(1) General. The grounding electrode conductor connection shall be made at any accessible point from the load end of the overhead service conductors, service drop, underground service conductors, or service lateral to and including the terminal or bus to which the grounded service conductor is connected at the service disconnecting means.

Informational Note: See definitions of *Service Conductors, Overhead; Service Conductors, Underground; Service Drop;* and *Service Lateral* in Article 100.

Proposal 5-68, 5-69, 5-70

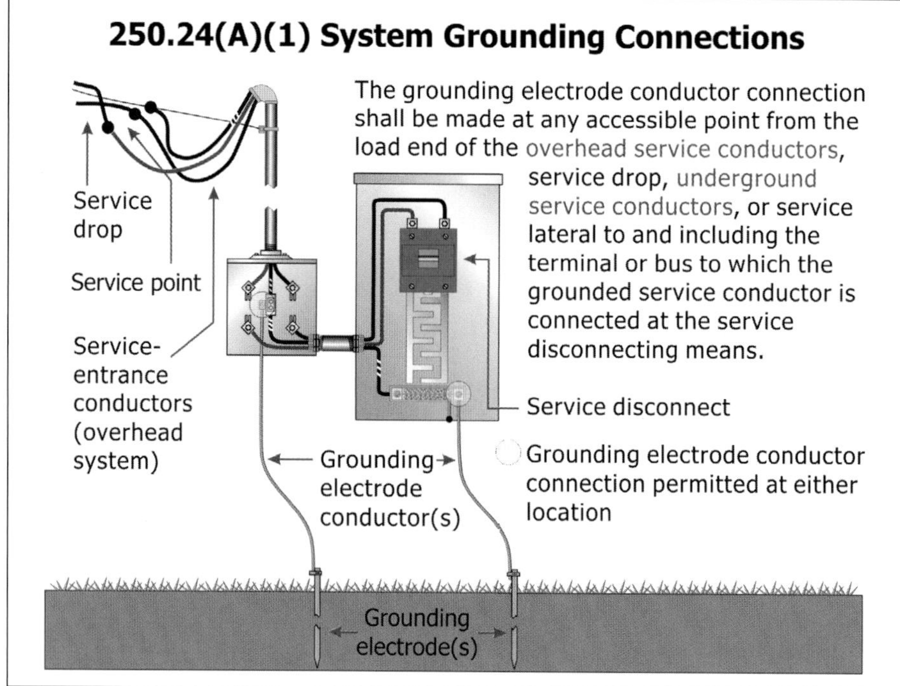
250.24(A)(1) System Grounding Connections
The grounding electrode conductor connection shall be made at any accessible point from the load end of the overhead service conductors, service drop, underground service conductors, or service lateral to and including the terminal or bus to which the grounded service conductor is connected at the service disconnecting means.
Service drop
Service point
Service-entrance conductors (overhead system)
Service disconnect
Grounding electrode conductor(s)
Grounding electrode conductor connection permitted at either location
Grounding electrode(s)

2011 *NEC* Requirement

All premises wiring systems supplied by a grounded ac service are required to have a grounding electrode conductor connected to the grounded service conductor at each service. For the 2011 *NEC*, this grounding electrode conductor connection could be made at any accessible point from the load end of the service drop or service lateral up to and including the grounded service conductor terminal bar at the service disconnecting means.

2014 *NEC* Change

The defined terms *overhead service conductors* and *underground service conductors* were added to load end accessible points where a grounding electrode conductor could be connected, in addition to service drops and service laterals.

Analysis of Change

The terms *overhead service conductor* and *underground service conductor* were added with definitions to Article 100 in the 2011 *NEC,* and used throughout Article 230 for service requirements. These terms were inadvertently omitted from Article 250 and needed to be added for proper application of these defined terms and their requirements. During the 2011 *NEC Code* cycle, the definitions dealing with services were added or revised to draw a clearer line of demarcation between the utility side which would not be within the scope of the *NEC* (as they would be under the exclusive control of electric utility companies) and the customer side of the *service point* and thus under the requirements of the *NEC*. The definitions for *overhead* and *underground service conductors* were added to define the conductors provided between the service point and the service-entrance conductors. The definition of *service drop* was revised to clearly identify these overhead conductors as being under the exclusive control of a serving utility.

The terms *overhead service conductors* and/or *underground service conductors* were added in other sections of Article 250 for clarity and to reflect changes to service definitions and terminology made in the 2011 *NEC*.

250.64(B)

Change at a Glance

New provisions were added to clarify that grounding electrode conductors and grounding electrode bonding jumpers are not required to comply with 300.5 for underground installations.

Code Language

250.64 Grounding Electrode Conductor Installation

Grounding electrode conductors at the service, at each building or structure where supplied by a feeder(s) or branch circuit(s), or at a separately derived system shall be installed as specified in 250.64(A) through (F).

(B) Securing and Protection Against Physical Damage. Where exposed, a grounding electrode conductor or its enclosure shall be securely fastened to the surface on which it is carried. Grounding electrode conductors shall be permitted to be installed on or through framing members. A 4 AWG or larger copper or aluminum grounding electrode conductor shall be protected if exposed to physical damage. A 6 AWG grounding electrode conductor that is free from exposure to physical damage shall be permitted to be run along the surface of the building construction without metal covering or protection if it is securely fastened to the construction; otherwise, it shall be protected in rigid metal conduit (RMC), intermediate metal conduit (IMC),

250.64(B) GEC Installation

New provisions added to clarify that grounding electrode conductors and grounding electrode bonding jumpers are not required to comply with 300.5 for underground installations.

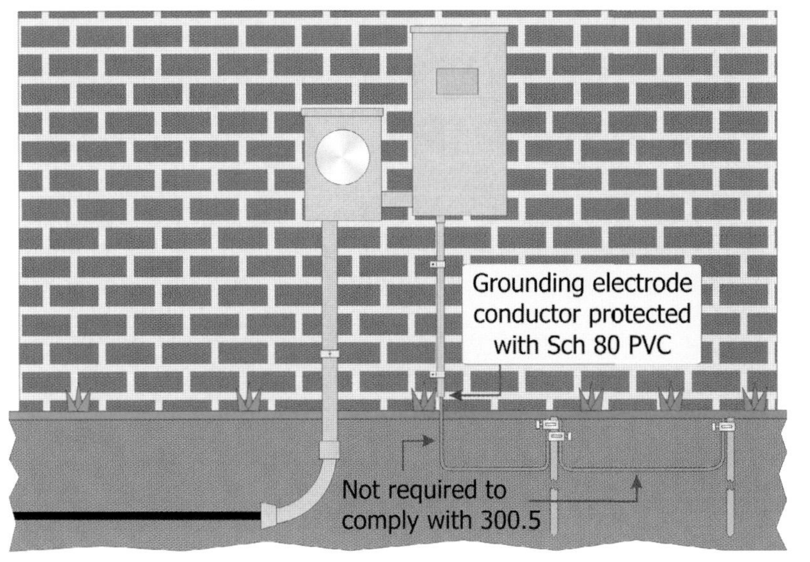

2011 *NEC* Requirement

Grounding electrode conductors are generally required to be secured and protected from physical damage where installed in an exposed manner. The 2011 *NEC* was silent on burial depth requirements for grounding electrode conductors.

2014 *NEC* Change

The same provisions for securing and protecting grounding electrode conductors against physical damage from the 2011 *NEC* were brought forward for the 2014 *NEC*. A new last sentence was added at 250.64(B) to alert users of the *Code* to the fact that grounding electrode conductors and grounding electrode bonding jumpers are not required to comply with 300.5 for underground installations.

Analysis of Change

Prior to this clarification concerning grounding electrode conductors and burial depth requirements of Table 300.5, the *Code* was unclear on this subject. Inconsistent interpretation was the result as some users of the *Code* would enforce or apply 300.5 burial depth requirements to grounding electrode conductors while others did not. Some enforcers of the *Code* would require grounding electrode conductors or grounding electrode bonding jumpers to be installed under the provisions of Column 1 of Table 300.5, which is for "Direct Buried Cables or Conductors." This added sentence at 250.64(B) will clarify that grounding electrode conductors or grounding electrode bonding jumpers are not subject to the burial depth requirements of 300.5 or Table 300.5.

In some cases, installing the grounding electrode conductor to comply with Table 300.5 would require the grounding electrode conductor to be routed down an exterior wall of a building, offset to the burial depth, and then back

250.64(B)

Continued

rigid polyvinyl chloride conduit (PVC), reinforced thermosetting resin conduit (RTRC), electrical metallic tubing (EMT), or cable armor. Grounding electrode conductors smaller than 6 AWG shall be protected in RMC, IMC, PVC, RTRC, EMT, or cable armor. Grounding electrode conductors and grounding electrode bonding jumpers shall not be required to comply with 300.5.

Proposal 3-39

Comment 3-13

up to be connected to a grounding electrode that might be installed close to the foundation wall. This could introduce sharp bends in the grounding electrode conductor that could decrease the effectiveness of this grounding electrode to dissipate over currents into the earth.

This added text at 250.64(B) was originally submitted to CMP-3 to be added as a note at the bottom of Table 300.5. CMP-3 rejected this proposal, understanding that this subject matter was better suited for CMP-5. The NEC Correlating Committee (NEC CC) directed that this provision be forwarded to CMP-5 for comment as CMP-5 has jurisdiction over grounding and bonding rules of Article 250. CMP-5 recommended that this information be located at 250.64(B) rather than at Table 300.5, as 250.64(B) includes the other requirements for the installation of grounding electrode conductors. The NEC CC agreed with the assessment of CMP-5.

250.64(D)(1)

Change at a Glance

"Common Grounding Electrode Conductor and Taps" was revised to address busbar specifications and where buildings or structures are supplied by a feeder or a service.

Code Language

250.64 Grounding Electrode Conductor Installation

Grounding electrode conductors at the service, at each building or structure where supplied by a feeder(s) or branch circuit(s), or at a separately derived system shall be installed as specified in 250.64(A) through (F).

(D) ~~Service~~ Building or Structure with Multiple Disconnecting Means in Separate Enclosures. ~~If~~ For a service ~~consists of more than a single enclosure as permitted in 230.71(A),~~ or feeder with two or more disconnecting means in separate enclosures supplying a building or structure, the grounding electrode connections shall be made in accordance with 250.64(D)(1), (D)(2), or (D)(3).

(1) Common Grounding Electrode Conductor and Taps. A common grounding electrode conductor and grounding electrode conductor taps shall be installed. The common grounding electrode conductor shall be sized in accordance with

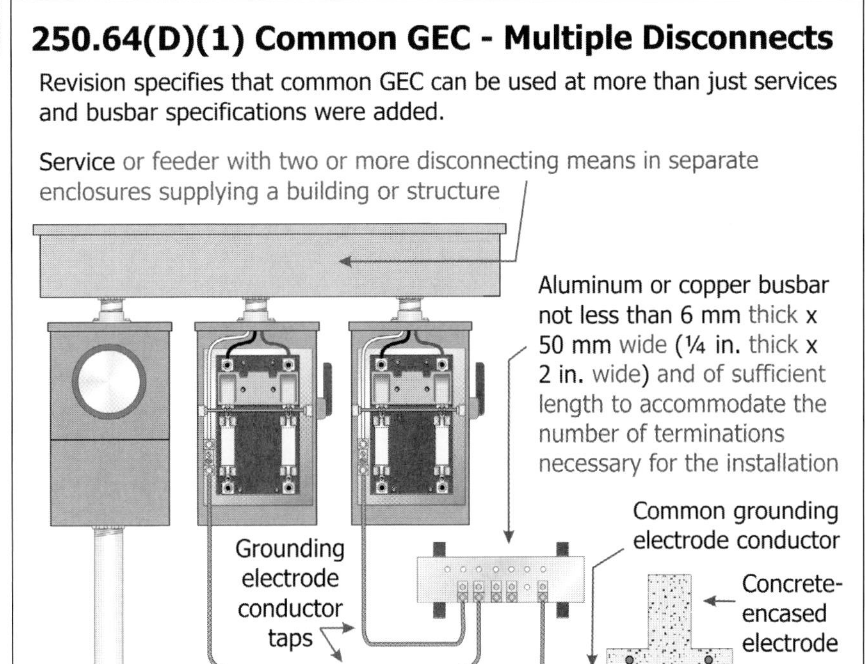

250.64(D)(1) Common GEC - Multiple Disconnects

Revision specifies that common GEC can be used at more than just services and busbar specifications were added.

2011 *NEC* Requirement

The *Code* permits up to six means of disconnect for services in accordance with 230.71(A). If a service consists of more than one disconnecting means, connections to the grounding electrode system(s) can be accomplished by three types of methods: (1) installing a common grounding electrode conductor and installing grounding electrode conductor taps to each of the service disconnects, (2) installing individual grounding electrode conductors to each service disconnect, or (3) connection of the grounding electrode conductor(s) at a common location, such as inside a wireway. Looking at the common grounding electrode conductor and taps in particular, the 2011 *NEC* language implied that the common grounding electrode conductor was to be sized based on the largest ungrounded *service-entrance conductor(s)* supplying the disconnecting means. This language also stated that the grounding electrode conductor taps were to extend to the inside of each *service* disconnecting means enclosure. When utilizing a common grounding electrode conductor busbar for making the conductor taps, the aluminum or copper busbar had to be not less than 6 mm × 50 mm (¼ in. × 2 in.)

2014 *NEC* Change

The title of 250.64(D) was changed from "Service with Multiple Disconnecting Means Enclosures" to "Building or Structure with Multiple Disconnecting Means in Separate Enclosures" to clarify that multiple disconnecting means can occur at a separate building or structure supplied by a feeder(s), not just at a building or structure supplied by a service. The language was revised at 250.64(D)(1), as well, to address the sizing requirements for the common grounding electrode conductor. This common grounding electrode conductor is to be sized based on the largest ungrounded conductor(s) supplying the disconnecting means, which could involve a feeder, not just a service. The grounding electrode conductor taps are to terminate inside of each disconnecting means enclosure which, again, does not necessarily have to be a

250.64(D)(1)

Continued

250.66, based on the sum of the circular mil area of the largest ungrounded ~~service-entrance~~ conductor(s) of each set of conductors that supply the disconnecting means. If the service-entrance conductors connect directly to overhead service conductors, ~~a~~ service drop, underground service conductors, or service lateral, the common grounding electrode conductor shall be sized in accordance with Table 250.66, Note 1.

A grounding electrode conductor tap shall extend to the inside of each ~~service~~ disconnecting means enclosure. The grounding electrode conductor taps shall be sized in accordance with 250.66 for the largest service-entrance or feeder conductor serving the individual enclosure. The tap conductors shall be connected to the common grounding electrode conductor by one of the following methods in such a manner that the common grounding electrode conductor remains without a splice or joint:

(1) Exothermic welding.
(2) Connectors listed as grounding and bonding equipment.
(3) Connections to an aluminum or copper busbar not less than 6 mm thick × 50 mm wide (¼ in. thick × 2 in. wide) and of sufficient length to accommodate the number of terminations necessary for the installation. The busbar shall be securely fastened and shall be installed in an accessible location. Connections shall be made by a listed connector or by the exothermic welding process. If aluminum busbars are used, the installation shall comply with 250.64(A).

Proposal 5-120, 5-121

Comment 5-44

service disconnect. The text was also revised to include some specifications for a common grounding electrode conductor busbar for making the conductor taps. This aluminum or copper busbar cannot be less than 6 mm thick × 50 mm wide (¼ in. thick × 2 in. wide) and it has to be "of sufficient length to accommodate the number of terminations necessary for the installation."

Analysis of Change

The parent text at 250.64 indicates that this section is intended to cover the installation of grounding electrode conductor(s) at services or buildings or structures where supplied by feeder(s) or branch circuit(s). However, a closer look at 250.64(D) in previous editions of the *Code* indicated that the installation of grounding electrode conductors with multiple disconnecting means only applied to buildings supplied by a service, and no language existed for buildings or structures supplied by feeders. Revisions in the 2014 *NEC* will make it clear that these provisions for grounding electrode conductor(s) connections apply to building or structures supplied by feeders or services.

Revisions were also made at 250.64(D)(1) to clarify that this common grounding electrode conductor busbar is a separate busbar and not an accessory terminal bar provided for a panelboard. This accessory terminal bar provided for a panelboard is not a busbar; it is terminal bar as noted. Revisions to this section add requirement that the common grounding electrode conductor busbar be of sufficient length to connect all grounding electrode conductors and/or bonding jumpers or conductors that must be attached.

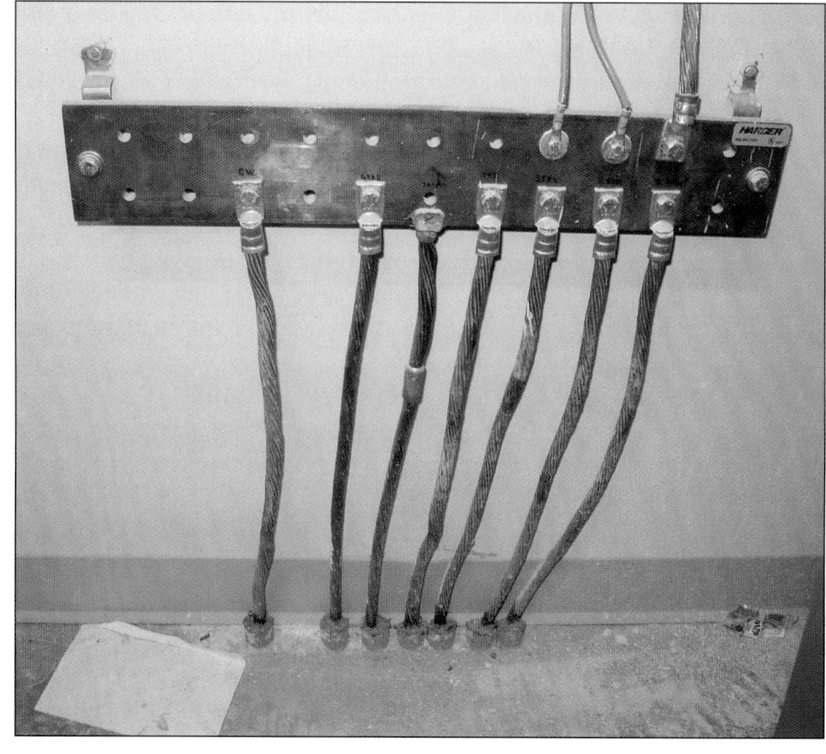

250.64(E)

Change at a Glance

Requirements for raceways and enclosures for grounding electrode conductors are broken into four (4) list items for clarity.

Code Language

250.64 Grounding Electrode Conductor Installation

(E) Raceways and Enclosures for Grounding Electrode Conductors.

(1) General. Ferrous metal raceways and enclosures for grounding electrode conductors shall be electrically continuous from the point of attachment to cabinets or equipment to the grounding electrode and shall be securely fastened to the ground clamp or fitting. Ferrous metal raceways and enclosures ~~that are not physically continuous from cabinets or equipment to the grounding electrode~~ shall be ~~made electrically continuous by bonding~~ bonded at each end of the raceway or enclosure to the grounding electrode or grounding electrode conductor. Nonferrous metal raceways and enclosures shall not be required to be electrically continuous.

(2) Methods. Bonding ~~methods shall be~~ in compliance with 250.92(B) ~~for installations at service equipment locations~~ and ~~with~~ ensured by one of the methods in 250.92(B)(2) through (B)(4) ~~for other than service equipment locations shall apply at each end and to all intervening ferrous raceways, boxes, and enclosures between the cabinets or equipment and the grounding electrode~~.

(3) Size. No Change

(4) Wiring Methods. No Change

See *NEC* for complete text.

Proposal 5-124

2011 *NEC* Requirement

Ferrous metal enclosures for grounding electrode conductors are required to be made electrically continuous from the point of attachment to cabinets or equipment to the grounding electrode, and are further required to be securely fastened to the ground clamp or fitting. These requirements for enclosures for grounding electrode conductors are found at 250.64(E); in the 2011 *NEC*, these requirements were located in one very long paragraph with six sentences.

2014 *NEC* Change

The existing long paragraph for enclosures for grounding electrode conductors was retitled "Raceways and Enclosures for Grounding Electrode Conductors," and was broken up into four (4) list items for readability and clarity. Provisions were added for ferrous metal raceways, not just ferrous metal enclosures.

Analysis of Change

The revisions made at 250.64(E) were intended to be editorial in nature, including breaking up a really long single-paragraph Level 1 subsection into list items and providing titles for the list items. There were not any technical changes to these provisions. Picking out specific requirements from a very long paragraph can often times prove to be difficult, at best. These revised list items will make this section of the *Code* more user-friendly. Language was also added to incorporate provisions for *ferrous metal raceways,* not just *ferrous metal enclosures*.

250.66(A) and (B)

Change at a Glance

Clarification to the term *sole connection* makes it clear that this sole connection is related to the grounding electrode conductor itself and not to the number of specified electrode(s) involved.

Code Language

250.66 Size of Alternating-Current Grounding Electrode Conductor

The size of the grounding electrode conductor at the service, at each building or structure where supplied by a feeder(s) or branch circuit(s), or at a separately derived system of a grounded or ungrounded ac system shall not be less than given in Table 250.66, except as permitted in 250.66(A) through (C).

~~**Informational Note:** See 250.24(C) for size of ac system conductor brought to service equipment.~~

(A) Connections to a Rod, Pipe, or Plate Electrode(s). Where the grounding electrode conductor is connected to a single or multiple rod, pipe, or plate electrode(s), or any combination thereof as permitted in 250.52(A)(5) or (A)(7), that portion of the conductor that is the sole connection to the grounding electrode(s) shall not be required to be larger than 6 AWG copper wire or 4 AWG aluminum wire.

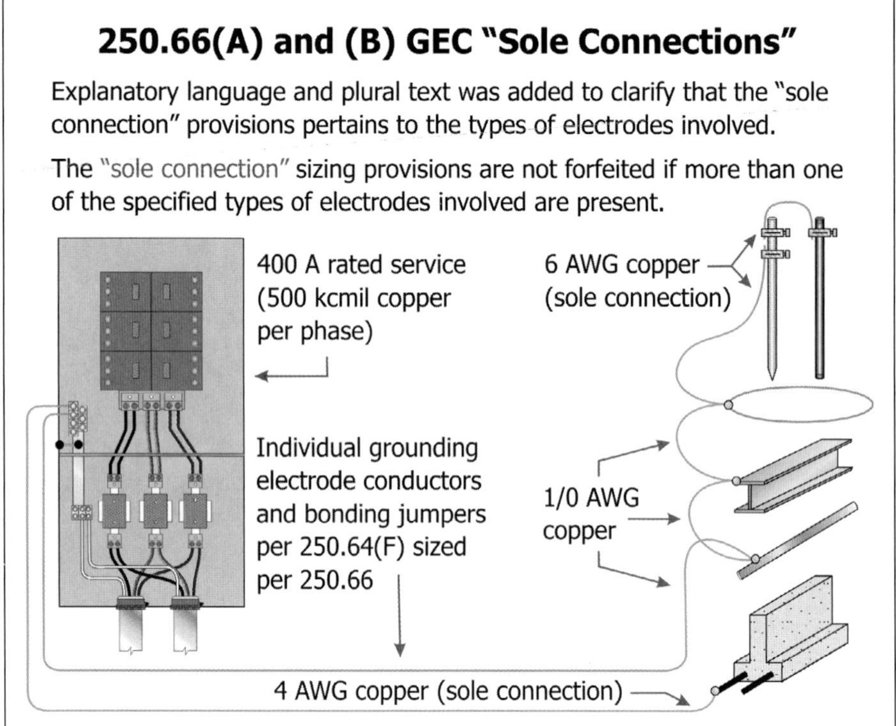

250.66(A) and (B) GEC "Sole Connections"
Explanatory language and plural text was added to clarify that the "sole connection" provisions pertains to the types of electrodes involved.
The "sole connection" sizing provisions are not forfeited if more than one of the specified types of electrodes involved are present.
400 A rated service (500 kcmil copper per phase)
6 AWG copper (sole connection)
Individual grounding electrode conductors and bonding jumpers per 250.64(F) sized per 250.66
1/0 AWG copper
4 AWG copper (sole connection)

2011 *NEC* Requirement

Grounding electrode conductors are required to be sized using Table 250.66, based on the size of the largest ungrounded service-entrance conductor or equivalent area for parallel conductors. A grounding electrode conductor with its sole connection to a rod, pipe, or plate electrode never has to be larger than a 6 AWG copper conductor or a 4 AWG aluminum conductor, regardless of the size of the ungrounded service-entrance conductors. A grounding electrode conductor with its sole connection to a concrete-encased electrode never has to be larger than a 4 AWG copper conductor.

2014 *NEC* Change

As far as sizing a grounding electrode conductor, the requirements are the same as they were for the 2011 *NEC*. Explanatory-type language and plural text were added to 250.66(A) and (B) to clarify that the *sole connection* provisions of these subsections pertain to the types of electrodes in these subsections, and the *sole connection* sizing provisions are not forfeited if more than one of the specified types of electrodes involved are present.

Analysis of Change

The revised language at 250.66(A) and (B) is an attempt to clarify that the *sole connection* sizing provisions for grounding electrode conductors to rod, pipe, plate, and concrete-encased electrodes are still relevant, even if more than one of these types of electrodes are installed or are present at a building or structure. As an example, let's say a single ground rod were installed to supplement a metal underground water piping system that qualified as a grounding electrode [3.0 m (10 ft) or more in contact with the earth]. The ungrounded service-entrance conductors involved are sized at 4/0 AWG copper, which would require a 2 AWG copper grounding electrode conductor. Installing a 2 AWG copper grounding electrode conductor from the service disconnecting means to the metal water piping system would be in order. Section 250.66(A) would permit a 6 AWG cop-

250.66(A) and (B)

Continued

(B) Connections to Concrete-Encased Electrode(s). Where the grounding electrode conductor is connected to a single or multiple concrete-encased electrode(s) as permitted in 250.52(A)(3), that portion of the conductor that is the sole connection to the grounding electrode(s) shall not be required to be larger than 4 AWG copper wire.

Proposal 5-131, 5-135, 5-128a, 5-130, 5-132, 5-134

per grounding electrode conductor from the service disconnecting means to the ground rod, or a 6 AWG copper grounding electrode conductor from the metal water piping system to the ground rod as this 6 AWG copper grounding electrode conductor would be the *sole connection* to the ground rod.

However, using this same scenario, with two ground rods involved and connected together with a bonding jumper [as required in 250.53(A)(2)], has caused some confusion as to whether or not the connection to the first ground rod is now the sole connection since both a grounding electrode conductor and a bonding jumper are now connected to this first ground rod. The plural language and revised text at both 250.66(A) and (B) should make it clear that the *Code* considers these two ground rods to be one electrode as far as the *sole connection* sizing provisions are concerned; and 6 AWG copper conductor could be used at both ground rods.

This revision should clarify that if a grounding electrode conductor is installed to multiple concrete-encased electrodes connected together with a bonding jumper(s), the maximum size grounding electrode conductor to the first concrete-encased electrode or any bonding jumper(s) between the multiple concrete-encased electrodes is not required to be larger than a 4 AWG copper conductor.

250.68(C)(2)

Change at a Glance

Provisions for metal structure steel used as a conductor to interconnect electrodes have been revised. The title of 250.68(C) has been changed to "Grounding Electrode Connections."

Code Language

250.68 Grounding Electrode Conductor and Bonding Jumper Connection to Grounding Electrodes

The connection of a grounding electrode conductor at the service, at each building or structure where supplied by a feeder(s) or branch circuit(s), or at a separately derived system and associated bonding jumper(s) shall be made as specified 250.68(A) through (C).

(C) ~~Metallic Water Pipe and Structural Metal~~ Grounding Electrode Connections. Grounding electrode conductors and bonding jumpers shall be permitted to be connected at the following locations and used to extend the connection to an electrode(s):

(1) Interior metal water piping located not more than 1.52 m (5 ft) from the point of entrance to the building...*(remainder of text and exception unchanged from 2011 text).*

(2) The metal structural frame of a building ~~that is directly connected~~

250.68(C) Grounding Electrode Connections

The title of 250.68(C) has been changed to "Grounding Electrode Connections."

Above-grade structural metal frame of a building can serve as a conductor without having to be connected directly to a grounding electrode or qualify as a grounding electrode as previously required.

Within the first 1.5 m (5 ft) of where pipe enters the building

Interior metal water piping and the metal structural frame of a building are permitted as a means of interconnecting electrodes that are part of the grounding electrode system.

2011 *NEC* Requirement

The structural frame of a building was permitted as a bonding conductor to interconnect electrodes that are part of the grounding electrode system. However, there was prescriptive language in this list item that the structural steel had to meet in order to qualify as a bonding conductor to interconnect electrodes. This prescriptive language was more appropriate for qualification as a grounding electrode rather than a bonding conductor.

2014 *NEC* Change

The metal structural frame of a building is still permitted as a means of interconnecting electrodes that are part of the grounding electrode system, but the prescriptive language has been removed.

Analysis of Change

The revised text clarifies that the structural metal frame of a building can be used to interconnect electrodes that are part of the grounding electrode system and should be treated the same as a metallic water piping system without having to meet qualifying conditions of a grounding electrode. The parent text at 250.68(C) makes it clear that structural metal can be used to connect wire type bonding jumpers or grounding electrode conductors to the structural metal as an extension of the wire type bonding conductors or grounding electrode conductors.

Changes made in the 2011 *NEC Code* cycle moved performance text for the metallic water piping system and the structural metal frame of the building from the qualifying text for grounding electrodes at 250.52(A) to 250.68(C), which more correctly qualifies them as a conductor. The relocated text for the metallic water piping system did not carry any requirement that the water pipe qualify as a grounding electrode. The provisions at 250.68(C)(1) allows a section of metallic water pipe within the first 1.52 m (5 ft) of entry to a building to be used as a connection or bonding point for other electrodes and to connect a wire type ground-

250.68(C)(2)

Continued

~~to a grounding electrode as specified in 250.52(A)(2) or 250.68(C)(2)(a), (b), or (c)~~ shall be permitted to be used as a ~~bonding~~ conductor to interconnect electrodes that are part of the grounding electrode system, or as a grounding electrode conductor.

a. By connecting the structural metal frame to the reinforcing bars of a concrete-encased electrode, as provided in 250.52(A)(3), or ground ring as provided in 250.52(A)(4)

b. By bonding the structural metal frame to one or more of the grounding electrodes, as specified in 250.52(A)(5) or (A)(7), that comply with 250.53(A)(2)

c. By other approved means of establishing a connection to earth

(3) A concrete-encased electrode extension... [*see Analysis of Changes for 250.68(C)(3)*].

Proposal 5-141

Comment 5-49

ing electrode conductor to this first 1.52 m (5 ft), even if the water service was not metallic or did not qualify as a grounding electrode per 250.52(A)(1). An above-grade structural metal frame of a building can act as a conductor without having to be connected directly to a grounding electrode or to qualify as a grounding electrode as previously required.

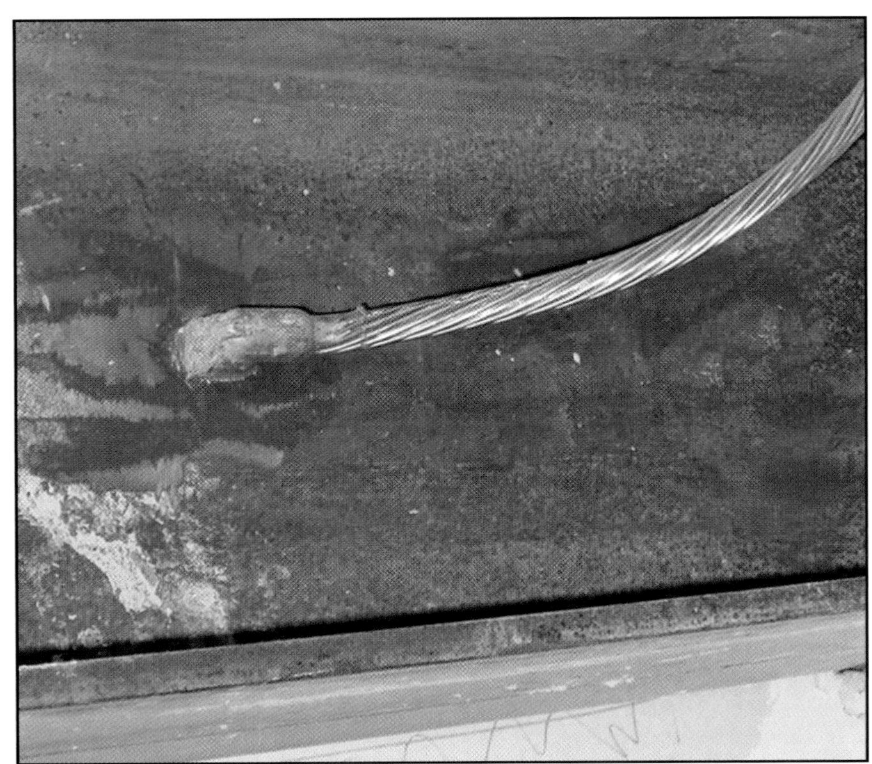

250.68(C)(3)

Change at a Glance

An extension from a concrete-encased electrode has been recognized for connection of grounding electrode conductors. The title of 250.68(C) has been changed to "Grounding Electrode Connections."

Code Language

250.68 Grounding Electrode Conductor and Bonding Jumper Connection to Grounding Electrodes

The connection of a grounding electrode conductor at the service, at each building or structure where supplied by a feeder(s) or branch circuit(s), or at a separately derived system and associated bonding jumper(s) shall be made as specified 250.68(A) through (C).

(C) ~~Metallic Water Pipe and Structural Metal~~ Grounding Electrode Connections. Grounding electrode conductors and bonding jumpers shall be permitted to be connected at the following locations and used to extend the connection to an electrode(s):

(1) Interior metal water piping located not more than 1.52 m (5 ft) from the point of entrance to the building... (*remainder of text and exception unchanged from 2011 text*).

(2) The metal structural frame of a building... [*see Analysis of*

250.68(C)(3) Concrete-Encased Electrode Extension

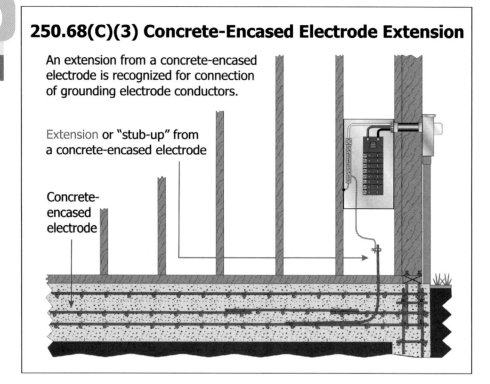

An extension from a concrete-encased electrode is recognized for connection of grounding electrode conductors.

Extension or "stub-up" from a concrete-encased electrode

Concrete-encased electrode

2011 *NEC* Requirement

The conditions or provisions that qualified a structural component as a concrete-encased electrode are described at 250.52(A)(3). This language does not mention an extension or "stub-up" from a concrete-encased electrode. Most users of the *Code* recognized that these extensions from a concrete-encased electrode are an acceptable means to make a connection to a concrete-encased electrode, but no language existed permitting (or not permitting) this practice.

2014 *NEC* Change

Language was added at 250.68(C)(3) to recognize an extension from a concrete-encased electrode as being suitable for the connection of grounding electrode conductor(s) to grounding electrodes, such as a concrete-encased electrode.

Analysis of Change

It has become a commonly accepted practice to extend a structural steel or rebar-type concrete-encased electrode out of the footing or foundation before the slab or foundation is poured by using another piece of rebar connected to the concrete-encased electrode and "stubbed-up" out of the poured concrete to provide an accessible point above the slab for use by the electrician to make a grounding electrode conductor connection at a later date after the foundation has been poured and cured. Although CMP-5 has publicly expressed no objection to this practice in past *Code* cycles, there was no *Code* language that addressed this practice until the 2014 *NEC*. Language was added at 250.68(C)(3) to recognize as permissible a concrete-encased electrode of either the conductor type, reinforcing rod or bar to be extended from the concrete-encased electrode location within the concrete to an accessible location above the concrete for connection of a grounding electrode conductor.

This practice of extending a piece of rebar (connected to a concrete-encased electrode) above the poured slab allows for construction activity to proceed in

250.68(C)(3)

Continued

Change for 250.68(C)(2)].

(3) A concrete-encased electrode of either the conductor type, reinforcing rod or bar installed in accordance with 250.52(A)(3) extended from its location within the concrete to an accessible location above the concrete shall be permitted.

Proposal 5-138, 5-137, 5-143

an orderly fashion (i.e., poured foundations, build-up of the walls and ceiling, etc., then the scheduling of the electrical contractor). It is important to note here that the extension or "stub-up" is not part of the concrete-encased electrode. A structural component meeting all of the conditions of 250.52(A)(3) must be present for the extension to be connected to same. The "stubbed-up" rebar adds to or takes away nothing from the structural component that qualifies as a concrete-encased electrode.

Table 250.102(C)

Change at a Glance

New Table 250.102(C) was added to be used for sizing grounded conductors, main bonding jumpers, system-bonding jumpers, and supply-side bonding jumpers, rather than Table 250.66.

Code Language

250.102 Bonding Conductors and Jumpers

(C) Size — Supply-Side Bonding Jumper.

(1) Size for Supply Conductors in a Single Raceway or Cable. The supply-side bonding jumper shall not be smaller than specified in ~~Table 250.66~~ Table 250.102(C) ~~for grounding electrode conductors. Where the ungrounded supply conductors are larger than 1100 kcmil copper or 1750 kcmil aluminum, the supply-side bonding jumper shall have an area not less than 121/2 percent of the area of the largest set of ungrounded supply conductors.~~

(2) Size for Parallel Conductor Installations in Two or More Raceways. Where the ungrounded supply conductors are paralleled in two or more raceways or cables, and an individual supply-side bonding jumper is used for bonding these raceways or cables, the size of the supply-side bonding jumper

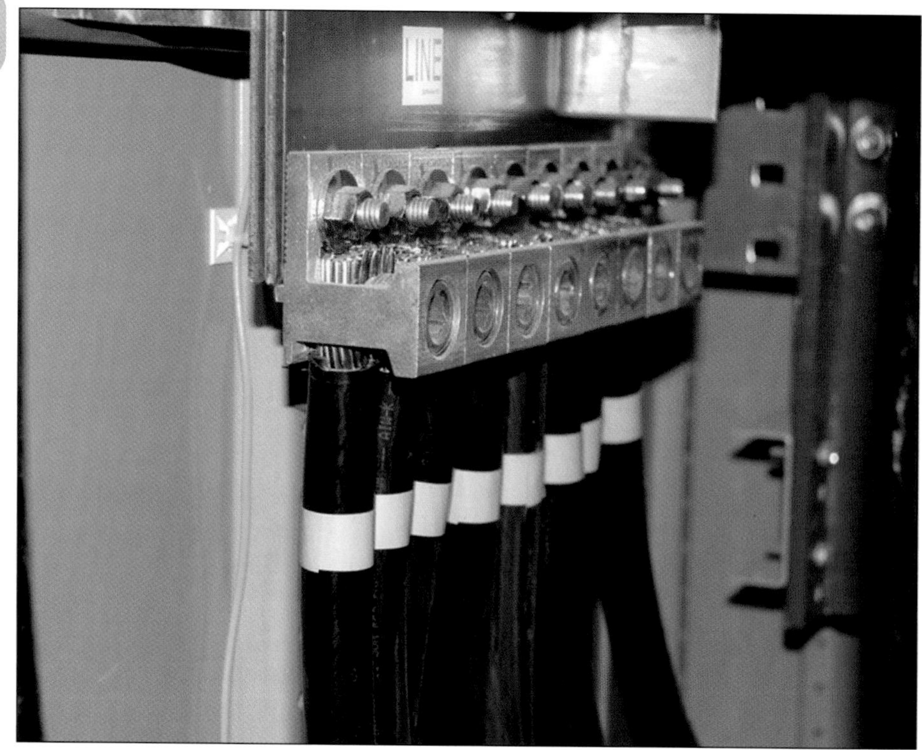

2011 *NEC* Requirement

Grounded conductors, main bonding jumpers, system-bonding jumpers, and supply-side bonding jumpers were required to be sized based on Table 250.66, which is titled, "Grounding Electrode Conductor for Alternating-Current Systems." Several *Code* sections in Article 250 of the 2011 *NEC* referenced Table 250.66 for sizing these conductors.

2014 *NEC* Change

A new Table 250.102(C) "Grounded Conductor, Main Bonding Jumper, System Bonding Jumper, and Supply-Side Bonding Jumper for Alternating-Current Systems" was added to the 2014 *NEC* to be used for sizing grounded conductors, main bonding jumpers, system-bonding jumpers, and supply-side bonding jumpers, rather than Table 250.66. References to this new table were revised throughout Article 250.

Analysis of Change

A new Table 250.102(C) was added with corresponding revisions to related sections in Article 250 to provide simplification to the sizing requirements for fault-return carrying conductors that are not sized using Table 250.122.
Previous *Code* language for multiple *Code* sections such as sizing requirements for main bonding jumpers, system bonding jumpers, supply-side bonding jumpers and grounded conductors referred to Table 250.66 for sizing these conductors or bonding jumpers. Table 250.66 is titled for grounding electrode conductors and has a maximum required conductor of 3/0 copper or 250 kcmil aluminum. Each *Code* reference for sizing these conductors or bonding jumpers contains similar language for sizing requirements above those Table 250.66 maximum sizing requirements, but the *Code* text was not always identical. Table 250.66 was designed for grounding electrode conductors and bonding conductors used to connect multiple electrodes.

Table 250.102(C)

Continued

for each raceway or cable shall be selected from ~~Table 250.66~~ Table 250.102(C) based on the size of the ungrounded supply conductors in each raceway or cable. A single supply-side bonding jumper installed for bonding two or more raceways or cables shall be sized in accordance with 250.102(C)(1).

Informational Note No. 1: The term *supply conductors* includes ungrounded conductors that do not have overcurrent protection on their supply side and terminate at service equipment or the first disconnecting means of a separately derived system.

Informational Note No. 2: See Chapter 9, Table 8, for the circular mil area of conductors 18 AWG through 4/0 AWG.

(See NEC and reproduction of Table 250.102(C) here for complete text of companion table.)

Proposal 5-42

Comment 5-56

Table 250.102(C) Grounded Conductor, Main Bonding Jumper, System Bonding Jumper, and Supply-Side Bonding Jumper for Alternating-Current Systems

Size of Largest Ungrounded Conductor or Equivalent Area for Parallel Conductors (AWG/kcmil)		Size of Grounded Conductor or Bonding Jumper* (AWG/kcmil)	
Copper	Aluminum or Copper-Clad Aluminum	Copper	Aluminum or Copper-Clad Aluminum
2 or smaller	1/0 or smaller	8	6
1 or 1/0	2/0 or 3/0	6	4
2/0 or 3/0	4/0 or 250	4	2
Over 3/0 through 350	Over 250 through 500	2	1/0
Over 350 through 600	Over 500 through 900	1/0	3/0
Over 600 through 1100	Over 900 through 1750	2/0	4/0
Over 1100	Over 1750	See Notes	

*For the purposes of this table, the term bonding jumper refers to main bonding jumpers, system bonding jumpers, and supply-side bonding jumpers.

Notes:

1. If the ungrounded supply conductors are larger than 1100 kcmil copper or 1750 kcmil aluminum, the grounded conductor or bonding jumper shall have an area not less than 12 ½ percent of the area of the largest ungrounded supply conductor or equivalent area for parallel supply conductors. The grounded conductor or bonding jumper shall not be required to be larger than the largest ungrounded conductor or set of ungrounded conductors.

2. If the ungrounded supply conductors and the bonding jumper are of different materials (copper, aluminum or copper-clad aluminum), the minimum size of the grounded conductor or bonding jumper shall be based on the assumed use of ungrounded supply conductors of the same material as the grounded conductor or bonding jumper and will have an ampacity equivalent to that of the installed ungrounded supply conductors.

3. If multiple sets of service-entrance conductors are used as permitted in 230.40, Exception No. 2, or if multiple sets of ungrounded supply conductors are installed for a separately derived system, the equivalent size of the largest ungrounded supply conductor(s) shall be determined by the largest sum of the areas of the corresponding conductors of each set.

4. If there are no service-entrance conductors, the supply conductor size shall be determined by the equivalent size of the largest service-entrance conductor required for the load to be served.

This new Table 250.102(C) and the included notes to the table will apply to other fault-return carrying conductors if the supply conductors do not have overcurrent protection on the supply side. Table 250.122 would continue to be used for sizing fault-return carrying conductors, such as equipment grounding conductors, if the supply conductors have overcurrent protection on the supply side.

The creation of this new table required revisions to the following *Code* sections for references back to this new table rather than to Table 250.66:

250.24(C)(1) for sizing of grounded conductors of ac systems installed in a single raceway.

250.28(D)(1)(1) for sizing main bonding jumpers and system bonding jumpers.

250.30(A)(3)(a) for sizing of grounded conductors of a separately derived system installed in a single raceway.

250.102(C)(1) for sizing supply-side bonding jumpers installed in a single raceway or cable.

250.102(C)(2) for sizing supply-side bonding jumpers for parallel conductors installed in two or more raceways.

A new Informational Note was added after 250.102(C)(2) to inform users of the *Code* what is intended by the term *supply conductors* as it is not defined in Article 100 or in 250.2.

250.122(B)

Change at a Glance

Wire-type equipment grounding conductors are required to be increased in size when the minimum sized ungrounded conductors are increased in size.

Code Language

250.122 Size of Equipment Grounding Conductors

(B) Increased in Size. Where ungrounded conductors are increased in size from the minimum size that has sufficient ampacity for the intended installation, wire-type equipment grounding conductors, where installed, shall be increased in size proportionately according to the circular mil area of the ungrounded conductors.

Proposal 5-199, 5-197, 5-198

250.122(B) EGC Increased in Size

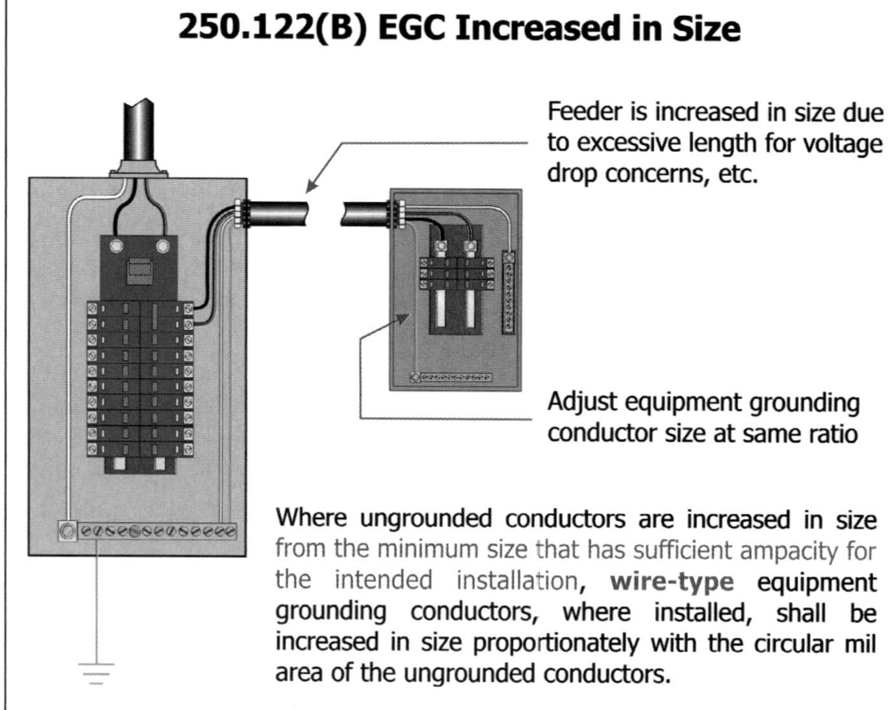

Feeder is increased in size due to excessive length for voltage drop concerns, etc.
Adjust equipment grounding conductor size at same ratio

Where ungrounded conductors are increased in size from the minimum size that has sufficient ampacity for the intended installation, **wire-type** equipment grounding conductors, where installed, shall be increased in size proportionately with the circular mil area of the ungrounded conductors.

2011 *NEC* Requirement

All equipment grounding conductors were required to be increased in size whenever the ungrounded conductors were increased in size for such things as voltage drop issues, etc.

2014 *NEC* Change

Revisions made to 250.122(B) to specify that the equipment grounding conductors were required to be increased in size whenever the ungrounded conductors were increased in size are limited to wire-type equipment grounding conductors only. Further revision indicates that the equipment grounding conductors are not required to be increased in size when the ungrounded conductors are already installed oversized or above the minimum sizes required for sufficient ampacity for the intended load.

Analysis of Change

The *Code* requires equipment grounding conductors to be increased in size at the same ratio whenever the ungrounded conductors of the associated circuit are increased for a variety of reasons such as ampacity adjustment and correction factors, voltage drop, overcurrent device performance, and other engineering factors. Where ampacity correction factors are applied, the ungrounded conductors are required to be protected at their ampacity after the adjustments; or these conductors can be increased in size. Ungrounded conductors are often increased in size when ampacity correction factors are necessary rather than reducing the size of the overcurrent protective device. The feeder or branch circuit equipment grounding in these cases is not impacted from a performance standpoint and, in a situation like this, the *Code* should not require more than the minimum sizes provided in Table 250.122. Revisions to 250.122(B) will make it plain that this "increase in size" for the equipment grounding conductors will apply only when the ungrounded conductors are increased in size from the minimum size required which will maintain sufficient ampacity for the intended installation.

250.122(B)

Continued

This requirement is not necessary when these ungrounded conductors are increased in size for ampacity correction factors rather than reducing the size of the overcurrent protective device.

Another revision to this subsection will make it clear that this "increased in size" requirement for equipment grounding conductors applies to *wire-type* equipment grounding conductors only and not to raceways such as electrical metallic tubing (EMT), which is a permitted equipment grounding conductor per the provisions for 250.118. In previous editions of the *Code*, when a 250.118 identified metallic raceway or conduit was used as the sole equipment grounding conductor and the ungrounded conductors involved were increased in size for something like a voltage drop issue, 250.122(B) would have literally required an "increase in size" of the metal raceway whether the existing metal raceway was sufficient to carry any imposed fault current or not. What formula or calculation would need to be used to increase the metallic raceway for adequate return of fault current?

250.130(C)(4)

Change at a Glance

Connection to an equipment grounding conductor that is part of another branch circuit that originates from the enclosure where the branch circuit for the receptacle or branch circuit originates is permitted for replacement of non-grounding-type receptacles with grounding-type receptacles and for branch-circuit extensions.

NEW

Code Language

250.130 Equipment Grounding Conductor Connections

(C) Non-grounding Receptacle Replacement or Branch Circuit Extensions. The equipment grounding conductor of a grounding-type receptacle or a branch-circuit extension shall be permitted to be connected to any of the following: [List items (1)-(3) and (5) and (6) remain unchanged.] See *NEC* for complete text.

(4) An equipment grounding conductor that is part of another branch circuit that originates from the enclosure where the branch circuit for the receptacle or branch circuit originates

Informational Note: See 406.4(D) for the use of a ground-fault circuit-interrupting type of receptacle.

Proposal 5-209

250.130(C) Nongrounding Extensions

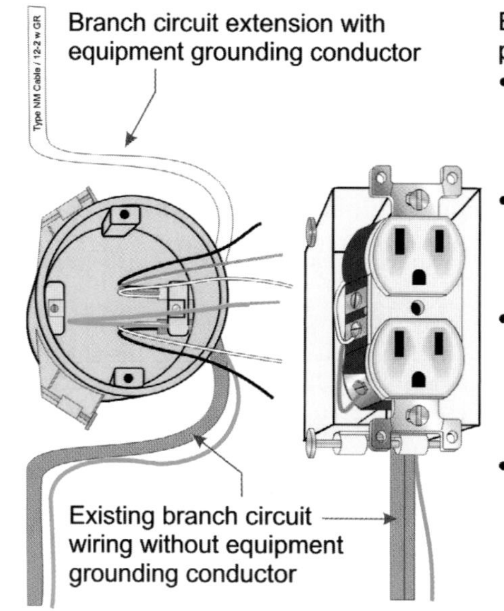
Branch circuit extension with equipment grounding conductor
Existing branch circuit wiring without equipment grounding conductor
Equipment grounding conductor permitted to connect to:
• Any accessible point on the grounding electrode system or the grounding electrode conductor
• The equipment grounding terminal bar within the enclosure where the branch circuit originates
• An EGC that is part of another branch circuit that originates from the enclosure where the branch circuit for the receptacle or branch circuit originates
• For grounded systems, the grounded service conductor within the service equipment enclosure or the grounding terminal bar for ungrounded systems

2011 *NEC* Requirement

For replacement of non-grounding-type receptacles with grounding-type receptacles and for branch-circuit extensions only in existing installations that do not have an equipment grounding conductor in the branch circuit, connections are permitted as indicated in 250.130(C), which had five provisions, any of which could be used to accomplish the equipment grounding conductor connection.

2014 *NEC* Change

A sixth provision was added in the form of item (4). This item will permit the connection of an equipment grounding conductor that is part of another branch circuit that originates from the enclosure where the branch circuit for the receptacle or branch circuit originates for replacement of non-grounding-type receptacles with grounding-type receptacles and for branch-circuit extensions only in existing installations that do not have an equipment grounding conductor in the branch circuit.

Analysis of Change

The addition of a sixth provision in item (4) to accomplish the connection of an equipment grounding conductor for replacement of non-grounding-type receptacles with grounding-type receptacles and for branch-circuit extensions is simply an extension of the present item (3) that allows connecting to the equipment grounding bar in the related panelboard. Allowing the connection of an equipment grounding conductor by the new item (4) will provide a more effective equipment grounding conductor path than do the current first two list items that permit connection to the grounding electrode system. Equipment grounding conductors are not grounding electrode conductors. While tying into the grounding electrode system does provide a connection to the grounding system of the building, it provides a rather high impedance path for equipment grounding due to its roundabout path. Allowing a connection back to the same enclosure or panelboard that serves the receptacle branch circuit would typically provide a shorter, more effective equipment grounding or ground-fault return path.

250.166

Change at a Glance

A maximum size requirement for grounding electrode conductor of dc systems was added.

Code Language

250.166 Size of the Direct-Current Grounding Electrode Conductor

The size of the grounding electrode conductor for a dc system shall be as specified in 250.166(A) and (B), except as permitted by 250.166(C) through (E). The grounding electrode conductor for a dc system shall meet the sizing requirements in this section but shall not be required to be larger than 3/0 copper or 250 kcmil aluminum.

(Remainder of text at 250.166(A) through (E) is unchanged. See NEC for complete text.)

Proposal 5-222

250.166 Size of DC Grounding Electrode Conductor

- A maximum size requirement for grounding electrode conductors of dc systems has been added at 250.166.
- The GEC for dc systems shall be sized per 250.166 but shall not be required to be larger than 3/0 copper or 250 kcmil aluminum.

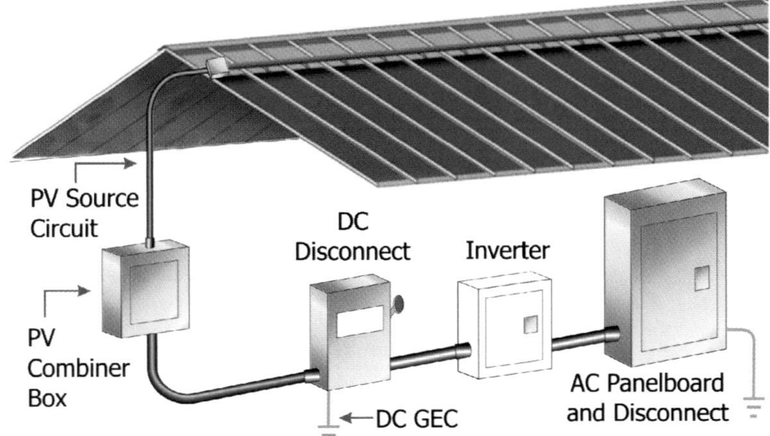

Note: 690.47(C) would required dc and ac GEC systems to be bonded together.

2011 *NEC* Requirement

The sizing requirements for grounding electrode conductor(s) for a dc system are required to be as specified in 250.166, but no maximum size for the dc system grounding electrode conductor(s) was specified. With an ac system grounding electrode conductor sizes are specified at 250.66 and Table 250.66.

2014 *NEC* Change

A maximum size requirement of 3/0 copper or 250 kcmil aluminum for grounding electrode conductor of dc systems was added at 250.166. This correlates with the maximum size requirements for ac system grounding electrode conductor as specified at 250.66 and Table 250.66.

Analysis of Change

For sizing of a dc system grounding electrode conductor, no maximum size was provided at 250.166, except for grounding electrode conductors that are the sole connection to grounding electrodes such as rods, ground rings, concrete-encased electrodes, etc., as provided in 250.166(C), (D), or (E). This new provision will limit the maximum size of a dc system grounding electrode conductor to 3/0 copper or 250 kcmil aluminum. In previous editions of the *Code*, where larger dc systems were installed, the grounding electrode conductor was not permitted to be smaller than the neutral conductor of the system or the largest conductor supplying the dc system. As an example, if a neutral of the largest conductor supplying the dc system, other than those covered in 250.166(A) for 3-wire balancer sets, is sized at (3) 350 kcmil copper per phase, the grounding electrode conductor for this dc system must be sized at 1050 kcmil copper at a minimum. This was more restrictive than necessary given that a grounding electrode conductor's primary purpose is to direct the dissipation of overcurrents, etc., and not for clearing ground-fault conditions.

250.167

Change at a Glance

New section requiring ground-fault detection on dc systems was added to "Direct-Current Ground-Fault Detection."

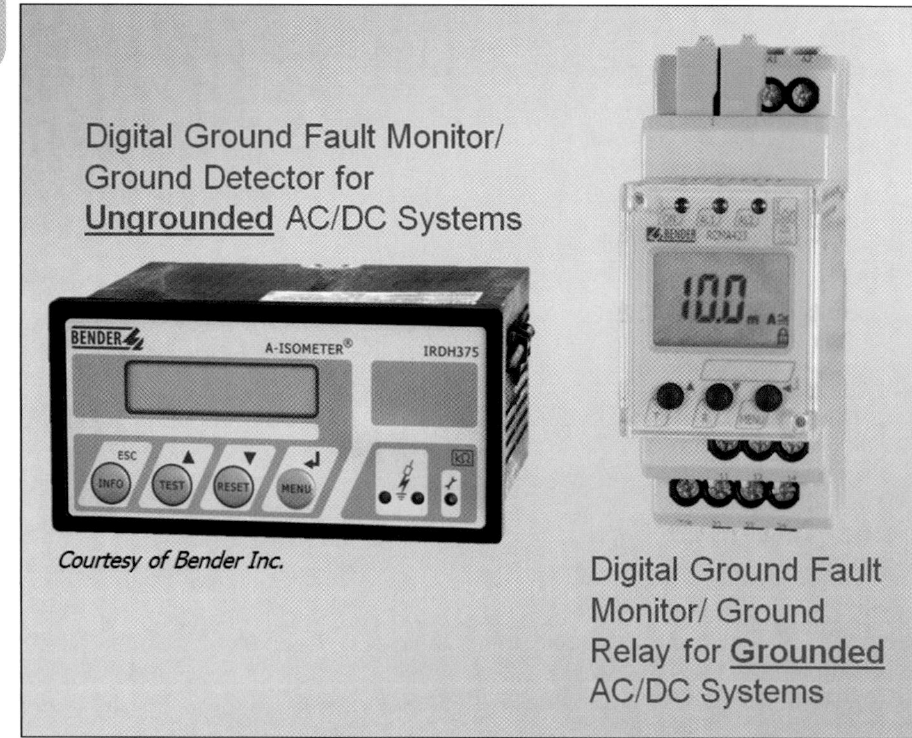

Courtesy of Bender Inc.

Code Language

250.167 Direct-Current Ground-Fault Detection

(A) Ungrounded Systems. Ground-fault detection systems shall be required for ungrounded systems.

(B) Grounded Systems. Ground-fault detection shall be permitted for grounded systems.

(C) Marking. Direct-current systems shall be legibly marked to indicate the grounding type at the dc source or the first disconnecting means of the system. The marking shall be of sufficient durability to withstand the environment involved.

Informational Note: NFPA 70E-2012 identifies four dc grounding types in detail.

Proposal 5-223

2011 *NEC* Requirement

There were no requirements for ground-fault detection for dc systems in the 2011 *NEC*.

2014 *NEC* Change

A new section was added to "Direct-Current Ground-Fault Detection" requiring ground fault detection on dc systems. These new requirements address grounded systems, ungrounded systems, and marking rules for each.

Analysis of Change

A new provision was added at 250.167 for ground-fault detection for dc systems for the 2014 *NEC*. These new provisions *require* ground-fault detection for ungrounded dc systems and *permit* ground-fault detection for grounded dc systems. Some dc applications cannot utilize a grounded system (with an intentionally grounded conductor). An unintentional voltage to ground or ground-fault can result in fires or shock hazards. Grounded systems are not all grounded or connected to earth (grounding electrode system) in the same manner. NFPA 70E, *Standard for Electrical Safety in the Workplace,* provides details on four different dc grounding methods. Ground-fault detection would not be appropriate for all of these different types of grounding methods.

New marking requirements were also put in place as these dc systems are required to be legibly marked to indicate the type of grounding provisions provided at the dc source or the first disconnecting means of the dc system. The marking must also be of sufficient durability to withstand the environment involved. The proposal that resulted in these new provisions was developed as a joint effort of the NEC DC Task Force of the NEC Correlating Committee and the IEEE Stationary Battery Codes Working Group.

250.186

Change at a Glance

New section for "Ground Fault Circuit Conductor Brought to Service Equipment" was added to require services over 1000 volts to have a grounded conductor to be brought to the service for a grounded system. Ungrounded systems (over 1000 volts) will require a supply side bonding jumper brought to the service.

NEW

Code Language

250.186 Ground-Fault Circuit Conductor Brought to Service Equipment

(A) Systems with a Grounded Conductor at the Service Point.
(1) Sizing for a Single Raceway or Overhead Conductor.
(2) Parallel Conductors in Two or More Raceways or Overhead Conductors.
(3) Delta-Connected Service.
(4) Impedance Grounded Neutral Systems.

(B) Systems without a Grounded Conductor at the Service Point.
(1) Sizing for a Single Raceway or Overhead Conductor.
(2) Parallel Conductors in Two or More Raceways or Overhead Conductors.
(3) Impedance Grounded Neutral Systems.

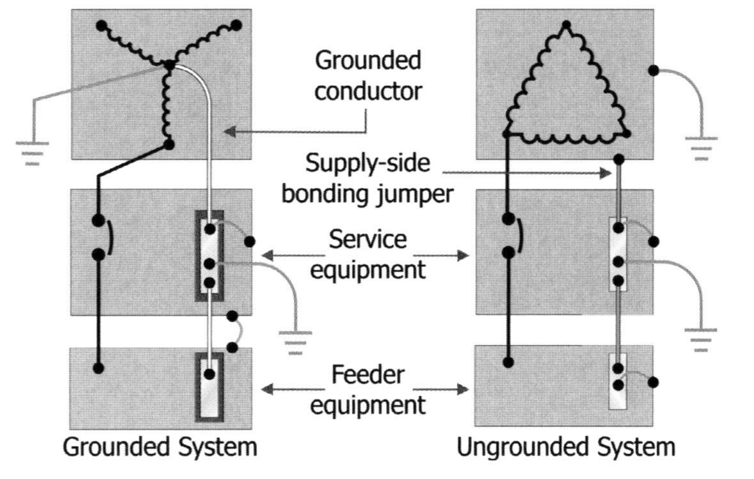
250.186 Ground-Fault Circuit Conductor Brought to Service Equipment
New 250.186 to require services (over 1000 volts) to have a grounded conductor brought to the service for a grounded system
Ungrounded systems (over 1000 volts) require a supply side bonding jumper brought to the service
Grounded conductor
Supply-side bonding jumper
Service equipment
Feeder equipment
Grounded System
Ungrounded System

2011 *NEC* Requirement

Section 250.24(C) requires a grounded (neutral) conductor to be brought to the service equipment for grounded systems, but this provision is limited to systems of 1000 volts or below.

2014 *NEC* Change

New 250.186 will now require services of over 1000 volts to have a grounded (neutral) conductor to be established at the service for a grounded system. Ungrounded systems (over 1000 volts) will require a supply side bonding jumper brought to the service equipment.

Analysis of Change

One of the main purposes for this grounded conductor being brought to the first means of disconnect(s) is to provide a low impedance return path in the event of imposed ground-fault current. At this point, the grounded conductors would serve and have the ability to return this faulted current from the point of the ground fault back to the utility supply source, back to the overcurrent device, and to clear the faulted condition. The same need for clearing ground faults exists for grounded systems of over 1000 volts, but these requirements did not exist until the 2014 *NEC* with this new requirement in 250.186. Some jurisdictions have relied on the performance requirements of 250.4(A)(5) for this provision for grounded systems of over 1000 volts, which requires all electrical equipment that is "likely to become energized" to be provided with an effective ground-fault current return path to facilitate the operation of the overcurrent device or ground detector for high-impedance grounded systems. These new provisions at 250.186 establish these low impedance fault-return path requirements for systems over 1000 volts, and also include provisions for situations where the serving utility company may or may not provide a neutral (grounded conductor) with their distribution system. Where the electrical utility provider does not provide a grounded (neutral) conductor, there

250.186

Continued

250.187 Impedance Grounded Neutral Systems.

(See NEC for complete text)

Proposal 5-234

Comment 5-99, 5-101, 5-103

is typically a static line or other ground-fault return path where a supply-side bonding jumper can be established to complete the fault-return path.

Typically, for a service supplied at over 1000 volts from the servicing electric utility company, the *NEC* does not have jurisdiction over this service until the service point comes into play. Section 250.186(A) establishes requirements where the servicing utility has a supply system and a grounded (neutral) conductor is provided to the service point (where the *NEC* application begins). This system may or may not be solidly grounded based on the local servicing utility practices and the user of the *Code* cannot assume what these servicing utility practices are in all cases. If there is no grounded (neutral) conductor provided, then 250.186(B) would apply where the servicing utility supply system does not have a grounded (neutral) conductor at the service point. In either situation, the primary concern is to provide a very low impedance ground-fault return path capable of safely carrying the maximum ground-fault current likely to be imposed from any point on the wiring system where a ground fault may occur to the electrical supply source.

Impedance grounded systems cannot be grounded as detailed in 250.186(A) or (B). The addition of new 250.186(A)(4) and (B)(3) will send users of the *Code* to 250.187 (*which was previously 250.186*) to provide clarity and prescriptive language for grounding requirements for impedance grounded neutral systems. Same requirements as 250.24(C) for services 1000 volts or below. The new provisions at 250.186 resulted from proposals created by a CMP-5 task group in addition to and intended to compliment the High Voltage Task Group work in the 2014 *NEC* cycle.

250.194

Change at a Glance

New section was added for bonding and grounding metal fences and other metal structures around substations.

Code Language

250.194 Grounding and Bonding of Fences and Other Metal Structures

Metallic fences enclosing, and other metal structures in or surrounding, a substation with exposed electrical conductors and equipment shall be grounded and bonded to limit step, touch, and transfer voltages.

(A) Metal Fences. Where metal fences are located within 5 m (16 ft) of the exposed electrical conductors or equipment, the fence shall be bonded to the grounding electrode system with wire-type bonding jumpers as follows:

(1) Bonding jumpers shall be installed at each fence corner and at maximum 50 m (160 ft) intervals along the fence.

(2) Where bare overhead conductors cross the fence, bonding jumpers shall be installed on each side of the crossing.

(3) Gates shall be bonded to the gate support post, and each gate support post shall be bonded to the grounding electrode system.

(4) Any gate or other opening in

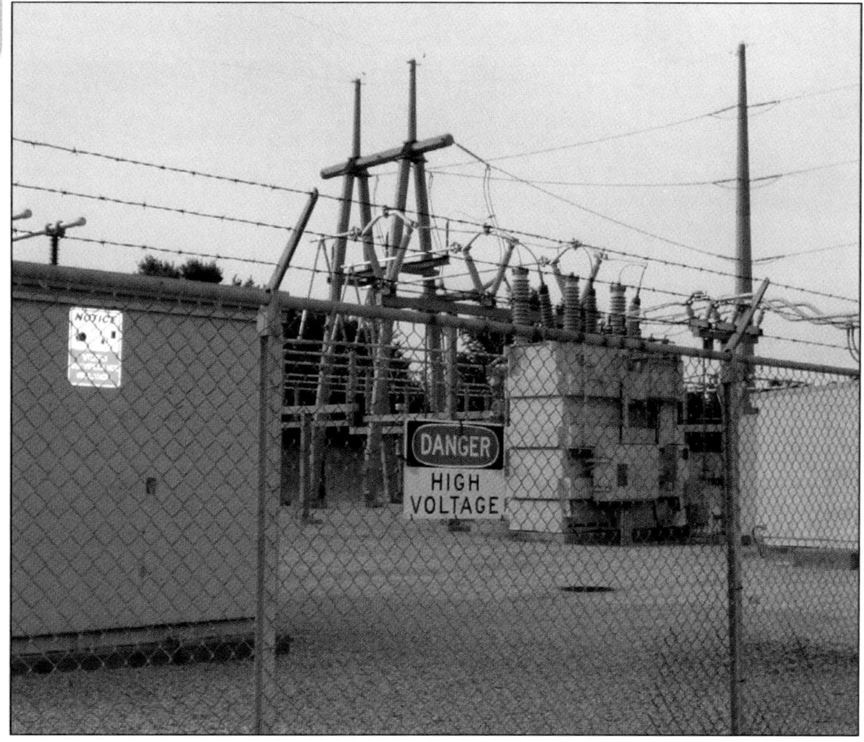

2011 *NEC* Requirement

No provisions existed in the 2011 *NEC* for grounding and bonding of metal fences and metal structures, particularly when the voltage is over 1000 volts.

2014 *NEC* Change

A new section was added to Part X, Grounding of Systems and Circuits of over 1000 Volts, of Article 250 entitled "Grounding and Bonding of Fences and Other Metal Structures." This new section provides new rules for bonding and grounding fences and other metal structures around substations.

Analysis of Change

For reasons of security and economics, metal fences are often built around substations. Due to the fact that these fences will be accessible to the general public, they must be grounded to limit the rise of hazardous voltage potential on the fence to the surrounding earth. This new provision in Part X of Article 250, Grounding of Systems and Circuits of over 1000 Volts, will establish basic prescriptive requirements for grounding and bonding of metal fences and metal structures built in and around substations. For situations where step and touch voltage potential considerations indicate that additional grounding and bonding design is necessary, alternate designs performed under engineering supervision are permitted. Informational Note No. 2 directs designers to the industry standard on the grounding of fences in and around substations (IEEE 80-2000, *Guide for Safety in AC Substation Grounding*). The proposal for this new section was created by a CMP-5 task group intended to add to and compliment the High Voltage Task Group work in the 2014 *NEC* cycle.

250.194

Continued

the fence shall be bonded across the opening by a buried bonding jumper.

(5) The grounding grid or grounding electrode systems shall be extended to cover the swing of all gates.

(6) The barbed wire strands above the fence shall be bonded to the grounding electrode system.

Alternate designs performed under engineering supervision shall be permitted for grounding or bonding of metal fences.

Informational Note No. 1: A nonconducting fence or section may provide isolation for transfer of voltage to other areas.

Informational Note No. 2: See IEEE 80-2000, *IEEE Guide for Safety in AC Substation Grounding*, for design and installation of fence grounding.

(B) Metal Structures. All exposed conductive metal structures, including guy wires within 2.5 m (8 ft) vertically or 5 m (16 ft) horizontally of exposed conductors or equipment and subject to contact by persons, shall be bonded to the grounding electrode systems in the area.

Proposal 5-241

285.13

Change at a Glance

Type 4 component assemblies and Type 5 SPDs are incomplete devices that are only acceptable when provided as part of listed equipment.

Code Language

285.13 Type 4 and Other Component Type SPDs

Type 4 component assemblies and other component type SPDs shall only be installed by the equipment manufacturer.

Proposal 5-244b

Comment 5-111

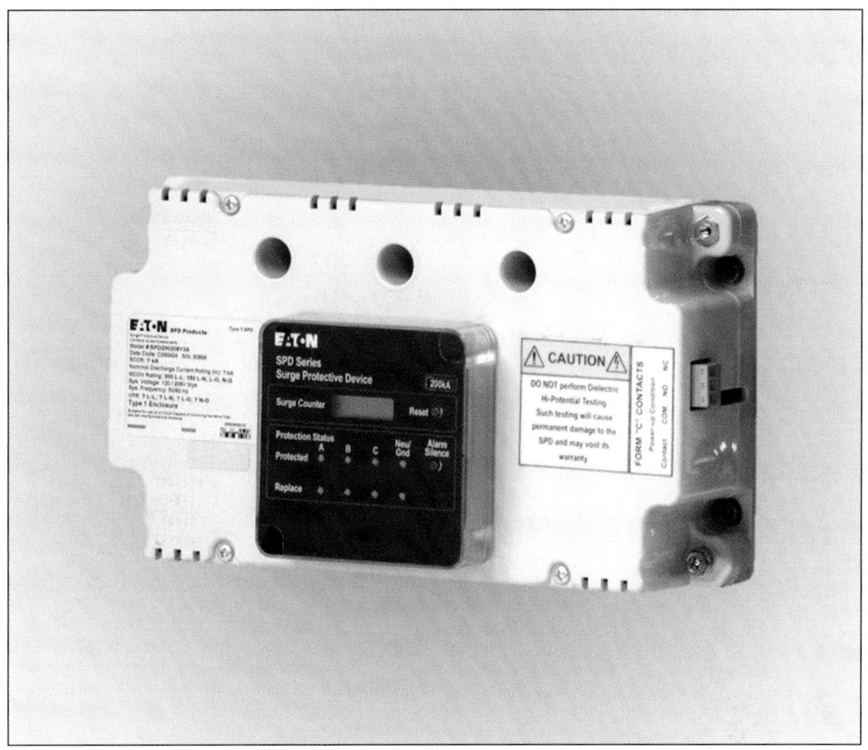

2011 *NEC* Requirement

Type 4 component assemblies and other component type SPDs were not addressed in the 2011 *NEC*.

2014 *NEC* Change

A new section, entitled "Type 4 and Other Component Type SPDs," was added to indicate that Type 4 component assemblies and Type 5 SPDs are incomplete devices that are only acceptable when provided as part of listed equipment. This new section will clarify that component SPD(s) are not to be installed in the field.

Analysis of Change

Article 285 covers surge-protective devices (SPDs) permanently installed on premises wiring systems of 1000 volts or less. A *surge-protective device* (SPD) is defined in Article 100 as "a protective device for limiting transient voltages by diverting or limiting surge current; it also prevents continued flow of follow current while remaining capable of repeating these functions." The term *transient voltage surge suppressor* (TVSS) was replaced by the term *surge protective devices* (SPDs) in the 2008 edition of the *NEC*. STPs are identified by Type 1, 2, 3, or 4 depending upon where the SPD will be incorporated within the power distribution system.

Type 1 also called *surge arresters* or *secondary surge arresters* are typically mounted on the line side of the main service disconnecting means and are intended to protect against external surges caused by lightning or utility capacitor bank switching, etc.

Type 2 are typically connected on the load side of the service disconnecting means serving a branch circuit and protects against residual lightning energy, motor driven surges, and other internally generated surges.

285.13

Continued

Type 3 SPDs are generally surge receptacles or cord-connected point-of-use devices. They are permitted to be installed anywhere on the load side of a branch circuit up to the equipment served. Type 3 STPs are typically used to protect equipment and to provide point-of-use protection; they are easily replaceable and provide the last line of defense against a lightning strike.

Type 4 SPDs are UL Recognized Components. They are typically component assemblies consisting of one or more component-type STPs together with a disconnect (integral or external). Type 4 STPs are designated equipment that is installed within other listed equipment denoted as *recognized component equipment*.

Type 4 component assemblies and component-type SPDs are incomplete devices that are only acceptable when provided as part of listed equipment. This section clarifies that component SPD(s) are not to be installed in the field.

Article 300, and 300.1(A)

Change at a Glance

Title to Article 300 has been revised. Similar revision to 300.1, Scope, was made to better reflect what is covered by Chapter 3 and Article 300.

Code Language

Article 300 General Requirements for Wiring Methods and Materials

300.1 Scope.

(A) All Wiring Installations. This article covers general requirements for wiring methods and materials for all wiring installations unless modified by other articles in Chapter 3.

Proposal 3-8, 3-9

Chapter 3 Wiring Methods and Materials

ARTICLE 300

General Requirements for Wiring Methods and Materials

I. General Requirements

300.1 Scope.

(A) All Wiring Installations. This article covers general requirements for wiring and materials for all wiring installations unless modified by other articles in Chapter 3.

2011 *NEC* Requirement

The title of Chapter 3 was "Wiring Methods and Materials" with the title of Article 300 being "Wiring Methods." The scope of Article 300 at 300.1(A) stated that Article 300 "covers wiring methods for all wiring installations unless modified by other articles."

2014 *NEC* Change

The title of Article 300 was revised from "Wiring Methods" to "General Requirements for Wiring Methods and Materials." The scope of Article 300 was revised to give a better understanding that the articles in Chapter 3 not only cover the wiring methods in Chapter 3, but the materials used in Chapter 3 as well.

Analysis of Change

This revision was intended to be editorial in nature as well as to enhance clarity and usability. With the previous title of Chapter 3 being, "Wiring Methods and Materials" and the previous title of Article 300 being "Wiring Methods," this indicated that what is covered in Article 300 are all of the wiring methods with the balance of Chapter 3 and the specific wiring method articles covering just wiring materials and not necessarily specific wiring methods for each remaining article. Wiring methods are generally recognized as the particular cable assemblies, conduits, and raceways covered in the individual Chapter 3 wiring method articles of the Code. These title changes better reflect what is covered by Chapter 3 and Article 300. Specific rules for each wiring method are part of every respective Chapter 3 wiring method article that follows Article 300.

300.6(A) IN

Change at a Glance

A new Informational Note was added indicating what constitutes "field-cut threads."

NEW

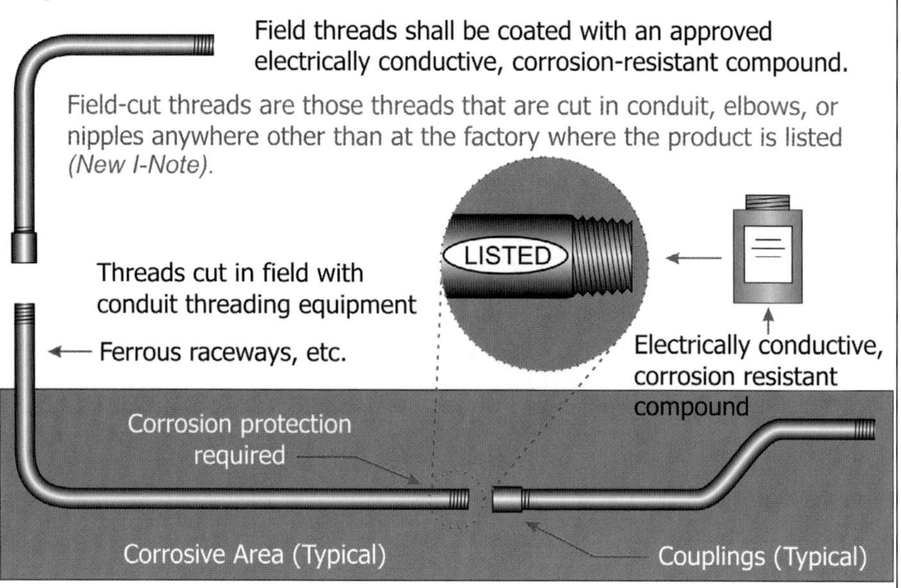
300.6(A) Protection Against Corrosion
Ferrous metal raceways, etc. are typically required to be suitably protected against corrosion inside and outside.
Field threads shall be coated with an approved electrically conductive, corrosion-resistant compound.
Field-cut threads are those threads that are cut in conduit, elbows, or nipples anywhere other than at the factory where the product is listed (New I-Note).
LISTED
Threads cut in field with conduit threading equipment
Ferrous raceways, etc.
Electrically conductive, corrosion resistant compound
Corrosion protection required
Corrosive Area (Typical)
Couplings (Typical)

Code Language

300.6 Protection Against Corrosion and Deterioration
Raceways, cable trays, cablebus, auxiliary gutters, cable armor, boxes, cable sheathing, cabinets, elbows, couplings, fittings, supports, and support hardware shall be of materials suitable for the environment in which they are to be installed.

(A) Ferrous Metal Equipment. Ferrous metal raceways, cable trays, cablebus, auxiliary gutters, cable armor, boxes, cable sheathing, cabinets, metal elbows, couplings, nipples, fittings, supports, and support hardware shall be suitably protected against corrosion inside and outside (except threads at joints) by a coating of approved corrosion-resistant material. Where corrosion protection is necessary and the conduit is threaded in the field, the threads shall be coated with an approved electrically conductive, corrosion-resistant compound.

Informational Note: Field-cut threads are those threads that are cut in conduit, elbows, or nipples anywhere other than at the factory where the product is listed.

Exception: *Stainless steel shall not be required to have protective coatings.*

2011 *NEC* Requirement

The provisions of 300.6 require electrical equipment such as raceways, cabinets, couplings, fittings, etc. to be made of materials suitable for the environment in which they will to be installed. Section 300.6(A) requires ferrous metal raceways and other electrical equipment such as boxes, elbows, etc., to be suitably protected against corrosion inside and outside by a coating of approved corrosion-resistant material. This subsection goes further to require conduits that are threaded in the field to have their threads coated with an approved electrically conductive, corrosion-resistant compound where necessary. An exception to this protective corrosion-resistant compound exists for stainless steel raceways and other electrical equipment.

2014 *NEC* Change

A new Informational Note was added after 300.6(A) detailing that field-cut threads are those threads that are field-applied or cut in conduit, elbows, or nipples anywhere other than at the factory where the product is produced and listed.

Analysis of Change

This new Informational Note will clarify for the user of the *Code* as to what constitutes field-cut threads and what is not a field-cut thread. This should also help alleviate confusion in the installation of field-cut threads in conduits and raceways concerning corrosion protection of these threads. There seems to be confusion as to whether corrosion protection only applies to straight lengths of ferrous metal raceways such as rigid steel conduit and intermediate metal conduit versus metal elbows, nipples, couplings and other fittings associated with ferrous metal raceways. Elbows, couplings and nipples associated with rigid steel conduit and intermediate metal conduit are listed to the same UL standards (UL 6 and UL 1242 respectively) for the applicable material type. Section 5.4.2 of UL 6 and 7.2 of UL 1242 entitled "Protection of Threads" require "threads that are cut after

Proposal: 3-51

Comment: 3-17

the protective coatings are applied shall be treated to keep corrosion from taking place before the conduit is installed." All field-cut threads, internal and external, are required to be corrosion protected, after cutting, as part of the product listing. Additionally, 300.10 states that protective coatings must not interfere with the electrical continuity or full engagements of the threads. The new Informational Note will emphasize the requirements for listed products.

300.11(B)(1)

Change at a Glance

Raceways can be used as a means of support where the raceway is identified "as a means of support."

Code Language

300.11 Securing and Supporting

(B) Raceways Used as a Means of Support. Raceways shall be used only as a means of support for other raceways, cables, or non-electrical equipment under any of the following conditions:

(1) Where the raceway or means of support is identified ~~for the purpose~~ as a means of support

(2) Where the raceway contains power supply conductors for electrically controlled equipment and is used to support Class 2 circuit conductors or cables that are solely for the purpose of connection to the equipment control circuits

(3) Where the raceway is used to support boxes or conduit bodies in accordance with 314.23 or to support luminaires in accordance with 410.36(E)

Proposal 3-65

2011 *NEC* Requirement

Raceways were permitted to be used as a means of support for other raceways, cables, or nonelectrical equipment where the raceway or means of support was "identified for the purpose."

2014 *NEC* Change

A revision to 300.11(B)(1) still permits raceways to be used as a means of support for other raceways, cables, or nonelectrical equipment, but the raceway or means of support must now be "identified as a means of support," not just "identified for the purpose."

Analysis of Change

An NEC Correlating Committee (NEC CC) Usability Task Group was assembled by the chairman of the NEC CC with the assignment of reviewing the use of the phrase "identified for the purpose" throughout the *NEC*. This is the completion of an ongoing process that was started in the 2005 edition of the *NEC* to identify specific locations throughout the *NEC* where the term *identified for the purpose* or *listed for the purpose* was used. Now the user of the *Code* will know the specific purpose that the item in question was identified or listed for, not just generically state that the item was "identified for the purpose." An example of this can be found at 680.23(A)(2) for underwater luminaries for a permanently installed swimming pool.

The word "identified" is defined in Article 100 of the *NEC* as "recognizable as suitable for the specific purpose..." The addition of "for the purpose" after the word identified is unnecessary and does not add clarity to the rule and does not state the specific purpose. For this situation here at 300.11(B)(1), deleting the phrase "for the purpose" would now require the raceway or means of support to only be "identified." Identified for what? Identified could be related to environment or other non-related functions. The intent of this revised text is to ensure that the raceway or means of support is identified as a "means of support."

300.22(C)(1)

Change at a Glance

Cable ties used to secure cables in plenums must be listed as having fire-resistant and low-smoke producing characteristics.

Code Language

300.22 Wiring in Ducts Not Used for Air Handling, Fabricated Ducts for Environmental Air, and Other Spaces for Environmental Air (Plenums)

The provisions of this section shall apply to the installation and uses of electrical wiring and equipment in ducts used for dust, loose stock, or vapor removal; ducts specifically fabricated for environmental air; and other spaces used for environmental air (plenums).

(C) Other Spaces Used for Environmental Air (Plenums). This section shall apply to spaces not specifically fabricated for environmental air-handling purposes but used for air-handling purposes as a plenum. This section shall not apply to habitable rooms or areas of buildings, the prime purpose of which is not air handling.
(See NEC for complete text and Informational Notes.)

Exception: *This section shall not apply to the joist or stud spaces of dwelling units where the wiring passes through such spaces perpendicular to the long dimension of such spaces.*

(1) Wiring Methods. The wiring methods for such other space shall be limited to totally enclosed, non-

300.22(C)(1) Wiring Methods (Plenums)

The wiring methods for environmental air-handling spaces shall be limited to Type AC cable, flexible metal conduit, EMT, etc.

Nonmetallic cable ties and other nonmetallic cable accessories used to secure and support cables shall be listed as having low smoke and heat release properties.

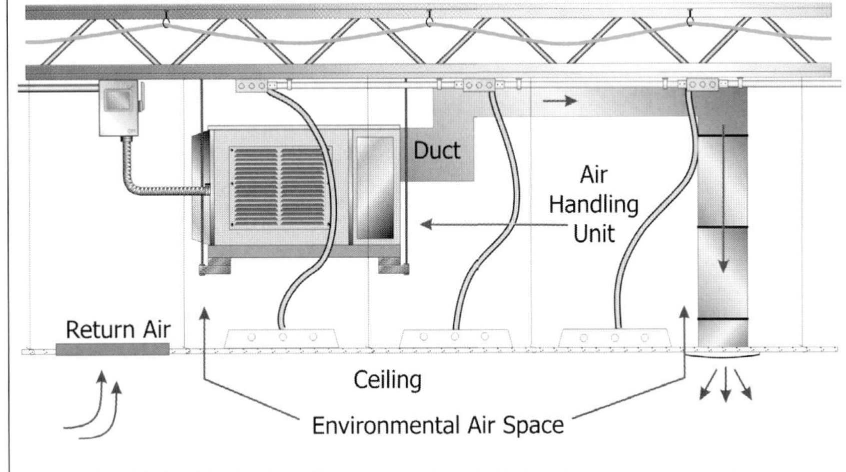

2011 *NEC* Requirement

Wiring methods used in spaces used for environmental air (plenums) have to be specifically listed for use within an air-handling space. A list of wiring methods identified for this use is provided at 300.22(C)(1). Even though the wiring methods were required to be "specifically listed for use within an air-handling space," the nonmetallic cable ties and other nonmetallic cable accessories used to secure and support cables in these plenums did not have to be listed for compliance within an air-handling space.

2014 *NEC* Change

A new sentence was added at the end of 300.22(C)(1) for wiring methods installed in spaces used for environmental air (plenums). This will require nonmetallic cable ties and other nonmetallic cable accessories used to secure and support cables in these spaces to be listed as having low-smoke and heat-release properties and characteristics. A new informational note was also added that will provide pertinent information related to low smoke and heat release properties for nonmetallic cable ties.

Analysis of Change

Revisions and new text were added at 300.22(C)(1) with the intent of bringing the *NEC* requirements for nonmetallic cable ties installed in spaces used for environmental air (plenums) into correlation with NFPA 90A, *Standard for the Installation of Air-Conditioning and Ventilating Systems*. This correlation will be achieved by requiring nonmetallic cable ties and other nonmetallic cable accessories used to secure and support cables in plenums to be listed as having low-smoke and heat-release properties. NFPA 90A-2012 has current requirements for cable ties in ceiling cavity plenums (4.3.11.2.6.5) and raised floor plenums (4.3.11.5.5.6) that correspond to these new provisions which have been added at this subsection of the *NEC*. Plenum grade nonmetallic cable ties are readily available in the marketplace today that can achieve compliance with this new provision.

300.22(C)(1)

Continued

ventilated, insulated busway having no provisions for plug-in connections, Type MI cable without an overall nonmetallic covering, Type MC cable without an overall nonmetallic covering, Type AC cable, or other factory-assembled multiconductor control or power cable that is specifically listed for use within an air-handling space, or listed prefabricated cable assemblies of metallic manufactured wiring systems without nonmetallic sheath. Other types of cables, conductors, and raceways shall be permitted to be installed in electrical metallic tubing, flexible metallic tubing, intermediate metal conduit, rigid metal conduit without an overall nonmetallic covering, flexible metal conduit, or, where accessible, surface metal raceway or metal wireway with metal covers. Nonmetallic cable ties and other nonmetallic cable accessories used to secure and support cables shall be listed as having low smoke and heat release properties.

Informational Note: One method to determine low smoke and heat release properties is that the nonmetallic cable ties and other nonmetallic cable accessories exhibits a maximum peak optical density of 0.50 or less, an average optical density of 0.15 or less and a peak heat release rate of 100 kW or less when tested in accordance with ANSI/UL 2043-2008, *Fire Test for Heat and Visible Smoke Release for Discrete Products and Their Accessories Installed in Air-Handling Spaces*.

Proposal 3-86, 3-84

Comment 3-24

Comment 3-24 which contributed to the final verbiage of these new provisions was developed by a CMP-3/CMP-16 Joint Task Group formed at the direction of the NEC Correlating Committee (NEC CC) to correlate the other requirements for cable ties in Articles 300, 770, 800, 820, and 830 with 300.22(C)(1).

300.38

Change at a Glance

Interior of raceways installed in wet locations above grade are now considered to be a wet location for installations of over 1000 volts, nominal.

Code Language

300.38 Raceways in Wet Locations Above Grade

Where raceways are installed in wet locations above grade, the interior of these raceways shall be considered to be a wet location. Insulated conductors and cables installed in raceways in wet locations above grade shall comply with 310.10(C).

Proposal 3-92

Comment 3-30

300.38 Raceways in Wet Locations Abovegrade

The interior of raceways installed in wet locations abovegrade shall be considered to be a wet location (regardless of the voltage).

The interior of enclosures or raceways installed underground shall be considered to be a wet location (regardless of the voltage).

Insulated conductors and cables installed in raceways in wet locations (abovegrade or underground) shall comply with 310.10(C).

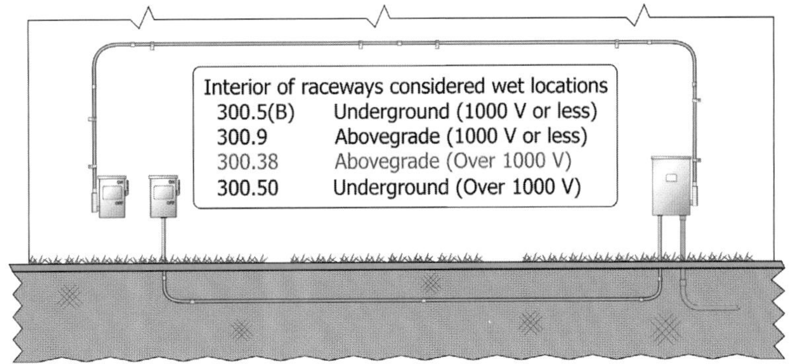

Interior of raceways considered wet locations
300.5(B) Underground (1000 V or less)
300.9 Abovegrade (1000 V or less)
300.38 Abovegrade (Over 1000 V)
300.50 Underground (Over 1000 V)

2011 *NEC* Requirement

The interior of enclosures or raceways installed underground are considered to be a wet location by 300.5(B) for installations of 600 volts (now 1000 volts) or less. The interior of raceways installed above ground are considered to be a wet location by 300.9 for installations of 600 volts (now 1000 volts) or less. The interior of enclosures or raceways installed underground are considered to be a wet location by 300.50(B) for installations over 600 volts (now 1000 volts), nominal. No provisions existed in the 2011 *NEC* dealing with the interior of a raceway installed above ground for installations over 600 volts (now 1000 volts), nominal.

2014 *NEC* Change

A new section was added to Part II (over 1000 volts, nominal) of Article 300 to indicate that the interior of raceways installed in wet locations above grade are now considered to be a wet location. This will bring aboveground installation requirements for over 1000 volts consistent with the requirements in 300.9 for 1000 volts and under.

Analysis of Change

With this new requirement at 300.38, the evolution of the fact that the interior of raceways being declared a wet location when the raceway is installed in wet locations is now complete. The 2008 edition of the *NEC* introduced the provisions to consider the interior of raceways installed in wet locations above grade as being a wet location at 300.9 for installations of 600 volts (now 1000 volts) or less. It was also in the 2008 *NEC* where the interior of enclosures or raceways installed underground were first considered to be a wet location at 300.5(B) for installations of 600 volts or less. For the 2011 *NEC*, the interior of enclosures or raceways installed underground were confirmed to be a wet location by 300.50(B) for installations over 600 volts, nominal. This new provision at 300.38 will complete the circle by identifying the interior of a raceway installed in a wet location above grade for installations over 1000 volts, nominal to be a wet location as well. The mere existence of condensation alone should render the interior of these raceways a wet location when these raceways are installed in wet locations, above grade or below, regardless of the voltage involved.

310.10(H)(2)

Change at a Glance

Parallel conductor installations were expanded to include grouping requirements for induction purposes.

Code Language

310.10 Uses Permitted

The conductors described in 310.104 shall be permitted for use in any of the wiring methods covered in Chapter 3 and as specified in their respective tables or as permitted elsewhere in this *Code*.

(H) Conductors in Parallel.

(1) General. Aluminum, copper-clad aluminum, or copper conductors, for each phase, polarity, neutral, or grounded circuit shall be permitted to be connected in parallel (electrically joined at both ends) only in sizes 1/0 AWG and larger where installed in accordance with 310.10(H)(2) through (H)(6). (*See NEC for exceptions and complete text.*)

(2) Conductor and Installation Characteristics. The paralleled conductors in each phase, polarity, neutral, grounded circuit conductor, equipment grounding conductor, or equipment bonding jumper shall comply with all of the following:

(1) Be the same length

(2) Consist of the same conductor material

(3) Be the same size in circular mil area

310.10(H)(2) Conductors in Parallel

Only conductors in sizes 1/0 AWG and larger, comprising each phase, polarity, neutral, or grounded circuit conductor shall be connected in parallel.

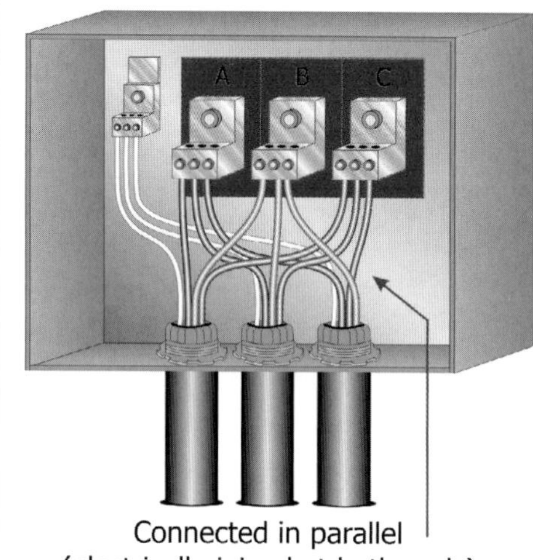

Where conductors of size 1/0 and larger are installed in parallel, must be installed as follows:

(1) Same length

(2) Consist of same conductor material

(3) Same circular mil area

(4) Same insulation type

(5) Terminated in same manner

(6) Grouped with all conductors of the same circuit to prevent heating effects from imbalances of current

2011 *NEC* Requirement

Conductors installed in parallel are generally required to be sized at 1/0 or larger. These parallel conductors are also required to be of the same length, consist of the same conductor material, be of the same size in circular mil area, have the same insulation type, and be terminated in the same manner.

2014 *NEC* Change

A new item (6) was added to not only require the conductor characteristics required by the previous *Code*, but also to require paralleled conductors installed in ferrous metal enclosures or raceways to be grouped with all conductors of the same circuit to prevent heating effects from imbalances of current.

Analysis of Change

A phenomenon known as *inductive heating* can occur with electrical circuits and surrounding metal such as metallic raceways, panelboard cabinets, etc., when all of the conductors of a branch circuit, feeder, etc., are not installed in the same enclosures or raceways. When current flows across a conductor, a magnetic field is built up around the conductor. When a magnetic field is generated near a metal or other conductive object, a flow of current (known as an *eddy current*) will be induced in the material and will generate heat. The heat generated is proportional to the amount of current involved multiplied by the resistance of the material. The more material or metal between the associated conductors (ungrounded, grounded, etc.), the greater the resistance involved. The effects of induction are used in transformers for converting voltages in all sorts of appliances. Most transformers have a metallic core and will therefore have eddy currents induced into them when in use. This induction heat is a good thing in transformers, but not such a good thing in service conductors, feeders, etc.

Documented failures have occurred due to induction and overheating involving paralleled conductors when these conductors were installed in different raceways

310.10(H)(2)

Continued

(4) Have the same insulation type
(5) Be terminated in the same manner
(6) Where paralleled in ferrous metal enclosures or raceways, conductors shall be grouped with all conductors of the same circuit to prevent heating effects from imbalances of current.

Informational Note: Where conductors are paralleled in enclosures or raceways, failure to group one conductor from each phase in each raceway or grouping within a wiring method may result in overheating and current imbalance.

(See NEC for remainder of 310.10(H) text.)

Proposal 6-15

Comment 6-4, 6-5, 6-6, 6-7

or wireways and were not grouped with all conductors of the same circuit. In addition to the requirement of each paralleled phase conductor being the same length, the proper grouping of phases in relation to one another can reduce inductive overheating and result in a more balanced load between each conductor of a paralleled phase. This new provision applies to magnetic (ferrous) enclosures, but the problem of inductive heating (as well as current imbalance) exists not only with parallel conductor sets installed in magnetic (ferrous) enclosures, but it can also be problematic in nonferrous enclosures as well, which is relative to improper grouping.

310.15(B)(3)(a) and Table 310.15(B)(3)(a)

Change at a Glance

Titles of 310.15(B)(3)(a) and corresponding table were changed to "More Than Three Current-Carrying Conductors ~~in a Raceway or Cable~~." Note to Table 310.15(B)(3)(a) was revised to make it clear that the table applies to spare conductors but does not apply to conductors that cannot be simultaneously energized.

Code Language

310.15 Ampacities for Conductors Rated 0–2000 Volts

(B) Tables. Ampacities for conductors rated 0 to 2000 volts shall be as specified in the Allowable Ampacity Table 310.15(B)(16) through Table 310.15(B)(19), and Ampacity Table 310.15(B)(20) and Table 310.15(B)(21) as modified by 310.15(B)(1) through (B)(7). The temperature correction and adjustment factors shall be permitted to be applied to the ampacity for the temperature rating of the conductor, if the corrected and adjusted ampacity does not exceed the ampacity for the temperature rating of the termination in accordance with the provisions of 110.14(C).

(See NEC for Informational Note and complete text.)

(3) Adjustment Factors.

(a) More Than Three Current-Carrying Conductors ~~in a Raceway or Cable~~. Where the number

Table 310.15(B)(3)(a) Adjustment Factors for More Than Three Current-Carrying Conductors ~~in a Raceway or Cable~~

Number of Conductors[1]	Percent of Values in Tables 310.15(B)(16) through 310.15(B)(19) as Adjusted for Ambient Temperature if Necessary
4-6	80
7-9	70
10-20	50
21-30	45
31-40	40
41 and above	35

[1]Number of conductors is the total number of conductors in the raceway or cable, including spare conductors. The count shall be adjusted in accordance with 310.15(B)(5) and (6), and shall not include conductors that are connected to electrical components but that cannot be simultaneously energized.

2011 *NEC* Requirement

The titles of both 310.15(B)(3)(a) and Table 310.15(B)(3)(a) indicated that adjustment factors for more than three current-carrying conductors applied only when this situation occurred within a raceway or cable. The parent text at 310.15(B)(3)(a) went on to specify that these adjustment factors applied where single conductors or multiconductor cables are installed without maintaining spacing for a continuous length longer than 600 mm (24 in.) and are not installed in raceways. The note following Table 310.15(B)(3)(a) stated that the table applied to the total number of conductors in the raceway or cable, but did not include the neutral conductor in certain conditions or the equipment grounding conductor adjusted in accordance with 310.15(B)(5) and (6).

2014 *NEC* Change

The titles of both 310.15(B)(3)(a) and Table 310.15(B)(3)(a) were changed from "More Than Three Current-Carrying Conductors in a Raceway or Cable" to "More Than Three Current-Carrying Conductors" to correspond to the text at 310.15(B)(3)(a). The note to Table 310.15(B)(3)(a) was revised to make it clear that the table applies to the total number of conductors in the raceway or cable, etc., as well as to spare conductors; but the table does not apply to conductors that cannot be simultaneously energized.

Analysis of Change

The ampacity values of Table 310.15(B)(16) are based on not more than three current-carrying conductors being installed in a raceway, or cable, etc. If more than three current-carrying conductors are involved, then the ampacity adjustment correction factors of Table 310.15(B)(3)(a) must be applied to the ampacity values of Table 310.15(B)(16). By deleting the words, "in a raceway or cable" in the titles of both 310.15(B)(3)(a) and Table 310.15(B)(3)(a), this should make it clear that an ampacity adjustment correction factor is required for three or more current-carrying conductors that are installed or bundled together without main-

310.15(B)(3)(a) and Table 310.15(B)(3)(a)

Continued

of current-carrying conductors in a raceway or cable exceeds three, or where single conductors or multiconductor cables are installed without maintaining spacing for a continuous length longer than 600 mm (24 in.) and are not installed in raceways, the allowable ampacity of each conductor shall be reduced as shown in Table 310.15(B)(3)(a). Each current-carrying conductor of a paralleled set of conductors shall be counted as a current-carrying conductor.
(See NEC for complete text.)

Proposal 6-44, 6-40, 6-32

Comment 6-33

taining spacing, as well as for those in a raceway or cable. The previous wording in the titles seemed to not be in harmony with the text in the parent language. This parent text indicates that where three or more conductors are installed in a raceway or cable, or where single conductors or multiconductor cables are installed without maintaining spacing for a continuous length longer than 600 mm (24 in.) and are not installed in raceways, the adjustment correction factors of Table 310.15(B)(3)(a) have to be applied. This language is clear that derating for conductors would apply to conductors that are not installed in a raceway or cable, thus the titles needed to be revised.

Another revision occurred at the note at the bottom of Table 310.15(B)(3)(a) to give users of the *Code* a better understanding as to exactly which conductors this table does and does not apply to. With the term *current-carrying conductors* being used, this brought into question as to whether or not a spare or extra conductor was under obligation to the ampacity adjustment rules of this table. That question was addressed in the 2011 *NEC* by removing the words "Number of Current-Carrying Conductors" from the first column heading and replacing the heading with "Number of Conductors." Added language in the note will make it clear that spare conductors are to be counted in the total number of conductors involved. Language was also added to this note to indicate that when two or more conductors cannot be simultaneously energized, only one of the conductors would be counted in the total number of conductors. The classic example of this type of situation would be one of the two travelers in a three-way switch loop. Both of these switch loop conductors cannot be energized simultaneously due to the intended function and design of a three-way switch.

310.15(B)(3)(c) EX and Table 310.15(B)(3)(c)

Change at a Glance

Title was revised for clarity and a new exception was added to permit the use of Type XHHW-2 conductors in raceways or cables on rooftops without having to apply an ambient temperature adjustment correction factor.

NEW

Code Language

310.15 Ampacities for Conductors Rated 0–2000 Volts

(B) Tables. Ampacities for conductors rated 0 to 2000 volts shall be as specified in the Allowable Ampacity Table 310.15(B)(16) through Table 310.15(B)(19), and Ampacity Table 310.15(B)(20) and Table 310.15(B)(21) as modified by 310.15(B)(1) through (B)(7). *(See NEC for complete text.)*

(3) Adjustment Factors.

(c) ~~Circular~~ Raceways and Cables Exposed to Sunlight on Rooftops. Where ~~conductors or cables are installed in circular~~ raceways or cables are exposed to direct sunlight on or above rooftops, the adjustments shown in Table 310.15(B)(3)(c) shall be added to the outdoor temperature to determine the applicable ambient temperature for application of the correction factors in Table 310.15(B)(2)(a) or Table 310.15(B)(2)(b).

Informational Note: One source for the ~~average~~ ambient temperatures in various locations is the

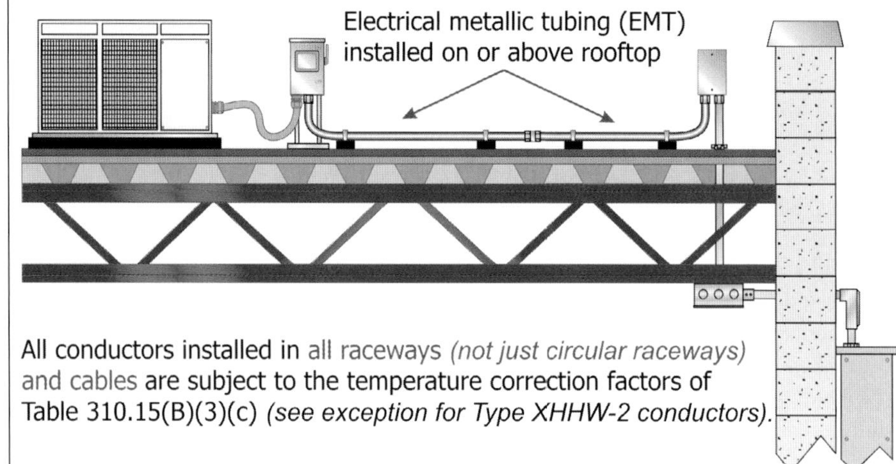
310.15(B)(3)(c) Raceways and Cables on Rooftops
Where raceways or cables are exposed to direct sunlight on or above rooftops, the adjustments shown in Table 310.15(B)(3)(c) shall apply.
By exception, Type XHHW-2 insulated conductors shall not be subject to this ampacity adjustment.
Electrical metallic tubing (EMT) installed on or above rooftop
All conductors installed in all raceways (not just circular raceways) and cables are subject to the temperature correction factors of Table 310.15(B)(3)(c) (see exception for Type XHHW-2 conductors).

2011 *NEC* Requirement

The 2011 *NEC* demanded an ambient temperature adjustment correction factor where conductors or cables are installed in circular raceways exposed to direct sunlight on or above rooftops. The adjustments shown in Table 310.15(B)(3)(c) had to be added to the average ambient outdoor temperatures to determine the applicable ambient temperature for application of the correction factors. These correction factors can be found in Table 310.15(B)(2)(a) for ambient temperatures other than 30°C (86°F) when the ampacity starting point is 30°C (86°F) from Table 310.15(B)(16). For ampacity values based on 40°C (104°F), correction factors for ambient temperatures other than 40°C (104°F) can be found at Table 310.15(B)(2)(b).

2014 *NEC* Change

The title and parent text at 310.15(B)(3)(c) was revised for clarity from "Circular Raceways Exposed to Sunlight on Rooftops" to "Raceways and Cables Exposed to Sunlight on Rooftops." The basic provisions for applying an ambient temperature adjustment correction factor where any type of raceway (not just circular raceways) is exposed to direct sunlight on or above rooftops have not changed. Provisions for cables installed on or above rooftops have been added as well. Cables were subject to these ambient temperature adjustment correction factors in the past, but the language indicated that the cable(s) had to be installed in a raceway.

A new exception was also added that will allow the employment of Type XHHW-2 conductors, which is a thermoset insulated conductor, to be installed in raceways or cables on rooftops without having to apply an ambient temperature adjustment correction factor for these conductors.

Analysis of Change

Revisions to the language and title of 310.15(B)(3)(c) and the title of Table

Continued

ASHRAE Handbook, Fundamentals.

***Exception:** Type XHHW-2 insulated conductors shall not be subject to this ampacity adjustment.*

Proposal 6-31, 6-41

Comment 6-29, 6-37

310.15(B)(3)(c) were in part the result of a UL Fact-Finding Report, File IN16969, by Underwriters Laboratories. This report detailed research on rooftop temperature adjustments involving Type MC cable, tray cable and other cable types plus all wiring methods currently subject to the ambient temperature adjustment correction factor required for rooftop installations. This would include rigid metal conduit (RMC), electrical metallic tubing (EMT), etc. According to this research, all conductors in all types of wiring methods experienced substantial ambient temperature increases above outdoor temperature when exposed to direct sunlight on rooftops. The word "circular" was removed from the term *circular raceway* as the ambient temperature adjustment correction factors should apply to all wiring methods, not just circular raceways.

Another change that occurred involving this portion of the *Code* and ambient temperature adjustment correction factors was the insertion of a new exception for Type XHHW-2 conductors installed in raceways or cables on rooftops. The abbreviation "XHHW" is the conductor designation with "X" meaning cross-linked synthetic polymer insulation, the "HH" meaning 90°C, with 30°C temperature rise over 60°C, and the "W" meaning moisture resistant. The "-2" designation allows the insulation to be suitable for use in both wet and dry locations up to 90°C. See *NEC* Table 310.104(A) for more information on conductor application and insulation ratings.

The concept behind ambient temperature adjustment correction factors at 310.15(B)(3)(c) center around the risk imposed due to potential damage to conductor insulation on conductors exposed to high ambient temperatures on rooftops. Melting of plastic insulation has been reported due to wiring methods being exposed to direct sunlight on rooftops. Melting of conductor insulation can only occur with thermoplastic type conductor insulations such as THWN-2, THW-2, etc. This melting of conductor insulation is not an issue and does not occur with thermoset type insulation such as XHHW-2, RHW-2, etc. Thermoset materials do not melt, but do begin to smolder and burn if sufficiently heated. In general, thermoset materials are more robust, with failure temperatures of approximately 350°C (662°F) or higher. Thermoplastic materials typically have failure temperatures much lower than 218°C (425 °F), where failure is typically associated with melting of the material. Even in the hottest areas of the country, fully loaded Type XHHW-2 thermoset insulated conductors show no signs of failure and demonstrate that there is no safety concern with thermoset insulation in these installations.

310.15(B)(7)

Change at a Glance

This revision deletes Table 310.15(B)(7) and replaces it with a provision allowing an 83% revision in ampacity for dwelling service and feeder conductors.

REVISION

delete

Code Language

310.15 Ampacities for Conductors Rated 0–2000 Volts

(B) Tables. Ampacities for conductors rated 0 to 2000 volts shall be as specified in the Allowable Ampacity Tables 310.15(B)(16) through Table 310.15(B)(19), and Ampacity Table 310.15(B)(20) and Table 310.15(B)(21) as modified by 310.15(B)(1) through (B)(7). *(See NEC for complete text.)*

(7) 120/240-Volt, Single-Phase Dwelling Services and Feeders. For ~~individual dwelling units~~ one-family dwellings and the individual dwelling units of two-family and multifamily dwellings, service and feeder conductors ~~as listed in Table 310.15(B)(7), shall be permitted as~~ supplied by a single-phase, 120/240-volt~~, 3-wire, service-entrance conductors, service-lateral conductors, and feeder conductors that serve as the main power feeder to each dwelling unit and are installed in raceway or cable with or without an equipment grounding conductor~~ system shall be permitted be sized in accordance with 310.15(B)(7)(a) through (d).
(1) For a service rated 100 through 400 amperes, the service conductors supplying the entire

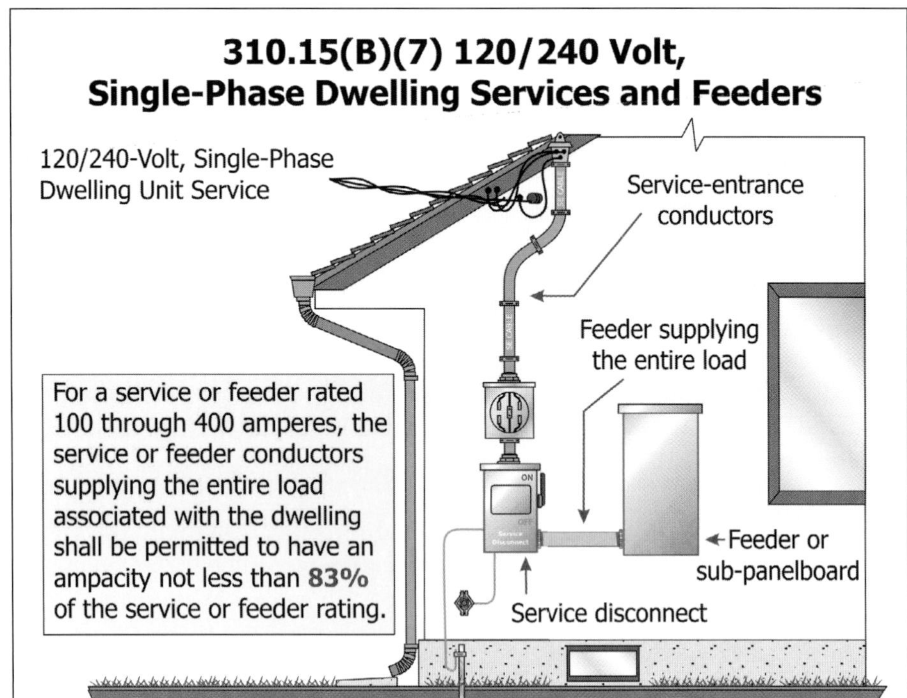
310.15(B)(7) 120/240 Volt,
Single-Phase Dwelling Services and Feeders
120/240-Volt, Single-Phase
Dwelling Unit Service
Service-entrance
conductors
Feeder supplying
the entire load
For a service or feeder rated 100 through 400 amperes, the service or feeder conductors supplying the entire load associated with the dwelling shall be permitted to have an ampacity not less than 83% of the service or feeder rating.
Feeder or
sub-panelboard
Service disconnect

2011 *NEC* Requirement

The service-entrance, service-lateral and the main power feeder conductors for dwelling units served at 120/240-volts, 3-wire, single-phase were permitted to be sized by 310.15(B)(7) and Table 310.15(B)(7). The table had an ampacity rating for the service or main power feeder from 100 to 400 amperes, with wire sizes from 4 AWG to 400 kcmil copper and 2 AWG to 600 kcmil aluminum. This table was also permitted to be used for the feeder conductors that serve as the main power feeder to a dwelling unit. The *main power feeder* being defined as "...the feeder between the main disconnect and the panelboard that supplies, either by branch circuits or by feeders, or both, all loads that are part or associated with the dwelling unit." To use Table 310.15(B)(7) for selection of the main power feeder, this feeder would have had to supply all loads associated with the dwelling unit.

2014 *NEC* Change

The existing Table 310.15(B)(7) has been deleted entirely. The parent text at 310.15(B)(7) has been revised and broken up into four list items. Rather than use previous Table 310.15(B)(7) for sizing service conductors and the main power feeder for dwelling units, the user of the *Code* is left with a calculation to perform. The ampacity values found at Table 310.15(B)(16) can be reduced by 17 percent (not less than 83 percent of the service or feeder rating), which will require the circular mils properties of Table 8 in Chapter 9 to be brought into the now required calculation. A new Informational Note will take users of the *Code* to Example D.7 in Annex D for an example of how to perform this dwelling unit service and feeder calculation.

Analysis of Change

From the publication of the 1956 *NEC*, residential service-entrance conductors have been permitted to be sized at a slightly higher ampacity values than the normal ampacity values found in the ampacity tables such as Table 310.15(B)(16)

Continued

load associated with a one-family dwelling or the service conductors supplying the entire load associated with an individual dwelling unit in a two-family or multifamily dwelling shall be permitted to have an ampacity not less than 83% of the service rating.
(2) For a feeder rated 100 through 400 amperes, the feeder conductors supplying the entire load associated with a one-family dwelling or the feeder conductors supplying the entire load associated with an individual dwelling unit in a two-family or multifamily dwelling shall be permitted to have an ampacity not less than 83% of the feeder rating.
(3) In no case shall a feeder for an individual dwelling unit be required to have an ampacity ~~rating~~ greater than ~~their service-entrance conductors~~ that of its 310.15(B)(7) (a) or (b) conductors.
(4) ~~The~~ Grounded conductors shall be permitted to be sized smaller than the ungrounded conductors provided the requirements of ~~215.2,~~ 220.61 and 230.42 for service conductors or the requirements of 215.2 and 220.61 for feeder conductors are met.

Informational Note No. 1: It is possible that the conductor ampacity will require other correction or adjustment factors applicable to the conductor installation.

Informational Note No. 2: See example D.7 in Annex D.

Proposal 6-49a, 6-53, 6-57, 6-58

Comment 6-52, 6-39, 6-51, 6-53, 6-54, 6-56, 6-58, 6-60

or some form thereof in previous editions of the *Code*. This higher ampacity allowance was permitted primarily due to the diversity loads associated with dwelling units. The genesis of 310.15(B)(7) can be traced to a note at the bottom of Table 1a of Chapter 10 of the 1956 *NEC*. In the 1959 *NEC*, this ampacity table and its associated notes were moved to Table 310-14. This provision stayed pretty much the same until the 1971 *NEC* when this ampacity table became Table 310-12 and the note became specific to 3-wire, single-phase *residential* services. In the 1975 *NEC*, this residential service ampacity provision became Note 3 to Table 310-16 through 310-19 titled, "Three-Wire Single-Phase Residential Services." The residential ampacity values first appeared in a table format in the 1978 *NEC* as a table under Note 3 to Tables 310-16 through 310-19. The 1978 *NEC* was where feeder conductors were first introduced to this residential ampacity value provision as well. This provision stayed basically the same until the 1993 *NEC* where feeder conductors utilizing this note were limited to "feeder conductors that supply the total load to a dwelling unit..." The 1999 *NEC* witnessed this residential ampacity provision moved from a note to its own subsection at 310-15(b)(6) and Table 310-15(b)(6) and finally to 310.15(B)(7) in the 2011 *NEC*.

This thirty-six-year-old table has been removed from the 2014 *NEC* and replaced with an ampacity reduction of not less than 83 percent of the service or feeder rating of the ampacity values of Table 310.15(B)(16). This 0.83 multiplier will result in basically the same ampacity values of previous Table 310.15(B)(7). In order to address the various proposals submitted suggesting changes to 310.15(B)(7), CMP-6 analyzed the existing language and determined that the conductor sizes in Table 310.15(B)(7) are equivalent to those that would be used if a 0.83 multiplier was applied to each service ampere rating. An informational note was added to indicate that adjustment and correction factors apply depending on conditions of use.

Do the ampacity provisions at 310.16(B)(7) override any ampacity adjustment factors (such as temperature or number of conductors in the same raceway or bundled together) or does any ampacity adjustment factors render 310.15(B)(7) noncompliant? Informational Note No. 1 to 310.15(B)(7) indicates that "it is possible that the conductor ampacity will require other correction or adjustment factors applicable to the conductor installation," but does not answer the question above. This informational note seems to insinuate that 310.15(B)(7) ampacity values are permitted to be applied on top of any ampacity adjustment factors, such as temperature or number of conductors in the same raceway or bundled together.

314.15

Change at a Glance

All outlet box hood covers are required to be listed for use in a wet location, not just *extra duty* outlet box hood covers installed in wet locations.

Code Language

314.15 Damp or Wet Locations

In damp or wet locations, boxes, conduit bodies, and fittings shall be placed or equipped so as to prevent moisture from entering or accumulating within the box, conduit body, or fitting. Boxes, conduit bodies, outlet box hoods, and fittings installed in wet locations shall be listed for use in wet locations. Approved drainage openings not larger than 6 mm (1/4 in.) shall be permitted to be installed in the field in boxes or conduit bodies listed for use in damp or wet locations. For installation of listed drain fittings, larger openings are permitted to be installed in the field in accordance with manufacturer's instructions.

Proposal 9-33

314.15 Damp or Wet Locations

Outlet box hood cover

"Extra-Duty" outlet box hood cover

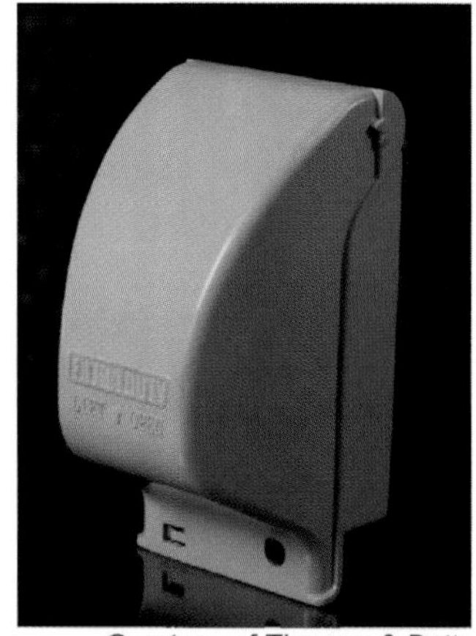

Courtesy of Thomas & Betts

Boxes, conduit bodies, outlet box hoods, and fittings installed in wet locations shall be listed for use in wet locations.

All "outlet box hood" covers are required to be listed for use in a wet location, not just "extra duty" outlet box hoods installed in a wet locations.

2011 *NEC* Requirement

Section 406.9(B)(1) required "extra duty" outlet box hoods installed in a wet location to be listed for use in a wet location. Section 314.15 required only boxes, conduit bodies, and fittings installed in wet locations to be listed for use in wet locations.

2014 *NEC* Change

The term *outlet box hoods* was added at this section. Boxes, conduit bodies, outlet box hoods, and fittings installed in wet locations are now required to be listed for use in wet locations.

Analysis of Change

Section 406.9(B)(1) of the 2011 *NEC* required "extra duty" outlet box hoods installed in a wet location to be listed for use in a wet location. All outlet box hoods should be required to be listed for use in a wet location when installed in a wet location as they are relied upon to provide environmental protection for enclosed devices such as GFCI receptacle outlet devices. Outlet box hood covers are used as a component of a weatherproof enclosure to protect other types of wiring devices, not just 15- and 20-ampere, 125- and 250-volt receptacles installed in a wet location covered by the requirements at 406.9(B)(1).

314.15

Change at a Glance

New provision was added to permit field-installed drainage openings in boxes or conduit bodies in accordance with the manufacturer's instructions.

NEW

Code Language

314.15 Damp or Wet Locations

In damp or wet locations, boxes, conduit bodies, and fittings shall be placed or equipped so as to prevent moisture from entering or accumulating within the box, conduit body, or fitting. Boxes, conduit bodies, outlet box hoods, and fittings installed in wet locations shall be listed for use in wet locations. Approved drainage openings not larger than 6 mm (1/4 in.) shall be permitted to be installed in the field in boxes or conduit bodies listed for use in damp or wet locations. For installation of listed drain fittings, larger openings are permitted to be installed in the field in accordance with manufacturer's instructions.

Proposal 9-35

Comment 9-26

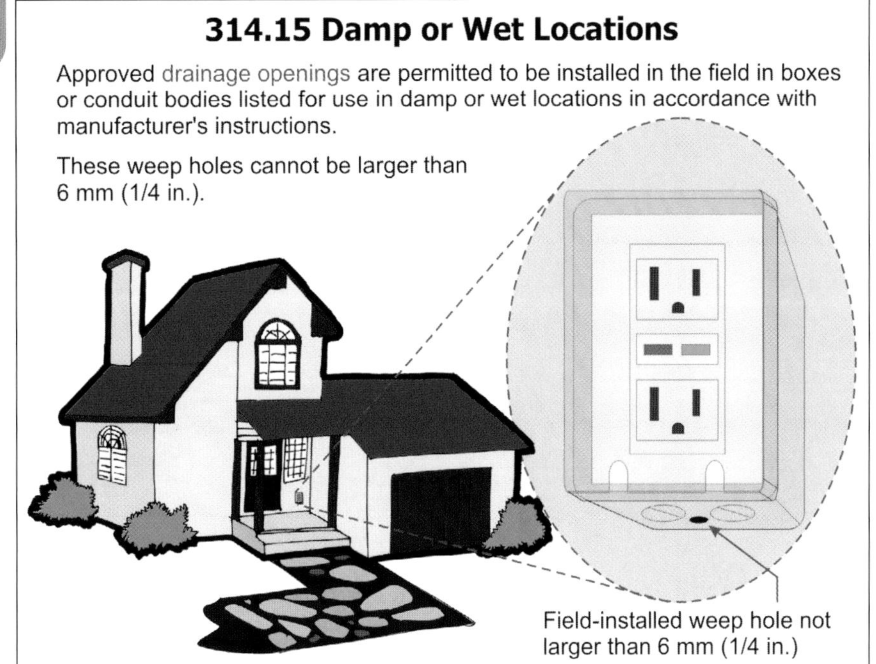
314.15 Damp or Wet Locations
Approved drainage openings are permitted to be installed in the field in boxes or conduit bodies listed for use in damp or wet locations in accordance with manufacturer's instructions.
These weep holes cannot be larger than 6 mm (1/4 in.).
Field-installed weep hole not larger than 6 mm (1/4 in.)

2011 *NEC* Requirement

The 2011 *NEC* had no language to allow field-installed weep holes to be installed in the bottom of boxes and conduit fittings, although this was a fairly common practice by installers.

2014 *NEC* Change

A new sentence was added at the end of 314.15 to permit approved drainage openings to be installed in the field in boxes or conduit bodies listed for use in damp or wet locations in accordance with manufacturer's instructions. These weep holes cannot be larger than 6 mm (1/4 in.).

Analysis of Change

The installation of weep holes in the bottom of boxes installed in wet locations improves the safety and durability of electrical installations. Without these weep holes, the inside of cast aluminum boxes and other metallic enclosures can degrade over time due to moisture condensation. Experienced installers will typically provide weep holes in the underside that provide enough ventilation to avoid such damage. Section 110.12(A) addressed a similar situation during the 1996 edition of the *NEC* to clarify that the required closure of unused cable and raceway openings did not apply to holes "intended for the operation of equipment" (such as weep holes) and "those intended for mounting purposes." Since the field orientation of cast aluminum or other such enclosures cannot be known at the time of manufacture, it would be impossible for such openings to be provided in advance by the manufacturer and, therefore, "as part of the design for listed equipment." Product evaluations include consideration for size and location of permitted drainage openings.

Language was added in the ROC stage to limit these field-installed weep holes to "boxes or conduit bodies for use in damp and wet locations." This ensures that these field-installed drilled holes are not intended for listed fittings and listed outlet box hoods. Substantiation was not provided for allowing such openings to be "field-installed" or drilled in these types of listed applications.

314.23(B)

Change at a Glance

Enclosures can be supported from any structural member, not just from a structural member of a building.

Code Language

(B) Structural Mounting

An enclosure supported from a structural member ~~of a building~~ or from grade shall be rigidly supported either directly or by using a metal, polymeric, or wood brace.

Proposal 9-1

314.23(B) Structural Mounting of Enclosures

The words "of a building" were removed to indicate that an enclosure within the scope of Article 314 could be supported from any structural member, not just a structural member of a building.

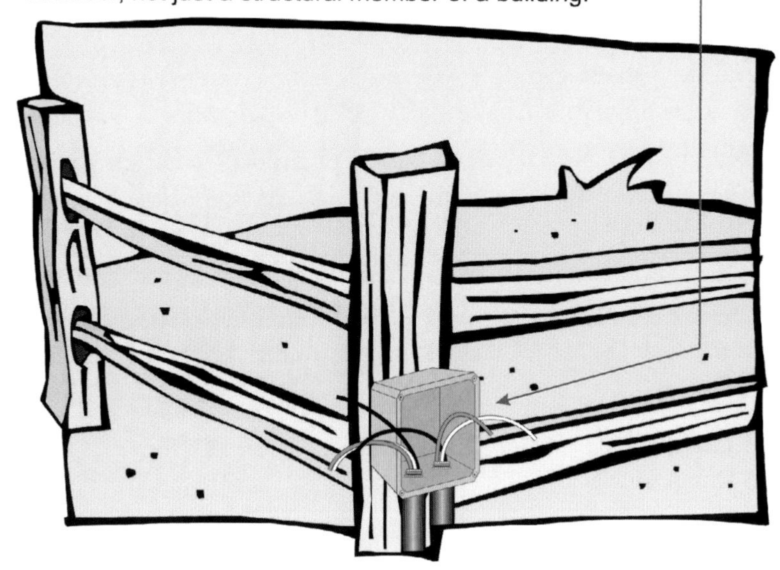

2011 *NEC* Requirement

Outlet, device, junction or pull boxes, conduit body, or fitting that were supported from a structural member had to be supported from a structural member of a building.

2014 *NEC* Change

The words "of a building" were removed to indicate that an enclosure within the scope of Article 314 could be supported from any structural member, not just a structural member of a building.

Analysis of Change

The term *building* is defined in Article 100 of the *NEC* as "a structure that stands alone or that is cut off from adjoining structures by fire walls with all openings therein protected by approved fire doors." This definition would not include such things as bridges, billboards, towers, tanks, etc. The intent of this section was never to exclude these types of structural members from possessing the ability to support an outlet box, junction box, etc. Removing the words "of a building" makes it clear that an enclosure within the scope of Article 314 could be supported from a structural member of a building as well as from any structural member, including bridges, billboards, towers, tanks, etc.

This change came about as a result of CMP-9 reviewing all instances of the use of the terms *building* or *buildings* within the articles under the responsibility of CMP-9. This also resulted in the change of the term *building* to *building or structure* at 314.29 where boxes, conduit bodies, and handhole enclosures are required to be accessible.

314.25

Change at a Glance

Drywall screws are not permitted to be used to attach box covers or other equipment fastened to a box. Cover and canopy screws need to be suitable for this purpose.

Code Language

314.25 Covers and Canopies

In completed installations, each box shall have a cover, faceplate, lampholder, or luminaire canopy, except where the installation complies with 410.24(B). Screws used for the purpose of attaching covers, or other equipment to the box, shall be either machine screws matching the thread gauge or size that is integral to the box or shall be in accordance with the manufacturer's instructions.

Proposal 9-55

2011 *NEC* Requirement

The requirement at 314.25 generally required boxes to have covers, faceplates, etc., installed for a complete installation; but the means of attachment for these covers was not addressed.

2014 *NEC* Change

A new sentence was added at the end of 314.25 addressing the attachment means for covers or other equipment attached to a box. Screws used for this purpose are now required to be either machine screws matching the thread gauge or of a size that is integral to the box. The screws and attachment process can also be installed in accordance with the manufacturer's instructions.

Analysis of Change

The use of screws not designed for the purpose, such as drywall screws, for attaching covers, luminaires, or other equipment to boxes has become a concern in the electrical industry. This practice is unacceptable and can result in damage to the box and inadequate support of the attached luminaire or equipment itself. Installers should always follow the manufacturer's installation instructions, but having *Code* language against this practice will help ensure proper support. The language to recognize that the screws or support means "be in accordance with the manufacturer's instructions" was inserted into this requirement to take into consideration nonmetallic products that do not have a thread form molded or machined into the attachment holes. The product standards for nonmetallic outlet boxes (UL 514C, *Standard for Nonmetallic Outlet Boxes, Flush-Device Boxes, and Covers*) allow for the use of thread forming screws for the attachment of covers, provided they can pass the performance requirements cited in the standard. This type of screw is typically used with nonmetallic junction boxes and is provided with the box.

Similar provisions have been introduced at 404.10(B) for mounting of switches (see Proposal 9-98 and Comment 9-52) and at 406.5 for mounting of receptacles (see Proposal 18-30 and Comment 18-20) restricting the use of such screws as drywall screws for installing or attaching these devices to boxes.

314.27(A)(1)

Change at a Glance

Requirements of 314.27(A)(1) apply to outlet boxes used to support luminaires and lampholders mounted on vertical surfaces (*not just on walls*).

Code Language

314.27 Outlet Boxes

(A) Boxes at Luminaire or Lampholder Outlets. Outlet boxes or fittings designed for the support of luminaires and lampholders, and installed as required by 314.23, shall be permitted to support a luminaire or lampholder.

(1) ~~Wall~~ Vertical Surface Outlets. Boxes used at luminaire or lampholder outlets in ~~a wall~~ or on a vertical surface shall be identified and marked on the interior of the box to indicate the maximum weight of the luminaire that is permitted to be supported by the box ~~in the wall,~~ if other than 23 kg (50 lb).

Exception: *A ~~wall-~~ vertically mounted luminaire or lampholder weighing not more than 3 kg (6 lb) shall be permitted to be supported on other boxes or plaster rings that are secured to other boxes, provided the luminaire or its supporting yoke, or the lampholder, is secured to the box with no fewer than two No. 6 or larger screws.*

Proposal 9-58

2011 *NEC* Requirement

Outlet boxes used to support luminaires and lampholders are divided into two subsections. Wall-mounted luminaires are addressed at 314.27(A)(1) and ceiling-mounted luminaires are covered at 314.27(A)(2). Outlet boxes or fittings used to support luminaires and lampholders must be designed (identified) for this support means. Outlet boxes mounted in a wall used to support luminaire or lampholder outlets must be marked on the interior of the box to indicate the maximum weight of the luminaire that is permitted to be supported by the box in the wall, if other than 23 kg (50 lb). An exception to the requirement that the box needs to be designed or identified for the support of a luminaire or lampholder allows a wall-mounted luminaire or lampholder weighing not more than 3 kg (6 lb) to be supported on "other boxes" or plaster rings that are secured to other boxes, provided that the luminaire or its supporting yoke, or the lampholder, is secured to the box with no fewer than two No. 6 or larger screws. An example of "other boxes" would be a box that is not designed to support a luminaire or lampholder such as a single-gang, nonmetallic outlet box typically used for the installation of a switch or a receptacle.

2014 *NEC* Change

The title of 314.27(A)(1) was changed from "Wall Outlets" to "Vertical Surface Outlets" as not all vertical surfaces where luminaires or lampholders are mounted are necessarily in a wall. Text was also revised in the subsection and the exception reflecting this vertical surface vs. wall surface fact. New language was also added to reflect that luminaires or lampholders can be mounted *on* a vertical service as well as *in* a vertical service.

Analysis of Change

Outlet boxes used to support luminaires and lampholders are often mounted *on* as well as *in* vertical surfaces that are not defined as a wall. The previous language at 314.27(A)(1) only addressed boxes mounted in a wall. An example of this type of vertical surface-mounted luminaire would be a luminaire mounted on the side of a square post in the middle of a large room or area. This type of post or pole would not be considered a wall, but rather a vertical surface. No previous or current *Code* language would or should prevent a luminaire or lampholder from being mounted on this type of vertical surface.

314.27(A)(2)

Change at a Glance

Outlet boxes used to support ceiling-mounted luminaires that weigh more than 23 kg (50 lb) are now required to be marked, on the interior of the box, with the maximum weight the box will support.

Code Language

314.27 Outlet Boxes

(A) Boxes at Luminaire or Lampholder Outlets. Outlet boxes or fittings designed for the support of luminaires and lampholders, and installed as required by 314.23, shall be permitted to support a luminaire or lampholder.

(2) Ceiling Outlets. At every outlet used exclusively for lighting, the box shall be designed or installed so that a luminaire or lampholder may be attached. Boxes shall be required to support a luminaire weighing a minimum of 23 kg (50 lb). A luminaire that weighs more than 23 kg (50 lb) shall be supported independently of the outlet box, unless the outlet box is listed and marked on the interior of the box to indicate ~~for~~ the maximum weight the box shall be permitted to ~~be supported~~ support.

Proposal 9-62

2011 *NEC* Requirement

Outlet boxes that support a ceiling-mounted luminaire or lampholder are required to be designed for that purpose. These boxes are required to support a luminaire weighing a minimum of 23 kg (50 lb). In cases where a luminaire weighs more than 23 kg (50 lb), the luminaire must be supported independently of the outlet box, unless the outlet box is listed and marked for the maximum weight to be supported.

2014 *NEC* Change

In situations where an outlet box is intended to support a luminaire weighing more than 23 kg (50 lb), a revision to 314.27(A)(2) will now require a ceiling-mounted outlet box to be listed and marked, on the interior of the box, for the maximum weight [*other than 23 kg (50 lb)*] that the outlet box is designed to support. Otherwise, the luminaire must be supported independently of the outlet box.

Analysis of Change

In order for a ceiling-mounted outlet box to support a luminaire weighing more than 23 kg (50 lb), that ceiling-mounted outlet box would be required to be listed and marked for the maximum weight that particular outlet box is designed to support. This maximum weight marking is now required to be on the interior of the box. This will allow the installer of the luminaire and the electrical inspector an opportunity to review this information at the time of installation, without having to climb into the attic to retrieve same. In some cases, the exterior of the outlet box is not accessible after a certain point in the building construction process, such as after the sheetrock or exterior finish of the walls and ceiling has been installed. From a practical standpoint, this is a necessary change to assist the installer and enforcement community.

324.41

Change at a Glance

Carpet squares that cover flat conductor cable (Type FCC) are required to be no larger than 1.0 m (39.37 in.) square.

Code Language

324.41 Floor Coverings

Floor-mounted Type FCC cable, cable connectors, and insulating ends shall be covered with carpet squares not larger than ~~914 mm (36 in.)~~ 1.0 m (39.37 in.) square. Carpet squares that are adhered to the floor shall be attached with release-type adhesives.

Proposal 7-23

2011 *NEC* Requirement

Floor-mounted flat conductor cable (Type FCC), their associated cable connectors, and insulating ends were permitted to be covered with standard-sized modular carpet squares. These carpet squares were not permitted to be larger than 914 mm (36 in.) square. Carpet squares that are adhered to the floor were required to be attached with release-type adhesives for access to the Type FCC cable after the initial installation.

2014 *NEC* Change

The maximum size modular carpet square permitted to cover floor-mounted flat conductor cable (Type FCC) has been increased to 1.0 m (39.37 in.) square. This will allow the use of standard-sized modular carpet products based on the International System of Units (SI units) of measure.

Analysis of Change

Flat conductor cable (Type FCC) has been recognized as an acceptable *NEC* wiring method since the 1981 *NEC*. *Type FCC cable* is defined as "three or more flat copper conductors placed edge-to-edge and separated and enclosed within an insulating assembly" at 324.2. A flat conductor cable system is designed to provide a completely accessible, flexible wiring system. This type of wiring system is also designed for installation under carpet squares where the carpet squares are adhered to the floor with release-type adhesives. The previous maximum size for these modular carpet squares was 914 mm (36 in.) square, which is based on the United States (US) Customary Units of Measurement (foot, pound, inches, etc.). This precluded the use of standard sized 1.0 m (39.37 in.) square modular carpet squares that are based on the International System of Units (SI units) of measure (metric meter, kilogram, etc.). Changing the maximum size of these modular carpet squares to match the common SI Units standard 1.0 m (39.37 in.) carpet square will allow these carpet squares to be used and will maintain accessibility to the Type FCC cable system. This revision will not disqualify the use of the readily available smaller 914 mm (36 in.) carpet squares, but will allow both US Customary Unit-sized as well as SI Unit-sized carpet squares to be utilized over floor-mounted Type FCC cable.

330.30(B)

Change at a Glance

Type MC cable is permitted to be secured in intervals not exceeding 3 m (10 ft) for vertical installations when listed and identified for such use.

Code Language

330.30 Securing and Supporting (Type MC cable)

(B) Securing. Unless otherwise provided, cables shall be secured at intervals not exceeding 1.8 m (6 ft). Cables containing four or fewer conductors sized no larger than 10 AWG shall be secured within 300 mm (12 in.) of every box, cabinet, fitting, or other cable termination. In vertical installations, listed cables with ungrounded conductors 250 kcmil and larger shall be permitted to be secured at intervals not exceeding 3 m (10 ft).

Proposal 7-29

Comment 7-5

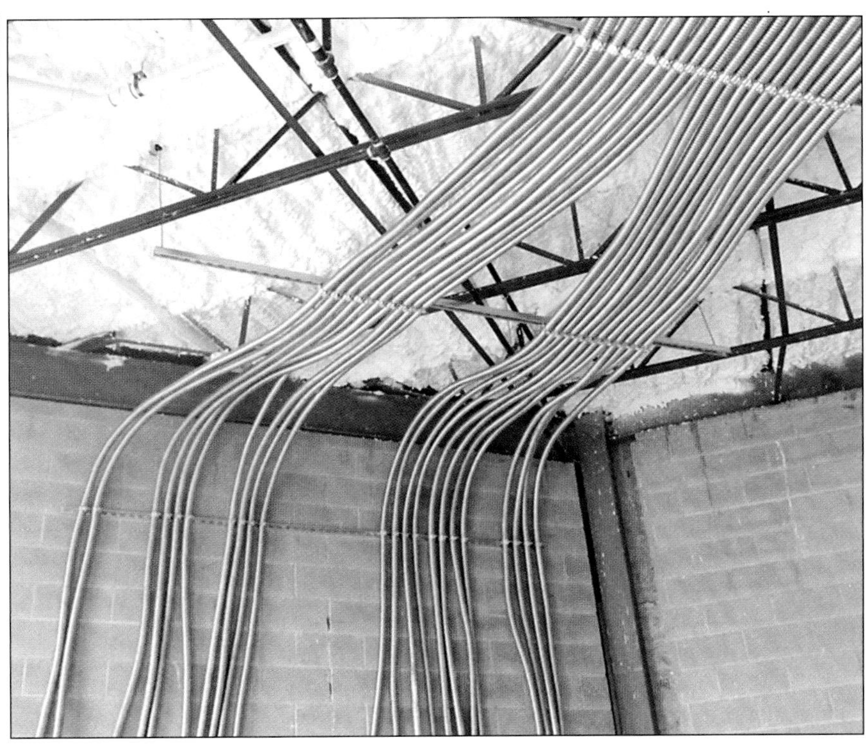

2011 *NEC* Requirement

Metal-clad cable (Type MC) is generally required to be secured at intervals not exceeding 1.8 m (6 ft) and is required to be secured within 300 mm (12 in.) of every box, cabinet, fitting, or other cable termination. No other securing provisions existed in the 2011 *NEC* for vertical installations.

2014 *NEC* Change

A new provision was added at the end of 330.30(B) to allow Type MC cable installed in vertical installations to be secured at intervals not exceeding 3 m (10 ft.) where listed and the Type MC cable contains ungrounded conductors 250 kcmil and larger.

Analysis of Change

It is not that uncommon to find Type MC cable with integral conductor supports used for high rise construction installations without offsets or directly securing the conductors under the armor. Cable manufacturers in conjunction with third-party testing agencies have conducted long-term testing on vertically-installed Type MC cable which showed no slipping of the internal conductors with internal integral conductor support. Information that brought about these revisions to increase the securing intervals for Type MC cable in vertical installations was a result of information supplied to CMP-7 from an Underwriters Laboratories (UL) Fact-Finding Report (Project 12ME07391).

For vertical installations, Type MC cable with integral conductor supports offers the installer an alternative and productive method for commercial vertical installs in high-rise buildings. Type MC cable with integral conductor supports eliminates the need for any type of special conductor supports or offsets because of an internal polymeric binder under the armor that holds the conductors in place.

330.30(D)(3)

Change at a Glance

Type MC cable now is permitted to be installed unsupported in lengths not exceeding 900 mm (3 ft) where necessary for vibration reasons or flexibility.

Code Language

330.30 Securing and Supporting

(D) Unsupported Cables. Type MC cable shall be permitted to be unsupported where the cable:

(1) Is fished between access points through concealed spaces in finished buildings or structures and supporting is impractical; or

(2) Is not more than 1.8 m (6 ft) in length from the last point of cable support to the point of connection to luminaires or other electrical equipment and the cable and point of connection are within an accessible ceiling. For the purpose of this section, Type MC cable fittings shall be permitted as a means of cable support.

(3) Is Type MC of the interlocked armor type in lengths not exceeding 900 mm (3 ft) from the last point where it is securely fastened and is used to connect equipment where flexibility is necessary to minimize the transmission of vibration from equipment or to provide flexibility for equipment that requires movement after installation.

Proposal 7-31

330.30(D)(3) Unsupported Type MC Cables

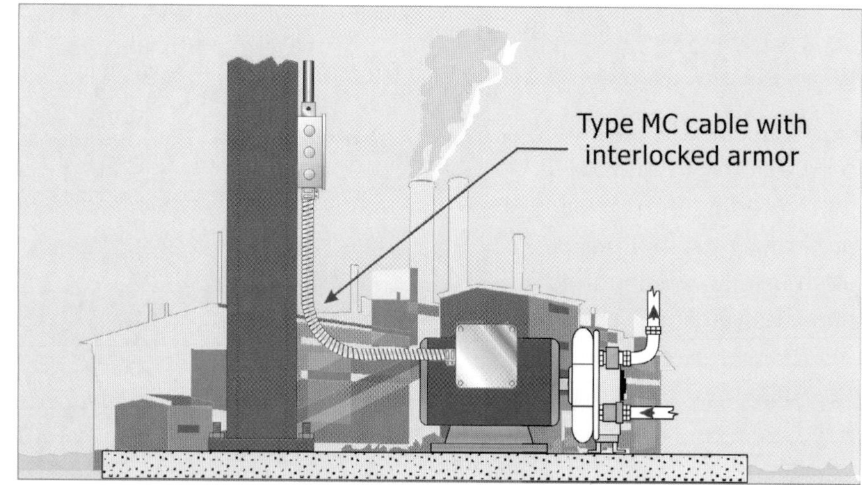

Interlocked armor Type MC cable is permitted to be unsupported in lengths not exceeding 900 mm (3 ft) from the last point where it is securely fastened and is used to connect equipment where flexibility is necessary to minimize transmission of vibration or to provide flexibility after installation.

2011 *NEC* Requirement

Metal-clad cable (Type MC) is permitted to be unsupported where the cable is fished in concealed spaces in finished buildings or structures and supporting is impractical; or where the cable is not more than 1.8 m (6 ft) in length from the last point of cable support to luminaires or other electrical equipment within an accessible ceiling. There were no provisions for Type MC cable concerning vibration or flexibility issues.

2014 *NEC* Change

A new provision was added at 330.30(D)(3) permitting Type MC cable to be unsupported where the cable is made of the interlocked armor type in lengths not exceeding 900 mm (3 ft) from the last point of support. This would apply where flexibility is necessary to minimize the transmission of vibration from equipment or to provide flexibility for equipment that requires movement after installation.

Analysis of Change

A new provision was added at 330.30(D)(3) permitting Type MC cable to be unsupported where the cable is made of the interlocked armor type in lengths not exceeding 900 mm (3 ft) from the last point of support. This would apply where flexibility is necessary to minimize the transmission of vibration from equipment or to provide flexibility for equipment that requires movement after installation.

334.40(B)

Change at a Glance

Nonmetallic-sheathed cable interconnectors have been recognized to be used without a box and concealed where used for "repair wiring" rather than "rewiring" in existing buildings.

334.40 Boxes and Fittings
(B) Devices of Insulating Material. Self-contained switches, self-contained receptacles ~~outlet~~, and nonmetallic sheathed cable interconnector ~~tap~~ devices of insulating material that are listed shall be permitted to be used without boxes in exposed cable wiring and for ~~rewiring~~ repair wiring in existing buildings where the cable is concealed ~~and fished~~. Openings in such devices shall form a close fit around the outer covering of the cable, and the device shall fully enclose the part of the cable from which any part of the covering has been removed. Where connections to conductors are by binding screw terminals, there shall be available as many terminals as conductors.

Proposal 7-49, 7-50, 7-51, 7-52

Comment 7-8, 7-9, 7-10

334.40(B) Devices of Insulating Material

Nonmetallic-sheathed cable interconnectors have been recognized to be used without a box and concealed where used for "repair wiring" rather than "rewiring" in existing buildings.

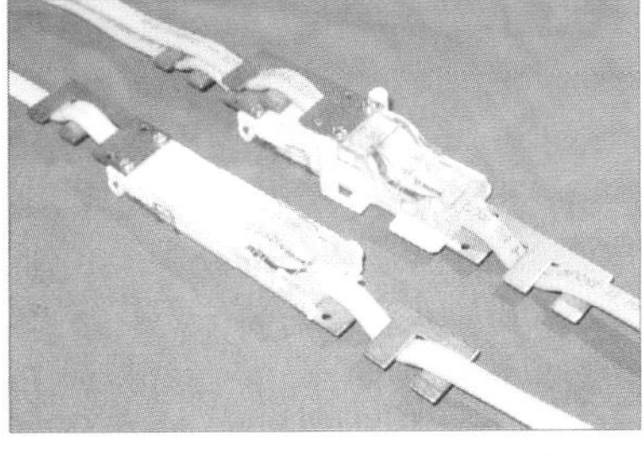

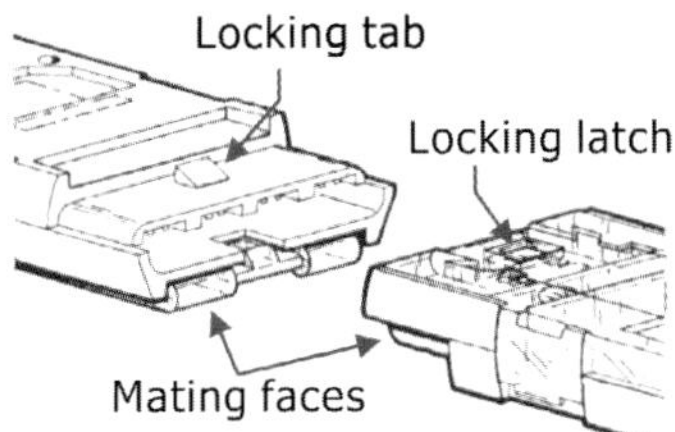

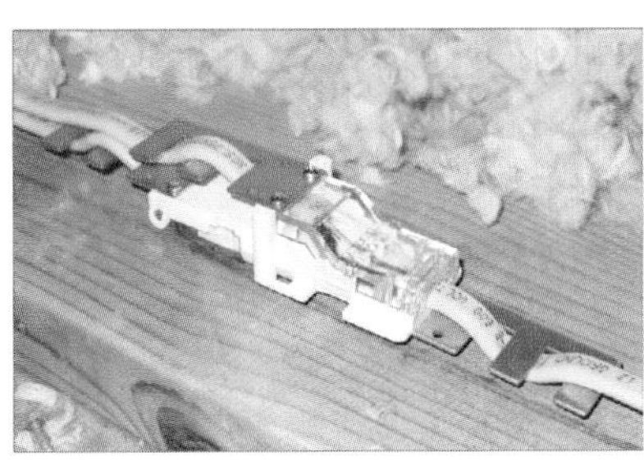

Courtesy of Tyco Electronics

2011 *NEC* Requirement

Switch, outlet, and tap devices of insulating material were permitted to be used without boxes in exposed cable wiring and for rewiring in existing buildings where the cable is concealed and fished.

2014 *NEC* Change

This subsection was revised to address the specific types of devices that are permitted to be used without boxes. Listed self-contained switches and listed self-contained receptacles are the devices permitted in this application, not just any switch or outlet. Listed *nonmetallic sheathed cable interconnector devices* replaces the term *tap devices* to zero in on the specific type of device permitted in this application as well. The specific type of situation where this application minus a box is permitted to occur was limited to "repair wiring" rather than "rewiring" in existing buildings where the cable is concealed.

Analysis of Change

When using nonmetallic-sheathed cable (Type NM), 300.15 generally requires a box to be installed at each conductor splice point, outlet point, switch point, junction point, termination point, or pull point. For the repair of Type NM cable, revised provisions at 334.40(B) have recognized a *nonmetallic-sheathed cable interconnector* for the purpose of concealment without an accessible junction box. These NM cable interconnectors are insulating enclosures which, when connected to Type NM cable, form both a mechanical and an electrical connection. These devices meet the requirements of 300.15(H) that are equivalent to Type NM cable and can be installed concealed if they are being used for "repair wiring" in existing buildings. These devices have been investigated for equivalency to Type NM cable in insulation and temperature rise, and for capability to withstand fault currents, vibration and mechanical shock. Previous text at 334.40(B) uses the broad term *tap* devices. Based on the use of the term *tap* in other locations across the *NEC*, and the fact that product standards refer to these devices as *nonmetallic-sheathed cable interconnector*, using that term in the *NEC* will clarify the permitted application and specific product for this requirement. See UL Guide Information for (QAAV).

Further revision to 334.40(B) made a clear distinction between "rewiring" and "repair wiring" in existing buildings. Rewiring is typically defined as replacing existing wiring with new wiring. If an electrician has the accessibility and availability to replace existing wiring with new wiring, there would be no need for a device such as a nonmetallic-sheathed cable interconnector. Justification for a concealed nonmetallic-sheathed cable interconnector for rewiring would seem to be difficult at best and unwarranted. Repair wiring, on the other hand, seems to be justified for the application of a nonmetallic-sheathed cable interconnector. A safe repair would be a practical solution for an unsafe, existing condition. A concealed nonmetallic-sheathed cable interconnector would always seem to be a last resort and this revision would limit this application to those situations.

An example of an area where these concealed nonmetallic-sheathed cable interconnectors might be used would be in flooded areas. With guidance from the AHJ, damaged or flooded wiring may be able to be removed in the wall cavity to a point where the Type NM cable was not exposed to flooding or syphoning effects. These devices, along with new wiring back to the device location, could then be installed, alleviating the need to replace the entire branch circuit cable.

344.2 and 344.100

Change at a Glance

Definition of *rigid metal conduit* was revised by removing the last two existing sentences and relocating this permitted construction material text to a new 344.100, Construction.

Code Language

344.2 Definition

Rigid Metal Conduit (RMC). A threadable raceway of circular cross section designed for the physical protection and routing of conductors and cables and for use as an equipment grounding conductor when installed with its integral or associated coupling and appropriate fittings. ~~RMC is generally made of steel (ferrous) with protective coatings or aluminum (nonferrous). Special use types are red brass and stainless steel.~~

344.100 Construction. RMC shall be made of one of the following:
(1) Steel (ferrous), with or without protective coatings
(2) Aluminum (nonferrous)
(3) Red Brass
(4) Stainless Steel

Proposal 8-47, 8-48, 8-52a

Comment 8-8, 8-9

2011 *NEC* Requirement

The definition of *rigid metal conduit* (RMC) had descriptive construction-type text at the end of the definition, which stated, "RMC is generally made of steel (ferrous) with protective coatings or aluminum (nonferrous). Special use types are red brass and stainless steel." This language did not define RMC but rather gave examples of RMC.

2014 *NEC* Change

The definition of *rigid metal conduit* was revised by removing the last two previous sentences. CMP-8 relocated these sentences with permitted construction materials to a new 344.100 titled "Construction."

Analysis of Change

The definition of *rigid metal conduit* was revised by deleting language that was repetitive by describing types of RMC that are already covered in Article 344 at 344.10, Uses Permitted. The information in 344.10 clarifies the uses permitted for RMC. Additionally, each of the specific types of RMC described at the previous text has special installation requirements according to the intended use and did not need to be located in a definition in accordance with the *NEC Style Manual*.

The four types of RMC were also placed in an improved and more user-friendly list format.

348.30(A) Ex. No. 4

Change at a Glance

Revision to Exception No. 4 for "Securely Fastened" clarifies that listed flexible metal conduit fittings are permitted as a support means for the purpose of applying this exception.

REVISION

Code Language

348.30 Securing and Supporting

FMC shall be securely fastened in place and supported in accordance with 348.30(A) and (B).

(A) Securely Fastened. FMC shall be securely fastened in place by an approved means within 300 mm (12 in.) of each box, cabinet, conduit body, or other conduit termination and shall be supported and secured at intervals not to exceed 1.4 m (4 ½ ft).

[*Exceptions No. 1 – 3 are unchanged. See NEC for complete text.*]

Exception No. 4: Lengths not exceeding 1.8 m (6 ft) from the last point where the raceway is securely fastened for connections within an accessible ceiling to luminaire(s) or other equipment. For the purposes of this exception, listed flexible metal conduit fittings shall be permitted as a means of support.

Proposal 8-54

Comment 8-11

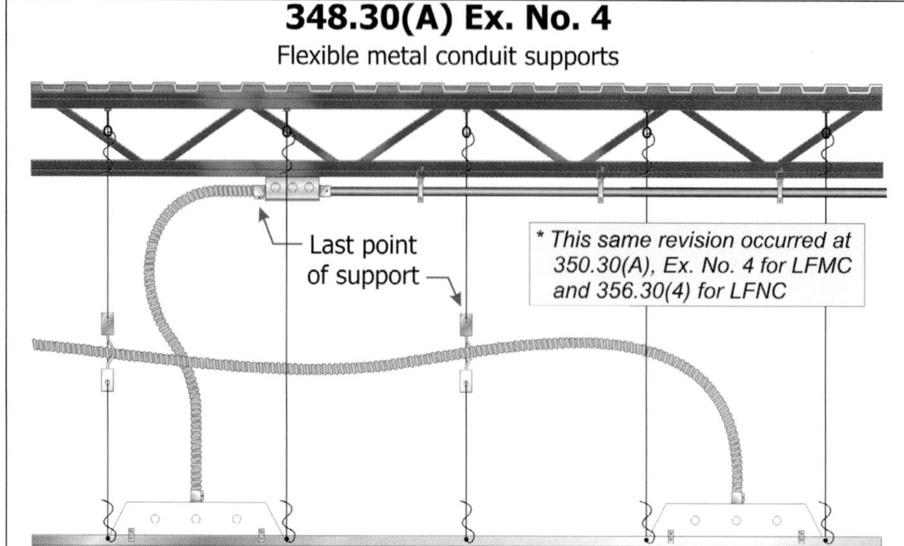
348.30(A) Ex. No. 4
Flexible metal conduit supports
Last point of support
* This same revision occurred at 350.30(A), Ex. No. 4 for LFMC and 356.30(4) for LFNC
Lengths not exceeding 1.8 m (6 ft) from the last point where the raceway is securely fastened for connections within an accessible ceiling to luminaires or other equipment
Listed flexible metal conduit fittings shall be permitted as a means of support.

2011 *NEC* Requirement

Flexible metal conduit (FMC) is typically required to be securely fastened in place within 300 mm (12 in.) of each box, cabinet, conduit body, etc., and to be supported and secured at intervals not to exceed 1.4 m (4 ½ ft). Four exceptions exist for this rule, with one of these exceptions permitting lengths not exceeding 1.8 m (6 ft) from the last point where the FMC is securely fastened for connections within an accessible ceiling to luminaire(s) or other equipment.

2014 *NEC* Change

A revision to Exception No. 4 for 348.30(A) was added to clarify that a flexible metal conduit fitting qualifies as the "last point of support" or as a support means at the luminaire for the purpose of applying Exception No. 4.

Analysis of Change

Flexible metal conduit (FMC) is often used above accessible drop ceilings for the purpose of connecting lay-in-type luminaires and other equipment. Section 348.30(A) Ex. No. 4 permits FMC to be installed where the length of the conduit does not exceed 1.8 m (6 ft) from the last point where the FMC is securely fastened to the luminaire itself. This type of FMC wiring installation is commonly referred to as a "fixture whip" from the junction box to the luminaire in suspended ceiling spaces. *Code* language exists at 320.30(D)(3) for armored cable (Type AC) and at 330.30(D)(2) for metal-clad cable (Type MC) to indicate that Type AC and Type MC cable fittings are permitted as a means of support. The requirements for supporting and securing flexible metal conduit (FMC) and its associated fittings installed above accessible suspended ceilings to luminaires should be the same as that for Type AC cable and Type MC cable. The performance requirements under the heading "Assembly, Resistance, and Pull" from the UL Product Standard for conduit, tubing, and cable fittings (UL 514B) are the same for FMC as the performance requirement for Type AC and Type MC fittings.

This same revision occurred at 350.30(A), Ex. No. 4 for liquidtight flexible metal conduit (LFMC) and at 356.30(4) for liquidtight flexible nonmetallic conduit (LFNC).

350.42

Change at a Glance

Only fittings listed for use with LFMC shall be used with LFMC. Straight LFMC fittings are permitted for direct burial where marked.

Code Language

350.42 Couplings and Connectors

Only fittings listed for use with LFMC shall be used. Angle connectors shall not be concealed. Straight LFMC fittings shall be permitted for direct burial where marked.

Proposal 8-58, 8-59

Comment 8-12, 8-13

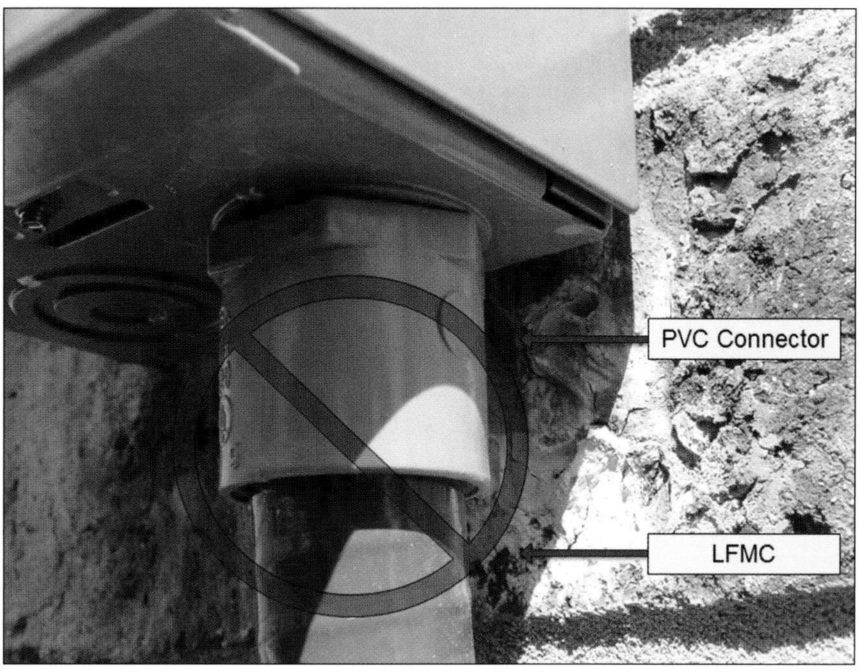

2011 *NEC* Requirement

The one and only provision at 350.42 stated that angle connectors used with liquidtight flexible metal conduit (LFMC) could not be installed or used where concealed.

2014 *NEC* Change

Two new provisions were put in place at 350.42. A new requirement was added to prohibit any type of fitting other than a fitting listed for use with LFMC from being used with LFMC. The second provision addresses straight fittings for LFMC. These straight fittings are permitted for direct burial, but only those straight fitting marked to indicate they have been identified for direct burial.

Analysis of Change

It has become somewhat commonplace to see rigid polyvinyl chloride conduit (PVC) fittings such as a PVC connector being used with liquidtight flexible metal conduit (LFMC). Because of the close proximity of the inner diameter of the PVC connector to the outside diameter of the LFMC conduit, some installers have been known to use PVC solvent cement to connect these PVC connectors to the end of LFMC conduit. This creates a problem with the inspection community as only LFMC fittings have been evaluated and listed to be used with LFMC conduit. This change at 350.42 harmonizes coupling and connector requirements for LFMC with the same provisions at 356.42 for liquidtight flexible nonmetallic conduit (LFNC).

Another change at 350.42 aligns the coupling and connector requirements for LFMC with the same provisions at 356.42 for LFNC. During the 2005 *NEC* Code development process, CMP-8 accepted provisions to allow straight LFNC fittings for direct burial. Where marked for the purpose, LFMC is permitted to be used for direct burial as is LFNC. A new last sentence was added to 350.42 to allow straight LFMC fittings for direct burial where the fitting is so marked.

356.12

Change at a Glance

Deletion of previous 356.12(4) will no longer limit LFNC to 600 volts and below applications.

Code Language

Article 356 Liquidtight Flexible Nonmetallic Conduit (LFNC)

356.12 Uses Not Permitted. LFNC shall not be used as follows:

(1) Where subject to physical damage

(2) Where any combination of ambient and conductor temperatures is in excess of that for which the LFNC is approved

(3) In lengths longer than 1.8 m (6 ft), except as permitted by 356.10(5) or where a longer length is approved as essential for a required degree of flexibility

~~(4) Where the operating voltage of the contained conductors is in excess of 600 volts, nominal, except as permitted in 600.32(A)~~

~~(5)~~ **(4)** In any hazardous (classified) location, except as permitted by other articles in this *Code*

Proposal 8-81a

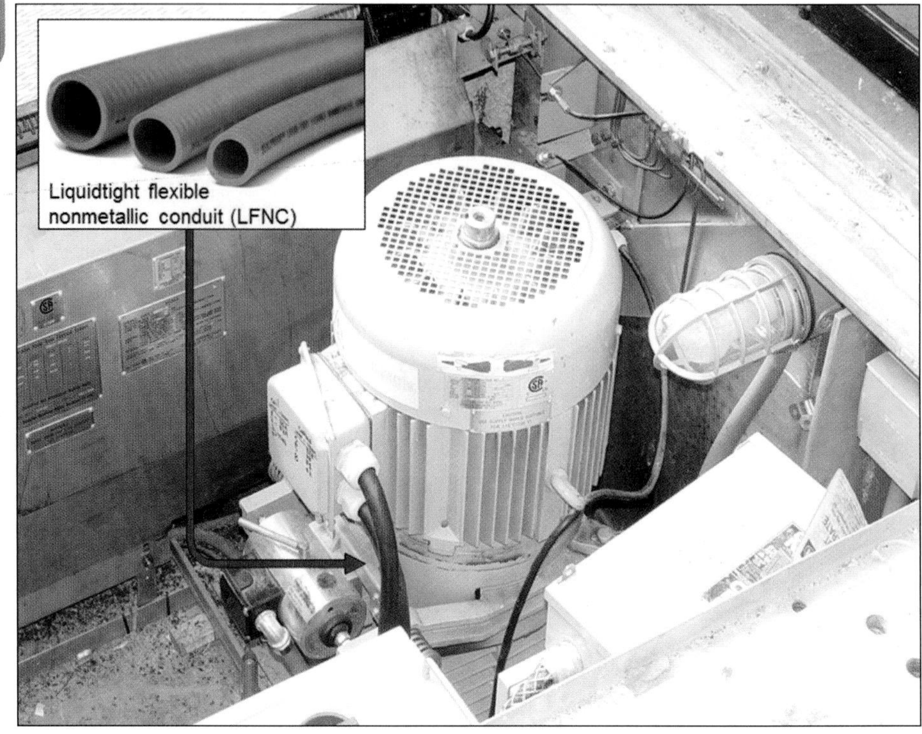

2011 *NEC* Requirement

The use of liquidtight flexible nonmetallic conduit (LFNC) is limited to areas where the wiring method will not be subject to physical damage. LFNC is prohibited where ambient and/or conductor temperatures are in excess of that for which the LFNC is approved. LNFC is generally limited to lengths not longer than 1.8 m (6 ft); and, in general, LFNC is also prohibited in any hazardous (classified) location. For the 2011 *NEC,* LFNC was prohibited in installations where the operating voltage of the contained conductors was in excess of 600 volts, nominal, except as permitted in 600.32(A) for a sign application.

2014 *NEC* Change

Previous item (4) at 356.12 for "Uses Not Permitted" for LFNC has been deleted. This will allow LFNC as an acceptable wiring method for applications where the voltage involved is greater than 600 volts.

Analysis of Change

Liquidtight flexible nonmetallic conduit (LFNC) is no longer limited to 600 volts and below applications. LFNC is listed per its own product standard, UL 1660, requiring LFNC to meet or exceed the very rigorous physical requirements such as impact and crush resistant test. In addition, *UL Certification Guide Information* (White Book), DXOQ, does not limit LFNC to 600 volts. LFNC has been an acceptable wiring method for signs with voltage ratings over 600 volts since the 1990 edition of the *NEC* [see 600.32(A)]. LFNC is also permitted as a wiring method enclosing leads to a motor from a separated junction box for all voltage applications [see 430.245(B)].

Article 370

Change at a Glance

Article 370, Cablebus, was reorganized to more closely follow the Chapter 3 parallel numbering system format.

Code Language

Article 370 Cablebus
Part I. General
370.1 Scope.
370.2 Definition.

Part II. Installation
370.10 Uses Permitted. [Was 370.3 Use.]

370.12 Uses Not Permitted. [Was 370.3 Use.]

370.18 Cablebus Installation. [Was 370.6 Support and Extension Through Walls and Floors.]
(A) Transversely Routed. [Was 370.6(B)]
(B) Through Dry Floors and Platforms. [Was 370.6(C)]
(C) Through Floors and Platforms in Wet Locations. [Was 370.6(D)]

370.20 Conductor Size and Termination. [Was 370.4 and 370.8]
(A) Conductors. [Was 370.4(A) Types of Conductors.]
(B) Termination.[Was 370.8 Conductor Terminations]

370.22 Number of Conductors. [Was 370.4(C) Size and Number of Conductors.]

Courtesy of MDF Cable Bus Systems

2011 *NEC* Requirement

The requirements for cablebus are found in Article 370 of the *NEC*. Refer to the 2011 *NEC* for complete text and article structure.

2014 *NEC* Change

Article 370 was restructured. See NEC for complete text and article structure.

Analysis of Change

Cablebus has been redefined in the 2014 *NEC* as "an assembly of units or sections with insulated conductors having associated fittings forming a structural system used to securely fasten or support conductors and conductor terminations in a completely enclosed, ventilated, protective metal housing. This assembly is designed to carry fault current and to withstand the magnetic forces of such current." Part of the existing language that was part of the previous definition at 370.2 was moved to a new Informational Note which states, "Cablebus is ordinarily assembled at the point of installation from the components furnished or specified by the manufacturer in accordance with instructions for the specific job."

Article 370 was reorganized in its entirety to more closely shadow the Chapter 3 parallel numbering system format that was introduced throughout the Chapter 3 wiring method articles during the 2002 *NEC Code* cycle. This system aligns common subject matters, such as "Definitions" (XXX.2), "Uses Permitted" (XXX.10), "Securing and Supporting" (XXX.30), "Marking" (XXX.120), etc., with the same numbering format throughout all of the wiring method articles where appropriate. This reformatted article now has a similar structure as Article 392 for Cable Tray, which is the other cable support system addressed in the *NEC*.

Article 370

Continued

370.23 Overcurrent Protection. [Was 370.5]

370.30 Securing and Supporting. [New]
(A) Cablebus Supports. [Was 370.6(A) Support.]
(B) Conductor Supports. [Was 370.4(D)]

370.42 Fittings. [Was 370.7]

370.60 Grounding. [Was 370.3 Use and 370.9 Grounding.]

370.80 Ampacity of Conductors. [Was 370.4(B)]

Part III. Construction Specifications

370.120 Marking. [Was 370.10]

(See NEC for complete text.)

Proposal 8-109a, 8-110 thru 8-117

Comment 8-34, 8-35, 8-36

The majority of the changes in Article 370 were reorganizational in nature with no technical impact, but there were a few technical revisions in the article as well. As stated previously, the definition of *cablebus* was revised by the actions of Proposal 8-113 and Comment 8-34. The voltage parameters at 370.80 for "Ampacity of Conductors" [previously 370.4(B)] were revised to match the voltages involved with the Article 310 ampacity tables that are referenced in this section. See Proposal 8-115 and Comment 8-35.

376.22(B)

Change at a Glance

Ampacity adjustment factors for more than three current-carrying conductors in a raceway shall only apply to metal wireways where the number of current-carrying conductors exceeds 30 at any cross section of the wireway.

Code Language

376.22 Number of Conductors and Ampacity

The number of conductors and their ampacity shall comply with 376.22(A) and (B).

A) Cross-Sectional Areas of Wireway. The sum of the cross-sectional areas of all contained conductors at any cross section of a wireway shall not exceed 20 percent of the interior cross-sectional area of the wireway.

(B) Adjustment Factors. The adjustment factors in 310.15(B)(3)(a) shall be applied only where the number of current-carrying conductors, including neutral conductors classified as current-carrying under the provisions of 310.15(B)(5), exceeds 30 at any cross section of the wireway. Conductors for signaling circuits or controller conductors between a motor and its starter and used only for starting duty shall not be considered as current-carrying conductors.

Proposal 8-137

2011 *NEC* Requirement

The ampacity adjustment factors of 310.15(B)(3)(a), More Than Three Current-Carrying Conductors in a Raceway or Cable, are applicable to metal wireway under certain conditions. These adjustment factors applied only where the number of current-carrying conductors, including current-carrying neutral conductors, exceeded 30. For this application, signaling and control conductors are not considered current-carrying conductors.

2014 *NEC* Change

The "30 current-carrying conductors" in question were identified as 30 current-carrying conductors at any cross section of the wireway — not just 30 or more current-carrying conductors total in the wireway.

Analysis of Change

Needed clarification was granted to this section for the number of conductors in a metal wireway and any ampacity adjustment correction factors involved. A revision to 376.22(B) clarifies that adjustment factors of 310.15(B)(3) only apply where the number of current-carrying conductors exceeds 30 at any cross sectional area of the wireway, as opposed to 30 conductors as a total number in the wireway itself.

Wireways were first recognized as a wiring method in the 1931 *NEC,* and the "30 current-carrying conductor" provision associated with wireways has been in the *Code* in some form since that time. In the 2002 *NEC Code* cycle, a change was accepted at 376.22 to editorially revise that section for clarity. The "at any cross section" language was separated from the "30 current-carrying conductors" as a result of that 2002 *NEC* change. This separation became even greater when 376.22 was divided into subsections (A) & (B) in the 2008 *NEC Code* cycle. It was never intended for the adjustment factors of 310.15(B)(3)(a) to apply once there were more than 30 conductors total in the wireway, as opposed to at a cross sectional area. The revisions to this section over the last few *Code* cycles were intended to be purely editorial in nature, not to change the required application of this section.

As an example of the issue involving the previous language at the section, consider a continuous wireway that is installed around corners in a "U" shape around a small electrical equipment room. The total length of this wireway is 6.7 m (22 ft) with several disconnects and panelboards feeding conductors in and out of this wireway. Besides the feeder conductors in this wireway, there are a total of (120) 12 AWG copper branch circuit conductors in the wireway. The fact is that there are never more than 30 current-carrying conductors at any cross section of this wireway, and there are actually cross sections of this wireway where there are no conductors. Without this revision and based on the previous language at this section, the ampacity of these conductors would literally have to be reduced to 35% of their Table 310.15(B)(16) ampacity values based on Table 310.15(B)(3)(a).

376.56(B)(1) and (B)(5)

Change at a Glance

Power distribution blocks installed in wireways ahead of the service main (line side) must be *listed for the purpose*. Also, conductors in wireways are required to be arranged so that power distribution block terminals are unobstructed after their installation.

Code Language

376.56 Splices, Taps, and Power Distribution Blocks

(B) Power Distribution Blocks.

(1) Installation. Power distribution blocks installed in metal wireways shall be listed. Power distribution blocks installed on the line side of the service equipment shall be listed for the purpose.

(2) Size of Enclosure. (*Text unchanged*)

(3) Wire Bending Space. (*Text unchanged*)

(4) Live Parts. (*Text unchanged*)

(5) Conductors. Conductors shall be arranged so the power distribution block terminals are unobstructed following installation.

Proposal 8-140, 8-141, 8-142

Comment 8-42, 8-43

376.56(B) Power Distribution Blocks (Wireways)

- Power distribution blocks installed in metal wireways shall be listed.
- Power distribution blocks installed in wireways ahead of the service main (line side) must be "listed for the purpose."
- Conductors in wireways are required to be arranged so that power distribution block terminals are unobstructed after their installation.

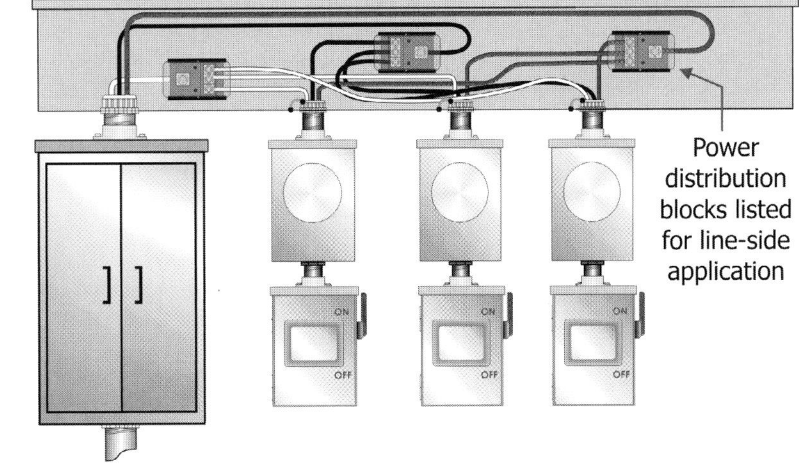

2011 *NEC* Requirement

Power distribution blocks (PDB) are permitted to be installed in metal wireways, provided the PDBs are listed for same. In addition to the wiring space required for splices and taps, wireways containing PDBs must meet the dimensions specified in the installation instructions of the PDBs. Sufficient wire bending space is required at the terminals of PDBs as specified at 312.6(B) for wire-bending space at terminals of cabinets, cutout boxes, and meter socket enclosures. PDBs cannot have uninsulated live parts exposed within a wireway, with or without the wireway cover installed. Clear plastic covers provided by the manufacturer of the PDBs typically can meet this last requirement.

2014 *NEC* Change

In addition to the requirements for power distribution blocks (PDB) required in the 2011 *NEC*, two new provisions were added to these requirements. A new sentence was added to item (1) requiring PDBs installed ahead of the service main (line side) to be *listed for the purpose*. The second change occurred by adding a new 376.56(B)(5) which requires PDBs installed in metal wireways to have all conductors arranged so that PDB terminals remain accessible and unobstructed after installation.

Analysis of Change

UL Product Standard 1953 and the UL White Book guide information "QPQS for power distribution blocks (PDB)" both state that PDBs are to be used only on the load side of service equipment. It is a fairly common practice to see PDBs used in metal wireways supplying multiple service disconnects. This new provision to require PDBs installed in wireways ahead of service equipment (line side) to be listed for the purpose will go a long way in alerting installers to the restrictions of these devices per their very listings.

376.56(B)(1) and (B)(5)

Continued

Another new provision for power distribution blocks (PDB) in metal wireways was the addition of new 376.56(B)(5) which requires PDBs installed in metal wireways to have all conductors arranged so that PDB terminals remain accessible and unobstructed after installation. This new provision in Article 376 for metal wireways will bring consistency with the provisions added by CMP-9 in the 2011 *NEC* at 314.28(E) for PDBs installed in pull or junction boxes. The concerns of obstructing the terminals of PDBs should be the same whether the PDB is installed in a wireway or a junction box.

386.120

Change at a Glance

Surface metal raceways are now required to have each length identified and marked according to 110.21(A) [manufacturer's marking requirements].

Code Language

Article 386 Surface Metal Raceways

386.120 Marking

386.120 Marking. Each length of surface metal raceways shall be clearly and durably identified as required in the first sentence of 110.21.

Proposal 8-154

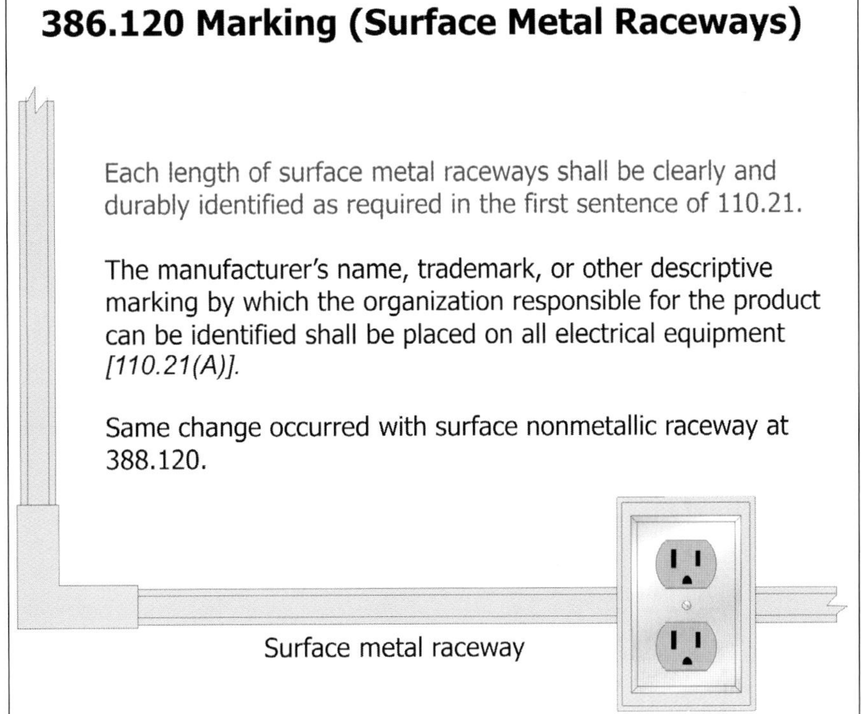

386.120 Marking (Surface Metal Raceways)
Each length of surface metal raceways shall be clearly and durably identified as required in the first sentence of 110.21.
The manufacturer's name, trademark, or other descriptive marking by which the organization responsible for the product can be identified shall be placed on all electrical equipment [110.21(A)].
Same change occurred with surface nonmetallic raceway at 388.120.
Surface metal raceway

2011 *NEC* Requirement

No marking requirements existed in Article 386 for surface metal raceways.

2014 *NEC* Change

A new section entitled "Marking" was added to Article 386 requiring each length of surface metal raceway to be identified and to be marked in accordance with the first part of 110.21(A) for manufacturer's marking requirements.

Analysis of Change

Surface metal raceway is defined at 386.2 as "a metallic raceway that is intended to be mounted to the surface of a structure, with associated couplings, connectors, boxes, and fittings for the installation of electrical conductors." A new product marking requirement was added at 386.120 for surface metal raceway. The addition of this new requirement provides consistency with other articles within the *Code* for similar products.

Part of the proposal that brought about this new marking requirement also sought to add language at 386.30 for securing and supporting of surface metal raceway. This proposal included language to recognize surface metal raceway installed suspended in a pendent style from a threaded rod, etc. This part of the proposal was rejected by CMP-8, stating that the scope of Article 386 "clearly states that surface metal raceways are intended to be mounted to the surface of a structure." CMP-8 encouraged the revisiting of this suspended mounting issue for future *Code* cycles and recommends that the submitter include a fact-finding report that technically supports the use of surface metal raceways in suspended applications.

These same changes occurred with surface nonmetallic raceway in Article 388. See Proposal 8-157 and Comment 8-46.

Table 392.10(A)

Change at a Glance

Table 392.10(A) was revised to reflect and clarify the permitted wiring methods that can be used in cable trays.

Code Language

Article 392 Cable Trays

392.10 Uses Permitted

Cable tray shall be permitted to be used as a support system for service conductors, feeders, branch circuits, communications circuits, control circuits, and signaling circuits. Cable tray installations shall not be limited to industrial establishments. Where exposed to direct rays of the sun, insulated conductors and jacketed cables shall be identified as being sunlight-resistant. Cable trays and their associated fittings shall be identified for the intended use.

(A) Wiring Methods. The wiring methods in Table 392.10(A) shall be permitted to be installed in cable tray systems under the conditions described in their respective articles and sections.
(See NEC for complete table text and revised Table 392.10(A) provided here.)

Proposal 8-158a

Comment 8-48

2011 *NEC* Requirement

The wiring methods permitted to be used in a cable tray are identified at Table 392.10(A). There were 32 types of wiring methods listed in this table that are permitted to be installed in cable tray systems under the conditions described in their respective articles and sections.

2014 *NEC* Change

Revisions were made to Table 392.10(A) with no substantial technical changes. The changes were more editorial in nature to properly identify the permitted wiring methods that can be supported by a cable tray. The common wiring method abbreviations were added to the end of the wiring methods where appropriate.

Analysis of Change

A proposal generated by CMP-8 revises Table 392.10(A) to clarify the permitted wiring methods for use in a cable tray. The wiring methods included in the table are described by the title of the corresponding articles, where appropriate, followed by the article numbers. Proper terminology was used were needed as "Polyvinyl chloride PVC conduit" and "Rigid nonmetallic conduit" were replaced with "Rigid polyvinyl chloride conduit: Type PVC." All other wiring methods in the table were addressed by name so the abbreviation "RTRC" was replaced with "Reinforced thermosetting resin conduit: Type RTRC." The terms *multiconductor service-entrance cable* and *multiconductor underground feeder and branch-circuit cable* were replaced with simply *service-entrance cable: Types SE and USE* and *underground feeder and branch-circuit cable: Type UF*.

Actions resulting from Comment 8-48 eliminated the terms *optical fiber raceways* and *signaling raceways* from the table. The submitter of the comment correctly pointed out that action taken by CMP-16 had resulted in the term *optical fiber raceways* being replaced with the term *communications raceways* (see Proposal

16-81). Similar action by CMP-3 eliminated the term *signaling raceways,* replacing it with *communications raceways* (see Proposal 3-156).

Table 392.10(A) Wiring Methods (Cable Trays)

Wiring Method	Article
Armored cable: Type AC	320
CATV cables	820
Class 2 and Class 3 cables	725
Communication cables	725, 770, and 800
Communication raceways	800
Electrical metallic tubing: Type EMT	358
Electrical nonmetallic tubing: Type ENT	362
Fire alarm cables	760
Flexible metal conduit: Type FMC	348
Flexible metallic tubing: Type FMT	360
Instrumentation tray cable: Type ITC	727
Intermediate metal conduit: Type IMC	342
Liquidtight flexible metal conduit: Type LFMC	350
Liquidtight flexible nonmetallic conduit: Type LFNC	356
Metal-clad cable: Type MC	330
Mineral-insulated, metal-sheated cable: Type MI	332
Network-powered broadband communication cable	830
Nonmetallic-sheathed cable: Types NM, NMC and NMS	334
Non-powered-limited fire alarm cable	760
Optical fiber cables	770
~~Optical fiber raceways~~	~~770~~
Other factory-assembled, multiconductor control, signal, or power cables that are specifically approved for the installation in cable trays	
Power and control tray cable: Type TC	336
Power-limited fire alarm cable	760
Power-limited tray cable	760
Rigid metal conduit: Type RMC	344
~~Rigid nonmetallic conduit~~	~~352~~
Rigid polyvinyl chloride ~~PVC~~ conduit: Type PVC	352
Reinforced thermosetting resin conduit: Type RTRC	355
~~Multiconductor~~ Service-entrance cable: Types SE and USE	338
~~Signaling raceways~~	~~725~~
~~Multiconductor~~ Underground feeder and branch-circuit cable: Type UF	340

392.18(H) and Exception

Change at a Glance

The marking requirement for cable trays containing conductors rated over 600 volts has been relaxed for industrial establishments with maintenance, supervision, and qualified persons servicing the installation.

Code Language

392.18(H) Cable Tray Installation

(H) Marking. Cable trays containing conductors rated over 600 volts shall have a permanent, legible warning notice carrying the wording "DANGER — HIGH VOLTAGE — KEEP AWAY" placed in a readily visible position on all cable trays, with the spacing of warning notices not to exceed 3 m (10 ft). The danger marking(s) or labels shall comply with 110.21(B).

Exception: *Where not accessible (as applied to equipment), in industrial establishments where the conditions of maintenance and supervision ensure that only qualified persons service the installation, cable tray system warning notices shall be located where necessary for the installation to assure safe maintenance and operation.*

Proposal 8-179, 8-180, 8-182

Comment 8-51

392.18(H) Cable Trays - Marking

Cable trays containing conductors rated over 600 volts are required to have warning notice (label) readily visible and spaced not to exceed 3 m (10 ft).

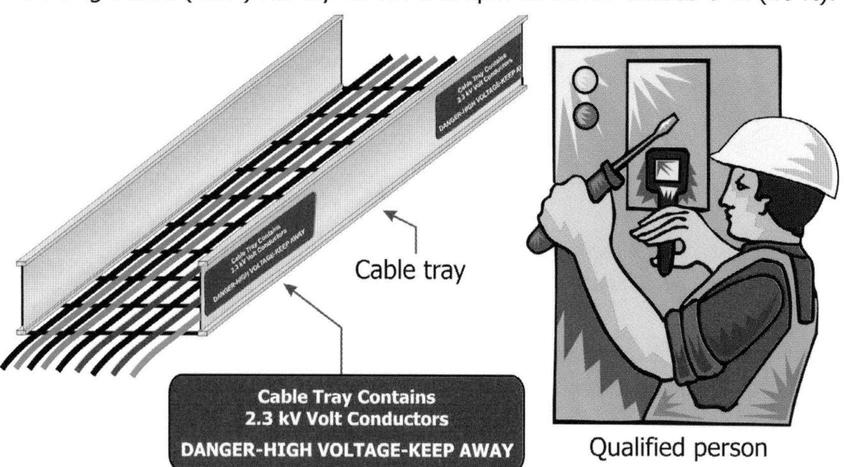

Exception was added for industrial establishments with maintenance, supervision, and qualified persons servicing the installation.

2011 *NEC* Requirement

The installation requirements for cable trays are covered at 392.18.

For the 2011 *NEC*, marking requirements were added to 392.18 for cable trays. This warning label is required when the cable tray contains conductors rated over 600 volts. This label or notice must to be permanent and legible with the phrase "DANGER—HIGH VOLTAGE—KEEP AWAY" located in a readily visible location. These warning labels are required to be located at least every 3 m (10 ft).

2014 *NEC* Change

An exception was added for the marking requirements of 392.18(H). In industrial establishments where the conditions of maintenance and supervision ensure that only qualified persons service the installation, cable tray system warning labels are not required for the installation of cable trays containing conductors rated over 600 volts where the cable tray is not accessible (as applied to equipment). A tag line was added at the end of the main rule at 392.18(H) directing installers to the new warning and danger label requirements at 110.21(B). The remainder of the 392.18 installation requirements for cable trays remained the same.

Analysis of Change

Because of the existence of trained, qualified persons at supervised industrial establishments, it may not always be necessary to provide warning labels at cable trays containing conductors rated over 600 volts. Electrical maintenance personnel in such industrial places as oil refineries and petrochemical plants are trained to recognize different voltage levels in their cable tray systems and are trained to not disturb them by walking on them or moving them while energized. In some industrial establishments, it is not always practical or necessary to place a warning label every 3 m (10 ft) along a cable tray. Some of these industrial cable tray installations may be at elevated locations where the warning labels cannot even be seen from the floor. Some industrial cable tray installations may extend thousands of feet; being required to post a warning label every 3 m (10 ft) can be burdensome, unnecessary, and costly in the eyes of some users of the *Code*.

Another change at 392.18(H) added a reference to the new warning and danger label requirements at 110.21(B). This was one of several coordinated changes throughout the *NEC* to provide consistency of danger, caution, and warning sign or markings as required in the *Code*. This additional information will correlate this danger marking requirement with 110.21(B) and the requirements in ANSI Z 535.4, *American National Standard for Product Safety Signs and Labels*.

392.20(A) and (B)

Change at a Glance

Cables installed in cable trays will be based upon the operating voltage and not the cable rating.

Code Language

392.20 Cable and Conductor Installation

(A) Multicondutor Cable ~~Rated~~ Operating at 600 Volts or Less. Multiconductor cables ~~rated~~ operating at 600 volts or less shall be permitted to be installed in the same cable tray.

(B) Cables ~~Rated~~ Operating at Over 600 Volts. Cables ~~rated~~ operating at over 600 volts and those ~~rated~~ operating at 600 volts or less installed in the same cable tray shall comply with either of the following:

(1) The cables ~~rated~~ operating at over 600 volts are Type MC.
(2) The cables ~~rated~~ operating at over 600 volts are separated from the cables ~~rated~~ operating at 600 volts or less by a solid fixed barrier of a material compatible with the cable tray.

Proposal 8-187

Comment 8-53

392.20 Cable and Conductor Installation (Cable Trays)

392.20 Cable and Conductor Installation
(A) Multicondutor Cable ~~Rated~~ Operating at 600 Volts or Less
(B) Cables ~~Rated~~ Operating at Over 600 Volts

- The term "rated" was replaced with the term "operating at" eight times within these two subsections
- These revisions were made to provide clarity that these cables installed in cable trays should be based upon the operating voltage rather than the actual rating of the cable
- Revisions bring the same provisions for conductors installed in raceway as those installed in a cable tray

2011 *NEC* Requirement

Cables rated 600 volts or less were permitted to be installed in the same cable tray as cables rated over 600 volts. However, cables rated over 600 volts had to meet one of two options. One was that the cables rated over 600 volts had to be of Type MC construction. The second was that cables rated over 600 volts had to be separated from the cables rated 600 volts or less by a solid fixed barrier within the cable tray.

2014 *NEC* Change

The word "rated" was replaced with the words "operating at" eight times within these two subsections. These revisions clarify that cables installed in cable trays should be based upon the operating voltage rather than the actual rating of the cable.

Analysis of Change

The previous language at 392.20 based all installations of cables in cable trays on insulation rating of the conductors or cables involved. *NEC* 300.3(C) permits conductors installed in raceways to be chosen based on the insulation rating of any of the conductors involved being equal to at least the maximum circuit voltage applied to any conductor within the enclosure, cable, or raceway, rather than the insulation rating itself. This change at 392.20 brings the same provisions for conductors installed in raceway as those installed in a cable tray.

There are times when cables rated over 600 volts are available for less than 600-volt system circuit or feeder installations. This revision will now make this practice acceptable.

Article 393

Change at a Glance

A new article was added to address low-voltage Class 2 equipment connected to ceiling grids and walls constructed for this purpose.

Code Language

Article 393 Low-Voltage Suspended Ceiling Power Distribution Systems

Part I. General

393.1 Scope.

393.2 Definitions.

393.6 Listing Requirements.
(A) Listed System.
(B) Assembly of Listed Parts.

Part II. Installation

393.10 Uses Permitted.

393.12 Uses Not Permitted.

393.14 Installation.
(A) General Requirements.
(B) Insulated Conductors.

393.21 Disconnecting Means.
(A) Location.
(B) Multiwire Branch Circuits.

393.30 Securing and Supporting.
(A) Attached to Building Structure.
(B) Attachment of Power Grid Rails.

393.40 Connectors and Enclosures.
(A) Connectors.
(B) Enclosures.

393.45 Overcurrent and Reverse Polarity (Backfeed) Protection.

Article 393 Low-Voltage Suspended Ceiling Power Distribution Systems

A new article was added to address low-voltage Class 2 ac and dc volt supplied equipment *(lighting and power)* connected to ceiling grids, floors and walls built for this purpose.

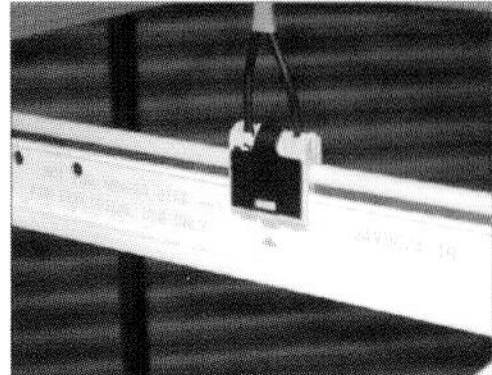

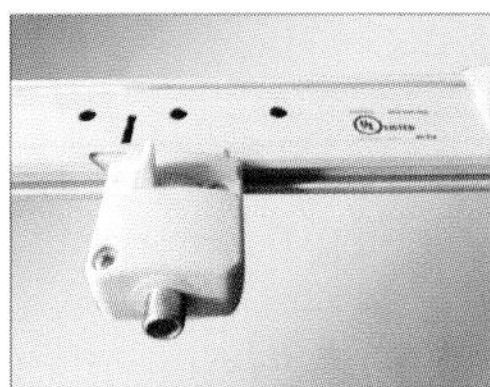

A system that serves as a support for a finished ceiling surface and consists of a busbar and busbar support system to distribute power to utilization equipment supplied by a Class 2 power supply.

2011 *NEC* Requirement

This subject matter was not addressed in the 2011 *NEC*.

2014 *NEC* Change

A new article entitled "Low-Voltage Suspended Ceiling Power Distribution Systems" was added to address low-voltage Class 2 supplied equipment (lighting and power) connected to ceiling grids, floors and walls built for this purpose. This article addresses equipment with similar characteristics to track lighting but includes the wiring and power supply requirements. This type of *low-voltage suspended ceiling power distribution system* is defined as "a system that serves as a support for a finished ceiling surface and consists of a busbar and busbar support system to distribute power to utilization equipment supplied by a Class 2 power supply."

Analysis of Change

A new article for "Low- Voltage Suspended Ceiling Power Distribution Systems" was added to address low-voltage Class 2 ac and dc volt equipment connected to ceiling grids and walls built specifically for this type of power distribution system. The growing interest in alternative energy sources (e.g., photovoltaics, wind turbines, batteries, fuel cells, etc.) and in the proliferation of low-voltage, low-power devices (sensors, LV lighting, IT equipment, AV equipment, etc.) has created a significant need for adequate language supporting the practical safeguarding of circuits and electrical equipment operating at 30 volts ac or 60 volts dc or less. This article addresses equipment with similar characteristics to track lighting but includes the wiring and power supply requirements as well. The article provides the specific requirements for the safe installation of low-voltage, power-limited power distribution providing power to lighting and non-lighting loads.

The previous *Code* has specific requirements for power distribution at 30

Article 393

Continued

(A) Overcurrent Protection.
(B) Interconnection of Power Sources.
(C) Reverse Polarity (Backfeed) Protection of Direct-Current Systems.

393.56 Splices.

393.57 Connections.

393.60 Grounding.
(A) Grounding of Supply Side of Class 2 Power Source.
(B) Grounding of Load Side of Class 2 Power Source.

Part III. Construction Specifications
393.104 Sizes and Types of Conductors.
(A) Load Side Utilization Conductor Size.
(B) Power Feed Bus Rail Conductor Size.

(See NEC for complete text)

Proposal 18-10a

Comment 18-7, 18-8, 18-9, 18-10, 18-10a

volts or less for listed lighting devices and their associated listed components (as covered by Article 411 with reference to Article 725). However, there were no similar requirements for power distribution at 30 volts or less for listed non-lighting systems and their associated listed components. This article provides the specific requirements for the safe installation of low-voltage, power-limited power distribution, providing power to lighting and non-lighting loads. Drawing largely from Articles 411 and 725, this article slightly expands the scope of these systems with the addition of low-voltage/power-limited (Class 2) non-lighting loads while maintaining the clear requirements necessary for safe installations. A low-voltage suspended ceiling power distribution system is a viable power distribution system, providing appropriate flexibility of power for lighting, sensors, temperature control, and other functional aspects of the newer building environment.

This proposal was developed as part of a larger effort to provide clear and specific requirements in NFPA 70 regarding the use of dc power. This proposal was developed by a subgroup of the NEC DC Task Force for the NEC Correlating Committee.

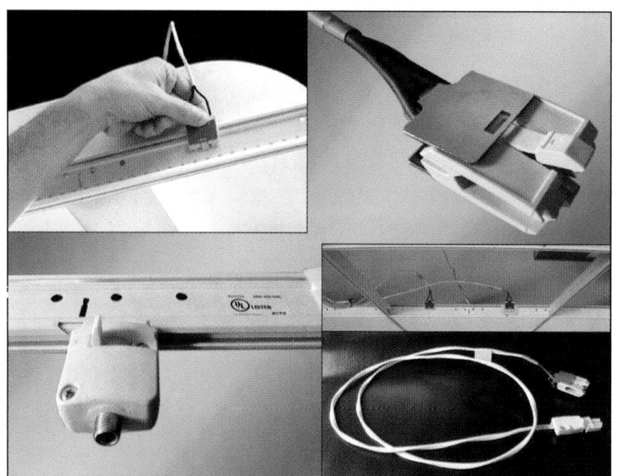

399.2

Change at a Glance

The definition of *outdoor overhead conductors* was revised to include the words "in free air" to ensure that the definition clearly indicated that wiring installed under the scope of Article 399 was not installed in raceways, etc.

Code Language

399.2 Definition. (Outdoor Overhead Conductors over ~~600~~ 1000 Volts)

Outdoor Overhead Conductors. Single conductors, insulated, covered, or bare, installed outdoors on support structures in free air.

Proposal 7-85, 7-87

Article 399 - Outdoor Overhead Conductors Over 1000 Volts

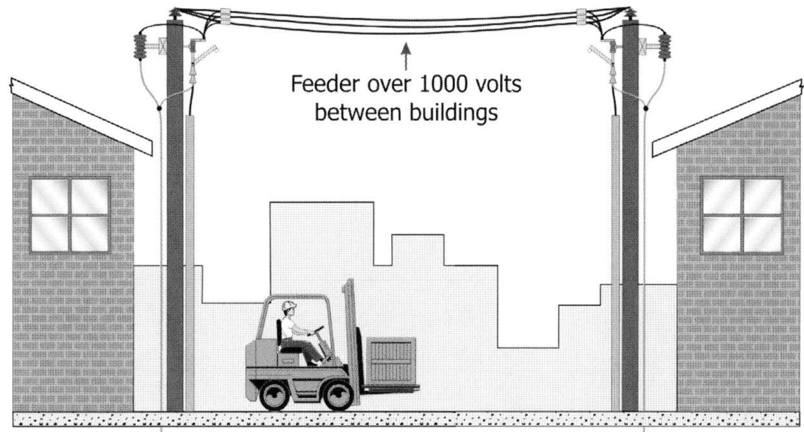

Outdoor Overhead Conductors - Single conductors, insulated, covered, or bare, installed outdoors on support structures in free air

Wiring installed under the scope of Article 399 is not installed in raceways, etc.

2011 *NEC* Requirement

The definition of an over-600-volt outdoor overhead conductor as it applied to Article 399 was "single conductors, insulated, covered, or bare, installed outdoors on support structures."

2014 *NEC* Change

The words "in free air" were added to the definition of *outdoor overhead conductors* as applied to Article 399, which now involves outdoor overhead conductors rated over 1000 volts due to the global changes pertaining to the 1000 volts parameter in the 2014 *NEC*.

Analysis of Change

Article 399, Outdoor Overhead Conductors Over 600 Volts, (600 volts at that time) was added in the 2011 *NEC*. This article was added to provide rules and installation requirements for premises wiring installations utilizing over 600 volt systems that exist in numerous locations and that have become more common as electrical usage has increased. Many of those installations utilize overhead bare conductors on insulators as feeders and branch circuits to safely distribute power to multiple buildings, structures and equipment locations. Article 399 provides prescriptive language to installers and designers for utilizing existing industry standards for the specific details of the installation and design of these outdoor overhead conductor installations, and, at the same time, provides the enforcement community a basis for approval of these installations.

This revised definition should clarify which conductors Article 399 represents as being the "conductors outside in free air" used for transmission and distribution of electrical power to utilization equipment that transitions from traditional indoor wiring methods such as wireways, raceways, busway conduit systems, etc.

A similar change adding the words "in free air" occurred at 399.10 for "Uses Permitted." See Proposal 7-87.

4

400.4

Change at a Glance

The use of flexible cords and flexible cables not described in Table 400.4 requires the permission of the AHJ.

Code Language

400.4 Types (Flexible Cords and Cables)

The use of flexible cords and flexible cables ~~shall conform to the description~~ other than those in Table 400.4 shall require permission by the authority having jurisdiction. ~~Types of flexible cords and flexible cables other than those listed in the table shall be the subject of special investigation.~~

Proposal 6-86

Comment 6-69

400.4 Types (Flexible Cords and Cables)

The use of flexible cords and flexible cables not described in Table 400.4 requires the permission of the AHJ.

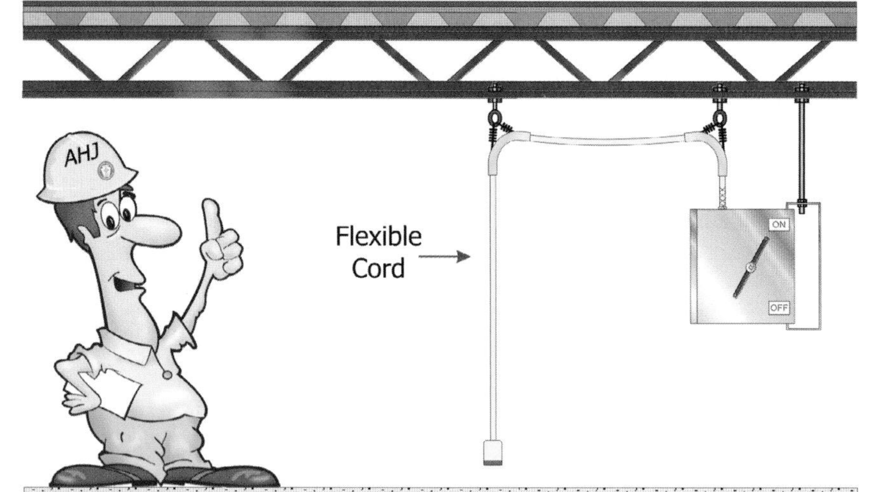

Requires "permission by the authority having jurisdiction" rather than requiring flexible cords and cables to be "subject of special investigation"

2011 *NEC* Requirement

The use of flexible cords and flexible cables was limited to those identified by Table 400.4. Any flexible cord or cable, other than those listed in the table, was to be the "subject of special investigation."

2014 *NEC* Change

A revision to 400.4 relaxed the rule for the use of flexible cords and flexible cables, other than those in Table 400.4, to require "permission by the authority having jurisdiction" rather than requiring these flexible cords and cables to be the "subject of special investigation."

Analysis of Change

A revision for the types of flexible cords and cables that can be used at 400.4 occurred for the 2014 *NEC*. In previous editions of the *Code*, the permitted flexible cords and cables were subject to Table 400.4; other types of flexible cords and cables were permitted but they were to be the "subject of special investigation." This "special investigation" language has been in the *Code* since the 1937 edition of the *NEC*. Up until the 1984 *NEC*, this language indicated that "…flexible cords and flexible cables other than those listed in the table shall be the subject of special investigation *and shall not be used before being approved*." Who approves? Who was to conduct this special investigation? For the 2014 *NEC*, the words "subject of special investigation" have been replaced with "shall require permission by the authority having jurisdiction (AHJ)." The AHJ is the person or organization that is responsible for enforcing the requirements of the *Code* or for "approving" equipment, materials, an installation, or a procedure.

400.5(A)

Change at a Glance

Temperature correction factors apply to ampacity values for flexible cords and cables in both Table 400.5(A)(1) and Table 400.5(A)(2).

Code Language

400.5 Ampacities for Flexible Cords and Cables

(A) Ampacity Tables.

Table 400.5(A)(1) provides the allowable ampacities, and Table 400.5(A)(2) provides the ampacities for flexible cords and cables with not more than three current-carrying conductors. These tables shall be used in conjunction with applicable end-use product standards to ensure selection of the proper size and type. Where cords and cables are used in ambient temperatures other than 30°C (86°F), the temperature correction factors from Table 310.15(B)(2)(a) that correspond to temperature rating of the cord or cable shall be applied to the ampacity in Table 400.5(A)(1) and Table 400.5(A)(2) Cords and cables rated 105°C shall use correction factors in 90°C column of Table 310.15(B)(2)(a) for temperature correction. Where the number of current-carrying conductors exceeds three, the allowable ampacity or the ampacity of each conductor shall be reduced from the 3-conductor rating as shown in Table 400.5(A)(3).

(Remainder of 400.5(A) text unchanged. See NEC for complete text.)

Proposal 6-93a, 6-94

400.5(A) Ampacity Tables for Cords and Cables

Temperature correction factors apply to ampacity values for flexible cords and cables in both Table 400.5(A)(1) and Table 400.5(A)(2).

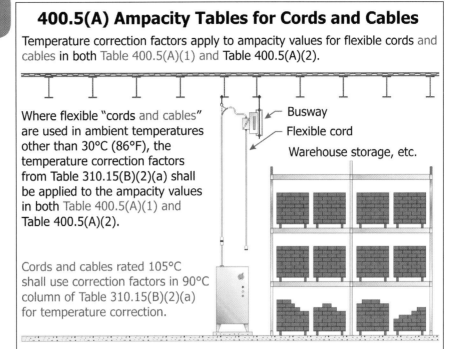

Where flexible "cords and cables" are used in ambient temperatures other than 30°C (86°F), the temperature correction factors from Table 310.15(B)(2)(a) shall be applied to the ampacity values in both Table 400.5(A)(1) and Table 400.5(A)(2).

Busway

Flexible cord

Warehouse storage, etc.

Cords and cables rated 105°C shall use correction factors in 90°C column of Table 310.15(B)(2)(a) for temperature correction.

2011 *NEC* Requirement

Provisions at 400.5(A) in the 2011 *NEC* indicated that where flexible cords are used in ambient temperatures other than 30°C (86°F), the temperature correction factors from Table 310.15(B)(2)(a) that correspond to the temperature rating of the flexible cord are to be applied to the ampacity values in Table 400.5(A)(2).

2014 *NEC* Change

Revisions to 400.5(A) clarified that where flexible cords and cables are used in ambient temperatures other than 30°C (86°F), the temperature correction factors from Table 310.15(B)(2)(a) that correspond to the temperature rating of the flexible cord and cables shall be applied to the ampacity values in both Table 400.5(A)(1) and Table 400.5(A)(2).

Analysis of Change

The previous language for ampacity tables and possible temperature correction factors for flexible cords and cables literally only applied to flexible cords and Table 400.5(A)(2). The literal language indicated that these provisions did not apply to flexible cables or to Table 400.5(A)(1). If temperature correction factors from Table 310.15(B)(2)(a) warrant being applied, there should be no difference in flexible cords or flexible cables. These temperature correction factors should apply to the ampacity values for both Table 400.5(A)(1) and Table 400.5(A)(2).

CMP-6 also added a sentence dealing with the use of correction factors for 105°C cords and cables as Table 310.15(B)(2)(a) does not include 105°C correction factors. In the absence of these values, 400.5(A) now indicates that it would be appropriate to use the ampacity values in the 90°C column from Table 310.15(B)(2)(a).

400.6(A)

Change at a Glance

Standard marking requirements for flexible cords and cables are now required to include the maximum operating temperature of the flexible cord or cable.

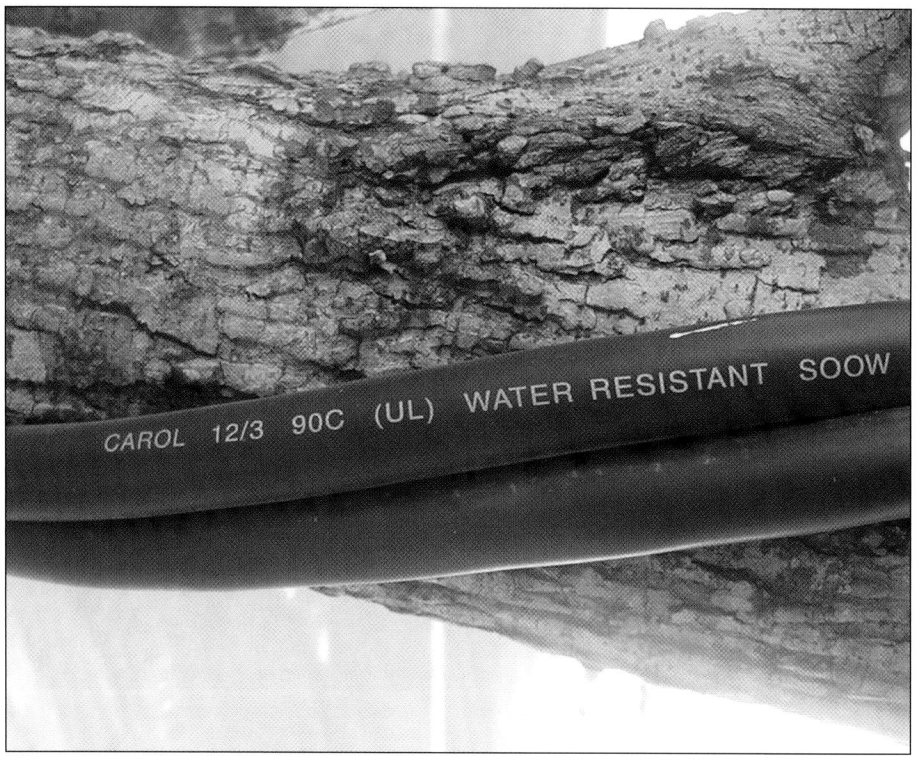

Code Language

400.6 Markings

(A) Standard Markings. Flexible cords and cables shall be marked by means of a printed tag attached to the coil reel or carton. The tag shall contain the information required in 310.120(A). Types S, SC, SCE, SCT, SE, SEO, SEOO, SJ, SJE, SJEO, SJEOO, SJO, SJT, SJTO, SJTOO, SO, SOO, ST, STO, STOO, SEW, SEOW, SEOOW, SJEW, SJEOW, SJEOOW, SJOW, SJTW, SJTOW, SJTOOW, SOW, SOOW, STW, STOW, and STOOW flexible cords and G, G-GC, PPE, and W flexible cables shall be durably marked on the surface at intervals not exceeding 610 mm (24 in.) with the type designation, size, and number of conductors. Required markings on tags, cords and cables shall also include the maximum operating temperature of the flexible cord or cable.

Proposal 6-100

2011 *NEC* Requirement

Flexible cords and cables are required to be marked by means of a printed tag attached to the coil reel or carton. This tag is required to identify the maximum rated voltage, the proper type letter or letters for the type of wire or cable involved, the manufacturer's name, trademark, or other distinctive marking, where the neutral conductor is smaller than the ungrounded conductors, and the AWG size or circular mil area. For most flexible cords or cables, the cord or cable is required to be durably marked on the surface at intervals not exceeding 610 mm (24 in.) with the type letter designation, size, and number of conductors.

2014 *NEC* Change

In addition to the standard marking requirements required in the previous *Code*, a new requirement was added to require flexible cords and cables or their associated tags to also include the maximum operating temperature of the flexible cord or cable.

Analysis of Change

A new requirement has been added at 400.6(A) Standard Marking to require markings on tags, flexible cords and cables to include the maximum operating temperature of the flexible cord or cable. Listed cords or cables may include a temperature marking, but not all flexible cords are required to be listed. With the maximum operating temperature marked on the flexible cord or cable, it would then be possible for an end user of this product to calculate the ampacity of a cord or cable in an ambient temperature if other than 30°C (86° F).

400.7(A)(11)

Change at a Glance

A flexible cord between an existing receptacle outlet and an inlet, where the inlet provides power to an additional single receptacle outlet as a listed assembly is now permitted.

NEW

Code Language

400.7 Uses Permitted

(A) Uses. Flexible cords and cables shall be used only for the following:

*[Items **(1)** through **(10)** unchanged. See NEC for complete text]*

(11) Between an existing receptacle outlet and an inlet, where the inlet provides power to an additional single receptacle outlet. The wiring interconnecting the inlet to the single receptacle outlet shall be a Chapter 3 wiring method. The inlet, receptacle outlet, and Chapter 3 wiring method, including the flexible cord and fittings, shall be a listed assembly specific for this application.

Proposal 6-101

Comment 6-71

400.7(A)(11) Uses Permitted (Flexible Cords)

A flexible cord between an existing receptacle outlet and an inlet, where the inlet provides power to an additional single receptacle outlet as a listed assembly is now permitted.

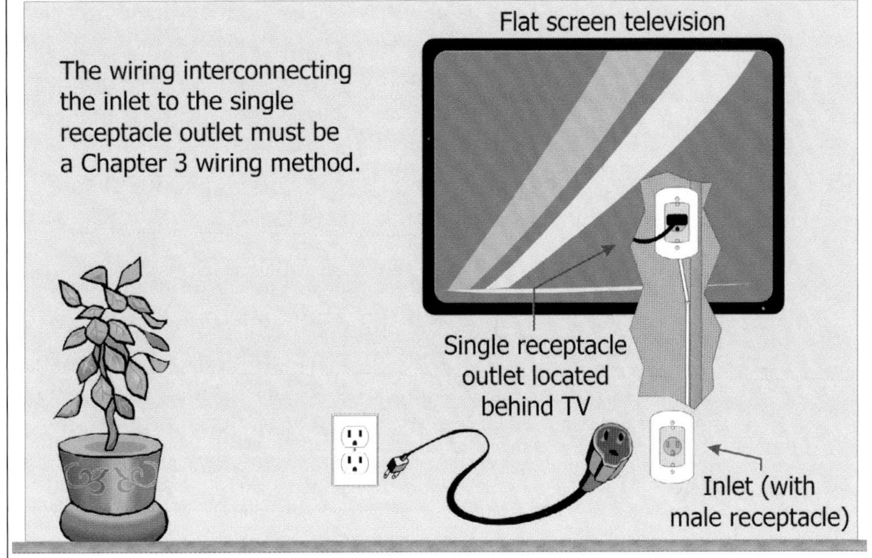
Flat screen television
The wiring interconnecting the inlet to the single receptacle outlet must be a Chapter 3 wiring method.
Single receptacle outlet located behind TV
Inlet (with male receptacle)

2011 *NEC* Requirement

Flexible cords and cables are permitted to be used with or for pendants, wiring of luminaires, connection of portable luminaires, portable and mobile signs, or appliances, elevator cables, wiring of cranes and hoists, connection of utilization equipment to facilitate frequent interchange, prevention of the transmission of noise or vibration, appliances where designed to permit ready removal and the appliance is intended or identified for flexible cord connection, connection of moving parts, and where specifically permitted elsewhere in the *Code*.

2014 *NEC* Change

In addition to the uses permitted in the previous edition of the *Code*, a new provision was added allowing a flexible cord to be used between an existing receptacle outlet and an inlet, where the inlet provides power to an additional single receptacle outlet. Part of this new allowance requires the wiring interconnecting the inlet to the single receptacle outlet to be a Chapter 3 wiring method. The inlet, receptacle outlet, and Chapter 3 wiring method, including the flexible cord and fittings, must be a "listed assembly" specific for this application.

Analysis of Change

This new provision is designed to allow newer and identified products primarily used for flat-screen televisions mounted on a wall. These products come as a listed assembly designed for this purpose. These listed assemblies typically come with a short flexible cord with a male cord cap to plug into an existing 120-volt receptacle outlet. The other end is typically a female cord cap designed to plug on to a male inlet outlet device that is part of the listed assembly. A 2.1 m (7 ft) nonmetallic-sheathed cable assembly is typically provided to connect from the inlet to a single inlet receptacle outlet located behind the wall-mounted flat-screen television. This 2.1 m (7 ft) nonmetallic-sheathed cable assembly is designed to be fished in the wall behind the finished wall surface and is provided with a nonmetallic-sheathed cable interconnector device in the middle of the assembly. These products are listed as an assembly, but there was no code language in the *NEC* that allowed the flexible cord from the existing receptacle outlet to the inlet device. The wiring in the wall from the inlet to the single receptacle outlet behind the flat-screen television would not be connected to the wiring system of the building, but would be energized only when the provided flexible cord (similar to a computer monitor power cord) is utilized to energize the listed flanged inlet. These products are typically listed with two sets of cords (with a Type NM interconnector device) and both flanged inlet and single outlet receptacle.

Without this new "Uses Permitted" provision, 400.8(1) could easily be interpreted by the AHJ as disallowing the use of this type of system as flexible cords or cables are not permitted as a substitute for the fixed wiring of a structure. The addition of 400.7(A)(11) removes any ambiguity and clearly allows these listed assemblies for powering and protecting the receptacle outlet used to energize a wall-mounted flat-screen television and other similar equipment.

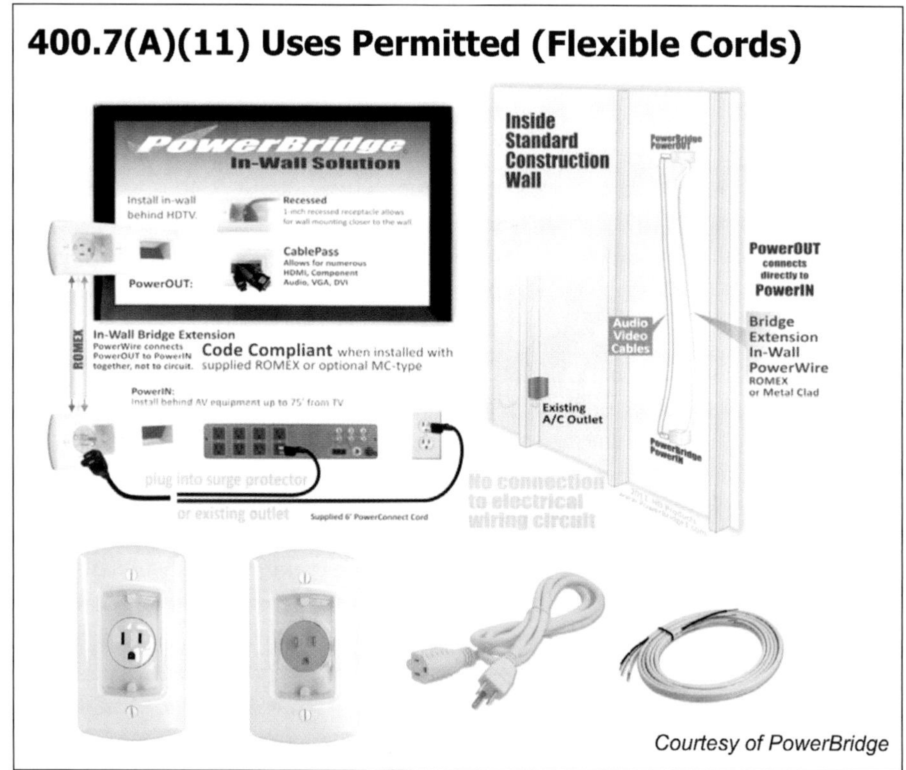

Courtesy of PowerBridge

404.2(C)

Change at a Glance

Requirements and exceptions for the grounded conductor at switching locations have been revised into positive text and rearranged into a list format.

Code Language

404.2 Switch Connections

(C) Switched Controlling Lighting Loads. The grounded circuit conductor for the controlled lighting circuit shall be provided at the ~~switch~~ location where switches control lighting loads that are supplied by a grounded general purpose branch circuit for other than the following:

1. Where conductors ~~for switches controlling lighting loads~~ enter the box enclosing the switch through a raceway, provided that the raceway is large enough for all contained conductors, including a grounded conductor. ~~The raceway shall have sufficient cross-sectional area to accommodate the extension of the grounded circuit conductor of the lighting circuit to the switch location whether or not the conductors in the raceway are required to be increased in size to comply with 310.15(B)(3)(a).~~

2. Where the box enclosing the switch is accessible for the installation of an additional or replacement cable without removing finish materials. ~~Cable assemblies for switches controlling lighting loads enter the box through a~~

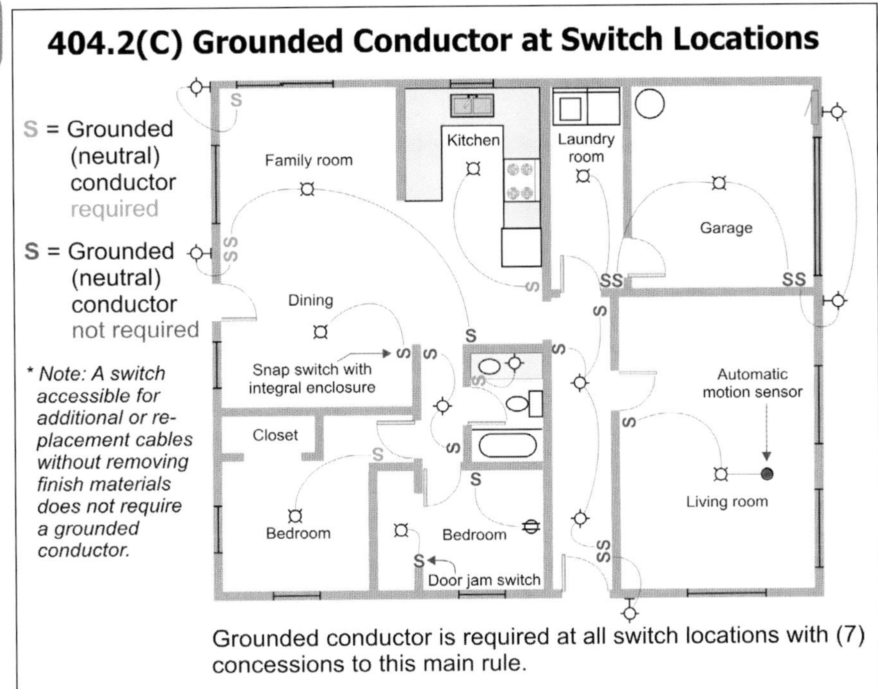

Grounded conductor is required at all switch locations with (7) concessions to this main rule.

2011 *NEC* Requirement

A grounded conductor was required at every switch location where switches control lighting loads supplied by a grounded general purpose branch circuit. This main rule had an exception with two specific conditions. The first exception permitted the grounded circuit conductor to be omitted from the switch enclosure where the wiring method employed was raceway systems that allow the grounded conductor to be added to the switch location at a later date, when and if needed. The raceway had to be of sufficient cross-sectional area to accommodate the addition of the grounded circuit conductor of the lighting circuit to the switch location. The other exception dealt with cable assemblies entering the switch box through a framing cavity that was open at the top or bottom on the same floor level, or through a wall, floor, or ceiling that is unfinished on one side.

2014 *NEC* Change

This subsection and the exception were revised to incorporate the exception (with two conditions) into positive text and to arrange the conditions to which a grounded conductor would not be required at the switch location into a simpler-to-use list format. Five new conditions were added along with two existing conditions described in the previous exception.

Analysis of Change

The provisions for requiring a grounded conductor at every switch location where switches control lighting loads supplied by a grounded general purpose branch circuit were added to the 2011 *NEC*. This 2011 *NEC* change requiring the presence of the grounded conductor was due in part to the influx of many electronic lighting control devices, such as occupancy sensors, that require a standby current to maintain a ready state of detection for the function of these devices. These devices typically require standby current even when they are in the "off" position. When the grounded conductor is not present, installers have been known to employ the equipment ground-

Continued

~~framing cavity that is open at the top or bottom on the same floor level, or through a wall, floor, or ceiling that is unfinished on one side.~~

3. Snap switches with integral enclosures complying with 300.15(E).

4. Where a switch does not serve a habitable room or bathroom.

5. Where multiple switch locations control the same lighting load such that the entire floor area of that room or space is visible from the single or combined switch locations.

6. Where lighting in the area is controlled by automatic means.

7. A switch controlling a receptacle load.

Proposal 9-89, 9-82, 9-83, 9-87, 9-88, 9-90, 9-91

Comment 9-44, 9-43, 9-45, 9-46

ing conductor for the standby current of these control devices. This is not a good practice due to the introduction of circulating current onto the equipment grounding conductor system.

For the 2014 *NEC*, there were several proposals and comments submitted to CMP-9 with suggested text and examples of switch locations where the presence of a grounded conductor might not be necessary. Some of these locations that are now incorporated into 404.2(C) included switch locations that do not serve a habitable room or bathroom, such as a closet light switch or a door-jam switch, where an occupancy sensor or other electronic device is highly unlikely to be installed. A room or area where two 3-way and/or 4-way switches are installed to serve the same area is another location where a grounded conductor is not required at every one of these switch locations. An occupancy or motion sensor would only be installed at one of these switch locations, not all of them. A grounded conductor installed at one of these switches would satisfy the requirements of 404.2(C).

Another switch location excused from the presence of a grounded conductor would be a switch controlling a receptacle outlet as allowed by 210.70(A)(1) Ex. No. 1. As no occupancy sensor will likely ever be listed for use with receptacle outlets, there is no need for a grounded conductor at this switch location. The connected load applied to receptacle outlets is inherently uncontrollable and unpredictable, in many aspects involving listing of occupancy sensors for same. Snap switches with integral enclosures complying with 300.15(E) are exempt from this grounded conductor requirement as well. Section 300.15(E) permits switches with integral enclosures "in lieu of a box or conduit body." These integral enclosure switches have no separate box for mounting other devices such as occupancy sensors or other electronic devices. One other switch location accepted that does not require a grounded conductor present was where automatic control of lighting has been provided. Some lighting designs use conventional snap switches at the conventional wall switch locations to turn lights on and off as needed, but in series with an occupancy sensor mounted in the ceiling. This allows for automatic lighting control when the room is unoccupied, but also allows a means to manually turn the lights off in an occupied room in order to project slides on a screen, etc.

Rather than add more exceptions to the existing exceptions, CMP-9 chose to incorporate the existing exceptions and the added provisions into a list format and to add positive language to this requirement. By addressing these issues, these additions and revisions should complete the action CMP-9 took for the 2011 *Code* cycle for grounded conductors at switch locations. An attempt was made to simplify the rule and to eliminate the lengthy and confusing exception. The opening paragraph to the main requirement was changed editorially to improve the structure and to complement the list of conditions that follow.

404.8(C)

Change at a Glance

Multipole snap switches that are rated not less than the system voltage (whether listed for multiple circuits or not) are no longer permitted to be fed from more than a single circuit.

Code Language

404.8 Accessibility and Grouping

(C) Multipole Snap Switches. A multipole, general-use snap switch shall not be permitted to be fed from more than a single circuit unless it is listed and marked as a two-circuit or three-circuit switch. ~~, or unless its voltage rating is not less than the nominal line-to-line voltage of the system supplying the circuits.~~

Proposal 9-97

Comment 9-47

404.8(C) Multipole Snap Switches

General-use multipole snap switches are not permitted to be fed from more than a single circuit unless listed and marked as a two-circuit or a three-circuit switch.

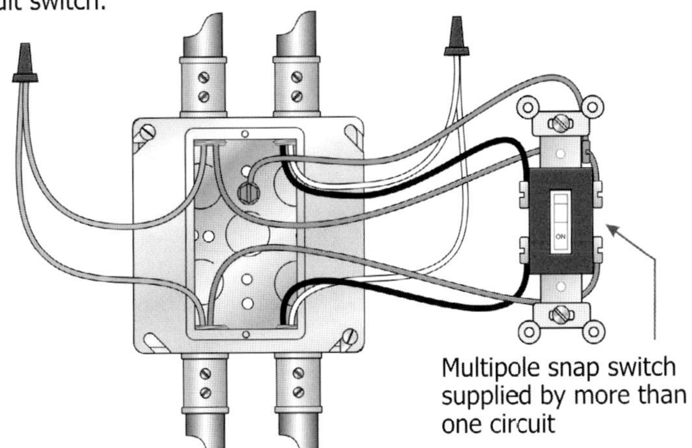

Multipole snap switches rated not less than the system voltage being allowed to be fed from more than a single circuit has been removed from 404.8(C).

2011 *NEC* Requirement

Multipole, general-use snap switches are not permitted to be fed from more than a single circuit unless listed and marked as a two-circuit or three-circuit switch. For the 2011 *NEC*, multipole snap switches rated not less than the system voltage were permitted to be fed from more than a single circuit.

2014 *NEC* Change

A multipole snap switch rated not less than the system voltage being allowed to be fed from more than a single circuit has been removed from the *Code*. Multipole, general-use snap switches listed and marked as a two-circuit or three-circuit switch are still permitted to be fed from more than a single circuit.

Analysis of Change

Previous language at 404.8(C) allowed a general-use multipole snap switch to be used for multi-circuit applications. Listed 2- and 3-pole general-use snap switches have not been evaluated for use in multi-circuit applications. In *UL Guide Information* (White Book), WJQR states, "Multi-pole, general-use snap switches have not been investigated for more than single-circuit operation unless marked '2-circuit' or '3-circuit.'" The reason this statement appears in the UL White Book is because there are different test requirements for 2- and 3-pole snap switches and 2- and 3-pole multi-circuit switches.

Multipole snap switches rated not less than the system voltage being allowed to be fed from more than a single circuit were added during the 2008 *Code* cycle. This addition generated discussions within the electrical industry and the UL Standards Technical Panel with responsibility for "General-Use Snap Switches" (STP 20) about including this allowance as an acknowledged use of these devices. It was concluded that a revision to STP 20 would be necessary and would need to include additional performance and marking re-

404.8(C)

Continued

quirements for this type of application. UL initiated a STP 20 Standards proposal that would include adding a definition of single-pole, 3-way, 4-way or 2-pole switches, and adding a definition of two- or three-circuit switches. The definitions were intended to identify that such switches are intended to be installed on multiple or multi-phase branch circuits controlling multiple or multi-phase loads of no more than 120 volts to ground and 240 volts line to line, 240 volts total per circuit. This STP proposal also sought to supplement the test requirements to indicate that marked "2-circuit and 3-circuit switches" are tested simultaneously with multiple supply and loads present to represent actual service conditions. The proposal was submitted to STP 20 members and consensus was achieved. The new requirements were published in February 2012. STP 20 now recognizes only snap switches marked "2-Circuit" or "3-Circuit" as suitable for use in a multi-circuit application. Products used in applications outside of their marked ratings would be a violation of *NEC* 110.3(B). The basic requirement for safety as stated in the initial sentence of 404.8(C) that multipole, general-use snap switches shall not be supplied from more than one circuit unless "listed and marked as a two-circuit or three-circuit switch." This is the only safe use of these products.

The proposal that generated this deletion first appeared as Comment 9-48 for Proposal 9-106 during the 2011 *NEC* procedures and was held for further study during that development process.

Change at a Glance

A new marking symbol for receptacle outlets controlled by an automatic control device or by an automatic energy management system. New requirement includes new Figure 406.3(E).

Code Language

406.3 Receptacle Rating and Type

(E) Controlled Receptacle Marking. All nonlocking-type, 125-volt, 15- and 20-ampere receptacles that are controlled by an automatic control device or incorporate control features that remove power from the outlet for the purpose of energy management or building automation shall be marked with the symbol shown below placed on the controlled receptacle outlet where visible after installation.

Figure 406.3(E) Controlled Receptacle Marking Symbol.

Exception: *The marking is not required for receptacles controlled by a wall switch as permitted by 210.70 to provide the required room lighting outlets.*

Proposal 18-15

406.3(E) Controlled Receptacle Marking

All nonlocking-type, 125-volt, 15- and 20-ampere receptacles controlled by an automatic control device, energy management, or building automation shall be marked with the "Controlled Receptacle Marking Symbol" from Figure 406.3(E) placed on the controlled receptacle outlet where visible after installation.

2011 *NEC* Requirement

Marking requirements for receptacles controlled by an automatic control device or by an automatic energy management system were not addressed in the 2011 *NEC*.

2014 *NEC* Change

A new subdivision entitled "Controlled Receptacle Marking" was added to 406.3, Receptacle Rating and Type. This subsection will require a new marking symbol for receptacle outlets controlled by an automatic control device or by an automatic energy management system. The new symbol was displayed in Figure 406.3(E). An exception follows this rule to indicate that this marking is not required for receptacle outlets controlled by a wall switch to provide the required room lighting outlet(s) as permitted by 210.70(A)(1) Ex. No. 1.

Analysis of Change

New energy management codes are currently being widely adopted. One such energy management code is ASHRAE 90.1 *Energy Standard for Buildings Except Low-Rise Residential Buildings*. This code requires that up to 50 percent of all 125-volt, 15- and 20-ampere receptacles be automatically controlled. The control could be an energy management system, a timer or a sensor. The occupant or end user needs to know which receptacle outlets will be automatically controlled and which receptacles will be energized continually. This will avoid plugging in loads, such as a refrigerator or appliance, and being unintentionally turned off for a period of time. Automated systems typically control identified loads such as lighting or HVAC equipment, with the consequences known and understood. The uncertainty of what is plugged into a controlled receptacle outlet can raise concerns regarding safety as well as convenience; thus it is important to be able to readily identify receptacle outlets that will be automatically powered on and off.

406.4(D)

Change at a Glance

AFCI- and GFCI-type replacement receptacles are required to be installed in a readily accessible location.

Code Language

406.4 General Installation Requirements

Receptacle outlets shall be located in branch circuits in accordance with Part III of Article 210. General installation requirements shall be in accordance with 406.4(A) through (F).

(D) Replacements. Replacement of receptacles shall comply with 406.4(D)(1) through (D)(6), as applicable. Arc- fault circuit-interrupter and ground-fault circuit-interrupter type receptacles shall be installed in a readily accessible location.

Proposal 18-18

406.4(D) Replacement Receptacles

AFCI and GFCI-type receptacles installed for replacement receptacles are required to be installed in a readily accessible location.

2011 *NEC* Requirement

When an existing receptacle is replaced, grounding-type receptacles are required to be used where a grounding means exists in the receptacle enclosure. Where an equipment grounding conductor does not exist in the receptacle enclosure, three options are available: (1) a non–grounding-type receptacle is permitted to be replaced with another non–grounding-type receptacle; (2) a non–grounding-type receptacle(s) is permitted to be replaced with a GFCI-type of receptacle; or (3) a non–grounding-type receptacle is permitted to be replaced with a grounding-type receptacle where supplied through a GFCI.

GFCI-protected receptacles are required where replacements are made at receptacle outlets that are required to be so protected elsewhere in the *Code*. Where a receptacle outlet is supplied by a branch circuit that requires AFCI protection as specified elsewhere in the *Code*, a replacement receptacle at this outlet must be provided with AFCI protection. Listed tamper-resistant receptacles and weather-resistant receptacles shall be provided where replacements are made at receptacle outlets that are required to be tamper-resistant or weather-resistant elsewhere in this *Code*.

2014 *NEC* Change

In addition to the replacement receptacle requirements of the previous edition of the *Code*, a new sentence was added to the main text at 406.4(D) to require arc-fault circuit-interrupter (AFCI) and ground-fault circuit-interrupter (GFCI) type replacement receptacles to be installed in a readily accessible location.

Analysis of Change

This new requirement for replacement of receptacles was initiated to align the "readily accessible" requirements for GFCI devices stated at 210.8 with the rules for GFCI and AFCI protective devices required at 406.4(D). The readily accessible requirement for GFCI receptacles governed at 210.8 was added to the 2011

NEC. Justification for the readily accessible rule at 210.8 was primarily related to occupant or user accessibility to the monthly testing and access to the reset features of the device. Just like GFCI protection, AFCI protection can also be accomplished by circuit breaker types or outlet-type devices which have the same monthly testing and reset features. Ready accessibility to these protective devices for replacement receptacles should not be different from that for GFCI devices covered at 210.8.

It should be noted that this readily accessible requirement pertains only to AFCI and GFCI outlet devices used for replacement of existing receptacles due to its placement at 406.4(D).

406.5(E)

Change at a Glance

Restrictions to prohibit receptacles from being installed in the face-up position expanded to all occupancies, not just dwelling units. Listed receptacle assemblies for countertop applications have been recognized for this application as well.

REVISION

Code Language

406.5 Receptacle Mounting

Receptacles shall be mounted in identified boxes or assemblies. ~~designed for the purpose, and such.~~ The boxes or assemblies shall be securely fastened in place unless otherwise permitted elsewhere in this *Code*. Screws used for the purpose of attaching receptacles to a box, shall be of the type provided with a listed receptacle, or machine screws having 32 threads per inch, or part of listed assemblies or systems, in accordance with the manufacturer's instructions.

(E) Receptacles in Countertops and Similar Work Surfaces ~~in Dwelling Units~~. Receptacles, unless listed as receptacle assemblies for countertop applications, shall not be installed in a face-up position in countertops or similar work surfaces. Where receptacles assemblies for countertop applications are required to provide ground-fault circuit-interrupter protection for personnel in accordance with 210.8, such assemblies shall be permitted to be

406.5(E) Receptacles in Countertops and Similar Work Surfaces ~~in Dwelling Units~~

Restriction to prohibit receptacles from being installed in the face-up position is expanded to all occupancies *(not just dwelling units)*

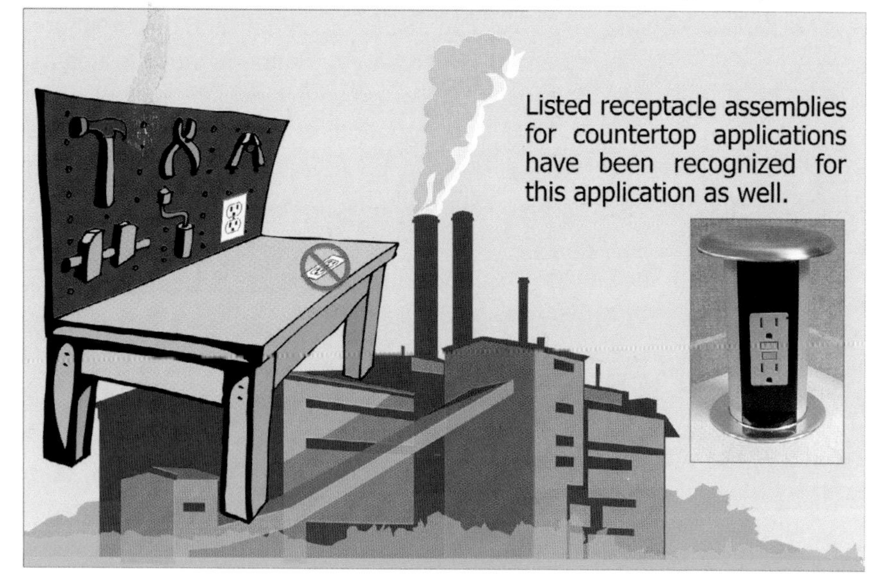
Listed receptacle assemblies for countertop applications have been recognized for this application as well.

2011 *NEC* Requirement

Receptacles were prohibited from being installed in a face-up position in countertops or similar work surfaces, but this prohibition applied to dwelling units only.

2014 *NEC* Change

The words "in Dwelling Units" were removed from the title of 406.5(E) to make it clear that receptacles cannot be installed in a face-up position in countertops or similar work surfaces of any type occupancy, not just dwelling units. Language was added to recognize listed receptacle assemblies for countertop applications.

Analysis of Change

If there is concern about receptacles installed in the face-up position at dwelling units countertops or similar work surfaces for such things as liquid spillage, these same concerns exist at countertops or similar work surfaces of non-dwelling units as well. Whereas 406.5(E) applied only to dwelling units in previous editions of the *Code*, this face-up prohibition now applies to all countertops or similar work surfaces, not just at dwelling units.

Section 406.5(E) also now recognizes "listed receptacle assemblies" for countertop applications. ANSI/UL 498-2012 *Standard for Safety for Attachment Plugs and Receptacles* in Sections 143, 144 and 146, and ANSI/UL 943-2012 *Standard for Safety for Ground-Fault Circuit-Interrupters* in Sections 6.28 – 6.29, specifically evaluate and list receptacle assemblies and GFCI receptacle assemblies for countertop applications. For assemblies that retract into the countertop, these evaluations include 6000 cycles of mechanical endurance of the retraction mechanism, followed by dielectric-voltage withstand (also leakage current if a GFCI receptacle), and a spill test using a half-gallon of saline solution tipped onto the same assembly. Further, if the assembly depends upon a self-closing

406.5(E)

Continued

listed as GFCI receptacle assemblies for countertop applications.

Proposal 18-32, 18-33, 18-34

Comment 18-21, 18-23

cover to achieve spill resistance and the receptacle (or GFCI receptacle) has more than one outlet, a single power supply cord is engaged in only one outlet and the cord exits the cover in its released natural resting position before conducting the spill test.

There is some new language in the main text of 406.5 pertaining to nonconforming screws, such as drywall screws, not being permitted to be used to mount or secure receptacles to a box. Similar provisions have been introduced in 314.25 for attaching box covers or other equipment fastened to a box (see Proposal 9-55), in 404.10(B) for mounting of switches (see Proposal 9-98 and Comment 9-52), and in 406.5 for mounting of receptacles (see Proposal 18-30 and Comment 18-20) restricting the use of nonconforming screws for installing or attaching these devices to boxes. This change is reported in full at 314.25 of this textbook.

406.5(F)

Change at a Glance

New provisions were added which prohibit receptacles from being installed in a face-up position in seating areas or similar surfaces unless they are part of an assembly listed for the application.

Code Language

406.5 Receptacle Mounting

Receptacles shall be mounted in identified boxes or assemblies ~~designed for the purpose, and such~~. The boxes or assemblies shall be securely fastened in place unless otherwise permitted elsewhere in this *Code*. Screws used for the purpose of attaching receptacles to a box, shall be of the type provided with a listed receptacle, or machine screws having 32 threads per inch, or part of listed assemblies or systems, in accordance with the manufacturer's instructions.

(F) Receptacles in Seating Areas and Other Similar Surfaces. In seating areas or similar surfaces, receptacles shall not be installed in a face-up position unless the receptacle is any of the following:
(1) Part of an assembly listed as a furniture power distribution unit, if cord-and-plug-connected
(2) Part of an assembly listed either as household furnishings or as commercial furnishings
(3) Listed either as a receptacle assembly for countertop applications or as a GFCI receptacle assembly for countertop applications.
(4) Installed in a listed floor box.

Proposal 18-34

Comment 18-23

406.5(F) Receptacles in Seating Areas and Other Similar Surfaces

New provisions added which prohibits receptacles from being installed in a "face-up" position in seating areas or similar surfaces unless they are part of an assembly listed for the application.

2011 *NEC* Requirement

No provisions existed in the 2011 *NEC* dealing with or prohibiting receptacles from being mounted in seating areas or similar surfaces.

2014 *NEC* Change

A new subdivision (F) Receptacles in Seating Areas and Other Similar Surfaces was added to 406.5 to prohibit receptacles from being installed in a face-up position in seating areas or similar surfaces unless they are part of an assembly listed for the application.

Analysis of Change

Receptacles are presently not permitted to be installed in a face-up position in countertops or similar work surfaces by the requirements at 406.5(E). Recently, receptacles are being installed in and on benches and seating areas in public locations such as airports. These are typically installed so that someone can sit on these benches and use the supplied 125-volt receptacle outlet for a laptop computer, or to charge a cell phone or other electronic hand-held device. In some cases, these receptacles are installed in the face-up position. This represents a hazard-in-waiting as it is possible, in some cases, to sit on the receptacle itself. Spillage of water, soft drinks, etc., is another issue involving these face-up receptacles. Where there is a need to install such receptacles in benches or other similar surfaces, it should be done with an assembly listed for the application to prevent damage and potential exposure to energized conductors or circuit parts.

For the 2014 *NEC*, strict language was adopted in 406.5(F) that will require receptacles in seating areas or similar surfaces to not be installed in the face-up position unless the receptacle is part of an assembly listed as a furniture power distribution unit (if cord-and-plug-connected) listed to UL Product Standard 962A, or as household or commercial furnishings listed to UL Product Standard 962. These seat-mounted receptacles can also be listed as a receptacle assembly, or as a GFCI receptacle assembly for countertop applications, or installed in a listed floor box.

406.9(B)(1)

Change at a Glance

Extra duty covers are now required for all 15- and 20-ampere, 125- and 250-volt receptacles installed in a wet location (not just for those supported from grade). This requirement also includes dwelling unit wet location receptacles as well.

Code Language

406.9 Receptacles in Damp or Wet Locations

(B) Wet Locations.

(1) 15- and 20-Ampere Receptacles in a Wet Location. 15- and 20-ampere, 125- and 250-volt receptacles installed in a wet location shall have an enclosure that is weatherproof whether or not the attachment plug cap is inserted. ~~For other than one- or two-family dwellings,~~ An outlet box hood installed for this purpose shall be listed, and ~~where installed on an enclosure supported from grade as described in 314.23(B) or as described in 314.23(F)~~ shall be identified as "extra-duty." All 15- and 20- ampere, 125- and 250-volt nonlocking-type receptacles shall be listed weather-resistant type.

Proposal 18-37, 18-38, 18-35, 18-36

2011 *NEC* Requirement

All 15- and 20-ampere, 125- and 250-volt receptacles installed in wet locations are required to have an enclosure and cover that are weatherproof whether a cord cap is inserted or not. An outlet box hood cover installed for this purpose must be listed, and where installed on an enclosure supported from grade, this outlet box hood cover had to be identified as an "extra-duty" type cover. This extra duty hood cover did not apply to dwelling unit receptacles in the 2011 *NEC*. All 15- and 20-ampere, 125- and 250-volt nonlocking-type receptacles installed in wet locations must also be of the listed weather-resistant type.

2014 *NEC* Change

All 15- and 20-ampere, 125- and 250-volt receptacles installed in a wet location still must have an enclosure and covers that are weatherproof whether an attachment plug cap is inserted or not. A revision now requires *all* enclosures and covers installed in wet locations for 15- and 20-ampere, 125- and 250-volt receptacles to be listed and of the "extra duty" type, not just boxes supported from grade. This requirement is now also required at dwelling units as well. The requirement for weather-resistant type receptacles in wet locations is still applicable in the 2014 *NEC*.

Analysis of Change

Revisions to 406.9(B)(1) have leveled the playing field for dwelling units and for non-dwelling unit wet locations as far as "extra duty" enclosures and covers are concerned. The "in-use" covers for wet location 15- and 20-ampere, 125- and 250-volt receptacles must all be of the extra duty type regardless of its occupancy type location. The requirements for these more rigidly-constructed extra duty covers or hoods at in-use covers for receptacles installed in wet locations were instituted in the 2011 *NEC*. The durability of the nonmetallic in-use cover hoods provided for compliance with these wet location requirements has been found to be less than desirable, especially

406.9(B)(1)

Continued

on construction sites. Breakage and hinge failure to these nonmetallic hood covers has been reported at dwelling units and at non-dwelling units, leaving the receptacles exposed to all weather conditions. The more rigorous performance requirements in UL Product Standard 514D *Standard for Cover Plates for Flush-Mounted Wiring Devices* for these extra duty in-use outlet box hood covers has improved the general durability of all listed in-use covers.

Another revision calls for these extra duty covers at all wet location 15- and 20-ampere, 125- and 250-volt receptacles, not just at the ones that are supported from grade. If the receptacle is installed in a wet location, it should make no difference how the enclosure or device box is installed or supported when determining the need for an extra duty hood cover.

Perhaps the next step in this extra duty hood cover journey would be to define what an extra duty hood cover is for installers, enforcers, and users of the *Code*.

406.12

Change at a Glance

Exception for tamper-resistant receptacles at dwelling units has been expanded to guest rooms and guest suites of hotels and motels and to child care facilities.

Code Language

406.12 Tamper-Resistant Receptacles ~~in Dwelling Units~~
Tamper resistant receptacles shall be installed as specified in 406.12(A) through (C).

(A) Dwelling Units. In all areas specified in 210.52, all nonlocking-type 125-volt, 15- and 20-ampere receptacles shall be listed tamper-resistant receptacles.

(B) Guest Rooms and Guest Suites of Hotels and Motels. All nonlocking-type 125-volt, 15- and 20-ampere receptacles located in guest rooms and guest suites of hotels and motels shall be listed tamper-resistant receptacles.

(C) Child Care Facilities. In all child care facilities, all nonlocking-type 125-volt, 15- and 20-ampere receptacles shall be listed tamper resistant receptacles.

Exception to (A), (B), and (C): *Receptacles in the following locations shall not be required to be tamper-resistant:*
(1) *Receptacles located more than 1.7 m (5 ½ ft) above the floor.*

406.12 Tamper-Resistant Receptacles

Exception for tamper-resistant receptacles at dwelling units has been expanded to guest rooms and guest suites of hotels and motels and child care facilities.

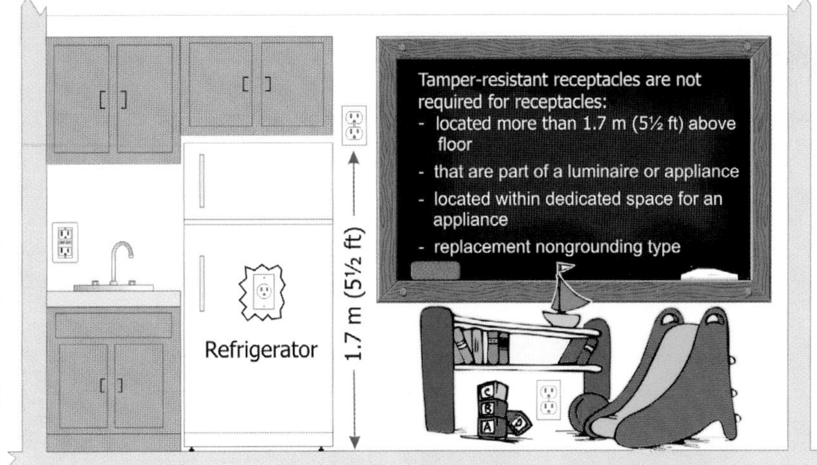

Tamper-resistant receptacles are not required for receptacles:
- located more than 1.7 m (5½ ft) above floor
- that are part of a luminaire or appliance
- located within dedicated space for an appliance
- replacement nongrounding type
Refrigerator
1.7 m (5½ ft)

All nonlocking type 125-volt, 15- and 20-ampere receptacles in hotel/motel guest rooms/suites and child care facilities are required to be listed tamper-resistant receptacles.

2011 *NEC* Requirement

In all areas specified in 210.52 (which are the majority of the areas of a dwelling unit), all nonlocking-type 125-volt, 15- and 20-ampere receptacles are required to be listed tamper-resistant receptacles with an exception for four specific locations or areas. Dwelling unit receptacles exempted from the tamper-resistant receptacle requirement are those located more than 1.7 m (5 ½ ft) above the floor, receptacles that are part of a luminaire or appliance, receptacles located in a dedicated appliance space, and non–grounding-type replacement receptacles. All nonlocking-type 125-volt, 15- and 20-ampere receptacles located in guest rooms and guest suites of hotels and motels and in child care facilities were required to be listed tamper-resistant receptacles.

2014 *NEC* Change

The exception for tamper-resistant receptacles with four specific locations or areas that applied only to dwelling units in the 2011 *NEC*, now applies to dwelling units, guest rooms and guest suites of hotels and motels, and to child care facilities.

Analysis of Change

Tamper-resistant receptacles for dwelling units were introduced in the 2008 *NEC* in an effort to prevent small children from inserting foreign objects (*paper clips, keys, etc.*) into energized electrical receptacles. In 2011 *NEC*, an exception (affecting four areas) was added to 406.12 for tamper-resistant receptacles. Tamper-resistant receptacle requirements for guest rooms and guest suites of hotels and motels [406.13] and for child care facilities [406.14] were also added to the 2011 *NEC*. These three sections for tamper-resistant receptacles were combined into one section, with the exception that applied to dwelling units being moved to apply to all three occupancies for the 2014 *NEC*. The exception with the four specified locations that was added to the 2011 *NEC* for dwelling units was warranted, but these exceptions are also needed for guest rooms and guest suites of hotels and

Continued

(2) Receptacles that are part of a luminaire or appliance.

(3) A single receptacle or a duplex receptacle for two appliances located within dedicated space for each appliance that, in normal use, is not easily moved from one place to another and that is cord-and plug-connected in accordance with 400.7(A)(6), (A)(7), or (A)(8).

(4) Nongrounding receptacles used for replacements as permitted in 406.4(D)(2)(a).

~~**406.13**~~ *(Deleted)*
~~**406.14**~~ *(Deleted)*

Proposal 18-41a, 18-44, 18-46, 18-48, 18-49, 18-50, 18-51, 18-52

Comment 18-25

motels and for child care facilities. These exempted locations — whether in a dwelling, hotel room, or a child care facility — are out of reach of small children and should be exempted for tamper-resistant receptacle provisions.

For guest rooms and guest suites, the words "of hotels and motels" were added for clarity to indicate exactly which type of guest rooms and guest suites are being discussed at 406.12(B).

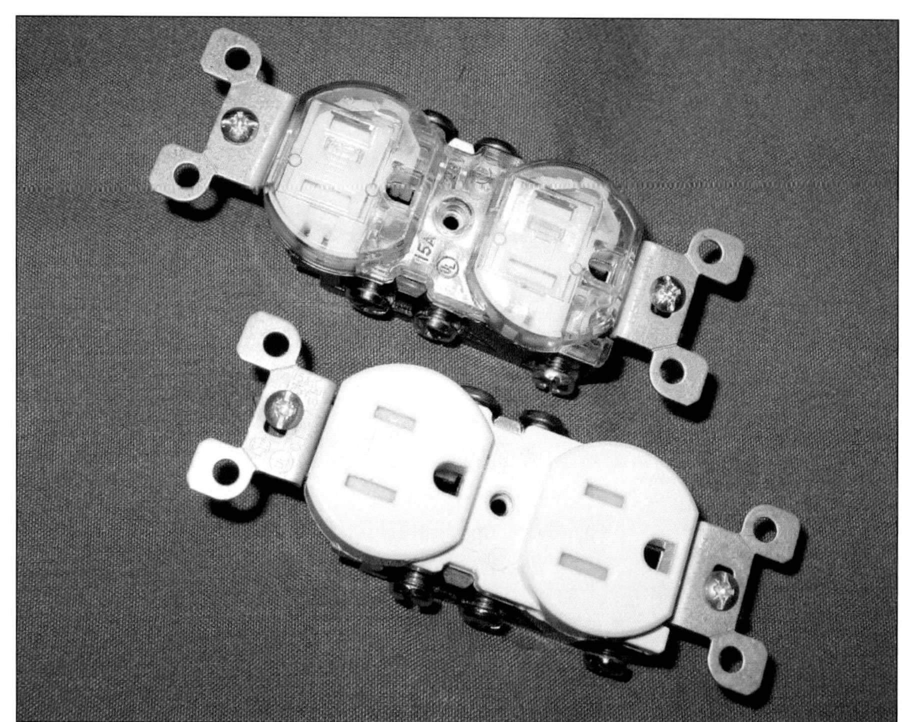

406.15

Change at a Glance

Dimmer-controlled receptacles are now permitted for a plug/receptacle combination in listed nonstandard configuration types.

Code Language

406.15 Dimmer Controlled Receptacles

A receptacle supplying lighting loads shall not be connected to a dimmer unless the plug/receptacle combination is a nonstandard configuration type that is specifically listed and identified for each such unique combination.

Proposal 18-53

406.15 Dimmer Controlled Receptacles

A receptacle supplying lighting loads shall not be connected to a dimmer unless the plug/receptacle combination is a nonstandard configuration type that is specifically listed and identified for each such unique combination.

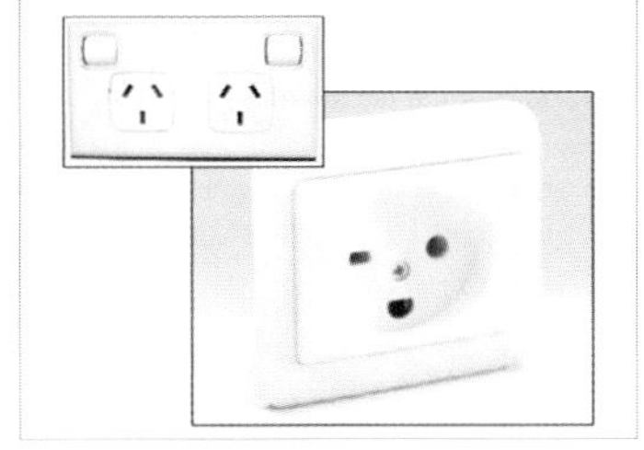

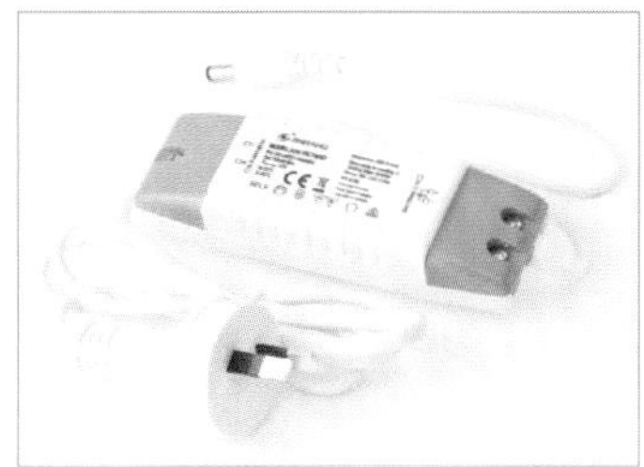

2011 *NEC* Requirement

Dimmer switches are generally to be used only to control permanently installed incandescent luminaires unless listed for the control of other loads and installed accordingly. Dimmer switches are generally not permitted to control receptacle outlets. This provision appears at 404.14(E). There was no language in Article 406 dealing with dimmer-controlled receptacles in the 2011 *NEC*.

2014 *NEC* Change

A new section was added at 406.15 to permit specific receptacles to be controlled by a dimmer under specific conditions. A receptacle supplying lighting loads can be connected to a dimmer if the plug/receptacle combination is a nonstandard configuration type and is specifically listed and identified for each such unique combination.

Analysis of Change

The electrical industry is starting to see 120-volt cord- and plug-connected lighting such as rope lighting being installed under shelving or under cabinets. To power this lighting, conventional 120-volt receptacle outlets are being employed. The concerns begin when the occupant complains that the lighting is too bright and wants to control this cord- and plug-connected lighting with a dimmer. Some of the manufacturers of these lighting sources provide a dimming feature that is listed with their product. Clear, concise code language was needed to ensure that standard grade receptacles cannot be controlled from any dimming or voltage dropping device. This new provision will require a receptacle supplying lighting loads from a dimmer, only if the plug/receptacle combination is a nonstandard configuration type and is specifically listed and identified for each such unique combination.

Article 408 and 408.1

Change at a Glance

The title of Article 408 was changed to "Switchboards, Switchgear, and Panelboards," and the scope of Article 408 was revised to reflect this revision.

Code Language

Article 408 Switchboards, Switchgear, and Panelboards

408.1 Scope: This article covers switchboards, switchgear, and panelboards. It does not apply to equipment operating at over ~~600~~ 1000 volts, except as specifically referenced elsewhere in the *Code*.

Proposal 9-104a, 9-103a, 9-104, 9-105, 9-106

Comment 9-55, 9-56

2011 *NEC* Requirement

Article 408 covered requirements for switchboards and panelboards operating at 600 volts or less. There was a definition of *metal-enclosed power switchgear* at Article 100, and this term was used intermittently throughout Article 408.

2014 *NEC* Change

The title of Article 408 was changed to "Switchboards, Switchgear, and Panelboards," and the scope of Article 408 was revised to reflect this revision. The definition of *metal-enclosed power switchgear* in Article 100 was revised and changed to *switchgear*. Wherever the term *metal-enclosed power switchgear* was used in Article 408, it was replaced with *switchgear*. The voltage limitation of 600 volts was replaced with 1000 volts in the scope and throughout the article to reflect the code-wide revision in this direction.

Analysis of Change

The previous definition in Article 100 for *metal-enclosed power switchgear* was modified and retitled simply *switchgear* to make it inclusive of all types of switchgear under the purview of the *NEC*. The new definition creates the opportunity to utilize the generic term in all locations where the term *switchboard* was previously mentioned, and where the use of the term *switchgear* is appropriate. The term *switchgear* includes *metal-enclosed low-voltage power circuit breaker switchgear, metal-clad switchgear,* and *metal-enclosed interrupter switchgear* according to ANSI C37.20 documents. This change also draws the distinction between a switchboard and switchgear by identifying the two pieces of equipment separately in the scope of Article 408.

408.3(E)

Change at a Glance

A new "DC Bus Arrangement" was added for dc ungrounded buses.

Code Language

408.3 Support and Arrangement of Busbars and Conductors

(E) ~~Phase~~ Bus Arrangement.

(1) AC Phase Arrangement. ~~The~~ AC phase arrangement on 3-phase buses shall be A, B, C from front to back, top to bottom, or left to right, as viewed from the front of the switchboard, switchgear, or panelboard. The B phase shall be that phase having the higher voltage to ground on 3-phase, 4-wire, delta-connected systems. Other busbar arrangements shall be permitted for additions to existing installations and shall be marked.

Exception: *Equipment within the same single section or multisection switchboard, switchgear, or panelboard as the meter on 3-phase, 4-wire, delta-connected systems shall be permitted to have the same phase configuration as the metering equipment.*

(2) DC Bus Arrangement. DC ungrounded buses shall be permitted to be in any order. Arrangement of dc buses shall be field marked as to polarity, grounding system, and nominal voltage.

Proposal 9-103a, 9-110

Comment 9-55, 9-62

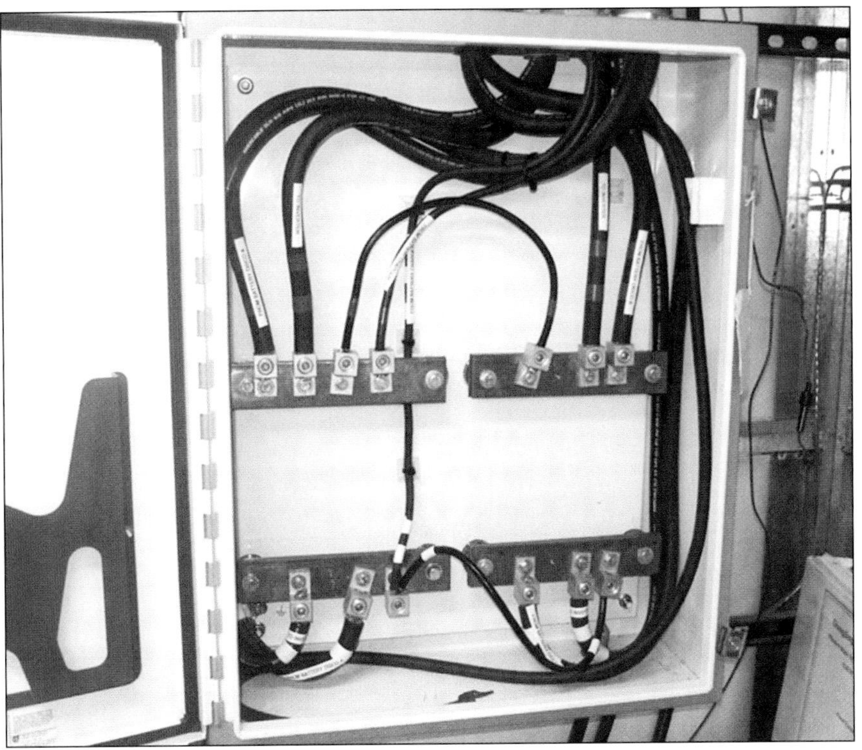

2011 *NEC* Requirement

Section 408.3(E) addressed the bus or phase arrangement for ac systems only. There were no provisions for the bus arrangement for dc systems in the 2011 *NEC*. The general phase arrangement requirement for an ac 3-phase bus system is phases A, B, C from front to back, top to bottom, or left to right, as viewed from the front of the switchboard or panelboard. The B phase shall be that phase having the higher voltage to ground on 3-phase, 4-wire, delta-connected systems.

2014 *NEC* Change

Provisions were added addressing dc bus arrangements. Ungrounded dc buses are permitted to be in any order. Arrangement of dc buses is to be field marked as to polarity, grounding system, and nominal voltage.

Analysis of Change

The previous edition of the *Code* dealing with specific requirements for ac bus arrangements left the user of the *Code* with vague information as to whether there was a proper arrangement in dc systems for the bus arrangement. Even if there is not a specific reason to have an exact dc bus arrangement, labeling of these busses is crucial for installers and maintenance personnel. Section 406.3(E)(2) now requires dc buses to be field marked with the applied polarity, grounding system, and nominal voltage. These are field marking requirements as the manufacturer may not know the grounding system. Voltage marking is required for both ac and dc systems (*see 408.58*). The proposal mainly responsible for this change was developed by a subgroup of the NEC DC Task Force of the NEC Correlating Committee.

408.4(B)

Change at a Glance

A revision was added to indicate that switchboards, switchgear, and panelboards can have more than one source of power.

REVISION

Code Language

408.4 Field Identification Required

(B) Source of Supply. All switchboards, switchgear, and panelboards supplied by a feeder(s) in other than one- or two-family dwellings shall be marked to indicate ~~the~~ each device or equipment where the power ~~supply~~ originates.

Proposal 9–116, 9–103a

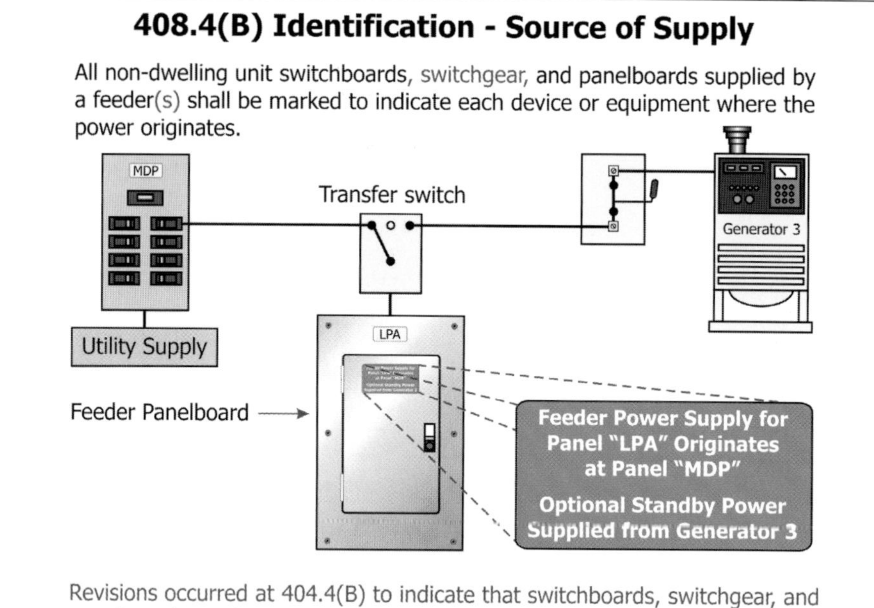
408.4(B) Identification - Source of Supply
All non-dwelling unit switchboards, switchgear, and panelboards supplied by a feeder(s) shall be marked to indicate each device or equipment where the power originates.
MDP
Transfer switch
Generator 3
Utility Supply
LPA
Feeder Panelboard
Feeder Power Supply for Panel "LPA" Originates at Panel "MDP"
Optional Standby Power Supplied from Generator 3

Revisions occurred at 404.4(B) to indicate that switchboards, switchgear, and panelboards can have more than one source of power.

2011 *NEC* Requirement

A new provision was added to the 2011 *NEC* to indicate that all switchboards and panelboards supplied by a feeder in other than one- or two-family dwellings shall be marked to indicate the device or equipment where the power supply originates. This language indicated (whether intended or not) that switchboards and panelboards could have only one source of power.

2014 *NEC* Change

The text at 408.4(B) was revised to add plural language such as "feeder(s)" to clarify that all switchboards, switchgear, and panelboards can have more than one source of power.

Analysis of Change

During the 2011 *NEC* development process, a provision was added to Article 408 for source of supply for all non-dwelling unit switchboards and panelboards supplied by a feeder to be marked as to the specific device or equipment where the power supply originates. Often in industrial and commercial occupancies, the facility will be supplied with multiple switchboards, switchgear, and panelboards located throughout the buildings or around the premises. This situation can make it difficult to locate the source of supply for individual switchboard, switchgear, or panelboard. This power supply identification practice enhances the safety for the electrical personnel who service these switchboards, switchgear, and panelboards.

It is not uncommon at all to see the electrical systems of today's electrical distribution network schemes utilizing optional standby systems, legally required standby systems or emergency systems for buildings such as hospitals and high rise office buildings. The one thing all these systems have in common is an additional source of electrical power, whether it is a generator, storage batteries, or a second electrical service. This revision to 408.4(B) clarifies that switchboards, switchgear, and panelboards that have more than one source of power must be clearly marked to indicate not only where the normal source of power originates, but any additional sources.

408.55

Change at a Glance

Section 408.55 was reorganized into a list format of types of bending spaces. Wire-bending space for rear entry, with a removable cover on the opposite wall of enclosure, is incorporated as well.

Code Language

408.55 Wire-Bending Space Within an Enclosure Containing a Panelboard

(A) Top and Bottom Wire-Bending Space. The enclosure for a panelboard shall have the top and bottom wire-bending space sized in accordance with Table 312.6(B) for the largest conductor entering or leaving the enclosure. ~~Side wire-bending space shall be in accordance with Table 312.6(A) for the largest conductor to be terminated in that space.~~

Exception No. 1 through Exception No. 4: *(Text unchanged. See NEC for complete text.)*

(B) Side Wire-Bending Space. Side wire-bending space shall be in accordance with Table 312.6(A) for the largest conductor to be terminated in that space.

(C) Back Wire-Bending Space. Where a raceway or cable entry is in the wall of the enclosure opposite a removable cover, the distance from that wall to the cover shall be permitted to comply with the distance required for one wire per terminal in Table 312.6(A). The distance between the center

408.55 Wire-Bending Space Within an Enclosure Containing a Panelboard

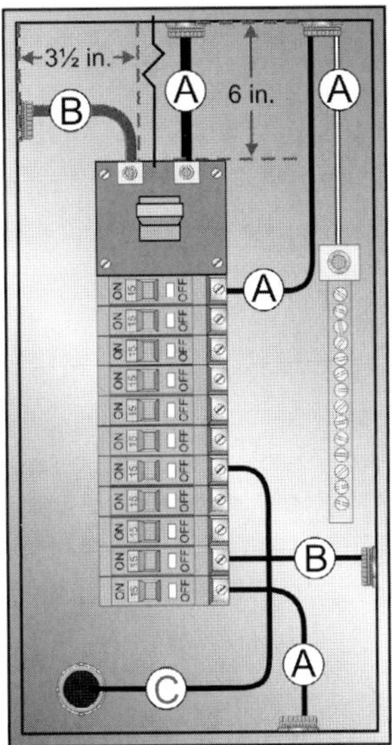

(A) Top and Bottom Wire-Bending Space
Minimum wire-bending space per Table 312.6(B) for the largest conductor entering or leaving the enclosure
(4 exceptions to top and bottom space)

(B) Side Wire-Bending Space
Minimum wire-bending space per Table 312.6(A) for the largest conductor entering or leaving the enclosure

(C) Back Wire-Bending Space
Minimum wire-bending space per Table 312.6(A) based on the "one wire per terminal" column.

The distance between the center of the rear entry and the nearest termination for the entering conductors shall not be less than the distance given in Table 312.6(B).

** Not all conductors shown*
** Distances shown are based on 2/0 AWG as largest conductors entering or leaving the enclosure.*

2011 *NEC* Requirement

The enclosures for a panelboards are required to have top and bottom wire-bending space sized in accordance with Table 312.6(B) (*conductors* ***entering*** *or leaving opposite walls*) for the largest conductor entering or leaving the enclosure.

Side wire-bending space is to be in accordance with Table 312.6(A) (*conductors not entering or leaving opposite walls*) for the largest conductor to be terminated in that space.

An example of these table requirements would be a 1/0 copper conductor with one wire per terminal would need 88.9 mm (3½ in.) of wire-bending space in accordance with Table 312.6(A), whereas the same 1/0 copper conductor with one wire per terminal would need 140 mm (5½ in.) of wire-bending space in accordance with Table 312.6(B).

Four exceptions exist for top and bottom wire-bending spaces. The first two exceptions permit either the top or bottom wire-bending space to be sized in accordance with Table 312.6(A) for a panelboard rated 225 amperes or less and designed to contain not over 42 overcurrent devices or where at least one side wire-bending space is sized in accordance with Table 312.6(B) for the largest conductor to be terminated in any side wire-bending space.

The third exception permits both the top and bottom wire-bending spaces to be sized in accordance with Table 312.6(A) if the panelboard is designed and constructed for wiring using only a single 90-degree bend for each conductor and the wiring diagram shows and specifies the method of wiring that is to be used.

The fourth exception permits either the top or the bottom wire-bending

408.55

Continued

of the rear entry and the nearest termination for the entering conductors shall not be less than the distance given in Table 312.6(B).

Proposal 9-130, 9-131

space, but not both, to be sized in accordance with Table 312.6(A) where there are no conductors terminated in that space.

2014 *NEC* Change

This section was reorganized into a list format for clarity. Besides the existing provisions for top, bottom, and side wire-bending spaces, provisions were added for "Back Wire-Bending Space." This new subsection (C) now addresses wire-bending space for rear entry with a removable cover on the opposite wall of the enclosure with the distance from that wall to the cover complying with the distance required for one wire per terminal in Table 312.6(A). The distance between the center of the rear entry and the nearest termination for the entering conductors cannot be less than the distance given in Table 312.6(B).

Analysis of Change

Section 408.55 gave specific language for minimum wire-bending space for conductors entering from the top, bottom, and side of the enclosure. However, when conductors entered the back of a panelboard or other enclosure, the *Code* was not clear-cut as to which requirements are warranted. This new language added at 408.55(C) will ensure a minimum required wire-bending space for conductors entering the enclosure from the rear similar to that required by 314.28(A)(2) for pull or junction boxes.

Enclosures for overcurrent devices such as panelboards are permitted to be used for feed-through conductors, splices, or taps similar to junction boxes or auxiliary gutters, if adequate space is provided (see 312.8), so the requirements of 314.28(A)(2) seem applicable here. This new provision is also comparable to 312.6(B)(2) Ex. No. 1 for prevention of insulation damage for a conductor bent 90 degrees and then pushed directly into a terminal or immediately bent another 90 degrees in order to accommodate the terminal orientation.

409.20

Change at a Glance

All heating loads — not just resistance heating loads — are required to be calculated when sizing the conductors which supply industrial control panels.

Code Language

409.20 Conductor – Minimum Size and Ampacity. (Industrial Control Panels)

The size of the industrial control panel supply conductor shall have an ampacity not less than 125 percent of the full-load current rating of all ~~resistance~~ heating loads plus 125 percent of the full-load current rating of the highest rated motor plus the sum of the full-load current ratings of all other connected motors and apparatus based on their duty cycle that may be in operation at the same time.

Proposal 11-13

2011 *NEC* Requirement

Industrial control panel supply conductors were required to have an ampacity not less than 125 percent of the full-load current rating of all resistance heating loads plus 125 percent of the full-load current rating of the highest rated motor plus the sum of the full-load current ratings of all other connected motors and apparatus. This was to be based on the duty cycle of the motors and apparatus that may be in operation at the same time.

2014 *NEC* Change

A revision to 409.20 removed the word, "resistance" to indicate that *all* heating loads were to be included in the ampacity equation for industrial control panels, not just resistance heating loads.

Analysis of Change

Industrial control panels are very often built in the field and manufactured on site to meet a specific process control need and/or explicit operational function(s). It is not uncommon for some of these control or operational tasks to be fulfilled using induction heating type equipment such as human machine interface (HMI) and information technology (IT) equipment. Induction heating loads were not previously required to be included as a load for determining the ampacity of the conductors that serve industrial control panels. These industrial control panel loads also need to be considered as part of the load a circuit serves when calculating the minimum ampacity of conductors that serve industrial control panels.

Article 409 for industrial control panels was introduced in the 2005 *NEC*. While introduced at the same time, the wording in 409.20 has remained unchanged until the 2014 *NEC*. An industrial control panel is an assembly of components intended to provide control logic and power distribution to a variety of loads in an assortment of occupancy types.

410.6

Change at a Glance

Listing requirements for luminaires and lampholders have been expanded to retrofit kits.

Code Language

410.6 Listing Required

All luminaires, lampholders, and retrofit kits shall be listed.

Proposal 18-59

410.6 Listing Required

Listing requirements for luminaires and lampholders have been expanded to "Retrofit Kits."

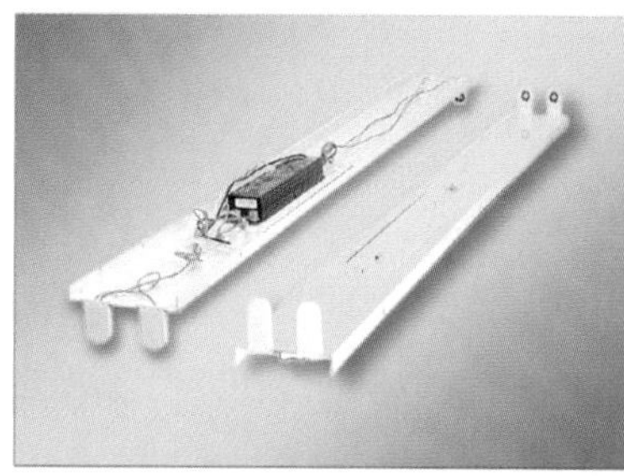

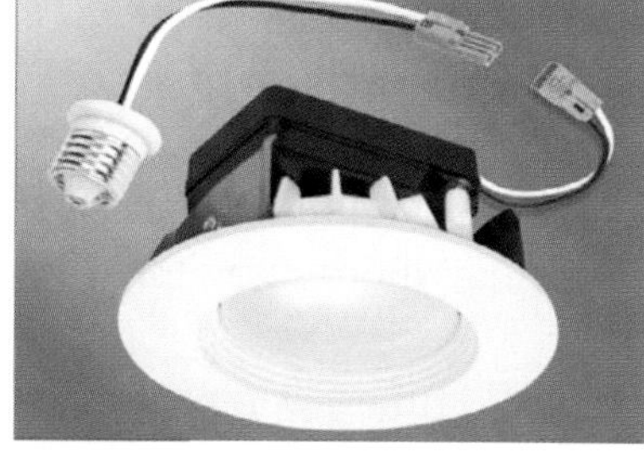

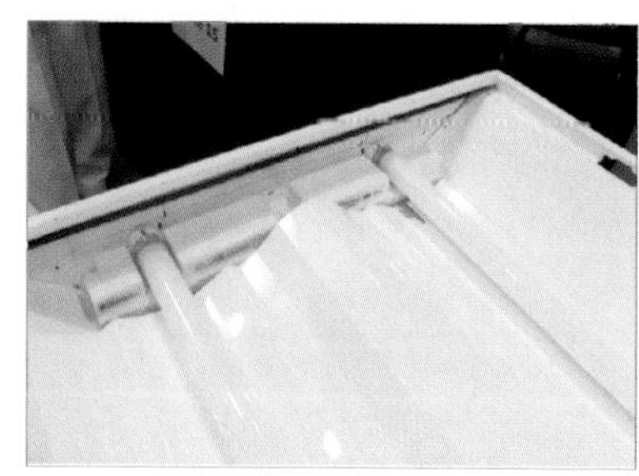

2011 *NEC* Requirement

All luminaires and lampholders are required be listed.

2014 *NEC* Change

Listing requirements in Article 410 were expanded to include retrofit kits as well as luminaires and lampholders.

Analysis of Change

A new definition for *retrofit kit* has been added to Article 100 of the *NEC*. This definition states that a retrofit kit is "a general term for a complete subassembly of parts and devices for field conversion of utilization equipment." Extensive upgrades are underway in the lighting and sign industries to achieve greater energy efficiency in luminaires and signs by replacing in-place illumination systems with light emitting diodes (LED) technology. In the case of Article 410, this will incorporate field modifications of existing luminaires. Testing laboratories, such as Underwriters' Laboratories (UL), have developed protocols for these field conversions such that, when done within the testing laboratory parameters, these kits do not compromise the safety profile of the listed luminaire. As an example, to ensure that the parts are compatible with the field modification, UL requires all the parts for luminaire conversions to be assembled into a kit that UL labels as Classified. By adding retrofit kits to the listing requirements of Article 410, this will drive the use of these classified kits and the use of conversion subassemblies.

The changing of illumination systems in luminaires presents a hazard for electricians doing maintenance after the conversion if the installers did not use one of these listed subassembly retrofit kits and properly follow the manufacturer's instructions.

410.10(F)

Change at a Glance

Luminaires are no longer permitted to be Installed within 38 mm (1½ in.) of the lowest metal deck surface.

Code Language

410.10 Luminaires in Specific Locations

(F) Luminaires Installed in or Under Roof Decking. Luminaires installed in exposed or concealed locations under metal-corrugated sheet roof decking, shall be installed and supported so there is not less than 38 mm (1½ in.) measured from the lowest surface of the roof decking to the top of the luminaire.

Proposal 18-66

2011 *NEC* Requirement

A cable, raceway, or box installed under metal-corrugated sheet roof decking is required to be installed and supported so there is not less than 38 mm (1½ in.) measured from the lowest surface of the roof decking to the top of the cable, raceway, or box. A cable, raceway, or box is prohibited from being installed in concealed locations in metal-corrugated sheet decking-type roofing. These provisions are covered at 300.4(E). For the 2011 *NEC*, there were no similar metal-corrugated roof decking prohibitions for luminaires.

2014 *NEC* Change

A new subsection (F) Luminaires Installed In or Under Roof Decking was added at 410.10 that will forbid luminaires from being installed within 38 mm (1½ in.) of the lowest metal roof decking surface.

Analysis of Change

New provisions were added at 410.10(F) that will bring luminaires in line with cables, raceways, and boxes as for as their location in proximity to metal-corrugated sheet roof decking. The process of laying down roofing materials and the re-roofing process can cause damage to wiring methods, boxes, and luminaires installed in close proximity to metal roof decking. The fastening devices used to hold down roofing materials are typically driven through the metal decking as a normal part of their installation. These roofing fastening devices are typically 32 mm (1¼ in.) in length. Where cables, raceways, and other electrical devices are installed on the underside of the decking and the required spacing is not maintained between the decking and the electrical components, these electrical components are vulnerable to damage by roof material fasteners that can penetrate the wiring method, luminaires, etc., during the roofing process.

This journey to prohibit electrically related items from being installed directly under metal roof decking started at 300.4(E) in the 2008 *NEC*, with

410.10(F)

Continued

cables and raceways being prohibited from installation within 38 mm (1½ in.) of corrugated sheet roof decking. For the 2011 *NEC*, boxes were added to this restriction. And now, luminaires. As required in previous editions of the *Code*, physical damage is not limited to only cables, raceways, and boxes installed beneath roof decking. Luminaires, conductors and associated equipment such as the ballast(s) and transformer within the luminaire are also subject to the same physical damage.

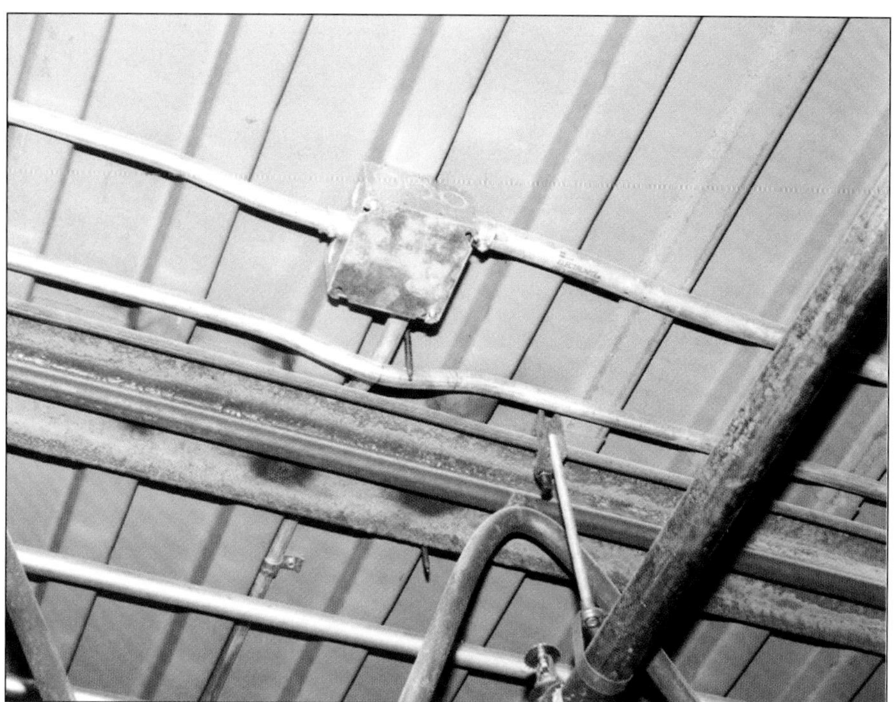

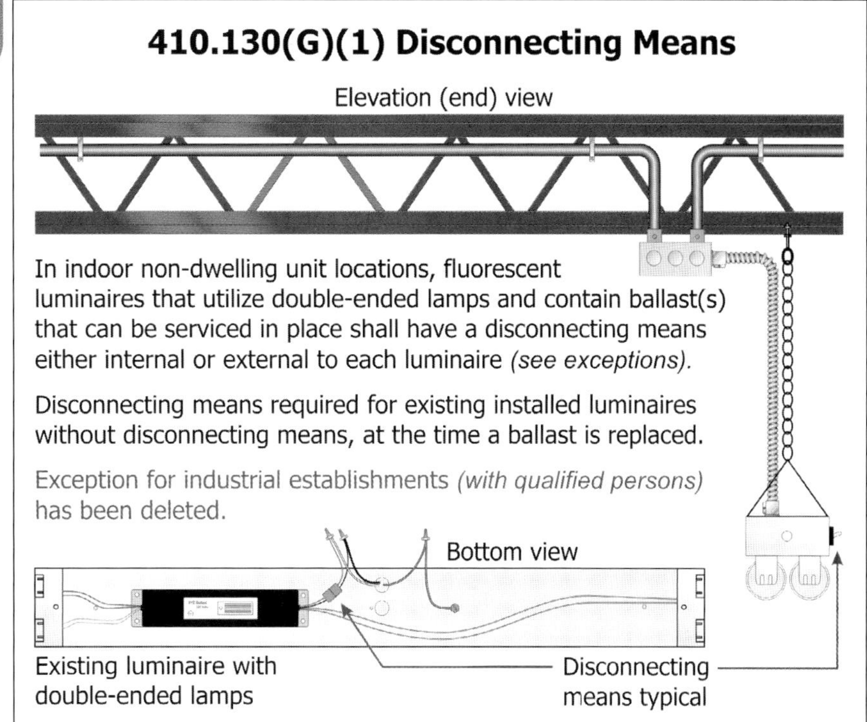
410.130(G)(1) Disconnecting Means
Elevation (end) view
In indoor non-dwelling unit locations, fluorescent luminaires that utilize double-ended lamps and contain ballast(s) that can be serviced in place shall have a disconnecting means either internal or external to each luminaire (see exceptions).
Disconnecting means required for existing installed luminaires without disconnecting means, at the time a ballast is replaced.
Exception for industrial establishments (with qualified persons) has been deleted.
Bottom view
Existing luminaire with double-ended lamps
Disconnecting means typical

Change at a Glance

Exception 4 has been deleted. This exception stated that disconnecting means were not required in industrial establishments that had limited public access and qualified personnel who serviced by written procedures.

delete

Code Language

410.130 General. (Electric-Discharge Lighting Systems of 1000 Volts or Less)

(G) Disconnecting Means.

(1) General. In indoor locations other than dwellings and associated accessory structures, fluorescent luminaires that utilize double-ended lamps and contain ballast(s) that can be serviced in place shall have a disconnecting means either internal or external to each luminaire. For existing installed luminaires without disconnecting means, at the time a ballast is replaced, a disconnecting means shall be installed. The line side terminals of the disconnecting means shall be guarded.

Exception No. 1: A disconnecting means shall not be required for luminaires installed in hazardous (classified) location(s).

Exception No. 2: A disconnecting means shall not be required for emergency illumination required in 700.16.

Exception No. 3: For cord-and-plug-connected luminaires, an accessible separable connector

2011 *NEC* Requirement

The parent text at 410.130(G)(1) requires fluorescent luminaires that utilize double-ended lamps and contain ballast(s) to have a local disconnecting means either internal or external to each luminaire. This would also include existing installed luminaires without disconnecting means, at the time ballast is replaced. This provision does not pertain to dwelling unit luminaires. Five exceptions existed for this local disconnecting means requirement. This local disconnecting means is not required for luminaires installed in hazardous (classified) location(s), for emergency illumination, or for industrial establishments with qualified service personnel. An accessible cord from a cord- and plug-connected luminaire can serve as the disconnecting means. Snap switches can serve as the local disconnecting means when these switches are designed such that the illuminated space cannot be left in total darkness.

2014 *NEC* Change

Exception No. 4 to 410.130(G)(1) has been deleted. This exception dealt with industrial establishments with restricted public access where conditions of maintenance and supervision ensure that only qualified persons service the installation by written procedures. These industrial areas will no longer be exempted from a local disconnecting means at indoor fluorescent luminaires (employing a ballast).

Analysis of Change

The provisions for requiring fluorescent luminaires that utilize double-ended lamps and contain ballast(s) to have a local disconnecting means either internal or external to each luminaire were introduced in the 2005 *NEC* at 410.73(G) [*later moved to 410.130(G)(1) in the 2008 NEC*]. Installers and maintenance personnel alike are often required to perform service work on fluorescent luminaires while energized. This would include replacement of ballasts. This type of service work often requires individuals to perform this

410.130(G)(1) Ex. No 4

Continued

or an accessible plug and receptacle shall be permitted to serve as the disconnecting means.

~~**Exception No. 4:** A disconnecting means shall not be required in industrial establishments with restricted public access where conditions of maintenance and supervision ensure that only qualified persons service the installation by written procedures.~~

Exception No. 5 4: Where more than one luminaire is installed and supplied by other than a multiwire branch circuit, a disconnecting means shall not be required for every luminaire when the design of the installation includes disconnecting means, such that the illuminated space cannot be left in total darkness.

Proposal 18-80, 18-78, 18-79

Comment 18-31, 18-35

work while standing on ladders which allows limited movement and limited ability to react to shock incidents where the worker might accidentally come in contact with energized parts. The practice of servicing these fluorescent luminaires while energized pre-sents a real danger to those having to perform this work. In an effort to provide a safer working environment for electrical personnel, these local disconnecting means provisions were introduced to the 2005 *NEC,* along with Exception No. 4 which removed the local disconnecting means for indoor fluorescent luminaires (employing a ballast) for industrial establishments (with qualified persons). Do electrical personnel in industrial establishments deserve any less safe working environment than their industry brothers and sisters?

There should not be an exception that permits a worker to perform an unsafe task in an industrial establishment that they would not perform in other locations. The requirements of NFPA 70E, *Standard for Electrical Safety in the Workplace* should be applied and followed. Applying the requirements of Article 130.2 of NFPA 70E, energized electrical conductors should be put into an electrically safe work condition before an electrical worker performs work. This is exactly what is being met by deleting Exception No. 4. Servicing luminaries while energized does not appear to meet the requirements of NFPA 70E. The purpose of the *Code* is the practical safeguarding of persons and property from hazards arising from the use of electricity. This exception should be deleted as it does not provide practical safeguarding for qualified persons. A person doing maintenance at a dwelling unit or an industrial establishment should have every possibility of safety in the performance of his or her job. The deletion of this exception adds another layer of safety.

There are quick and easy local disconnecting means that have been developed in direct response to this requirement from the time it was added to the 2005 *NEC*. With the development of the in-line disconnecting means and other safety features provided by manufacturers, this exception needs to be deleted.

422.5

Change at a Glance

GFCI devices providing protection to appliances in Article 422 are required to be installed in readily accessible locations.

Code Language

422.5 Ground-Fault Circuit-Interrupter (GFCI) Protection

The device providing GFCI protection required in this article shall be readily accessible.

Proposal 17-19

422.5 GFCI Protection (Appliances)

GFCI devices providing protection to appliances in Article 422 are required to be installed in readily accessible locations.

Drinking fountains

Vending machines

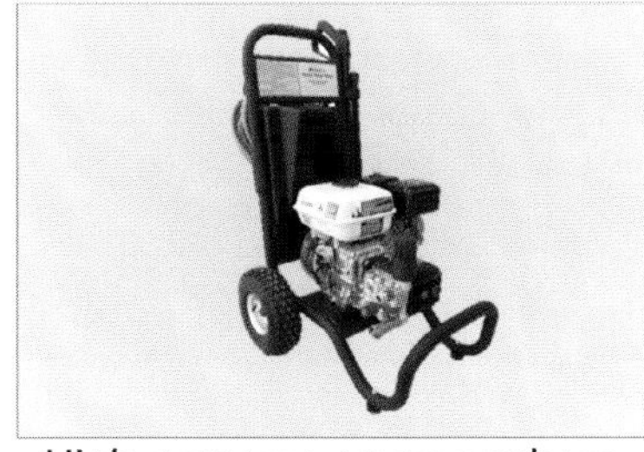

High-pressure spray washers

Tire inflation/auto vac machines

2011 *NEC* Requirement

GFCI devices installed to meet the requirements of 210.8 are required to be installed in a readily accessible location. This "readily accessible" location provision did not exist in Article 422 for appliances in the 2011 *NEC*.

2014 *NEC* Change

A new section 422.5 has been added to require all devices providing GFCI protection for appliances to be installed in a readily accessible location.

Analysis of Change

The new 422.5 requires all ground-fault circuit-interrupter (GFCI) devices for appliances to be installed in a readily accessible location (see definition of *readily accessible* in Article 100). Manufacturers of GFCI protective devices routinely require that their GFCI device be tested on a monthly basis to ensure it is providing the life-safety protection intended. These provisions can typically be found in the manufacturer's specifications that accompany the GFCI product. When a GFCI device is installed in locations that are not readily accessible, such as behind a refrigerator or behind a vending machine, the ability for someone, such as the homeowner or maintenance personnel at a shopping mall, to test the GFCI device is greatly impaired. Installation of these devices in a readily accessible location will greatly aid in this monthly testing process and, at the very least, not hinder this testing process.

A very similar requirement demanding that the GFCI devices be located in a readily accessible location was added to 210.8 for branch-circuit GFCI requirements for dwelling units and other than dwelling units during the 2011 *NEC* development process. This same accessibility provision should be provided for the appliances requiring GFCI protection in Article 422.

422.5

Continued

As a matter of note, a proposal was submitted to CMP-1 (see Proposal 1-131) to add a provision in Article 110 to require all GFCI and AFCI receptacle outlet devices to be installed in a readily accessible location. Inclusion in Article 110 would make this provision mandatory across the entire *Code* and it would not be necessary to repeat this provision in different articles. CMP-1 accepted this proposal but requested that the NEC Correlating Committee refer this proposal to CMP-2, CMP-3, CMP-19 and CMP-18 for comment. CMP-19 came back with a comment (see Comment 1-46) to CMP-1 recommending a rejection of Proposal 1-131 stating that, "GFCI receptacles have been around for decades and, as a matter of course, GFCI receptacles are not always periodically tested. Making them readily accessible will not change this fact." CMP-1 accepted the recommendation of CMP-19 reversing their decision from the proposal stage, removing this "readily accessible" provision from the proposed text for the 2014 *NEC* in Article 110.

422.11(F)(3)

422.11(F)(3) Water Heaters and Steam Boilers

Resistance-type immersion electric heating elements for low-pressure water heater tanks or open-outlet water heater vessels are now permitted to be subdivided into 120 ampere circuits and protected at not more than 150 amperes.

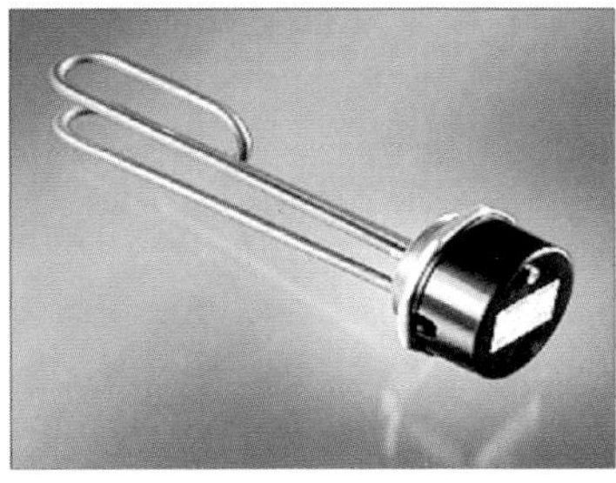

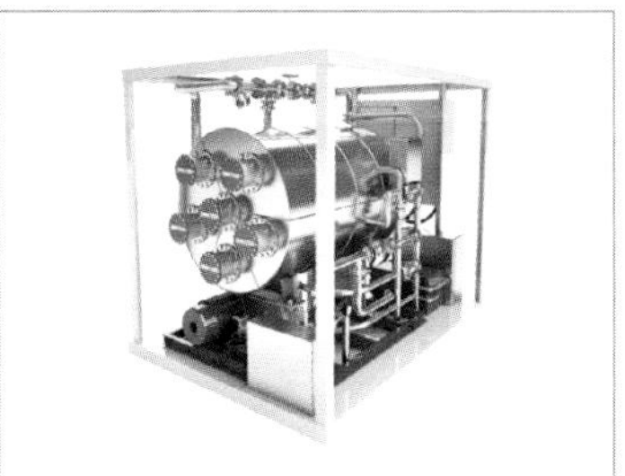

Change at a Glance

Resistance-type immersion electric heating elements for low-pressure water heater tanks or open-outlet water heater vessels are permitted to be subdivided into 120-amperes circuits and protected at not more than 150 amperes.

Code Language

422.11 Overcurrent Protection

Appliances shall be protected against overcurrent in accordance with 422.11(A) through (G) and 422.10.

(F) Electric Heating Appliances Employing Resistance-Type Heating Elements Rated More Than 48 Amperes.

(1) Electric Heating Appliances. *(Text unchanged, see NEC for complete text.)*

(2) Commercial Kitchen and Cooking Appliances. *(Text unchanged, see NEC for complete text.)*

(3) Water Heaters and Steam Boilers. ~~Water heaters and steam boilers employing~~ Resistance-type immersion electric heating elements ~~contained in an ASME-rated and stamped vessel or listed instantaneous water heaters~~ shall be permitted to be subdivided into circuits not exceeding 120 amperes and protected at not

2011 *NEC* Requirement

Overcurrent protection of appliances is covered at 422.11. Electric heating appliances employing resistance-type heating elements rated more than 48 amperes, generally are required to have their heating elements subdivided. Each subdivided load cannot exceed 48 amperes and must be protected at not more than 60 amperes. Water heaters and steam boilers employing resistance-type immersion electric heating elements contained in an **American Society of Mechanical Engineers (ASME)**-rated and stamped vessel or listed instantaneous water heaters are permitted to be subdivided into circuits not exceeding 120 amperes and protected at not more than 150 amperes.

2014 *NEC* Change

For the 2014 *NEC*, 422.11(F)(3) was revised into a list format and low-pressure water heater tanks or open-outlet water heater vessels were added to this provision. This revision will now allow low-pressure water heater tanks or open-outlet water heater vessels to be subdivided into 120-ampere circuits instead of the 48 amperes restriction in the parent text of 422.11(F).

Analysis of Change

Section 422.11(F) covered electric heating appliances employing resistance-type heating elements rated more than 48 amperes, but did not include appropriate regulations for electric immersion water heaters used for heating water or solutions in either vented industrial process tanks (low-pressure water heaters) or in flow-through vessels with the outlet connected directly to vented tanks without valves or restrictions (open-outlet water heaters). Similar "closed water heaters" were and are covered in Article 422 [see 422.11(F), 422.13, and 422.47], but not specifically these low-pressure water heater tanks or open-outlet water heater vessels. There are three physical risks associated with electric immersion heaters for water: (1) If the heaters are powered while not immersed in water, damage can occur to the heating

422.11(F)(3)

Continued

more than 150 amperes as follows:
(1) Where contained in ASME rated and stamped vessels
(2) Where included in listed instantaneous water heaters
(3) Where installed in low-pressure water heater tanks or open-outlet water heater vessels

Informational Note: Low-pressure and open-outlet heaters are atmospheric-pressure water heaters as defined in IEC 60335-2-21 Household and similar electrical appliances – Safety – Particular requirements for storage water heaters.

Proposal 17-21

vessel and a potential fire can result; (2) If the heaters are powered while immersed in water, high pressure can cause an explosion (*but the temperature will not exceed the boiling point of the water*); (3) And, like any other electrical load, overcurrent and overloads in the electrical supply conductors can damage the insulation resulting in a short circuit and the potential exists for a fire to occur.

Part of the reasoning for the different circumstances for 120 amperes versus 48 amperes subdivided circuits in 422.11(F)(3) is to limit the momentary pressure built up in the tank by limiting the additional energy that is likely to be delivered to the water during an overcurrent event. It should be noted that a similar 120-amperes rule exists at 424.72(A) for boilers, for which there are no comparable appliances like instantaneous or vented water heaters. The use of 120-amperes subdivided loads has a lower overpressure risk for vented systems than for any closed systems. Restricting circuits to 48 amperes can only mitigate the overpressure risk without necessarily mitigating the effects that overloads can have on the internal wiring of a water heater product, or on the field wiring that connects heater elements to their controller. For the field wiring conductors and connections, the permitted wiring methods in *NEC* Chapter 3 should be sufficient for any circuit size.

The overcurrent subdivision requirement was introduced in the 1975 *NEC* with the justification that heaters with "small internal conductors might be protected by unspecified sizes of overcurrent devices." Instantaneous water heaters were added to 422.11(F)(3) in the 2002 *NEC*. CMP-17 allowed 120-amperes subdivisions for explosion-risk-free vented systems, using the same 120-amperes subdivisions that are currently allowed for low-explosion-risk closed systems.

422.23

Change at a Glance

GFCI protection is now required for all tire inflation and automotive vacuum machines provided for public use.

Code Language

422.23 Tire Inflation and Automotive Vacuum Machines

Tire inflation machines and automotive vacuum machines provided for public use shall be protected by a ground-fault circuit-interrupter.

Proposal 17-31

422.23 Tire Inflation and Auto Vacuum Machines

GFCI protection is now required for all tire inflation and automotive vacuum machines provided for public use.

2011 *NEC* Requirement

There was no provision in the 2011 *NEC* requiring GFCI protection for tire inflation and automotive vacuum machines.

2014 *NEC* Change

A new section 422.33 was added to require ground-fault circuit-interrupter (GFCI) protection for all tire inflation machines and automotive vacuum machines provided for public use.

Analysis of Change

Tire inflation and automotive vacuum machines are generally located in commercial establishments, such as convenience stores and car wash areas, where they are heavily used by the general public. This type of public-use equipment is typically exposed to the elements and is often misused to the point of abuse. This type of equipment will typically be used outdoors in rain, snow, and puddles of accumulated standing water. Abused, deteriorated electrical equipment combined with a wet environment are recognized as contributing factors that increase the risk of an electrical shock hazard. Reports from the U.S. Consumer Product Safety Commission (CPSC) submitted with the substantiation for this new requirement detailed fatalities that had occurred in conjunction with tire inflation and vacuum machines, whether these appliances were coin-operated, credit-card-reader-operated, or free to the public. Requiring GFCI protection for this type of equipment will greatly reduce future electrical shock hazard related incidents.

Over the years since the introduction of GFCI protection in the 1968 *NEC*, GFCI devices have demonstrated their value in preventing electrocution in exactly these types of conditions. CMP-17 has recognized the value of GFCI protection and has instilled this protection for coin-operated equipment and appliances used by the public in past editions of the *Code*. An example of this protection would be vending machines (see 422.51). Vending machines are subject to the same type of abuse by users and can also be located in wet or damp areas.

422.49

Change at a Glance

GFCI protection in the cord or the plug of high-pressure spray washing machines was expanded to three-phase equipment rated 208Y/120 volts and 60 amperes or less.

REVISION

Code Language

422.49 High-Pressure Spray Washers

422.49 High-Pressure Spray Washers. ~~All single-phase~~ Cord- and plug-connected high-pressure spray washing machines ~~rated at 250 volts or less~~ as specified in (1) or (2) shall be provided with factory-installed ground-fault circuit-interrupter protection for personnel ~~The ground-fault circuit interrupter shall be~~ that is an integral part of the attachment plug or ~~shall be~~ that is located in the supply cord within 300 mm (12 in.) of the attachment plug.

(1) All single-phase equipment rated 250 volts or less
(2) All three-phase equipment rated 208Y/120 volts and 60 amperes or less.

Proposal 17-37, 17-18a

Comment 17-13, 17-14

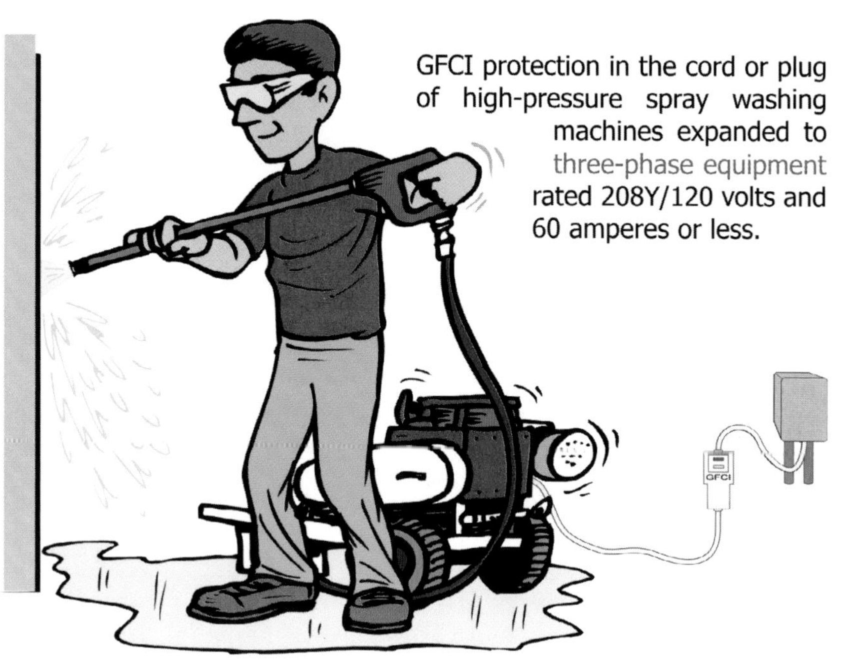
422.49 High-Pressure Spray Washers
GFCI protection in the cord or plug of high-pressure spray washing machines expanded to three-phase equipment rated 208Y/120 volts and 60 amperes or less.
GFCI

2011 *NEC* Requirement

All single-phase cord- and plug-connected high-pressure spray washing machines rated at 250 volts or less are required to be provided with factory-installed ground-fault circuit-interrupter (GFCI) protection for personnel. The GFCI for this purpose is also required to be an integral part of the attachment plug or it must be located in the supply cord within 300 mm (12 in.) of the attachment plug.

2014 *NEC* Change

The requirement for cord- and plug-connected high-pressure spray washing machines to be provided with factory-installed GFCI protection for personnel was expanded to three-phase equipment rated 208Y/120 volts and 60 amperes or less, as well as to single-phase equipment rated 250 volts or less.

Analysis of Change

The requirements for providing GFCI protection for high-pressure spray washers were instituted at 422-8(d)(3) in the 1987 edition of the *NEC*. The proposal was submitted by the U.S. Consumer Product Safety Commission (CPSC) with the following substantiation: "At least ten documented electrocutions have been linked to nonindustrial high pressure spray washing machines of the type purchased by, or rented to consumers. These appliances dispense pressurized water or water/detergent mixtures through a nozzle for cleaning purposes. Although provided with equipment grounding conductors, these cord- and plug-connected machines present shock hazards to users in the presence of very wet surroundings."

The same shock hazard exists for three-phase machines as for single-phase. The technology and product standards exist today that can offer ground-fault protection for personnel for three-phase applications at 250 volts and 60 amperes or less. At this date, there are no three-phase 240-volt listed GFCI devices, or listed GFCI devices intended for use on circuits rated greater than 150 volts to ground. Three-phase 208Y/120-volt GFCI devices are recognized in UL Product Standard

Continued

943 *Ground-Fault Circuit-Interrupters* and UL 489 *Molded-Case Circuit Breakers, Molded-Case Switches and Circuit-Breaker Enclosures*. Listed products are available that meet this requirement, but there are no listed products that provide the GFCI protection to be located in the attachment plug or in the cord of the appliance as prescribed in the new text at 422.49.

This new provision for three-phase high-pressure spray washing machines rated 208Y/120 volts and 60 amperes or less could prove to be difficult at best in compliance and enforcement when dealing with the GFCI protection having to be located in the attachment plug or in the cord of the appliance. While the product standard may permit attachment plug or cord type three-phase GFCI protection, (*probably a portable type device*), it is not obvious this product exists today. While having the protection in the cord will better ensure the GFCI protection is provided at any location where the high-pressure spray washer is used, it will obviously require a revision to the product standard for high-pressure spray washing machines and will require a GFCI manufacturer to develop that specific product. Based on previous experience with product standards, such as with vending machines, a revision and implementation of the revision to the product standard could take years to complete. Meanwhile, designers, contractors, electricians, and the enforcement community could be forced to revise or ignore this requirement as they wait for the product to become available.

422.51

Change at a Glance

GFCI protection has been expanded to hard-wired vending machines as well as to cord- and plug-connected vending machines.

Code Language

422.51 ~~Cord-and-Plug-Connected~~ Vending Machines

(A) Cord- and Plug-Connected. Cord-and plug connected vending machines manufactured or remanufactured on or after January 1, 2005, shall include a ground fault circuit interrupter identified for portable use as an integral part of the attachment plug or be located within 300 mm (12 in.) of the attachment plug. Older vending machines manufactured or remanufactured prior to January 1, 2005, shall be connected to a GFCI-protected outlet.

(B) Other Than Cord-and Plug-Connected. Vending machines not utilizing a cord-and plug connection shall be connected to a ground fault circuit interrupter protected circuit.

Informational Note: For further information, see ANSI/UL 541-~~2005~~ 2010, Standard for Refrigerated Vending Machines, or ANSI/UL 751-~~2005~~ 2010, Standard for Vending Machines.

Proposal 17-38, 17-18a, 17-41, 17-39, 17-40

Comment 17-3

422.51 Vending Machines

GFCI protection has been expanded to hard-wired vending machines as well as cord-and-plug-connected vending machines.

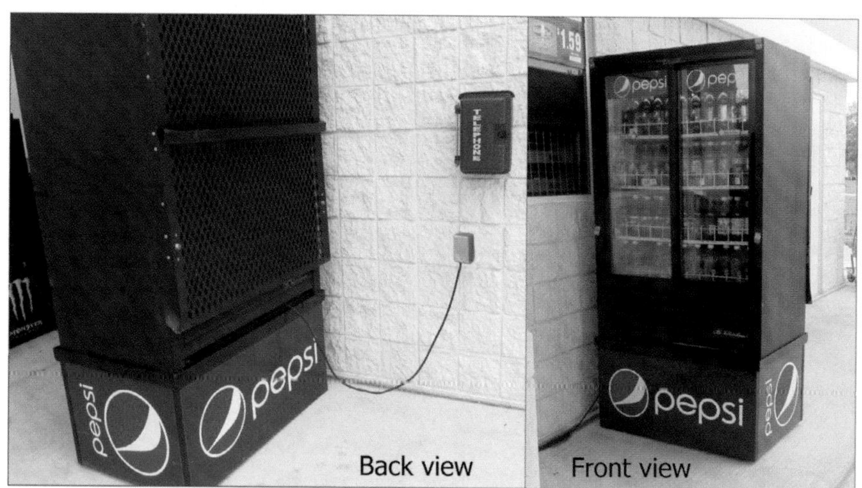

Vending machines not utilizing a cord-and-plug connection are required to be connected to a GFCI-protected circuit.

2011 *NEC* Requirement

Cord- and plug-connected vending machines are required to be provided with a ground-fault circuit interrupter (GFCI) as an integral part of the attachment plug or to be located within 300 mm (12 in.) of the attachment plug. This GFCI requirement applies to vending machines manufactured or remanufactured on or after January 1, 2005. Older vending machines manufactured or remanufactured prior to January 1, 2005, are required to be connected to a GFCI-protected outlet.

2014 *NEC* Change

The requirement for GFCI protection for vending machines was expanded to other than cord- and plug-connected vending machines, such as direct hard-wired vending machines. For cord- and plug-connected vending machines, the GFCI protection must be provided by a GFCI device that is "identified for portable use."

Analysis of Change

GFCI protection for cord- and plug-connected vending machines was a requirement that first appeared in the 2005 *NEC*. Cord- and plug-connected vending machines are often located in areas where they are accessible to a large number of people. They can be found in public locations, both indoors and outdoors. When located outdoors, they are often exposed to wet or damp locations; and the people accessing their use are often standing on concrete or some other conductive surface. The original substantiation for requiring GFCI protection for vending machines reported incidents where individuals were subject to shock hazards by coming in contract with energized conductive surfaces of vending machines; and, unfortunately, some resulted in fatalities by electrocution. The same hazard can exist regardless whether the vending machine is cord- and plug-connected or direct hard-wired. Adding a provision to require GFCI protection for any and all vending machines, regardless of the connection method, will provide a significant level of increased safety for users of these machines.

When it comes time to provide GFCI protection for a vending machine, keep in mind the new provision in 422.5 that all GFCI devices required by Article 422 are now required to be installed in a readily accessible location. A GFCI receptacle outlet can no longer be installed behind a vending machine. Under previous editions of the *Code*, if the GFCI receptacle outlet for a vending machine was installed outdoors, it had to be installed in a readily accessible location in accordance of 210.8(B)(4); but this new readily accessible provision at 422.5 would require *all* GFCI devices to be installed in a readily accessible location (indoors or outdoors).

424.19

Change at a Glance

Fixed electric space-heating equipment can be supplied by more than one source that can include more than one feeder or branch circuit.

REVISION

Code Language

424.19 Disconnecting Means. (Fixed Electric Space-Heating Equipment)

Means shall be provided to simultaneously disconnect the heater, motor controller(s), and supplementary overcurrent protective device(s) of all fixed electric space-heating equipment from all ungrounded conductors. Where heating equipment is supplied by more than one source, feeder, or branch circuit, the disconnecting means shall be grouped and marked. The disconnecting means specified in 424.19(A) and (B) shall have an ampere rating not less than 125 percent of the total load of the motors and the heaters and shall be lockable in accordance with 110.25. ~~The provision for locking or adding a lock to the disconnecting means shall be installed on or at the switch or circuit breaker used as the disconnecting means and shall remain in place with or without the lock installed.~~

Proposal 17-49

Comment 17-17

424.19 Disconnecting Means (FESH)

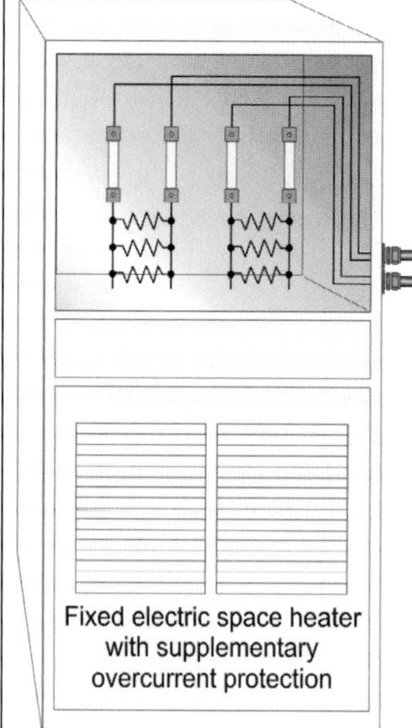
Fixed electric space heater with supplementary overcurrent protection
Fixed electric space-heating equipment can be supplied by more than one source that can include more than one feeder or branch circuit.
Disconnecting means within sight of motor controller and supplementary overcurrent protection
Simultaneous disconnecting means required
If supplied by more than one source, feeder, or branch circuit, disconnecting means shall be grouped and marked.
Disconnecting means shall have ampere rating not less than 125% of the total load of the motors and the heaters.

2011 *NEC* Requirement

Simultaneous disconnecting means has to be provided to the heater, motor controller(s), and supplementary overcurrent protective device(s) of all fixed electric space-heating equipment. The disconnecting means generally has to have an ampere rating not less than 125 percent of the total load of the motors and the heaters. A provision for locking or adding a lock to the disconnecting means has to be installed on or at the disconnecting means and shall remain in place with or without the lock installed. Where heating equipment is supplied by more than one source, the disconnecting means is required to be grouped and marked. The sources supplying the heating equipment were not defined in the 2011 *NEC*.

2014 *NEC* Change

Language was added at 424.19 to clarify that the source of power supplying fixed electric space-heating equipment could be in the form of either feeders or branch circuits. A reference to the new 110.25 was added to take the place of the existing provisions addressing a lockable disconnecting means.

Analysis of Change

The word "source" implies several different meanings and is used more than once in the *Code* with no definition, such as in Article 695, Article 700, Article 701, and Article 702. Fixed electric space-heating equipment such as an electric furnace often requires more than one feeder or branch circuit supplying the unit. The requirement for a simultaneous disconnecting means has been contentious, based on the interpretation of the word "source," with some users of the *Code* interpreting this to mean a requirement of a single disconnecting means at the unit. This additional wording should help clarify that more than one disconnecting means is permissible.

It should be noted that whenever the *Code* allows more than one disconnecting means (*especially in separate enclosures*) and at the same time requires "simul-

424.19

Continued

taneous disconnecting means," careful consideration should be in order. It would seem to be virtually impossible to achieve "simultaneous disconnection" with more than one disconnecting means in separate enclosures. Simultaneous disconnection can easily be achieved with more than one disconnecting means located in the same enclosure with identified handle ties, etc. Perhaps this is a subject in the *Code* that deserves a well-crafted proposal in future editions of the *Code*.

424.66(A) and (B)

Change at a Glance

New provisions were put in place to require limited forms of working space about duct heaters for fixed electric space-heating equipment.

Code Language

424.66 Installations

(A) (Duct Heaters) Duct heaters shall be installed in accordance with the manufacturer's instructions in such a manner that operation does not create a hazard to persons or property. Furthermore, duct heaters shall be located with respect to building construction and other equipment so as to permit access to the heater. Sufficient clearance shall be maintained to permit replacement of controls and heating elements and for adjusting and cleaning of controls and other parts requiring such attention. See 110.26.

Working space about electrical enclosures for resistance heating element type duct heaters which are mounted on duct systems and contain equipment that requires examination, adjustment, servicing, or maintenance while energized shall comply with Section 424.66(B).

(B) Limited Access. Where the enclosure is located in a space above a ceiling, all of the following shall apply:

(1) The enclosure shall be accessible through a lay in type ceiling or access panel(s).

2011 *NEC* Requirement

As far as access or working space for duct heaters is concerned, 424.66 required duct heaters to be located with respect to building construction and other equipment so as to permit "access to the heater." This section goes on to indicate that sufficient clearance must be maintained to permit replacement of controls and heating elements, and for adjusting and cleaning of controls and other parts requiring such attention. One of the shortest sentences in the entire section simply states, "See 110.26." This does not necessarily indicate that the working space requirements of 110.26 must be met for duct heaters and other equipment installed in areas, such as above a suspended drop ceiling.

2014 *NEC* Change

The same provisions stated above of the 2011 *NEC* still exist at new 424.66(A), with new language added to send users of the *Code* to new 424.66(B) for working space provisions for electrical enclosures for duct heaters, which are mounted on duct systems and contain equipment that requires examination, adjustment, servicing, or maintenance while energized. The new language at 424.66(B) requires these enclosures, if located in a space above a ceiling, to be accessible through a lay in type ceiling or access panel(s). The width of the required working space must be equal to the width of the enclosure or a minimum of 762 mm (30 in.), whichever is greater. Any and all doors or hinged panels are required to have the ability to open at least 90 degrees. And, finally, the space in front of the enclosure must comply with Table 110.26(A)(1) working space depth requirements, with horizontal T-bar ceiling grid permitted in this space.

Analysis of Change

Installers and maintenance personnel often must work, while standing on a ladder, on duct heating equipment that is located above suspended ceilings with very limited space available. These duct heaters are typically energized and can be supplied by up to 480-volt circuits. Electrical workers may be required to test

Continued

(2) The width of the working space shall be the width of the enclosure or a minimum of 762 mm (30 in.), whichever is greater.
(3) All doors or hinged panels shall open to at least 90 degrees.
(4) The space in front of the enclosure shall comply with Table 110.26(A)(1) depth requirements. Horizontal ceiling T-bar is permitted in this space.

Informational Note: For additional installation information, see NFPA 90A-2009, *Standard for the Installation of Air-Conditioning and Ventilating Systems*, and NFPA 90B- 2009, *Standard for the Installation of Warm Air Heating and Air-Conditioning Systems*.

Proposal 17-75

Comment 17-19

or examine these units while energized. Many of these types of enclosures have hinged doors, which necessitates the need to open these doors up to 90 degrees in order to access all components of the equipment. It is not unusual at all for electrical personnel to encounter metal piping or metal structural members installed or located directly in front of this equipment enclosure. This all contributes to an unsafe working condition for electrical workers due in part to grounded metal parts in front of the equipment being worked on while energized.

A working clearance violation of this magnitude would not be tolerated for something like a 480-volt switchboard or panelboard installed at floor level. The new provisions added at 424.66(A) and (B) seek to level the playing field for duct heaters installed above a suspended ceiling as far as adequate working space is concerned. This new language will improve safety for electrical workers and will provide enforceable *Code* language for the enforcement community, as far as duct heaters are concerned.

It should be noted that this new limited working space provision is restricted to duct heaters. What about other types of electrical equipment and utilization equipment installed above a suspended ceiling that could require examination, adjustment, servicing, or maintenance while energized? Perhaps this is a direction that will be addressed in future editions of the *Code*.

430.22(G)

Change at a Glance

The current referred to within 430.22(G) is the current of the motor and not of the conductors. The term *ampacity* was removed as motors do not have ampacities; they have current values.

Code Language

430.22 Single Motor

Conductors that supply a single motor used in a continuous duty application shall have an ampacity of not less than 125 percent of the motor full-load current rating, as determined by 430.6(A)(1), or not less than specified in 430.22(A) through (G).

(G) Conductors for Small Motors. Conductors for small motors shall not be smaller than 14 AWG unless otherwise permitted in 430.22(G)(1) or (G)(2).

(1) 18 AWG Copper. Where installed in a cabinet or enclosure, 18 AWG individual copper conductors, copper conductors that are part of a jacketed multiconductor cable assembly, or copper conductors in a flexible cord shall be permitted, under either of the following sets of conditions:

(1) The circuit supplies a motor ~~circuits~~ with a full-load current rating, as determined by 430.6(A)(1), ~~ampacity~~ greater than 3.5 amperes or less than or equal to 5 amperes and ~~if~~ all the following conditions are met:

430.22(G) Conductors for Small Motors

Conductors for small motors shall not be smaller than 14 AWG unless otherwise permitted in 430.22(G)(1) or 430.22(G)(2).

Where installed in a cabinet or enclosure, 18 or 16 AWG individual copper conductors, or copper conductors of either a jacketed multiconductor cable assembly or a flexible cord shall be permitted, under specific conditions.

Current referred to within 430.22(G) is the current of the motor and not the conductors.

The word "ampacity" was removed as motors do not have "ampacities" *(they have current values).*

2011 *NEC* Requirement

Conductors for small motors are generally not permitted to be smaller than 14 AWG. Where installed in a cabinet or enclosure, specific 18 AWG copper conductors were permitted to be used for small motors (full-load ampacity greater than 3.5 up to 5 amperes). These small motors had to have circuits protected in accordance with 430.52, be provided with maximum Class 10 overload protection in accordance with 430.32, and have overcurrent protection provided in accordance with 240.4(D)(1)(2). These same provisions applied to small motors with full-load ampacities of 3.5 amperes or less when provided with maximum Class 20 overload protection. Similar provision for the use of 16 AWG copper conductors were given at 430.22(G)(2).

2014 *NEC* Change

Section 430.22(G) was revised to clarify that the current referred to within 430.22(G) is the current of the motor and not of the conductors. Further clarification was added to indicate that the 125 percent multiplier for continuous duty required by the parent text at 430.22 is not required to be calculated in determining the conductor sizing for these small motors, due to the fact the motor full-load current rating cannot exceed the values given in these subsections for 16 and 18 AWG conductors. The 125 percent multiplier is already included due to the limitations imposed on the maximum current rating of the motor allowed for the 16 and 18 AWG conductors. The term *ampacity* was removed throughout this subsection as it is only permitted to be used in conjunction with the ability of a conductor to carry current. Motors, devices, circuits, and utilization equipment do not have ampacities; they have current values.

Analysis of Change

Section 430.22(G) was added to the 2011 *NEC* to establish guidelines for allowing 18 AWG and 16 AWG copper conductors for small motors under specific conditions. Several changes were instituted in 430.22(G) for the 2014 *NEC*.

430.22(G)

Continued

a. The circuit is protected in accordance with 430.52.
b. The circuit is provided with maximum Class 10 or Class 10A overload protection in accordance with 430.32.
c. Overcurrent protection is provided in accordance with 240.4(D)(1)(2).

(2) The circuit supplies a motor ~~circuits~~ with a full-load current rating, as determined by 430.6(A)(1), ~~ampacity~~ of 3.5 amperes or less ~~if~~ and all the following conditions are met:
a. The circuit is protected in accordance with 430.52.
b. The circuit is provided with maximum Class 20 overload protection in accordance with 430.32.
c. Overcurrent protection is provided in accordance with 240.4(D)(1)(2).

(2) 16 AWG Copper. *(Same changes for 16 AWG copper. See NEC for complete text.)*

Proposal 11-29a, 11-30

These changes were primarily for editorial purposes and for compliance with the *NEC Style Manual*. In conjunction with the circuit supplying a motor, the term *ampacity* was replaced with "current rating, as determined by 430.6(A)(1)," which is the motor table ampacity values. The term *ampacity* is only permitted to be used in conjunction with the ability of a conductor to carry current. Motors, devices, circuits, and utilization equipment do not have ampacities; they have current values, and rules should not be written that assume they can have such ampacity values.

In order to permit 18 AWG or 16 AWG copper conductors to supply these smaller motors, three specific conditions must be met (see *NEC* text for conditions). All of these conditions must be satisfied, not just some of them. At these qualifying conditions, revisions replace the conditional phrase "*if* all the following conditions are met" with "*and* all the following conditions are met" simply because all such requirements must be simultaneously true; there is nothing conditional about the subsequent conditions.

The previous text at 430.22(G)(1)(1)b and (2)(1)b only specified the use of Class 10 overload relays as *one* of the provisions for allowing these smaller conductors for small motors having a full-load ampacity greater than 3.5 up to 5 amperes. Revisions for the 2014 *NEC* will now recognize Class 10A overload relays as well, as most of the thermally adjustable, bi-metallic overload relays used in the industry today could be classified as Class 10A overload relays per the relevant UL product standards. Like Class 10 overload relays, all Class 10A overload relays that are certified per UL product standards meet the motor overload tripping requirements of 430.32 and also operate in less than 10 seconds at locked rotor conditions.

Note: A Class 10A overload relay has also been added to the Informational Note following 430.32(C). The previous text in this Informational Note only specified Class 10 overload relays as well. See Proposal 11-33a.

430.52(C)(5)

Change at a Glance

Semiconductor fuses intended to protect bypass contactors, isolation contactors, and conductors in a solid-state motor control system are permitted in lieu of devices listed in Table 430.52.

Code Language

430.52 Rating or Setting for Individual Motor Circuit

(C) Rating or Setting.

(5) Power Electronic Devices. ~~Suitable~~ Semiconductor fuses intended for the protection of electronic devices shall be permitted in lieu of devices listed in Table 430.52 for power electronic devices, associated electromechanical devices (such as bypass contactors and isolation contactors) and conductors in a solid-state motor controller system, provided that the marking for replacement fuses is provided adjacent to the fuses.

Proposal 11-35a

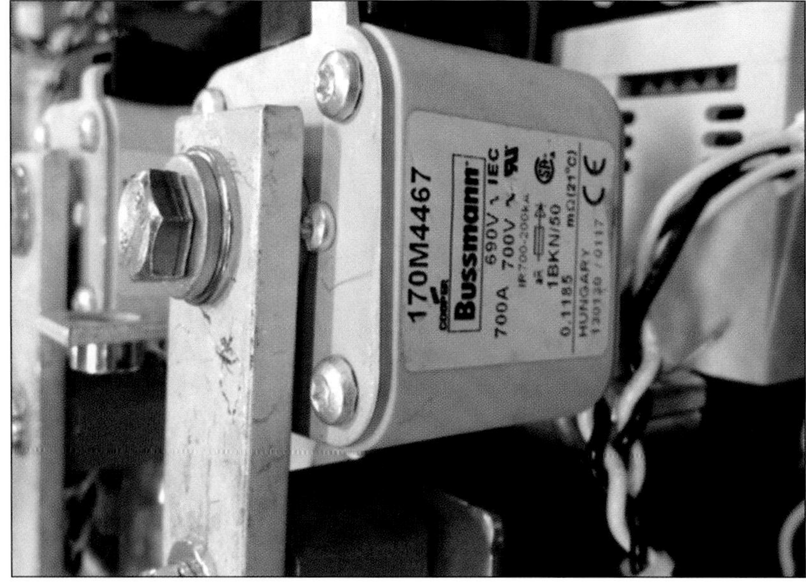

2011 *NEC* Requirement

"Suitable" fuses were permitted in lieu of devices listed in Table 430.52 for power electronic devices in a solid-state motor controller system. The suitable replacement fuse had to be marked "suitable" adjacent to the fuse.

2014 *NEC* Change

"Suitable fuses" were replaced with "semiconductor fuses" and their purpose was clarified as "intended for the protection of electronic devices." Examples of "power electronic devices," such as bypass and isolation contactors, were added along with their conductors.

Analysis of Change

Clarification was made at 430.52(C)(5) as to the specific type of fuses permitted in place of devices listed in Table 430.52 for the protection of certain electronic devices. Semiconductor fuses replace "suitable" fuses as the word "suitable" is vague and unenforceable. The revised wording clarifies the type of fuses that are permitted in this application. Semiconductor fuses are evaluated to UL Product Standard 248-13. This revision also clarifies that semiconductor fuses are permitted in systems which contain non-electronic power devices, such as contactors.

Semiconductor fuses are typically used to protect against overcurrent conditions in semiconductor devices. Because of their fast action, semiconductor fuses help to limit short-circuit current significantly. Semiconductor fuses are intended for short-circuit protection only, and are not designed to be used as traditional current-limiting fuses. Special purpose semiconductor fuses provided for branch-circuit short-circuit protection of solid-state motor controller systems must be evaluated as part of a listed combination motor controller in order to ensure their proper use and coordination.

430.53(D)

Change at a Glance

Revisions clarify that the 3 m (10 ft) and the 7.5 m (25 ft) tap conductors measurements for a motor are intended to begin from the point of the tap.

REVISION

Code Language

430.53 Several Motors or Loads on One Branch Circuit
Two or more motors or one or more motors and other loads shall be permitted to be connected to the same branch circuit under conditions specified in 430.53(D) and in 430.53(A), (B), or (C). The branch-circuit protective device shall be fuses or inverse time circuit breakers.

(D) Single Motor Taps. For group installations described above, the conductors of any tap supplying a single motor shall not be required to have an individual branch-circuit short-circuit and ground-fault protective device, provided they comply with one of the following:

(1) No conductor to the motor shall have an ampacity less than that of the branch-circuit conductors.

(2) No conductor to the motor shall have an ampacity less than one-third that of the branch-circuit conductors, with a minimum in accordance with 430.22. The conductors from the point of the tap to the motor overload device shall be ~~being~~ not more than 7.5 m (25 ft) long and be ~~being~~ pro-

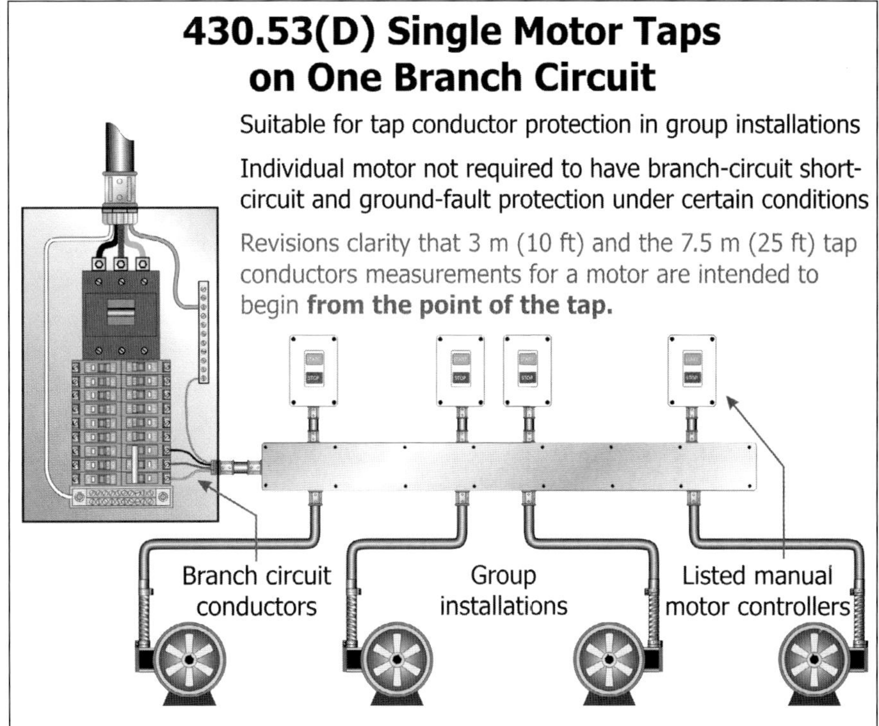
430.53(D) Single Motor Taps on One Branch Circuit
Suitable for tap conductor protection in group installations
Individual motor not required to have branch-circuit short-circuit and ground-fault protection under certain conditions
Revisions clarity that 3 m (10 ft) and the 7.5 m (25 ft) tap conductors measurements for a motor are intended to begin **from the point of the tap.**
Branch circuit conductors
Group installations
Listed manual motor controllers

2011 *NEC* Requirement

Two or more motors, or one or more motors and other loads, are permitted to be connected to the same branch circuit under specified conditions. For these group installations, the conductors of any tap supplying a single motor is permitted to omit individual branch-circuit short-circuit and ground-fault protection, provided they comply with one of the following:

(1) Conductors to the motor shall have an ampacity equal to that of the branch-circuit conductors.

(2) Conductors to the motor shall have an ampacity not less than one-third that of the branch-circuit conductors, with a minimum in accordance with 430.22 Single Motor. Under this condition, the conductors to the motor overload device cannot be more than 7.5 m (25 ft) long and must be protected from physical damage by being enclosed in an approved raceway or other approved means.

(3) Conductors are permitted to have an ampacity not less than one-tenth the rating or setting of the branch-circuit short-circuit and ground-fault protective device under specific conditions. Under this condition, conductors from the controller to the motor must have an ampacity in accordance with 430.22 Single Motor.

Additionally, these conductors from the branch-circuit short-circuit and ground-fault protective device to the controller must be suitably protected from physical damage, enclosed either by an enclosed controller or by a raceway and be not more than 3 m (10 ft) long, or have an ampacity not less than that of the branch-circuit conductors.

2014 *NEC* Change

These same provisions exist for the 2014 *NEC*, with language added to

430.53(D)

Continued

tected from physical damage by being enclosed in an approved raceway or by use of other approved means.

(3) Conductors from the branch-circuit short-circuit and ground-fault protective device to a listed manual motor controller additionally marked "Suitable for Tap Conductor Protection in Group Installations," or to a branch circuit protective device, shall be permitted to have an ampacity not less than one-tenth the rating or setting of the branch-circuit short-circuit and ground-fault protective device. The conductors from the controller to the motor shall have an ampacity in accordance with 430.22. The conductors from the point of the tap ~~branch-circuit short-circuit and ground-fault protective device~~ to the controller(s) shall (1) be suitably protected from physical damage and enclosed either by an enclosed controller or by a raceway and be not more than 3 m (10 ft) long or (2) have an ampacity not less than that of the branch-circuit conductors.

Proposal 11-36b

clarify as to where the 3 m (10 ft) and the 7.5 m (25 ft) tap conductors measurements are intended to begin. The 3 m (10 ft) and the 7.5 m (25 ft) tap conductors measurements for a motor are intended to begin from the point of the tap.

Analysis of Change

Installation of multiple motors on a single branch circuit that is protected by a single branch-circuit short-circuit and ground-fault protective device is a common industry practice. This is typically referred to as a "group motor installation." In its simplest form, group motor installation means that multiple motors and their conductors, or one motor and other loads and their conductors, are protected by a single branch-circuit short-circuit and ground-fault protective device. However, numerous requirements must be met for a group motor installation to be compliant with the *NEC*. Establishing the conductor size of the group motor branch circuit taps can be found in 430.53. Section 430.53(D) prescribes that any tap supplying a single motor is not required to be protected by a single branch-circuit short-circuit and ground-fault protective device as long as it meets one of three requirements specified. Clarification was needed at these tap conditions to remove any doubt as to where the measurement of these taps was to begin and to end. For not more than 7.5 m (25 ft) long single motor taps, the tap is to be measured from the "point of the tap" to the motor overload device. For not more than 3 m (10 ft) long single motor taps, the measurement runs from the "point of the tap" to the controller(s).

430.233

Change at a Glance

The minimum voltage levels for live parts of motors or controllers requiring guarding against accidental contact by insulating mats or platforms were lowered from 150 volts to ground to 50 volts to ground.

Code Language

430.233 Guards for Attendants

Where live parts of motors or controllers operating at over ~~150~~ 50 volts to ground are guarded against accidental contact only by location as specified in 430.232, and where adjustment or other attendance may be necessary during the operation of the apparatus, suitable insulating mats or platforms shall be provided so that the attendant cannot readily touch live parts unless standing on the mats or platforms.

Informational Note: For working space, see 110.26 and 110.34.

Proposal 11-68

430.233 Guards for Attendants

The minimum voltage levels for live parts of motors or controllers requiring guarding against accidental contact by insulating mats or platforms were lowered from 150 volts to ground to 50 volts to ground.

Courtesy of Vardhman Electrical Insulating Mats

Any voltage above 50 volts is considered an electrical shock hazard according to NFPA 70E (Standard for Electrical Safety in the Workplace), the *NEC*, and the U.S. Occupational Safety and Health Administration (OSHA).

2011 *NEC* Requirement

Provisions at 430.232 require exposed live parts of motors and controllers operating at 50 volts or more between terminals to be guarded against accidental contact by their enclosures or by their locations. These locations include (1) a room or enclosure that is accessible only to qualified persons, (2) a suitable balcony, gallery, or platform, elevated and arranged so as to exclude unqualified persons, or (3) by elevation 2.5 m (8 ft) or more above the floor.

In the 2011 *NEC*, where live parts of motors or controllers operating at over 150 volts to ground were guarded against accidental contact only by the location described above, suitable insulating mats or platforms were required to be provided. Another requirement for the inclusion of these insulating mats or platforms is the necessity of adjustment or other attendance being necessary during the operation of the apparatus. These insulating mats or platforms were required at this over 150 volts to ground level so that electrical personnel cannot readily touch live exposed parts unless standing on the insulating mats or platforms.

2014 *NEC* Change

The same provisions for guarding against accidental contact from exposed live parts of motors and controllers and insulating mats or platforms exist as in the 2011 *NEC*, but the minimum voltage levels for inclusion of the insulating mats or platforms were lowered from 150 volts to ground to 50 volts to ground.

Analysis of Change

Any voltage above 50 volts is considered an electrical shock hazard according to NFPA 70E *Standard for Electrical Safety in the Workplace*, the *NEC*, and the U.S. Occupational Safety and Health Administration (OSHA). Section 430.233 was one place in previous editions of the *Code* where the voltage to ground was allowed to be greater than 50 volts. It was perceived by some users of the *Code* that this 150-volt level at 430.233 sent a mixed message about the safe voltage level and the types of protection that need to be provided for the qualified person working around exposed live parts of motors and controllers. This lowering of the minimum voltage level will ensure the same level of safety for qualified persons as afforded to unqualified persons.

It should be noted that two separate situations are addressed at 430.232 and 430.233. Section 430.232 addresses accidental contact; while 430.233 addresses workers' safety while adjusting energized equipment.

440.9

Change at a Glance

A wire type equipment grounding conductor is now required for outdoor HVAC equipment in the outdoor portion of the wiring method of LFMC or EMT.

Code Language

440.9 Grounding and Bonding

Where air-conditioning and refrigeration equipment are installed outdoors with wiring methods consisting of liquidtight flexible metal conduit or electrical metallic tubing, a wire type equipment grounding conductor, as specified in 250.118(1), shall be provided in the outdoor portion of the raceway.

Proposal 11-83

Comment 11-32, 11-29, 11-30

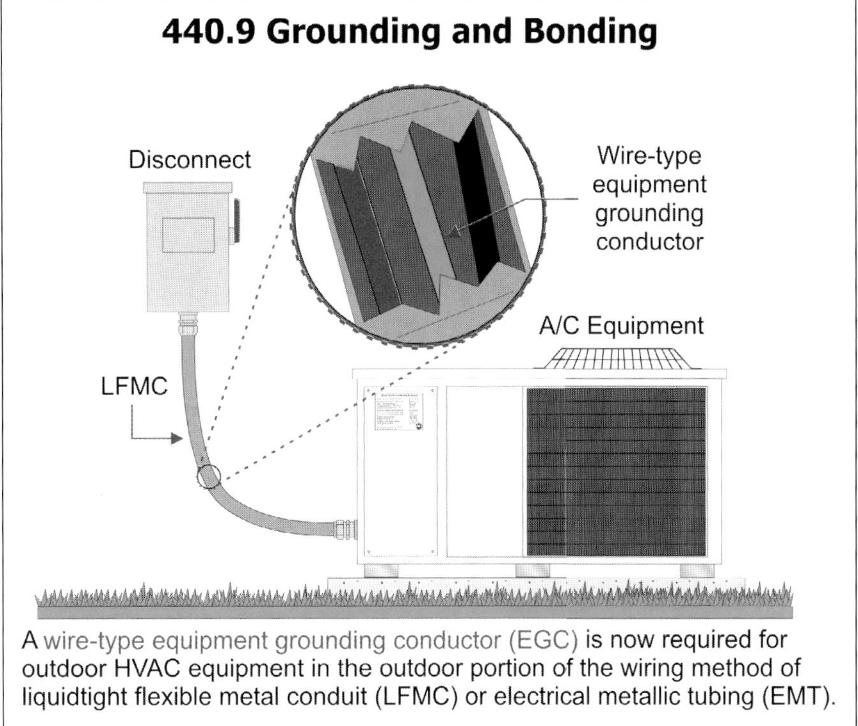

A wire-type equipment grounding conductor (EGC) is now required for outdoor HVAC equipment in the outdoor portion of the wiring method of liquidtight flexible metal conduit (LFMC) or electrical metallic tubing (EMT).

2011 *NEC* Requirement

By their own respective articles, liquidtight flexible metal conduit (LFMC) and electrical metallic tubing (EMT) are both permitted as an acceptable wiring method for outdoor heating and air-conditioning equipment. For the 2011 *NEC*, these two wiring methods were also permitted as their own equipment grounding conductor (EGC) from the unit disconnecting means to the AC units themselves in accordance with 250.118. No wire type EGC was required in addition to these wiring methods.

2014 *NEC* Change

A new section 440.9 now requires a wire type equipment grounding conductor, as specified in 250.118(1), to be provided in the outdoor portion of the raceway at outdoor air-conditioning and refrigeration equipment when the wiring method consists of liquidtight flexible metal conduit (LFMC) or electrical metallic tubing (EMT).

Analysis of Change

A proposal recommending action similar to this new wire type equipment grounding conductor (EGC) provision was actually accepted in principal by CMP-11 in the proposal stage of the 2011 *NEC*. The NEC Correlating Committee (NEC CC) directed that the proposal be referred to Code-Making Panels 5, 7, and 8 for information (see 2011 *NEC* Proposal 11-129). Two comments were submitted to CMP-11 to continue this action and both were accepted in principal by CMP-11 (see 2011 *NEC* Comment 11-52 and Comment 11-60). The NEC CC directed that Proposal 11-129 and Comment 11-52 both be reported as "Reject" (with reference to NEC CC action taken at Comment 11-52 for Comment 11-60), stating that "the CMP with jurisdiction over the individual wiring method is the panel that decides the necessity of an equipment grounding conductor." The NEC CC went further to direct that the chairs of

Continued

CMPs 7, 8 and 11 form a Task Group to develop proposals for the 2014 edition of the *NEC* to correlate this issue.

The basis of the 2011 *NEC* proposal detailed the fatality of a young boy who was killed when he stepped on top of an air-conditioning unit and touched a chain link fence. Other deaths and injuries have been reported by the U.S Consumer Product Safety Commission (CPSC) involving HVAC equipment with improper grounding. Installers and inspectors alike have witnessed problems at these outside AC systems with conduits and connectors separating from either abuse or lack of maintenance where they have been installed at these locations. The intent of this new provision is to require an equipment grounding conductor of the wire type for non-threaded metallic conduit that supplies power to air-conditioning and refrigeration equipment where located outside. The equipment grounding conductor serves to bond all metal parts together and to connect these same metal parts to the service or separately derived system's grounding electrode system. The equipment grounding conductor provides both a grounding and a bonding function. The primary purpose of this all-important conductor is to facilitate the operation of overcurrent devices under ground-fault current conditions. It is critical to maintain this grounding and bonding continuity. This redundant grounding provision has precedents in the *NEC*. An example would be at wiring methods for patient care areas of health care facilities in accordance with 517.13(B).

The addition of this new requirement will help prevent electrocution and shock hazards from occurring around air-conditioning and refrigerating equipment located outdoors by requiring a more specific and intentional type of equipment grounding conductor that has the potential to maintain a grounding and bonding connection even under duress. Companion proposals were submitted and accepted at 350.60 for LFMC and at 358.60 for EMT. These proposals, along with this one, were developed by the NEC CC Task Group consisting of members of CMPs 7, 8 and 11, which was developed from the action of the NEC CC during the 2011 *NEC* code cycle.

Note to Reader: At the time of publication of this textbook, a Certified Amending Motion (CAM) had been presented to the voting body of NFPA 70 at the NFPA Annual meeting in Chicago, IL. (see CAM 70–19). This CAM sought to accept Comment 11-28 to remove this requirement at 440.9 and return to the 2011 *NEC* provisions. This CAM was accepted by the voting body by a vote of 137 to 136. If approved by the NEC Correlating Committee (NEC CC) and the NFPA Standards Council at their meeting in late July 2013 (after the publication of this textbook), this provision at 440.9 will not be a part of the 2014 *NEC*.

445.11

Change at a Glance

Marking is required for generators to indicate when the neutral of a generator is bonded to the generator frame.

Code Language

445.11 Marking

Each generator shall be provided with a nameplate giving the manufacturer's name, the rated frequency, ~~power factor~~ the number of phases if of ac ~~alternating current, the subtransient and transient impedances~~, the rating in kilowatts or kilovolt-amperes, the normal volts and amperes corresponding to the rating, the rated revolutions per minute, ~~insulation system class~~ and the rated ambient temperature or rated temperature rise~~, and time rating~~.

Nameplates for all stationary generators and portable generators rated more than 15 kW shall also give the power factor, the subtransient and transient impedances, the insulation system class, and the time rating.

Marking shall be provided by the manufacturer to indicate whether or not the generator neutral is bonded to the generator frame. Where the bonding of a generator is modified in the field, additional marking shall be required to indicate whether the generator neutral is bonded to the generator frame.

2011 *NEC* Requirement

Marking requirements for generators required each generator to be provided with a nameplate. This nameplate was to indicate the manufacturer's name, the rated frequency, power factor, number of phases if of alternating current, the subtransient and transient impedances, the rating in kilowatts or kilovolt amperes, the normal volts and amperes corresponding to the rating, rated revolutions per minute, insulation system class and rated ambient temperature or rated temperature rise, and time rating. This applied to all generators, with no distinction between sizes of the generator.

2014 *NEC* Change

These same marking provisions held true for the 2014 *NEC*, but the power factor, the subtransient and transient impedances, the insulation system class, and the time rating markings are now required only for stationary and portable generators rated more than 15 kW. A new manufacturer's marking provision was also added requiring indication as to whether or not the generator neutral is bonded to the generator frame. This new neutral bonding provision goes further to require additional marking to indicate whether the generator neutral is bonded to the generator frame, whenever the bonding of a generator is modified in the field.

Analysis of Change

Article 250 of the *NEC* allows a generator to be installed as a separately derived system, or provisions can be implemented where a generator is not a separately derived system (*see 250.30 and Informational Notes*). What determines if a generator is not a separately derived system is, if the grounded conductor is solidly interconnected to a service-supplied system grounded conductor. An example of such a situation is where alternate source transfer equipment does not include a switching action in the grounded conductor, and allows it to remain solidly connected to the service-supplied grounded

Continued

Proposal 13-10, 13-11

Comment 13-2

conductor when the alternate source is operational and supplying the load served. In order to determine if a generator is a separately derived system or not, installers, enforcers, and users of the *Code* must be able to determine if the neutral conductor of the generator is bonded to the generator frame, in order to select appropriate transfer equipment and implement applicable wiring method requirements. This new requirement for the manufacturer to identify the neutral conductor bonding provisions will greatly aid and facilitate that adequate equipment selection. Since the generator neutral bonding point could be modified in the field, a second sentence was added to require additional marking when such events occur.

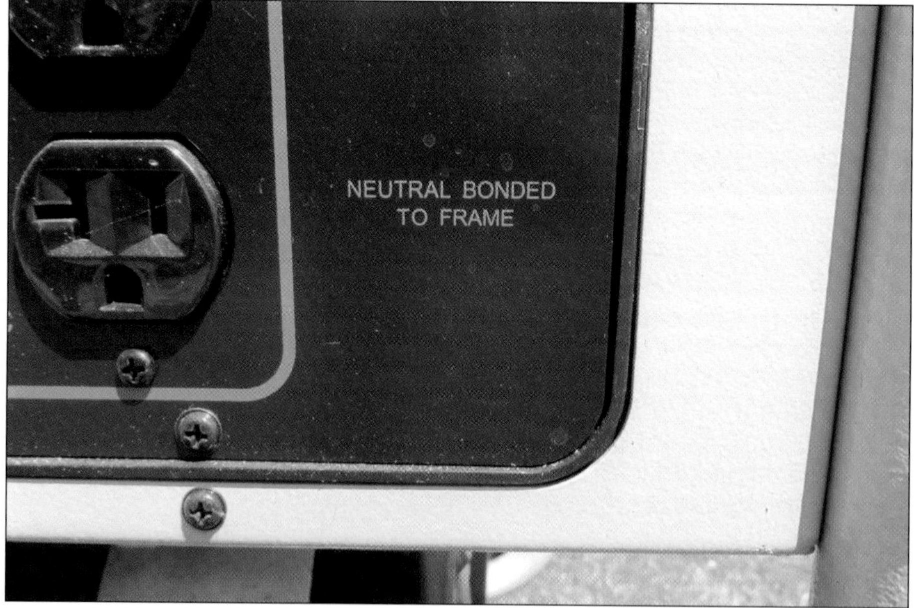

445.18

Change at a Glance

Portable generators that employ a cord and plug connection have been added as an acceptable disconnecting means for a generator.

Code Language

445.18 Disconnecting Means Required for Generators Informational Note

445.18 Disconnecting Means Required for Generators. Generators shall be equipped with disconnect(s), lockable in the open position, by means of which the generator and all protective devices and control apparatus are able to be disconnected entirely from the circuits supplied by the generator except where ~~both of~~ the following conditions apply:

(1) Portable generators that are cord and plug connected or

(2) Where both of the following conditions apply:

(a) The driving means for the generator can be readily shut down, rendered incapable of restarting and is lockable in the OFF position in accordance with 110.25.

(b) The generator is not arranged to operate in parallel with another generator or other source of voltage.

Informational Note: See UL 2200 Standard for Safety of Stationary Engine Generator Assemblies.

2011 *NEC* Requirement

Generators are required to be equipped with disconnect(s) that are lockable in the open position. This lockable disconnecting means must be able to disconnect the generator and all protective devices, and to control apparatus entirely from the circuits supplied by the generator. Two conditions existed in the 2011 *NEC* that overrode this generator disconnecting means rule: (1) if the driving means for the generator can be readily shut down; and (2) the generator is not arranged to operate in parallel with another generator or other source of voltage.

2014 *NEC* Change

A few more conditions were added to the circumstances that permit the disconnecting means requirements for generators to be omitted. For portable generators that supply power from a self-contained receptacle outlet which would accept a cord and plug connection, the cord and plug can serve as the disconnecting means. For generators where the driving means can be readily shut down, they must also be rendered incapable of restarting and be lockable in the off or "open" position in accordance with the new locking provisions of 110.25 in order to suspend the requirement for a disconnecting means.

Analysis of Change

Generators typically require a disconnecting means. Language has been added at 445.18 to eliminate a disconnecting means for a portable generator since, by their very design, these portable generators provide a cord- and plug-type connection. Power from the generator can be readily disconnected by removal of the cord from the portable generator's outlet.

The other revision at 445.18(2)(a) for generators where the driving means can be readily shut down occurred primarily to coincide with revisions for

445.18

Continued

Proposal 13-16

Comment 13-18a, 13-5, 13-6, 13-7

generators at 700.12(B)(6), Emergency Systems; at 701.12(B)(5), Legally Required Standby Systems; and at 702.12, Optional Standby Systems. This section in Article 445 had to be revised to also require the generator be rendered incapable of restarting and to be lockable in the off or "open" position, as the sections mentioned above in Chapter 7 now reference 445.18 for requirements for outdoor generator sets. These Chapter 7 changes are partially based on UL 2200, *Standard for Safety of Stationary Engine Generator Assemblies*, which mandates a means to stop the driving means, prevent restarting, and requires this means to be lockable in the off position. A new Informational Note at 445.18 points users of the *Code* to this UL standard reference. Without this revision at 445.18, there would only be a control device like a "mushroom" start-stop button to stop the generator driving means, and nothing more would be required for these Chapter 7 generator sets. This revision was needed for the safety of installers and maintainers. It should be noted that the Occupational Safety and Health Administration (OSHA) does not permit an emergency stop button to be used to lockout electrical equipment.

445.20

Change at a Glance

New GFCI requirements were added for portable generators and associated 125-volt, single-phase, 15- or 20-amperes receptacles.

Code Language

445.20 Ground-Fault Circuit-Interrupter Protection for Receptacles on 15-kW or Smaller, Portable Generators. All 125-volt, single-phase, 15-and 20 ampere receptacle outlets, that are a part of a 15 kW or smaller, portable generator, either shall have ground-fault circuit interrupter protection for personnel integral to the generator or receptacle, or shall not be available for use when the 125/250 volt locking-type receptacle is in use. If the generator does not have a 125/250 volt locking-type receptacle, this requirement shall not apply.

Proposal 13-19

Comment 13-16

445.20 GFCI Protection for Receptacles on 15-kW or Smaller, Portable Generators

All 125-volt, single-phase, 15-and 20 ampere receptacle outlets, on 15 kW or smaller, portable generators shall have GFCI protection for personnel:
- integral to the generator or receptacle, or...
- receptacle outlets shall not be available for use when the 125/250 volt locking-type receptacle is in use

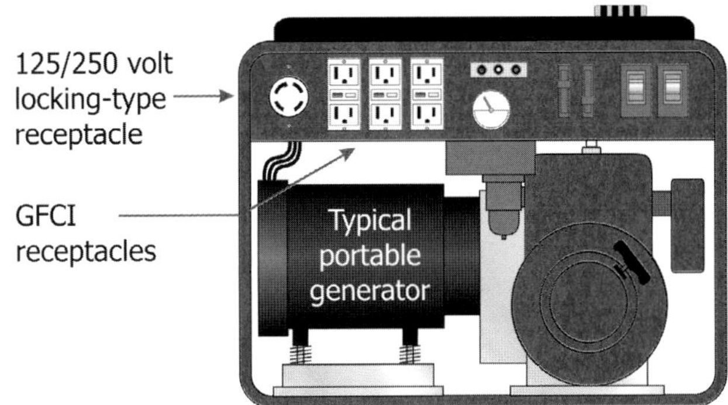

If the generator does not have a 125/250-volt locking-type receptacle, GFCI requirements are not required.

2011 *NEC* Requirement

The 2011 *NEC* added provisions for all 125-volt and 125/250-volt, single-phase, 15-, 20-, and 30-ampere receptacle outlets that are a part of a 15-kW or smaller portable generators to have listed ground-fault circuit-interrupter (GFCI) protection for personnel for temporary installations, at 590.6(A)(3). These GFCI provisions for portable generators did not exist in Article 445 in the 2011 *NEC*.

2014 *NEC* Change

A new section entitled, "Ground-Fault Circuit-Interrupter Protection for Receptacles on 15-kW or Smaller, Portable Generators" was added in Article 445. This new provision will require all 125-volt, single-phase, 15-and 20-ampere receptacle outlets that are a part of a 15 kW or smaller, portable generator to either be equipped with GFCI protection integral to the generator or receptacle, or the generator must be capable of rendering the 125-volt, single-phase, 15- and 20-ampere receptacle outlets unavailable for use when the 125/250-volt locking-type receptacle is in use. This new requirement also indicates that if the generator does not have a 125/250-volt locking-type receptacle, this GFCI requirement is not applicable.

Analysis of Change

For the 2011 *NEC* code development process, a very similar proposal seeking GFCI requirements for portable generators was submitted to CMP-13 (see 2011 *NEC* Proposal 13-19), and was accepted by CMP-13 during the proposal stage. This accepted action was reversed during the 2011 *NEC* comment stage and was not included in the 2011 *NEC*. Interestingly enough, a companion proposal (see 2011 *NEC* Proposal 3-139) was accepted by CMP-3, and was adopted into 590.6(A)(3), requiring GFCI protection for portable generators used for temporary installations. The requirements for portable generators in Article 445 and the provisions for portable generators used for temporary installations in Article 590 need to support and coincide with one another.

Small portable generators sized at 15 kW or smaller are used for many different applications. Portable generators are used extensively for temporary power at construction sites, but other applications apply as well, such as on camping trips, for temporary connection of electrical circuits in a home, or for small commercial buildings during power outages, and for power for all different types of installations during emergency situations due to natural disasters such as hurricanes. In all of these applications, there are many potential hazards that can be associated with these temporary installations. Accidental cuts, abraded wire and cable, standing water, and wet locations are just a few examples of these potentially hazardous applications. During power outages from storms and other natural disasters, personnel who may not be familiar with adequate safety procedures often use these small portable generators to supply power in less than optimal conditions. Requiring all 125-volt, single-phase, 15- and 20-ampere receptacles on 15 kW or smaller generators to be integrally GFCI-protected will help eliminate the possibilities of shock hazards from damaged circuits, damaged equipment, or the use of equipment in wet locations.

By limiting GFCI protection to only 15- and 20-ampere, single-phase, 120-volt circuits, these small generators can still be used for supplying standby power for non-GFCI-protected 30-ampere, and larger 120/240 single-phase, 3-wire with ground as well as 3-phase circuits of all sizes for houses and small commercial buildings. Typically, the duplex receptacles on the portable generator are not used when powering the entire building or large portions of the building because the occupants want as much power to the building as possible through the locking 125/250-volt receptacle which is typically used to power the building.

Note to Reader: At the time of production and publishing of this *Analysis* text, a proposed Tentative Interim Amendment (TIA) was being published for public comment in the May 3, 2013 issue of *NFPA News* with a Public Comment Closing Date of June 14, 2013. Any public comments received will be circulated to CMP-13. The Standards Council will consider the issuance of this TIA at their July 29–August 1, 2013, meeting. This proposed TIA is seeking to limit this new GFCI requirement to 15 kW or smaller, portable generators that are manufactured or remanufactured after January 1, 2015. According to the substantiation submitted with the proposed TIA, without this proposed text, this GFCI provision would apply to the use of any 15 kW or smaller portable generator, regardless of its date of manufacture. This retroactive application of this NEC rule would effectively ban the use of millions of portable generators that have been, and continue to be, used safely on a daily basis. See NFPA 70- Proposed 2014 *National Electrical Code* TIA Log No. 1097 (Reference: 445.20) for more information.

450.10

Change at a Glance

A grounding and bonding terminal bar in transformer enclosures is not permitted to be installed on or over the vent screen portion of the enclosure.

Code Language

450.10 Grounding

(A) Dry-Type Transformer Enclosures. Where separate equipment grounding conductors and supply-side bonding jumpers are installed, a terminal bar for all grounding and bonding conductor connections shall be secured inside the transformer enclosure. The terminal bar shall be bonded to the enclosure in accordance with 250.12 and shall not be installed on or over any vented portion of the enclosure.

Exception: *Where a dry-type transformer is equipped with wire-type connections (leads), the grounding and bonding connections shall be permitted to be connected together using any of the methods in 250.8 and shall be bonded to the enclosure if of metal.*

(B) Other Metal Parts. Where grounded, exposed non– current-carrying metal parts of transformer installations, including fences, guards, and so forth, shall be grounded and bonded under the conditions and in the manner

445.10(A) Violation

2011 *NEC* Requirement

Section 450.10 of the 2011 *NEC* addressed grounding and bonding of exposed non–current-carrying metal parts of transformer installations. This might include fences, guards, etc. A grounding and bonding terminal bar inside the transformer enclosure was not addressed in Article 450 in the 2011 *NEC*.

2014 *NEC* Change

New provisions were put in place for terminating grounding and bonding conductors inside a transformer enclosure. These conductors could include equipment grounding conductors, supply-side bonding jumpers, etc. A grounding and bonding terminal bar for the purpose of landing these grounding and bonding conductors must be bonded to the transformer enclosure, but cannot be mounted on or over any vented opening or vented screens provided by the manufacturer of the transformer enclosure. A new exception to this new grounding and bonding main rule addresses transformers equipped with wire-type connections (pig-tail leads). Under this wire-type connection condition, the grounding and bonding connections are permitted to be connected together using any of the methods in 250.8, Connection of Grounding and Bonding Equipment, and shall be bonded to the enclosure (*if the enclosure is metal*). The existing rule for grounding and bonding of other metal parts associated with the installation of a transformer has become 450.10(B).

Analysis of Change

The need to terminate grounding and bonding conductors, such as supply-side bonding jumpers, in enclosures for dry-type transformers creates problematic concerns if a grounding and bonding terminal bar is not supplied by the manufacturer. The *Code* has not provided clear and concise requirements to deal with this issue. Often, it is common practice to see installers

450.10

Continued

specified for electrical equipment and other exposed metal parts in Parts V, VI, and VII of Article 250.

Proposal 9-144

mounting a grounding and bonding terminal bar on top of the vented openings in the bottom of the transformer enclosure, with the terminal bar attached to the enclosure with a common nut, bolt, and fender washer through one of the vented openings. This can result in a less than effective connection — using a method that has not been evaluated as grounding and bonding equipment and should not be depended upon to serve as an effective ground-fault current return path. This new requirement calling for a grounding and bonding terminal bar and prohibiting this terminal bar from being installed on or over the vented openings will eliminate the inconsistencies and will provide needed direction for installers and the enforcement community alike.

450.11

Change at a Glance

Marking requirements for transformers were revised into a list format. Transformers can be supplied at the secondary voltage (reversed wired) only in accordance with manufacturer's instructions.

Code Language

450.11 Marking

(A) General. Each transformer shall be provided with a nameplate giving the following information:

(1) Name of manufacturer
(2) Rated kilovolt-amperes
(3) Frequency
(4) Primary and secondary voltage
(5) Impedance of transformers 25 kVA and larger
(6) Required clearances for transformers with ventilating openings
(7) Amount and kind of insulating liquid where used
(8) For dry-type transformers, temperature class for the insulation system

(B) Source Marking. A transformer shall be permitted to be supplied at the marked secondary voltage, provided that the installation is in accordance with the manufacturer's instructions.

Proposal 9-145

Comment 9-73

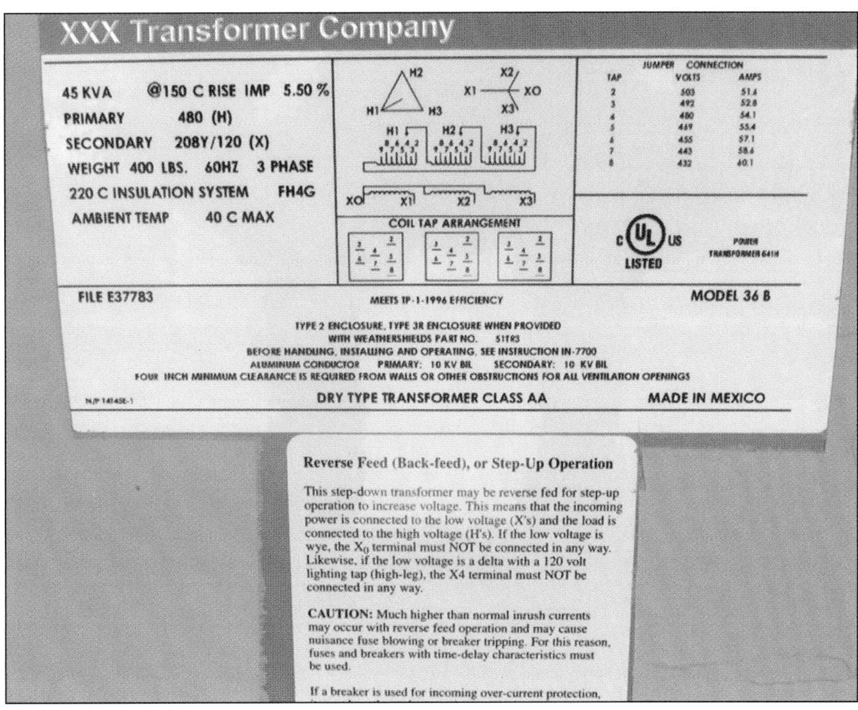

2011 *NEC* Requirement

In the 2011 *NEC*, the required information was provided in a paragraph format.

2014 *NEC* Change

The required nameplate information for transformers was formatted into a more user-friendly list format. A new subsection (B) was added to require transformers that are supplied at the secondary voltage (reversed wired) to be installed in accordance with manufacturer's instructions. Transformers supplied at their secondary voltage are only permitted if identified as such by the manufacturer.

Analysis of Change

Dry-type transformers that are permitted to be supplied from either direction (primary or secondary) are typically marked by the manufacturer as "Bi-Directional." The manufacturer of these "Bi-Directional" transformers will also provide installation instructions detailing specific information as to how the transformer should be connected when the primary and secondary are reversed. Although it is common industry practice to reverse wire dry-type transformers, the product standard for dry-type transformers (UL 1561 *Dry-Type General Purpose and Power Transformers*) does not support this practice for any and all dry-type transformers. Unless identified for "reverse wiring," UL 1561 requires the supply to a transformer be connected to the primary, and the load to be connected to the secondary side of the transformer. The new provisions at 450.11(B) will require transformers supplied at the secondary voltage only to be so in accordance with manufacturer's instructions.

Article 480

Change at a Glance

Several changes occurred in Article 480 that resulted in the article's being restructured. New 480.3 was added for "Battery and Cell Terminations." New 480.6 was added for "DC Disconnect Methods." Section 480.9 was revised from "Working Space" to "Battery Locations."

Code Language

Article 480 Storage Batteries

480.1 Scope

480.2 Definitions

480.3 Battery and Cell Terminations

480.4 Wiring and Equipment Supplied from Batteries

480.5 Overcurrent Protection for Prime Movers

480.6 DC Disconnect Methods

480.7 Insulation of Batteries Not Over 250 Volts

~~**480.7 Insulation of Batteries of over 250 Volts**~~

480.8 Racks and Trays

480.9 Battery Locations

480.10 Vents

(See *NEC* for complete text).

Proposal 13-3, 13-22, 13-24 thru 13-33, 13-37, 13-38, 13-42, 13-44, 13-45

Comment 13-21 thru 13-29

2011 *NEC* Requirement

The requirements for storage batteries are found in Article 480. Refer to the 2011 *NEC* for complete text and article structure.

2014 *NEC* Change

Article 480, Storage Batteries, was restructured. See the 2014 *NEC* for complete text and article structure.

Analysis of Change

Rules for storage batteries have been part of the *NEC* since its inception in 1897. Several changes were implemented in Article 480, Storage Batteries, for the 2014 *NEC*. Some of the more noteworthy changes occurred at new 480.3, Battery and Cell Terminations, which will provide needed guidance for dissimilar metals at battery connections, for intercell and intertier conductors and connectors, and for electrical connections to the battery terminals. Another change occurred at 480.8(C), Accessibility, which adds requirements for terminals and transparent battery containers to be readily accessible. Another change of note occurred at 480.9(D), Top Terminal Batteries, under battery locations; this subsection addresses working space requirements for top-terminal batteries and requires them to be in accordance with the manufacturer's instructions.

490.48

Change at a Glance

Requirements for substations were removed from 225.70 in their entirety and relocated at new 490.48(B). New provisions for substations were added at 490.48(A) and (C).

Code Language

490.48 Substations

(A) Documentation

(1) General
(2) Protective Grounding
(3) Guarding Live Parts
(4) Transformers and Regulators
(5) Conductors
(6) Circuit Breakers, Switches, and Fuses
(7) Switchgear Assemblies
(8) Metal-Enclosed Bus
(9) Surge Arresters

(B) Warning Signs

(1) General
(2) Isolating Equipment
(3) Fuse Locations
(4) Backfeed
(5) ~~Metal-Enclosed and Metal-Clad~~ Switchgear

(C) Diagram

(See NEC for complete text)

Proposal 4-86 thru 4-94, 9-179

Comment 9-9 thru 9-17

2011 *NEC* Requirement

Requirements for substations were located at 225.70 in the 2011 *NEC*. Section 225.70 dealt with warning signs for substations only.

2014 *NEC* Change

Requirements for substations were removed from 225.70 in their entirety and relocated at new 490.48(B). New provisions documentation requirements for substations were added at 490.48(A). Also new for the 2014 *NEC* are provisions for a permanent, single-line diagram of the switchgear to be provided in a readily visible location within the same room or enclosed area with the switchgear. This diagram must also identify interlocks, isolation means, and all possible sources of voltage to the installation under normal or emergency conditions with companion markings on the switchgear itself. A new exception was added for 490.48(C) to allow this diagram to be omitted where the equipment consists of a single cubicle or metal-enclosed unit substation containing only one set of high-voltage switching devices.

Analysis of Change

The previous language at 225.70 did not adequately address the installation of substations. The relocated and new text at 490.48 will provide the user of the *Code* with a performance based outline of items that must be designed by a qualified licensed professional engineer engaged primarily in the design of substations. This new Article 490 will include minimum requirements for substations. Developing prescriptive requirements for substations is infeasible due to the wide range of equipment, characteristics and design. These new substation requirements are similar in nature to Article 399, Outdoor Overhead Conductors over 1000 Volts, which was added to the 2011 *NEC*.

Section 225.70 was removed from Article 225, Outside Branch Circuits and Feeders, in its entirety and inserted into a new 490.48 as none of its contents

490.48

Continued

was within the scope of Article 225. These provisions were the result of proposals by the High Voltage Task Group appointed by the NEC Correlating Committee.

It should also be noted that separate proposals and comments resulted in similar language being accepted by CMP-4 and CMP-9 at two different sections of Article 490. New 490.25 and new 490.48(B)(4) are very similar in nature pertaining to warning labels for backfeed isolating switches or disconnecting means for equipment, over 1000 volts, nominal. See Proposal 9-165 for the changes at 490.25. This may be something that will need to be addressed in future editions of the *Code*.

501.40 and Exception

501.40 Multiwire Branch Circuits

501.40 and the exception were deleted entirely as the requirements for simultaneous disconnection of all ungrounded conductors of multiwire branch circuits are already provided at 210.4(B).

~~In a Class I, Division 1 location, a multiwire branch circuit shall not be permitted.~~

~~Exception: Where the disconnect device(s) for the circuit opens all ungrounded conductors of the multiwire circuit simultaneously.~~

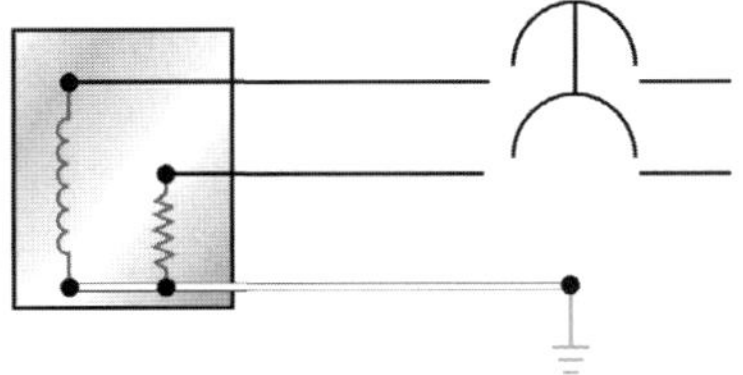

Note: *Same deletion at 502.40, 505.21, and 506.21*

Change at a Glance

Section 501.40 and the associated exception dealing with multiwire branch circuits in Class I, Division 1 were deleted entirely.

Code Language

~~**501.40 Multiwire Branch Circuits**~~

~~In a Class I, Division 1 location, a multiwire branch circuit shall not be permitted.~~

~~***Exception:*** *Where the disconnect device(s) for the circuit opens all ungrounded conductors of the multiwire circuit simultaneously.*~~

Proposal 14-59

2011 *NEC* Requirement

The main rule of this section of Article 501 prohibited a multiwire branch circuit from being installed in a Class I, Division 1 location. Then the exception, which followed the main rule, permitted a multiwire branch circuit in a Class I, Division 1 location if the disconnect means for the multiwire branch circuit opened all ungrounded conductors simultaneously.

2014 *NEC* Change

NEC 501.40 and the exception were deleted entirely. The requirements for simultaneous disconnection of all ungrounded conductors of multiwire branch circuits are already provided at 210.4(B).

Analysis of Change

Requirements and provisions for multiwire branch circuits have gone through several revisions throughout the *NEC* over the last few *Code* cycles. Language at 210.4 dealing with multiwire branch circuits has itself gone through significant changes recently. The requirement for simultaneous disconnection of all ungrounded conductors of multiwire branch circuits was revised in the 2008 *NEC*. Prior to this revision, simultaneous disconnection of all ungrounded conductors of multiwire branch circuits was only required when the ungrounded conductors terminated on the same yoke or mounting strap. This change seemed to be lost when it came to multiwire branch circuits in hazardous (classified) locations until the 2014 *NEC*. With the 2008 *NEC* revised language at 210.4(B), this language at 501.40, besides being a bit contradictive with its own exception, was redundant and no longer necessary. It should be pointed out that the requirements in Article 210 apply to all electrical installations, except as modified or amended by Chapter 5, 6, or 7 in accordance with 90.3.

The same deletion of text with very similar requirements for multiwire branch circuits occurred at the following locations:

502.40	Class II, Division 1 Locations	Proposal 14-92
505.21	Class I, Zone 1 Locations	Proposal 14-184
506.21	Zone 20 and Zone 21 Locations	Proposal 14-255a

Article 504

Change at a Glance

Article 504 was revised to align with intrinsically safe products standards.

Code Language

Article 504 Intrinsically Safe Systems

504.1 Scope

504.2 Definitions

504.3 Application of Other Articles

504.4 Equipment

504.10 Equipment Installation

~~504.20 Wiring Methods~~

504.30 Separation of Intrinsically Safe Conductors

504.50 Grounding

504.60 Bonding

504.70 Sealing

504.80 Identification

(See NEC for complete text)

Proposal 14-112, 14-116, 14-117, 14-120, 14-123 through 14-125

Comment 14-33, 14-34, 14-36

2011 *NEC* Requirement

Article 504 covered intrinsically safe systems. An *intrinsically safe system* is defined as, "an assembly of interconnected intrinsically safe apparatus, associated apparatus, and interconnecting cables, in that those parts of the system that may be used in hazardous (classified) locations are intrinsically safe circuits."

2014 *NEC* Change

Article 504 was revised to align with intrinsically safe products standards. New subsections were added such as 504.10(C) for "Enclosures"; 504.10(D) for "Simple Apparatus"; and 504.30(C) for separation of intrinsically safe conductors "From Grounded Metal." Revision also resulted in deletion of some duplication within Article 504.

Analysis of Change

Revisions took place in Article 504 to align with intrinsically safe products standards such as ANSI/ISA-60079-11 *Explosive Atmospheres – Part 11* and ANSI/UL 913 *Standard for Safety, Intrinsically Safe Apparatus and Associated Apparatus for Use in Class I, II, and III, Division 1, Hazardous (Classified) Locations*. Revision also resulted in deletion of some duplication within Article 504, such as 504.20 for "Wiring Methods."

A new 504.10(C) was added for general-purpose enclosures containing intrinsically safe apparatus and associated apparatus, and duplicate text was removed from 504.10(B). A new 504.10(D) entitled, "Simple Apparatus" resulted from deletion of matching text at 504.10(B) that deals with the locations of intrinsically safe apparatus.

Table 514.3(B)(1), Footnote 2 and Figures 514.3(a) and 514.3(b)

Change at a Glance

Footnote 2 following Table 514.3(B)(1) now references Figure 514.3(a) and new Figure 514.3(b).

Code Language

Table 514.3(B)(1) Class 1 Locations – Motor Fuel Dispensing Facilities

Footnote 2 to Table: Refer to Figure 514.3(a) and Figure 514.3(b) for an illustration of classified location around dispensing devices.

Figure 514.3(a) Classified Areas Adjacent to Dispensers ~~as Detailed in Table 514.3(B)(1)~~. [30A: Figure 8.3.2(a)]

Figure 514.3(b) Classified Areas Adjacent to Dispenser Mounted on Aboveground Storage Tank [30A: Figure 8.3.2(b)]

(See NEC for complete table and figures.)

Proposal 14-237

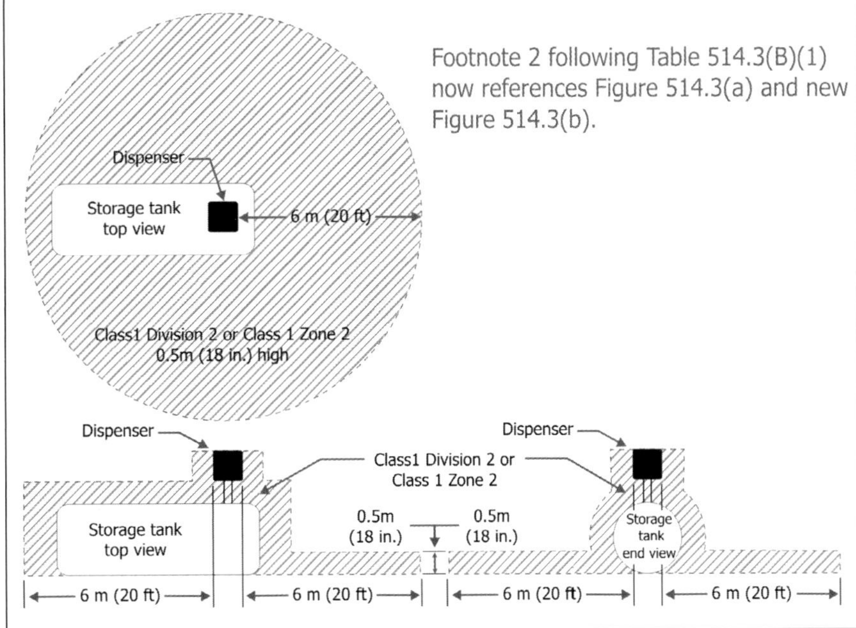

Figure 514.3(b) Classified Areas Adjacent to Dispenser Mounted on Aboveground Storage Tank

Footnote 2 following Table 514.3(B)(1) now references Figure 514.3(a) and new Figure 514.3(b).

2011 *NEC* Requirement

Table 514.3(B)(1) gives a list of areas where Class 1 liquids are stored, handled, or dispensed and is used to delineate and classify motor fuel dispensing facilities, commercial garages, and aboveground tanks. Footnote 2 to this table referred to Figure 514.3 for an illustration of classified locations around dispensing devices.

2014 *NEC* Change

Footnote 2 to Table 514.3(B)(1) refers to the existing and renamed Figure 514.3(a) for illustrations of classified areas adjacent to dispensers, in addition to referencing the new Figure 514.3(B) for illustrations of classified areas adjacent to dispensers mounted on aboveground storage tanks.

Analysis of Change

A new Figure 514.3(b) was added in Article 514 and is referenced at Table 514.3(B)(1), Footnote 2. The existing Figure 514.3(a) and the new Figure 514.3(b) were updated to reflect the information conveyed at Figure 8.3.2(a) and Figure 8.3.2(b) of NFPA 30A, *Code for Motor Fuel Dispensing Facilities and Repair Garages*. New Figure 514.3(b) illustrates classified areas adjacent to dispensers mounted on aboveground storage tanks. These aboveground storage tanks with dispensers are becoming more and more commonplace and needed to be reflected in Article 514.

Article 516

Change at a Glance

Article 516 was revised and reorganized for the 2014 *NEC*, including a new title of "Spray Application, Dipping, and Coating, and Printing Processes Using Flammable or Combustible Materials."

Code Language

Article 516 Spray Application, Dipping, ~~and~~ Coating, and Printing Processes Using Flammable or Combustible Materials

See *NEC* for complete text.

Proposal 14-243, 14-244

Comment 14-67

2011 *NEC* Requirement

Article 516 covers the regular or frequent application of flammable liquids, combustible liquids, and combustible powders by spray operations and the application of flammable liquids, or combustible liquids at temperatures above their flashpoint, by dipping, coating, or other means.

2014 *NEC* Change

Article 516 was revised and rewritten to correlate with the 2011 editions of NFPA 33 *Standard for Spray Application Using Flammable and Combustible Materials* and NFPA 34 *Standard for Dipping, Coating, and Printing Processes Using Flammable or Combustible Liquids*.

Analysis of Change

For the 2011 *NEC*, the Informational Notes in Article 516 were revised to the 2011 editions of NFPA 33 and NFPA 34. However, the actual text in Article 516 remained the extracted text from 2007. Proposal 14-244 and other proposals suggested partial revisions to Article 516, but no proposal addressed all of the parts of Article 516 that were 2007 NFPA 33 and 34 extracted text. The NEC Correlating Committee directed that a task group be formed to resolve correlation issues/conflicts, rather than refer to an outdated material. This task group came up with a total re-write of Article 516.

The proper maintenance and operation of processes and process area where flammable and combustible materials are handled and applied are critical with respect to the protection of life and property from fire and explosion. Experience has shown that the largest fire losses and frequency of fires have occurred where the proper codes and standards have not been used or applied properly. This makes the revision of Article 516 critical to the process of providing a safe working environment in and around spray application, dipping, and coating, and printing processes using flammable or combustible materials.

517.2 Definitions

Change at a Glance

Several definitions in Article 517 were revised, deleted, or added.

517.2 Definitions (Health Care Facilities)

Several definitions in Article 517 were revised, deleted or added as a result of the re-organization of the make-up of the "Essential Electrical System" of a hospital.

New Definitions:
Support Space
Wet Procedure Location

Revised Definitions:
Critical Branch
Equipment ~~System~~ Branch
Life Safety Branch
Patient Care ~~Area~~ Space
General Care ~~Area~~ Space
Patient Care Vicinity

Deleted Definitions:
~~Emergency System~~
~~Wet Procedure Locations~~
(from definition of Patient Care Space)

2011 *NEC* Requirement

Definitions related to health care facilities are located at 514.2.

2014 *NEC* Change

Several definitions in Article 517 were revised, deleted or added. This was the result of the re-organization of the make-up of the "Essential Electrical System" of a hospital. *(See NEC and 517.2 for complete text)*

Analysis of Change

As a result of an NFPA Standards Council Decision regarding the scoping issues of electrical requirements in NFPA 99 *Health Care Facilities Code*, it was determined that coordination of the electrical requirements was needed between the *NEC* and NFPA 99. In an effort to coordinate the *NEC* —and, in particular, Article 517— with NFPA 99, several definitions had to be revised. Some definitions were deleted, and others were added. Some of the definition revisions resulted from the re-organization of the make-up of the "Essential Electrical System" of a hospital. This action eliminates the term *emergency system*, leaving only the essential system with the three separate branches: the critical, the life safety, and the equipment branch. In some definitions and other locations in Article 517, CMP-15 changed words such as "room" or "area" to "space" or "location." This is an effort to have Article 517 remain consistent with NFPA 99.

Code Language

517.2 Definitions

Critical Branch. A ~~subsystem of the emergency system consisting~~ system of feeders and branch circuits supplying ~~energy to~~ power for task illumination, ~~special power circuits,~~ fixed equipment, select receptacles, and select power circuits serving areas and functions related to patient care and that ~~are~~ is connected to alternate power sources by one or more transfer switches during interruption of normal power source. ~~[99:3.3.26]~~ [99:3.3.30] *[ROP 15-12] [ROC 15-5]*

~~**Emergency System.** A system of circuits and equipment intended to supply alternate power to a limited number of prescribed functions vital to the protection of life and safety. [99:3.3.41]~~ *[ROP 15-13]*

Equipment ~~System~~ Branch. A system of feeders and branch circuits ~~and equipment~~ arranged for delayed, automatic, or manual connection to the alternate power source and that

Continued

serves primarily 3-phase power equipment. [99:3.3.46]. *[ROP 15–14]*

Life Safety Branch. A ~~subsystem of the emergency system consisting~~ system of feeders and branch circuits~~, meeting the requirements of Article 700 and intended to provide adequate power needs to ensure safety to patients and personnel, and~~ supplying power for lighting, receptacles, and equipment essential for life safety that ~~are~~ is automatically connected to alternate power sources by one or more transfer switches during interruption of the normal power source. ~~[99:3.3.96]~~ [99:3.3.94] *[ROP 15–16] [ROC 15–10]*

Patient Care ~~Area~~ Space. ~~Any portion of~~ Space within a health care facility wherein patients are intended to be examined or treated. ~~Areas of a health care facility in which patient care is administered are classified as general care areas or critical care areas. The governing body of the facility designates these areas in accordance with the type of patient care anticipated and with the following definitions of the area classification.~~ [ROP 15–19] *[ROC 15–12]*
Basic Care Space. Space in which failure of equipment or a system is not likely to cause injury to the patients or caregivers but may cause patient discomfort. *[ROP 15–19]*
General Care ~~Area~~ Space. ~~Patient bedrooms, examining rooms, treatment rooms, clinics, and similar areas in which it is intended that the patient will come in contact with ordinary appliances such as a nurse call system, electric beds, examining lamps, telephones, and entertainment devices. [99, 2005]~~ Space in which failure of equipment or a system is likely to cause minor injury to patients or caregivers. *[ROP 15–19]*
Critical Care ~~Areas~~ Space. ~~Those special care units, intensive care units, coronary care units, angiography laboratories, cardiac catheterization laboratories, delivery rooms, operating rooms, and similar areas in which patients are intended to be subjected to invasive procedures and connected to line-operated, electromedical devices.~~ Space in which failure of equipment or a system is likely to cause major injury or death to patients or caregivers. *[ROP 15–19]*
~~Wet Procedure Locations.~~ *(Deleted from definition of Patient Care Space).*
Support Space. Space in which failure of equipment or a system is not likely to have a physical impact on patients or caregivers. *[ROP 15–19]*

Patient Care Vicinity. ~~In an area in which patients are normally cared for, the patient care vicinity is the space with surfaces likely to be contacted by the patient or an attendant who can touch the patient.~~ A space, within a location intended for the examination and treatment of patients, extending 1.8 m (6 ft) beyond the ~~perimeter of the bed in its nominal location~~ normal location of the patient bed, chair, table, treadmill, or other device that supports the patient during examination and treatment and extending vertically to 2.3 m (7 ft 6 in.) above the floor. ~~[99:3.3.140]~~ [99:3.3.139] *[ROP 15–21]*

Wet Procedure Location. The area in a patient care space where a procedure is performed that is normally subject to wet conditions while patients are present, including standing fluids on the floor or drenching of the work area, either of which condition is intimate to the patient or staff. *[ROP 15–24]*

Informational Note: Routine housekeeping procedures and incidental spillage of liquids do not define a wet procedure location. *[ROP 15–24]*

(See NEC and 517.2 for complete text)

Proposal 15-3, 15-12, 15-13, 15-14, 15-16, 15-19, 15-21, 15-24

Comment 15-5, 15-6, 15-8, 15-10, 15-11, 15-12

517.16

Change at a Glance

Isolated grounding type receptacles are not permitted within patient care vicinity *(rather than the entire health care facility)*.

REVISION

Code Language

517.16 Use of Isolated Ground Receptacles ~~with Insulated Grounding Terminals~~. An ~~Receptacles with~~ insulated grounding receptacle ~~terminals, as permitted in 250.146(D),~~ shall not be ~~permitted~~ installed within a patient care vicinity. [99:6.3.2.2.7.1(B)]

Proposal 15-31

Comment 15-22

517.16 Use of Isolated Ground Receptacles

Isolated grounding type receptacles are now not permitted within a patient care vicinity only *(rather than the entire health care facility).*

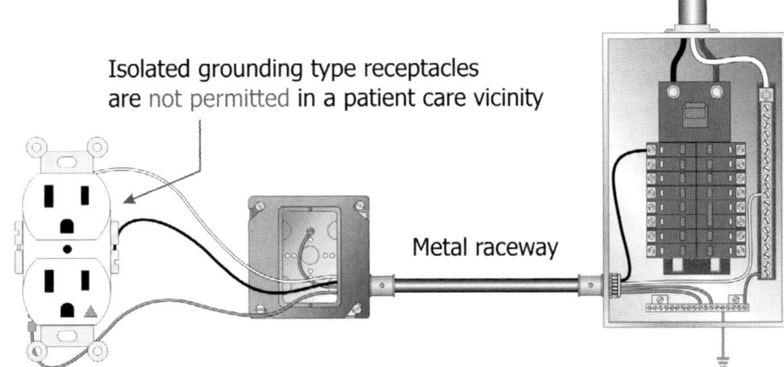
Isolated grounding type receptacles
are not permitted in a patient care vicinity
Metal raceway

517.16 Use of Isolated Ground Receptacles. An isolated ground receptacle shall not be installed within a patient care vicinity.

2011 *NEC* Requirement

Receptacles with insulated grounding terminals, as described in 250.146(D), were not permitted within a health care facility.

2014 *NEC* Change

The requirement to prohibit isolated ground receptacles in health care facilities was condensed to prohibit these receptacles from only the patient care vicinity of a health care facility.

Analysis of Change

The previous language at 517.16 would prohibit the use of isolated ground receptacles in the entire health care facility. Section 517.16 is located in Part II of Article 517 and, as such, applies to the entire health care facility. The 2012 edition of NFPA 99 *Health Care Facilities Code* affirms the use of isolated ground receptacles in health care facilities while continuing to forbid their use only within patient care vicinities [see NFPA 99 6.3.2.2.7.1(A) and 6.3.2.2.7.1(B)]. Listed cord- and plug-connected medical instrumentation used in health care facilities outside of patient care vicinities, typically at nurses' monitoring stations, often require connection to isolated ground receptacles to insure measurement accuracy by mitigating electrical noise or interference, which is essential to patient medical safety. Allowing isolated ground receptacles away from patient care vicinity would allow this mitigation against equipment interference without affecting patient safety.

The issue and concern with isolated ground receptacles within patient care vicinity is the assurance of the equipment grounding conductor redundancy requirement of 517.13(A) and (B) for wiring methods at patient care vicinity. This "redundant grounding" provision in a patient care space or area requires two equipment grounding paths to always insure one is functioning at all times. This is usually accomplished with a wire-type equipment grounding conductor within a metallic wiring method that meets the equipment grounding conductor provisions of 250.118. This redundant grounding provision cannot be accomplished with an isolated ground receptacle.

517.18(A)

Change at a Glance

All receptacles or the cover plate supplied from the critical branch are required to have a distinctive color or marking so as to be readily identifiable. Marking is also to indicate the panelboard and branch circuit number supplying them.

Code Language

517.18 General Care Areas

(A) Patient Bed Location. Each patient bed location shall be supplied by at least two branch circuits, one from the ~~emergency system~~ critical branch and one from the normal system. All branch circuits from the normal system shall originate in the same panelboard. The electrical receptacles or the cover plate for the electrical receptacles supplied from the critical branch shall have a distinctive color or marking so as to be readily identifiable and shall also indicate the panelboard and branch circuit number supplying them.

~~The~~ B~~b~~ranch circuits serving patient bed locations shall not be part of a multiwire branch circuit.

Proposal 15-34

517.18(A) Patient Bed Location (General Care)

Cover plates for the receptacles or the electrical receptacles themselves are required to have a distinctive color or marking so as to be readily identifiable as being supplied from the critical branch.

Covers or receptacles must also indicate the panelboard and branch circuit number supplying them.

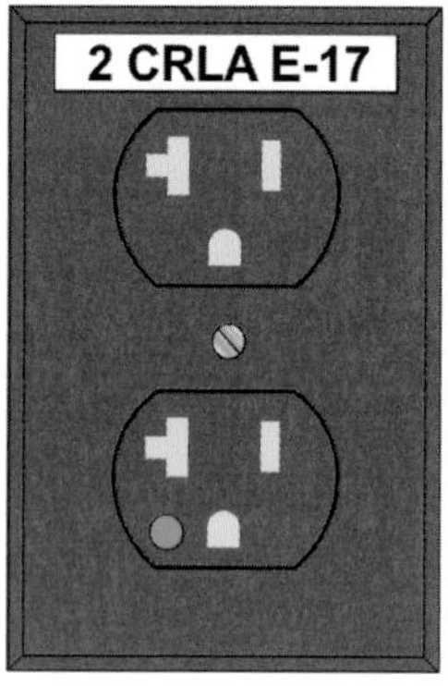

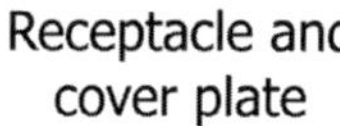

Receptacle and cover plate

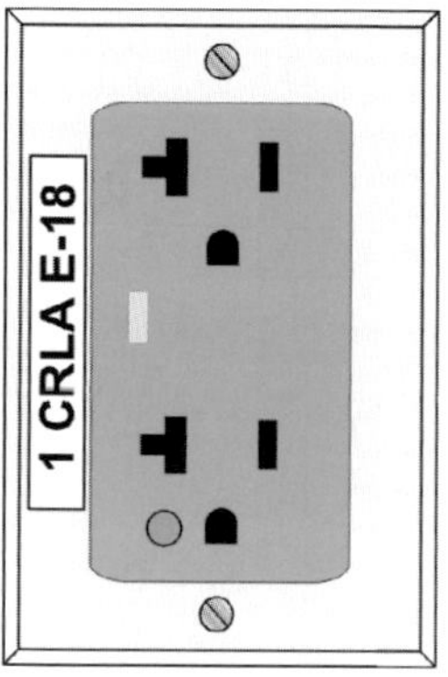

Receptacle only

Cover plate only

2011 *NEC* Requirement

Each patient bed location shall be supplied by at least two branch circuits; one of these branch circuits is required to be supplied from the normal system. In the 2011 *NEC*, one of these branch circuits was required to be supplied from the emergency system. These branch circuits serving patient bed locations cannot be part of a multiwire branch circuit. All branch circuits from the normal system must originate from the same panelboard. Three exceptions exist for these requirements.

2014 *NEC* Change

The term *emergency system* was removed from Article 517. Therefore, one of the two branch circuits to supply patient bed locations is now required to be supplied from the *critical branch* rather than from the emergency system. The branch circuit serving patient bed locations still cannot be part of a multiwire branch circuit and the normal system branch circuits must continue to originate from the same panelboard. A new requirement for all receptacles or the cover plate supplied from the critical branch is to have a distinctive color or marking so as to be readily identifiable. These markings are also required to indicate the panelboard and branch circuit number supplying these receptacles. The three existing exceptions for these requirements remain in place.

Analysis of Change

This change is a continuation to align *NEC* Article 517 with NFPA 99, *Health Care Facilities Code*. Distinctive color or marking of receptacles or the cover plate supplied from the critical branch in patient bed locations is a requirement of NFPA 99. Requiring the same at 517.18(A) will make the *NEC* consistent with NFPA 99 regarding branch circuit identification requirements. For the 2014 *NEC*, the term *emergency system* was removed from Article 517 to once again be consistent with NFPA 99, and also to remove confusion from these circuits in health care facilities from those circuits described in Article 700, Emergency Systems.

517.18(B)

Change at a Glance

The minimum number of receptacles required for general care area patient bed locations of health care facilities was increased from four to eight.

REVISION

Code Language

517.18 General Care Areas

(B) Patient Bed Location Receptacles. Each patient bed location shall be provided with a minimum of ~~four~~ eight receptacles. They shall be permitted to be of the single, duplex, or quadruplex type, or any combination of the three. All receptacles~~, whether four or more,~~ shall be listed "hospital grade" and shall be so identified. The grounding terminal of each receptacle shall be connected to an insulated copper equipment grounding conductor sized in accordance with Table 250.122.

Exception No. 1: *The requirements of 517.18(B) shall not apply to psychiatric, substance abuse, and rehabilitation hospitals meeting the requirements of 517.10(B)(2).*

Exception No. 2: *Psychiatric security rooms shall not be required to have receptacle outlets installed in the room.*

Proposal 15-35, 15-36

517.18(B) Patient Bed Location Receptacles

The minimum number of receptacles required for general care area patient bed locations of health care facilities was increased from four to eight receptacles.

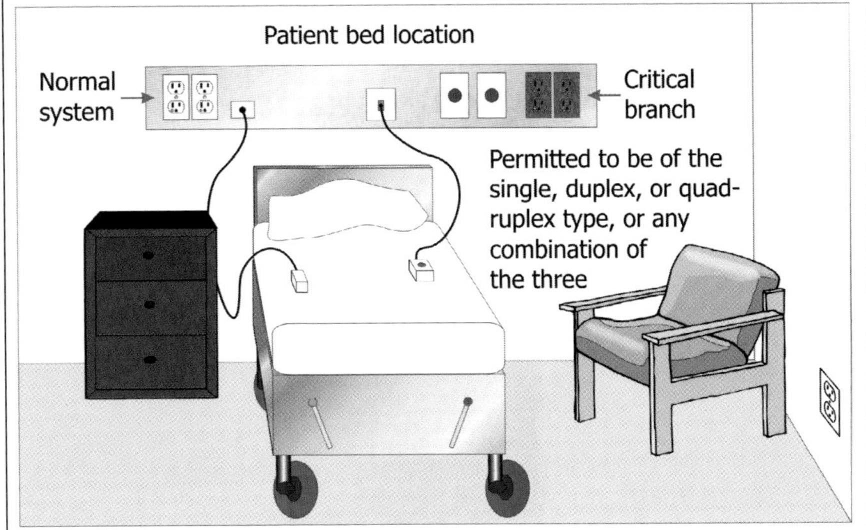
Patient bed location
Normal system
Critical branch
Permitted to be of the single, duplex, or quadruplex type, or any combination of the three

2011 *NEC* Requirement

Each general care area patient bed location was required to be provided with a minimum of four receptacles. These receptacles are permitted to be supplied from a configuration of single, duplex, or quadruplex type, or any combination of the three. All of these patient bed location receptacles are required to be listed hospital grade-type receptacles and so identified. The grounding terminal of each receptacle is also required to be connected to an insulated copper equipment grounding conductor sized in accordance with Table 250.122. Two exceptions to these requirements deal with psychiatric, substance abuse, and rehabilitation hospitals.

2014 *NEC* Change

These same provisions for receptacles in general care area patient bed locations still apply, with the provision for the number of required receptacles being expanded from four to eight.

Analysis of Change

The minimum number of receptacles required for general care area patient bed locations of a health care facility was increased from four to eight to align the *NEC* with NFPA 99, *Health Care Facilities Code*. The 2012 edition of NFPA 99 underwent some major modification, one of which eliminated all occupancy chapters within the document and adopted a risk-based approach as far as the patient is concerned. A new process detailing building systems categories in healthcare facilities was introduced. Category 1 covers facility systems in which failure of such equipment or system is likely to cause major injury or death of patients or caregivers. Category 2 is facility systems in which failure of such equipment is likely to cause minor injury to patients or caregivers. Category 3 is facility systems in which failure of such equipment is not likely to cause injury to patients or caregivers but can cause patient discomfort. Category 4 is facility systems in which failure of such equipment would have no impact on patient care. These categories are determined by documenting a defined risk-assessment procedure found in NFPA 99.

NFPA 99 Section 6.3.2.2.6.2 requires each patient bed location in general care areas, where considered a Category 2 application, to be provided with a minimum of eight receptacles. Section 517.18(B) in the 2011 *NEC* required only four receptacles. CMP-15 revised the number of receptacles from four to eight to bring 517.18(B) in line with NFPA 99. Similar revisions for the number of required receptacles occurred at 517.19(B) for critical care areas and at new 517.19(C) for operating room receptacles. Two separate "Analysis of Change" forms have been provided for these changes in this publication.

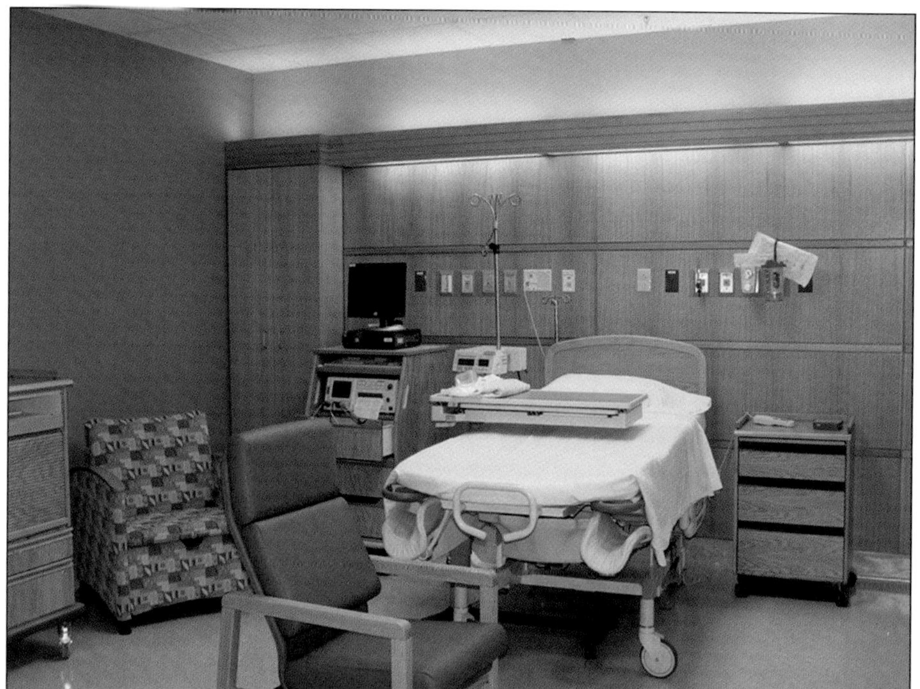

517.19(B)

Change at a Glance

The minimum number of receptacles required for critical care area patient bed locations of health care facilities was increased from six to fourteen.

Code Language

517.19 Critical Care Areas

(B) Patient Bed Location Receptacles.

(1) Minimum Number and Supply. Each patient bed location shall be provided with a minimum of ~~six~~ fourteen receptacles, at least one of which shall be connected to either of the following:

(1) The normal system branch circuit required in 517.19(A)

(2) ~~An emergency system~~ critical branch circuit supplied by a different transfer switch than the other receptacles at the same patient bed location.

(2) Receptacle Requirements. The receptacles required in 517.19(B)(1) shall be permitted to be single, duplex, or quadruplex type or any combination thereof. All receptacles shall be listed "hospital grade" and shall be so identified. The grounding terminal of each receptacle shall be connected to the reference grounding point by means of an insulated copper equipment grounding conductor.

Proposal 15-39

517.19(B) Patient Bed Location Receptacles

The minimum number of receptacles required for critical care area patient bed locations of health care facilities was increased from six to fourteen receptacles.

2 CBLA E-17

Normal branch

Critical branch

Minimum of fourteen receptacles

Listed hospital grade

Permitted to be single, duplex, or quadruplex type or any combination thereof

Permitted to be connected to either the normal system branch or the critical branch

Critical care patient bed locations

2011 *NEC* Requirement

Each critical care area patient bed location was required to be provided with a minimum of six receptacles. At least one of these six receptacles must be supplied by either the normal system or by the emergency system supplied by a different transfer switch than the other receptacles at the same patient bed location. These receptacles are permitted to be supplied from a configuration of single, duplex, or quadruplex type, or any combination of the three. All of these patient bed location receptacles are required to be listed hospital grade-type and be so identified. The grounding terminal of each receptacle is also required to be connected to the reference grounding point by means of an insulated copper equipment grounding conductor.

2014 *NEC* Change

These same provisions for receptacles in critical care area patient bed locations still apply, with the provision for the number of required receptacles being expanded from six to fourteen. The systems required to supply at least one of these receptacles was changed from the emergency system to the critical branch, as the term *emergency system* has been removed from Article 517 in the 2014 *NEC*.

Analysis of Change

The minimum number of receptacles required for critical care area patient bed locations of a health care facility was increased from six to fourteen. NFPA 99 Section 6.3.2.2.6.2 requires each patient bed location in critical care areas, where considered a Category 1 application, to be provided with a minimum of fourteen receptacles. Section 517.19(B) in the 2011 *NEC* required only six receptacles. CMP-15 revised the number of receptacles from six to fourteen to bring 517.19(B) in line with NFPA 99, *Health Care Facilities Code*.

517.19(C)

Change at a Glance

New 517.19(C) was added requiring a minimum number of 36 receptacles in an operating room of health care facilities.

Code Language

517.19 Critical Care Areas

(C) Operating Room Receptacles.

(1) Minimum Number and Supply. Each operating room shall be provided with a minimum of 36 receptacles, at least 12 of which shall be connected to either of the following:

(1) The normal system branch circuit required in 517.19(A)

(2) A critical branch circuit supplied by a different transfer switch than the other receptacles at the same location

(2) Receptacle Requirements. The receptacles required in 517.19(C)(1) shall be permitted to be of the single or duplex types or a combination of both. All receptacles shall be listed hospital grade and so identified. The grounding terminal of each receptacle shall be connected to the reference grounding point by means of an insulated copper equipment grounding conductor.

Proposal 15-41

517.19(C) Operating Room Receptacles

New 517.19(C) was added requiring a minimum number of **thirty-six** receptacles in an operating room of a health care facilities.

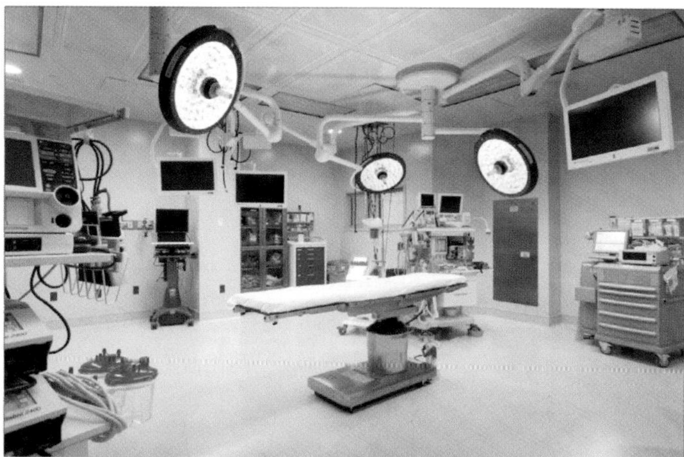

At least twelve of the thirty-six receptacles are required to be connected to either the normal system branch or the critical branch circuit supplied by a different transfer switch than the other receptacles at the same location.

2011 *NEC* Requirement

The minimum number of receptacles required in an operating room of a health care facility was not addressed.

2014 *NEC* Change

New subdivision (C) of 517.19 was added to address the minimum number of receptacles required in an operating room of a health care facility. A minimum number of thirty-six receptacles is now required in an operating room, with at least twelve of the thirty-six receptacles required to be connected to either the normal system branch or the critical branch circuit supplied by a different transfer switch than the other receptacles at the same location. Being consistent with 517.18(B) and 517.19(B), all of these receptacles are permitted to be supplied from a configuration of single, duplex, or quadruplex type, or any combination of the three. All of these operating room receptacles are required to be listed hospital grade-type receptacles and so identified. The grounding terminal of each receptacle is also required to be connected to the reference grounding point by means of an insulated copper equipment grounding conductor.

Analysis of Change

The minimum number of receptacles for an operating room of a health care facility is now thirty-six. NFPA 99 Section 6.3.2.2.6.2 requires each operating room, where considered a Category 1 application, to be provided with a minimum of thirty-six receptacles. There were no provisions in the 2011 *NEC* to address the minimum number of required receptacles. CMP-15 added a new 517.19(C) and a minimum number of operating room receptacles of thirty-six to bring the *NEC* in line with NFPA 99, *Health Care Facilities Code*.

517.30(B)

Change at a Glance

The use of, and term, *emergency systems* has been eliminated from Article 517, leaving only the essential system with the three separate branches: critical, life safety and equipment. The diagram in Figure 517.30, No. 1 has been re-worked to reflect these changes as well.

Code Language

517.30 Essential Electrical Systems for Hospitals

(B) General.

(1) Separate Branches ~~Systems~~. Essential electrical systems for hospitals shall be comprised of three ~~two~~ separate branches ~~systems~~ capable of supplying a limited amount of lighting and power service that is considered essential for life safety and effective hospital operation during the time the normal electrical service is interrupted for any reason. These three ~~two~~ branches ~~systems~~ are life safety, critical, and ~~shall be the emergency system and the~~ equipment ~~system~~.

~~**(2) Emergency Systems.** The emergency system shall be limited to circuits essential to life safety and critical patient care. These are designated the life safety branch and the critical branch. [99:4.4.2.2.1.1]~~

517.30(B) Essential Electrical System (Hospital)

- Essential electrical systems for hospitals shall be comprised of three separate branches capable of supplying a limited amount of lighting and power service that is considered essential for life safety and effective hospital operation during the time the normal electrical service is interrupted for any reason.

Normal source
Alternate power source
Nonessential loads
Automatic switching equipment
Delayed automatic switching equipment
Life Safety Branch
Critical Branch
~~Emergency System~~
Equipment Branch
Essential Electrical System

- The three branches are life safety, critical, and equipment branches.

2011 *NEC* Requirement

The general applications of an essential electrical system for hospitals are described at 517.30(B). There were six list items addressed at this subsection. (1) Separate Systems demanded that the essential electrical systems for hospitals be comprised of two separate systems capable of supplying a limited amount of lighting and power considered essential for life safety and effective hospital operation during the time the normal electrical service is interrupted for any reason. These two systems were to be considered the *emergency system* and the *equipment system*. (2) Emergency System was to be limited to circuits essential to life safety and critical patient care and was designated as the life safety branch and the critical branch. (3) Equipment Systems supplied major electrical equipment necessary for patient care and basic hospital operation.

(4) Transfer Switches described the number of transfer switches to be used, based on reliability, design, and load considerations. (5) Optional Loads were not covered in Article 517. These loads required their own transfer switch(es); and there had to be provisions so the transfer wouldn't take place if the generator would be overloaded, or the loads had to be shed if the generator became overloaded.

(6) Contiguous Facilities required hospital power sources and alternate power sources to be permitted to serve the essential electrical systems of contiguous or same site facilities.

2014 *NEC* Change

The requirements for the "Essential Electrical Systems for Hospitals" were revised by removing references to the emergency system. Section 517.30()B) (3) Equipment System was also removed. This action leaves only the essential system with the three separate branches: critical, life safety and equipment branch.

517.30(B)

Continued

~~**(3) Equipment System.** The equipment system shall supply major electrical equipment necessary for patient care and basic hospital operation.~~

~~(4)~~ **(2) Transfer Switches.** The number of transfer switches to be used shall be based on reliability, design, and load considerations. Each branch of the essential electrical ~~emergency~~ system ~~and each equipment system~~ shall have one or more transfer switches. One transfer switch and downstream distribution system shall be permitted to serve one or more branches ~~or systems~~ in a facility with a maximum demand on the essential electrical system of 150 kVA.

***Informational Note No. 1*:** See NFPA 99-2012 ~~2005~~, ~~Standard for~~ Health Care Facilities Code, 6.4.3.2 ~~4.4.3.2~~, Transfer Switches ~~Operation Type I~~; 6.4.2.1.5 ~~4.4.2.1~~.4,Automatic Transfer Switch Features; 6.4.2.1.5.15, Nonautomatic Transfer Switch Features, and 6.4.2.1.7 ~~4.4.2.1.6~~, Nonautomatic Transfer Device Features.

***Informational Note No. 2*:** See Informational Note Figure 517.30, No. 1.

***Informational Note No. 3*:** See Informational Note Figure 517.30, No. 2.

~~(5)~~ **(3) Optional Loads** *(text unchanged)*

~~(6)~~ **(4) Contiguous Facilities.** *(text unchanged)*

Proposal 15-52, 15-51

Comment 15-46

Analysis of Change

In an effort to correlate the requirements of the *NEC* and, in particular, Article 517 with NFPA 99, *Health Care Facilities Code*, section 517.30(B) was re-organized for the make-up of the essential system of a hospital. This action eliminated references to the *emergency system* as this is not addressed to NFPA 99; this removes major confusion resulting from the previous use of the word "emergency" in similar, yet sometimes quite different, ways in Article 517 and in Article 700. These changes also required the re-working of the diagram in Figure 517.30, No. 1 as well.

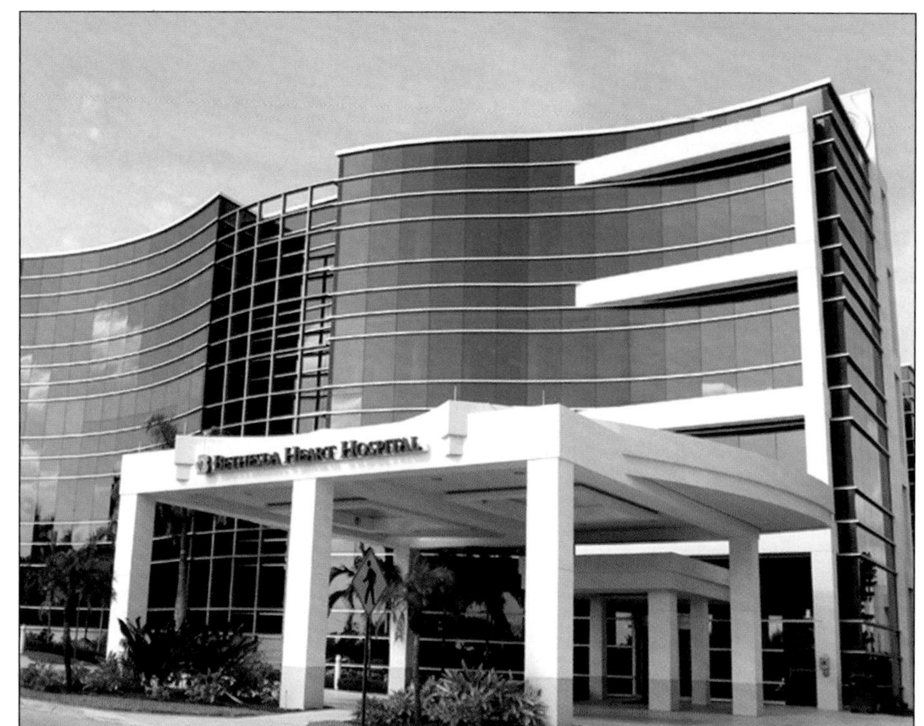

517.30(E)

Change at a Glance

Cover plates or the receptacles supplied from the essential electrical system are required to have a distinctive color or marking, and must also be supplied with an illuminated face or an indicator light to indicate that there is power to the receptacle.

Code Language

517.30 Essential Electrical Systems for Hospitals

(E) Receptacle Identification. The cover plates for the electrical receptacles or the electrical receptacles themselves supplied from the ~~emergency~~ essential electrical system shall have a distinctive color or making so as to be readily identifiable. [~~99:4.4.2.2.4.2(B)~~ 99:6.4.2.2.6.2(C)] Nonlocking-type, 125-volt, 15- and 20-ampere receptacles shall have an illuminated face or an indicator light to indicate that there is power to the receptacle.

Proposal 15-64, 15-65

Comment 15-57

Receptacles courtesy of Pass & Seymour/Legrand

2011 *NEC* Requirement

The cover plates or the electrical receptacles themselves that are supplied from the emergency system were required to have a distinctive color or marking so as to be readily identifiable.

2014 *NEC* Change

All references to the *emergency system* were removed from Article 517. These receptacles are now required to be supplied from the *essential electrical system*. The cover plates or the electrical receptacles themselves are still required to have a distinctive color or marking so as to be readily identifiable, but they now must also be supplied with an illuminated face or an indicator light to indicate that there is power to the receptacle.

Analysis of Change

Receptacles that are supplied from the essential electrical system must be clearly identified to insure that vital health care equipment and instrumentation continue to function in the event of power interruption. However, the previous language at 517.30(E) required no method of indicating that the receptacles on these essential electrical circuits were, in fact, continually supplying power to the equipment. While the "distinctive color or marking" requirement identifies that the receptacle is connected to the essential electrical system, requiring that the receptacle be supplied with an illuminated face or an indicator light will insure that there is clear indication that the receptacle is providing power. The increased visibility of an illuminated face or an indicator light will insure that a receptacle that is providing power can be quickly accessed in an emergency situation, especially when power failures result in diminished illumination. Furthermore, reliance solely on some distinctive color in an emergency situation may be ineffective for health care personnel who might be color blind.

517.30(E)

Continued

Such illuminated indication of the powered state of receptacles at essential electrical systems is consistent with the requirement for pilot light indicators of switch position in 2012 NFPA 99, clauses 6.4.2.1.5.12 and 6.4.2.1.5.15(B). This "illuminated face or an indicator light" requirement will aid in maintenance replacements of cover plates and receptacles on circuits intended for nonessential electrical loads where red cover plates or receptacles have been used for the replacements. In these situations, the "distinctive color" intended for essential electrical system circuits has been compromised at this point.

This 517.30(E) "distinctive color" requirement was added in the 2002 *NEC* Code cycle. During that same cycle, proposals were made to make the "distinctive color" requirement be prescriptively assigned to a specific color (red). These proposals were rejected by CMP-15 as any color that was "distinctive" from the normal power receptacles would meet this *Code* requirement.

This same change for an illuminated face or an indicator light occurred at 517.41(E) nursing homes and limited care facilities. See Proposal 15-80 and Comment 15-70.

Note to Reader: At the time of publication of this textbook, an appeal had been submitted to the NFPA Standards Council seeking to reject Proposal 15-64 and to remove this illumination requirement from 517.30(E) and to return to the 2011 NEC provisions. If this appeal is upheld by the NFPA Standards Council at their meeting in late July 2013 (after the publication of this textbook), this provision at 517.30(E) will not be part of the 2014 NEC.

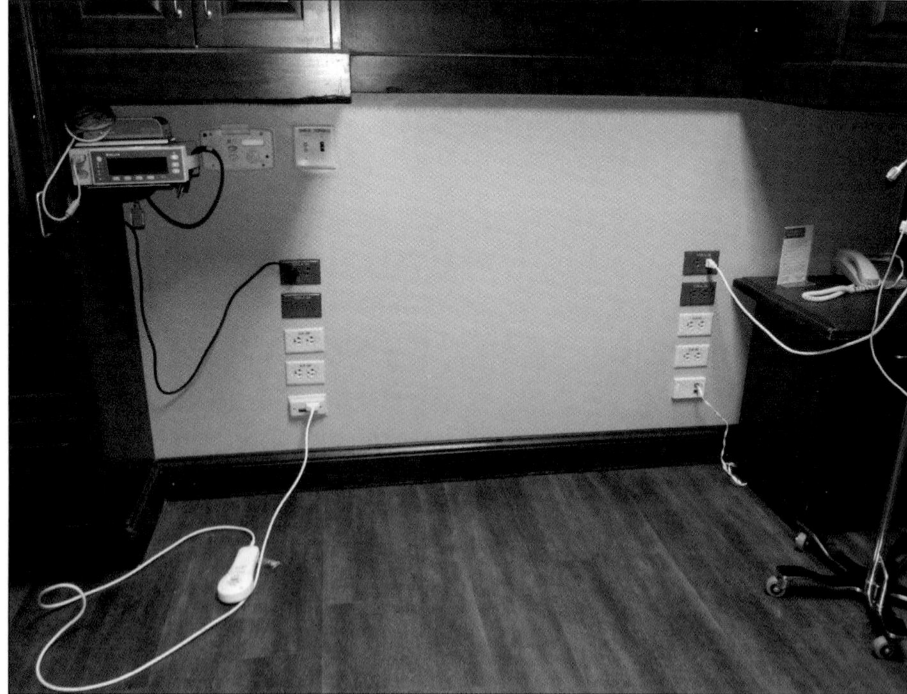

517.30(G)

Change at a Glance

Overcurrent devices for the essential electrical system do not need to be fully selectively coordinated but only required "coordination" for fault events that exceed 0.1 seconds.

Code Language

517.30 Essential Electrical Systems for Hospitals

(G) Coordination. Overcurrent protective devices serving the essential electrical system shall be selectively coordinated for the period of time that a fault's duration extends beyond 0.1 second.

***Exception No. 1*:** Between transformer primary and secondary overcurrent protective devices, where only one overcurrent protective device or set of overcurrent protective devices exist on the transformer secondary.

***Exception No. 2*:** Between over current protective devices of the same size (ampere rating) in series.

***Informational Note*:** The terms "Coordination" and "Coordinated" as used in this section do not cover the full range of overcurrent conditions.

Proposal 15-66

Comment 15-58 thru 15-65

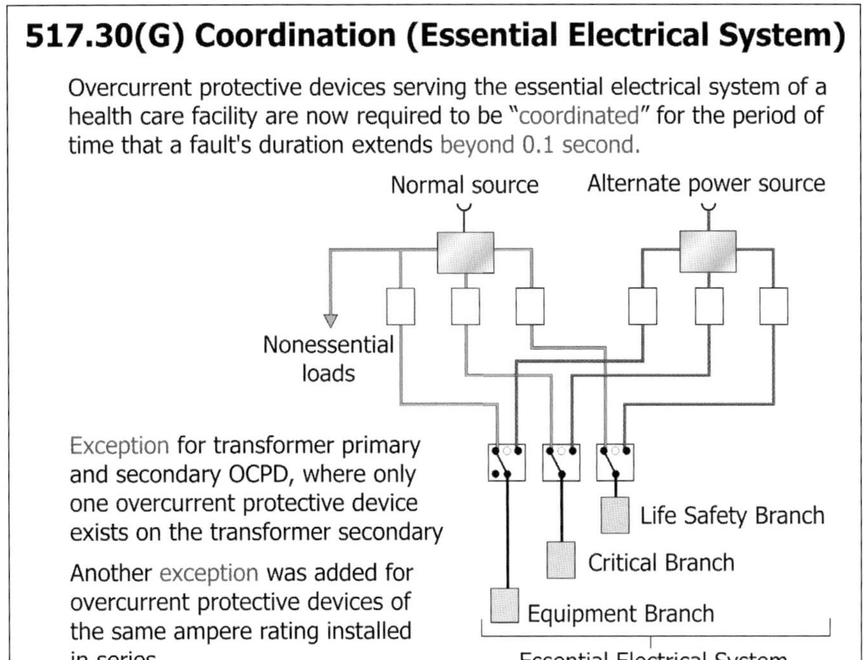

2011 *NEC* Requirement

Selective coordination provisions for a health care facility exist at 517.17(C) in the 2011 *NEC*. No requirements existed in Article 517 for simply "coordination" for the essential electrical system in the 2011 *NEC*.

2014 *NEC* Change

Overcurrent protective devices serving the essential electrical system of a health care facility are now required to be coordinated for the period of time that a fault's duration extends beyond 0.1 second. An exception exists for this new rule for transformer primary and secondary overcurrent protective devices, where only one overcurrent protective device exists on the transformer secondary. Another exception was added for overcurrent protective devices of the same ampere rating installed in series.

Analysis of Change

This is another change that is designed to bring Article 517 in line with NFPA 99, *Health Care Facilities Code*. This new 517.30(G) permits overcurrent devices installed to achieve selective coordination of the essential electrical system to only operate for episodes longer than 1/10th of a second. Allowing the circuit protection to function that late in the cycle of an overcurrent event will mean that only overload conditions will be interrupted by the nearest overcurrent protection device.

Eleven different proposals were submitted to CMP-15 by the Committee on Electrical Systems to eliminate the term *emergency systems* from Article 517. These moves remove the critical branch from the requirement for selective coordination and allow the coordination of the overcurrent protective devices for the life safety branch to be reduced to faults greater than .1 second.

The new Informational Note following this new requirement reports that "the terms *coordination* and *coordinated* as used in this section do not cover the full range of overcurrent conditions."

520.2 Definitions

Change at a Glance

Three new definitions were added to Article 520 to meet demands of new theatre stage lighting technology.

Code Language

520.2 Definitions (Theaters, Audience Areas of Motion Picture and Television Studios, Performance Areas, and Similar Locations)

Stage Equipment. Equipment at any location on the premises integral to the stage production including, but not limited to, equipment for lighting, audio, special effects, rigging, motion control, projection, or video.

Stage Lighting Hoist. A motorized lifting device that contains a mounting position for one or more luminaires, with wiring devices for connection of luminaires to branch circuits, and integral flexible cables to allow the luminaires to travel over the lifting range of the hoist while energized.

Stage Switchboard. A switchboard, panelboard, or rack containing dimmers or relays with associated overcurrent protective devices, or overcurrent protective devices alone, used primarily to feed stage equipment.

Proposal 15-98, 15-99

520.2 Definitions (Theaters, TV Studios, Etc.)

Three new definitions were added to Article 520 to meet demands of new theater stage lighting technology.

- Stage Equipment
- Stage Lighting Hoist
- Stage Switchboard

2011 *NEC* Requirement

These new definitions were not part of the 2011 *NEC*.

2014 *NEC* Change

Three new definitions were added to Article 520. New definitions were added for *stage equipment*, *stage lighting hoist*, and *stage switchboard*.

Analysis of Change

Three new definitions were added to Article 520 to meet demands of new theatre stage lighting technology. Theatre technology is changing with other technology and these new definitions will help apply the appropriate rules to newer, more advanced stage lighting equipment. This advanced stage lighting equipment has moved rapidly from tungsten luminaires fed from dimmers and now can include arc-source or LED luminaires controlled by a data connection directly to the luminaire. Modern stage lighting switchboards may be a relay cabinet or a panel of circuit breakers used as a dimming system. Stage equipment is no longer simply the stage lighting and controller. These new definitions were needed in the *NEC* to cover these types of modern applications and uses.

Stage equipment is no longer limited to lighting equipment. Stage switchboards are required to supply a wide variety of production-related equipment, not just lighting equipment. A new section for "Stage Lighting Hoist" was added at 540.40, thus a new definition was needed. According to the submitter of the proposal, a new listed "packaged" stage lighting hoist has emerged in the theater world over the past few years. These devices contain a movable mounting position for one or more luminaires, a connector strip with wiring devices for connection of luminaires to branch circuits, and integral flexible round or flat cables to allow the luminaires and connector strip to travel over the lifting range of the hoist while energized. These cables are permanently connected at both ends and contained in a cable handling system that controls the path of the cable while gathering or folding as the hoist ascends. Such a design often requires a flat cable to insure controlled gathering of the cable. These cables are an integral part of a listed product.

547.2 Definition

Change at a Glance

Equipotential plane for agriculture buildings is to minimize (not prevent) voltage potentials within the plane and between the plane, grounded equipment, and the earth.

Code Language

547.2 Definitions

Equipotential Plane. An area where wire mesh or other conductive elements are embedded in or placed under concrete, bonded to all metal structures and fixed nonelectrical equipment that may become energized, and connected to the electrical grounding system to ~~prevent a difference in~~ minimize voltage ~~from developing~~ potentials within the plane and between the plane, grounded equipment, and the earth.

Proposal 19-11a

Comment 19-5

547.2 Definition: Equipotential Plane (Agricultural Buildings)

Equipotential Plane. An area where wire mesh or other conductive elements are embedded in or placed under concrete, bonded to all metal structures and fixed nonelectrical equipment that may become energized, and connected to the electrical grounding system to ~~prevent~~ minimize voltage potentials within the plane and between the plane, grounded equipment, and the earth.

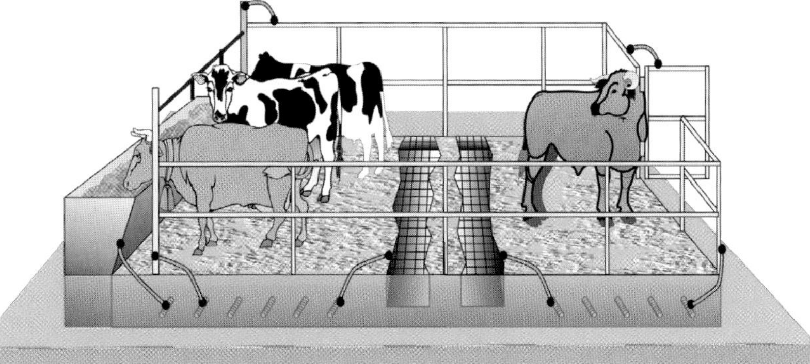

The bonding conductor for the equipotential bonding plane is required to be a solid copper, insulated, covered or bare conductor, not smaller than 8 AWG.

2011 *NEC* Requirement

The definition of an *equipotential plane* for agriculture buildings was defined at 547.2 as a plane to "prevent" a difference in voltage from developing within the plane for livestock.

2014 *NEC* Change

The definition of an *equipotential plane* for agriculture buildings was revised to indicate that this plane is intended to "minimize" voltage potentials within the plane and between the plane, the grounded equipment, and the earth.

Analysis of Change

The definition of *equipotential plane* for agriculture buildings was revised to more closely represent the level of voltage reduction obtained with an equipotential plane. As was indicated with the previous wording, the equipotential plane never completely eliminates all of the voltage granulates or stray voltage that could be present between the earth, grounded metal equipment, and a concrete floor of something like a dairy barn.

Stray voltage is a difference in voltage potential between two metal objects. These voltages are termed "stray voltage" when they can be measured between two metal objects that are contacted simultaneously by livestock or people. If this voltage reaches sufficient levels, animals coming into contact with grounded devices may receive a mild electrical shock. Animals that become conditioned to the fact that they are going to be tingled when entering or exiting an agricultural building due to the effects of a difference of voltage potential between the concrete floor of the building and the earth soon become reluctant to enter or leave the building. It is a particular problem with milk cows, whose productivity may be altered when this tingle voltage causes them to produce less milk. A properly installed equipotential plane will protect animals and people from stray voltage and other electrical hazards by minimizing different voltage potentials in livestock confinement areas.

547.5(F)

Change at a Glance

An insulated or covered aluminum or copper equipment grounding conductor is now permitted for underground agricultural building installations.

REVISION

Code Language

547.5 Wiring Methods

(F) Separate Equipment Grounding Conductor. Where an equipment grounding conductor is installed underground within a location falling under the scope of Article 547, it shall be ~~a copper conductor. Where an equipment grounding conductor is installed underground, it shall be~~ insulated or covered ~~copper~~.

Proposal 19-20

Comment 19-8

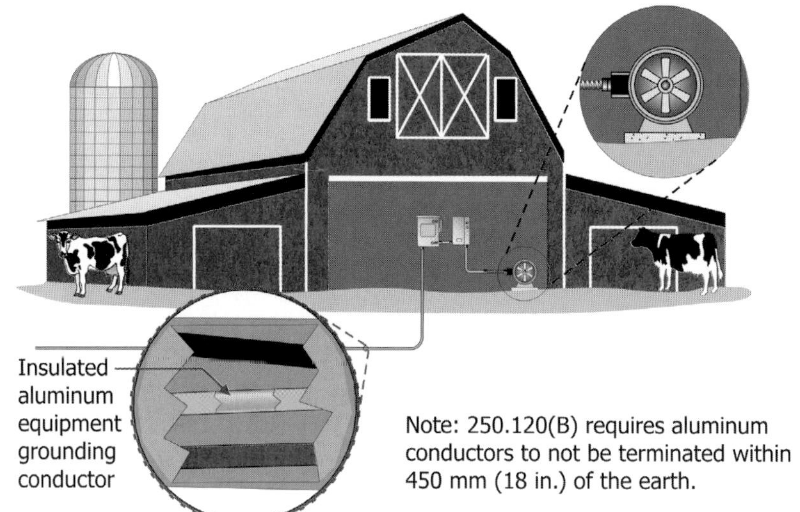
547.5(F) Separate EGC (Agricultural Buildings)
An insulated or covered aluminum or copper equipment grounding conductor is now permitted for underground agricultural building installations.
Insulated aluminum equipment grounding conductor
Note: 250.120(B) requires aluminum conductors to not be terminated within 450 mm (18 in.) of the earth.

2011 *NEC* Requirement

Where an equipment grounding conductor was installed underground at an agricultural building location, it had to be an insulated or covered copper conductor.

2014 *NEC* Change

Revisions were made to 547.5(F) to now permit an equipment grounding conductor installed underground at an agricultural building location to be an insulated or covered aluminum or copper conductor.

Analysis of Change

Revisions to 547.5(F) will now permit the use of an aluminum equipment grounding conductor as well as copper for underground installations at agricultural buildings or structures falling under the scope of Article 547. Previous language only permitted a copper equipment grounding conductor due to considerations regarding corrosion and oxidation, and exposure to the many contaminates present in and around livestock facilities. While all metals corrode, aluminum is highly corrosion-resistant. Since aluminum conductor connections in meters and panelboards are common, the use of aluminum conductors is beneficial in preventing galvanic reactions. Additionally, the equipment grounding conductors required at 547.5(F) for underground use must be insulated or covered; therefore, the metal used inside the insulated material is irrelevant since the conductor is protected by this insulation.

Aluminum conductors are used in many agricultural applications, including power conductors, irrigation pipe, watering troughs, fencing, etc. Aluminum conductors have a proven track record of being suitable for agricultural applications. Aluminum ungrounded and grounded conductors have operated satisfactorily for decades in agricultural installations. The prohibition of insulated or covered aluminum equipment grounding conductors in these underground installations was not warranted.

It should be noted that 250.120(B) requires aluminum conductors to not be terminated within 450 mm (18 in.) of the earth.

550.15(H)

Change at a Glance

"Under-Chassis Wiring (Exposed to Weather)" has been revised to allow any raceway or conduit "approved" for a wet location or where subject to physical damage.

Code Language

550.15 Wiring Methods and Materials

Except as specifically limited in this section, the wiring methods and materials included in this *Code* shall be used in mobile homes. Aluminum conductors, aluminum alloy conductors, and aluminum core conductors such as copper-clad aluminum shall not be acceptable for use as branch-circuit wiring.

(H) Under-Chassis Wiring (Exposed to Weather). Where outdoor or under chassis line-voltage (120 volts, nominal, or higher) wiring is exposed to moisture or physical damage, it shall be protected by ~~rigid metal conduit or intermediate metal conduit, except as provided in (1) or (2)~~ a conduit or raceway approved for use in wet locations or where subject to physical damage. The conductors shall be ~~suitable~~ listed for use in wet locations.

~~(1) Where closely routed against frames and equipment enclosures, reinforced thermosetting resin conduit (RTRC) listed for aboveground use, Type MI cable, electrical~~

550.15(H) Under-Chassis Wiring

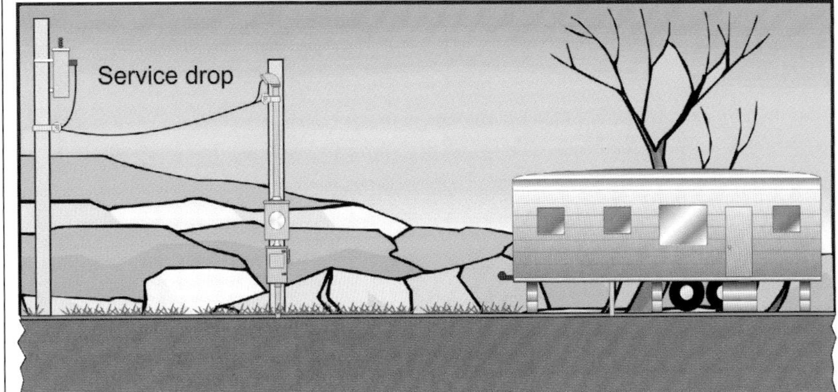

Revisions now permit mobile home line-voltage wiring *(120 volts, nominal, or higher)* installed outdoor or under the chassis of the mobile home, exposed to moisture or physical damage, to be protected by a conduit or raceway "approved" for use in wet locations or where subject to physical damage.

Rather than the conductors having to be "suitable" for use in a wet location, the conductors must now be "listed" for use in wet locations.

2011 *NEC* Requirement

Where mobile home line-voltage wiring (120 volts, nominal, or higher) was installed outdoors or under the chassis of the mobile home, exposed to moisture or physical damage, this wiring had to be protected by rigid metal conduit or intermediate metal conduit, and the conductors must be "suitable" for wet locations. Two conditions existed that precluded the use of rigid metal conduit or intermediate metal conduit. Reinforced thermosetting resin conduit (RTRC) listed for aboveground use, Type MI cable, electrical metallic tubing, or rigid polyvinyl chloride conduit (PVC) was permitted as a wiring method where "closely routed against frames and equipment enclosures." The second condition allowed Schedule 80 PVC or RTRC listed for exposure to physical damage as a wiring method where this wiring method extended vertically from a direct-burial depth of at least 457 mm (18 in.) below grade and terminated to a factory-installed conduit or enclosure. These two conditions were added to the 2011 *NEC*.

2014 *NEC* Change

Revisions to 550.15(H) now permit mobile home line-voltage wiring (120 volts, nominal, or higher) installed outdoors or under the chassis of the mobile home, exposed to moisture or physical damage, to be protected by a conduit or raceway "approved" for use in wet locations or where subject to physical damage. Rather than the conductors having to be "suitable" for use in a wet location, the conductors must now be "listed" for use in wet locations.

Analysis of Change

Wiring methods from the service power supply to mobile and manufactured homes is addressed at 550.15. When this supply circuit is run exposed to physical damage or to the weather conditions under the chassis of the mobile home, the wiring method and materials must comply with 550.15(H).

550.15(H)

Continued

~~metallic tubing, or rigid polyvinyl chloride conduit (PVC) shall be permitted.~~
~~(2) Where extending vertically from a direct-burial depth of at least 457 mm (18 in.) below grade and terminated to a factory-installed conduit or enclosure, Schedule 80 PVC or RTRC listed for exposure to physical damage.~~

Proposal 19-37, 19-38, 19-39

A revision to this subsection took place in the 2011 *NEC* to clarify the use of nonmetallic products for line-voltage circuits under mobile or manufactured homes. Nonmetallic wiring methods such as Schedule 80 PVC conduit had been used for feeders to these mobile home types for years; but based on 2008 *NEC* text, the use of nonmetallic wiring methods was limited only to areas where the wiring method was "closely routed against frames and equipment enclosures." Further revisions have occurred at 550.15(H) for the 2014 *NEC* to allow any raceway or conduit "approved" for a wet location or "approved" to afford physical protection where subject to physical damage. There are multiple types of conduits identified for use in locations where the wiring method may be subject to damage and/or in wet locations, not just rigid metal conduit or intermediate metal conduit.

The feeder requirements at 550.33 do not limit feeder wiring methods to nonmetallic wiring methods. The text at 550.15(H) should not be limited to nonmetallic wiring methods either. The area under the mobile home was not considered to be subject to physical damage by many AHJs. Schedule 40 PVC is not identified to be used where subject to damage; but in areas not subject to physical damage (such as under the chassis of a mobile home), Schedule 40 PVC is identified for use in a wet location.

It should be noted that "approved" might not have been the best choice of words in this revised application. Article 100 defines *approved* as "acceptable to the authority having jurisdiction." The AHJ could approve rubber garden hose as an "approved" wiring method for this application. Perhaps a better choice of terms would have been "identified," or perhaps "a conduit or raceway listed for use in wet locations or listed to provide protection against to physical damage."

551.4(C)

Change at a Glance

New subsection was added to standardize label requirements in Article 551 at one location.

Code Language

551.4 General Requirements

(C) Labels. Labels required by Article 551 shall be made of etched, metal-stamped, or embossed brass; stainless steel; plastic laminates not less than 0.13 mm (0.005 in.) thick; or anodized or alclad aluminum not less than 0.5 mm (0.020 in.) thick or the equivalent.

Informational Note: For guidance on other label criteria used in the recreational vehicle industry, refer to 2011 ANSI Z535, Product Safety Signs and Labels.

Proposal 19-50

Comment 19-23

551.4(C) Labels (Recreational Vehicles)

Labels required by Article 551 must be made of etched, metal-stamped, or embossed brass, stainless steel, or plastic laminates 0.005 in. (0.13 mm) minimum thick, or anodized or alclad aluminum not less than 0.020 in. (0.5 mm) thick or equal.

2011 *NEC* Requirement

There are four label requirements within Article 551: 551.46(D); 551.46(Q); 551.46(R)(4); and 551.46(S)(3). In the 2011 *NEC*, 551.46(D) was identified as the "label criteria" for Article 551. The other three Article 551 label requirements referred back to 551.46(D) for specifics of the label.

2014 *NEC* Change

A new subsection for "Labels" for recreational vehicles and recreational vehicle parks was added to the general requirements of 551.4. This new provision will require labels required by Article 551 to be made of etched, metal-stamped, or embossed brass, stainless steel, or plastic laminates 0.005 in. (0.13 mm) minimum thick, or anodized or alclad aluminum not less than 0.020 in. (0.5 mm) thick or equal.

Analysis of Change

The standard for RV label requirements was located at 551.46(D) in the 2011 *NEC*. This labeling requirement was located under a provision for "Means for Connecting to Power Supply." All other labeling requirements within Article 551 referred back to this 551.46(D) provision. In an effort to consolidate and simplify all labeling information in Article 551, a new 551.4(C) was added to place all the current label criteria found in 551.46(D) under the "General Requirements" heading of Article 551. A companion Informational Note alerts users of the *Code* to pertinent labeling information found in the ANSI nationally recognized standard, ANSI Z535 *Product Safety Signs and Labels*. These new provisions will enable the RV industry to provide a set of RV labels that will be uniform and more recognizable for the RV consumer.

Corresponding proposals were submitted and accepted to make appropriate reference to the new 551.4(C) at four locations within Article 551 with labeling requirements: 551.46(D); 551.46(Q); 551.46(R)(4); and 551.46(S)(3).

551.71

Change at a Glance

Every recreational vehicle site equipped with a 50-ampere receptacle is now required to also be equipped with a 30-ampere, 125-volt receptacle.

Code Language

551.71 Type Receptacles Provided. (Recreational Vehicle Parks)

Type Receptacles Provided. Every recreational vehicle site with electrical supply shall be equipped with at least one 20-ampere, 125-volt receptacle. A minimum of 20 percent of all recreational vehicle sites, with electrical supply, shall each be equipped with a 50-ampere, 125/250 volt receptacle conforming to the configuration as identified in Figure 551.46(C). Every recreational vehicle site equipped with a 50-ampere receptacle shall also be equipped with a 30-ampere, 125-volt receptacle conforming to Figure 551.46(C).

(Remainder of text unchanged.) See NEC for complete text.

Proposal 19-77

2011 *NEC* Requirement

In accordance with the requirements of 551.71, every recreational vehicle site (with electrical power provided) must be equipped with a certain number and type of receptacles. Every recreational vehicle site must be provided with at least one 20-ampere, 125-volt receptacle. At least 20 percent of all recreational vehicle sites are required to be supplied with a 50-ampere, 125/250-volt receptacle. A minimum of 70 percent of all recreational vehicle sites must be equipped with a 30-ampere, 125-volt receptacle. All of the RV sites mentioned above are also permitted to include additional receptacles that have configurations such as 50-ampere, 125/250-volt, 3-pole, 4-wire receptacle or other configurations conforming to 551.81.

The remainder of the RV sites (with electrical power supplied) are required to be equipped with one or more of the receptacle configurations conforming to 551.81. Dedicated tent sites with a 15- or 20-ampere electrical supply are permitted to be excluded when determining the percentage of recreational vehicle sites with 30- or 50-ampere receptacles.

2014 *NEC* Change

In addition to all of the numbers and types of receptacle provisions required by the 2011 *NEC*, every recreational vehicle site equipped with a 50-ampere receptacle must also be equipped with a 30-ampere, 125-volt receptacle.

Analysis of Change

More and more recreational vehicles are being provided with a 30-ampere, 125-volt, 2-pole, 3-wire electrical supply cord. At RV sites supplied with only a 50-ampere receptacle, a 50-ampere to 30-ampere "cheater" cord is being sold to connect a 30-ampere RV supply cord to a 50-ampere receptacle. Proper connection of the grounding and bonding connections is only one concern with these "cheater" cords.

555.15(B) and (C)

Change at a Glance

An insulated aluminum or copper equipment grounding conductor is now permitted at marinas and boatyards.

Code Language

555.15 Grounding

Wiring and equipment within the scope of this article shall be grounded as specified in Article 250 and as required by 555.15(A) through (E).

(B) Type of Equipment Grounding Conductor. The equipment grounding conductor shall be an insulated ~~copper~~ conductor with a continuous outer finish that is either green or green with one or more yellow stripes. The equipment grounding conductor of Type MI cable shall be permitted to be identified at terminations. For conductors larger than 6 AWG, or where multiconductor cables are used, re-identification of conductors as allowed in 250.119(A)(2)(b) and (A)(2)(c) or 250.119(B)(2) and (B)(3) shall be permitted.

(C) Size of Equipment Grounding Conductor. The insulated ~~copper~~ equipment grounding conductor shall be sized in accordance with 250.122 but not smaller than 12 AWG.

2011 *NEC* Requirement

For wiring and equipment at marinas and boatyards, equipment grounding conductors were required to consist of an insulated copper conductor with a continuous outer finish that is either green or green with one or more yellow stripes. The insulated copper equipment grounding conductor is to be sized in accordance with 250.122 but not smaller than 12 AWG. Where the wiring method is Type MI cable, the equipment grounding conductor is permitted to be identified at terminations. For conductors larger than 6 AWG, or where multiconductor cables are used, re-identification of conductors is allowed.

2014 *NEC* Change

The 2011 *NEC* provisions at 555.15(B) and (C) hold true in the 2014 *NEC*, only the insulated equipment grounding conductor can be either copper or aluminum.

Analysis of Change

Limiting equipment grounding conductors used in marina and boatyard wiring systems to copper only is not justifiable. Aluminum conductors are well-suited for the application and commonly available. Many of the terminations used at marinas and boatyards are primarily aluminum and are, in all likelihood, better suited for use with aluminum conductors in these locations. Aluminum ungrounded and grounded neutral conductors have operated satisfactorily for decades in marina and boatyard installations. Additionally, when properly insulated, aluminum has been proven to be highly resistant to corrosion in marinas and boatyards. Aluminum conductors are used successfully and reliably in North American environments as diverse as Alaska to Mexico City, clearly indicating their suitability for use when subjected to temperature fluctuations that might be associated with marinas and boatyards.

The inherent corrosion resistance of aluminum is due to the thin, tough, oxide coating that forms directly after a fresh surface of metallic aluminum is ex-

Proposal 19-106

Comment 19-36

posed to air. Another reason for the excellent corrosion resistance of aluminum conductors in ordinary atmospheres is that the alloy components are selected so as to minimize corrosion. Thus, suitable alloys of the 6000-series aluminum conductors, though not listed as "marine" alloys, are well-suited for ocean/shore applications.

590.4(D)(2)

Change at a Glance

"Extra duty" covers are now required for all 15- and 20-ampere, 125- and 250-volt receptacles installed at temporary installations in a wet location (not just those supported from grade). This requirement now also includes dwelling unit temporary installation wet location receptacles as well.

Code Language

590.4 General

(D) Receptacles.

(2) Receptacles in Wet Locations. All 15- and 20-ampere, 125- and 250-volt receptacles installed in a wet location shall comply with 406.9(B)(1).

[See revisions at 406.9(B)(1) for changes for "Extra Duty" covers]

Proposal 3-102

Comment 3-33

590.4(D)(2) Receptacles (Temporary Installations)

"Extra duty" covers are now required for all 15- and 20-ampere, 125- and 250-volt receptacles installed at temporary installations in a wet location *(not just those supported from grade).*

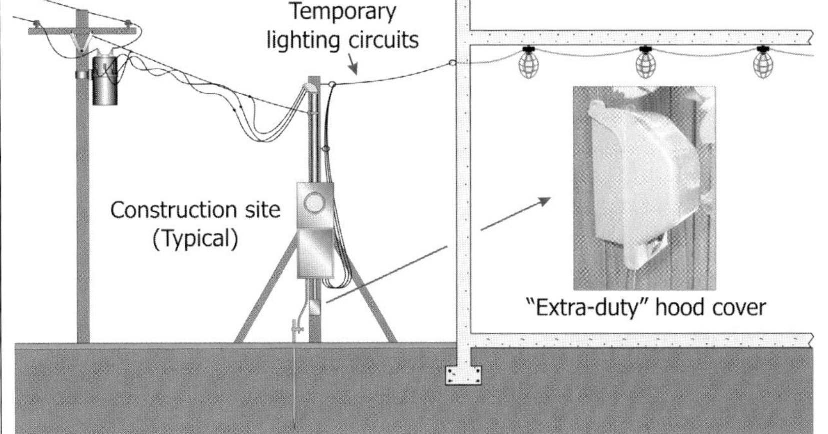

All 15- and 20-ampere, 125- and 250-volt receptacles installed in a wet location shall comply with 406.9(B)(1) *[see changes for "extra duty" covers at 406.9(B)(1)].*

2011 *NEC* Requirement

All 15- and 20-ampere, 125- and 250-volt receptacles installed in a temporary installation wet location are required to comply with 406.9(B)(1). This Article 406 requirement called for these receptacles to have an enclosure and cover that are weatherproof whether a cord cap is inserted or not. An outlet box hood cover installed for this purpose must be listed; and where installed on an enclosure supported from grade, this outlet box hood cover has to be identified as an "extra-duty" type cover. This extra duty hood cover did not apply to dwelling unit receptacles in the 2011 *NEC*. All 15- and 20-ampere, 125- and 250-volt nonlocking-type receptacles installed in wet locations must also be of the listed weather-resistant type.

2014 *NEC* Change

The language and text at 590.4(D)(2) remains the same from the 2011 *NEC* to the 2014 *NEC*. What has changed is the referenced text and requirements at 406.9(B)(1). For the 2014 *NEC*, a revision at 406.9(B)(1) now requires all enclosures and covers installed in wet locations for 15- and 20-ampere, 125- and 250-volt receptacles to be listed and of the "extra duty" type, not just boxes supported from grade. This requirement is now also required at dwelling units as well. All 15- and 20-ampere, 125- and 250-volt receptacles installed in a wet location must still have an enclosure and covers that are weatherproof whether an attachment plug cap is inserted or not. The requirement for weather-resistant type receptacles in wet locations is still applicable in the 2014 *NEC* as well.

Analysis of Change

A proposal was accepted by CMP-3 to add language at 590.4(D)(2) to require "extra duty" hood covers at temporary installations at one- and two-family dwellings 15- and 20-ampere, 125- and 250-volt receptacles installed in a wet location. This revision in Article 590 became unnecessary as CMP-18 made a similar revision to the referenced text at 406.9(B)(1). Revisions to

406.9(B)(1) have leveled the playing field for dwelling units and for non-dwelling unit wet locations as far as extra duty enclosures and covers are concerned.

The "in-use" covers for wet location 15- and 20-ampere, 125- and 250-volt receptacles must all be of the "extra duty" type regardless of occupancy type location. The requirements for these more rigidly-constructed extra duty covers or hoods at in-use covers for receptacles installed in wet locations was instituted in the 2011 *NEC*. The durability of the nonmetallic in-use cover hoods provided for compliance with these wet location requirements has been found to be less than desirable, especially on construction sites. Breakage and hinge failure to these nonmetallic hood covers have been reported at dwelling unit and non-dwelling unit construction sites as well, leaving the receptacles exposed to all weather conditions. The more rigorous performance requirements in UL Product Standard 514D, *Standard for Cover Plates for Flush-Mounted Wiring Devices* for these extra duty in-use outlet box hood covers have improved the general durability of all listed in-use covers.

Another revision at 406.9(B)(1), which also affects 590.4(D)(2) calls for these extra duty covers at all wet location 15- and 20-ampere, 125- and 250-volt receptacles, not just the ones that are supported from grade. If the receptacle is installed in a wet location, it should make no difference how the enclosure or device box is installed or supported when determining the need for an extra duty hood cover.

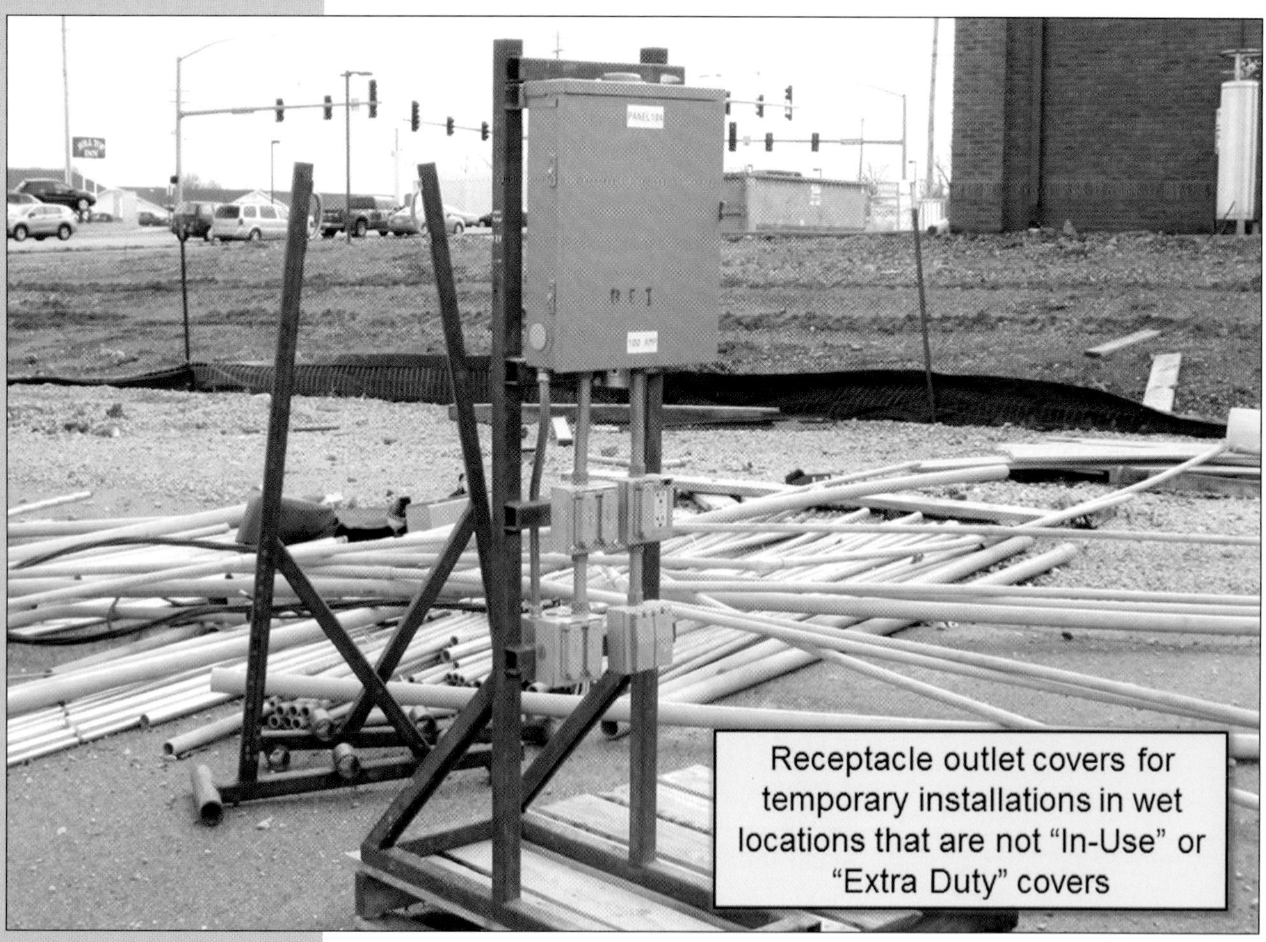
Receptacle outlet covers for temporary installations in wet locations that are not "In-Use" or "Extra Duty" covers

590.4(I)

Change at a Glance

Flexible cords and cables must be secured to boxes with fittings "listed for connecting flexible cords and cables to boxes."

Code Language

590.4 General

(I) Termination(s) at Devices. Flexible cords and cables entering enclosures containing devices requiring termination shall be secured to the box with fittings listed for connecting flexible cords and cables to boxes ~~designed for the purpose~~.

Proposal 3-104

2011 *NEC* Requirement

Flexible cords and cables entering enclosures containing devices requiring termination were required to be secured to the box with fittings "designed for the purpose."

2014 *NEC* Change

Flexible cords and cables entering enclosures containing devices requiring termination are now required to be secured to the box with fittings "listed for connecting flexible cords and cables to boxes."

Analysis of Change

An NEC Correlating Committee (NEC CC) Usability Task Group was assembled by the chairman of the NEC CC with the assignment of reviewing the use of the phrase "designed for the purpose" throughout the *NEC*. This is the completion of an ongoing process that was started in the 2005 edition of the *NEC* to identify specific locations throughout the *NEC* where the terms *identified for the purpose* or *listed for the purpose* were used. Now the user of the *Code* will know the specific purpose that the item in question was identified or listed for, not just generically stated that the item was "designed for the purpose." An example of this can be found at 680.23(A)(2) for underwater luminaries for a permanently installed swimming pool. This *Code* rule previously stated that transformers and power supplies used for the supply of underwater luminaires had to be "listed for the purpose." Current language at this location now states that these transformers and power supplies used for the supply of underwater luminaires must be "listed for swimming pool and spa use."

For this situation at 590.4(I), deleting the phrase "designed for the purpose" would now require flexible cords and cables entering enclosures containing devices to be secured to the box with fittings "listed for connecting flexible cords and cables to boxes."

590.4(J)

Change at a Glance

Cable assemblies and flexible cords installed as branch circuits or feeders are now prohibited from being installed or laid on the floor or the ground for temporary installations such as construction sites. (This does not include extension cords.)

Code Language

590.4 General

(J) Support. Cable assemblies and flexible cords and cables shall be supported in place at intervals that ensure that they will be protected from physical damage. Support shall be in the form of staples, cable ties, straps, or similar type fittings installed so as not to cause damage. Cable assemblies and flexible cords and cables installed as branch circuits or feeders shall not be installed on the floor or on the ground. Extension cords shall not be required to comply with 590.4(J). Vegetation shall not be used for support of overhead spans of branch circuits or feeders.

Exception: *(unchanged)*

Proposal 3-105

Comment 3-35, 3-34

590.4(J) Support (Temporary Installations)

Cable assemblies and flexible cords installed as branch circuits or feeders are now prohibited from being installed or laid on the floor or the ground for temporary installations such as constriction sites *(does not include extension cords).*

Cable assemblies and flexible cords and cables shall be supported in place at intervals that ensure that they will be protected from physical damage.

2011 *NEC* Requirement

When installed for temporary lighting, branch circuits, etc., at construction sites, cable assemblies and flexible cords and cables are required to be supported by staples, cable ties, straps, or similar type fittings at intervals that ensure that they will be protected from physical damage. Vegetation is also not permitted to be used for support of overhead spans of branch circuits or feeders, with an exception for temporary holiday lighting.

2014 *NEC* Change

The same requirements for the 2011 *NEC* still apply, with a new provision for cable wiring methods. Cable assemblies and flexible cords and cables installed as branch circuits or feeders cannot be installed on the floor or on the ground. This new rule does not apply to extension cords.

Analysis of Change

It is not uncommon to see temporary wiring at construction sites to be run on the floor and on the ground. In some cases, the wiring method enlisted for this temporary wiring is nonmetallic-sheathed cable (Type NM cable). This can be a very dangerous practice. It is also not uncommon to see these cable assemblies laying on the ground or concrete floor and damaged by normal construction activity. This is a real potential shock hazard for construction workers and anyone else in the work area. Construction site locations can quickly become a wet location, particularly during the time of construction when the complete roof and windows are not installed.

The rules and regulations at 590.6 for GFCI protection provide excellent safeguards for workers utilizing cord- and plug-connected tools, but this GFCI protection is only in effect on the load side of the temporary receptacle outlet. There is no GFCI protection on the feeder or branch circuit supplying these receptacle outlets. New provisions at 590.4(J) will require these feeders and branch circuits

Continued

to be installed where they are not installed on the floor or on the ground. The OSHA standards for construction do not allow these feeders or branch circuits to be run on the floor or ground [see 1926.405(a)(2)(ii)(b)]. This new requirement would not impact the normal construction site use of extension cords that are normally connected and disconnected to a construction site branch circuit. Extension cord use would still be subject to protection from physical damage during its transient use.

6

600.4(E)

Change at a Glance

All signs, outline lighting, skeleton tubing systems and retrofit kits are required to be marked to indicate that field-wiring and installation instructions are required (not just section signs).

Code Language

600.4 Markings

(E) ~~Section Signs~~ Installation Instructions. ~~Section~~ All signs, outline lighting, skeleton tubing systems and retrofit kits shall be marked to indicate that field wiring and installation instructions are required.

Exception: Portable, cord connected signs are not required to be marked.

Proposal 18-93

2011 *NEC* Requirement

Section signs were required to be marked to indicate that field-wiring and installation instructions are required.

2014 *NEC* Change

Revisions to 600.4(E) changed the title of this subsection from "Section Signs" to "Installation Instructions." This subsection now requires all signs, outline lighting, skeleton tubing systems and retrofit kits to be marked to indicate that field-wiring and installation instructions are required (not just section signs). An exception was added to exclude portable, cord-connected signs from this requirement.

Analysis of Change

The marking requirements for electric signs and outline lighting systems have been revised to include additional marking requirements to indicate when field-wiring and installation instructions are required. The previous wording at this subsection only applied to section signs. Section 110.3(B) requires listed or labeled equipment to be installed and used in accordance with any manufacturer's instructions included in the listing or labeling. Listing and labeling of equipment serves as the primary basis for approvals by the authority having jurisdiction (AHJ). Without indication from the manufacturer, it becomes difficult, particularly for the AHJ to know precisely when field-wiring is necessitated and when a sign component is part of a packaged assembly. The UL *Guide Information for Electrical Equipment* (White Book), under category UXYT for signs, clearly indicates, "...the acceptability of the assembled sections in the field rests with the authority having jurisdiction." To carry out the approval process, AHJs should verify that the installed listed sign component is installed in accordance with its associated installation instructions. This revision will require manufacturers of listed signs components to provide installation instructions for the field installer. This revision should provide sign installers with reasonable assurances of attaining approvals from the AHJ for these listed signs components where installa-

Continued

tion instructions are provided, and the installation is consistent with those instructions.

This revision establishes continuity between requirements in 600.3 and listing requirements for signs and UL 48, *Electric Signs*, the product standard for electric signs. Except for portable cord-connected signs, all listed signs, outline lighting and skeleton tubing systems require installation instructions to be in harmony with UL 48, 15th Edition, 8.1 – 8.1.5. This marking requirement and installation instructions requirement were needed for more than just section signs as installation instructions are required by UL Subject 879A, *Outline of Investigation for LED Kits*. Additionally, 600.12 requires field-installed secondary circuit wiring for electric signs, retrofit kits, outline lighting systems, and skeleton tubing systems to be installed in accordance with installation instructions.

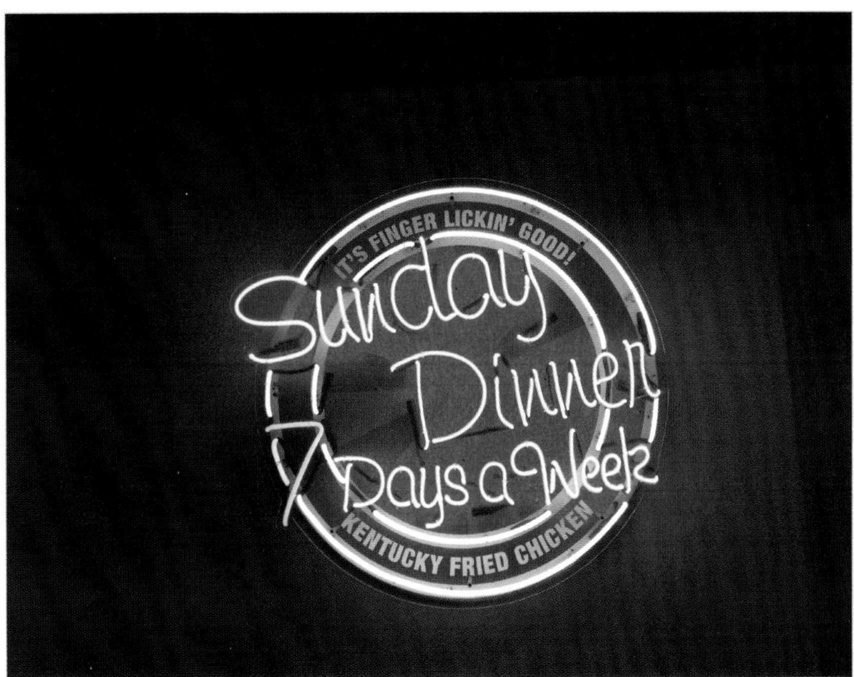

600.6(A)(1)

Change at a Glance

Disconnect is required to be located at the point feeder(s) or branch circuit(s) supplying a sign or outline lighting system enters a sign enclosure or pole. This new language requires disconnection of all wiring where it enters the enclosure of the sign or pole.

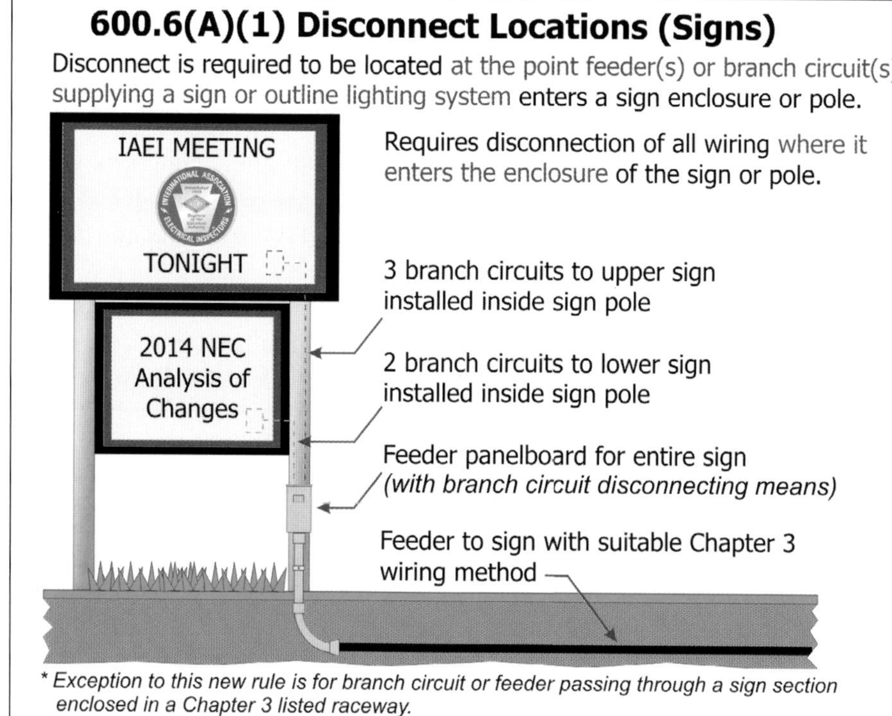

600.6(A)(1) Disconnect Locations (Signs)
Disconnect is required to be located at the point feeder(s) or branch circuit(s) supplying a sign or outline lighting system enters a sign enclosure or pole.
IAEI MEETING
TONIGHT
2014 NEC
Analysis of
Changes
Requires disconnection of all wiring where it enters the enclosure of the sign or pole.
3 branch circuits to upper sign installed inside sign pole
2 branch circuits to lower sign installed inside sign pole
Feeder panelboard for entire sign (with branch circuit disconnecting means)
Feeder to sign with suitable Chapter 3 wiring method
* Exception to this new rule is for branch circuit or feeder passing through a sign section enclosed in a Chapter 3 listed raceway.

Code Language

600.6 Disconnects

Each sign and outline lighting system, feeder circuit or branch circuit supplying a sign, outline lighting system, or skeleton tubing shall be controlled by an externally operable switch or circuit breaker that opens all ungrounded conductors and controls no other load. The switch or circuit breaker shall open all ungrounded conductors simultaneously on multi-wire branch circuits in accordance with 210.4(B). *(See NEC for remainder of text)*

(A) Location.

(1) **At Point of Entry to a Sign Enclosure.** The disconnect shall be located at the point the feeder circuit or branch circuit(s) supplying a sign or outline lighting system enters a sign enclosure or a pole in accordance with 600.5(C)(3) and shall disconnect all wiring where it enters the enclosure of the sign or pole.

2011 *NEC* Requirement

Section 600.6 requires each sign and outline lighting system, feeder circuit or branch circuit supplying a sign, outline lighting system, or skeleton tubing to be controlled by an externally operable switch or circuit breaker that opens all ungrounded conductors. Section 600.6(A)(1) and (A)(2) require the disconnecting means to be within sight of the sign and the controller. No provisions existed in the 2011 *NEC* as to the disconnecting means being required to be located ahead of the point of entry of electrical circuits before these circuits enter the sign enclosure.

2014 *NEC* Change

A new 600.6(A)(1) entitled, "At Point of Entry to a Sign Enclosure" has been added to this subsection. This addition will require the sign disconnect to be located at the point the feeder(s) or branch circuit(s) supplying a sign or outline lighting system enters a sign enclosure or pole and will require disconnection of all wiring where it enters the enclosure of the sign or pole. The existing provisions for the disconnecting means to be within sight of the sign and the controller have been pushed to 600.6(A)(2 and (A)(3) respectively.

Analysis of Change

It has become common practice in the electrical sign industry to attach or install a sign disconnecting means on a sign body or sign enclosure without respect to the location where supply conductors enter the sign in relationship to the disconnecting means. Installing these disconnecting means randomly without taking into consideration where the supply source enters these same sign enclosure can create a false sense of security for service personnel. It is also common practice and *Code*-compliant to install exposed insulated conductors in sign sections and sign poles. Sections 600.5(C)(3) and 410.30(B) both permit metal or nonmetallic poles to be used as a raceway to enclose supply conductors. It is easy to assume that the disconnect(s) de-energizes all conductors within the sign enclosure

600.6(A)(1)

Continued

Exception: A disconnect shall not be required for branch or feeder circuits passing through the sign where enclosed in a Chapter 3 listed raceway.

Proposal 18-99

Comment 18-47, 18-46

once the disconnecting means has been put in the open or "OFF" position. Without the provisions of this new requirement, exposed, insulated supply conductors to these disconnecting means can navigate within the sign enclosure, cabinets, poles, etc., to the supply side of the randomly located disconnect and remain energized, with the supplied disconnecting means in the open or closed position. This new disconnection of all wiring where it enters the enclosure of the sign or pole requirement will help protect those who work on signs by removing live conductors present after the disconnect switch has been de-energized.

Previous language at 210.4(B) and 600.6 already required multiwire branch circuits to be de-energized where the branch circuit originates in the same spirit of this new provision. The current and previous language at the main text of 600.6 mandates that a feeder circuit or branch circuit supplying a sign shall have a single disconnecting means that "opens all ungrounded conductors." However, this provision stops short of requiring the ungrounded conductors to be de-energized before they enter a sign body or enclosure. Occupational Safety & Health Administration (OSHA) rules covered in NFPA 70E, *Standard for Electrical Safety in the Workplace,* preclude working on energized equipment except under emergency and special circumstances. This new requirement will aid and assist in this process as well.

An exception to this new rule will allow a branch circuit or feeder to pass through a sign where enclosed in a *NEC* Chapter 3 listed raceway, allowing the disconnecting means at each section of a large sign. This will allow an extremely large sign with an extremely large structure provided with multiple feeders, branch circuits with perhaps multiple 200-ampere panelboards provided at each level of the sign structure, to qualify as the required disconnecting means. The circuit breaker(s) in each of these panelboards will act as the disconnecting means before the circuits enter each sign section or enclosure.

600.7(A)(1)

Change at a Glance

Metal parts of skeleton tubing as well as signs and outline lighting systems are required to be grounded by connection to the equipment grounding conductor of the supply branch circuit(s) or feeder.

REVISION

Code Language

600.7 Grounding and Bonding

(A) Grounding.

(1) Equipment Grounding. ~~Signs and m~~Metal Equipment of signs, outline lighting, and skeleton tubing systems shall be grounded by connection to the equipment grounding conductor of the supply branch circuit(s) or feeder using the types of equipment grounding conductors specified in 250.118.

Exception: *Portable cord-connected signs shall not be required to be connected to the equipment grounding conductor where protected by a system of double insulation or its equivalent. Double insulated equipment shall be distinctively marked.*

Proposal 18-103

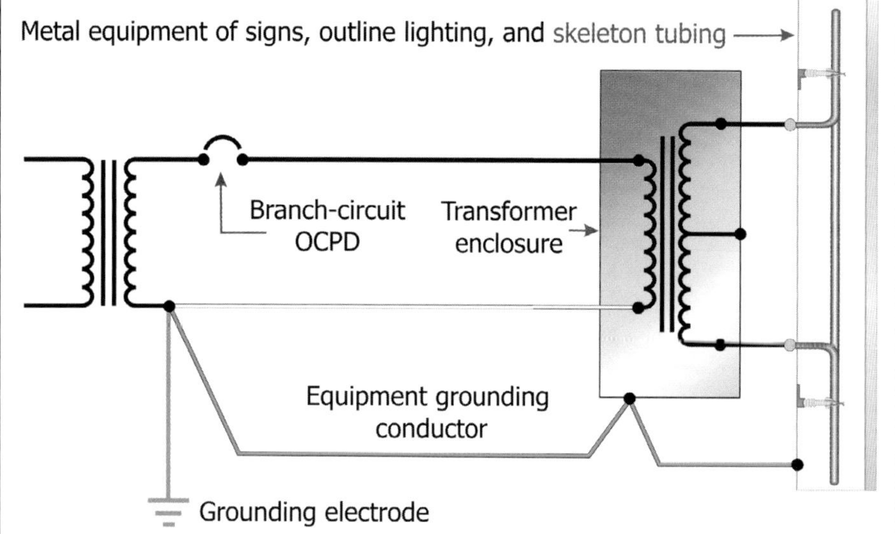
600.7(A)(1) Equipment Grounding (Signs)
Metal parts of skeleton tubing as well as signs and outline lighting systems are required to be grounded by connection to the equipment grounding conductor of the supply branch circuit(s) or feeder.
Metal equipment of signs, outline lighting, and skeleton tubing
Branch-circuit OCPD
Transformer enclosure
Equipment grounding conductor
Grounding electrode

2011 *NEC* Requirement

Signs and metal equipment of outline lighting systems were required to be grounded by connection to the equipment grounding conductor of the supply branch circuit(s) or feeder using any of the types of equipment grounding conductors specified in 250.118. Metal parts of skeleton tubing were not included in this grounding provision.

2014 *NEC* Change

Revisions occurred at 600.7(A)(1) to include metal parts of skeleton tubing as well as metal parts of signs and outline lighting systems requiring grounding by connection to the equipment grounding conductor of the supply branch circuit(s) or feeder.

Analysis of Change

Skeleton neon tubing systems operate at voltages over 1000 volts and are field assembled similar to section signs with neon illumination. Remote non–current-carrying metal parts, such as through-wall neon tubing receptacles, transformer enclosures, and metallic raceways used for secondary conductors have potential to be energized. These metal parts need to be properly bonded to the equipment grounding conductor of the supply branch circuit(s) or feeder for electrical continuity and safety the same as metal parts of section signs and outline lighting systems.

Skeleton tubing is defined at 600.2 as "neon tubing that is itself the sign or outline lighting and not attached to an enclosure or sign body."

610.31

Change at a Glance

New reference to 430.109, Types of Disconnecting Means, replaces the previous laundry list of types of disconnecting means which was incomplete.

REVISION

NEW

Code Language

610.31 Runway Conductor Disconnecting Means. ***(Cranes and Hoists)***

610.31 Runway Conductor Disconnecting Means. A disconnecting means that has a continuous ampere rating not less than that calculated in 610.14(E) and (F) shall be provided between the runway contact conductors and the power supply. The disconnecting means shall comply with 430.109. ~~Such disconnecting means shall consist of a motor-circuit switch, circuit breaker, or molded-case switch.~~ This disconnecting means shall be as follows:

(1) Readily accessible and operable from the ground or floor level

(2) Lockable in accordance with 110.25. ~~Capable of being locked in the open position. The provision for locking or adding a lock to the disconnecting means shall be installed on or at the switch or circuit breaker used as the disconnecting means and shall remain in place with or without the lock installed. Portable means for adding a lock to the switch or circuit breaker shall not be permitted as the means required to be installed at and remain with the equipment.~~

610.31 Runway Conductor Disconnecting Means

New reference to 430.109 *(Types of Disconnecting Means)* replaces the previous "laundry list" of types of disconnecting means, which was incomplete.

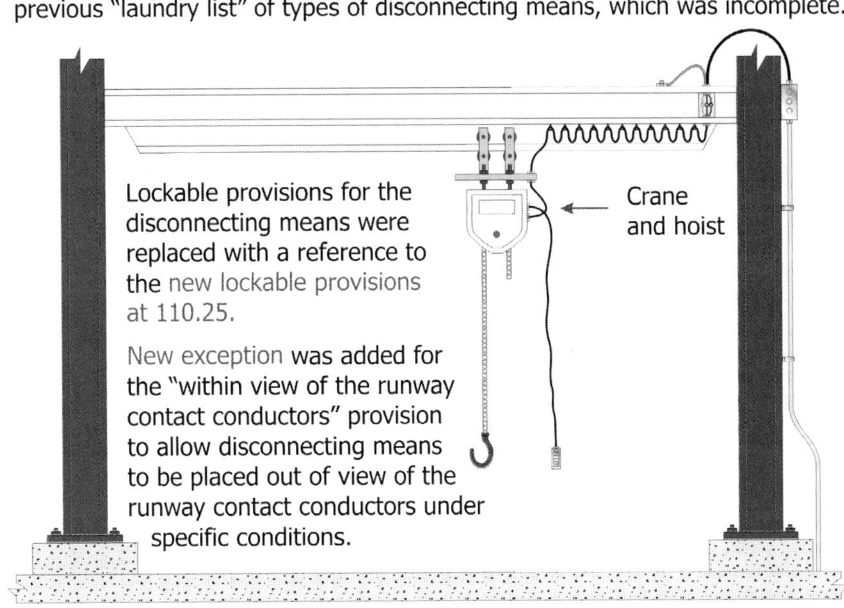
Lockable provisions for the disconnecting means were replaced with a reference to the new lockable provisions at 110.25.
New exception was added for the "within view of the runway contact conductors" provision to allow disconnecting means to be placed out of view of the runway contact conductors under specific conditions.
Crane and hoist

2011 *NEC* Requirement

A disconnecting means for a crane or hoist must be provided somewhere between the runway contact conductors and the power supply. This disconnecting means was required to consist of a motor circuit switch, circuit breaker, or molded-case switch. This disconnecting means had to comply with four specific conditions. (1) Installed in a readily accessible location and be operable from the ground or floor level. (2) Capable of being locked in the open position with specific conditions for the locking means. (3) Open all ungrounded conductors simultaneously, and (4) Placed within view of the runway contact conductors.

2014 *NEC* Change

This section was revised by removing the incomplete laundry list of types of disconnecting means permitted for cranes and hoists and replacing this previous list with a new reference to 430.109, Types of Disconnecting Means. The lockable provisions for the disconnecting means were replaced with a reference to the new lockable provisions at 110.25. A new exception was added for the "within view of the runway contact conductors" provision to allow the disconnecting means to be placed out of view of the runway contact conductors under specific conditions.

Analysis of Change

Previous language at 610.31 required the disconnecting means runway contacts of a crane or hoist to consist of a motor-circuit switch, circuit breaker, or molded-case switch. Proposals were submitted to CMP-12 to add to this laundry list of permitted types of disconnecting means, "fuseable-type disconnects." Rather than add to the laundry list, CMP-12 instead choose to remove the list of types of disconnecting means entirely and to replace the incomplete list with a reference to 430.109. This Article 430 reference gives a complete list of allowable types of disconnecting means for motors

610.31

Continued

(3) Open all ungrounded conductors simultaneously

(4) Placed within view of the runway contact conductors

Exception: The runway conductor disconnecting means or electrolytic cell lines shall be permitted to be placed out of view of the runway contact conductors where either of the following conditions are met:
(a) Where a location in view of the contact conductors is impracticable or introduces additional or increased hazards to persons or property
(b) In industrial installations, with written safety procedures, where conditions of maintenance and supervision ensure that only qualified persons service the equipment

---

Proposal 12-10, 12-11, 12-12, 12-12a

Comment 12-1

and motor controllers, which is sufficient for this provision here in Article 610 of cranes and hoists.

This disconnecting means has to comply with four specific conditions. One of these conditions called for the disconnecting means to be "capable of being locked in the open position" with specific conditions for the locking means. The details for this locking means were removed and replaced with a reference to the new locking provisions at 110.25. This new 110.25, which was added in Article 110, provides consistent requirements at one location for "Lockable Disconnecting Means" rules.

The fourth condition for the crane or hoist disconnecting means requires the disconnecting means to be "placed within view of the runway contact conductors." An exception to this rule was added for locations where placing the disconnecting means in view of the contact conductors is impracticable or introduces additional or increased hazards to persons or property or in industrial installations, with written safety procedures, where conditions of maintenance and supervision ensure that only qualified persons service the equipment. Many cranes and hoists run entire lengths of industrial and commercial buildings at such distances that "within view" does not serve a purpose or address any specific hazard. Restricting the location of the disconnecting means to "within view" as opposed to a dedicated and protected location makes the design less able to protect the disconnecting means from overhead loads served by the cranes. Providing an exception to the "within view" requirement will make this Article 610 requirement consistent with other similar industrial installations such as allowed in Article 430 for motors.

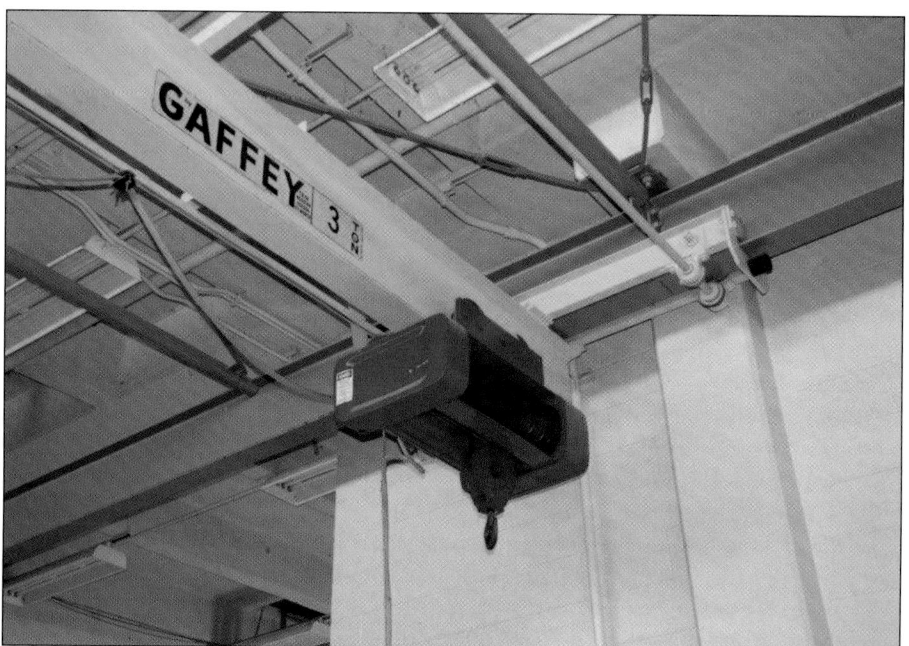

620.21, EX

Change at a Glance

The cords and cables of listed cord- and plug-connected equipment are not required to be installed in a raceway in hoistways, escalators, moving walkways, etc.

Code Language

620.21 Wiring Methods *(Elevators, Escalators, Etc.)*

Conductors and optical fibers located in hoistways, in escalator and moving walk wellways, in platform lifts, stairway chairlift runways, machinery spaces, control spaces, in or on cars, in machine rooms and control rooms, not including the traveling cables connecting the car or counterweight and hoistway wiring, shall be installed in rigid metal conduit, intermediate metal conduit, electrical metallic tubing, rigid nonmetallic conduit, or wireways, or shall be Type MC, MI, or AC cable unless otherwise permitted in 620.21(A) through (C).

***Exception:** Cords and cables of listed cord- and plug connected equipment shall not be required to be installed in a raceway.*

Proposal 12-28

Comment 12-13, 12-12

2011 *NEC* Requirement

All conductors and optical fiber cables located in and for hoistways, elevators, escalators, etc., were generally required to be installed in rigid metal conduit, intermediate metal conduit, electrical metallic tubing, rigid nonmetallic conduit, or wireways, or to be Type MC, MI, or AC cable. This does not include the traveling cables connecting the car or counterweight and hoistway wiring.

2014 *NEC* Change

An exception was added to this existing raceway rule for cords and cables of listed cord- and plug-connected equipment.

Analysis of Change

All conductors and optical fiber cables associated with wiring methods for elevators, escalators, etc., are generally required to be installed in some form of a raceway system. In many cases, listed cord- and plug-connected equipment is used within these installations, such as computer displays, power supplies, etc. The wiring methods typically employed for this type of equipment are flexible cords and cables not intended by the manufacturer to be run in a raceway. Listed cord- and plug-connected equipment is intended and should be allowed to be run without a raceway. Recognizing this fact, CMP-12 added an exception for cords and cables of listed cord- and plug-connected equipment to this wiring method section for the 2014 *NEC*.

620.51(C)(1)

Change at a Glance

Both fused and non-fused motor circuit switches are allowed when motor controllers are installed within the elevator hoistway and are not supplied with a means for protection from internal short circuits.

Code Language

620.51 Disconnecting Means

A single means for disconnecting all ungrounded main power supply conductors for each unit shall be provided and be designed so that no pole can be operated independently. *(See NEC for complete text).*

(C) Location. The disconnecting means shall be located where it is readily accessible to qualified persons.

(1) On Elevators Without Generator Field Control. On elevators without generator field control, the disconnecting means shall be located within sight of the motor field controller. Where the motor controller is located in the elevator hoistway, the disconnecting means required by 620.51(A) shall be located in a machinery space, machine room, control space or control room outside the hoistway; and an additional, fused or non-fused externally operable motor circuit switch that is lockable in accordance with 110.25 ~~capable of being locked in the open position~~ to disconnect all ungrounded main power-

620.51(C)(1) Disconnecting Means

Both fused and non-fused motor circuit switches are allowed when motor controllers are installed within the elevator hoistway and not supplied with a means for protection from internal short circuits.

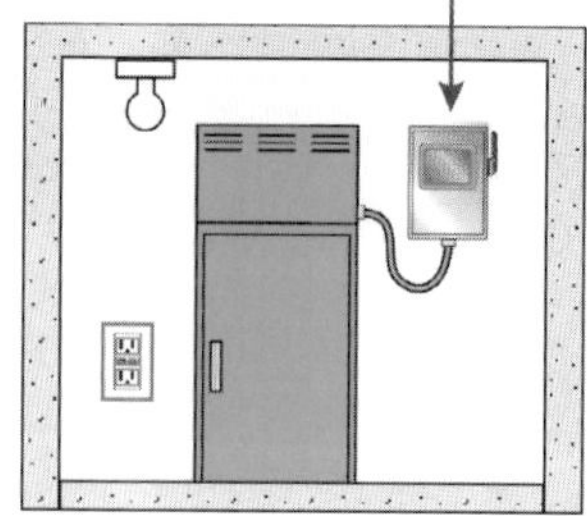

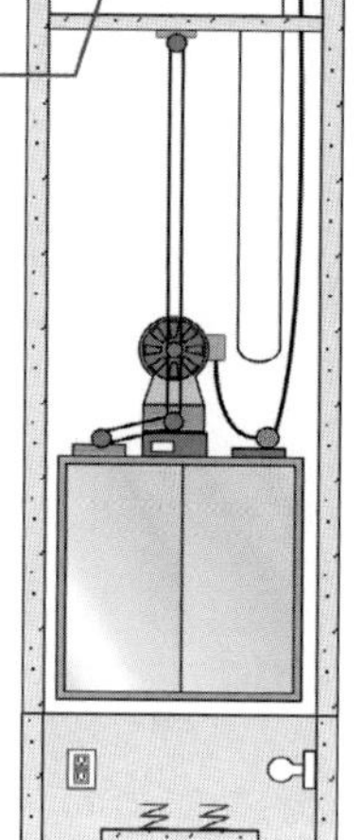

2011 *NEC* Requirement

On elevators without generator field control, the disconnecting means is required to be located within sight of the motor controller. Where the motor controller is located in the elevator hoistway, the disconnecting means is also required to be located in a machinery space, machine room, control space or control room outside the hoistway. In addition to these requirements, a non-fused, enclosed externally, operable motor-circuit switch, capable of being locked in the open position, to disconnect all ungrounded main power-supply conductors was required to be located within sight of the motor controller.

2014 *NEC* Change

In conjunction with the above provisions that were carried forward from the 2011 *NEC*, the enclosed externally operable motor-circuit switch for disconnection of all ungrounded main power-supply conductors is now permitted to be either a fused or non-fused motor-circuit switch.

Analysis of Change

The previous text at 620.51(C)(1) required a motor-circuit switch, capable of being locked in the open position, to disconnect all ungrounded main power-supply conductors to be located within sight of the motor controller. This motor circuit switch was required to be a "non-fused" motor-circuit switch. Proposals were submitted to CMP-12 to suggest that this motor-circuit switch could be either "fused or non-fused." The option to add fuses to this additional motor-circuit switch would provide a safe and clearly recognized means to access fuses dedicated for protection of that motor controller. It should be noted that selective coordination of overcurrent protection is still required for this elevator application.

A reference to new 110.25 was also added at this subsection. This new 110.25 was added in Article 110 for the 2014 *NEC* to provide consistent requirements

620.51(C)(1)

Continued

supply conductors shall be located within sight of the motor controller. The additional switch shall be a listed device and shall comply with 620.91(C). *(See NEC for remainder of text).*

Proposal 12-37, 12-39

Comment 12-16, 12-17

at one location for "Lockable Disconnecting Means" rules. This is one of several locations in the *NEC* where a reference to 110.25 replaces separate rules for lockable disconnecting means rules. These separate and individual lockable disconnecting means rules varied widely in their uniformity.

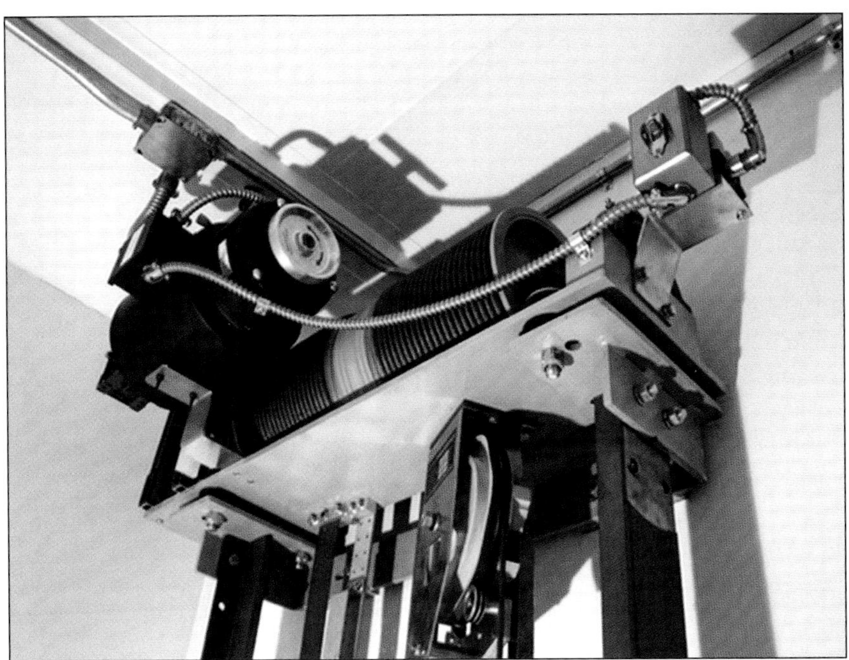

Article 625

Change at a Glance

Article 625 was renumbered and reorganized to provide a logical sequence and arrangement.

Code Language

Article 625 Electric Vehicle Charging System

I. General
625.1 Scope.
625.2 Definitions.
625.4 Voltages.
625.5 Listed ~~or Labeled~~.

II. Equipment Construction ~~Wiring Methods~~
625.10 Electric Vehicle Coupler. *[Was 625.9]*

~~III. Equipment Construction~~
~~625.13 Electric Vehicle Supply Equipment.~~ *[Now 625.44(B)]*
~~625.14 Rating~~. *[Now 625.41]*
625.15 Marking.
625.16 Means of Coupling.
625.17 Cords and Cables.
625.18 Interlock.
625.19 Automatic De-Energization of Cable.

~~IV. Control and Protection~~
~~625.21 Overcurrent Protection.~~ *[Now 625.40]*
625.22 Personnel Protection System.
~~625.28 Hazardous (Classified) Locations.~~
~~625.29 Indoor Sites.~~
~~625.30 Outdoor Sites.~~

III. Installation
625.40 Overcurrent Protection. *[Was 625.21]*

Article 625 Electric Vehicle Charging System

Article 625 was renumbered and reorganized to provide a logical sequence and arrangement.

Article 625 now consists of three parts: Part I General, Part II Equipment Construction, and Part III Installation.

2011 *NEC* Requirement

Article 625, Electric Vehicle Charging Systems, was arranged with five parts; Part I. General; Part II. Wiring Methods; Part III. Equipment Construction; Part IV. Control and Protection; and Part V. Electric Vehicle Supply Equipment Locations.

2014 *NEC* Change

Article 625 was renumbered and reorganized into three parts; Part I. General; Part II. Equipment Construction; and Part III. Installation.

Analysis of Change

Article 625 has been renumbered and reorganized to provide a more logical structure and arrangement. The titles for the various parts of Article 625 did not fit the requirements found within those parts and needed to be revised in order to enhance the comprehensiveness of this EV charging station article. Article 625 had installation requirements scattered throughout the article, even under parts that are found in the construction parts. New definitions are now found at 625.2. Clarification of cord- and plug-connected supply equipment is now located at 625.44. Revisions occurred for specific criteria for cords and cables at 625.17.

Article 625 and provisions for EV charging stations were added to the 1996 *NEC*. An *EV charging station* is an element in an infrastructure that supplies electric energy for the recharging of plug-in electric vehicles, including all-electric cars, neighborhood electric vehicles and plug-in hybrids. As plug-in hybrid electric vehicles and battery/electric vehicle ownership is expanding, there is a growing need for widely distributed publicly accessible charging stations, some of which support faster charging at higher voltages and currents than are available from domestic supplies. As this need grows, so must the *NEC* expand to encompass these ever-changing EV charging demands. As of March 2013, the United States had approximately 5,678 charging stations across the country, with over 16,200

Continued

625.41 Rating. *[Was 625.14]*
625.42 Disconnecting Means. *[Was 625.23]*
625.44 Electric Vehicle Supply Equipment Connection.
625.46 Loss of Primary Source. *[Was 625.25]*
625.48 Interactive Systems. *[Was 625.26]*

~~**V. Electric Vehicle Supply Equipment Locations**~~
625.50 Location. *[Was 625.29(A) and (B) and 625.30(A)(and (B)]*
625.52 Ventilation. *[Was 625.29(C) and (D)]*

Proposal 12-52

public charging points. Of these public charging points, 26 percent are located in California, with 10 percent located in Texas, and 7.4 percent in Washington state.

These revisions and the reorganization were primarily the result of the work of a CMP-12 Task Group on Electric Vehicles.

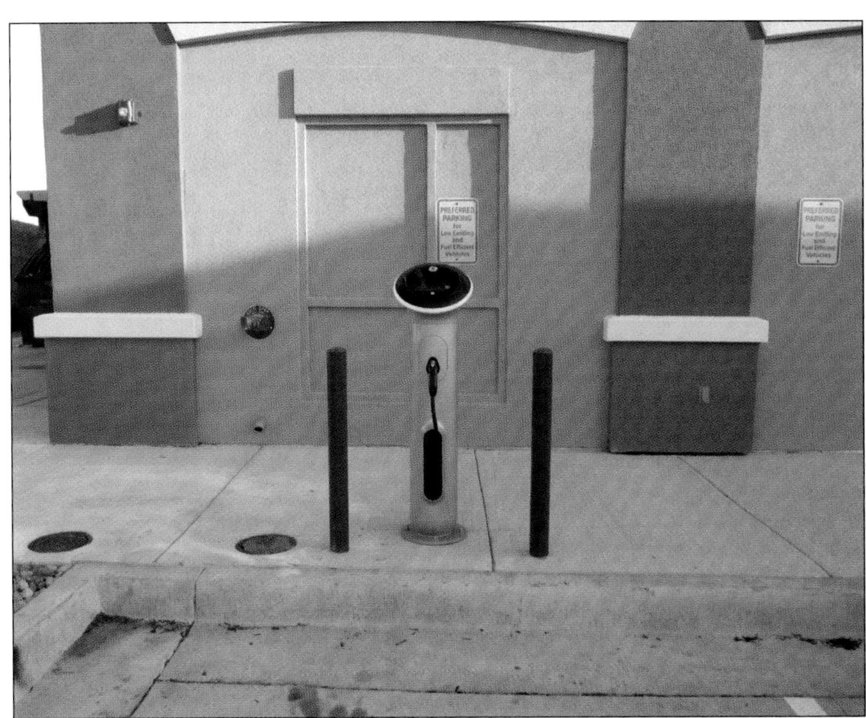

630.13

Change at a Glance

Revision requires the arc welder disconnect be marked to "identify" what the disconnect actually disconnects rather than requiring the disconnect be "identified."

Code Language

630.13 Disconnecting Means

630.13 Disconnecting Means. A~~n~~ ~~identified~~ disconnecting means shall be provided in the supply circuit for each arc welder that is not equipped with a disconnect mounted as an integral part of the welder. The disconnecting means identity shall be marked in accordance with 110.22(A). The disconnecting means shall be a switch or circuit breaker, and its rating shall be not less than that necessary to accommodate overcurrent protection as specified under 630.12.

Proposal 12-93

Comment 12-53

630.13 Disconnecting Means (Electric Welders)

Revision requires arc welder disconnecting means shall be marked to "identify" what the disconnect actually disconnects rather than require the disconnect be "identified."

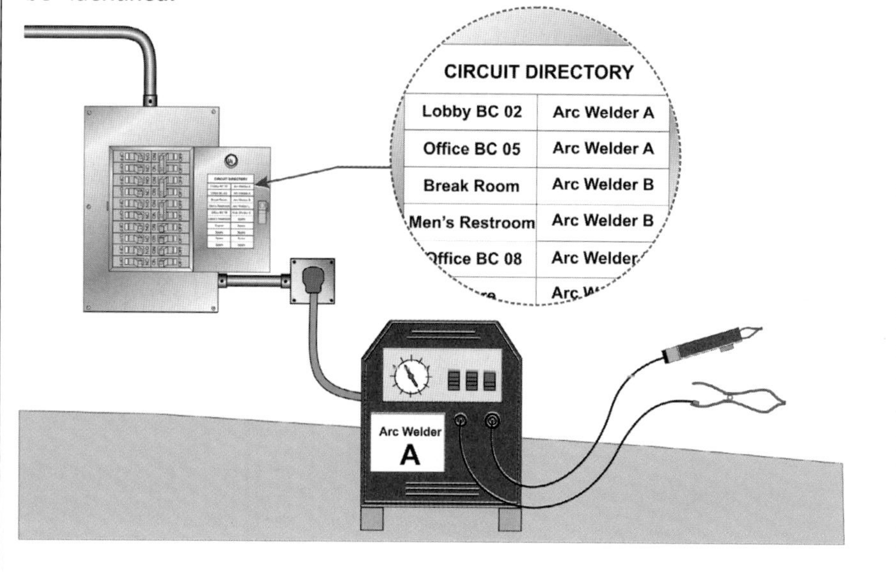

2011 *NEC* Requirement

At 630.13 in the 2011 *NEC*, the *Code* called for an "identified" disconnecting means in the supply circuit for each arc welder that is not equipped with a disconnect mounted as an integral part of the welder. "Identified" for what?

2014 *NEC* Change

A disconnecting means is still required in the supply circuit for each arc welder that is not equipped with a disconnect mounted as an integral part of the welder, but language was added to specify that this disconnecting means is required to be marked to "indicate its purpose" or "identify" what it supplies.

Analysis of Change

Previous language at 630.13 called for an "identified" disconnecting means when, in fact, this requirement intended for this disconnecting means to "identify" what it supplies. *Identified* is defined in Article 100 and appeared to be misapplied at 630.13 in the context of the previous text. This "identified" disconnecting means text was added in the 2011 *NEC* with the intent to require the disconnect be marked to identify what it disconnects. The literal wording of the previous text using the defined term *identified* seemed to require that the disconnect be "recognizable as suitable for the specific purpose, function, use, environment, application..." rather than the intended application that the disconnect be marked to identify what it disconnects.

645.14 and 645.15

Change at a Glance

This revision divides the grounding requirements for information technology equipment into two separate sections: one for equipment grounding and bonding, and new provisions for systems grounding.

Code Language

645.14 System Grounding. (Information Technology Equipment)

645.15 Equipment Grounding and Bonding

645.14 System Grounding. Separately derived power systems shall be installed in accordance with Part I and II of Article 250. Power systems derived within listed information technology equipment that supply information technology systems through receptacles or cable assemblies supplied as part of this equipment shall not be considered separately derived for the purpose of applying 250.30.

645.15 Equipment Grounding and Bonding. All exposed non-current-carrying metal parts of an information technology system shall be bonded to the equipment grounding conductor in accordance with Parts I, V, VI, VII, and VIII of Article 250 or shall be double insulated. ~~Power systems derived within listed information technology equipment that supply information technology systems through receptacles or cable assemblies supplied as part of this~~

645.14 System Grounding and 645.15 Equipment Grounding and Bonding (IT Equipment)

Revision divides the grounding requirements for information technology equipment into two separate sections, one for equipment grounding and bonding and new provisions for systems grounding.

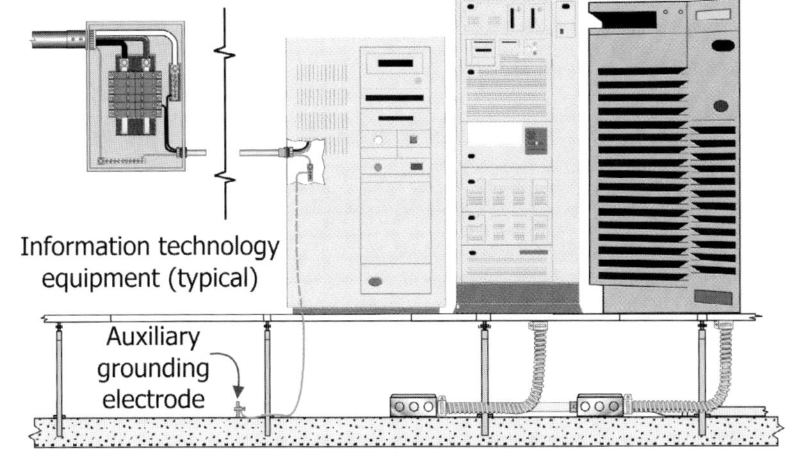

Any auxiliary grounding electrode(s) installed for information technology equipment shall be installed in accordance with the provisions of 250.54.

2011 *NEC* Requirement

Section 645.15 entitled, "Grounding" required all exposed non–current-carrying metal parts of an information technology system to be bonded to the equipment grounding conductor in accordance with the entire Article 250, unless it was a double insulated system. Power systems derived within listed information technology equipment that supply information technology systems through receptacles or cable assemblies supplied as part of this equipment are not to be considered separately derived for the purpose of applying 250.30 *(requirements for grounding a separately derived system)*. Where signal reference structures are installed, they are required to be bonded to the equipment grounding conductor provided for the information technology equipment.

2014 *NEC* Change

New 645.14 entitled, "System Grounding" was added, and existing 645.15 was retitled, "Equipment Grounding and Bonding" and revised. This revision divides the grounding requirements into two different sections: one for equipment grounding and bonding (645.15), and one for systems grounding (645.14). The provisions for separately derived power systems were moved to new 645.14. A new reference to 250.54 for auxiliary grounding electrode(s) was added to 645.15 as well.

Analysis of Change

In the comment stage of the 2014 *NEC*, under the advisement of an Article 645 Task Group, CMP-12 divided the grounding requirements for information technology (IT) equipment into two distinct sections. New 645.14 provides requirements for systems grounding; and 645.15 deals with equipment grounding and bonding for IT equipment. The previous requirements at 645.15 necessitated that all exposed non–current-carrying metal parts of an IT system be bonded to the equipment grounding conductor in accordance

645.14 and 645.15

Continued

~~equipment shall not be considered separately derived for the purpose of applying 250.30.~~ Where signal reference structures are installed, they shall be bonded to the equipment grounding conductor provided for the information technology equipment. Any auxiliary grounding electrode(s) installed for information technology equipment shall be installed in accordance with the provisions of 250.54.

Informational Note No. 1: The bonding requirements in the product standards governing this listed equipment ensure that it complies with Article 250.

Informational Note No. 2: Where isolated grounding-type receptacles are used, see 250.146(D) and 406.3(D).

Proposal 12-138, 12-139

Comment 12-68

with "Article 250." The 2011 *NEC Style Manual (see 4.1.1)* states that "references shall not be made to an entire article, such as 'grounded in accordance with Article 250' unless additional conditions are specified. References to parts within articles shall be permitted." This *NEC Style Manual* violation was corrected by referencing "Parts I, V, VI, VII, and VIII of Article 250" for this equipment grounding conductor requirement.

A new sentence was added to the existing provisions in 645.15 for equipment grounding and bonding of IT equipment. This new sentence refers to 250.54 for auxiliary grounding electrode(s). There is much confusion in the electrical industry and the IT world as to what constitutes an isolated ground as it relates to computer installations. Installing a separate grounding electrode *(connected to the earth)* that is not connected to the equipment grounding conductor of the branch circuits and feeders supplying IT equipment is not a "isolated ground," and is, in fact, a violation of the general requirements in 250.4(A)(5) and (B)(4) as well as in 250.54. The earth should never serve as a ground-fault current return path. This new sentence will provide clear direction and correlation for users of the *Code* about required connections between auxiliary grounding electrodes and equipment grounding conductors of the branch circuits and feeders supplying IT equipment.

645.27

Change at a Glance

All overcurrent devices in critical operations data systems are required be selectively coordinated with all supply-side overcurrent devices.

Code Language

645.27 Selective Coordination

Critical operations data system(s) overcurrent devices shall be selectively coordinated with all supply side overcurrent protective devices.

Proposal 12-143

645.27 Selective Coordination

All overcurrent devices in critical operations data systems are required be selectively coordinated with all supply-side overcurrent devices.

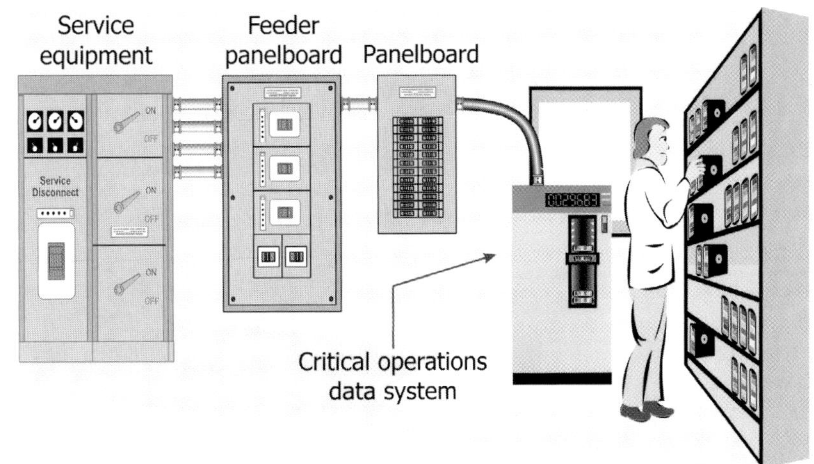

Critical Operations Data Systems: "An information technology equipment system that requires continuous operation for reasons of public safety, emergency management, national security, or business continuity."

2011 *NEC* Requirement

There were no selective coordination requirements in Article 645 for information technology equipment in the 2011 *NEC*.

2014 *NEC* Change

A new 645.27 was added that will now require all critical operations data system(s) overcurrent protective devices to be selectively coordinated with all supply-side overcurrent protective devices.

Analysis of Change

Critical operations data systems are defined at 645.2 as "An information technology equipment system that requires continuous operation for reasons of public safety, emergency management, national security, or business continuity." A lack of selective coordination reduces the reliability of these systems and negates the benefits of selective coordination provisions that are typically designed into these systems. *Selective coordination* is defined in Article 100 as "Localization of an overcurrent condition to restrict outages to the circuit or equipment affected, accomplished by the selection and installation of overcurrent protective devices and their ratings or settings for the full range of available overcurrents, from overload to the maximum available fault current, and for the full range of overcurrent protective device opening times associated with those overcurrents."

Article 646

Change at a Glance

A new article was added entitled, "Modular Data Centers."

Code Language

Article 646 Modular Data Centers

I. General

II. Equipment

III. Lighting.

IV. Work Space

Proposal 12-147

Comment 12-71, 12-72, 12-74, 12-75, 12-76, 12-77, 12-78, 12-80, 12-81, 12-82, 12-83

Article 646 Modular Data Centers

New Article was added to draw a distinction between data centers that currently fall under the scope of Article 645 *(Information Technology Equipment)* and those described in this new article.

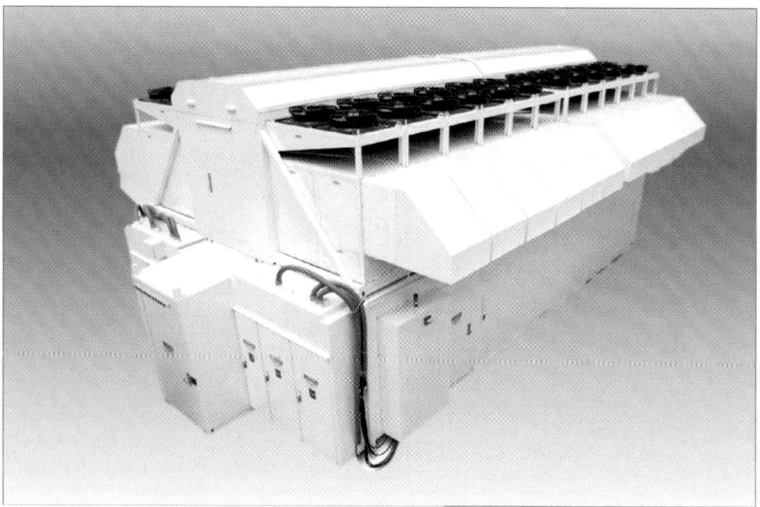

New article identifies those areas of the *NEC* that should be applied to MDCs and also includes additional new requirements where necessary.

2011 *NEC* Requirement

Information technology equipment is addressed at Article 645. Modular data centers were not specifically addressed in the 2011 *NEC*.

2014 *NEC* Change

A new Article 646 entitled, "Modular Data Centers" was added to the 2014 *NEC*.

Analysis of Change

A new article for "Modular Data Centers" was added in Chapter 6 to draw a distinction between data centers that currently fall under the scope of Article 645, Information Technology Equipment, and those described in this new article. Modular Data Centers (MDCs) are an important emerging trend in data center architecture. Their construction, installation and use result in a unique hybrid piece of equipment that falls somewhere in between a large enclosure and a pre-fabricated building. The contained equipment in the enclosures or prefabricated buildings would be fully customizable and scalable to provide data center operations, but typically would not be permanently installed. Article 645 for IT equipment is only applicable to installations that meet the criteria of 645.4. Otherwise, Article 645 would not be applicable to these modular data centers, and the other articles of the *Code* would have to be applied. However, it is not always obvious what requirements in the *NEC* are applicable or how they should be applied given the complexity, customization and scalability of modular data centers. This new article identifies those areas of the *NEC* that should be applied to MDCs and also includes additional new requirements where necessary.

This new article provides requirements that enhance safety, supports the design and development of safe products and provides clarity for installers, end users and the authorities having jurisdiction (AHJs). This new article was numbered 646, so that it is in close proximity to current Article 645 covering Information Technology Equipment.

680.2

Change at a Glance

Definition for *storable swimming, wading, or immersion pools* has been revised to include *storable/portable spas and hot tubs.*

Code Language

680.2 Definitions: Storable Swimming, Wading, or Immersion Pools, or Storable/ Portable Spas and Hot Tubs

Those that are constructed on or above the ground and are capable of holding water to a maximum depth of 1.0 m (42 in.), or a pool, spa, or hot tub with nonmetallic, molded polymeric walls or inflatable fabric walls regardless of dimension.

Proposal 17-90

680.2 Definitions: Storable Swimming, Wading, or Immersion Pools; or Storable/Portable Spas and Hot Tubs

Definition for "Storable Swimming, Wading, or Immersion Pools" has been revised to include "Storable/Portable Spas and Hot Tubs."

It includes those that are constructed on or above the ground and are capable of holding water to a maximum depth of 1.0 m (42 in.), or a pool, spa, or hot tub with nonmetallic, molded polymeric walls or inflatable fabric walls regardless of dimension.

2011 *NEC* Requirement

For the 2011 *NEC*, the definition for *storable or portable spas or hot tubs* was not included in the definition for a *storable swimming, wading, or immersion pool.* This definition did include pools that are constructed on or above the ground and are capable of holding water to a maximum depth of 1.0 m (42 in.). This definition also included any pool with nonmetallic, molded polymeric walls or inflatable fabric walls regardless of dimension.

2014 *NEC* Change

The definition remained the same with the inclusion of *storable or portable spas and hot tubs* in the definition.

Analysis of Change

The definition of *storable swimming, wading, or immersion pools* at 680.2 was revised to include *storable or portable spas and hot tubs*. These portable spas and hot tub systems are very much similar in design, structure, and installation as storable pools. They also bring the same concerns as storable pools,such as, ground-fault circuit-interrupter (GFCI) protection, listing requirements, etc. The revision to this definition will clarify such things as the requirement at 680.42(C), which describes the need for underwater luminaires to comply with 680.23 and 680.33 for storable or portable spas, and hot tubs and storable pools. Without this revised definition, it becomes difficult for the enforcement community to apply Article 680 safety regulations to storable or portable spas and hot tubs.

680.12

Change at a Glance

Fountains were added to requirements for "Maintenance Disconnecting Means."

Code Language

680.12 Maintenance Disconnecting Means

One or more means to simultaneously disconnect all ungrounded conductors shall be provided for all utilization equipment other than lighting. Each means shall be readily accessible and within sight from its equipment and shall be located at least 1.5 m (5 ft) horizontally from the inside walls of a pool, spa, fountain, or hot tub unless separated from the open water by a permanently installed barrier that provides a 1.5 m (5 ft) reach path or greater. This horizontal distance is to be measured from the water's edge along the shortest path required to reach the disconnect.

Proposal 17-96

680.12 Maintenance Disconnecting Means

"Fountains" added to requirements for "Maintenance Disconnecting Means."

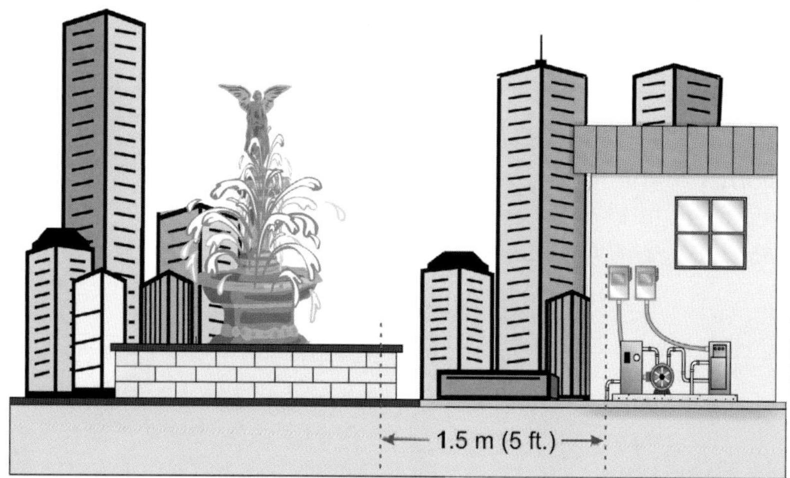

Each means shall be readily accessible and within sight from its equipment and shall be located at least 1.5 m (5 ft) horizontally from the inside walls of a pool, spa, fountain, or hot tub.

2011 *NEC* Requirement

A disconnecting mean(s) is required to simultaneously disconnect all ungrounded conductors for all utilization equipment (other than lighting) for a pool, spa, or hot tub. This disconnecting mean(s) must be readily accessible and within sight from its equipment. This disconnecting mean(s) must also generally be located at least 1.5 m (5 ft) horizontally from the inside walls of a pool, spa, or hot tub (unless separated by a permanently installed barrier).

2014 *NEC* Change

The same 2011 *NEC* maintenance disconnecting means rules at 680.12 were extended to fountains as well as to pools, spas, or hot tubs.

Analysis of Change

Section 680.12 provides requirements for installing a maintenance disconnecting means for all utilization equipment *(other than lighting)* associated with pools or similar bodies of water covered by Article 680. A revision occurred at this section in the 2008 *NEC* to clarify where the distances must be measured from when applying this rule to field-installed equipment. This disconnecting mean(s) must generally be located at least 1.5 m (5 ft) horizontally from the inside walls of the body of water. This 2008 *NEC* revision also identified "pools, spas, and hot tubs" concerning the types of equipment that were required to be provided with a maintenance disconnecting means.

Whatever concerns there might be to require a maintenance disconnecting means for a pool, spa, or hot tub would also hold true for a fountain. The previous text at 680.12 did not contain a disconnecting means provision for signs and outlines lighting installed within fountains as outlined at 600.6. This requirement at 600.6 also contains a reference back to 680.12. Without requiring the maintenance disconnecting means for a fountain to be located at least 1.5 m (5 ft) horizontally from the inside walls of a fountain, hazards can exist for maintenance personnel attempting to make contact with a disconnect while standing in a fountain filled with water.

680.21(C)

Change at a Glance

All single-phase, 120-volt through 240-volt outlets supplying pool pump motors now require GFCI protection *(regardless of ampacity)*.

Code Language

680.21 Motors

(C) GFCI Protection. Outlets supplying pool pump motors connected to single-phase, 120 volt through 240 volt branch circuits, ~~rated 15 or 20 amperes,~~ whether by receptacle or by direct connection, shall be provided with ground-fault circuit interrupter protection for personnel.

Proposal 17-100

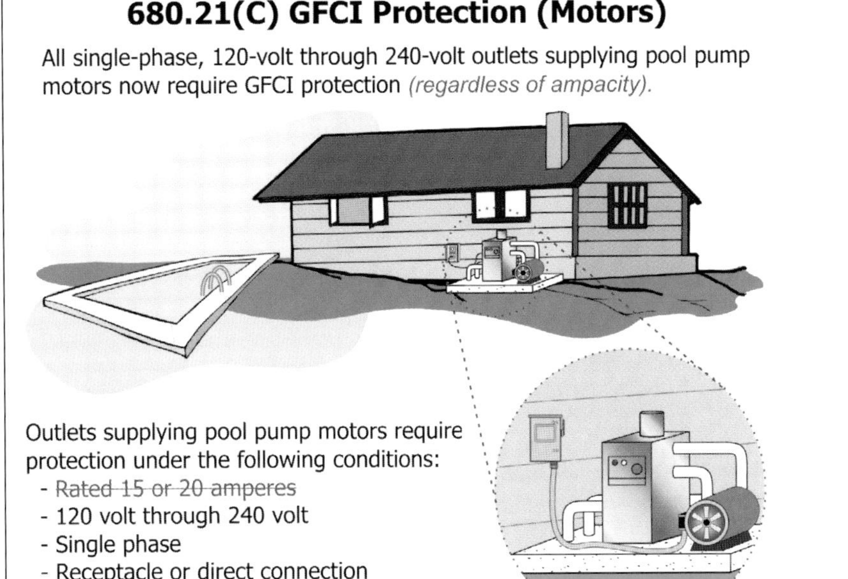

680.21(C) GFCI Protection (Motors)
All single-phase, 120-volt through 240-volt outlets supplying pool pump motors now require GFCI protection (regardless of ampacity).
Outlets supplying pool pump motors require protection under the following conditions:
- ~~Rated 15 or 20 amperes~~
- 120 volt through 240 volt
- Single phase
- Receptacle or direct connection
- Regardless of location

2011 *NEC* Requirement

The outlet(s) supplying pool pump motors for permanently installed pools, connected to single-phase, 120-volt through 240-volt branch circuits, rated 15 or 20 amperes required ground-fault circuit interrupter (GFCI) protection for personnel. This GFCI protection rule applies whether the pool pump motor is supplied by receptacle or by direct connection.

2014 *NEC* Change

These GFCI protection rules at 680.21(C) still apply to permanently installed pool pump motors, but for the 2014 *NEC*, the applicable limitation of motors "rated 15 or 20 amperes" has been removed.

Analysis of Change

The requirements for ground-fault circuit-interrupter (GFCI) protection for permanently installed pool pump motors are located at 680.21(C). This GFCI provision for permanently installed pool pump motors has gone through some type of revision every *Code* cycle since the re-write of Article 680 in the 2002 *NEC* code cycle. Revisions have included such things as GFCI requirements for "125-volt *or* 240-volt" to "120-volt *through* 240-volt" limitations. Further past revisions included expanding these GFCI provisions to hard-wired pool pump motors, not just cord- and plug-connected pool pump motors. Further revision has now occurred at this subsection for the 2014 *NEC* by removing the 15- or 20-ampere rating of pool pump motors as the only pool pump motors applicable to this GFCI provision.

Under the previous requirements at 680.21(C), a 1.5 hp, 230-volt pool pump motor would have been permitted to be installed on a 25-ampere rated branch circuit without GFCI protection; whereas a 1 hp, 230-volt pool pump motor requiring a 20-ampere overcurrent device would require GFCI protection for personnel. Any concerns of shock hazard potential for 20-ampere branch circuits feeding pool pump motors are also present for a 25-ampere branch circuits or any size branch circuits feeding single-phase pool pump motors.

680.22(A)(1)

Change at a Glance

At least one 125-volt, 15- or 20-ampere receptacle on a general-purpose branch circuit must to be located not less than 1.83 m (6 ft) from, and not more than 6.0 m (20 ft) from, the inside wall of all permanently installed pools *(not just dwelling unit pools)*.

Code Language

680.22 Lighting, Receptacles, and Equipment

(A) Receptacles.

~~(3)~~ (1) ~~Dwelling Unit(s)~~ Required Receptacle, Location. Where a permanently installed pool is installed ~~at a dwelling unit(s),~~ no fewer than one 125-volt, 15- or 20-ampere receptacle on a general-purpose branch circuit shall be located not less than 1.83 m (6 ft) from, and not more than 6.0 m (20 ft) from, the inside wall of the pool. This receptacle shall be located not more than 2.0 m (6 ft 6 in.) above the floor, platform, or grade level serving the pool.

Proposal 17-106

Comment 17-31

680.22(A)(1) Required Receptacle - Location

At least one 125-volt, 15- or 20-ampere receptacle on a general-purpose branch circuit must be located not less than 1.83 m (6 ft) from, and not more than 6.0 m (20 ft) from, the inside wall of all permanently installed pools *(not just dwelling unit pools).*

VOLTS HOTEL

Welcome IAEI Section Meeting

This required receptacle outlet requirement was expanded to all permanently installed pools, not just dwelling unit permanently installed pools.

2011 *NEC* Requirement

At least one 125-volt, 15- or 20-ampere receptacle on a general-purpose branch circuit was required to be located not less than 1.83 m (6 ft) from, and not more than 6.0 m (20 ft) from, the inside wall of all permanently installed pools at dwelling units. This receptacle(s) could not be located more than 2.0 m (6 ft 6 in.) above the floor, platform, or grade level serving the pool. This convenience receptacle was only applicable to dwelling unit and did not apply to "other than dwelling unit" permanently installed pools. This provision was also located at 680.22(A)(3) in the 2011 *NEC*.

2014 *NEC* Change

This provision for a required 125-volt, 15- or 20-ampere receptacle on a general-purpose branch circuit was moved to 680.22(A)(1). The requirement was expanded to all permanently installed pools, not just dwelling unit permanently installed pools. The title was revised from, "Dwelling Unit(s)" to "Required Receptacle, Location."

Analysis of Change

For permanently installed pools, at least one 125-volt, 15- or 20-ampere receptacle must be installed in the vicinity of the pool. This receptacle must be GFCI-protected, be on a general purpose branch circuit, and must be located not closer than 1.83 m (6 ft) and not farther than 6.0 m (20 ft) from the inside wall of the pool. This receptacle shall be located not more than 2.0 m (6½ ft) above the same floor, platform or grade on which the pool is installed. Prior to the 2014 *NEC*, this required receptacle was only required at permanently installed pools at dwelling units. The requirement to have at least one 125-volt, 15- or 20-ampere receptacle at permanently installed dwelling unit pools was introduced in the 1978 *NEC*. At that time, the receptacle was required to be installed within 3.0 m (10 ft) and 4.5 m (15 ft). For the 1984 *NEC*, this provision was changed to 3.0 m (10 ft) and 6 m (20 ft).

This receptacle outlet(s) is commonly used for ordinary devices such as radios, electric grills, bug zappers, etc., servicing the pool area. This receptacle's primary function is to limit the use of extension cords around and near the pool's water edge. If no convenience receptacle can be found and an extension cord is employed, untrained users of these extension cords typically would not stop at the 1.83 m (6 ft) barrier within the pool's edge. This requirement has been expanded to all permanently installed pools, not just permanently installed pools at dwelling units. A permanently installed pool location, be it at a dwelling unit, commercial, or public location, should not be the determining factor as to this issue of safety and a convenience receptacle required or not. At least one general purpose GFCI-protected receptacle outlet should be installed at all permanent pool locations.

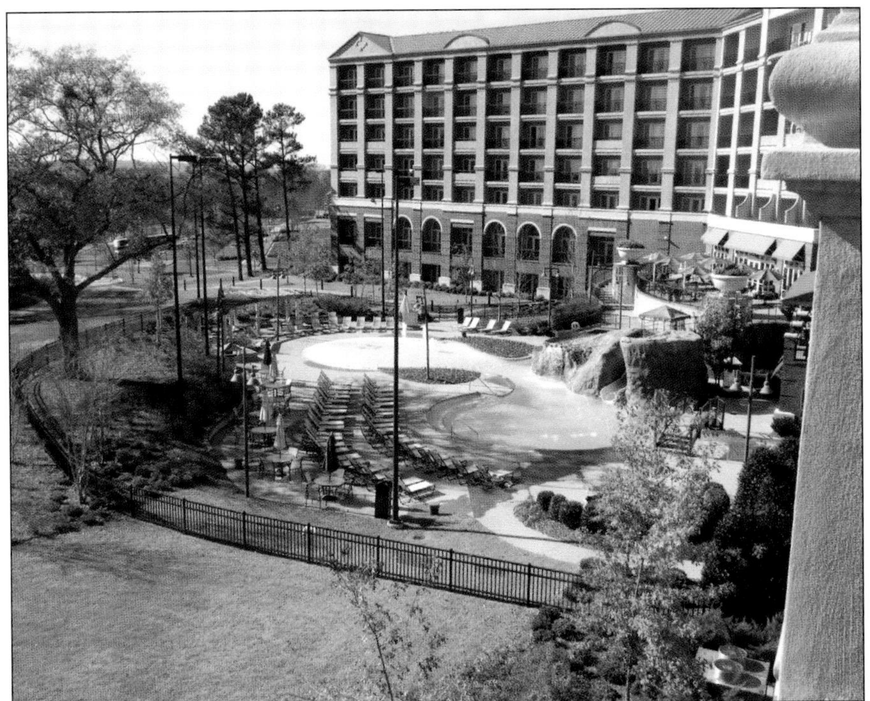

680.22(A)(2)

Change at a Glance

Receptacles that provide power for pool pump motors located between 3.0 m (10 ft) and 1.83 m (6 ft) from the pool no longer are required to "employ a locking configuration."

REVISION

Code Language

680.22 Lighting, Receptacles, and Equipment

(A) Receptacles.

~~**(1)**~~ **(2) Circulation and Sanitation System, Location.** Receptacles that provide power for water-pump motors or for other loads directly related to the circulation and sanitation system shall be located at least 3.0 m (10 ft) from the inside walls of the pool, or not less than 1.83 m (6 ft) from the inside walls of the pool if they meet all of the following conditions:

(1) Consist of single receptacles

~~(2) Employ a locking configuration~~

~~(3)~~ (2) Are of the grounding type

~~(4)~~ (3) Have GFCI protection

Proposal 17-101, 17-104, 17-105, 17-106

Comment 17-31

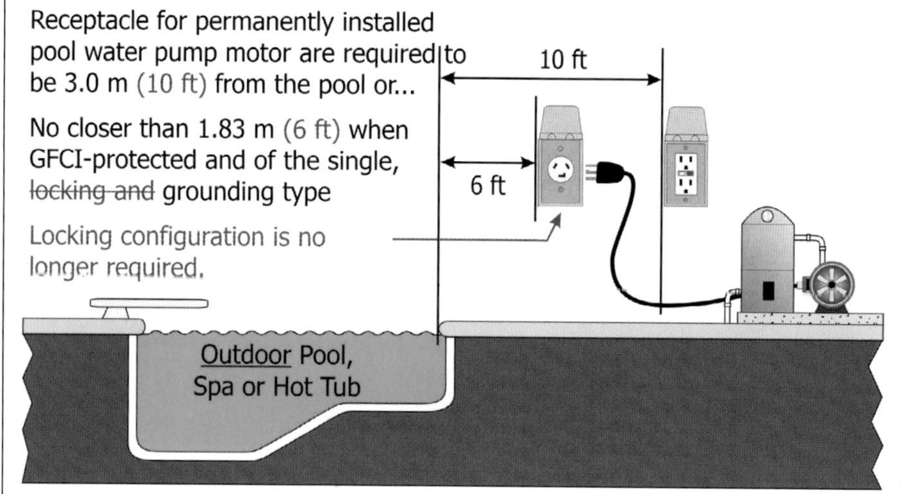
680.22(A)(2) Circulation and Sanitation Receptacle - Location
Receptacles that provide power for pool pump motors located between 3.0 m (10 ft) and 1.83 m (6 ft) from the pool no longer are required to "employ a locking configuration."
Receptacle for permanently installed pool water pump motor are required to be 3.0 m (10 ft) from the pool or...
10 ft
No closer than 1.83 m (6 ft) when GFCI-protected and of the single, ~~locking and~~ grounding type
6 ft
Locking configuration is no longer required.
Outdoor Pool, Spa or Hot Tub

2011 *NEC* Requirement

Receptacles that supply power for pool pump motors or other loads directly related to the circulation and sanitation system were addressed at 680.22(A)(1) in the 2011 *NEC*. This provision required the receptacle(s) to be located at least 3.0 m (10 ft) from the inside walls of the pool. Permission was granted at 680.22(A)(1) to allow the circulation and sanitation receptacle(s) to be located not less than 1.83 m (6 ft) from the inside walls of the pool, if the receptacle(s) complied with all of the following conditions: (1) consist of single receptacles, (2) employ a locking configuration, (3) are of the grounding type, and (4) be provided with GFCI protection.

2014 *NEC* Change

The requirements for receptacles that supply power for pool pump motors or other loads directly related to the circulation and sanitation system were moved to 680.22(A)(2). The same provisions in the 2011 *NEC* at 680.22(A)(1) were brought forward to 680.22(A)(2), with the exception of the requirement for "employ a locking configuration" being deleted.

Analysis of Change

Prior to the 2008 *NEC*, receptacles were not permitted to be located within 3.0 m (10 ft) from the inside wall of a permanently installed pool. This distance changed in the 2008 *NEC* to permit receptacles to be located not less than 1.83 m (6 ft) from the inside walls of the pool. Revisions occurred at several sections in the 2008 *NEC* to change the minimum or maximum distances mentioned from either 1.5 m (5 ft) or 3.0 m (10 ft) to a consistent 1.83 m (6 ft) distance. When the minimum distance was 3.0 m (10 ft) rather than 1.83 m (6 ft), this provision for the circulation and sanitation system receptacle(s) tied in well with the rest of Part II of Article 680. When the minimum distance for all receptacle(s) was reduced to 1.83 m (6 ft), this left this circulation and sanitation receptacle(s) pro-

Continued

vision, which was still required to be at least 3.0 m (10 ft) from the pool (if conditioned provisions were not employed) — rather confusing at best.

The requirements of 680.22(A)(2) [now 680.22(A)(3)] permits a 125-volt, 15- or 20-ampere convenience receptacle to be located not less than 1.83 m (6 ft) from the inside walls of the pool with no restriction of a locking configuration. If these convenience receptacles do not require a locking configuration, why would the circulation and sanitation receptacle need a locking configuration? Any 15- and 20-ampere, single-phase, 125-volt receptacles located within 6.0 m (20 ft) of the inside walls of a pool must be provided with ground-fault circuit interrupter (GFCI) protection.

680.22(B)(6)

Change at a Glance

Specific low-voltage luminaires are now permitted to be installed within 1.5 m (5 ft) of the inside walls of permanently installed pools.

Code Language

680.22 Lighting, Receptacles, and Equipment

(B) Luminaires, Lighting Outlets, and Ceiling-Suspended (Paddle) Fans.

(6) Low-Voltage Luminaires. Listed low-voltage luminaires not requiring grounding, not exceeding the low-voltage contact limit, and supplied by listed transformers or power supplies that comply with 680.23(A)(2) are permitted to be located less than 1.5 m (5 ft) from the inside walls of the pool.

Proposal 17-108

Comment 17-32, 17-33

680.22(B)(6) Low-Voltage Luminaires

Specific low-voltage luminaires are now permitted to be installed within 1.5 m (5 ft) of the inside walls of permanently installed pools.

2011 *NEC* Requirement

Requirements at 680.22(B)(1) through (B)(5) generally prohibited luminaires from being installed within 1.5 m (5 ft) horizontally of the inside of a pool. These provisions did not quantify the voltage type of these luminaires. No provisions existed at 680.22(B) for low-voltage luminaires in the 2011 *NEC*. Section 411.4(B) stated that "Lighting systems shall be installed not less than 3 m (10 ft) horizontally from the nearest edge of the water, unless permitted by Article 680."

2014 *NEC* Change

A new list item was added at 680.22(B)(6) to address low-voltage luminaires around permanently installed pools. Specific low-voltage luminaires will now be permitted to be located less than 1.5 m (5 ft) from the inside walls of the pool under certain conditions. These luminaires must be of the type that does not require connection to an equipment grounding conductor. These luminaires cannot exceed the voltage limitations defined in the definition of *low voltage contact limit* at 680.2. These luminaires must also be supplied by listed transformers or power supplies that comply with 680.23(A)(2) for transformers or power supplies listed for swimming pool and spa use.

Analysis of Change

A new definition for *low voltage contact limit* was introduced at 680.2 in the 2011 *NEC*. This definition pertains to low-voltage luminaires installed around swimming pools, fountains, and spas. Low-voltage lighting systems are referenced several times within Article 680 for requirements for low-voltage luminaires and this definition will assist users of the *Code* in determining the voltage limitations for these applications. Even though this new definition was added at 680.2, previous language at 680.22(B) did not allow low-voltage lighting to be installed in close proximity to swimming pools. The new provisions at 680.22(B)(6) will permit low-voltage installations that are already being installed around numerous swimming pools. Without this new language these low-voltage luminaires would not be *Code*-compliant.

Continued

In Article 411 for "Lighting Systems Operating at 30 Volts or Less," the provisions of 411.4(B) low-voltage lighting systems may be installed in close proximity to swimming pools if "permitted by Article 680." This new allowance at 680.22(B)(6) will give this needed Article 680 permission. Low-voltage landscape lighting power units complying with UL 1838, *Low Voltage Landscape Lighting Systems*. Some of these systems are also marked "For Use with Submersible Fixtures,"and are listed as swimming pool and spa transformers or power supplies as specified in 680.23(A)(2), and also comply with the low voltage contact limit of 680.2.

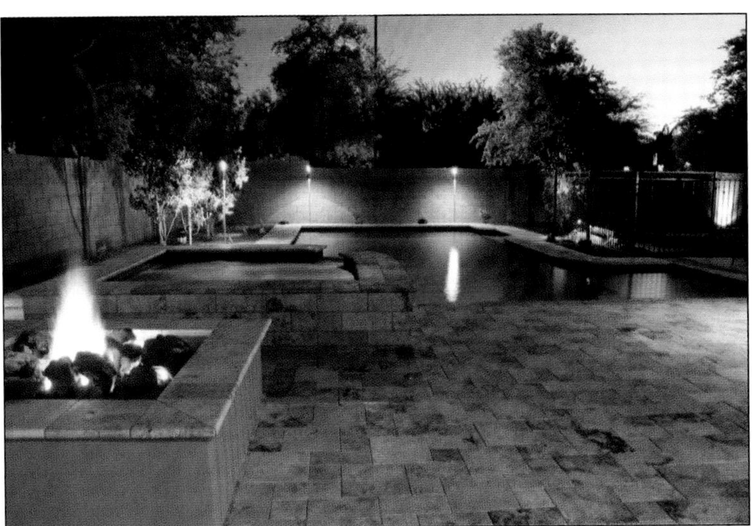

680.25(A)(1), EX

Change at a Glance

The exception allowing an "existing" feeder between an "existing" remote swimming pool panelboard and service equipment to be run in flexible metal conduit or an approved cable assembly has been revised to allow this exception for any feeder and remote swimming pool panelboard. Cable assembly is required to have an "insulated" EGC.

Code Language

680.25 Feeders

These provisions shall apply to any feeder on the supply side of panelboards supplying branch circuits for pool equipment covered in Part II of this article and on the load side of the service equipment or the source of a separately derived system.

(A) Wiring Methods.

(1) Feeders. Feeders shall be installed in rigid metal conduit or intermediate metal conduit. The following wiring methods shall be permitted if not subject to physical damage:

(1) Liquidtight flexible nonmetallic conduit

(2) Rigid polyvinyl chloride conduit

(3) Reinforced thermosetting resin conduit

(4) Electrical metallic tubing where installed on or within a building

680.25(A)(1) Exception: Wiring Methods (Feeders)

Exception for an "existing" feeder between an "existing" remote panelboard and service equipment was revised to include all feeders to remote panelboards *(not just existing feeders and existing remote panelboards).*

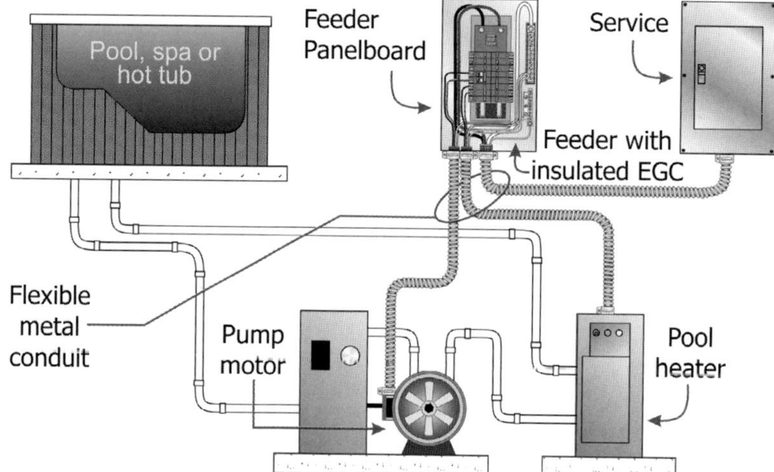

Feeder is permitted to run in flexible metal conduit or an approved cable assembly that includes an insulated equipment grounding conductor within its outer sheath.

2011 *NEC* Requirement

The wiring methods for feeders on the supply side of panelboards supplying branch circuits for pool equipment are required to be installed in rigid metal conduit or intermediate metal conduit. Where not subject to physical damage, six specific wiring methods with conditions are permitted for this feeder installation, including EMT and PVC. An exception to this feeder wiring method rule permitted an existing feeder between an existing remote panelboard and service equipment to be run in flexible metal conduit or an approved cable assembly that includes an equipment grounding conductor within its outer sheath.

2014 *NEC* Change

The requirements for wiring methods for swimming pool panelboard feeders did not change at the main text of 680.25()A(1), but the exception for an existing feeder between an existing remote panelboard and service equipment was deleted.

Analysis of Change

For the 2011 *NEC*, an exception to 680.25(A)(1) permitted an existing feeder between an existing remote panelboard and service equipment to be run in flexible metal conduit or an approved cable assembly that included an equipment grounding conductor (EGC) within its outer sheath. Installers and inspectors alike have struggled with the word "existing" in this exception. What does "existing" mean? At new construction, a new feeder is "existing" the next day after it has been installed. In order to determine the wiring method for a feeder to a swimming pool panelboard, what difference should it make if the feeder and the remote panelboard are "existing" or not?

The grounding and bonding requirements for pools and spas are in place for the safety of the users involved. The previous exception for "existing" feeders allowed the installation of the feeder without an insulated EGC and after some

680.25(A)(1), EX

Continued

(5) Electrical nonmetallic tubing where installed within a building
(6) Type MC cable where installed within a building and if not subject to corrosive environment

Exception: *~~An existing~~ A feeder between a ~~an existing~~ remote panelboard and service equipment shall be permitted to run in flexible metal conduit or an approved cable assembly that includes an insulated equipment grounding conductor within its outer sheath. The equipment grounding conductor shall comply with 250.24(A)(5).*

Proposal 17-119, 17-120

Comment 17-37, 17-38

arbitrary time period the installation becomes "existing." The pool equipment could then be installed without this important electrical safety requirement of an insulated EGC. This inconsistency has been removed for the 2014 *NEC* by requiring an insulated EGC to be installed with the permitted wiring methods identified at the exception for 680.25(A)(1). Under these revised provisions, nonmetallic-sheathed cable (Type NM cable) would not be an acceptable wiring method as Type NM cable typically does not employ an insulated EGC. This could now possibly require the use of wiring methods for this feeder that are typically foreign to the construction of a dwelling unit if this feeder passes through the interior of the dwelling.

680.26(C)

Change at a Glance

The requirement for "bonding" of pool water has been revised.

Code Language

680.26 Equipotential Bonding

(C) Pool Water. ~~An intentional bond of a minimum conductive surface area of 5800 mm² (9 in²) shall be installed in contact with the pool water. This bond shall be permitted to consist of parts that are required to be bonded in 680.26(B). Pool water shall have an electrical connection to one or more of the bonded parts described in 680.26(B).~~ Where none of the bonded parts is in direct connection with the pool water, the pool water shall be in direct contact with an approved corrosion-resistant conductive surface that exposes not less than 5800 mm² (9 in.²) of surface area to the pool water at all times. The conductive surface shall be located where it is not exposed to physical damage or dislodgement during usual pool activities, and it shall be bonded in accordance with 680.26(B).

Proposal 17-131, 17-130

680.26(C) Equipotential Bonding (Pool Water)

The requirement for "bonding" of pool water has been revised by removing the term "intentional bond" or "bond."

Where none of the required bonded parts *(ladders, metal forming shells, etc.)* is in direct connection with the pool water, the pool water shall be in direct contact with a conductive surface that exposes not less than 5800 mm² (9 in.²) of surface area to the pool water at all times.

2011 *NEC* Requirement

The 2011 *NEC* text called for an "intentional bond" to the pool water from some conductive surface with a minimum surface area of 5800 mm² (9 in.²) in contact with the pool water. This bond to the conductive surface from the pool water was permitted to consist of parts that are required to be bonded in 680.26(B), such as metal ladders, metal railings, metal underwater luminaire housings, etc.

2014 *NEC* Change

The same provisions that were found in the 2011 *NEC* are still in place, but are worded differently to avoid the terms *intentional bond* or *bond*.

Analysis of Change

The bonding of pool water was first described in the 2008 edition of the *NEC*. This provision was put in the *Code* to ensure a good undisputable connection (bonding) between the equipotential bonding grid described at 680.26(B) and the actual pool water. The original substantiation for this 2008 *NEC* requirement included information about testing performed by the National Electric Energy Testing Research and Application Center (NEETRAC), which identified that shock hazard potentials increase where the chemically treated pool water is not in contact with the equipotential bonding grid of the pool. This can occur where the pool water is isolated by an insulated pool shell and there are no conductive elements such as metal ladders, etc., in contact with the pool water. These reports indicate that potential shock hazards are increased for persons that can form a bridge between the isolated water and electrically conductive parts within the vicinity of the pool water.

Since the inception of this requirement, some users of the *Code* have had trouble visualizing the aspect of bonding with respect to a liquid such as the pool water. This subsection has been rewritten for the 2014 *NEC* to purposely avoid the terms *intentional bond* or *bond*. The most important aspect of this requirement

Continued

is to have the pool water in physical contact with "an approved corrosion-resistant conductive surface that exposes not less-than 5800 mm^2 (9 $in.^2$) of surface area to the pool water at all times." As with the previous language at 680.26(C), this can be accomplished with any of the bonded metal parts that are required to be bonded to the equipotential bonding grid of the pool such as metal ladders, conductive underwater luminaire housing shells, etc. A simple method to achieve this connection or bonding from the pool water to the equipotential bonding grid of the pool is through the installation of a short, bonded metal nipple in the drain piping system. This nipple can be comprised of stainless steel or brass (depending in part on the pool chemicals intended to be used). This metal nipple functions to make contact with every drop of water circulating to and from the pool itself and does not require any penetrations of the pool wall, but would not be generally listed for this purpose, but could be "an approved corrosion-resistant conductive surface that exposes not less-than 5800 mm^2 (9 $in.^2$) of surface area to the pool water at all times."

The inclusion of the term *intentional bond* has apparently caused some concerns with the uniform enforcement of this requirement. Because 680.26(C) said "intentional," some inspectors and contractors were not allowing the methods in 680.26(B) (metal ladders, etc.) to be used for the bonding of the pool water if the water bond was not completed first and intentional even though, to make this assumption, one would have to completely ignore the last sentence of the previous text at 680.26(C). The avoidance of the terms *intentional bond* or *bond* in the 2014 *NEC* should remove this misapplication of the *Code* for future users of the *Code*.

680.42(B)

Change at a Glance

Equipotential bonding of perimeter surfaces is not required for outdoor spas and hot tubs with (4) specific conditions that must be meet.

NEW

Code Language

680.42 Outdoor Installations

A spa or hot tub installed outdoors shall comply with the provisions of Parts I and II of this article, except as permitted in 680.42(A) and (B), that would otherwise apply to pools installed outdoors.

(B) Bonding. Bonding by metal-to-metal mounting on a common frame or base shall be permitted. The metal bands or hoops used to secure wooden staves shall not be required to be bonded as required in 680.26. Equipotential bonding of perimeter surfaces in accordance with 680.26(B)(2) shall not be required to be provided for spas and hot tubs where all of the following conditions apply:

(1) The spa or hot tub shall be listed as a self-contained spa for aboveground use.

(2) The spa or hot tub shall not be identified as suitable only for indoor use.

(3) The installation shall be in accordance with the manufacturer's instructions and shall be located on or above grade.

(4) The top rim of the spa or hot tub shall be at least 71 cm (28 in.) above all perimeter surfaces

680.42(B) Outdoor Spas and Hot Tubs (Bonding)

Equipotential bonding of perimeter surfaces is not required for outdoor spas and hot tubs with (4) specific conditions that must be meet:

(1) Listed as a self-contained spa for aboveground use

(2) Not be identified as suitable only for indoor use

(3) Installation per manufacturer's instructions and located on or above grade

(4) Top rim located at least 71 cm (28 in.) above all perimeter surfaces that are within 76 cm (30 in.) (horizontally) from the spa or hot tub

2011 *NEC* Requirement

A spa or hot tub installed outdoors is required to comply with the provisions of Parts I and II of Article 680. Section 680.42(A) and (B) gives some specific conditions that would supersede the provisions of Parts I and II of Article 680; but, otherwise, an outdoor spa or hot tub is to be treated like a permanently installed pool installed outdoors. Section 680.42(B) states that bonding by metal-to-metal mounting on a common frame or base is permitted, and the metal bands or hoops used to secure wooden staves are not required to be bonded as required in 680.26 for equipotential bonding.

There was no text at 680.42(B) in the 2011 *NEC* to supplant the provisions of 680.26 and equipotential bonding for outdoor spas or hot tubs, since outdoor spas or hot tubs were required to comply with the provisions of Parts I and II of Article 680. However, it should be noted that a Tentative Interim Amendment 70-11-1 (Log #1005) was issued by the Standards Council on March 1, 2011, for 680.42(B). This TIA introduced language that would exempt self-contained listed spas and hot tubs from the provisions of equipotential bonding in Part II of Article 680. A Tentative Interim Amendment (TIA) is tentative because it has not been processed through the entire *Code*-making procedures. It is interim because it is effective only between editions of the *Code*. A TIA automatically becomes a proposal of the proponent for the next edition of the *Code*; as such, it then is subject to all of the procedures of the code-making process.

2014 *NEC* Change

The concepts of TIA 70-11-1 were incorporated and added to 680.42(B) for the 2014 *NEC*. These new provisions eliminate equipotential bonding requirements for listed self-contained spas or hot tubs for aboveground use. In order for these listed self-contained spas or hot tubs to avoid 680.26 equipotential bonding requirements, four specific conditions must be satisfied *(see actual NEC text provided on this page for specific conditions)*.

Continued

that are within 76 cm (30 in.), measured horizontally from the spa or hot tub. The height of nonconductive external steps for entry to or exit from the self-contained spa shall not be used to reduce or increase this rim height measurement.

Informational Note: For information regarding listing requirements for self-contained spas and hot tubs, see ANSI/UL 1563 - 2010, *Standard for Electric Spas, Equipment Assemblies, and Associated Equipment.*

Proposal 17-142, 17-141, 17-144

Comment 17-46

Analysis of Change

New language was added at 680.42(B) that will eliminate equipotential bonding requirements for listed self-contained spas or hot tubs for aboveground use under specific conditions. This new text was the result of a Tentative Interim Amendment [TIA 70-11-1 (Log # 1005)] that was issued by the Standards Council on March 1, 2011, for 680.42(B). Outdoor listed self-contained spas and hot tubs are essentially manufactured appliance units tested and listed under UL 1563, *Electric Spas, Equipment Assemblies, and Associated Equipment*, and designed and intended to be installed on or above grade. These listed self-contained units have very different concerns of safety and enforcement than that of custom in-ground spas and built-in permanently installed swimming pools. This difference has been recognized by CMP-17 for indoor spas and hot tubs and for storable pools, both of which are excluded from perimeter bonding requirements of 680.26. It was argued by some users of the *Code* that the application of 680.26 equipotential bonding requirements in the previous *NEC* text created undue expense and extreme difficulty for homeowners who wish to simply set up a portable spa in their backyard, while adding no additional documented safety benefit. This had the potential to result in increased numbers of unpermitted self-installations of these listed self-contained spas and hot tubs, significantly increasing safety risks and nullifying the very intent of this *Code* provision.

680.57(B)

Change at a Glance

GFCI protection is required for *either* the branch circuit *or* feeder supplying electric signs installed within a fountain, but not both.

Code Language

680.57 Signs

(A) General. This section covers electric signs installed within a fountain or within 3.0 m (10 ft) of the fountain edge.

(B) Ground-Fault Circuit-interrupter Protection for Personnel. ~~All~~ Branch circuits or feeders supplying the sign shall have ground-fault circuit-interrupter protection for personnel.

Proposal 17-147

Comment 17-48

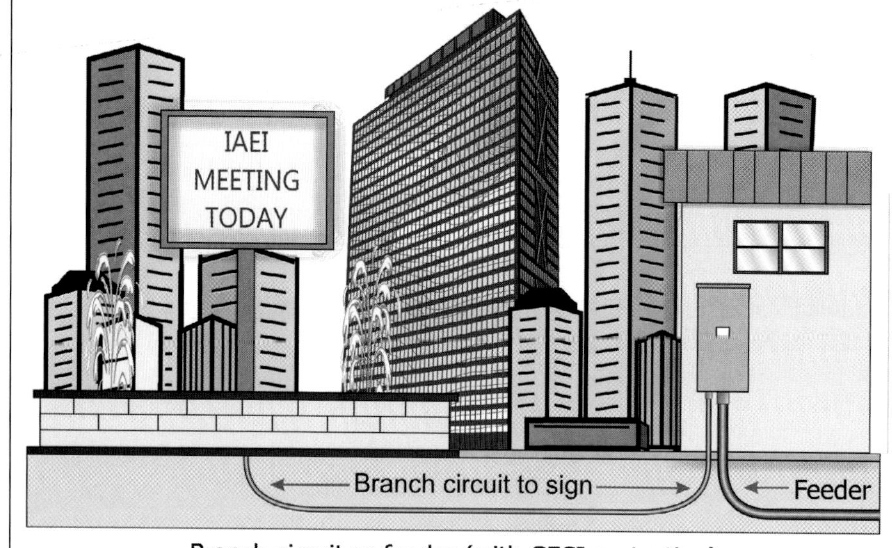

Branch circuit or feeder (with GFCI protection)

2011 *NEC* Requirement

All circuits supplying electric signs within a fountain or within 3.0 m (10 ft) of the fountain's edge were required to provide ground-fault circuit-interrupter (GFCI) protection for personnel.

2014 *NEC* Change

This subsection was revised to clarify that the required GFCI protection for fountain signs had to be provided in either the branch circuit or feeder supplying the sign, but not both.

Analysis of Change

Signs installed in or within close proximity to fountains are becoming more commonplace. When this situation occurs, the supply circuits to these signs must provide GFCI protection for personnel. The provisions for signs in fountains were first addressed in the 1999 *NEC*. This is the genesis of the "all" circuits supplying electric signs within a fountain requiring GFCI protection addressed at 680.57. Prior to this 1999 *NEC* text, the *Code* called for GFCI protection to be installed in the branch circuit supplying fountain equipment. A revision to the text at 680.57(B) now requires GFCI protection in either the branch circuit or the feeder supplying the sign, but not both.

In a scenario where a sign in a fountain is supplied from a branch circuit from a remote panelboard with that remote panelboard being supplied from a feeder, the literal reading of the previous text at 680.57(B) would have required GFCI protection in *both* the branch circuit *and* the feeder supplying this sign. It would be redundant at best to provide GFCI protection at both the branch circuit and the feeder supplying the branch circuit panelboard. The provisions at 215.9 are one location where GFCI protection is not necessary on both the feeder and the branch circuits if the feeder has been provided with GFCI protection. In requiring

Continued

GFCI protection on "all" circuits supplying these signs, this would literally require GFCI protection on communication circuits or Class 2 control circuits that simply transfer data to and from the sign. This revision will make it clear that GFCI protection for these fountain signs was intended for power circuits only and the required GFCI protection was not intended for the feeder *and* the branch circuit simultaneously.

690.2 Definitions

Change at a Glance

Two new definitions were added to Article 690: *DC to DC Converter* and *Direct Current (dc) Combiner.*

Code Language

690.2 Definitions

DC to DC Converter. A device installed in the PV source circuit or PV output circuit that can provide an output dc voltage and current at a higher or lower value than the input dc voltage and current.

Direct Current (dc) Combiner. A device used in the PV source and PV output circuits to combine two or more dc circuit inputs and provide one dc circuit output.

Proposal 4-172, 4-173

Comment 4-81, 4-83

690.2 Definitions

Two new definitions were added to Article 690: "DC to DC Converter" and "Direct Current (dc) Combiner."

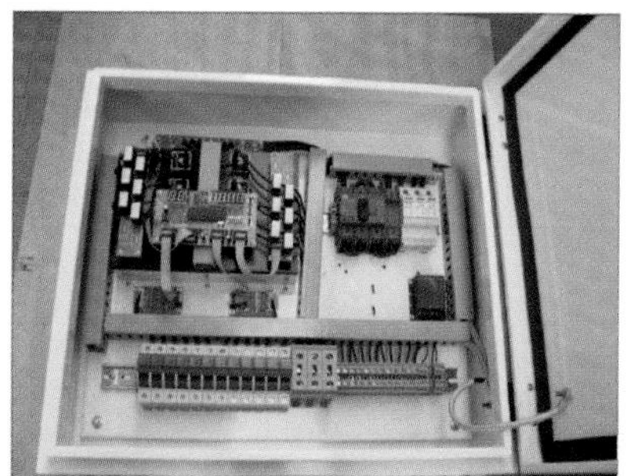

Direct Current (dc) Combiner

DC to DC Converters

DC to DC Converters: A device installed in the PV source circuit or PV output circuit that can provide an output dc voltage and current at a higher or lower value than the input dc voltage and current.

Direct Current (dc) Combiner: A device used in the PV source and PV output circuits to combine two or more dc circuit inputs and provide one dc circuit output.

2011 *NEC* Requirement

These two terms were used in the 2011 *NEC*, but they were not defined in the 2011 *NEC*.

2014 *NEC* Change

Two new definitions were added to define two terms being used in quite a few locations in Article 690. *DC to DC converter* is a device that can be installed in either the PV source circuit or PV output circuit that can provide an output dc voltage and current at a higher or lower value than the input dc voltage and current. A *direct current (dc) combiner* is a device used in the PV source and PV output circuits to combine two or more dc circuit inputs, providing one dc circuit output.

Analysis of Change

Prior to this new definition, there was no definition in Article 690 for dc to dc converters. These devices are becoming more common and have specific unique requirements. Since the output parameters of these devices can be different from the input parameters, users of the *Code* need to be aware that the rating of equipment on the output side may need to be different from that on the input. This definition will also make it clear that the PV source or output circuit ends at the input to the device by defining it as dc utilization equipment. This will prevent the application of 690.7(A), Maximum PV System Voltage, requirements to the output of these devices.

Once again, the term, *dc combiner* is used in more than a couple of locations in Article 690 with no definition, until now. In the PV industry, dc combiners are referred to under several different monikers: source circuit combiners, recombiners, and subcombiners just to name a few. Since the requirements should be the same regardless of where in the circuit the combiner is located, there needs to be a defined term that covers all dc combiners.

690.5(A)

Change at a Glance

Requirements for ground-fault protection devices or systems for PV systems were revised into a list format. This ground-fault protection device or system must also be listed for providing PV ground-fault protection.

Code Language

690.5 Ground-Fault Protection

Grounded dc PV arrays shall be provided with dc ground-fault protection meeting the requirements of 690.5(A) through (C) to reduce fire hazards. Ungrounded dc PV arrays shall comply with 690.35.

Exception ~~No 1~~: Ground-mounted or pole-mounted PV arrays with not more than two paralleled source circuits and with all dc source and dc output circuits isolated from buildings shall be permitted without ground-fault protection.

~~***Exception No. 2:*** *Photovoltaic arrays installed at other than dwelling units shall be permitted without ground-fault protection if each equipment grounding conductor is sized in accordance with 690.45.*~~

(A) Ground-Fault Detection and Interruption. The ground-fault protection device or system shall: **(1)** Be capable of detecting a

690.5(A) Ground-Fault Detection and Interruption

Requirements for ground-fault protection devices or systems for PV systems were revised into a list format.

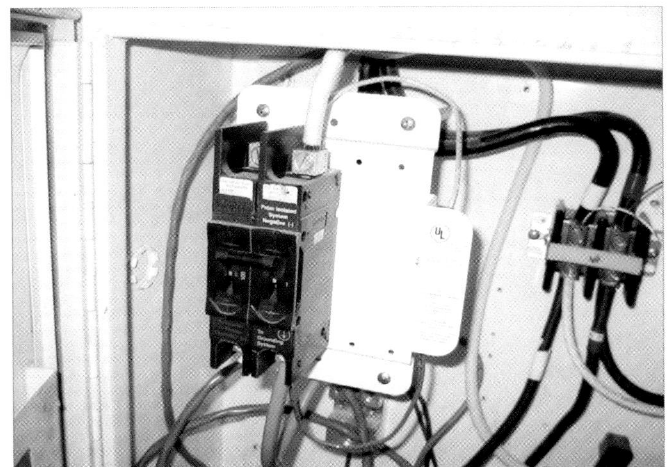

Ground-fault protection devices or systems must be "listed" for providing PV ground-fault protection.

2011 *NEC* Requirement

Grounded dc photovoltaic arrays are required to be provided with dc ground-fault protection (GFP) for the reduction of fire hazards. Ungrounded dc photovoltaic arrays are required to comply with 690.35, which are the provisions for ungrounded PV power systems. There were two exceptions to this GFP rule. The first exception dealt with ground-mounted or pole-mounted PV arrays having not more than two paralleled source circuits and with all dc source and dc output circuits isolated from buildings. The second exception: PV arrays installed at other than dwelling units with equipment grounding conductor is sized in accordance with 690.45.

The GFP device or system had to be capable of detecting a ground-fault current, interrupting the flow of fault current, and providing an indication of the fault. Automatically opening the grounded conductor of the faulted circuit to interrupt the ground-fault current path shall be permitted if all conductors of the faulted circuit automatically and simultaneously open as well. Manual operation of the main PV dc disconnect cannot activate the GFP device or result in grounded conductors becoming ungrounded.

2014 *NEC* Change

The provisions for dc ground-fault protection (GFP) for grounded dc photovoltaic arrays were brought forward with some revisions. The second exception for other than dwelling units was deleted. The conditions for the GFP device or system were formatted into a list format. A fourth condition was added requiring the GFP device or system to be "listed" for providing PV ground-fault protection. A change allowing the automatic opening of the grounded conductor "for measurement purposes" or to interrupt the ground-fault current path allows for interruption of the grounded conductor to make the isolation measurement.

690.5(A)

Continued

ground-fault in the PV array dc current carrying conductors and components, including any intentionally grounded conductors,

(2) Interrupt the flow of fault current,

(3) Provide an indication of the fault, and

(4) Be listed for providing PV ground-fault protection.

Automatically opening the grounded conductor ~~of the faulted circuit~~ for measurement purposes or to interrupt the ground-fault current path shall be permitted. If a grounded conductor is opened to interrupt the ground-fault current path, all conductors of the faulted circuit shall be automatically and simultaneously opened.

Manual operation of the main PV dc disconnect shall not activate the ground-fault protection device or result in grounded conductors becoming ungrounded.

Proposal 4-212, 4-214

Comment 4-85, 4-86, 4-87

Analysis of Change

Several revisions were implemented by CMP-4 at 690.5 and 690.5(A) for the 2014 *NEC*. These revisions are intended to revise the ground-fault protection (GFP) requirements and add an additional array isolation measurement prior to export of current. Recent information on existing ground-fault protection techniques has indicated that additional protection is necessary to provide protection against high impedance and multiple ground faults on PV systems. Ground faults that occur in the grounded conductors of traditional grounded PV arrays can pose detection challenges for existing GFI equipment.

The first of these revisions resulted in Exception No. 2 to 690.5 being deleted. This exception permitted the deletion of ground-fault protection (GFP) for grounded dc photovoltaic arrays if each equipment grounding conductor were sized to have an ampacity of at least two times the temperature and conduit fill corrected circuit conductor ampacity. This exception was deleted in part due to the fact that research on actual fires due to ground faults indicates that oversizing the equipment-grounding conductors would not reduce the potential fire hazard. The same basic revision also occurred at 690.45 where this previous equipment grounding conductor oversizing rule was found.

The conditions that PV system GFP devices or systems had to meet are found at 690.5(A). These conditions were revised into an easier-to-read list format. The first condition previously stated that the PV GFP devices or systems "shall be capable of detecting a ground-fault current." This condition was revised to require the GFP devices or systems to be capable of detecting a ground-fault "in the PV array dc current-carrying conductors and components, including any intentionally grounded conductors."

The previous text detection methods were not always the most effective GFP solutions for all PV system designs. Some inspectors view the 2011 *NEC* 690.5(A) text as not allowing for insulation resistance measurements on grounded conductors in solidly grounded systems because it would require disconnecting these conductors from ground during the measurement. Insulation resistance measurements can be a very effective GFP method in some system designs and will help improve detection of grounded conductor ground faults. This reasoning also invoked the change in test at the "automatically opening the grounded conductor" text below these conditions as well.

And lastly, a new condition was added to 690.5(A) requiring the GFP device or system to be listed for providing PV ground-fault protection. This requirement will insure that a GFP device or system used in this application has been identified by a third-party testing agency as capable of delivering the important ground-fault protection for grounded dc photovoltaic arrays.

690.7(F)

Change at a Glance

A new subsection was added for "Disconnects and Overcurrent Protection" at 690.7, Maximum Voltage, dealing with batteries and other energy storage devices.

Code Language

690.7 Maximum Voltage

(F) Disconnects and Overcurrent Protection. Where energy storage device output conductor length exceeds 1.5 m (5 ft), or where the circuits pass through a wall or partition the installation shall comply with (1) through (5):

(1) A disconnecting means and overcurrent protection shall be provided at the energy storage device end of the circuit. Fused disconnecting means or circuit breakers are acceptable.

(2) Where fused disconnecting means are used, the "Line" terminals of the disconnecting means shall be connected toward the energy storage device terminals.

(3) Overcurrent devices or disconnecting means shall not be installed in energy storage device enclosures where explosive atmospheres can exist.

(4) A second disconnecting means located at the connected equipment shall be installed where the disconnecting means

690.7(F) Disconnects and Overcurrent Protection

New subsection was added for "Disconnects and Overcurrent Protection" at the section for "Maximum Voltage" dealing with batteries and other energy storage devices.

Where energy storage device output conductor length exceeds 1.5 m (5 ft), or where the circuits pass through a wall or partition, the installation is now required to comply with five specific provisions.

2011 *NEC* Requirement

Storage batteries are addressed at Part VIII of Article 690. No provisions for disconnects and overcurrent protection existed in the 2011 *NEC* for other types of storage devices.

2014 *NEC* Change

Where energy storage device output conductor length exceeds 1.5 m (5 ft), or where the circuits pass through a wall or partition, the installation is now required to comply with five specific provisions added to the 2014 *NEC*. See *Code* language provided for specific conditions.

Analysis of Change

New provisions were added to 690.7 to provide requirements for disconnects and overcurrent protection for batteries and other energy storage devices frequently used in the PV industry. Batteries and other energy storage devices represent significant sources of current (10,000 amps or more). Circuits connected to these sources must be protected with overcurrent protection. These circuits are bidirectional and confusion exists as to where the disconnect(s) and overcurrent protection are required since there are two supply sources. Operating voltages for residential systems can operate above 300 volts dc. A switched disconnecting means is required to allow rapid disconnection of the batteries from the circuit under connected equipment failure and during maintenance. It can be difficult to install this disconnecting equipment when the cable lengths are short, such as under 1.5 m (5 ft).

Where energy storage device output conductor length exceeds 1.5 m (5 ft), or where the circuits pass through a wall or partition, the installation is now required to comply with five specific provisions. The maximum distance that the product standard and Underwriters Laboratories (UL) generally allows for unprotected cable lengths when testing PV power centers is 1.5 m (5 ft). Any

690.7(F)

Continued

required by (1) is not within sight of the connected equipment.

(5) Where the energy storage device disconnecting means is not within sight of the PV system ac and dc disconnecting means, placards or directories shall be installed at the locations of all disconnecting means indicating the location of all disconnecting means.

Proposal 4-325

Comment 4-91

penetration of a wall or partition necessitates the installation of a disconnecting means and overcurrent protection at the energy storage device of the circuit to protect the circuit as it passes through the wall and to allow the energy storage device, such as a battery, to be disconnected at the source. Overcurrent protection is generally required at the battery or energy storage device end of the circuit since this is the source of the highest continuous currents and the source of the highest fault currents in the circuit. Where the disconnecting means at the energy storage device is not within sight of the connected equipment (such as where a wall is involved), disconnects are now required at each end of the circuit.

690.9

Change at a Glance

"Overcurrent Protection" requirements were revised for clarity by grouping similar overcurrent protection requirements for PV systems together in order to make Article 690 easier to use.

Code Language

690.9 Overcurrent Protection

(A) Circuits and Equipment.

(B) ~~Power Transformers~~ Overcurrent Device Ratings.

(C) ~~Photovoltaic Source Circuits~~ Direct-Current Rating.

(D) ~~Direct-Current Rating~~ Photovoltaic Source and Output Circuits.

(E) Series Overcurrent Protection.

(F) Power Transformers.

(See NEC for complete text)

Proposal 4-232a, 4-233 thru 4-237, 4-239, 4-241, 4-242

Comment 4-93 thru 4-96

690.9 Overcurrent Protection (PV Systems)

"Overcurrent Protection" requirements for PV systems were revised for clarity by grouping similar overcurrent protection requirements together.

Circuits Required to be Protected. PV source circuits, PV output circuits, inverter output circuits, and battery circuit conductors	690.9(A), Article 240
Circuits Connected to Current-Limited Supplies. Circuits (ac or dc) connected to current-limited supplies (e.g., PV modules, ac output of utility-interactive inverters), or connected to sources having significantly higher current availability (e.g., parallel strings of modules, utility power), shall be protected at the source from overcurrent	690.9(A)
Rating. OCPDs are required to be rated for not less than 125% of the maximum currents calculated or determined in 690.8(A)	690.9(B), 240.4
DC Rating. OCPDs in DC circuits are required to be listed for such use and have the appropriate voltage, current, and interrupt ratings	690.9(C)
PV Source and Output Circuits. Listed PV overcurrent devices required for overcurrent protection in PV source and output circuits	690.9(D)
Series Overcurrent Protection-Grounded PV source circuits. A single OCPD (where required) permitted to protect the PV modules and the interconnecting conductors. **Ungrounded.** OCPD (where required) shall be installed in each ungrounded circuit conductor and permitted to protect the PV modules and the interconnecting cables	690.9(E)
Transformers. Overcurrent protection required for transformers in accordance with 450.3	690.9(F), 450.3

2011 *NEC* Requirement

The requirements for overcurrent protection for PV source circuits were identified at 690.9. However, not all overcurrent protection requirements were addressed at this one 2011 *NEC* location.

2014 *NEC* Change

This section for "Overcurrent Protection" was revised for clarity. This was part of a series of revisions to group similar requirements for PV systems together in order to make Article 690 easier to use. Overcurrent device requirements from previous 690.8(B)(1) for "Overcurrent Device Ratings" were moved to 690.9(B) to group them with other overcurrent protection requirements.

Analysis of Change

This revision was part of a series of revisions and re-origination which sought to group similar requirements for PV systems together in order to make Article 690 more user friendly. Language was added to insure that listed equipment be used to provide this overcurrent protection. Overcurrent protection devices in PV source and output circuits are subject to wide operating current and temperature cycling, high ambient temperatures, low clearing currents and high open-circuit voltages. Product standards have been created specifically for PV dc system overcurrent protection (both fuses and circuit breakers). The added language in these revisions will make it clear to the inspector and installer that devices specifically designed for these systems are required.

New and revised language was added at 690.9(E) to distinguish between a grounded PV source circuit and an ungrounded PV source circuit. Ungrounded PV arrays are being installed in increasing numbers to permit the use of the newer non-transformer utility interactive inverters. These

690.9

Continued

ungrounded PV source circuits require overcurrent devices in each of the ungrounded conductors, whereas the grounded PV source circuit requires an overcurrent device in only the single ungrounded conductor. In some cases, overcurrent protection is not required in either grounded or ungrounded PV source circuits (see 690.9(A), Exception). The addition of the word "grounded" and the reference to 690.35 and the ungrounded PV source circuit clarifies these differing requirements.

690.10(E)

Change at a Glance

"Utility-interactive systems" were removed from the requirements of having to have back-fed circuit breakers secured in place by an additional fastener. "Multimode" inverter output in stand-alone systems was added to the requirement.

Code Language

690.10 Stand-Alone Systems

The premises wiring system shall be adequate to meet the requirements of this *Code* for a similar installation connected to a service. The wiring on the supply side of the building or structure disconnecting means shall comply with the requirements of this *Code*, except as modified by 690.10(A) through (E).

(E) Back-fed Circuit Breakers. Plug-in type back-fed circuit breakers connected to a stand-alone or multimode inverter output in ~~either~~ stand-alone ~~or utility-interactive~~ systems shall be secured in accordance with 408.36(D). Circuit breakers ~~that are~~ marked "line" and "load" shall not be back-fed.

Proposal 4-245, 4-246, 4–243

Comment 4-97, 4-98, 13–31

690.10(E) Back-Fed Circuit Breakers (PV Systems)

Plug-in type back-fed circuit breakers connected to stand-alone or multimode inverter output in stand-alone ~~or utility-interactive~~ systems shall be secured in place by an "additional fastener" that requires other than a pull to release the device from the mounting means on the panelboard *[408.36(D)]*.

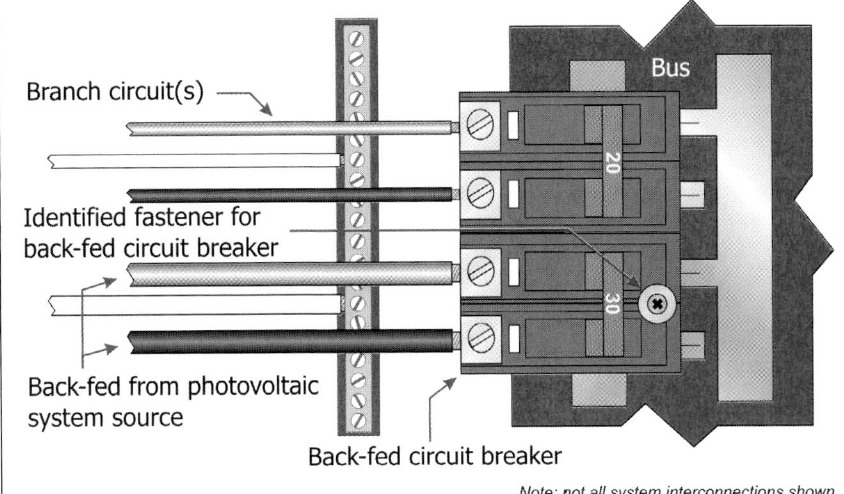

Note: not all system interconnections shown

2011 *NEC* Requirement

Plug-in type back-fed circuit breakers connected to a stand-alone inverter output in *either* stand-alone or utility-interactive systems were required to be secured in place by an additional fastener in accordance with 408.36(D). Circuit breakers that are marked "line" and "load" are not permitted to be back-fed.

2014 *NEC* Change

The requirement for a utility-interactive system to have its back-fed circuit breakers secured in place by an additional fastener was removed from 690.10(E). Multimode inverter output in stand-alone systems was added to the requirement.

Analysis of Change

The requirements for back-fed circuit breakers for stand-alone solar photovoltaic (PV) systems were added to the 2011 *NEC* at 690.10(E). These requirements were put in place to ensure that plug-in type back-fed circuit breakers used with PV systems are secured in place in a panelboard. Language at 690.64(B)(6) of the 2008 *NEC* specified that listed plug-in type circuit breakers back-fed from utility-interactive inverters were permitted to omit the additional fastener normally required by 408.36(D), Panelboard Back-Fed Devices. The added provisions at 690.10(E) of the 2011 *NEC* required plug-in type back-fed circuit breakers connected to a stand-alone inverter output to be secured in accordance with 408.36(D), which requires plug-in type overcurrent protection devices that are back-fed and used to terminate field-installed ungrounded supply conductors to be secured in place by an "additional fastener" that requires other than a pull to release the device from the mounting means on the panel. The inclusion of utility-interactive systems in this back-fed provision of 690.10(E), actually conflicted with the permissive rules in Article 705 for such applications. Section

Continued

705.12(D)(6) [now 705.12(D)(5)] permits listed plug-in-type circuit breakers that are back-fed from utility-interactive inverters to omit the additional fastener normally required by 408.36(D) for such applications. These listed plug-in-type circuit breakers must also be listed and identified as interactive and for a back-fed use. To make 690.10(E) compatible with 705.12(D)(5), utility-interactive systems were removed from 690.10(E) in the 2014 *NEC*.

Multimode inverter output in stand-alone systems was added to the back-fed requirement of 690.10(E). A new definition for *multimode inverter* was added to 690.2: "Equipment having the capabilities of both the utility-interactive inverter and the stand-alone inverter" (see Proposal 4-181). Multimode inverters have characteristics of both the utility-interactive inverter and the stand-alone, off-grid inverter with features that are unique to the multimodal inverter. These inverters will be listed to UL 1741, *Inverters, Converters, Controllers and Interconnection System Equipment for Use With Distributed Energy Resources*. These inverters will have two sets of ac input/output terminals and a connection for the battery bank. One characteristic of most multimode inverters is that they can pass power from the utility through to the protected load circuits at a greater power level than they can supply power to the utility in the utility interactive mode. Certified/listed multimode inverters ensure safety for the power line and utility personnel anytime the utility is shutdown or operates abnormally.

690.12

Change at a Glance

New provisions were added for rapid shutdown of PV systems on buildings.

NEW

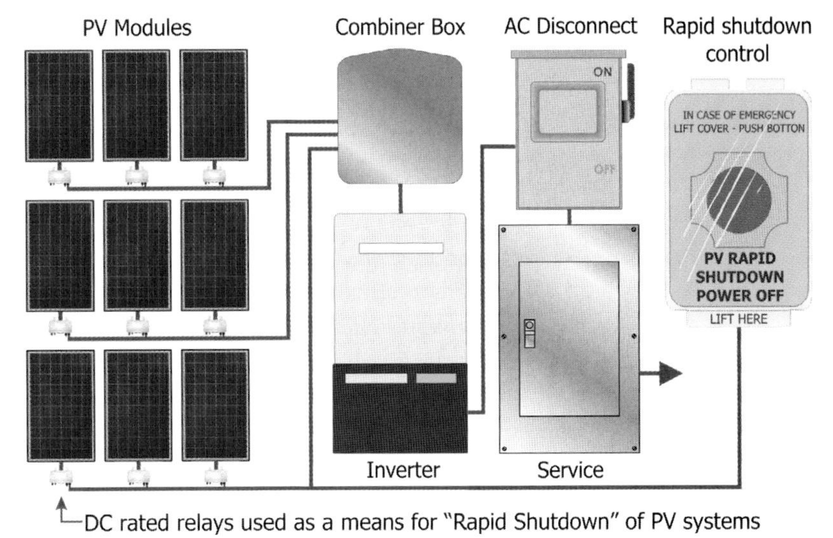
690.12 Rapid Shutdown of PV Systems on Buildings
PV source circuits to be de-energized from all sources within 10 seconds of when the utility supply is de-energized or when the PV power source disconnecting means is opened
PV Modules
Combiner Box
AC Disconnect
Rapid shutdown control
ON
OFF
IN CASE OF EMERGENCY LIFT COVER - PUSH BOTTON
PV RAPID SHUTDOWN POWER OFF
LIFT HERE
Inverter
Service
DC rated relays used as a means for "Rapid Shutdown" of PV systems

Code Language

690.12 Rapid Shutdown of PV Systems on Buildings
PV system circuits installed on or in buildings shall include a rapid shutdown function that controls specific conductors in accordance with 690.12(1) through (5) as follows.

(1) Requirements for controlled conductors shall apply only to PV system conductors of more than 1.5 m (5 ft) in length inside a building, or more than 3 m (10 ft) from a PV array.

(2) Controlled conductors shall be limited to not more than 30 volts and 240 VA within 10 seconds of rapid shutdown initiation.

(3) Voltage and power shall be measured between any two conductors and between any conductor and ground.

(4) The rapid shutdown initiation methods shall be labeled in accordance with 690.56(B).

(5) Equipment that performs the rapid shutdown shall be listed and identified.

2011 *NEC* Requirement

Disconnecting means provisions for PV systems are addressed in Part III of Article 690, but no provisions for a rapid shutdown of PV systems existed in the 2011 *NEC*.

2014 *NEC* Change

A new 690.12 entitled "Rapid Shutdown of PV Systems on Buildings" was added. This new section applies to PV systems installed on building roofs and would require that PV source circuits be de-energized from all sources within 10 seconds of when the utility supply is de-energized or when the PV power source disconnecting means is opened.

Analysis of Change

In an effort to increase the electrical and fire safety of PV systems on buildings, new "rapid shutdown" provisions have been incorporated into Article 690. This will incorporate a significant improvement in safety for rooftop PV systems based on the safety concerns of the first and second responders of the emergency and fire service communities during emergency operations on PV-equipped buildings and structures. Under the United States Department of Homeland Security (DHS) Assistance to Firefighter grant program, Underwriters Laboratories (UL) examined concerns of photovoltaic (PV) systems and potential impacts on firefighting operations. Key concerns included firefighter vulnerability to electrical and casualty hazards when attempting to extinguish a fire involving a PV system. This research project by UL provided evidence of the need for the ability to de-energize PV-generated power sources in the event of an emergency. The use of PV systems is increasing at a rapid pace. As a result of greater utilization, traditional firefighter tactics for suppression, ventilation, and overhaul have been complicated, leaving firefighters vulnerable to severe hazards.

Continued

Proposal 4-253, 4-167

Comment 4-113, 4-107, 4-108, 4-110

This new section will address the de-energizing of rooftop wiring, leaving only the module wiring and internal conductors of the module still energized. PV source circuit conductors include all wiring between modules or modular electronic devices up to the combining point. In order to meet these new requirements, an electronic means will be necessary to shut down the module at the source circuit level. This shutdown must coincide with a utility outage, or manual inverter shutdown. A PV module-level dc-dc converter, single-module micro-inverter, and ac module can all meet this requirement at the module end of the circuit. Simple remotely controlled electronic switches can also meet this requirement. A voltage limit of 30-volts and a power limit of 240 volt/amperes (watts) were established as a safe power limited environment. This is consistent with international standards including IEC 61730, *Photovoltaic (PV) Module Safety Qualification*, which establish safety procedures for PV modules. This also allows for 24-volt control circuits throughout the array that are currently used in products that employ contactors for shutting down combiner boxes. CMP-4 has taken a huge step to reduce hazards for first and second responders by accepting these new rapid shutdown provisions into 690.12 of the 2014 *NEC*.

These new rapid shutdown provisions were integrated into the 2014 *NEC* as a result of combined efforts from three different groups, all with concerns for safety of emergency responders at buildings or structures with PV systems involved. These groups included the CMP-4 Firefighter Safety Task Group, the Solar Energy Industries Association (SEIA) Codes and Standards Working Group, and the PV Industry Forum.

690.31

Change at a Glance

Section 690.31 was revised and reorganized for clarity and to bring PV wiring methods to one location.

Code Language

690.31 Methods Permitted. ***(Wiring Methods)***
(A) Wiring Systems.

(B) Identification and Grouping. ***[Was 690.4(B)]***

(C) Single-Conductor Cable. ***[Was 690.31(B)]***

(D) Multiconductor Cable. ***[New]***

(E) Flexible Cords and Cables. ***[Was 690.31(C)]***

Table 690.31(E) Correction Factors. ***[New]***

(F) Small-Conductor Cables. ***[Was 690.31(D)]***

(G) Direct-Current Photovoltaic Source and DC Output Circuits On or Inside a Building. ***[Was 690.31(E)]***

(H) Flexible, Fine-Stranded Cables. ***[Was 690.31(F)]***

(I) Bipolar Photovoltaic Systems. ***[Was 690.4(G)]***

(J) Module Connection Arrangement. ***[Was 690.4(C)]***

690.31 Methods Permitted (Wiring Methods)

690.31 was revised and re-organized for clarity and to bring PV wiring methods to one location.

(A) Wiring Systems
(B) Identification and Grouping
(C) Single-Conductor Cable
(D) Multiconductor Cable
(E) Flexible Cords and Cables
Table 690.31(E) Correction Factors
(F) Small-Conductor Cables
(G) Direct-Current Photovoltaic Source and DC Output Circuits On or Inside a Building
(H) Flexible, Fine-Stranded Cables
(I) Bipolar Photovoltaic Systems
(J) Module Connection Arrangement

2011 *NEC* Requirement

Wiring methods permitted for PV systems were located at 690.31. Other wiring method provisions were located at 690.4 for "Installation"; and other wiring method provisions were located at 690.14 for "Additional Provisions."

2014 *NEC* Change

Section 690.31 was revised and reorganized to incorporate various wiring method provisions from previous 690.4 and 690.14. The previous and revised portions of 690.14 were variously incorporated into 690.13, 690.31, and others.

Analysis of Change

Numerous and various proposals and comments were submitted to CMP-4 to add to, revise, and reorganize wiring method provisions for PV systems in Article 690. Proposal 4-284a was created by CMP-4 to incorporate these various proposals and to move all wiring method provisions to one location in Article 690 and in particular, 690.31.

Some of the changes that occurred with these revised requirements included adding "inverter output circuits" at 690.31(B) to the PV circuits that cannot be contained in the same raceway, cable tray, cable, outlet box, junction box, or similar fitting as other non-PV systems, unless the conductors of the different systems are separated by a partition. This revision was needed as multiple interpretations of this requirement were an issue with the previous text. Without this required separation, in the event that the insulation on a PV output circuit and an inverter output circuit became damaged and came in contact with each other, dc currents could be present on the inverter output circuit conductors even with the inverter shut down due to a lack of ac power.

690.31

Continued

Proposal 4-194, 4-284a, 4-285, 4-287, 4-301, 4-295, 4-296, 4-300

Comment 4-84, 4-114, 4-136, 4-232

New provisions were also added at 690.31(D) pertaining to multiconductor cables (Type TC-ER or USE-2) permitted in outdoor locations in PV inverter output circuits when used with utility-interactive inverters mounted in not-readily-accessible locations. Previous text at 690.31 had no specific cable designation for the ac wiring between microinverters. This multiconductor cable is typically installed in outdoor locations, attached to, or within, photovoltaic system racking.

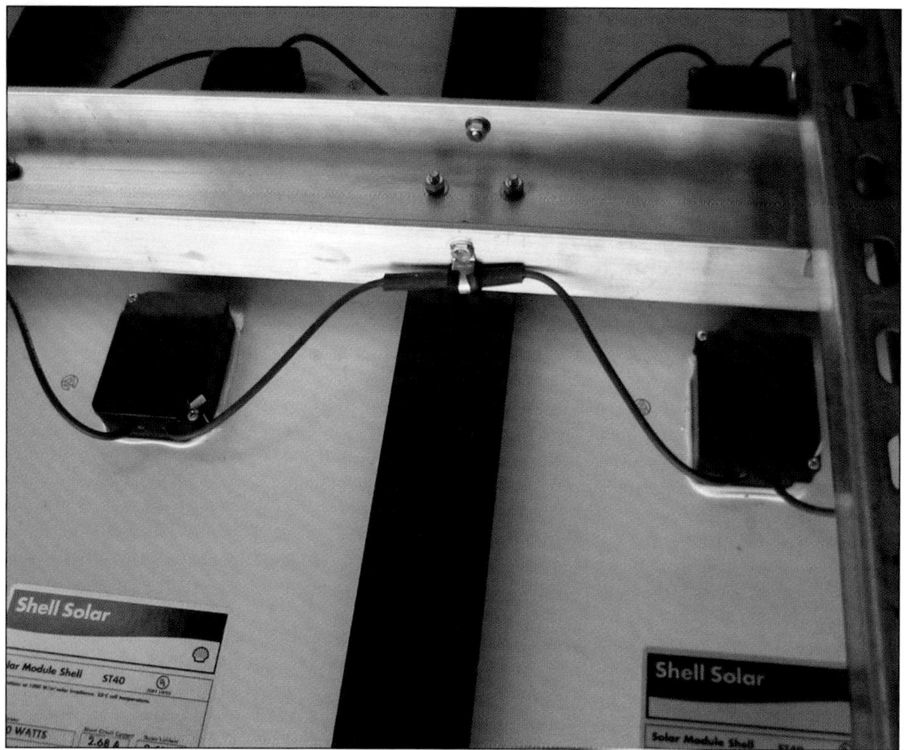

690.35(C)

Change at a Glance

Ground-fault protection for ungrounded PV systems is required to be listed.

Code Language

690.35 Ungrounded Photovoltaic Power Systems

Photovoltaic power systems shall be permitted to operate with ungrounded PV source and output circuits where the system complies with 690.35(A) through (G).

(C) Ground-Fault Protection. All photovoltaic source and output circuits shall be provided with a ground-fault protection device or system that complies with (1) through (4):

(1) Detects ~~a~~ ground fault(s) in the PV array dc current carrying conductors and components

(2) Indicates that a ground fault has occurred

(3) Automatically disconnects all conductors or causes the inverter or charge controller connected to the faulted circuit to automatically cease supplying power to output circuits

(4) Be listed for providing PV ground fault protection.

Proposal 4-302

Comment 4-139, 4-140, 4-141

690.35(C) GFP (Ungrounded PV Systems)

"Ground-Fault Protection" for ungrounded PV systems is required to be listed.

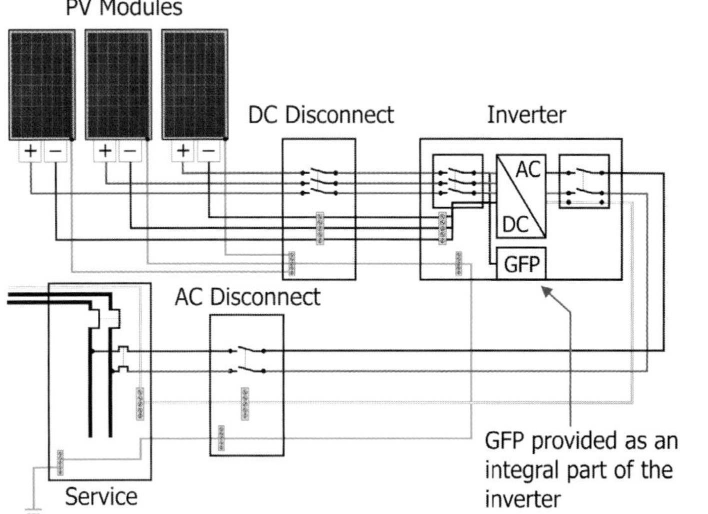

GFP device or system must possess the ability to detect ground fault(s) in the PV array dc current carrying conductors and components.

2011 *NEC* Requirement

Photovoltaic power systems are permitted to operate with ungrounded PV source and output circuits where the system complies with the specific conditions of 690.35(A) through (G). The requirements of 690.35(C) necessitates all PV source and output circuits be provided with a ground-fault protection (GFP) device or system that detects a ground fault, indicates that a ground fault has occurred, and automatically disconnects all conductors, or causes the inverter or charge controller connected to the faulted circuit to automatically cease supplying power to output circuits.

2014 *NEC* Change

The same GFP provisions for ungrounded PV power systems from the 2011 *NEC* were brought forward with one modification and a new provision for the GFP device or system to be listed for providing PV ground-fault protection. Clarification was given at 690.35(C)(1) to specify that the GFP device or system must possess the ability to detect ground fault(s) in the PV array dc current-carrying conductors and components.

Analysis of Change

Existing ground-fault protection (GFP) techniques have indicated that additional protection is necessary against high ground faults that can readily occur on PV systems. Inadequate GFP protection has resulted in several fires in PV systems over the last few years. GFP device or system is now required to detect ground fault(s) in the PV array dc current-carrying conductors and components. This adds an additional array isolation measurement prior to export of current.

New provisions were also added to require the GFP device or system to be listed for providing PV ground-fault protection. This will allow the authority having jurisdiction (AHJ) to rely upon the listing to verify the functionality of this extremely important protection system. This will also improve the enforceability of the GFP requirements for ungrounded PV systems.

690.41

Change at a Glance

System grounding requirements for PV systems have been revised into a list format for clarity.

Code Language

690.41 System Grounding

Photovoltaic systems shall comply with one of the following:

(1) Ungrounded systems shall comply with 690.35

(2) Grounded 2-wire systems ~~with voltage over 50 volts~~ shall have one conductor ~~solidly~~ grounded or be impedance grounded, and the system shall comply with 690.5

(3) Grounded bipolar systems shall have the reference (center tap) conductor ~~solidly~~ grounded or be impedance grounded, and the system shall comply with 690.5

(4) Other methods that accomplish equivalent system protection in accordance with 250.4(A) ~~that utilize~~ with equipment listed and identified for the use.

Exception: *Systems complying with 690.35.*

Proposal 4-307

Comment 4-144, 4-145, 4-147

690.41 System Grounding (PV Systems)

This section for "System Grounding" was revised into a list format for clarity.

Reference to "over 50" volts was deleted (applies to all PV systems at any voltage).

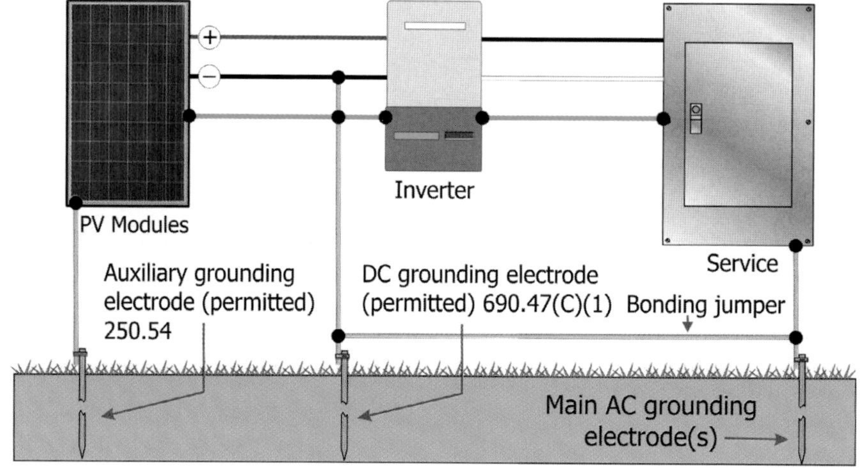

The term "solidly" grounded was removed for consistency.

An allowance for impedance grounding and the reference the 690.5 (GFP) was also added for clarity when grounded 2-wire and bipolar PV systems are installed.

2011 *NEC* Requirement

For a photovoltaic power source, one conductor of a 2-wire system with a PV system voltage over 50 volts and the reference (center tap) conductor of a bipolar system were required to be solidly grounded or to use other methods that accomplish equivalent system protection in accordance with 250.4(A). These provisions also called for utilizing equipment listed and identified for the use. An exception was present in the 2011 *NEC* which exempted PV systems complying with 690.35 (ungrounded PV systems with ground-fault protection).

2014 *NEC* Change

This section for "System Grounding" was revised into a list format for clarity. The reference to "over 50" volts was deleted since the list now includes all types of PV systems at any voltage. The term *solidly* grounded was removed for consistency. An allowance for impedance grounding and the reference to 690.5, Ground-Fault Protection, were also added for clarity when grounded 2-wire and bipolar PV systems are installed.

Analysis of Change

System grounding requirements for PV systems have been revised into a list format for clarity, and further revision also makes the intent of this section clearer. The original proposal for these revisions (which was accepted at the Proposal stage) was seeking to limit the use of solidly grounded systems to only those below 300 volts to be consistent with 250.162, which generally calls for all dc circuits and systems to be grounded. This requirement was removed at the Comment stage, as restricting PV systems operating over 300 volts to have only ungrounded PV arrays does not improve safety and imposes severe constraints on the design and development of future PV systems where other renewable resources will be interacting with PV systems. Grounded electrical systems at 600 volts and higher have been successfully and safely operated for several years.

690.41

Continued

The previous reference to "over 50" volts was deleted to remove this restriction as the new list format at 690.41 now includes all types of PV systems at any voltage. The term *solidly* grounded was also deleted in an effort to make this *Code* language consistent with the PV inverters and other equipment product standards where an overcurrent device is allowed to make the dc bonding jumper as a part of the required ground-fault protective device. Additional text was added to allow impedance grounding; and references to 690.5 (ungrounded PV systems with ground-fault protection) were also added for clarity when grounded 2-wire and bipolar PV systems are installed.

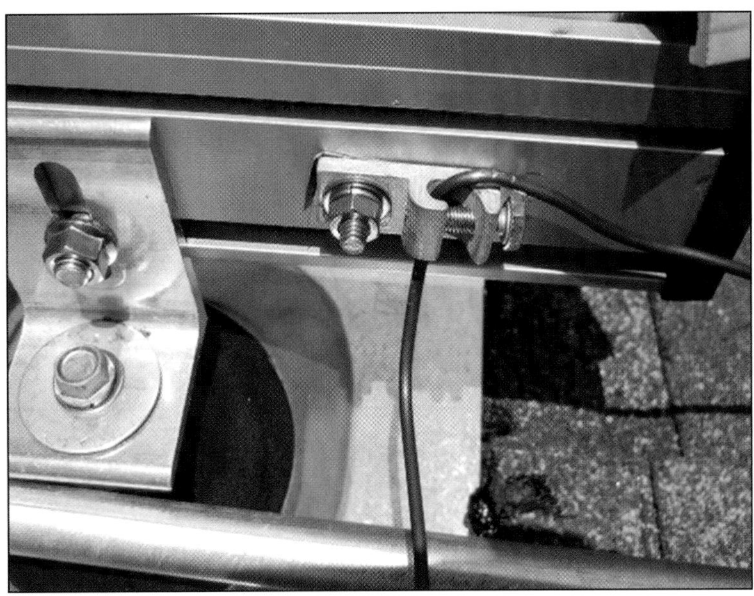

690.47(D)

Change at a Glance

An auxiliary grounding electrode system is required to be installed in accordance with 250.52 and 250.54 at all ground- and pole-mounted PV arrays and as close as practicable to roof-mounted PV arrays.

NEW

Code Language

690.47 Grounding Electrode System

(D) Additional Auxiliary Electrodes for Array Grounding. A grounding electrode shall be installed in accordance with 250.52 and 250.54 at the location of all ground- and pole-mounted photovoltaic arrays and as close as practicable to the location of roof-mounted photovoltaic arrays. The electrodes shall be connected directly to the array frame(s) or structure. The dc grounding electrode conductor shall be sized according to 250.166. Additional electrodes are not permitted to be used as a substitute for equipment bonding or equipment grounding conductor requirements. The structure of a ground- or pole-mounted photovoltaic array shall be permitted to be considered a grounding electrode if it meets the requirements of 250.52. Roof mounted photovoltaic arrays shall be permitted to use the metal frame of a building or structure if the requirements of 250.52(A)(2) are met.

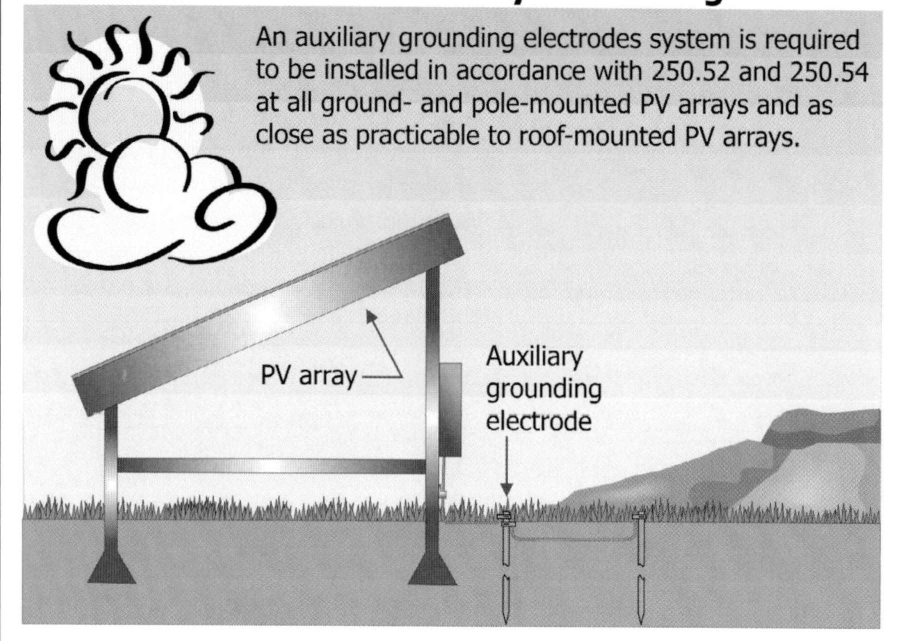
690.47(D) Additional Auxiliary Electrodes for Array Grounding
An auxiliary grounding electrodes system is required to be installed in accordance with 250.52 and 250.54 at all ground- and pole-mounted PV arrays and as close as practicable to roof-mounted PV arrays.
PV array
Auxiliary grounding electrode

2011 *NEC* Requirement

This language at 690.47(D) was inadvertently removed from the 2011 *NEC* as it appeared in the 2008 *NEC*.

2014 *NEC* Change

New provisions were added at 690.47(D) for "Additional Auxiliary Electrodes for Array Grounding." This *Code* language appeared in some form from the 1996 to the 2008 *NEC*. Requirements for auxiliary grounding electrodes and 250.54 were added to the 2014 *NEC* that did not appear in the previous 2008 *NEC*. This subsection revived from the 2008 *NEC* requires a grounding electrode system to be installed at the location of all ground- and pole-mounted PV arrays and as close as practicable to the location of roof-mounted PV arrays. This grounding electrode system must meet the requirements of 250.52 for grounding electrodes and 250.54 for auxiliary grounding electrodes. These grounding electrodes are required to be connected directly to the array frame(s) or structure. See 690.47(D) *Code* text for additional requirements and two exceptions.

Analysis of Change

A grounding electrode system has been required to be established for PV systems and PV arrays since the 1996 *NEC*. This PV grounding electrode system was required in some form or fashion until the 2008 *NEC*. During the 2011 *NEC* code-making process, a proposal was submitted to delete this provision (see 2011 NEC Proposal 4-238). This proposal was rejected by CMP-4 and never received affirmative voting from CMP-4 to remove this requirement. Several revisions and changes occurred in Article 690 and, in particular, 690.47 during the 2011 *NEC*. During the rewrite of 690.47 for the 2011 *NEC*, 690.47(D) for "Additional Electrodes for Array Grounding" was inadvertently removed and did not appear in the 2011 *NEC*. This subsection has been revised for the 2014 *NEC* and is needed to make it clear that ground- and pole-mounted PV arrays require a grounding electrode system.

690.47(D)

Continued

Exception No. 1: *Array grounding electrode(s) shall not be required where the load served by the array is integral with the array.*
Exception No. 2: *Additional array grounding electrode(s) shall not be required if located within 1.8 m (6 ft) of the premises wiring electrode.*

Note to Reader: Gray shaded text at this *Code* language is compared to 2008 *NEC* text at 690.47(D).

Proposal 4-314, 4-315

Comment 4-155, 4-156, 4-157

The large quantity of conductive material that is added to a roof when a PV system is installed increases the likelihood of a lightning strike. This PV grounding electrode system would help to minimize the effects of such a lightning strike. The purpose of this PV grounding electrode is two-fold. The primary purpose is to maintain the frames of the PV array to as close to local earth voltage potential as possible. This is preferable to relying on a potentially long equipment grounding conductor back to a grounding electrode, perhaps on another structure. This situation presents a potential shock hazard and necessitates these PV arrays be grounded to a local grounding electrode. The secondary purpose of this PV grounding electrode is to provide a simple and direct path to earth for any static charge that may build up in storm or lightning activities.

The word "Auxiliary" was added to the title and referenced in the text, along with a reference to 250.54, to indicate that this PV grounding electrode system is not required to be tied into the premises grounding electrode system. This tie-in with auxiliary grounding electrodes will also make it clear that if multiple PV auxiliary grounding electrodes are installed, they do not need to be bonded together by a dedicated bonding jumper. These grounding electrode(s) will be permitted to be connected to the equipment grounding conductors of the branch circuit(s) or feeder(s) to these PV arrays.

690.81

Change at a Glance

New 690.81 was added for listing requirements for PV wire used with systems over 600 volts but not exceeding 2000 volts.

Code Language

690.81 Listing

Products listed for photovoltaic systems shall be permitted to be used and installed in accordance with their listing. Photovoltaic wire that is listed for direct burial at voltages above 600 volts but not exceeding 2000 volts shall be installed in accordance with Table 300.50, Column 1.

Proposal 4-227

Comment 4-92

690.81 Listing (PV Systems over 1000 Volts)

Products listed for photovoltaic systems are permitted to be used and installed in accordance with their listing.

PV wire that is listed for direct burial at voltages above 600 volts but not exceeding 2000 volts are required to be installed in accordance with Table 300.50, Column 1.

2011 *NEC* Requirement

This listing requirement did not exist in the 2011 *NEC*.

2014 *NEC* Change

Products listed for photovoltaic systems are permitted to be used and installed in accordance with their listing. PV wire that is listed for direct burial at voltages above 600 volts but not exceeding 2000 volts is required to be installed in accordance with Table 300.50, Column 1.

Analysis of Change

It has become common practice in large utility-scale solar PV installations to direct bury 2000-volts rated conductors used to deliver power from combiner boxes to the inverter. Since these installations are not accessible to the public, and maintenance and supervision ensure that only qualified persons service the installed cable, direct-buried single-conductor installations are appropriate for these installations. There are currently listed PV wire products available that are rated at up to 2000 volts that are also listed for direct burial. New product standards are being developed for above 600-volts equipment and other electrical systems components; and this new Article 690 listing requirement will allow these products to be used where applicable and available.

A companion proposal was submitted to CMP-3 and accepted at 300.50(A)(2) to simultaneously revise 300.50 just for listed direct burial, nonshielded, single conductor cables up to 2000 volts (see Proposal 3-96). Without these companion changes, the previous requirements at 690.80 and 300.50 were likely to be interpreted as being in conflict with the listed use of 2000-volts direct burial PV wire. Chapters 1–4 of the *NEC* apply generally. Since this is a wiring method specific to Article 690 and the PV industry, it is necessary to recognize it at 690.81 and at 300.50(A)(2) in order to ensure appropriate installation methods are followed.

Article 694

Change at a Glance

The title, scope and appropriate text throughout Article 694 were revised by removing the word "small," leaving the subject of the article simply "Wind Electric Systems."

Code Language

Article 694 ~~Small~~ Wind Electric Systems

694.1 Scope. The provisions of this article apply to ~~small~~ wind (turbine) electric systems that consist of one or more wind electric generators ~~with individual generators having a rated power up to and including 100 kW~~. These systems can include generators, alternators, inverters, and controllers.

Informational Note: ~~Small~~ Wind electric systems can be interactive with other electrical power production sources or might be stand-alone systems. ~~Small~~ Wind electric systems can have ac or dc output, with or without electrical energy storage, such as batteries. See Informational Note Figures 694.1(a)~~, No. 1~~ and 694.1(b)~~, No. 2~~.

Proposal 4-345, 4-346

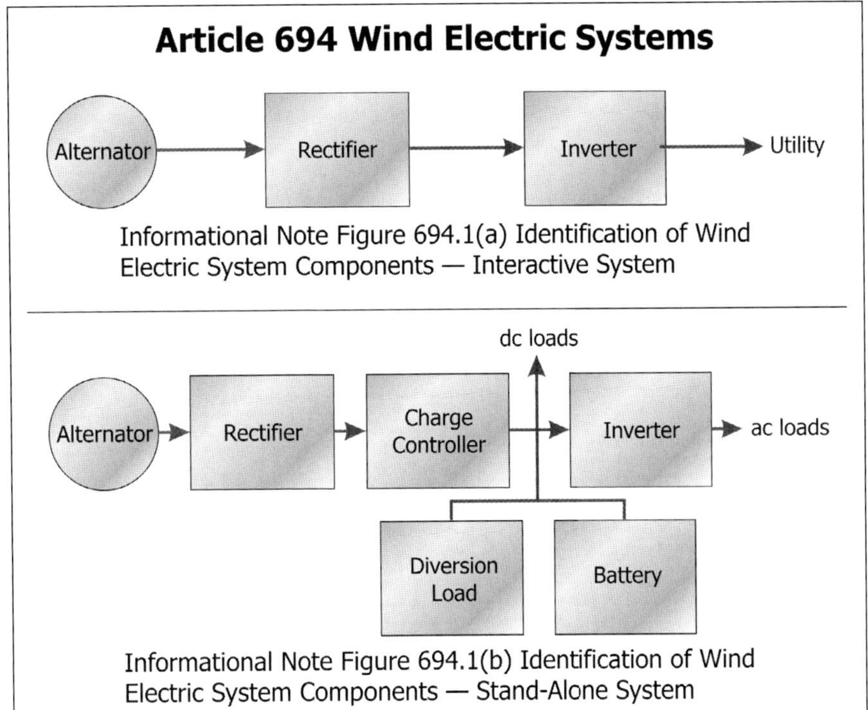

Informational Note Figure 694.1(a) Identification of Wind Electric System Components — Interactive System

Informational Note Figure 694.1(b) Identification of Wind Electric System Components — Stand-Alone System

2011 *NEC* Requirement

Article 694 applied to small wind (turbine) electric systems that consist of one or more wind electric generators with individual generators having a rated power up to and including 100 kW.

2014 *NEC* Change

Article 694 now applies to wind (turbine) electric systems that consist of one or more wind electric generators. This article is no longer limited to wind (turbine) electric systems rated 100 kW and below.

Analysis of Change

Article 694 for "Small Wind Electric Systems" was introduced in the 2011 *NEC*. With the increasing number of wind turbines being installed across the country, there was no specific article to address the particular characteristics of these unique electrical systems. The electrical safety of these installations was improved by adding clear requirements for grounding and other aspects of the electrical installation. Since wind turbine towers are typically tall structures, other considerations needed to be addressed such as lightning strikes and as such deserve special attention when connected to a premises electrical system.

Experience over the last *Code* cycle has also shown that there is no significant difference between an electrical installation for a wind turbine sized at 100 kW or less and that for one rated above 100 kW. The requirements developed for "small" wind turbine systems should have, and now have been, applied for intermediate and large wind turbines as well. The product standards for wind turbines, UL 6141, *Wind Turbine Converters and Interconnection Systems Equipment* and UL 6142, *Small Wind Turbine Systems* both draw the same conclusion: there is no need to draw a distinction between small, intermediate, and large wind electric systems. Rules for the larger wind turbines previously did not exist in Article 694 due to the limitation of the scope of the article to 100 kW or less.

700.8

Change at a Glance

Listed surge protective devices (SPD) are now required for emergency systems.

Code Language

700.8 Surge Protection. ***(Emergency Systems)***

A listed SPD shall be installed in or on all emergency systems switchboards and panelboards.

Proposal 13-98

Comment 13-69, 13-68

700.8 Surge Protection (Emergency Systems)

A listed surge protective device (SPD) shall be installed in or on all emergency systems switchboards and panelboards.

Emergency system switchboard

Service

Transfer switch

Listed SPD

Generator

2011 *NEC* Requirement

Surge protection devices were not required for emergency systems in the 2011 *NEC*.

2014 *NEC* Change

A new 700.8 was added requiring a listed surge protective device (SPD) in or on all emergency systems switchboards and panelboards.

Analysis of Change

New requirements were added to Article 700 requiring all emergency systems switchboards and panelboards to be supplied with a listed surge protective device (SPD). An SPD is defined in Article 100 as, "A protective device for limiting transient voltages by diverting or limiting surge current; it also prevents continued flow of follow current[1] while remaining capable of repeating these functions." There are four types of SPDs that are described in the Article 100 definition as well. A spike or surge in current that goes unarrested can cause great damage to such things as appliances and electronic equipment. This damage can result from such things as the starting and stopping of power electronic equipment, direct or indirect lightning strikes, and imposition of a higher voltage on a lower voltage system. SPDs have proven to provide benefits for components and systems against the damages of voltage surges. SPDs are readily available to protect against these types of surges.

Surge protection will now be required for emergency systems since electronics are embedded within the infrastructure of facilities involving these emergency systems. These emergency system electronics monitor and control several aspects of the building involving such components as fire alarm systems, emergency lighting and exit lighting, generator and transfer equipment, and automatic load control relays. As our buildings and infrastructures become more reliant on electronic control and communication, surge protection has the opportunity to

700.8

Continued

ensure critical safety systems are not compromised and property damage within these infrastructures become less and less common.

Article 285 covers general requirements, installation and connection requirements for surge-protective devices (SPDs) permanently installed on premises wiring systems of 1000 volts or less. For further information on Type 1, Type 2, Type 3, and Type 4 SPDs, see UL 1449, *Standard for Surge Protective Devices*.

[1]**Follow current.** The current at power frequency that passes through a surge diverter or other discharge path after a high-voltage surge has started the discharge.
— *McGraw-Hill Science of Technology Dictionary*

700.12(F)

Change at a Glance

Section 700.12(F) was reformatted into a list. For emergency systems, a separate branch circuit for unit equipment that is permitted (by exception) in a separate and uninterrupted area supplied by a minimum of three normal lighting circuits cannot be part of a multiwire branch circuit.

Code Language

700.12 General Requirements. ***(Sources of Power for Emergency Systems)***

Current supply shall be such that, in the event of failure of the normal supply to, or within, the building or group of buildings concerned, emergency lighting, emergency power, or both shall be available within the time required for the application but not to exceed 10 seconds. *(See NEC for complete text)*.

(F) Unit Equipment.

(1) Components of Unit Equipment. Individual unit equipment for emergency illumination shall consist of the following:

(1) A rechargeable battery

(2) A battery charging means

(3) Provisions for one or more lamps mounted on the equipment, or shall be permitted to have terminals for remote lamps, or both

(4) A relaying device arranged to

700.12(F)(2)(3) Exception
Installation of Unit Equipment

The branch circuit feeding emergency lighting unit equipment shall be the same branch circuit as that serving the normal lighting in the area and connected ahead of any local switches.

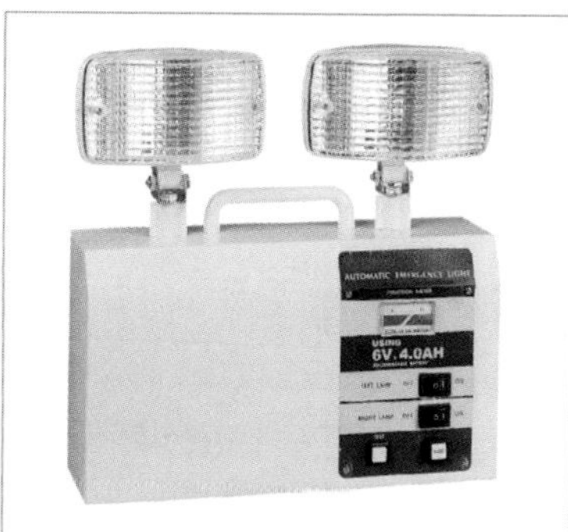

Exception: In a separate and uninterrupted area supplied by a minimum of three normal lighting circuits that are not part of a multiwire branch circuit, a separate branch circuit for unit equipment is permitted if it originates from the same panelboard as that of the normal lighting circuits and is provided with a lock-on feature.

2011 *NEC* Requirement

Section 700.12 covers the general requirements for sources of power for emergency systems. Section 700.12(F) covers individual unit equipment for the emergency system. One of the provisions for the installation of emergency unit equipment requires the branch circuit feeding this unit equipment to be on the same branch circuit as that serving the normal lighting in the area and connected ahead of any local switches. An exception to this rule permits a separate branch circuit for unit equipment in a separate and uninterrupted area supplied by a minimum of three normal lighting circuits. This exception for a separate branch circuit can only be applied if it originates from the same panelboard as that of the normal lighting circuits and is provided with a lock-on feature. A second exception permits remote heads providing lighting for the exterior of an exit door to be supplied by the unit equipment serving the area immediately inside the exit door.

2014 *NEC* Change

The provisions for 700.12(F) were reformatted into a list format. A revision occurred with the exception [now 700.12(F)(2)(3), Exception] that permits a separate branch circuit for unit equipment in a separate and uninterrupted area supplied by a minimum of three normal lighting circuits. The revision to this exception makes it clear that this separate branch circuit cannot be part of a multiwire branch circuit. The previous second exception permitting remote heads providing lighting for the exterior of an exit door to be supplied by the unit equipment serving the area immediately inside the exit door has been revised into positive language and is now found at 700.12(F)(2)(6).

Analysis of Change

The text at 700.12(F) has been reformatted by adding titles to the two new subsections and adding numbering changes to the list items of components under 700.12(F)(1) and (F)(2). The previous Exception No 2 has been changed to posi-

700.12(F)

Continued

energize the lamps automatically upon failure of the supply to the unit equipment

(2) Installation of Unit Equipment. Unit equipment shall be installed in accordance with 700.12(F)(2)(1) through (6).
(1) The batteries shall be of suitable rating and capacity to supply and maintain at not less than 87 ½ percent of the nominal battery voltage for the total lamp load associated with the unit for a period of at least 1 ½ hours, or the unit equipment shall supply and maintain not less than 60 percent of the initial emergency illumination for a period of at least 1 ½ hours. Storage batteries, whether of the acid or alkali type, shall be designed and constructed to meet the requirements of emergency service.
(2) Unit equipment shall be permanently fixed in place (i.e., not portable) and shall have all wiring to each unit installed in accordance with the requirements of any of the wiring methods in Chapter 3. Flexible cord-and plug connection shall be permitted, provided that the cord does not exceed 900 mm (3 ft) in length.
(3) The branch circuit feeding the unit equipment shall be the same branch circuit as that serving the normal lighting in the area and connected ahead of any local switches.

Exception ~~No. 1~~: *In a separate and uninterrupted area supplied by a minimum of three normal lighting circuits that are not part of a multiwire branch circuit, a separate branch circuit for unit equipment shall be permitted if it originates from the same panelboard as that of the normal lighting circuits and is provided with a lock-on feature.*
(4) The branch circuit that feeds unit equipment shall be clearly identified at the distribution panel.
(5) Emergency luminaires that obtain power from a unit equipment and are not part of the unit equipment shall be wired to the unit equipment as required by 700.10 and by one of the wiring methods of Chapter 3.
(6) ~~***Exception No. 2:***~~ Remote heads providing lighting for the exterior of an exit door shall be permitted to be supplied by the unit equipment serving the area immediately inside the exit door.

Proposal 13-114, 13-116

tive text from an exception since this is part of an installation and is better formulated as positive text.

A revision occurred with the previous first exception [now 700.12(F)(2)(3), Exception]. This exception permits a separate branch circuit for unit equipment in a separate and uninterrupted area to be supplied by a minimum of three normal lighting circuits. The main rule at 700.12(F)(3) requires the branch circuit feeding this unit equipment to be on the same branch circuit as that serving the normal lighting in the area and connected ahead of any local switches. The revision to this exception prohibits this separate branch circuit from being part of a multiwire branch circuit. Section 210.4(B) requires each multiwire branch circuit to be provided with a means to simultaneously disconnect all ungrounded conductors at the point where the branch circuit originates. This can be accomplished using multi-pole circuit breakers or single-pole circuit breakers with identified handle ties. If a multiwire branch circuit were allowed to be used to comply with this exception, there would be an increased possibility of leaving the area in total darkness. If one circuit of a multiwire branch circuit were to trip, both circuits would trip due to the "simultaneous" disconnecting means requirement. This revision will improve consistency with other *NEC* rules that restrict multiwire branch circuit in areas where similar hazards have been identified, such as 517.18(A) and 517.19(A).

700.19

Change at a Glance

Branch circuits for emergency power or lighting are restricted from being part of a multiwire branch circuit.

NEW

Code Language

700.19 Multiwire Branch Circuits.
The branch circuit serving emergency lighting and power circuits shall not be part of a multiwire branch circuit.

Proposal 13-118

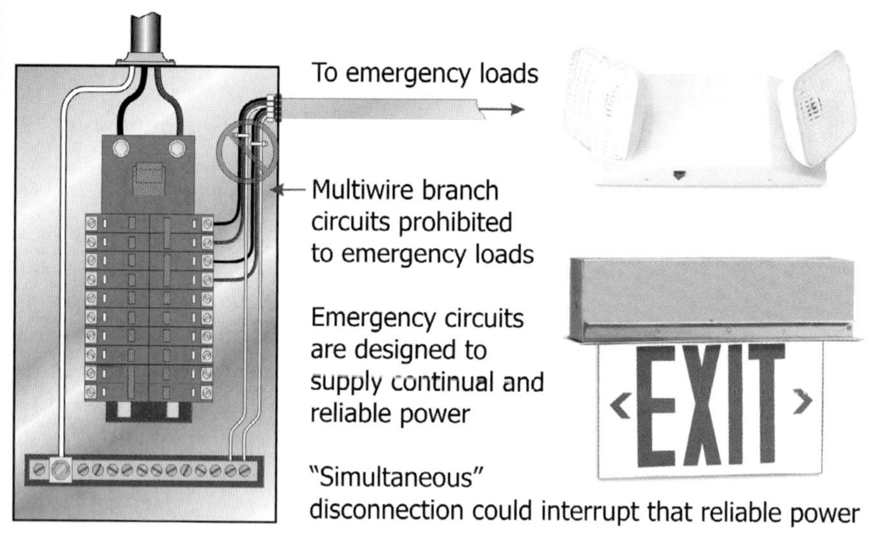
700.19 Multiwire Branch Circuits
The branch circuit serving emergency lighting and power circuits shall not be part of a multiwire branch circuit.
To emergency loads
Multiwire branch circuits prohibited to emergency loads
Emergency circuits are designed to supply continual and reliable power
"Simultaneous" disconnection could interrupt that reliable power
EXIT

2011 *NEC* Requirement

There were no provisions for multiwire branch circuits in Article 700 in the 2011 *NEC*.

2014 *NEC* Change

New provisions were added at 700.19 to prohibit multiwire branch circuits from serving emergency lighting and power circuits.

Analysis of Change

Emergency systems, circuits, and equipment are intended to supply, distribute, and control electricity for illumination, power, or both, to required facilities when the normal electrical supply or system is interrupted. As such, it is critical that these emergency circuits are built and maintained to supply continual and reliable power. To assist in this reliable source, new provisions were added at 700.19 to prohibit multiwire branch circuits from serving emergency lighting and power circuits. This new Article 700 requirement is similar in nature to the requirements added to 517.18(A) and 517.19(A) in the 2011 *NEC*. It should be noted that 210.4(B) requires each multiwire branch circuit be provided with a means to simultaneously disconnect all ungrounded conductors at the point where the branch circuit originates. This new requirement and those added to Article 517 were added to prevent the unnecessary opening of all poles of a multiwire branch circuit when an overload, ground-fault, or short-circuit occurs on one pole of the multiwire branch circuit. Emergency power and lighting circuits have the same need for continuity of service as those circuits at a health care facility.

700.24

Change at a Glance

Emergency system luminaires and all external bypass controls are required to be individually listed for use in emergency systems.

Code Language

700.24 Directly Controlled Luminaires

Where emergency illumination is provided by one or more directly controlled luminaires that respond to an external control input to bypass normal control upon loss of normal power, such luminaires and external bypass controls shall be individually listed for use in emergency systems.

Proposal 13-121

Comment 13-81

700.24 Directly Controlled Luminaires

Emergency system luminaire and all external bypass controls are required to be individually listed for use in emergency systems.

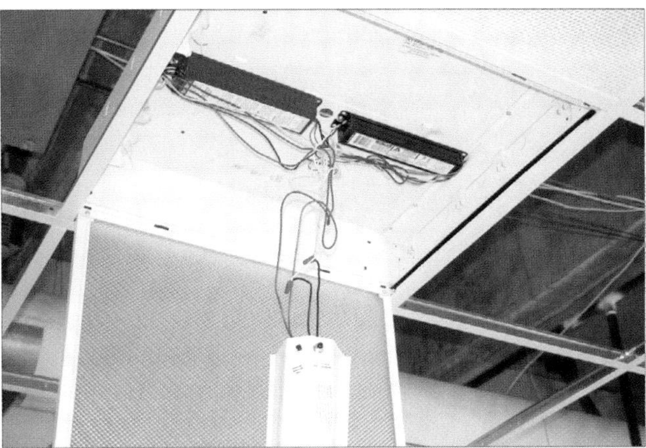

Where emergency illumination is provided by one or more directly controlled luminaires that respond to an external control input to bypass normal control upon loss of normal power, such luminaires and external bypass controls shall be individually listed for use in emergency systems.

2011 *NEC* Requirement

Lighting loads and circuits for emergency system lighting and power are covered in Part IV of Article 700. Control of emergency lighting circuits such as switching and dimmer controls are specified in Part V of Article 700. No provisions for directly controlled luminaires were included in Article 700; Section 700.24 addressed "Automatic Load Control Relay" in the 2011 *NEC*.

2014 *NEC* Change

A new section was added at 700.24 for "Directly Controlled Luminaires." This new provision requires emergency luminaires and the external bypass controls to be individually listed for use in emergency systems where emergency illumination is provided by one or more directly controlled luminaires. These directly controlled luminaires respond to an external control input to bypass normal control upon loss of normal power.

Analysis of Change

Emergency illumination in Article 700 is required to include all means of egress lighting, illuminated exit signs, and all other lights specified as necessary to provide required illumination in an emergency situation. Emergency lighting systems are required to be designed and installed so that the failure of any individual lighting element, such as the burning out of a lamp, cannot leave in total darkness any space that requires emergency illumination. In accordance with 700.23, a dimmer or relay system containing more than one dimmer or relay and listed for use in emergency systems is permitted to be used as a control device for energizing emergency lighting circuits. In recent years, a new class of light-emitting diode (LED) luminaire has emerged and is being used in emergency lighting systems. These luminaires are typically dimmable LED luminaires that operate on constant power with an analog or digital input connected to an analog or digital control system to provide a dimming or switching function in the luminaire when normal power is present.

This luminaire will also have a separate analog or dry-closure "emergency" control input which can be actuated by an upstream transfer switch. When this emergency input is accessed upon loss of normal power, transfer of power is switched from the luminaire's normal branch circuit to emergency power. At this point, the luminaire turns on full, regardless of the control setting of the normal control system. These LED luminaires are currently not listed for this emergency application and may or may not have sufficient reliability or predictable performance for use in emergency systems. LED luminaires contain multifaceted electronics and just like other critical components in the emergency system, should be listed for use for emergency systems.

It should be noted that this new provision not only requires the emergency system luminaire to be listed, but the external bypass controls are required to be individually listed for use in emergency systems as well.

700.27

Change at a Glance

A licensed professional engineer or other qualified persons must design and select the selective coordination of the overcurrent protective devices for emergency systems.

Code Language

700.27 Selective Coordination

Emergency system(s) overcurrent devices shall be selectively coordinated with all supply-side overcurrent protective devices. Selective coordination shall be selected by a licensed professional engineer or other qualified persons engaged primarily in the design, installation, or maintenance of electrical systems. The selection shall be documented and made available to those authorized to design, install, inspect, maintain, and operate the system.

Exception: Selective coordination shall not be required between two overcurrent devices located in series if no loads are connected in parallel with the downstream device.

Proposal 13-126

Comment 13-85

700.27 Selective Coordination (Emergency Systems)

A licensed professional engineer or other qualified persons must now design and select the selective coordination of the overcurrent protective devices for emergency systems.

Documentation is required to be made available to those authorized to design, install, inspect, maintain, and operate the system.

This same new "licensed professional engineer or other qualified persons" selective coordination provision was implemented at the following locations:

620.62 Elevators, Escalators, (Etc.)

701.27 Optional Standby Systems

708.54 Critical Operations Power Systems (COPS)

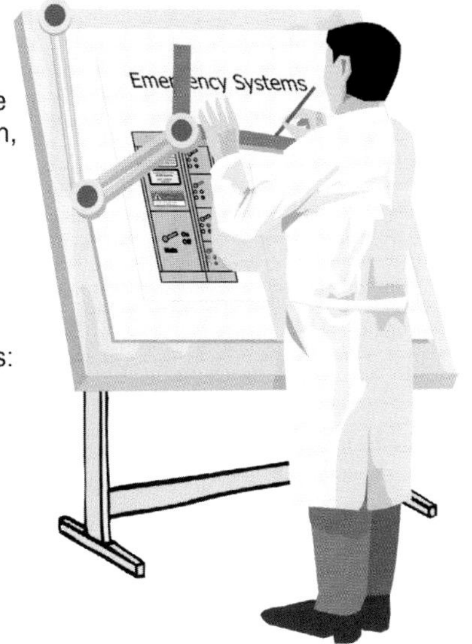

2011 *NEC* Requirement

The overcurrent devices for emergency system(s) are required to be selectively coordinated with all supply side overcurrent protective devices. An exception to this rule would exempt selective coordination between two overcurrent devices located in series if no loads are connected in parallel with the downstream device.

2014 *NEC* Change

A provision was added to the "Selective Coordination" requirements for emergency systems to require this selective coordination be designed and selected by a licensed professional engineer or other qualified persons engaged primarily in the design, installation, or maintenance of electrical systems.

Analysis of Change

Selective coordination is defined in Article 100 as "Localization of an overcurrent condition to restrict outages to the circuit or equipment affected, accomplished by the selection and installation of overcurrent protective devices and their ratings or settings for the full range of available overcurrents, from overload to the maximum available fault current, and for the full range of overcurrent protective device opening times associated with those overcurrents." Some users of the *Code* feel that selective coordination is not being uniformly enforced, or is not being enforced at all. In an effort to aid in the enforcement of this essential issue with emergency systems, this new language seeks to identify who is responsible for the design and selection of the overcurrent protective devices for selective coordinated for emergency systems. This new requirement will also provide verified selective coordination documentation as part of the construction documents available to the AHJ. This design professional described in the new text is the only person who has overall control of the selective coordination system at the implementation stage.

700.27

Continued

Without this new provision, the electrical switchboard or switchgear manufacturer is often relied upon to provide this selective coordination. In most cases, the electrical switchboard or switchgear manufacturer only has control of the coordination of their own equipment. This can result in no coordination on other electrical equipment such as generators and automatic transfer switches. It should be noted that this new text would not prohibit the switchgear manufacturer from designing the total selective coordination as long as this person is "a licensed professional engineer or other qualified person(s) engaged primarily in the design, installation, or maintenance of electrical systems." Emergency systems are an important enough aspect of the overall electrical system that justification is warranted to selective coordination being performed by a licensed professional engineer or a qualified person.

This same new "licensed professional engineer or other qualified persons" selective coordination provision was implemented at the following locations during the 2014 *NEC* development process:

620.62	Elevators, Escalators, (Etc.)	Proposal 12-50	
701.27	Optional Standby Systems	Proposal 13-139	Comment 13-92
708.54	Critical Operations Power Systems (COPS)	Proposal 13-176	Comment 13-110

702.7(C)

Change at a Glance

Where an optional standby systems power inlet is used for a temporary connection to a portable generator, a warning sign is required to be placed near the inlet to indicate the type of derived system involved (bonded neutral or floating neutral).

NEW

Code Language

702.7 Signs

(C) Power Inlet. Where a power inlet is used for a temporary connection to a portable generator, a warning sign shall be placed near the inlet to indicate the type of derived system that the system is capable of based on the wiring of the transfer equipment. The sign shall display one of the following warnings:

WARNING:
FOR CONNECTION OF A SEPARATELY DERIVED
(BONDED NEUTRAL) SYSTEM ONLY

or

WARNING:
FOR CONNECTION OF A NON-SEPARATELY DERIVED
(FLOATING NEUTRAL) SYSTEM ONLY

Proposal 13-146

Comment 13-96

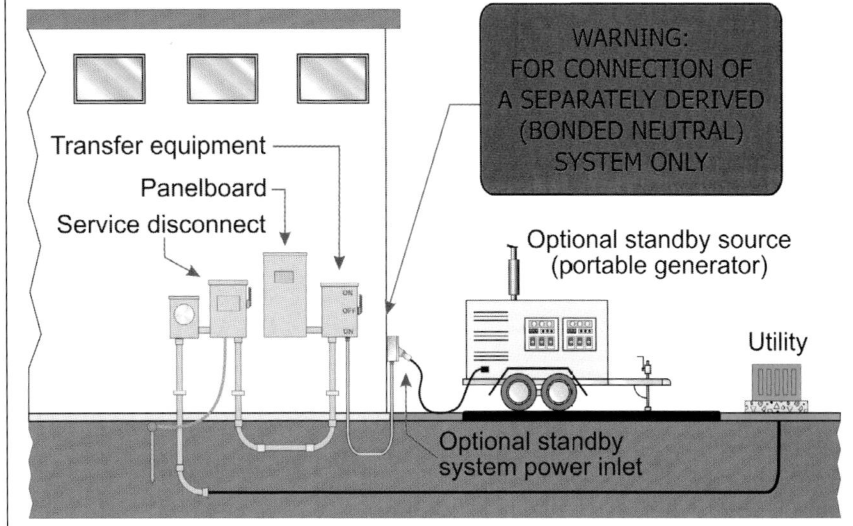
702.7(C) Signs for Power Outlets
Optional standby system power inlets used for temporary connection to a portable generator require a warning sign to be placed near the inlet to indicate the type of derived system involved (bonded or floating neutral).
WARNING:
FOR CONNECTION OF
A SEPARATELY DERIVED
(BONDED NEUTRAL)
SYSTEM ONLY
Transfer equipment
Panelboard
Service disconnect
Optional standby source
(portable generator)
Utility
Optional standby
system power inlet

2011 *NEC* Requirement

A sign is required to be placed at the service-entrance equipment that indicates the type and location of on-site optional standby power sources. A warning sign is also required where the removal of a grounding or bonding connection in normal power source equipment interrupts the grounding electrode conductor connection to the alternate power source(s) grounded conductor. These signage requirements are found at 702.7(A) and (B). No provision appeared in the 2011 *NEC* for signage at power inlets.

2014 *NEC* Change

A new provision was added at 702.7(C) for "Power Inlet" which requires a warning sign to be placed near the inlet when an optional standby systems power inlet is used for a temporary connection to a portable generator. This warning sign must indicate the type of derived system that the system is capable of delivering. The warning sign would indicate a separately derived (bonded neutral) system or a nonseparately derived (floating neutral) system.

Analysis of Change

Article 250 of the *NEC* allows a generator installation to be installed as separately derived systems or provisions can be implemented where a generator is not a separately derived system (see 250.30 and Informational Notes). What determines if a generator is not a separately derived system is if the grounded (neutral) conductor is solidly interconnected to a service-supplied system grounded conductor. A new manufacturer's marking provision has been added at 445.11 in the 2014 *NEC* requiring indication whether or not the generator neutral is bonded to the generator frame. This new neutral bonding provision goes further to require additional marking to indicate whether the generator neutral is bonded to the generator frame whenever the bonding of a generator is modified in the field. Along these same lines, new provisions were added at 702.7(C) requiring a warning sign to be placed

702.7(C)

Continued

near the inlet when an optional standby system's power inlet is used for a temporary connection to a portable generator. This warning sign must indicate the type of derived system that the system is capable of delivering. The warning sign must indicate if the source delivered is a separately derived (bonded neutral) system or a nonseparately derived (floating neutral) system.

Portable generators may or may not be part of an electrical inspection. Depending on what type of portable generator is involved (bonded neutral vs. floating neutral), an unsafe environment can be created such as paralleling grounded currents on both the equipment grounding conductor and the grounded conductor, or circulating currents on the equipment grounding conductor system. This new warning sign requirement will give clear indication as to the type of required electrical connection to the portable generator inlet to achieve optimal electrical safety.

702.12

Change at a Glance

Portable generator (rated 15 kW or less) using a flanged inlet or other cord- and plug-type connection is not required to have a disconnecting means where ungrounded conductors serve or pass through a building or structure.

Code Language

702.12 Outdoor Generator Sets

(A) Permanently Installed Generators and Portable Generators Greater Than 15 kW. Where an outdoor housed generator set is equipped with a readily accessible disconnecting means in accordance with 445.18, and the disconnecting means is located within sight of the building or structure supplied, an additional disconnecting means shall not be required where ungrounded conductors serve or pass through the building or structure. Where the generator supply conductors terminate at a disconnecting means in or on a building or structure, the disconnecting means shall meet the requirements of 225.36.

(B) Portable Generators 15 kW or Less. Where a portable generator, rated 15 kW or less, is installed using a flanged inlet or other cord- and plug-type connection, a disconnecting means

702.12 Outdoor Generator Sets

Portable generator (rated 15 kW or less) using a flanged inlet or other cord- and plug-type connection is not required to have a disconnecting means where ungrounded conductors serve or pass through a building or structure.

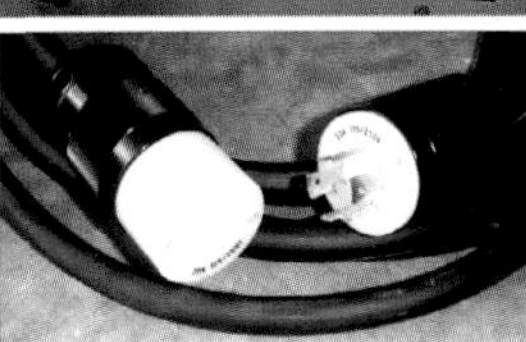

Outdoor generator sets have been divided into two subsections:

702.12(A) Permanently Installed Generators and Portable Generators Greater Than 15 kW

702.12(B) Portable Generators 15 kW or Less

2011 *NEC* Requirement

Where an outdoor housed generator set is equipped with a readily accessible disconnecting means located within sight of the building or structure supplied, an additional disconnecting means was not required where ungrounded conductors serve or pass through the building or structure. This disconnecting means had to meet the requirements of 225.36 for having to be suitable for use as service equipment.

2014 *NEC* Change

This section for outdoor generator sets was divided into two subsections. Section 702.12(A), Permanently Installed Generators and Portable Generators Greater Than 15 kW, incorporated the previous previsions from 702.12 of the 2011 *NEC*. Section 702.12(B), Portable Generators 15 kW or Less, is new. This new subsection permits portable generators (rated 15 kW or less) using a flanged inlet or other cord- and plug-type connection to omit a disconnecting means where ungrounded conductors serve or pass through a building or structure.

Analysis of Change

The requirements for outdoor generator sets covered at 702.12 were divided into two new subsections. New subsection 702.12(A) Permanently Installed Generators and Portable Generators Greater Than 15 kW incorporated a new reference to 445.18 for an outdoor housed generator set equipped with a readily accessible disconnecting means located within sight of the building or structure supplied. Section 445.18 generally requires a disconnecting means for a generator, and this disconnecting means is required to be equipped with a disconnect(s), lockable in the open position, capable of disconnecting entirely the circuits supplied by the generator. Section 445.18 also provides two conditions where a disconnecting means is not required. Provisions were added to 455.18 for the 2014 *NEC* to permit a portable

Continued

shall not be required where ungrounded conductors serve or pass through a building or structure.

Proposal 13-111, 13-148, 13-110

Comment 13-97

generator that employs a cord and plug connection as an acceptable disconnecting means for a generator. This disconnecting means is also required to meet the requirements of 225.36 for having to be suitable for use as service equipment where the generator supply conductors terminate at a disconnecting means in or on a building or structure. Similar revisions for outdoor generator sets were also implemented at 700.12(B)(6) for emergency systems and at 701.12(B)(5) for legally required standby systems.

New requirements were added at 702.12(B) for "Portable Generators 15 kW or Less." This new subsection permits portable generator (rated 15 kW or less) using a flanged inlet or other cord- and plug-type connection to not require a disconnecting means where ungrounded conductors serve or pass through a building or structure. This new provision in Article 702 also correlates with the new provisions added at 445.18 for cord- and plug-type portable generators. When portable generators were added to the scope of Article 702 in the 2002 *NEC,* small portable generators connected by means of a flanged inlet and a flexible cord- and plug-type connection were not considered with regard to the disconnecting means at the building or other structure supplied required by 225.31. These small portable generators (found mostly in residential applications) are often installed without a disconnecting means other than the above-mentioned flanged inlet and flexible cord. This new provision will bring the requirements for portable generators rated 15 kW or less in line with typical installation practices that are already being implemented by manufacturers and today's work force.

705.12(D)

Change at a Glance

Section 705.12(D) covering "Utility-Interactive Inverters" was reorganized for clarity.

Code Language

705.12 Point of Connection. ***(Interconnected Electric Power Production Sources)*** The output of an interconnected electric power source shall be connected as specified in 705.12(A), (B), (C), or (D).

(D) Utility-Interactive Inverters.
(1) Dedicated Overcurrent and Disconnect.

(2) Bus or Conductor Ampere Rating.
(1) Feeders.
(2) Taps.
(3) Busbars.
~~**(3) Ground-Fault Protection.**~~ *[See 705.32]*

(3) Marking. *[Was 705.12(D)(4)]*

(4) Suitable for Backfeed. *[Was 705.12(D)(5)]*

(5) Fastening. *[Was 705.12(D)(6)]*

(6) Wire Harness and Exposed Cable Arc-Fault Protection.
~~**(7) Inverter Output Connection.**~~
[Much of this text was incorporated into 705.12(D)(2)(1), (2), and (3)]
(See NEC for complete text)

705.12(D) Point of Connection (Utility-Interactive Inverters)

705.12(D) was rearranged and reorganized for clarity as there are multiple options for connection to the load side of the service disconnecting means *(overcurrent protection devices, taps, busbar, etc.).*

Revisions were made to provide a safe and systematic approach for the design and installation of utility-interactive inverter connections.

2011 *NEC* Requirement

Section 705.12(D) covered the point of connection requirements for utility-interactive inverters. See 2011 *NEC* for complete text.

2014 *NEC* Change

Section 705.12(D) was rearranged and reorganized for clarity. There are multiple options for connection to the load side of the service disconnecting means (overcurrent protection devices, taps, busbar, etc.). These revisions were made to provide a safe and systematic approach for the design and installation of these connections. See 2014 *NEC* for complete text.

Analysis of Change

Utility-interactive inverters are an important key for unlocking future growth of alternative energy projects. This equipment has the ability to export energy back to the local utility. This fact makes utility-interactive inverters unusual in that they require not only the local AHJ's (electrical inspector) approval, but typically, the local utility company's approval as well. It is this blending of electrical safety issues and utility performance concerns that makes this equipment unique from both an inspector approval and testing lab evaluation standpoint. This bridging of jurisdictional concerns has been incorporated into the standard used to evaluate this equipment, UL 1741, *Inverters, Converters and Controllers for Use in Independent Power Systems*, and is also evident in Article 705. The level of electronic sophistication of a typical utility-interactive inverter is considerably high as these devices not only convert dc electricity into ac, but they also have the capability to supply their own ac energy in a form suitable for back feeding the local utility grid.

Section 705.12(D) contains the provisions for utility-interactive inverters and their point of connection for an interconnected electric power source. Several changes and revisions occurred at this subsection for the 2014 *NEC*.

705.12(D)

Continued

Proposal 4-375a, 9-181g, 4-391, 4-392, 4-394, 4-396, 4-397, 4-399a, 4-400, 4-401, 4-402, 4-403, 4-404

Comment 4-199, 4-203, 4-204, 4-206

Among the more notable revisions was a rearrangement of this subsection for usability and clarity. Other revisions included dividing 705.12(D)(2) for "Bus or Conductor Ampere Rating" into three parts and separating the requirements for connection to the load side of the service disconnecting means. These new parts include requirements for feeders, taps, and busbars. Some of the key concerns for these new provisions are the addition of a utility-interactive inverter supply which presents a potential overload condition for the feeder and main lug only (MLO) panelboards on the load side of the inverter interconnection point. By making sure that the ampacity of the feeder is sufficient for both sources, or by installing an overcurrent device ahead of the feeder on the load side of the inverter interconnection point, the feeder is protected. The busbar of the MLO panelboard can be protected by the overcurrent device installed at the interconnection point or by installing a main overcurrent device in the panelboard to prevent busbar overcurrent. Some of the language at previous 705.12(D)(7) Inverter Output Connection was incorporated into these three new list items at 705.12(D)(2) as well.

The previous requirements of 705.12(D)(3) Ground-Fault Protection were deleted as they were found to be redundant as these GFP requirements are covered at 705.32.

A new list item was added at 705.12(D)(6) Wire Harness and Exposed Cable Arc-Fault Protection. This new requirement calls for utility interactive inverter(s) that have a wire harness or cable output circuit (rated 240 volts, 30 amperes or less), that is not installed within an enclosed raceway, to be provided with listed ac AFCI protection. Single and multiple utility interactive inverter systems such as ac modules and micro inverters can have significant amounts of exposed PV ac wiring (harnesses and cables) that are often exposed to movement, abuse, and degradation due to such things as weather environments and rodents. These factors can lead to insulation breakdown and broken conductors that can lead to series and parallel arc faults. AFCI protection is warranted in these applications.

708.52(D)

Change at a Glance

Section 708.52(D) was revised to require separation of GFP time-current characteristics to conform to manufacturer's recommendations.

Code Language

708.52 Ground-Fault Protection of Equipment. ***[Critical Operations Power System(COPS)]***

(D) Selectivity. Ground-fault protection for operation of the service and feeder disconnecting means shall be fully selective such that the feeder device, but not the service device, shall open on ground faults on the load side of the feeder device. ~~A six-cycle minimum separation between the service and feeder ground-fault tripping bands shall be provided. Operating time of the disconnecting devices shall be considered in selecting the time spread between these two bands~~ Separation of ground-fault protection time-current characteristics shall conform to manufacturer's recommendations and shall consider all required tolerances and disconnect operating time to achieve 100 percent selectivity.

Informational Note: See 230.95, Informational Note No. 4, for transfer of alternate source where ground-fault protection is applied.

Proposal 13-175

708.52(D) Ground-Fault Protection of Equipment [Critical Operations Power System (COPS)]

708.52(D) was revised to require separation of GFP time-current characteristics to conform to manufacturer's recommendations.

Feeder OCPD and GFP devices

GFP for operation of the service and feeder disconnecting means shall be fully selective such that the feeder device *(but not the service device)* shall open on ground faults on the load side of the feeder device.

Separation of GFP time-current characteristics shall conform to manufacturer's recommendations and shall consider all required tolerances and disconnect operating time to achieve 100 percent selectivity.

2011 *NEC* Requirement

Ground-fault protection (GFP) for operation with critical operations power systems (COPS) service and feeder disconnecting means is required to be fully selective such that the feeder device (but not the service device) will open on ground faults on the load side of the feeder device. For the 2011 *NEC*, a six-cycle minimum separation between the service and feeder ground-fault tripping bands had to be provided. Operating time of the disconnecting devices was required to be considered in selecting the time spread between these two bands to achieve 100 percent selectivity.

2014 *NEC* Change

For the 2014 *NEC*, the "six-cycle minimum separation between the service and feeder ground-fault tripping bands" and the "time spread between these two bands" was removed and replaced with provisions for the separation of GFP time-current characteristics required to conform to the manufacturer's recommendations. Consideration of all required tolerances and disconnect operating time is also required to achieve 100 percent selectivity.

Analysis of Change

Revisions occurred at 708.52(D) for selectivity of ground-fault protection (GFP) for operation with critical operations power systems (COPS) service and feeder disconnecting means. This revision requires separation of GFP time-current characteristics to conform to manufacturer's recommendations. This revision in Article 708 will bring 708.52(D) into alignment with 517.17(C) for ground-fault protection (GFP) at health care facilities. Prior to the 2011 *NEC*, 517.17(C) and 708.52(D) were identical in text and requirements. During the 2011 *NEC Code* cycle, 517.17(C) was revised to include text identical to the new text here in Article 708. However, this revision was overlooked for 708.52(D) during the 2011

708.52(D)

Continued

NEC revisions. This revision to 708.52(D) will bring improvement in GFP and selective coordination with critical operations power systems (COPS).

The 6-cycle separation requirement is not universally required and is a carryover from the days of electromechanical relays operating on separate switching mechanisms. In most cases today, ground-fault protection is integral to the disconnect devices upon which the ground-fault relay operates. Manufacturer's recommended curves include all applicable tolerances and mechanical operating time. It is not required to add artificial clearance between curves. Adding artificial delays where they are not required complicates the process of designing selective systems and slows down protection unnecessarily, potentially increasing exposure to arc-flash hazard. GFP system designers should and do routinely consider manufacturer's recommendations in the selection and setting of these protective devices.

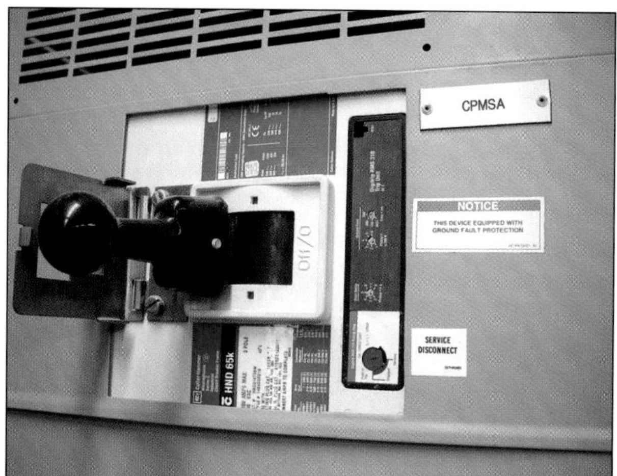

725.2

Change at a Glance

New definition was added for *power-limited tray cable (PLTC)*.

Code Language

725.2 Definitions: *(Class 1, Class 2, and Class 3 Remote-Control, Signaling, and Power-Limited Circuits)*

Power-Limited Tray Cable (PLTC). A factory assembly of two or more insulated conductors rated at 300 volts, with or without associated bare or insulated equipment grounding conductors, under a nonmetallic jacket.

Proposal 7-15

Comment 3-45a

725.2 Definitions: Power-Limited Tray Cable (PLTC)

New definition was added in Article 725 (Class 1, Class 2, and Class 3 Remote-Control, Signaling, and Power-Limited Circuits) for "Power-Limited Tray Cable."

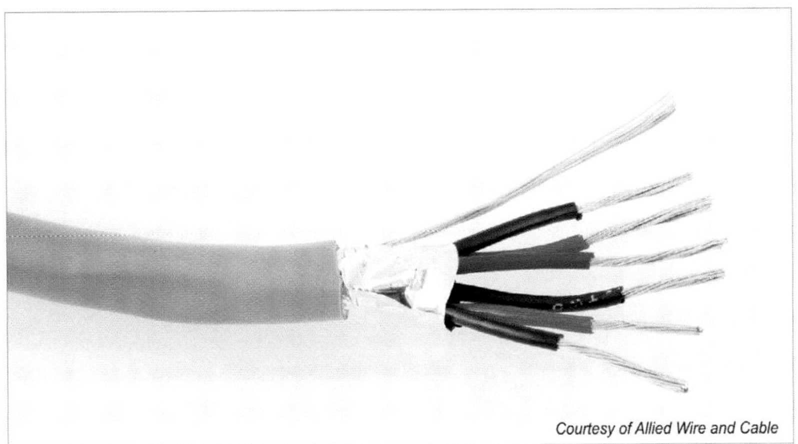

Courtesy of Allied Wire and Cable

Power-Limited Tray Cable (PLTC). A factory assembly of two or more insulated conductors rated at 300 volts, with or without associated bare or insulated equipment grounding conductors, under a nonmetallic jacket.

2011 *NEC* Requirement

The terms *power-limited tray cable* or *PLTC* were used dozens of time in Article 725, such as at 725.179(E), but neither the term nor acronym was defined in the 2011 *NEC*.

2014 *NEC* Change

A new definition was added for *power-limited tray cable* (*PLTC*) in Article 725. This wiring method is defined as "a factory assembly of two or more insulated conductors rated at 300 volts, with or without associated bare or insulated equipment grounding conductors, under a nonmetallic jacket."

Analysis of Change

Power-limited tray cables (PLTC) are commonly used in power-limited circuits and for applications such as in the mass transit industry. Other common applications include: burglar alarms, computer interconnects, business machines, intercom systems, and cash registers. Unshielded PLTC cable is a power limited control cable rated at 300 volts with the option of 2 or 3 conductors per cable. These unshielded cables are typically manufactured in sizes 22 AWG through 12 AWG. PLTC cable typically has PVC insulation on the conductors and PVC gray outer sheathing. The outer sheathing has a sunlight-resistant jacket to protect it when used outdoors.

A new definition was added for *power-limited tray cable* (*PLTC*) in Article 725 as this term is used several times in Article 725. A great deal of information about PLTC can be found at 725.179(E).

725.3(K) and (L)

Change at a Glance

Two new conditions were added to "Other Articles" applying to Class 1, Class 2, and Class 3 remote-control, signaling, and power-limited circuits.

Code Language

725.3 Other Articles. ***(Class 1, Class 2, and Class 3 Remote-Control, Signaling, and Power-Limited Circuits)***

725.3 Other Articles. Circuits and equipment shall comply with the articles or sections listed in 725.3(A) through ~~(J)~~ (L). Only those sections of Article 300 referenced in this article shall apply to Class 1, Class 2, and Class 3 circuits.

(A) Number and Size of Conductors in Raceway.

(B) Spread of Fire or Products of Combustion.

(C) Ducts, Plenums, and Other Air-Handling Spaces.

(D) Hazardous (Classified) Locations.

(E) Cable Trays.

(F) Motor Control Circuits.

(G) Instrumentation Tray Cable.

725.3 Other Articles

725.3(K) - Installation of conductors with other systems shall comply with 300.8 (Raceways or cable trays containing electrical conductors shall not contain any pipe, tube, or equal for steam, water, air, gas, drainage, or any service other than electrical).

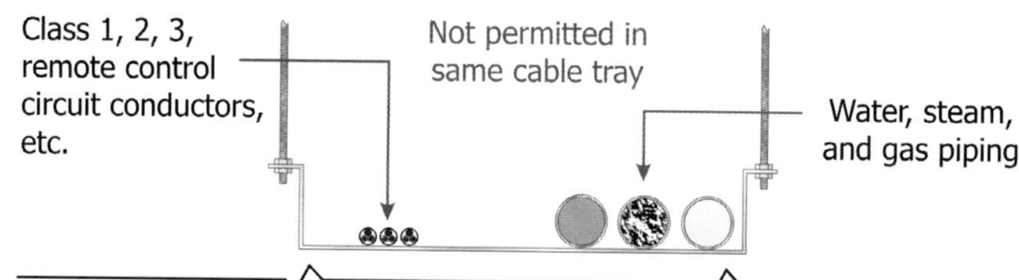

725.3(L) - Class 2 and Class 3 cables, installed in corrosive, damp, or wet locations, shall comply with the applicable requirements in 110.11, 300.5(B), 300.6, 300.9, and 310.10(G).

Class 1 Class 2, and Class 3 circuits installed in corrosive, damp, and wet locations are required to be identified for these conditions.

Type CL2R-CI Cable

2011 *NEC* Requirement

Ten specific conditions of items were listed in the 2011 *NEC* at 725.3 for "Other Articles" that applied to Class 1, Class 2, and Class 3 circuits. See 2011 *NEC* for complete text.

2014 *NEC* Change

Two new conditions were added to "Other Articles" applying to Class 1, Class 2, and Class 3 circuits: Subsection (K) for "Installation of Conductors with Other Systems" and Subsection (L) for "Corrosive, Damp, or Wet Locations."

Analysis of Change

The arrangement of the *Code* is specified at 90.3 of the *NEC*. This section stipulates that Chapters 1 through 4 apply generally to all electrical installations; whereas, Chapters 5, 6, and 7 apply to special occupancies, special equipment, or other special conditions. These latter chapters supplement or modify the general rules in Chapters 1 through 4. The requirements for Class 1, Class 2, and Class 3 remote-control, signaling, and power-limited circuits are addressed in Article 725 (Chapter 7). Section 725.3 gives users of the *Code* specific conditions and *Code* references where this Chapter 7 article is to apply to articles and *Code* sections other than in Article 725. Two new conditions with Code references were added to the existing ten conditions identified at 725.3 for the 2014 *NEC*.

The addition of Subsection (K) for "Installation of Conductors with Other Systems" gives a *Code* reference of 300.8. This *Code* reference will assure that cables installed in compliance of Article 725 in raceways or cable trays will not be run with any pipe, tube, or equal for steam, water, air, gas, drainage, or any service other than electrical.

The addition of Subsection (L) for "Corrosive, Damp, or Wet Locations" requires compliance with 110.11; 300.5(B); 300.6; 300.9; and 310.10(G). Section 110.11

725.3(K) and (L)

Continued

(H) Raceways Exposed to Different Temperatures.

(I) Vertical Support for Fire-Rated Cables and Conductors.

(J) Bushing.

(K) Installation of Conductors with Other Systems. Installations shall comply with 300.8.

(L) Corrosive, Damp, or Wet Locations. Class 2 and Class 3 cables, installed in corrosive, damp, or wet locations, shall comply with the applicable requirements in 110.11, 300.5(B), 300.6, 300.9, and 310.10(G). *(See NEC for complete text)*

Proposal 3-122a, 3-154, 3-163

Comment 3-46

addresses conductors or equipment required to be identified for the application where exposed to gases, fumes, vapors, liquids, or other agents that have a deteriorating effect on the conductors or equipment. Section 300.5(G) declares the interior of enclosures or raceways installed underground to be a wet location. Section 300.6 requires raceways, cable trays, boxes, etc., to be of materials suitable for the environment in which they are to be installed (protection against corrosion and deterioration). Section 300.9 stipulates that the interior of raceways are to be considered a wet location where raceways are installed in wet locations abovegrade. Section 310.10(G) requires conductors exposed to oils, greases, vapors, gases, fumes, liquids, or other substances having a deleterious effect on the conductor or insulation to be of a type suitable for the application. New 725.3(L) will assure that Class 2, and Class 3 circuits installed in corrosive, damp, and wet locations are identified for these conditions. These two new subsections were necessary to insure safe and compliant applications where Class 1, Class 2, and Class 3 cables and conductors are installed in any of the referenced conditions.

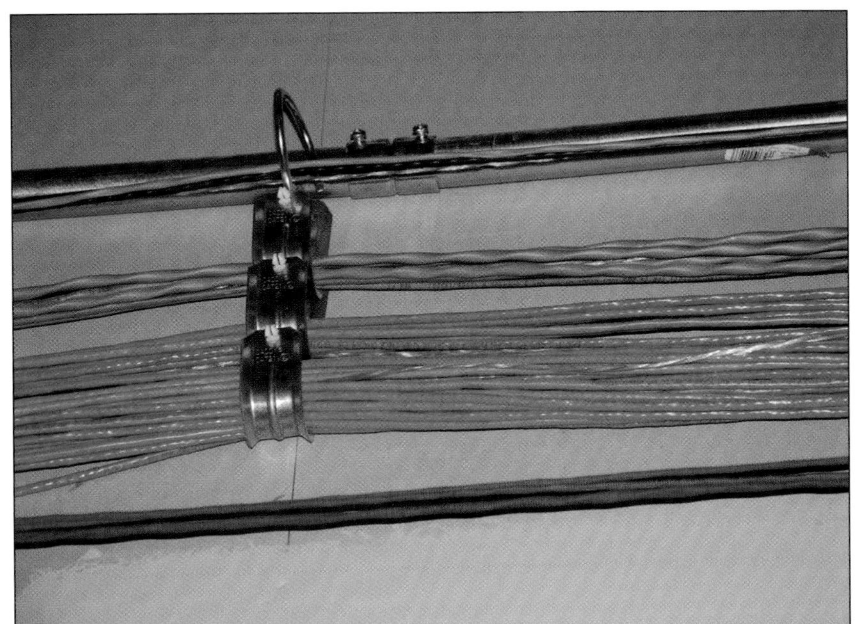

725.154 and Table 725.154

Change at a Glance

Section 725.154 and subsections were revised and reference new Table 725.154 entitled "Applications of Listed Class 2, Class 3 and PLTC Cables in Buildings."

Code Language

725.154 Applications of Listed Class 2, Class 3, and PLTC Cables.

725.154 Applications of Listed Class 2, Class 3, and PLTC Cables. Class 2, Class 3, and PLTC cables shall comply with any of the requirements described in 725.154(A) through ~~(I)~~ (C) and as indicated in Table 725.154.

~~**(A) Plenums.**~~ ***[Now 725.135(B) and (C)]***

~~**(B) Risers.**~~ ***[Now 725.135(D),)F), and (G)]***

~~**(C) Cable Trays.**~~ ***[Now 725.135(H)]***

~~**(D) Industrial Establishments.**~~ ***[Now 725.135(J)]***

~~**(E) Other Wiring Within Building.**~~ ***[Now 725.135(K), (L), and (M)]***

~~**(F) Cross-Connect Arrays.**~~ ***[Now 725.135(I)]***

~~(G)~~ (A) Class 2 and Class 3 Cable Substitutions.

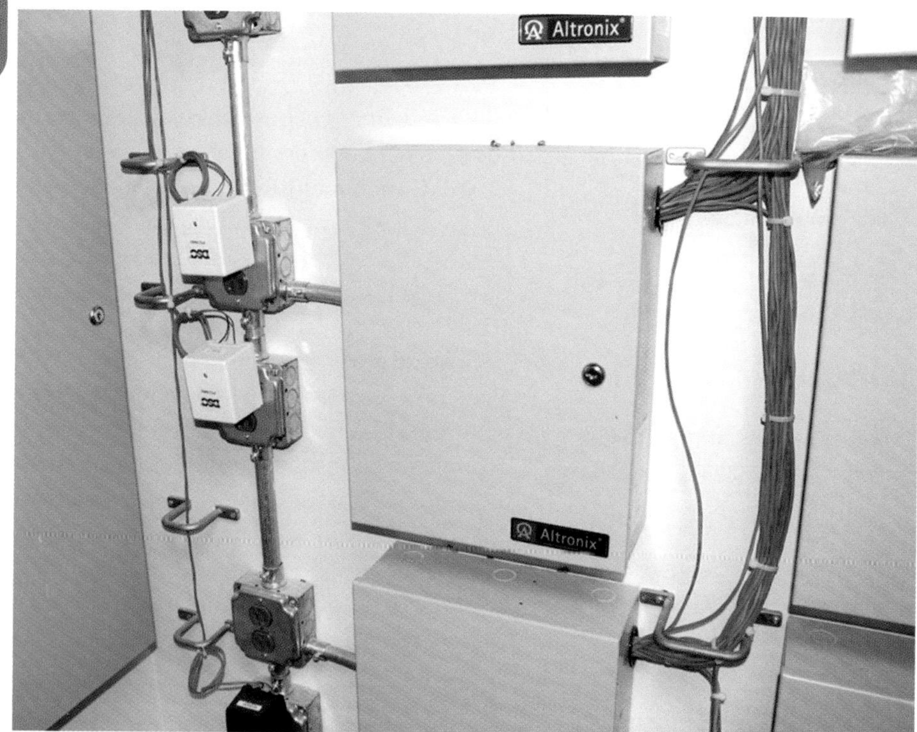

2011 *NEC* Requirement

The application requirements for Class 2, Class 3, and power-limited tray cables (PLTC) were addressed at 725.154(A) through (I). These subsections addressed plenums, risers, cable trays, industrial establishments, other wiring within buildings, cross-connect arrays, Class 2 and Class 3 cable substitutions, Class 2, Class 3, PLTC circuit integrity (CI) cable or electrical circuit protective systems, and thermocouple circuits.

2014 *NEC* Change

The application requirements for Class 2, Class 3, and power-limited tray cables (PLTC) were revised for clarity and reduced to 725.154(A) through (C). What remains at 725.154 covers Class 2 and Class 3 cable substitutions; Class 2, Class 3, PLTC circuit integrity (CI) cable or electrical circuit protective systems; and thermocouple circuits. The remainder of the previous requirements at former 725.154 was re-located to new 725.135 entitled, "Installation of Class 2, Class 3 and PLTC Cables." A new Table 725.154 entitled, "Applications of Listed Class 2, Class 3 and PLTC Cables in Buildings" follows these requirements with simplified, descriptive requirements in an easy-to-read table format.

Analysis of Change

The title of 725.154 is "Applications of Listed Class 2, Class 3, and PLTC Cables," yet the section contains numerous installation rules for Class 2, Class 3, and PLTC cables and raceways. The revision of 725.154 separated the application rules from the installation rules by re-locating the installation rules to a new 725.135 entitled, "Installation of Class 2, Class 3 and PLTC Cables." A new Table 725.154 entitled, "Applications of Listed Class 2, Class 3 and PLTC Cables in Buildings" was also added to present the application rules in table format to improve the readability and usability of the *Code*. A note at the bottom of the new table indicates: "An "N" in the table indicates that the cable type shall not be permitted to be installed in the application. A "Y*" indicates that the cable shall

725.154 and Table 725.154

Continued

~~(H)~~ (B) Class 2, Class 3, PLTC Circuit Integrity (CI) Cable or Electrical Circuit Protective System.

~~(I)~~ (C) Thermocouple Circuits.

See NEC for complete text and new Table 725.154.

Proposal 3-154a

Comment 3-63, 3-60, 3-61

be permitted to be installed in the application, subject to the limitations described in 725.130 through 725.143." This new table clearly identifies the permitted and prohibited applications for Class 2, Class 3, and PLTC cables. The previous text only stated the permitted applications and left the user of the *Code* to interpret whether an application is prohibited or simply overlooked. The prohibited applications for Class 2 and Class 3 cables correlate with the prohibited applications of communications cables in Table 800.154(a). This revision at 725.154 makes the application requirements for Class 2, Class 3, and PLTC cables consistent with application rules in Articles 770, 800, 820 and 830.

Table 725.154
Applications of Listed Class 2, Class 3 and PLTC Cables

Applications		Wire and Cable Type					
		CL2P & CL3P	CL2R & CL3R	CL2 & CL3	CL2X & CL3X	CMUC	PLTC
In fabricated ducts as described in 300.22(B)	In fabricated ducts	Y*	N	N	N	N	N
	In metal raceway that complies with 300.22(B)	Y*	Y*	Y*	Y*	N	Y*
In Other Spaces Used for Environmental Air as Described in 300.22(C)	In other spaces used for environmental air	Y*	N	N	N	N	N
	In metal raceway that complies with 300.22(C)	Y*	Y*	Y*	Y*	N	Y*
	In plenum communications raceways	Y*	N	N	N	N	N
	In plenum cable routing assemblies	NOT PERMITTED					
	Supported by open metal cable trays	Y*	N	N	N	N	N
	Supported by solid bottom metal cable trays with solid metal covers	Y*	Y*	Y*	Y*	N	Y*
In Risers	In vertical runs	Y*	Y*	N	N	N	N
	In metal raceways	Y*	Y*	Y*	Y*	N	Y*
	In fireproof shafts	Y*	Y*	Y*	Y*	N	Y*
	In plenum communications raceways	Y*	Y*	N	N	N	N
	In plenum cable routing assemblies	Y*	Y*	N	N	N	N
	In riser communications raceways	Y*	Y*	N	N	N	N
	In riser cable routing assemblies	Y*	Y*	N	N	N	N
	In one- and two-family dwellings	Y*	Y*	Y*	Y*	N	Y*
Within buildings in other than air-handling spaces and risers	General	Y*	Y*	Y*	Y*	N	Y*
	In one- and two-family dwellings	Y*	Y*	Y*	Y*	Y*	Y*
	In multifamily dwellings	Y*	Y*	Y*	Y*	Y*	Y*
	In nonconcealed spaces	Y*	Y*	Y*	Y*	Y*	Y*
	Supported by cable trays	Y*	Y*	Y*	N	N	Y*
	Under carpet	N	N	N	N	Y*	N
	In cross-connect arrays	Y*	Y*	Y*	N	N	Y*
	In any raceway recognized in Chapter 3	Y*	Y*	Y*	Y*	N	Y*
	In plenum communications raceways	Y*	Y*	Y*	N	N	Y*
	In plenum cable routing assemblies	Y*	Y*	Y*	N	N	Y*
	In riser communications raceways	Y*	Y*	Y*	N	N	Y*
	In riser cable routing assemblies	Y*	Y*	Y*	N	N	Y*
	In general-purpose communications raceways	Y*	Y*	Y*	N	N	Y*
	In general-purpose cable routing assemblies	Y*	Y*	Y*	N	N	Y*

Note: An "N" in the table indicates that the cable type shall not be permitted to be installed in the application. A "Y*" indicates that the cable shall be permitted to be installed in the application, subject to the limitations described in 725.130 and 725.143.

725.179(F)

Change at a Glance

Section 725.179(F) has been split into two list items for establishing cable survivability. Cables are tested either as CI cables or as part of an electrical circuit protective system.

Code Language

725.179 Listing and Marking of Class 2, Class 3, Type PLTC Cables, and Signaling Raceways.

Class 2, Class 3, and Type PLTC cables, nonmetallic ~~signaling~~ communications raceways, and cable routing assemblies installed as wiring methods within buildings shall be listed as being resistant to the spread of fire and other criteria in accordance with 725.179(A) through ~~(K)~~ (I) and shall be marked in accordance with 725.179~~(L)~~ (I).

(F) Circuit Integrity (CI) Cable or Electrical Circuit Protective System. Cables that are used for survivability of critical circuits under fire conditions shall ~~be listed as circuit integrity (CI) cable~~ meet either 725.179(F)(1) or (F)(2) as follows:

(1) Circuit Integrity (CI) Cables. Circuit Integrity (CI) cables, specified in 725.154(A), (B), (D)(1), and (E), and used for survivability of critical circuits, shall have the additional classification using the suffix "-CI." Circuit integrity (CI) cables shall only be permitted to be installed in a raceway where

725.179(F) Listing and Marking of Circuit Integrity (CI) Cable or Electrical Circuit Protective System

725.179(F) has been split into two list items for establishing cable survivability.

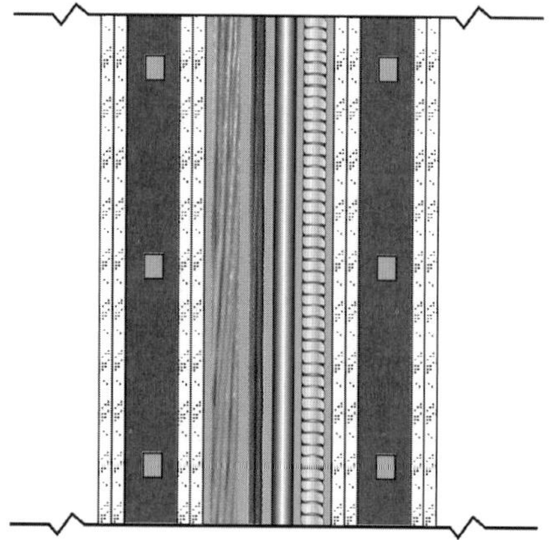

Electrical Circuit Protective System

Circuit Integrity (CI) Cable

Cables are either tested as a circuit integrity (CI) cables or tested as part of an electrical circuit protective system.

2011 *NEC* Requirement

Class 2, Class 3, and Type PLTC cables along with nonmetallic signaling raceways installed as wiring methods within buildings are required to be listed as being resistant to the spread of fire. These cables and wiring methods had to meet the provisions of 725.179(A) through (L). Cables used for survivability of critical circuits had to be listed as circuit integrity (CI) cable. Cables that are part of a listed electrical circuit protective system are considered to meet the requirements of survivability.

2014 *NEC* Change

The two cable survivability methods at 725.179(F) were divided into two separate list items. Provisions for circuit integrity (CI) cables are now found at 725.179(F)(1), and requirements for electrical circuit protective systems are now addressed at 725.179(F)(2).

Analysis of Change

Two methods of establishing cable survivability for Class 2, Class 3, and Type PLTC cables are described at 725.179(F). The requirements for each method were separated into two list items for the 2014 *NEC*. These two methods are circuit integrity (CI) cables and electrical circuit protective systems. *Circuit integrity (CI)* cables are defined at 725.2 as "Cable(s) used for remote-control, signaling, or power-limited systems that supply critical circuits to ensure survivability for continued circuit operation for a specified time under fire conditions." *Electrical circuit protective systems* are defined at both 770.2 and 800.2 as "A system consisting of components and materials intended for installation as protection for specific electrical wiring systems with respect to the disruption of electrical circuit integrity upon exterior fire exposure."

These survivability cables are tested and identified as either *circuit integrity (CI) cable,* or are tested and identified as part of an *electrical circuit protective*

725.179(F)

Continued

specifically listed and marked as ~~that are~~ part of ~~a listed~~ an electrical circuit protective system as covered in 725.179(F)(2) ~~shall be considered to meet the requirements of survivability~~.

(2) Electrical Circuit Protective System. Cables specified in 725.154(A), (B), (D)(1), (E), and (F)(1) that are part of an electrical circuit protective system shall be identified with the protective system number and hourly rating printed on the outer jacket of the cable and installed in accordance with the listing of the protective system.

Informational Note No. 1: One method of defining circuit integrity (CI) cable or an electrical circuit protective system is by establishing a minimum 2-hour fire-~~resistance~~ resistive rating when tested in accordance with UL 2196-2012, Standard for Tests of Fire Resistive Cables.

Informational Note No. 2: UL guide information for electrical circuit protective systems (FHIT) contains information on proper installation requirements to maintain the fire rating.

Proposal 3-165

Comment 3-74, 3-75

system. The UL Guide Information (White Book), under the category code (FHIT) Electrical Circuit Protective Systems states that "CI cable is tested on steel rings to simulate installation in free air. If CI cable is intended to be installed in a raceway it is so tested. CI cable that has been tested in a raceway will be specified in the system." The FHIT category covers Electrical Circuit Protective Systems consisting of components and materials intended for installation as protection for specific electrical wiring systems, with respect to the disruption of electrical circuit integrity upon external fire exposure. This category deals with systems designed to maintain circuit integrity under fire conditions.

The new text at the two separate list items clarifies the two cable options and marking separate requirements for same. Similar changes occurred at 760.179(G) for fire alarm systems. See Proposal 3-210 and Comment 3-111.

Article 728

Change at a Glance

New article entitled "Fire-Resistive Cable Systems" has been added to address installations of fire-resistive cables.

Code Language

Article 728 Fire-Resistive Cable Systems

728.1 Scope.

728.2 Definition.

728.3 Other Articles.

728.4 General.

728.5 Installations.

(A) Mounting.
(B) Supports.
(C) Raceways and Couplings.
(D) Cable Tray.
(E) Boxes.
(F) Pulling Lubricants.
(G) Vertical Supports.
(H) Splices.

728.60 Grounding.

728.120 Marking.

(See NEC for complete text)

Proposal 3-170

Comment 3-79 thru 3-83, 3-83a, 3-83b

Article 728 Fire-Resistive Cable Systems

A new article titled "Fire Resistive Cable Systems" had been added to the 2014 *NEC* to address installations of fire resistive cables.

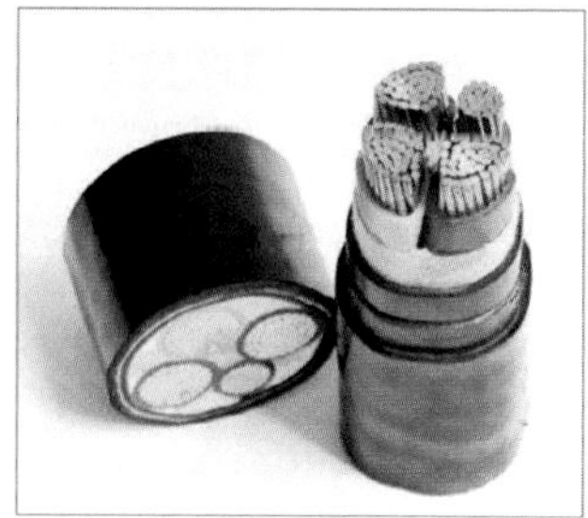

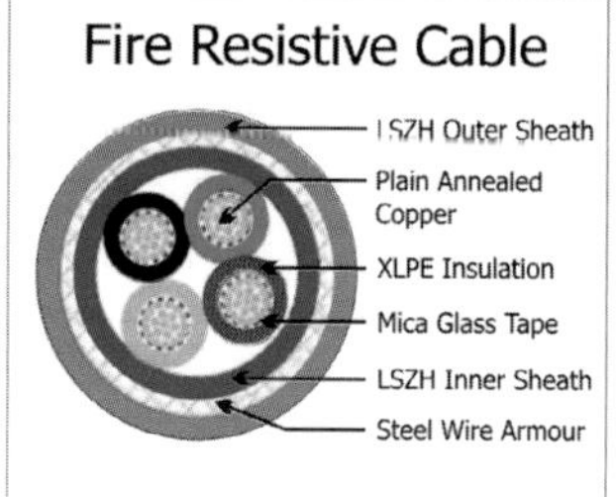

2011 *NEC* Requirement

This is a new article that did not appear in the 2011 *NEC*.

2014 *NEC* Change

A new article entitled "Fire-Resistive Cable Systems" has been added to address installations of fire-resistive cables. This new article informs the installer that there are different details when installing fire rated cables. These systems must be installed in accordance with very specific materials, supports, and requirements and are critical for the survivability of life safety circuits.

Analysis of Change

A new article for "Fire-Resistive Cable Systems" has been added in the 2014 *NEC* to address installations of fire-resistive cables. The installations of these cables are critical to their ability to function during a fire. These systems must be installed in accordance with very specific materials, supports, and requirements and are critical for the survivability of life safety circuits. There are diverse details for installing fire rated cables that differ from other type cables. Some of these variances pertain to conduit, conduit supports, type of couplings, vertical supports and boxes and splices. This new article is intended to help the user of the *Code* with installation requirements for these cable systems. Without these details being included in the *NEC,* the installer and the enforcement community could be left uninformed.

In addition to the marking required in 310.120, fire-resistive cable system cables and conductors are required to be surface marked with the suffix "-FRR" (Fire Resistive Rating). These fire-resistive cables must also be marked with the circuit integrity duration in hours and with the system identifier.

Article 750

Change at a Glance

New article, "Energy Management Systems," was added to address the types of loads permitted to be controlled through energy management systems.

Code Language

Article 750 Energy Management Systems

750.1 Scope.

750.2 Definitions.

750.20 Alternate Power Sources.

750.30 Load Management.

(A) Load Shedding Controls.

(B) Disconnection of Power.

(C) Capacity of Branch Circuit, Feeder, or Service.

750.50 Field Markings.

Proposal 13-180

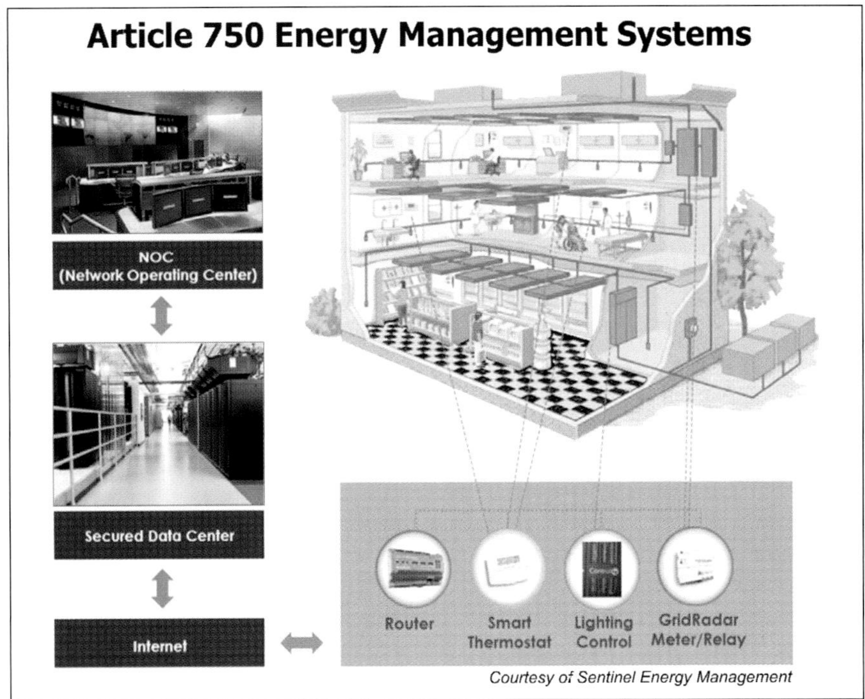

Courtesy of Sentinel Energy Management

2011 *NEC* Requirement

This did not exist in the 2011 *NEC*.

2014 *NEC* Change

A new article was added, which includes definitions, requirements for alternative-power sources, load-management provisions and field-marking requirements. The article provides a good basis for inclusion of general requirements to address the types of loads permitted to be controlled through energy management.

Analysis of Change

This new article for "Energy Management Systems" provides some general requirements to address the types of loads permitted to be controlled through an energy management system. Energy management has become commonplace in today's electrical infrastructure through the control of utilization equipment, energy storage, and power production. Installation codes currently establish requirements for utilization equipment, energy storage, and power production that serve to address facility and personnel safety. However, limited consideration has been given in installation codes to actively managing these systems as a means to reduce energy cost or to support peak power needs for a much broader electrical infrastructure demand. An important aspect to consider in regards to an energy management system is to make sure an overall energy management system does not override a system specific to addressing load shedding for an alternate power source for such things as fire pumps and emergency systems. Restricting the control of certain basic functions in a building by the energy management system becomes critical to ensure safety. As an example, turning off ventilation systems for hazardous materials or de-energizing a moving walkway, causing someone to fall, are examples of where energy load management control needs to be restricted in the *NEC*.

This article resulted from the work of the Smart Grid Task Group appointed by the NEC Correlating Committee.

760.24

Change at a Glance

"Mechanical Execution of Work" requirements for fire alarm systems have been divided into two subsections and requirements for circuit integrity (CI) cables added.

Code Language

760.24 Mechanical Execution of Work

(A) General. Fire alarm circuits shall be installed in a neat workmanlike manner. Cables and conductors installed exposed on the surface of ceilings and sidewalls shall be supported by the building structure in such a manner that the cable will not be damaged by normal building use. Such cables shall be supported by straps, staples, cable ties, hangers, or similar fittings designed and installed so as not to damage the cable. The installation shall also comply with 300.4(D).

(B) Circuit Integrity (CI) Cable. Circuit integrity (CI) cables shall be supported at a distance not exceeding 610 mm (24 in.). Where located within 2.1 m (7 ft) of the floor, as covered in 760.53(A)(1) and 760.130(B)(1), as applicable, the cable shall be fastened in an approved manner at intervals of not more than 450 mm (18 in.). Cable supports and fasteners shall be steel.

Proposal 3-178

760.24 Mechanical Execution of Work

"Mechanical Execution of Work" requirements for fire alarm systems have been divided into two subsections and requirements for circuit integrity (CI) cables added.

Structure
Steel cable supports
Ductwork
Ceiling
Heat detector
Smoke detector
FACP
FIRE
Horn and light
FIRE
PULL
Pull station

2011 *NEC* Requirement

Fire alarm circuits have to be installed in a neat workmanlike manner. Fire alarm cables and conductors installed exposed on the surface of ceilings and sidewalls are required to be supported by the building structure in such a manner that the cable(s) will not be damaged by normal building use. These cables must also be supported by straps, staples, cable ties, hangers, or similar fittings designed and installed so as not to damage the cable. The installation of these cables must also comply with 300.4(D) for cables and raceways installed parallel to framing members (metal nail protectors).

2014 *NEC* Change

The 2011 *NEC* general provisions for mechanical execution of work for fire alarm systems were brought forward for the 2014 *NEC*. New provisions for "Circuit Integrity (CI) Cable" were added to new 760.24(B). Circuit integrity (CI) cables for fire alarm systems are required to be supported at a distance not exceeding 610 mm (24 in.). Where these cables are located within 2.1 m (7 ft) of the floor, the cable must be fastened in an approved manner at intervals of not more than 450 mm (18 in.). The fire alarm cable supports and fasteners must be made of steel.

Analysis of Change

Section 760.24 has been revised into two separate list items with the existing general "Mechanical Execution of Work" text becoming new 760.24(A). New 760.24(B) addresses "Circuit Integrity (CI) Cable" which references 760.53(A)(1) and 760.130(B)(1) to provide direction to the user when installing circuit integrity cables in an exposed application located within 2.1 m (7 ft) of the floor. *Fire alarm circuit integrity* (CI) *cable* is defined at 760.2 as "Cable used in fire alarm systems to ensure continued operation of critical circuits during a specified time under fire conditions."

760.24

Continued

The circuit integrity cable listing requirements provide support distances not exceeding 610 mm (24 in.) on the surface of the structure. This distance of 610 mm (24 in.) is the distance that the support or steel rings are spaced during the product standard circuit integrity fire test. The supports need to be steel because plastic or aluminum supports would melt under fire conditions. The UL product standard for fire-resistive cables, UL 2196, *Tests for Fire Resistive Cables* requires CI cable to be supported every 610 mm (24 in.) on steel rings. In order for CI cables to survive and continue to function during a fire, the cable must be supported more frequently than normal fire alarm cables and must be attached to a fire rated surface or structure that has an equivalent hourly fire rating as the CI cable.

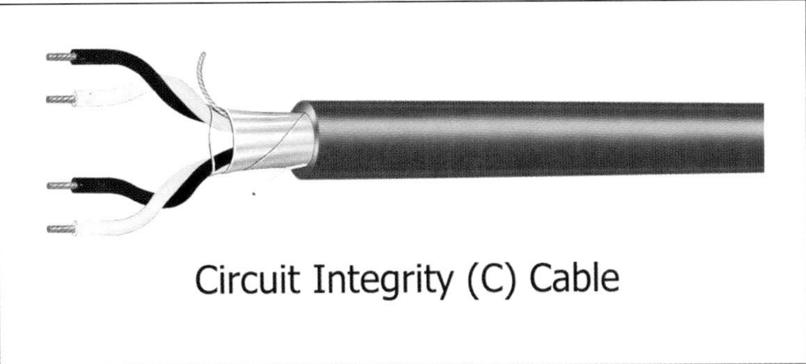

770.110

Change at a Glance

The title of 770.110 was revised to "Raceways and Cable Routing Assemblies for Optical Fiber Cables." New 770.110(C) was added to include provisions for "Cable Routing Assemblies."

Code Language

770.110 Raceways and Cable Routing Assemblies for Optical Fiber Cables.

(A) Types of Raceways.
(1) Raceways Recognized in Chapter 3.
(2) Communications ~~Other Permitted~~ Raceways.

(B) Raceway Fill for Optical Fiber Cables.
(1) Without Electric Light or Power Conductors.
(2) Nonconductive Optical Fiber Cables with Electric Light or Power Conductors.

(C) Cable Routing Assemblies.
(1) Horizontal Support.
(2) Vertical Support.

(See *NEC* for complete text)

Proposal 16-57, 16-58

Comment 16-31, 16-28, 16-29, 16-30, 16-32, 16.33

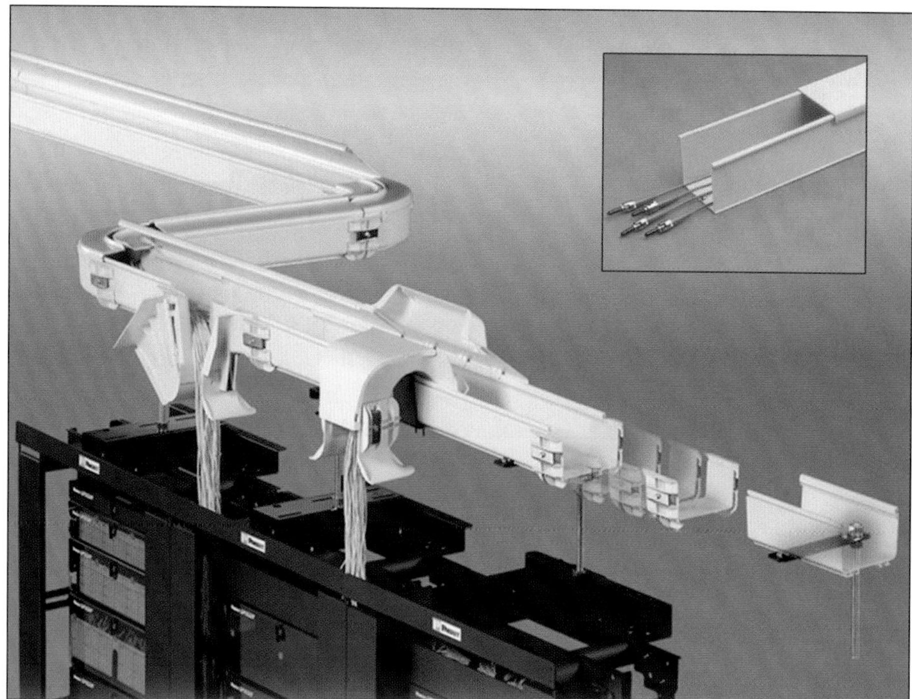

2011 *NEC* Requirement

For the 2011 *NEC*, 770.110 addressed raceways for optical fiber cables installed within a building. These provisions dealt with the types of raceways permitted to be used with optical fiber cables. These raceways included raceways recognized in Chapter 3 as well as other permitted raceways such as listed plenum optical fiber raceways, listed plenum communications raceways, listed riser optical fiber raceways, listed riser communications raceways, listed general-purpose optical fiber raceways, or listed general-purpose communications raceways. Section 770.110(B) contains rules for raceway fill for optical fiber cables. Where optical fiber cables are installed in raceway without electric light or power conductors, the raceway fill requirements of Chapters 3 and 9 shall not apply.

2014 *NEC* Change

Besides the existing requirements for raceways for optical fiber cables installed within a building, provisions were added at 770.110(C) for "Cable Routing Assemblies." These new provisions make it clear that optical fiber cables are permitted to be installed in plenum cable routing assemblies, riser cable routing assemblies, and general-purpose cable routing assemblies. The existing title of "Other Permitted Raceways" used at 770.110(A)(2) has been replaced with the title "Communication Raceways." *Communication raceway* is a defined term in Article 800 that was added for the 2011 *NEC*.

Analysis of Change

In Chapters 7 and 8 of the *NEC*, several types of raceways are addressed: such as, optical fiber raceways, communication raceways, and CATV raceways. These raceways are actually identical raceways with different markings. During the 2011 *NEC* development process, CMP-16 eliminated *CATV raceways* and replaced this term with *communication raceway*. The existing title of "Other Permitted Raceways" used at 770.110(A)(2) has been replaced with the title "Communication Raceways." *Communications raceway* is defined at 800.2 as

770.110

Continued

"An enclosed channel of nonmetallic materials designed expressly for holding wires and cables, typically communications wires and cables and optical fiber and data (Class 2 and Class 3) cables in plenum, riser, and general-purpose applications." This revision, along with other companion proposals will delete *optical fiber raceways* and leave one type of raceway, *communications raceways*, to be used for optical fiber, communications, and CATV cable use. This will simplify the types of raceways specified in Articles 770, 800 and 820.

Another change that occurred at 770.110 was the addition of Subsection (C) to include provisions for "Cable Routing Assemblies." A revised definition was relocated to Article 100 for *cable routing assemblies*, which is defined as "A single channel or connected multiple channels, as well as associated fittings, forming a structural system that is used to support and route communications wires and cables, optical fiber cables, data cables associated with information technology and communications equipment, Class 2 and Class 3 cables, and power-limited fire alarm cables." The term *cable routing assemblies* was introduced in the 2011 *NEC* at 770.2 with installation rules described at 770.113; 800.113; 820.113; and 830.113. These installation rules at 770.113 have been removed from that section and inserted at 770.110(C). In order to separate the installation rules for optical fiber cables from the installation rules from raceways for optical fiber cables, the rules for raceways for optical fiber cables were expanded to include cable routing assemblies.

770.154 and Table 770.154(a)

Change at a Glance

Revisions to 770.154 and Table 770.154(a) delete references to raceways and cable routing assemblies.

Code Language

770.154 Applications of Listed Optical Fiber Cables

770.154 Applications of Listed Optical Fiber Cables ~~and Raceways, and Cable Routing Assemblies~~.

Permitted and nonpermitted applications of listed optical fiber cables ~~and raceways, and cable routing assembly types~~ shall be as indicated in Table 770.154(a) ~~on the following page~~. The permitted applications shall be subject to the installation requirements of 770.110 and 770.113. The substitutions for optical fiber cables in Table 770.154(b) and illustrated in Figure 770.154 shall be permitted.

Table 770.154(a) Applications of Listed Optical Fiber Cables ~~and Raceways, and Cable Routing Assemblies~~ in Buildings

[See NEC for revised Table 770.154(a)] The following are Informational Notes to Table 770.154(a).

Informational Note 1: Part V of Article 770 covers installation methods within buildings. This table covers the applications of listed optical fiber cables ~~and raceways and cable routing as-~~

770.154 and Table 770.154(a) Applications of Listed Optical Fiber Cables

Revisions to 770.154 and Table 770.154(a) delete references to raceways and cable routing assemblies.

770.154 Applications of Listed Optical Fiber Cables ~~and Raceways, and Cable Routing Assemblies~~

Table 770.154(a) Applications of Listed Optical Fiber Cables ~~and Raceways, and Cable Routing Assemblies~~ in Buildings

References to optical fiber raceways, and cable routing assemblies were relocated to other appropriate sections of Article 770.

2011 *NEC* Requirement

For the 2011 *NEC*, Section 770.154 and Table 770.154(a) had permitted and non-permitted applications for listed optical fiber cables and raceways, and cable routing assembly types.

2014 *NEC* Change

References to optical fiber raceways, and cable routing assemblies were removed from 770.154 and Table 770.154(a) and were relocated to other appropriate sections of Article 770. A new Informational Note to Table 770.154(a) was added to inform users of the *Code* that cable routing assemblies are not addressed in NFPA-90A-2012, *Standard for the Installation of Air Conditioning and Ventilation Systems*.

Analysis of Change

Revisions to 770.154 and Table 770.154(a) deleted references to optical fiber raceways and cable routing assemblies. A revised definition was relocated to Article 100 for *cable routing assemblies*, which are defined as "A single channel or connected multiple channels, as well as associated fittings, forming a structural system that is used to support and route communications wires and cables, optical fiber cables, data cables associated with information technology and communications equipment, Class 2 and Class 3 cables, and power-limited fire alarm cables." The term *cable routing assemblies* was introduced in the 2011 *NEC* at 700.2 with installation rules described at 770.113; 800.113; 820.113; and 830.113. The listing of cable routing assemblies was covered twice in the 2011 *NEC*: in 770.182 and in 800.182. Deleting 770.182 removed this redundancy. Since the listing requirements for cable routing assemblies are covered at 800.182 and have been deleted from 770.182, the applications of cable routing assemblies have be moved from 770.154 to 800.154. Table 770.154(a) has been revised by deleting the five columns on the right (riser and general-purpose cable routing assemblies and plenum, riser and general-purpose optical fiber race-

770.154 and Table 770.154(a)

Continued

~~semblies~~ in buildings. The definition of Point of Entrance is in 770.2. Optical fiber entrance cables that have not emerged from the rigid metal conduit (RMC) or intermediate metal conduit (IMC) are not considered to be in the building.

Informational Note No. 2: For information on the restrictions to the installation of optical fiber cables in fabricated ducts, see 770.113(B).

Informational Note No. 3: Cable routing assemblies are not addressed in NFPA-90A-2012, *Standard for the Installation of Air Conditioning and Ventilation Systems.*

Proposal 16-71, 16-72, 16-73, 16-74

ways). Applications have been added at this table for plenum cable routing assemblies. Applications of optical fiber raceways have been deleted.

770.180

Change at a Glance

New 770.180, Grounding Devices has been added for listing requirements (*or be part of listed equipment*) for grounding devices used for optical fiber cables.

Code Language

770.180 Grounding Devices. Where bonding or grounding is required, devices used to connect a shield, sheath, or non–current-carrying metallic members of a cable to a bonding conductor or grounding electrode conductor shall be listed or be part of listed equipment.

Proposal 16-80

770.180 Grounding Devices

New 770.180 "Grounding Devices" has been added for listing requirements (or be part of listed equipment) for grounding devices used for optical fiber cables.

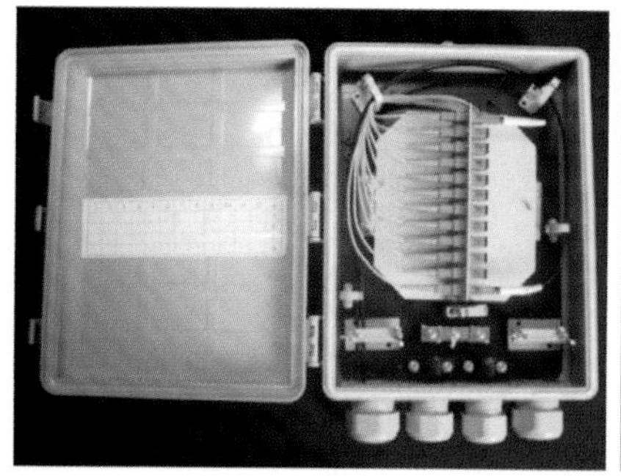

This same new listing requirement (Grounding Devices) has been implemented at the following locations:

800.180	Communications Circuits
810.7	Radio and Television Equipment
820.180	Community Antenna Television and Radio Distribution Systems
830.180	Network-Powered Broadband Communications Systems
840.180	Premises-Powered Broadband Communications Systems

2011 *NEC* Requirement

Grounding devices for optical fiber cables and listing of same was not covered in Article 770 in the 2011 *NEC*.

2014 *NEC* Change

A new section was added to Article 770 with requirements for grounding devices used for optical fiber cables. This new section stipulates that devices used to connect a shield, sheath, or non–current-carrying metallic members of an optical fiber cable to a bonding conductor or grounding electrode conductor (where bonding or grounding is required) must be listed or be part of listed equipment.

Analysis of Change

Proper, effective, and reliable grounding and bonding are critical for "the practical safeguarding of persons and property from hazards arising from the use of electricity." This is required and demonstrated throughout the *NEC*. Although requirements exist in Article 770 that specify when grounding or bonding of a shield, sheath or non–current-carrying metallic members of an optical fiber cable are required, there was no requirement that the devices used for this grounding and bonding application should be listed for that purpose. There are currently listed devices and grounding devices that are part of listed equipment that comply with UL 467, *Grounding and Bonding Equipment* that ensures the grounding or bonding connection meets construction and performance criteria necessary for reliable bonding and grounding. Without this new listing requirement at 770.180, the grounding and bonding connection would go undefined. Without using a device listed for this application, poor connections due to questionable installation methods (e.g., wrapping the conductor around a cable sheath) can increase twofold. Employing devices that do not have the necessary strength to maintain a solid connection, or utilizing materials unsuitable for the application can add to unsatisfactory connections as well.

770.180

Continued

This same new listing requirement (Grounding Devices) has been implemented at the following locations:

800.180	Communications Circuits	Proposal 16-139
810.7	Radio and Television Equipment	Proposal 16-145
820.180	Community Antenna Television and Radio Distribution Systems	Proposal 16-211
830.180	Network-Powered Broadband Communications Systems	Proposal 16-258
840.180	Premises-Powered Broadband Communications Systems	Proposal 16-285

8

800.2

Change at a Glance

Definition of *point of entrance* has been revised by deleting "connected by a bonding conductor or grounding electrode in accordance with 800.100(B)."

Code Language

800.2 Definitions: Point of Entrance

The point within a building at which the communication wire or cable emerges from an external wall, from a concrete floor slab, or from a rigid metal conduit (Type RMC) or an intermediate metal conduit (Type IMC) ~~connected by a bonding conductor or grounding electrode in accordance with 800.100(B)~~.

Proposal 16-88, 16-89, 16-90

800.2 Definitions: Point of Entrance

Definition of "Point of Entrance" has been revised by deleting grounding and bonding requirement "connected by a bonding conductor or grounding electrode in accordance with 800.100(B)" from definition.

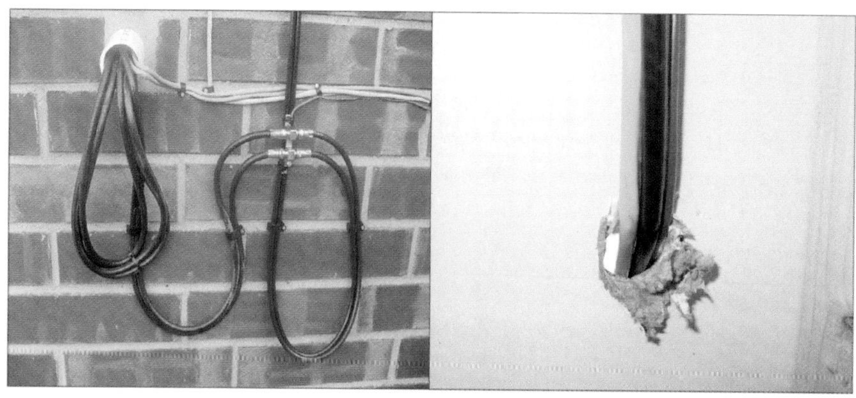

This same revision occurred at the definition of "Point of Entrance" at the following locations:

820.2	Community Antenna Television and Radio Distribution Systems
830.2	Network-Powered Broadband Communications Systems

2011 *NEC* Requirement

Point of entrance was defined at 800.2 in the 2011 *NEC* as "The point within a building at which the wire or cable emerges from an external wall, from a concrete floor slab, or from a rigid metal conduit (Type RMC) or an intermediate metal conduit (Type IMC) connected by a bonding conductor or grounding electrode in accordance with 800.100(B)."

2014 *NEC* Change

This definition was revised to identify that the wire or cable that emerges from an external wall is indeed a "communication" wire or cable. The phrase, "connected by a bonding conductor or grounding electrode in accordance with 800.100(B)" has been removed as well.

Analysis of Change

The *NEC Style Manual* prohibits a definition from containing requirements or recommendations in the said definition (see Section 2.2.2 of the *NEC Style Manual*). Some users of the *Code* viewed the 2011 *NEC* definition of *point of entrance* as having a grounding requirement in the last part of the definition. A CMP-16 Definitions Task Group reviewed all definitions in Articles 770; 800; 810; 820; 830; and 840 to correct errors and to establish new definitions where needed. This task group recommended to CMP-16 to remove this grounding requirement from 800.2 and to relocate this needed requirement to a new 800.49 entitled, "Metallic Entrance Conduit Grounding." Further revision occurred to this definition by identifying the wire or cable that emerges from an external wall as a "communication" wire or cable.

This same revision occurred at the definition of *point of entrance* at 820.2 for Community Antenna Television (CATV) and Radio Distribution Systems (see Proposal 16-159), and at 830.2 for Network-Powered Broadband Communications Systems (see Proposal 16-217).

800.12

Change at a Glance

A new definition and new provisions have been added for *Innerduct*.

Code Language

800.12 Innerduct.

Listed plenum communications raceway, listed riser communications raceway, and listed general-purpose communications raceway selected in accordance with the provisions of Table 800.154(b) shall be permitted to be installed as innerduct in any type of listed raceway permitted in Chapter 3.

800.2 Definitions.

Innerduct. A nonmetallic raceway placed within a larger raceway.

Proposal 16-97, 16–87

Comment 16-42

800.12 Innerduct

A new definition and new section for "Innerduct" have been added permitting listed communications raceways to be installed as innerduct in any type of listed raceway permitted in Chapter 3.

800.2 Definitions: Innerduct - A nonmetallic raceway placed within a larger raceway

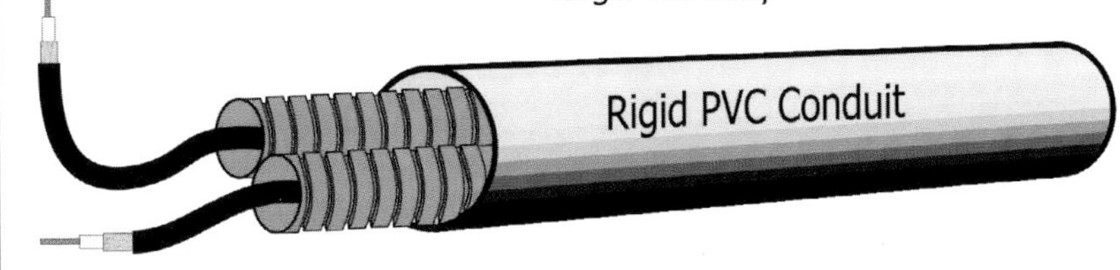

2011 *NEC* Requirement

In the 2011 *NEC*, the term, *innerduct* appeared at 770.12 for optical fiber cable and raceways. There was no definition for *innerduct.*

2014 *NEC* Change

A new requirement for "Innerduct" was added at 800.12. This new provision permits the different types of listed communications raceways to be installed as innerduct in any type of listed raceway permitted in Chapter 3. A new definition for *innerduct* was introduced at 800.2 as, "A nonmetallic raceway placed within a larger raceway," (Building Industry Consulting Service International dictionary).

Analysis of Change

Innerduct is typically manufactured from high density polyethylene (HDPE) and is intended to be placed inside of existing conduits or other innerducts. This product is designed to reduce surface contact when pulling cable. This lightweight product offers maximum flexibility, and allows for installation in small or restricted areas. Innerduct is available in a variety of sizes with 1 in., 1¼ in., and 1½ in. sizes being most common. The standard color is orange, but it is offered in a variety of other colors. Communications raceways are permitted to substitute for optical fiber raceways. Optical fiber raceways are permitted to be used as innerduct; but in previous editions of the *Code*, this permission was only given in Article 770 at 770.12. For the 2014 *NEC*, this permissive text was introduced in Article 800 as well. This change was brought about primarily from the efforts of the CMP-16 Special Editorial Task Group. One of the goals of this task group was to improve the parallelism between related articles such that similar requirements are stated the same way in each article, and that requirements are placed in the appropriate sections.

800.179(G)

Change at a Glance

A revision to 800.179(G) will now contain listing requirements for an "Electrical Circuit Protective System." A new definition for *electrical circuit protective system* has also been added to 800.2.

Code Language

800.179 Communications Wires and Cables.

Communications wires and cables shall be listed in accordance with 800.179(A) through (I) and marked in accordance with Table 800.179. *(See NEC for complete text)*

(G) ~~Communications~~ Circuit Integrity (CI) Cable or Electrical Circuit Protective System. Cables ~~suitable for use in communications systems to ensure~~ that are used for survivability of critical circuits ~~during a specified time~~ under fire conditions shall be listed and meet either 800.179)(G)(1) or (G)(2) as follows:

(1) Circuit Integrity (CI) Cables.

(2) Fire-Resistive Cables.

(See NEC for complete text)

800.2 Definitions: Electrical Circuit Protective System. A system consisting of components and materials intended for installation as protection for specific electrical wiring systems with respect to the disruption of electrical circuit

800.179(G) Communications Circuit Integrity (CI) Cable or Electrical Circuit Protective System

800.179(G) has been revised by adding requirements for "electrical circuit protective systems" and adding two new list items for establishing cable survivability.

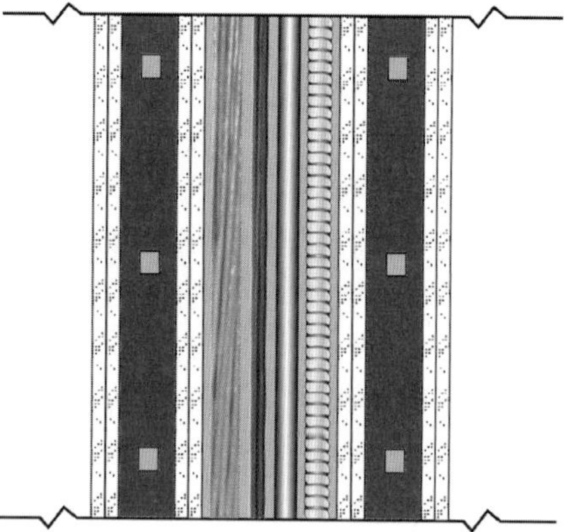

Electrical Circuit Protective System

Fire-Restrictive Communication Cable

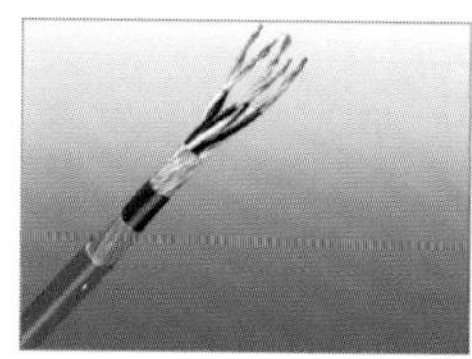

Circuit Integrity (CI) Communication Cable

A revision to 800.179(G) will now contain listing requirements for an "Electrical Circuit Protective System" and a new definition for same has been added to 800.2.

2011 *NEC* Requirement

Cables suitable for use in communications systems to ensure survivability of critical circuits during a specified time under fire conditions were required to be listed as circuit integrity (CI) cable. Cables identified at 800.179(A) through (E) that meet the requirements for circuit integrity must have the additional classification, using the suffix "CI." A definition of *electrical circuit protective system* did not exist in the 2011 *NEC*.

2014 *NEC* Change

The requirements at 800.179(G) were revised by adding requirements for electrical circuit protective systems and by adding two new list items. Section 800.179(G)(1) now covers requirements for "Circuit Integrity (CI) Cables." In addition to an additional classification using the suffix "CI," this new provision specifies that in order to maintain its listed fire rating, circuit integrity (CI) cable shall only be installed in free air. Section 800.179(G)(2) now addresses "Fire-Resistive Cables." This provision requires circuit integrity (CI) cables that are part of an *electrical circuit protective system* to be fire-resistive cables identified with the protective system number and installed in accordance with the listing of the protective system. A new definition for *electrical circuit protective system* was also added to 800.2.

Analysis of Change

The term, *electrical circuit protective system* and its application has been added to the requirements of 800.179(G). The requirements of this subsection were divided into two new list items which separates them into two methods of establishing cable survivability. In accordance with the *UL Guide Information* under the category code FHIT for "Electrical Circuit Protective Systems," communications wires and cables are either tested as circuit integrity (CI) cables or tested as part of an electrical circuit protective system. Circuit integrity (CI) cable is tested on steel rings to simulate installation in free air. If CI cable is intended to be in-

800.179(G)

Continued

integrity upon exterior fire exposure.

Proposal 16-85a, 16-137

Comment 16-40, 16-65

stalled in a raceway, it is so tested as an electrical circuit protective system. The main purpose of this revision is to clarify what an electrical circuit protective system is and what type of circuit integrity (C) cable is part of an electrical circuit protective system.

To coincide with the revisions at 800.179(G), a new definition of *electrical circuit protective system* was also added at 800.2. This new definition states that an *electrical circuit protective system* is "A system consisting of components and materials intended for installation as protection for specific electrical wiring systems with respect to the disruption of electrical circuit integrity upon exterior fire exposure."

800.182

Change at a Glance

Revisions have occurred at 800.182(A), (B), and (C) as to the specific cable routing assembly being discussed in each subsection. Three Informational Notes have been deleted and replaced with one Informational Note.

Code Language

800.182 Communications Raceways and Cable Routing Assemblies.
Communications raceways and cable routing assemblies shall be listed in accordance with 800.182(A) through (C).

Informational Note: For information on listing requirements for both communications raceways and cable routing assemblies, see ANSI/UL 2024-2011, Signaling, Optical Fiber and Communications Raceways and Cable Routing Assemblies.

(A) Plenum Communications Raceways and Plenum Cable Routing Assemblies. Plenum communications raceways and plenum cable routing assemblies ~~listed as plenum optical fiber raceways~~ shall be ~~permitted for use in ducts, plenums, and other spaces used for environmental air and shall also be~~ listed as having adequate fire-resistant and low smoke-producing characteristics.

800.182 Communications Raceways and Cable Routing Assemblies

800.182(A), (B), and (C) were revised to reference the specific cable routing assembly being discussed in each subsection.

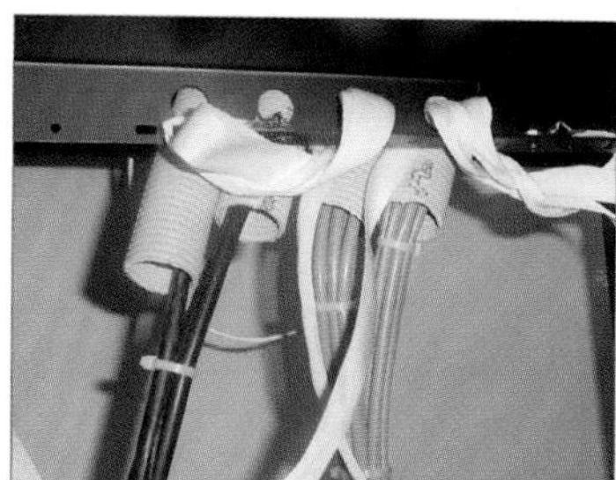

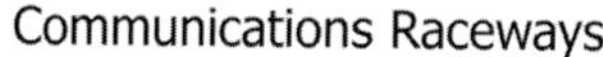
Communications Raceways

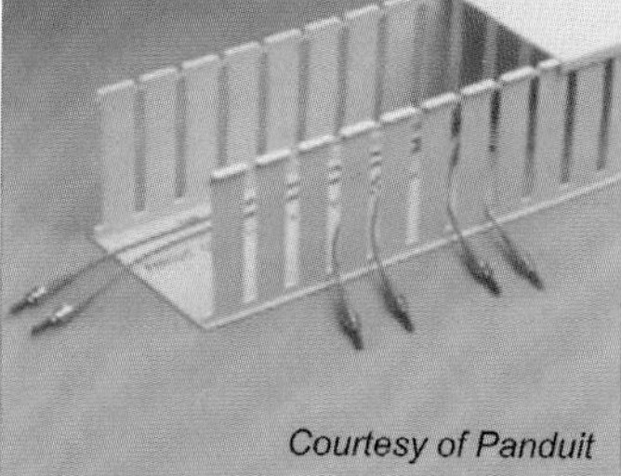
Courtesy of Panduit
Cable Routing Assembly

800.182(A) Plenum Communications Raceways and Plenum Cable Routing Assemblies

800.182(B) Riser Communications Raceways and Riser Cable Routing Assemblies

800.182(C) General-Purpose Communications Raceways and General-Purpose Cable Routing Assemblies

2011 *NEC* Requirement

The title of 800.182 was revised in the 2011 *NEC* to include both communications raceways and cable routing assemblies, but the subsequent subsection did not properly address cable routing assemblies specifically. All three subsections were followed by an informational note that basically referenced the same UL product standards for optical fiber raceways or optical fiber cable routing assemblies.

2014 *NEC* Change

Section 800.182(A), (B), and (C) were revised to reference the specific cable routing assembly being discussed in each subsection. Section 800.182(A) now addresses "Plenum Communications Raceways and Plenum Cable Routing Assemblies." Section 800.182(B) now addresses "Riser Communications Raceways and Riser Cable Routing Assemblies." Section 800.182(C) is specific for "General-Purpose Communications Raceways and General-Purpose Cable Routing Assemblies." Three repetitive Informational Notes have been deleted and replaced with a new Informational Note located in the main section as it applies to 800.180(A) (B) and (C).

Analysis of Change

Cable routing assemblies have been added to the main text of 800.182 and to the title of 800.182(A). The text of 800.182(A) has been simplified for clarity as well. Throughout this revised text at 800.182, cable routing assemblies are, wherever feasible, referred to as plenum cable routing assemblies, riser cable routing assemblies, and general-purpose cable routing assemblies. This was needed in order to avoid the possible interpretation that "communications raceways and cable routing assemblies" refers to "communications raceways" and "communications cable routing assemblies." There is actually no "communications cable routing assemblies," only "cable routing assemblies" that are simply plenum, riser, or general-purpose cable routing assemblies. This revised text now

800.182

Continued

~~**Informational Note:** One method of defining that an optical fiber raceway is a low smoke producing raceway and a fire-resistant raceway is that the raceway exhibits a maximum peak optical density of 0.5 or less, an average optical density of 0.15 or less, and a maximum flame spread distance of 1.52 m (5 ft) or less when tested in accordance with the plenum test in UL 2024-2004, Standard for Optical Fiber Cable Raceway.~~

(B) Riser Communications Raceways and Riser Cable Routing Assemblies. Riser communications raceways and riser cable routing assemblies shall be listed as having adequate fire-resistant characteristics capable of preventing the carrying of fire from floor to floor.

~~**Informational Note:** One method of defining fire-resistant characteristics capable of preventing the carrying of fire from floor to floor is that the raceways pass the requirements of the test for Flame Propagation (riser) in UL 2024- 2004, Standard for Optical Fiber Cable Raceway, or UL~~ 2024a-~~2008, Outline of Investigation for Optical Fiber Cable Routing Assemblies, as applicable.~~

(C) General-Purpose Communications Raceways and General-Purpose Cable Routing Assemblies. General-purpose communications raceways and general-purpose cable routing assemblies shall be listed as being resistant to the spread of fire.

~~***Informational Note:*** One method of defining resistance to the spread of fire is that the raceways pass the requirements of the Vertical-Tray Flame Test (General Use) in UL 2024- 2004, Standard for Optical Fiber Cable Raceway, or UL 2024a-2008, Outline of Investigation for Optical Fiber Cable Routing Assemblies, as applicable.~~

Proposal 16-140

includes plenum cable routing assemblies, in order to provide for applications in *plenums* (other space used for environmental air), particularly under raised floors in raised floor plenums. Companion proposals were submitted elsewhere in the *Code* where appropriate to provide applications and installation rules for plenum cable routing assemblies.

The previous informational notes, that followed the three subsections to 800.182, referenced two different Underwriters Laboratories (UL) product standards. UL has merged the requirements for listing cable routing assemblies (formerly UL 2024a-2008, *Outline of Investigation for Optical Fiber Cable Routing Assemblies*), and the requirements for listing communications and optical fiber raceways (formerly UL 2024-2004, *Standard for Optical Fiber Cable Raceway*), into one UL product standard. The new product standard is UL 2024-2011, *Signaling, Optical Fiber and Communications Raceways and Cable Routing Assemblies*. This new product standard has listing requirements for plenum, riser, and general-purpose grades of signaling, optical fiber and communications raceways; as well as plenum, riser, and general-purpose grades of cable routing assemblies. The new Informational Note following the main text of 800.182 simplifies the listing requirements by utilizing one informational note referring to the new UL 2024 and deleting the previous three informational notes.

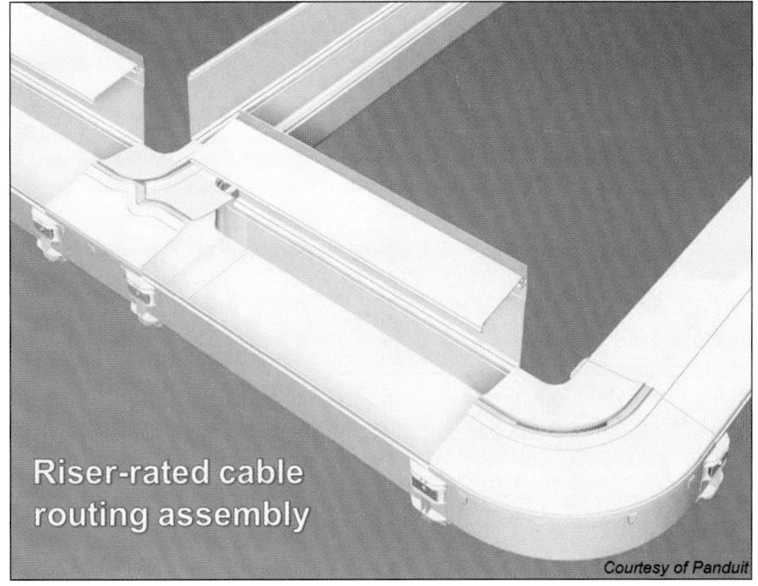

Riser-rated cable routing assembly

Courtesy of Panduit

810.6

Change at a Glance

Listing requirements for "Antenna Lead-In Protectors" have been added to Article 810.

Code Language

810.6 Antenna Lead-In Protectors

Where an antenna lead-in surge protector is installed, it shall be listed as being suitable for limiting surges on the cable that connects the antenna to the receiver/transmitter electronics and shall be connected between the conductors and the grounded shield or other ground connection. The antenna lead-in protector shall be grounded using a bonding conductor or grounding electrode conductor installed in accordance with 810.21(F).

Informational Note: For requirements covering protectors for antenna lead-in conductors, refer to UL Subject 497E, *Outline of Investigation for Protectors for Antenna Lead-In Conductors*.

Proposal 16-144

Comment 16-74

810.6 Antenna Lead-In Protectors

New provisions were added at 810.6 requiring radio and television equipment antenna lead-in surge protectors *(when installed)* to be listed as being suitable for limiting surges on the cable that connects the antenna to the receiver/transmitter electronics.

Antenna lead-in surge protector is required to be connected between the conductors and the grounded shield or other ground connection.

2011 *NEC* Requirement

There were no provisions in Article 810 for antenna lead-in surge protection.

2014 *NEC* Change

New provisions were added at 810.6 that require radio and television equipment antenna lead-in surge protectors (when installed) to be listed as being suitable for limiting surges on the cable that connects the antenna to the receiver/transmitter electronics. This antenna lead-in surge protector is required to be connected between the conductors and the grounded shield or other ground connection. Grounding must be accomplished using a bonding conductor or grounding electrode conductor installed in accordance with 810.21(F) through the intersystem bonding termination (if present).

Analysis of Change

Radio and television equipment antenna lead-in surge protectors can be subject to high energy lightning surges in the range of 5–50 kA or higher. Listing and compliance with appropriate product standards ensure that the antenna lead-in protector can withstand these surges without introducing a risk of fire or personal injury. These antenna lead-in protectors will continue to provide surge protection after being subjected to various environmental and surge conditions that may be expected in a typical installation.

Radio and television equipment antenna lead-in surge protectors are designed to protect personnel and customer premises electronic equipment from lightning and power induced surges in community antenna television (CATV) systems. Costly digital stereos and home entertainment systems, sensitive internet cable modems, home networking components and interfaces, personal computers, digital satellite TV systems, digital video recorders, big screen flat-screen televisions and high-end HDTV sets are just a few examples of electronic equipment shielded from these potentially damaging surges by antenna lead-in surge protectors. Radio and television equipment antenna lead-in surge protectors will greatly increase system reliability and reduce service outages by protecting against induced high voltage surges that may appear at the center conductor of a CATV cable. These antenna lead-in protectors typically are designed to be virtually transparent to all analog or digital bi-directional signals transmitted from dc to 1.5 GHz.

Article 810 already requires various devices that may be connected to antenna systems to be listed. This new requirement for antenna lead-in protectors is in line with those listing requirements. An example if this listing requirement can be found at 810.5 for radio noise suppressors. Several requirements in Chapter 8 typically require listing for surge protectors used in various applications. As an example, 800.170(A) has listing requirements for primary protectors for communications circuits.

A new informational note was also added following this new antenna lead-in protector requirement. This new Informational Note gives users of the *Code* direction to UL Subject 497E, *Outline of Investigation for Protectors for Antenna Lead-In Conductors*.

820.3

Change at a Glance

New subsections for "Wiring in Ducts for Dust, Loose Stock, or Vapor Removal" and "Equipment in Other Space Used for Environmental Air" have been added to 820.3.

Code Language

820.3 Other Articles

Circuits and equipment shall comply with 820.3(A) through ~~(G)~~ (J).

(A) Hazardous (Classified) Locations. CATV equipment installed in a location that is classified in accordance with 500.5 and 505.5 shall comply with the applicable requirements of Chapter 5.

(B) Wiring in Ducts for Dust, Loose Stock, or Vapor Removal. The requirements of 300.22(A) shall apply.

(C) Equipment in Other Space Used for Environmental Air. The requirements of 300.22(C)(3) shall apply.

~~(B)~~ (D) Installation and Use. The requirements of 110.3(B) shall apply.

~~(C)~~ (E) Installations of Conductive and Nonconductive Optical Fiber Cables. The requirements of Article 770 shall apply.

~~(D)~~ (F) Communications Circuits. The requirements of Article 800 shall apply.

820.3 Other Articles

New subsections for "Wiring in Ducts for Dust, Loose Stock or Vapor Removal" and "Equipment in Other Spaces Used for Environmental Air" have been added to 820.3.

References and requirements of 300.22(A) and 300.22(C)(3) were added for CATV systems.

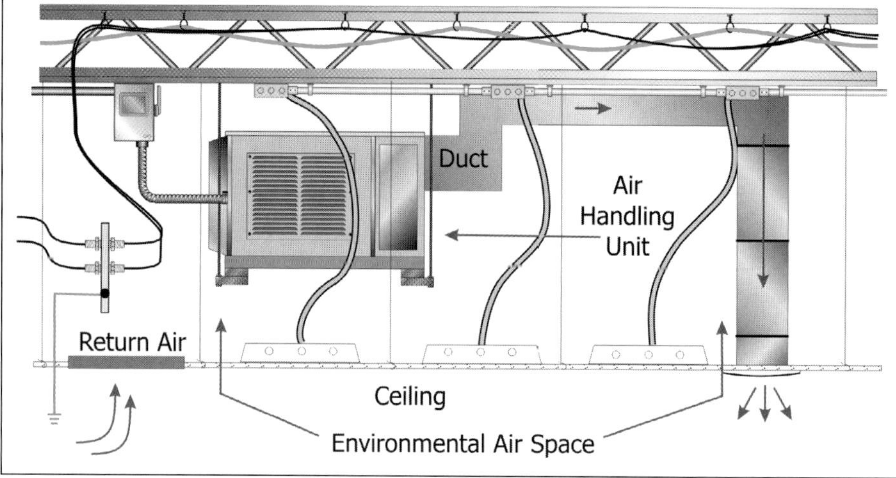

2011 *NEC* Requirement

Section 820.3 for "Other Articles" covered hazardous (classified) locations requirements of Chapter 5; installation and use requirements of 110.3; installations of conductive and nonconductive optical fiber cables of Article 770; communications circuit requirements of Article 800; network-powered broadband communications system requirements of Article 830; premises-powered broadband communications system requirements of Article 840; the alternate wiring methods of Article 830 being permitted to substitute for the wiring methods of Article 820; and the definition and the application requirements of Article 770 being permitted to apply to Article 820.

2014 *NEC* Change

Besides the 2011 *NEC* requirements brought forward, two new provisions were added to 820.3. Requirements of 300.22(A) were added for wiring in ducts for dust, loose stock, or vapor removal. Section 300.22(A) basically states that no wiring systems of any type shall be installed in ducts used to transport dust, loose stock, or flammable vapors. The other new provision at 820.3 added the requirements of 300.22(C)(3) for equipment in other space used for environmental air. Section 300.22(C)(3) states that electrical equipment with a metal enclosure, or electrical equipment with a nonmetallic enclosure listed for use within an air-handling space and having low-smoke and heat release properties shall be permitted to be installated in such space unless prohibited elsewhere. Proper *Code* references for cable routing assemblies were updated to coincide with changes in the 2014 *NEC* pertaining to cable routing assemblies.

Analysis of Change

The arrangement of the *Code* is specified at 90.3 of the *NEC*. This section stipulates that Chapters 1 through 4 apply generally to all electrical installations; whereas Chapters 5, 6, and 7 apply to special occupancies, special equipment, or other special conditions. These latter chapters (Chapters 6, 7 and 8) supple-

820.3

Continued

~~(E)~~ (G) Network-Powered Broadband Communications Systems. The requirements of Article 830 shall apply.

~~(F)~~ (H) Premises-Powered Broadband Communications Systems. The requirements of Article 840 shall apply.

~~(G)~~ (I) Alternate Wiring Methods. The wiring methods of Article 830 shall be permitted to substitute for the wiring methods of Article 820.

Informational Note: Use of Article 830 wiring methods will facilitate the upgrading of Article 820 installations to network-powered broadband applications.

~~(H)~~ (J) Cable Routing Assemblies. The definition in Article 100 ~~770.2~~, the applications in Table 800.154(c) ~~770.154~~, and installation requirements ~~rules~~ in 800.110 and 800.113 ~~770.113~~ shall apply to Article 820.

Proposal 16-161, 16-162, 16-163

Comment 16-75

ment or modify the general rules in Chapters 1 through 4. The requirements for community antenna television (CATV) systems are addressed in Article 820 (Chapter 8). Section 820.3 gives users of the *Code* specific conditions and *Code* references where this Chapter 8 article is to apply to other articles and *Code* sections other than in Article 820. Two new conditions with *Code* reference were added to the existing seven conditions identified at 820.3 for the 2014 *NEC*.

At 820.3(B), requirements of 300.22(A) were added for wiring in ducts for dust, loose stock, or vapor removal. Section 300.22(A) basically states that no wiring systems of any type can be installed in ducts used to transport dust, loose stock, or flammable vapors. At 820.3(C), the requirements of 300.22(C)(3) for equipment in other space used for environmental air were added. Section 300.22(C)(3) states that electrical equipment with a metal enclosure, or electrical equipment with a nonmetallic enclosure listed for use within an air-handling space and having low-smoke and heat release properties.

This is one of a group of changes to reference 300.22(A) and 300.22(C)(3) and to prohibit wiring in ducts used for dust and vapor removal. This is one of a group of proposals prepared by the CMP-16 Special Editorial Task Group. Part of the goals of this CMP-16 task group was to improve the parallelism between related articles such that similar requirements are stated the same way in each article and requirements are placed in the appropriate sections.

Similar revisions with these 300.22(A) and 300.22(C)(3) references were implemented at the following locations:

770.3	Optical Fiber Cables and Raceways	Proposal 16-36
800.3	Communications Circuits	Proposal 16-91
830.3	Network-Powered Broadband Communications Systems	Proposals 16-219, 16-220
840.3	Premises-Powered Broadband Communications Systems	Proposals 16-269, 16-270

820.47(A)

Change at a Glance

Underground coaxial cables are required to be sectioned off from electric light, power, Class 1, or "non–power-limited fire alarm" circuit conductors.

REVISION

Code Language

820.47 Underground Coaxial Cables Entering Buildings

Underground coaxial cables entering buildings shall comply with 820.47(A) and (B).

(A) Underground Systems with Electric Light, ~~and~~ Power, Class 1, or Non-Power-Limited Fire Alarm Circuit Conductors. Underground coaxial cables in a duct, pedestal, handhole enclosure, or manhole that contains electric light, ~~or~~ power, Class 1, or non-power-limited fire alarm circuit conductors shall be in a section permanently separated from such conductors by means of a suitable barrier.

(B) Direct-Buried Cables and Raceways. *(Text unchanged, see NEC for complete text).*

Proposal 16-171

820.47(A) Underground Coaxial Cables Entering Buildings

Underground coaxial cables in a duct, pedestal, handhole enclosure, or manhole that contains electric light, power, Class 1, or non-power-limited fire alarm circuit conductors shall be in a section permanently separated from such conductors by means of a suitable barrier.

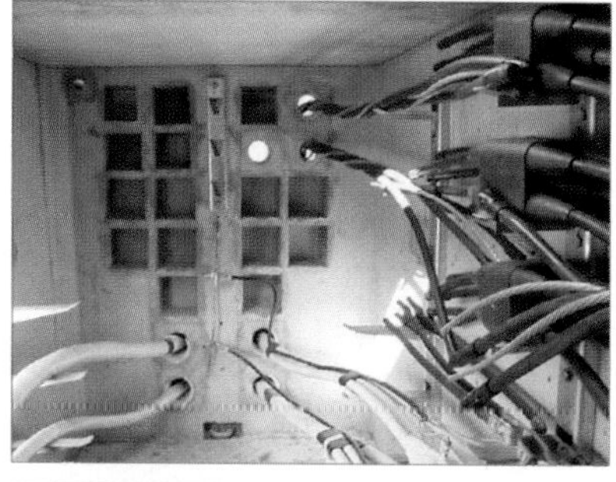

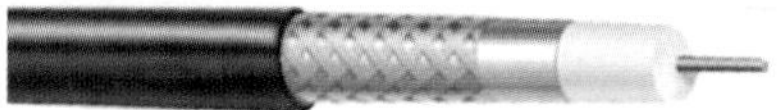

Underground coaxial cable

Non-Power Limited Fire Alarm Cable

2011 *NEC* Requirement

Underground coaxial cables were required to be in a separate section permanently separated by a suitable barrier from electric light or power conductors or Class 1 circuits when installed in a duct, pedestal, handhole enclosure, or manhole.

2014 *NEC* Change

"Non–power-limited fire alarm circuit conductors" were added to the type of conductors which underground coaxial cables are required to be sectioned off from when installed in a duct, pedestal, handhole enclosure, or manhole.

Analysis of Change

Previous editions of the *Code* required underground coaxial cables in a pedestal, handhole enclosure, etc., to be in a separate section permanently separated from exposed electric light, power, or Class 1 circuit conductors by a suitable barrier. For the 2014 *NEC*, "non–power-limited fire alarm circuit conductors" were added to the type of conductors which underground coaxial cables are required to be sectioned off from when installed in a duct, pedestal, handhole enclosure, or manhole. *Non–power-limited fire alarm circuit* (NPLFA) is defined at 760.2 as, "A fire alarm circuit powered by a source that complies with 760.41 and 760.43. Section 760.41 states that the power source of non–power-limited fire alarm circuits must comply with Chapters 1 through 4, and the output voltage cannot be more than 600 volts, nominal. Section 760.43 states that the overcurrent protection for conductors 14 AWG and larger must be provided in accordance with the conductor ampacity without applying the ampacity adjustment and correction factors of 310.15 to the ampacity calculation. As noted in the definition and the referenced text, NPLFA circuit conductors are capable of carrying as much or more voltage as Class 1 or power conductors. The revisions to 820.47 fix this issue by adding NPLFA circuit conductors to the conductors required to be separated from underground coaxial cables.

830.24

Change at a Glance

Nonmetallic cable ties and other nonmetallic cable accessories used to secure and support network-powered broadband communications cables are required to be listed as having low smoke and heat release properties.

Code Language

830.24 Mechanical Execution of Work

Network-powered broadband communications circuits and equipment shall be installed in a neat and workmanlike manner. Cables installed exposed on the surface of ceilings and sidewalls shall be supported by the building structure in such a manner that the cable will not be damaged by normal building use. Such cables shall be secured by hardware including straps, staples, cable ties, hangers, or similar fittings designed and installed so as not to damage the cable. The installation shall also conform to ~~300.4(D) and~~ 300.11. Nonmetallic cable ties and other nonmetallic cable accessories used to secure and support cables shall be listed as having low smoke and heat release properties.

Proposal 16-225, 16-226, 16-227

Comment 16-17, 16-89

830.24 Mechanical Execution of Work

Nonmetallic cable ties and other nonmetallic cable accessories used to secure and support network-powered broadband communications cables are required to be listed as having low smoke and heat release properties.

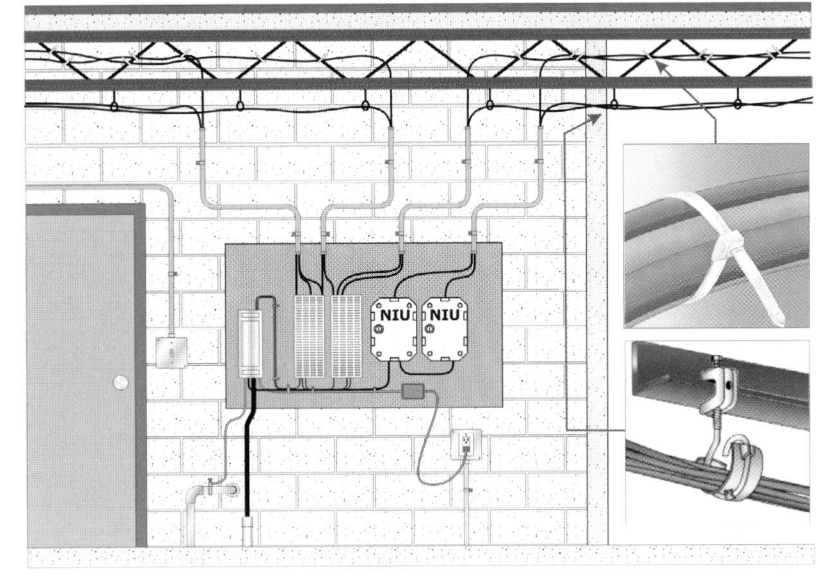

2011 *NEC* Requirement

Network-powered broadband communications (NPBC) circuits and equipment are required to be installed in a neat and workmanlike manner. NPBC cables installed exposed on the surface of ceilings and sidewalls are required to be supported by the building structure in such a manner that the cable will not be damaged by normal building use. Such cables are also required to be secured by hardware including straps, staples, cable ties, hangers, or similar fittings designed and installed so as not to damage the cable. In the 2011 *NEC*, these NPBC cable installations had to also conform to 300.4(D) Cables and Raceways Parallel to Framing Members and Furring Strips, and 300.11 Wiring Methods Securing and Supporting.

2014 *NEC* Change

A new last sentence was added to the existing "Mechanical Execution of Work" requirements of 830.24. This new provision calls for nonmetallic cable ties and other nonmetallic cable accessories used to secure and support NPBC cables to be listed as having low smoke and heat release properties. The reference to 300.4(D) was also dropped from 830.24, as 830.3(F) already includes a requirement to comply with 300.4.

Analysis of Change

New text was added at 830.24 with the intent of bringing the *NEC* requirements for nonmetallic cable ties installed in spaces used for environmental air (plenums) into correlation with NFPA 90A, *Standard for the Installation of Air-Conditioning and Ventilating Systems*. This correlation will be achieved by requiring nonmetallic cable ties and other nonmetallic cable accessories used to secure and support cables in plenums to be listed as having low smoke and heat release properties. NFPA 90A-2012 has current requirements for cable ties in ceiling cavity plenums (4.3.11.2.6.5) and raised floor plenums (4.3.11.5.5.6) that correspond to these new provisions which have been added at this subsection of the *NEC*. Plenum grade nonmetallic cable ties are readily available in the marketplace today that can achieve compliance with this new provision.

It should be noted that the original proposed language for this section stated that "Cable ties used to secure network-powered broadband plenum cables "in other space used for environmental air (plenums)" shall be listed as having low smoke and heat release properties." In the comment stage, the language was reverted to "Nonmetallic cable ties and other nonmetallic cable accessories used to secure and support cables shall be listed as having low smoke and heat release properties" with a Panel Statement from CMP-16 stating that, "The panel action correlates with the CMP-3 action on Comment 3-24 that added "and other nonmetallic cable accessories" following "cable ties." This comment added the "low smoke and heat release properties" requirement to 300.22(C)(1). A closer look at this Article 300 requirement reveals that this section deals with "the installation and uses of electrical wiring and equipment in ducts used for dust, loose stock, or vapor removal; ducts specifically fabricated for environmental air; and other spaces used for environmental air (plenums)." By removing the "in other space used for environmental air (plenums)" from 830.24, this "low smoke and heat release properties" requirement for cable ties is no longer limited to nonmetallic cable ties and other nonmetallic cable accessories in plenums.

This same change occurred at 770.24; 800.24; 820.24; and 830.24.

Chapter 9 Tables: Table 1

Change at a Glance

Table was revised to include provisions for cables as well as conductors.

Code Language

Chapter 9 Tables

Table 1 Percent of Cross Section of Conduit and Tubing for Conductors and Cables

(See illustrated Table 1 on this page and *NEC* for complete table text).

Proposal 8-202

Chapter 9 Tables: Table 1

Table 1: Percent of Cross Section of Conduit and Tubing for Conductors and Cables

Number of Conductors and/or Cables	Cross Sectional Area (%) ~~All Conductor Types~~
1	53%
2	31%
Over 2	40%

53% 31% 40%

2011 *NEC* Requirement

Table 1 of Chapter 9 was entitled, "Percent of Cross Section of Conduit and Tubing for Conductors."

2014 *NEC* Change

The title of Chapter 9, Table 1 was renamed, "Percent of Cross Section of Conduit and Tubing for Conductors and Cables."

Analysis of Change

The first table in Chapter 9 has been revised for the 2014 *NEC* to recognize that cables as well as conductors can be installed in raceways. Table 1 gives the user of the *Code* the percentage fill of conductors and, now, cables when installed in a raceway. For example, if more than 2 conductors or cables are installed in a raceway, those conductors or cables cannot occupy more than 40 percent of the total cross sectional area of the inside of that raceway. The title of the table was changed to "Percent of Cross Section of Conduit and Tubing for Conductors and Cables" from "Percent of Cross Section of Conduit and Tubing for Conductors." The first column heading was changed to "Number of Conductors and/or Cables" from simply "Number of Conductors." The second column heading was changed to "Cross Sectional Area (%)" from "All Conductor Types."

Table 1 fill requirements apply to both conductors and cables such as optical fiber cables. The term *cables* should be included since optical fiber cables are not considered to be conductors. Note 9 to the Chapter 9 tables also gives direction for situations where cables are installed in a raceway. This note states that for cables that have elliptical cross sections (such as Type NM cable), the cross-sectional area calculation shall be based on using the major diameter of the ellipse as a circle diameter.

Change at a Glance

New Note (10) was added addressing the values for approximate conductor diameter and area shown in Table 5.

Code Language

Chapter 9 Tables

Notes to Tables

(10) The values for approximate conductor diameter and area shown in Table 5 are based on worst-case scenario and indicate round concentric-lay-stranded conductors. Solid and round concentric-lay-stranded are grouped together for the purpose of Table 5. Round compact-stranded conductor values are shown in Table 5A. If the actual values of the conductor diameter and area are known, they shall be permitted to be used.

Proposal 6-112

Comment 6-77

Chapter 9 Tables: Notes to Tables - Note (10)

New Note (10) was added addressing the values for approximate conductor diameter and area shown in Table 5.

Solid Conductor	Standard Stranding	Compact Stranding
	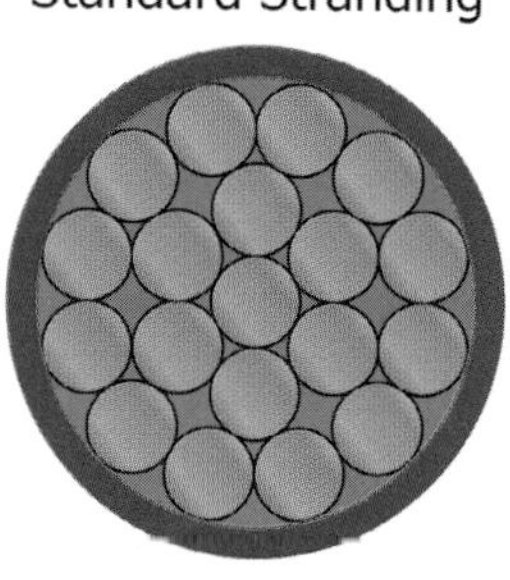	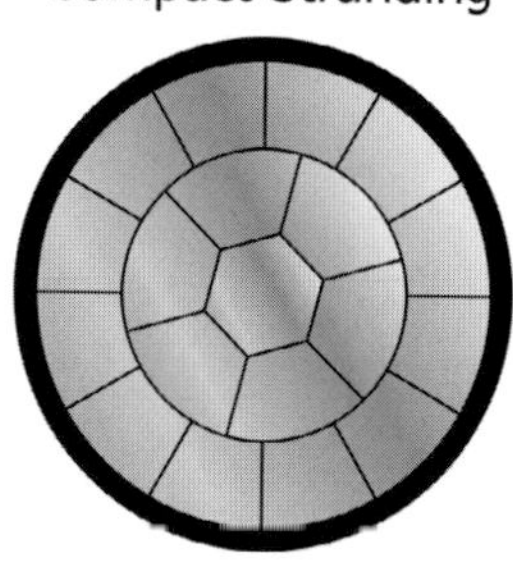
8 AWG THWN Dia = 5.486 mm (0.216 in.) Area = 23.61 mm^2 (0.0366 $in.^2$)	8 AWG XHHW Dia = 5.994 mm (0.236 in.) Area = 28.19 mm^2 (0.0437 $in.^2$)	8 AWG XHHW Dia = 5.690 mm (0.224 in.) Area = 25.42 mm^2 (0.0394 $in.^2$)

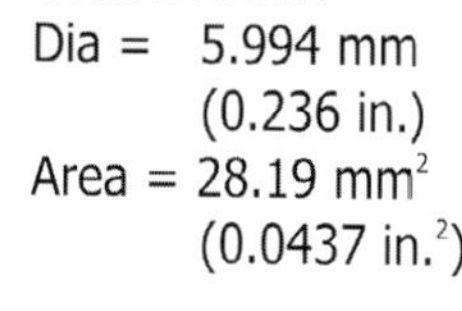

2011 *NEC* Requirement

There were nine (9) notes to the Chapter 9 Tables in the 2011 *NEC*. None of these notes addressed approximate conductor diameter and area shown in Table 5.

2014 *NEC* Change

A new Note (10) was added to the Chapter 9 Notes to Tables. This new note indicates that the values for approximate conductor diameter and area shown in Table 5 are based on worst-case scenario. The information here goes on to indicate that Table 5 is based on round concentric-lay-stranded conductors. Solid and round concentric-lay-stranded conductors are to be grouped together for the purpose of Table 5, while round compact-stranded conductor values are shown in Table 5A. This new note gives the user of the *Code* permission to use the actual values of the conductor diameter and area if they are known.

Analysis of Change

During the 2002 *NEC Code* cycle, some of the insulation thickness approximate diameter and area values at Table 5 were revised by CMP-6. At the same time, CMP-8 rejected proposals to revise Informative Annex C for these same conductor types. This rejection was primarily based on conductors, manufactured prior to the effective date, that were still being installed. This left Informative Annex C with the "maximum number of conductors" values based on the old Table 5 approximate diameter and area values. Doing a straight calculation for Table 5 would leave the user of the *Code* with a different number of permitted conductors allowed in a particular conduit than the number of conductors permitted by Informative Annex C.

For the 2011 *NEC*, proposals and comments were submitted to both CMP-6 and CMP-8 to coordinate the numbers and values of Table 5 and Informative Annex C. The end result of these recommendations was a review of both Table 5 and Informative Annex C, which was needed to confirm the accuracy of both of these

Continued

tables. CMP-8 recommended a task group be formed comprised of CMP-6 and CMP-8 members to review for accuracy the tables in Informational Annex C and Table 5. This task group was to come back to the Code-Making Panels with their findings for the 2014 *NEC*, as these new values would require public review before publication.

As a result of the finding of this task group, it was determined that before updating the tables of Informative Annex C, a review of Table 4, Table 5, and Table 5a was required. All of the insulation types of Table 5 were reviewed against multiple UL product standards. Table 5a was left unchanged as these values are denoted as from industry sources, not from specific UL standards. For the 2014 *NEC*, Proposal 6-114 resulted in revisions to Table 5. Proposal 204a resulted in revisions to some of the tables in Informative Annex C. Proposal 6-112 and Comment 6-77 resulted in a new Note (10) to the Notes to the Tables of Chapter 9. This new note clarifies that stranded, not solid, values are used in Table 5. This new note was needed to point out this fact to the user of the *Code* and to give direction when solid conductors are encountered.

Change at a Glance

Table 4 was rearranged with "Over 2 Wires 40%" as the first column after "Trade Size."

Code Language

Table 4 Dimensions and Percent Area of Conduit and Tubing

(See 2014 NEC for remainder of Table)

Proposal 8-204

Chapter 9 Tables: Table 4

Table 4: Dimensions and Percent Area of Conduit and Tubing

(2014 NEC)

Article 352 - Rigid PVC Conduit (PVC), Schedule 80

Metric Designator	Trade Size	Over 2 Wires 40%		60%		1 Wire 53%		2 Wires 31%		Norminal Internal Diameter		Total Area 100%	
		mm²	in²	mm²	in²	mm²	in²	mm²	in²	mm	in	mm²	in²
12	⅜	—	—	—	—	—	—	—	—	—	—	—	—
16	½	56	0.087	85	0.130	75	0.115	44	0.067	13.4	0.526	141	0.217
21	¾	105	0.164	158	0.246	139	0.217	82	0.127	18.3	0.722	263	0.409
27	1	178	0.275	267	0.413	236	0.365	138	0.213	23.8	0.936	445	0.688
35	1¼	320	0.495	480	0.742	424	0.656	248	0.383	31.9	1.255	799	1.237
41	1½	442	0.684	663	1.027	585	0.907	342	0.530	37.5	1.476	1104	1.711
53	2	742	1.150	1113	1.725	983	1.523	575	0.891	48.6	1.913	1855	2.874

(2011 NEC)

Article 352 - Rigid PVC Conduit (PVC), Schedule 80

Metric Designator	Trade Size	Norminal Internal Diameter		Total Area 100%		60%		1 Wire 53%		2 Wires 31%		Over 2 Wires 40%	
		mm	in	mm²	in²	mm²	in²	mm²	in²	mm²	in²	mm²	in²
12	⅜	—	—	—	—	—	—	—	—	—	—	—	—
16	½	13.4	0.526	141	0.217	85	0.130	75	0.115	44	0.067	56	0.087
21	¾	18.3	0.722	263	0.409	158	0.246	139	0.217	82	0.127	105	0.164
27	1	23.8	0.936	445	0.688	267	0.413	236	0.365	138	0.213	178	0.275
35	1¼	31.9	1.255	799	1.237	480	0.742	424	0.656	248	0.383	320	0.495
41	1½	37.5	1.476	1104	1.711	663	1.027	585	0.907	342	0.530	442	0.684
53	2	48.6	1.913	1855	2.874	1113	1.725	983	1.523	575	0.891	742	1.150

Reproduction of NEC Table 4 (Chapter 9) (in part)

2011 *NEC* Requirement

Table 4 of Chapter 9 gives dimensions and percent area of different types of conduits and tubing. It covers 13 articles and 12 different types of conduits and tubing covering four pages in the 2011 *NEC*. Each of these tables list "Metric Designator" and "Trade Size" as the first and second columns. The following columns from left to right were; "Nominal Internal Diameter," "Total Area 100%," "60%," "1 Wire 53%," "2 Wires 31%," and "Over 2 Wires 40%."

2014 *NEC* Change

Some of the internal diameter values changed in some of the tables due to the overall review of the tables for accuracy (see Proposal 8-92). The main change that happened to Table 4 was the rearrangement of the columns. "Metric Designator" and "Trade Size" are still the first and second columns. For the 2014 *NEC*, the next column is now "Over 2 Wires 40%." This is followed by "60%," "1 Wire 53%," and "2 Wires 31%." The last two columns in the revised arrangement are "Nominal Internal Diameter," and "Total Area 100%."

Analysis of Change

Table 4 in its previous arrangement was felt to be difficult to use accurately by some users of the *Code*. This was due in part to the orientation of the columns. The columns most often utilized for conductor fill calculations are the "Over 2 Wires 40%" and "60%" respectively, were previously located on the extreme right of the table. Other columns that are not used as much in the plan review process or in the installation or inspection processes such as "Nominal Internal Diameter" and "Total Area 100%" were located closest to the metric designator and trade sizes of the raceways. Conduit fill calculations require great care and detail. The need to access and re-access these 4-digit decimal values is paramount in making accurate calculations. By repositioning the most commonly used conduit fill columns closer to the metric designator and trade size column sizes will allow for easier and more accurate use of Table 4.

Chapter 9 Tables: Table 5

Change at a Glance

Table 5 has been rearranged by repositioning the "Approximate Area" column next to "Size (AWG or kcmil)" column.

Code Language

Table 5 Dimensions of Insulated Conductors and Fixture Wires

Approximate Area

Approximate Diameter

(See 2014 NEC for remainder of Table)

Proposal 6-113

Comment 6-78

Chapter 9 Tables: Table 5

Table 5: Dimensions of Insulated Conductors and Fixture Wires

(2014 NEC)

Type	Size (AWG or kcmil)	Approximate Area mm²	Approximate Area in²	Approximate Diameter mm²	Approximate Diameter in²
RFH-2, FFH-2	18	9.355	0.0145	3.454	0.136
	16	11.10	0.0172	3.759	0.148
RHH, RHW, RHW-2	14	18.90	0.0293	4.902	0.193
	12	22.77	0.0353	5.385	0.212
	10	28.19	0.0437	5.994	0.236

(2011 NEC)

Type	Size (AWG or kcmil)	Approximate Diameter mm²	Approximate Diameter in²	Approximate Area mm²	Approximate Area in²
RFH-2, FFH-2	18	3.454	0.136	9.355	0.0145
	16	3.759	0.148	11.10	0.0172
RHH, RHW, RHW-2	14	4.902	0.193	18.90	0.0293
	12	5.385	0.212	22.77	0.0353
	10	5.994	0.236	28.19	0.0437

Reproduction of NEC Table 5 (Chapter 9) (in part)

2011 *NEC* Change

Table 5 of Chapter 9 gives dimensions of insulated conductors and fixture wires. This information is needed to determine the maximum number of conductors that can be installed in a raceway or conduit in conjunction with Table 4. This table provides approximate area and diameter information on all insulation types for conductors installed in raceways and conduits. This table covers four pages in the 2011 *NEC*. The table has four main columns, with "Type" listed as the first column. This refers to the type of insulation. "Size (AWG or kcmil)" is the second column. In the 2011 *NEC*, the third column is "Approximate Diameter" followed by "Approximate Area" as the last column on the far right of the table.

2014 *NEC* Change

Some of the approximate diameter and area values changed in the tables due to the overall review of the Chapter 9 tables for accuracy. Some missing insulation types were also added to the table (see Proposal 6-114 and Comment 6-79). Another important change that occurred with Table 5 was the rearrangement of the columns. "Type" and "Size (AWG or kcmil)" are still the first and second columns. For the 2014 *NEC*, the next column is now "Approximate Area" followed by "Approximate Diameter."

Analysis of Change

Table 5 of Chapter 9 in its previous arrangement was felt to be difficult to use accurately by some users of the *Code*. This was due in part to the orientation of the columns. The column most often utilized for conductor fill calculations in Table 5 is the "Approximate Area" column. This column was previously located on the extreme right of the table. The other column, "Approximate Diameter," which is not used as much in the plan review process or the installation or inspection process, was located closest to the type of insulation and size columns. Conductor fill calculations require great care and detail. The need to access and re-access these 4-digit decimal values is paramount in making accurate calculations. By repositioning the most commonly used "Approximate Area" column closer to the size of conductor column will allow for easier and more accurate use of Table 5. This rearrangement of the columns of Table 5 will make the tables more user-friendly and the likelihood of errors will be diminished.

Example D7 [Example using 310.15(B)(7)]

Change at a Glance

New Example D7 was added to Informative Annex D describing how to apply revised 310.15(B)(7) by using a .83 percentage factor rather than the former Table 310.15(B)(7).

NEW

Code Language

Informative Annex D: Examples

Example D7 Sizing of Service Conductors for Dwelling(s) [see 310.15(B)(7)]

Service conductors and feeders for certain dwellings are permitted to be sized in accordance with 310.15(B)(7).

If a 175-ampere service rating is selected, a service conductor is then sized as follows: 175 amperes × 0.83 = 145.25 amperes per 310.15(B)(7).

If no other adjustments or corrections are required for the installation, then, in accordance with Table 310.15(B)(16), a 1/0 AWG copper or a 3/0 AWG aluminum would meet this rating at 75°C (167°F).

Proposal 6-117a

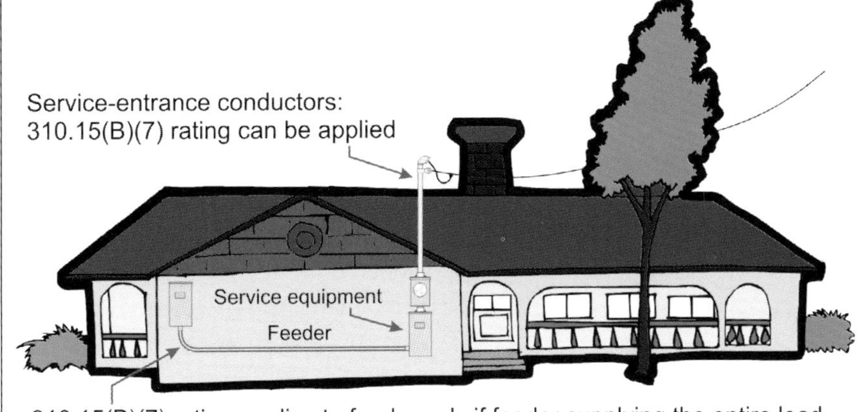
Example D7 [Example using 310.15(B)(7)]
Sizing of Service Conductors for Dwelling(s)
New Example D7 was added to Informative Annex D describing how to apply revised 310.15(B)(7) to dwelling unit services and the main power feeder by using a .83 percentage factor rather than the former Table 310.15(B)(7).
Service-entrance conductors: 310.15(B)(7) rating can be applied
Service equipment
Feeder
310.15(B)(7) rating applies to feeder only if feeder supplying the entire load associated with the dwelling unit.

2011 *NEC* Requirement

Service-entrance, service-lateral and the main power feeder conductors for dwelling units served at 120/240 volts, 3-wire, single-phase were permitted to be sized by 310.15(B)(7) and Table 310.15(B)(7). The table had an ampacity rating for the service or main power feeder from 100 to 400 amperes, with wire sizes from 4 AWG to 400 kcmil copper and 2 AWG to 600 kcmil aluminum. This table was also permitted to be used for the feeder conductors that serve as the main power feeder to a dwelling unit. To use Table 310.15(B)(7) for selection of the main power feeder, this feeder would have had to supply all loads associated with the dwelling unit. There was no "Example D7" giving an example of sizing service-entrance conductors for dwelling units in the 2011 *NEC*.

2014 *NEC* Change

Table 310.15(B)(7) has been eliminated entirely, primarily by the actions of Proposal 6-49a and Comment 6-52. The parent text at 310.15(B)(7) has been revised and broken up into four list items. Rather than use previous Table 310.15(B)(7) for sizing service conductors and the main power feeder for dwelling units, the user of the *Code* is left with a calculation to perform. The ampacity values found at Table 310.15(B)(16) can be reduced by 17 percent (not less than 83 percent of the service or feeder rating), which will require the circular mils properties of Table 8 in Chapter 9 to be brought into the now required calculation. A new Informational Note will take users of the *Code* to this new Example D7 in Annex D for an example of how to perform this dwelling unit service and feeder calculation.

Analysis of Change

Table 310.15(B)(7) has been removed from the 2014 *NEC*. See the "Analysis of Changes" at 310.15(B)(7) of this text for further information concerning this deletion. This previous table was replaced with an ampacity reduction of

Continued

not less than 83 percent of the service or feeder rating of the ampacity values of Table 310.15(B)(16). This 0.83 multiplier will result in basically the same ampacity values of previous Table 310.15(B)(7). In order to address the various proposals submitted suggesting changes to 310.15(B)(7), CMP-6 analyzed the existing language and determined that the conductor sizes in Table 310.15(B)(7) are equivalent to those that would be used if a 0.83 multiplier was applied to each service ampere rating.

As a result of these revisions and deletions at 310.15(B)(7), CMP-6 determined that an example for calculating service-entrance conductors for dwelling units was warranted to be placed in Informative Annex D to assist users of the *Code* in this calculation. It should be noted that the text at Example D7 indicates that, "service conductors and 'feeders' for certain dwellings are allowed to be sized per 310.15(B)(7)." A close read of the revised text at 310.15(B)(7) will indicate that 310.15(B)(7) can only be applied to "a feeder rated 100 through 400 amperes supplying the entire load associated with a one-family dwelling or an individual dwelling unit in a two-family or multifamily dwelling." This would mean that only one feeder in the entire dwelling could qualify for this reduction in ampacity rating at 310.15(B)(7). This feeder (that supplies the entire load of the dwelling) was referred to as the *main power feeder* in previous editions of the *Code*.

Annex J

Change at a Glance

New Informative Annex J, ADA Standards for Accessible Design, was added to assist in usability and to provide information about ADA electrical device mounting heights, etc.

Code Language

Informative Annex J: ADA Standards for Accessible Design

J.1 Protruding Objects.

J.2 Protrusion Limits.

J.3 Post-Mounted Objects.

J.4 Vertical Clearance.

J.5 Required Clear Width.

J.6 Forward Reach.

J.6.1 Unobstructed.

J.6.2 Obstructed High Reach.

J.7 Side Reach.

J.7.1 Unobstructed.

J.7.2 Obstructed High Reach.

(See Informative Annex J of 2014 NEC for complete text)

Proposal 1-191a

Informative Annex J:
ADA Standards for Accessible Design

New Informative Annex J (ADA Standards for Accessible Design) was added to assist in usability and provide information about ADA electrical device mounting heights, etc.

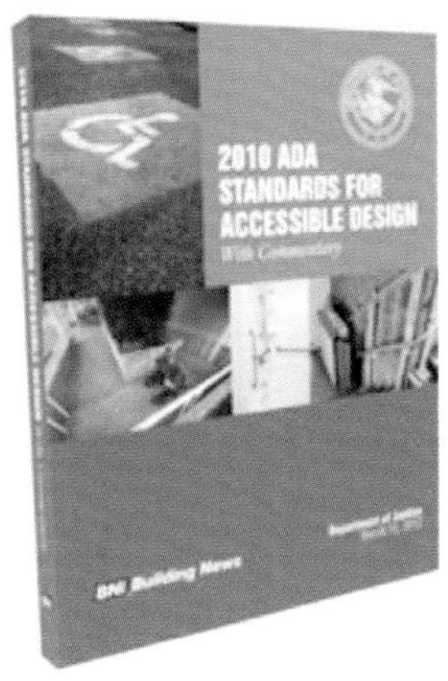

2011 *NEC* Requirement

This Informative Annex did not exist in the 2011 *NEC*.

2014 *NEC* Change

This new Informative Annex J, ADA Standards for Accessible Design, was added to assist installers and designers in usability requirements and to provide information about ADA electrical device mounting heights, etc.

Analysis of Change

Being part of the informative annexes of the *NEC*, this new informative Annex J is not a part of the requirements of the *NEC*, but is included for informational purposes only. The provisions cited in Informative Annex J are included to assist the users of the *Code* in properly considering various electrical design constraints of other building systems, and are part of the 2010 ADA Standards for Accessible Design, and are the same as those found in ANSI/ICC A117.1-2009, *Accessible and Usable Buildings and Facilities*. This is not the complete set of requirements adopted by the US Department of Justice, but rather some of the sections that may be frequently used by the electrical industry. A new Informational Note was added after 110.1, the scope of the general requirements of the *NEC*. This important information is needed to comply with Federal Accessibility requirements for location of such electrical equipment such as devices, switches, receptacles, disconnects, controls, etc. Inclusion of this annex will assist installers, inspectors, and designers to understand and comply with these vital regulations.

IAEI MEMBERSHIP HAS VALUE

When you join IAEI, you receive exclusive member benefits as well as enjoy the satisfaction of helping to support a broad range of IAEI initiatives that affect everyone who cares about electrical safety.

Along with being part of a community of electrical professionals, your member benefits include:

- Free Code book after three consecutive years of membership ($89.50 value)
- Free Subscription to IAEI print and digital magazine ($112.95 value)
- Free UL White Book ($45.00 value)
- Discounts on IAEI publications
- Discounts on IAEI education training / seminar
- Certification Programs
- Membership Rewards Discount Program

Member Type	1-Year Membership	3-Year Membership
Associate Members	$102.00	$286.00
Inspector Members*	$102.00	$286.00
Student Members**	$78.00	N/A

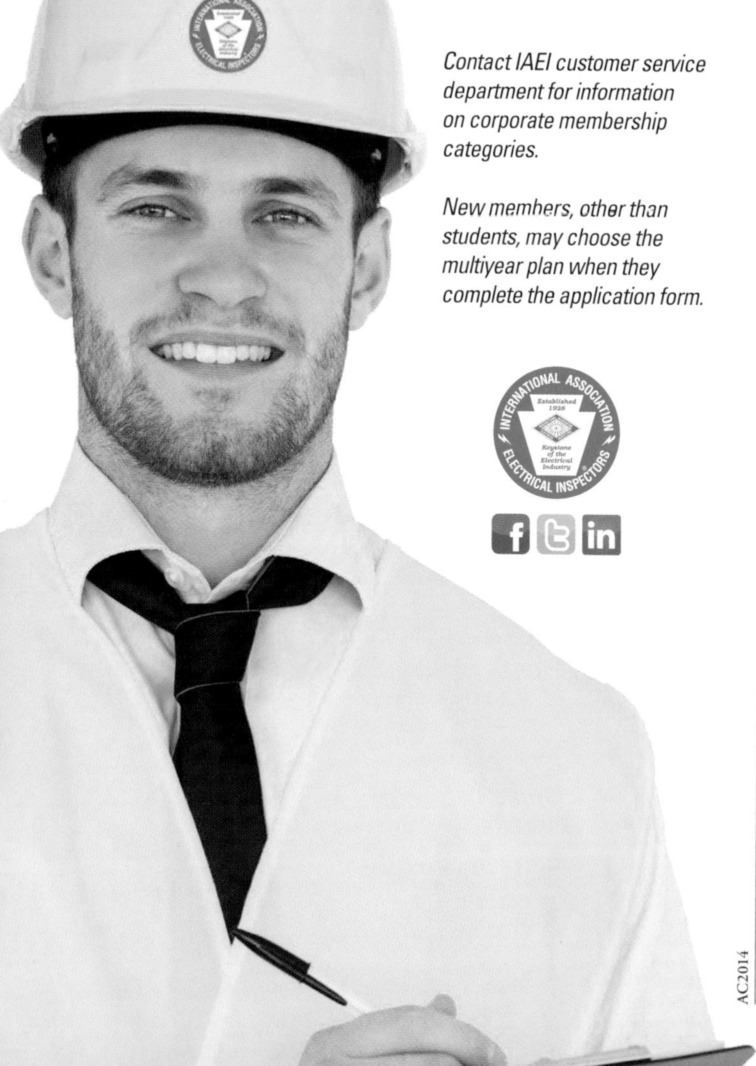

Contact IAEI customer service department for information on corporate membership categories.

New members, other than students, may choose the multiyear plan when they complete the application form.

AC2014

MEMBERSHIP APPLICATION | PLEASE PRINT

Name - Last First M.I.

Title

Employer

Address of Applicant

City State or Province ZIP or Postal Code

(Area Code) Telephone Number

Email Date of Birth

How did you hear about IAEI?

Student applicants give school attending** Graduation date

Applicant's Signature

Chapter, where you live or work, if known (Division, where appropriate).

If previous member, give last membership number and last year of membership.

Endorsed by Endorser's Membership Number

☐ MasterCard ☐ Visa ☐ AMEX ☐ Money Order
☐ Discover ☐ Diners Club ☐ Check

Name on Card

Charge Card Number Expiration Date

Inspector ☐ Associate ☐ Student ☐ Other ☐
Amount Paid $ Specify member type

Inspector Member MUST sign below:

I, ______________________________

meet the qualification for inspector member as described below.

*Inspector members must regularly make electrical inspections for preventing injury to persons or damage to property on behalf of a governmental agency, insurance agency, rating bureau, recognized testing laboratory or electric light and power company.
** Student member must be currently enrolled in an approved college, university, vocational technical school or trade school specializing in electrical training or approved electrical apprenticeship school.

MAIL TO: IAEI
P.O. Box 830848, Richardson
TX 75083-0848
For information call:
(972) 235-1455 (8–5 CST)

ONLINE: Join by scanning the QR Code ▸ or at iaei.org

Section	Chapter No.	Division No.

Analysis of Changes *NEC*-2014

Editor-in-Chief	David Clements
Director of Education	Keith L. Lofland
Education, Codes and Standards Coordinator	Joseph Wages Jr.
Director of Marketing	Melody Schmidt
Director of Publishing	Kathryn Ingley
Creative Director / Cover Design	John Watson
Research Editor & Webmaster	Laura Hildreth

IAEI representatives to 2014 *NEC* Code-Making Panels:

CMP-1 Susan Newman-Scearce and Paul Sood
CMP-2 Mark Hilbert and Bill McGovern
CMP-3 Robert Walsh and Joseph Wages, Jr.
CMP-4 James Rogers and Glenn Soles
CMP-5 David Williams and William Pancake, III
CMP-6 Rick Maddox and John Stacey
CMP-7 Charles Palmieri and Allen Turner
CMP-8 James Imlah and Pete Jackson
CMP-9 David Humphrey and L. Keith Lofland
CMP-10 Robert Kauer and Christopher Mark Jensen
CMP-11 Robert Fahey and Rodney Jones
CMP-12 Phil Clark and Phillip Yehl
CMP-13 Peter Olney and Steve Froemming
CMP-14 Vacant and Jack Jamison, Jr.
CMP-15 Marcus R. Sampson and Joe Dupriest
CMP-16 Tom Moore and Larry Chan
CMP-17 Donny Cook and Ira Lee Douglas
CMP-18 Amos Lowrance, Jr. and Rick Hollander
CMP-19 Ron Chilton and Dean Hunter

Principal Author: L. Keith Lofland

Technical Review: L. Keith Lofland, Mark Earley, Jeff Sargent, James Rogers, Joseph Wages, Jr., Mark Hilbert, Donny Cook

Photographs by:
Pass and Seymore/Legrand
Hubbell
PowerBridge
Allied Wire and Cable, Inc.
Bridgeport Fittings
Mohawk Cable
Belden Cable
Armstrong Building Products
Eaton Corporation
Bender Incorporated
Schneider Electric/Square D Company
Southwire Company, Inc.
Cooper Lighting
Erico International
RSCC Wire and Cable
Copper Bussman
Thomas and Betts
Underwriters Laboratories, Inc.
IAEI Archives

L. Keith Lofland
Joseph Wages, Jr.
Bill McGovern
Darrell Hefley
Chad Kennedy
Steve Rood
Brian Rock
Dale Missey
David Kendall
Chris DeCesare
Jessica Buck
Jeff Fecteau
Dustin Hostetter
Karin Martin
Jim Pistol
James Conrad
Donny Cook
Rick Maddox
Mark Hilbert
Michael J. Johnston
John Wiles
James Rogers

Composed at International Association of Electrical Inspectors in Optima LT Standard by Adobe® and Arial Narrow by TrueType®.

Printed by Walsworth Print Group on 70# Book. Bound in 12 pt. Cover.